60 YEARS OF THE UNIVERSAL DECLARATION OF HUMAN RIGHTS IN EUROPE

VINODH JAICHAND
MARKKU SUKSI
(EDS)

INTERSENTIA
Antwerp — Oxford — Portland

Distribution for the UK:
Hart Publishing Ltd.
16C Worcester Place
Oxford OX1 2JW
UK
Tel.: +44 1865 51 75 30
Fax: +44 1865 51 07 10

Distribution for the USA and Canada:
International Specialized Book Services
920 NE 58th Ave Suite 300
Portland, OR 97213
USA
Tel.: +1 800 944 6190 (toll free)
Tel.: +1 503 287 3093
Fax: +1 503 280 8832
Email: info@isbs.com

Distribution for Switzerland and Germany:
Schulthess Verlag
Zwingliplatz 2
CH-8022 Zürich
Switzerland
Tel.: +41 1 251 93 36
Fax: +41 1 261 63 94

Distribution for other countries:
Intersentia Publishers
Groenstraat 31
BE-2640 Mortsel
Belgium
Tel.: +32 3 680 15 50
Fax: +32 3 658 71 21

60 Years of the Universal Declaration of Human Rights in Europe
Vinodh Jaichand and Markku Suksi (eds)

ISBN 978-90-5095-880-6
D/2009/7849/18
NUR 828

TABLE OF CONTENTS

PREFACE ix
LIST OF AUTHORS xiii

1. INTRODUCTION (Vinodh Jaichand, Markku Suksi) 1

PART I: EUROPEAN STATES IN THE DRAFTING BODIES OF THE UDHR

2. BELGIUM: A REFERENCE INSTRUMENT, BUT WITHOUT BINDING FORCE (Paul Lemmens, Ludovic Hennebel, Arnaud Van Waeyenberge, Evelien Vandeven) 7
3. FRANCE: THE ORIGINS, WITH THE PROSPECT OF INCREASING EFFECT (Florence Benoît-Rohmer) 19
4. THE UNITED KINGDOM: DEVELOPING A HUMAN RIGHTS CULTURE (Rory O'Connell, Tom Obokata) 27

PART II: EUROPEAN STATES THAT WERE MEMBERS OF THE UN BY THE TIME OF THE ADOPTION OF THE UDHR

5. DENMARK: A DOCUMENT OF IDEOLOGICAL IMPORTANCE (Eva Maria Lassen) 43
6. GREECE: MORE VERBALISM, LESS EFFECTIVENESS? (Stelios Perrakis) 59
7. LUXEMBOURG: CONTENT WITHOUT REFERENCE? (Jean-Paul Lehners, Fabienne Rossler) 73
8. THE NETHERLANDS: RELIGIOUS INSPIRATION, BUT LITTLE DOMESTIC IMPACT (Fons Coomans, Willemijn Noordhoek) 85
9. POLAND: FROM OBLIVION TO LEGAL USE (Roman Wieruszewski) 101
10. SWEDEN: UNDERESTIMATION OF RIGHTS (Jonas Grimheden) 111

PART III: EUROPEAN STATES THAT BECAME MEMBERS OF THE UN IN THE DEAL OF 1955

11. AUSTRIA: KEEPING A LOW PROFILE (Wolfgang Benedek, Manfred Nowak) 137
12. BULGARIA: EVOLVING INTO DEMOCRACY UNDER THE UDHR TEMPLATE (Maria Mandova) 147
13. FINLAND: POLITICAL, NOT LEGAL (Markku Suksi) 161
14. HUNGARY: THE IMPACT ON THE FREEDOM OF EXPRESSION (Gábor Halmai, Eszter Polgári) 179

15. IRELAND: FROM DOMESTIC PRE-OCCUPATIONS TO WIDER RECEPTION (Attracta Ingram, Vinodh Jaichand) 197
16. ITALY: A LEGAL PUZZLE, BUT THE CIVIL SOCIETY HAS TAKEN THE BALL AND RUNS WITH IT (Paolo De Stefani) 213
17. PORTUGAL: HUMAN RIGHTS GUIDELINES FROM THE CONSTITUTION TO SUGAR BAGS (Tereza Pizarro Beleza, Helena Pereira de Melo) 231
18. ROMANIA: SIDELINED TO THE MARGINS OF LEGAL PLURALISM (Iulia Voina-Motoc) 241
19. SPAIN: FROM TOTALITARIANISM TO FULFILMENT (Felipe Gómez Isa, Carmen Márquez Carrasco) 247

PART IV: EUROPEAN STATES THAT BECAME MEMBERS OF THE UN BETWEEN 1955 AND 1989

20. CYPRUS: FROM AN INTERESTING COLONIAL LEGACY TO POST-CONFLICT CONTEXTUALISATION (Kalliope Agapiou-Josephides) 265
21. GERMANY: FROM IMPOSITION TO ADHERENCE (Anja Mihr) 281
22. MALTA: A TENUOUS LINK IN HUMAN RIGHTS PRACTICE AND PROCEDURE (Ian Refalo) 293

PART V: EUROPEAN STATES THAT BECAME MEMBERS OF THE UN AFTER 1989

23. THE CZECH REPUBLIC: FROM LIP SERVICE TO CONCRETE APPLICATION (Jan Holzer, Hubert Smekal) 305
24. ESTONIA: TRANSITION THROUGH HUMAN RIGHTS (Katre Luhamaa) 325
25. LATVIA: BINDING FORCE THROUGH COURT PRACTICE (Maris Burbergs, Arturs Kucs) 343
26. LITHUANIA: SUBTLE MATERIAL IMPACT (Vygantė Milašiūtė) 357
27. THE SLOVAK REPUBLIC: POLITICAL SIGNIFICANCE, NOT LEGAL (Mária Patakyová, Katarína Galdunová) 373
28. SLOVENIA: INDIRECT BUT INCREASING IMPACT (Milan Brglez, Bojko Bučar) 385

PART VI: THE EUROPEAN ORGANISATIONS

29. THE COUNCIL OF EUROPE: FIRST STEPS AND THEN SOME — COLLECTIVE ENFORCEMENT OF THE UNIVERSAL DECLARATION (Antti Korkeakivi) 399
30. THE EUROPEAN UNION: IN SEARCH OF LEGITIMACY (Allan Rosas) 415
31. THE OSCE: A COMMITMENT TO HUMAN RIGHTS (Robert-Jan Uhl, Bernhard Knoll) 433

PART VII: FINAL COMMENTS

32. A VIEW FROM THE OUTSIDE (Hurst Hannum) 445
33. CONCLUDING REMARKS ON EUROPE: DIVERSITY WITHIN THE UNITY
(Vinodh Jaichand, Markku Suksi) 453

SUBJECT INDEX 469

PREFACE

It is self-evident that the Universal Declaration of Human Rights (UDHR) constitutes a centrepiece of the activities of all those persons who in one way or another participate in the European Master's Programme in Human Rights and Democratisation (often referred to as the E.MA programme or the Venice programme). The subject matter taught in the Master's Programme deals with virtually all of the provisions of the UDHR and the Declaration can therefore be regarded the intellectual springboard of our activities. What often strikes us is the fact that the UDHR has managed to maintain its topicality and freshness, even after 60 years since its adoption. One reason for this is, of course, that the work for human rights is still largely unfinished, even in the European space. Nonetheless, 60 years is long enough to warrant a look back in order to assess the current status of the UDHR as regards its reception and implementation in individual states and in international organisations in Europe.

When the Universal Declaration became 50 years old in 1998, several volumes studying the UDHR primarily from the point of view of public international law were published. However, the UDHR identifies rights that the individual should have in any state, and therefore, the specific forms of the national reception, implementation and usage of the UDHR should attract more interest. With a view to the 60th anniversary, the idea was conceived to engage the E.MA network in a joint effort to compile a commentary or a narrative from the point of view of national law, politics and implementation so that each of the 27 member states of the European Union and the three European international organisations (the Council of Europe, the European Union and the Organisation for Security and Cooperation in Europe) would feature in the book with one article each on the reception and understanding of the UDHR in the legal and social order of that country or international organisation.

The idea of compiling this volume was first hatched during a salubrious dinner in Venice in December 2007 at which the E.MA professors were making use of the first part of Article 24 of the UDHR ("Everyone has the right to rest and leisure, including reasonable limitation of working hours ..."). We were in a relaxed, leisurely environment at a nice restaurant after having worked from 9 a.m. until 7 p.m. Once again, it was proven that academics may be productive even when not doing anything particular: others might say this was food for thought. The discussion in our corner of the table dealt with all sorts of matters such as family, travel and health. For a moment, we also paused on the potential of our network that had not yet been entirely tapped into with the innocuous question: "I wonder how the UDHR was received in Europe?" The specific potential was to carry out comparative research in each of the participating countries concerning, for instance, different legal mechanisms, such as the implementation of the UDHR and its different articles in the participating countries.

When the same group of persons was attending the Assembly meeting of the European Inter-University Centre of Human Rights and Democratisation (EIUC) the following day, the chair of that meeting, professor Horst Fischer, solicited commitments from the E.MA network concerning suitable ways to commemorate the 60th anniversary of the UDHR. Several proposals were tabled and supported, among them the one that the reception of the UDHR should be studied from a national perspective. The idea was enthusiastically received by the participants in the E.MA, and all the participating universities in all the countries involved were quick to commit themselves towards contributing to this book.

It is our understanding that the idea resulted in a truly unique project to which all 27 EU member countries and the European organisations who had much in common willingly contributed in order to honour the 60th anniversary of the UDHR. The book is original not only in its approach to the UDHR but also as concerns the contributions, because it seems that not many of the European contributors had ever written anything on this specific issue. Every country, big or small, tells a different story about human rights and democratisation in this book, and taken together, this is the European Story of Human Rights and Democratisation, very much conditioned by the fact that the UDHR was approved 60 years ago, in 1948, in the aftermath of the denial of the rights and the belittlement of the individual brought about by the Second World War.

We, the participating universities in the E.MA programme, hereby wish to congratulate the United Nations on one of its most significant achievements. On the occasion of the celebration of the 60 years of the UDHR on 10 December 2008, two exclusive copies of this book were presented with congratulations to the United Nations, one to the United Nations High Commissioner on Human Rights, H.E. Mrs. Pillay, and another to the President of the General Assembly of the United Nations, H.E. Mr. d'Escoto Brockmann.

The production of this book would not have been possible without the commitments of the contributing authors who set aside so much of their time for this joint initiative. Therefore, we first and foremost thank the authors featuring in this volume for their contributions. In addition to professor Fischer, we also wish to thank Mr. George Ulrich, Secretary General of the EIUC, for their support for the project, and Ms. Raija Hanski of the Institute for Human Rights at Åbo Akademi University for the technical editing of the entire text and the Foundation for Åbo Akademi University for funding the last stages of the technical editing as well as Intersentia for accepting the book for publication.

Galway and Åbo on 30 December 2008
Vinodh Jaichand and Markku Suksi

LIST OF AUTHORS

Kalliope Agapiou-Josephides, PhD in Political Science (Paris I Panthéon-Sorbonne), MA in Advanced European Studies and MA in History of the XXth Century (International Relations) (the University Robert Schuman STRASBOURG III), Assistant Professor at the Department of Social and Political Sciences of the University of Cyprus; Cyprus.

Wolfgang Benedek, Dr., Professor, Institute for International Law and International Relations, Karl-Franzens-Universität, Graz; Austria.

Florence Benoît-Rohmer, PhD in Law, Professor at the University of Strasbourg; President of the University of Strasbourg; France.

Milan Brglez, PhD, Assistant Professor and Head of the International Relations Department of the Faculty of Social Sciences at the University of Ljubljana; Slovenia.

Bojko Bučar, PhD, Professor and Vice-Dean for International Cooperation, the Faculty of Social Sciences at the University of Ljubljana; Slovenia.

Maris Burbergs, E.MA, Lecturer at the Department of the International and European Law, Faculty of Law, University of Latvia; Latvia.

Fons Coomans, PhD, UNESCO Chair on Human Rights and Peace at Maastricht University, Coordinator of the Maastricht Centre on Human Rights; the Netherlands.

Paolo De Stefani, Human Rights PhD School of the University of Padua, Lecturer in International Law at the Faculty of Political Sciences and the Human Rights Centre, the University of Padua. Advisor to the Children's Ombudsperson Office of the Veneto Region, Venice; Italy.

Katarína Galdunová, JUDr., Faculty of Law, Comenius University in Bratislava; part-time PhD student; Slovakia.

Felipe Gómez Isa, Dr., Professor of Public International Law at the Institute of Human Rights of the University of Deusto (Bilbao); Spain.

Jonas Grimheden, BA, LLB, LLM, LLD, all from Lund University, Senior Researcher, Deputy Head of the Academic Department at the Raoul Wallenberg Institute of Human Rights and Humanitarian Law; Sweden.

Gábor Halmai, Dr., Professor of Law, Director of the Institute for Political and International Studies at the Eötvös Lóránd University, Budapest; Hungary.

Hurst Hannum, A.B. and J.D. (University of California, Berkeley), Professor of International Law, Fletcher School of Law and Diplomacy, Tufts University.

Ludovic Hennebel, Global Research Fellow affiliated with New York University (B.A.E.F. Fellow), the Magna Carta Institute and the Perelman Centre of Legal Philosophy of the Brussels University (Université Libre de Bruxelles); Belgium.

Jan Holzer, PhD, Doc., Vice-Dean of the Faculty, Department of Political Science, Faculty of Social Studies, Masaryk University; the Czech Republic.

Attracta Ingram, Professor, BA, PhD, MRIA, School of Politics and International Relations, UCD, Dublin; Professor of Political Theory; Ireland.

Vinodh Jaichand, BA (UD-W), STD (UD-W), LLB (Natal) LLM (Miami), LLM *(magna cum laude)*, J.S.D (Notre Dame); Deputy Director, Irish Centre for Human Rights, National University of Ireland, Galway; Ireland.

Bernhard Knoll, MA, JHU/SAIS, PhD/EUI, Special Adviser to the Director of the ODIHR, Warsaw; Organisation for Security and Cooperation in Europe.

Antti Korkeakivi, LLM (the University of Helsinki), LLM (Columbia University), Head of the Secretariat of the Framework Convention for the Protection of National Minorities, Council of Europe, Strasbourg (until the end of 2008), Adjunct Professor, Columbia University, School of International and Public Affairs (2007–2008), Head of the UN OHCHR's Unit on Indigenous Peoples and Minorities (from January 2009 on); Council of Europe.

Arturs Kucs, Dr.iur., Docent at the Department of the International and European Law, Faculty of Law, University of Latvia; Latvia.

Eva Maria Lassen, Exam.art; Mag.art.; PhD in History; Research Director and Senior Researcher at the Danish Institute for Human Rights; Denmark.

Jean-Paul Lehners, Dr., Professor of Global History, Director of the Human Rights Observatory, the University of Luxembourg, President of the Advisory Commission on Human Rights of the Grand Duchy of Luxembourg; Luxembourg.

Paul Lemmens, Judge in the *Conseil d'Etat* (Supreme Administrative Court) of Belgium, Professor of International Human Rights Law at the Catholic University of Leuven; Belgium.

Katre Luhamaa, magister iuris (Tartu University), baccalaureus artium (Tartu University), Doctoral student at the University of Helsinki, Lecturer of international law, human rights and EU law at the Faculty of Law of Tartu University; Estonia.

Maria Mandova, BA in International Relations (Agnes Scott College, GA, USA), European Master's Degree in Human Rights and Democratisation (Venice, Italy); Bulgaria.

Carmen Márquez Carrasco, Dr., Professor of Public International Law and International Relations at the University of Seville, Spain, Chairperson of the European Master's Programme in Human Rights and Democratisation since December 2007; Spain.

Anja Mihr, PhD, Visiting Professor for Human Rights at Peking University Law School in China of the Raoul Wallenberg Research Institute and Senior Fellow at the European Inter-University Center for Human Rights and Democratization (EIUC) in Venice, Italy; Germany.

Vygantė Milašiūtė, LLM (Vilnius), M.I.L. (Lund), PhD (Vilnius), Lecturer at the Department of International and EU Law, Faculty of Law, Vilnius University; Lithuania.

Willemijn Noordhoek, MA in International Business Studies (Maastricht University), Student-Assistant at the Department of International and European Law; the Netherlands.

Manfred Nowak, Dr., Professor for International Human Rights Protection at the University of Vienna, Visiting Professor, Swiss Chair on Human Rights, Graduate Institute, Geneva (since 2008), Director of the Ludwig Boltzmann Institute of Human Rights (Vienna); Austria.

Tom Obokata, Lecturer in Law at the Human Rights Centre, Queen's University Belfast; the United Kingdom.

Rory O'Connell, Senior Lecturer in Law at the Human Rights Centre, Queen's University, Belfast; the United Kingdom.

Mária Patakyová, JUDr., PhD., Assisting Professor, Faculty of Law, Comenius University in Bratislava; Vice-Dean for International Relations and Grant Policy; Slovakia.

Helena Pereira de Melo, LLB (Coimbra), M.Phil. in Law (Lisbon), PhD in Law (Lisbon), Assistant Professor at the Faculty of Law, New University of Lisbon; Portugal.

Stelios Perrakis, Professor of International and European Institutions in Panteion University of Athens; J. Monnet Chair 'ad personam' 'Democracy and human rights in the EU'; Director of the European Centre of Research and Training on Human Rights and Humanitarian Action; Greece.

Tereza Pizarro Beleza, BA in Law (Coimbra), M.Phil in Criminology (Cantabrigia), PhD in Law (Lisbon), Agregate Professor at the Faculty of Law of the New University of Lisbon; Portugal.

Eszter Polgári, European Master's Degree in Human Rights and Democratisation (Venice, Italy), Special Project Officer, Central European University; Hungary.

Ian Refalo, BA, LLD, Dip.I.L.(Cantab.), Professor of Law at the Department of Public Law, Dean of the Faculty of Laws of the University of Malta; Malta.

Allan Rosas, Dr.iur, Judge, Court of Justice of the European Communities; European Union.

Fabienne Rossler, MA in Translation, E.MA in Human Rights and Democratisation, Chief Executive of the Commission of Human Rights of Luxembourg; Luxembourg.

Hubert Smekal, PhD, Lecturer at the Department of International Relations and European Studies, Faculty of Social Studies, Masaryk University; the Czech Republic.

Markku Suksi, Dr., Professor of Public Law, Åbo Akademi University; Finland.

Robert-Jan Uhl, LLM, Leiden University and E.MA, Venice, Human Rights Officer at the OSCE Office for Democratic Institutions and Human Rights (ODIHR) in Warsaw; Organisation for Security and Cooperation in Europe.

Evelien Vandeven, Researcher at the Catholic University of Leuven, Graduate Student at the Northwestern University School of Law (Chicago); Belgium.

Arnaud Van Waeyenberge, Researcher at the Perelman Centre of Legal Philosophy of the Brussels University (Université Libre de Bruxelles); Belgium.

Iulia Voina-Motoc, Dr., Professor of International Law, University of Bucharest; Romania.

Roman Wieruszewski, Professor, Poznan Centre for Human Rights, Institute of Legal Studies, Polish Academy of Sciences; Poland.

1. INTRODUCTION

Vinodh Jaichand
Markku Suksi

While it is clear that human rights conventions signed and ratified by a state should be duly implemented in the domestic legal order of the state that assumes the obligation, it remains unclear exactly what a state should do in relation to the Universal Declaration of Human Rights (UDHR). On the basis of the Preamble of the UDHR,[1] it can be said that it was proclaimed in 1948 as a "common standard of achievement for all peoples and all nations", and by the time of adoption, it was understood to be a non-binding document. At that point, the intention was to draft and adopt a binding set of human rights norms as soon as possible, something that was realised only in 1966, when the two Covenants were adopted. At the same time the UDHR is a unique document which reflects the most solemn expression of international commitments by states to human rights.

As a non-binding standard, the UDHR directed itself to "every individual and every organ of society" and asked them to keep the Declaration constantly in mind. In addition, it requested them to "strive by teaching and education to promote respect for these rights and freedoms and by progressive measures, national and international, to secure their universal and effective recognition and observance, both among the peoples of Member States themselves and among the peoples of territories under their jurisdiction". Hence actions to be taken for the promotion of the UDHR by the individuals and every organ of society were to be taken also at the national level, not only at the international level.[2]

The request to take action at the national level was sustained by a recommendation by the General Assembly in another part of the resolution[3]

---

1 General Assembly resolution 217 A (III) of 10 December 1948.

2 Although the UDHR is generally understood as a relatively complete enumeration of human rights, it should be mentioned that there were two areas that were considered in the context but not included in the UDHR, namely the issue of minorities, which the UN felt was too difficult an issue to be dealt with in the context, and the issue of the right of petition, which the General Assembly recognized as an essential human right but chose provisionally to drop from the list of rights included in the UDHR. See General Assembly resolution 217 B (III) and General Assembly resolution 217 C (III) of 10 December 1948.

3 General Assembly resolution 217 D (III) of 10 December 1948.

concerning the publicity to be given to the UDHR. The recommendation that was directed to the Governments of Member States was "to show their adherence to Article 56 of the Charter by using every means within their power solemnly to publicize the text of the Declaration and to cause it to be disseminated, displayed, read and expounded principally in schools and other educational institutions, without distinction based on the political status of countries or territories".

Against this background and 60 years after the adoption of the UDHR, it is of great interest to study the reception of the UDHR in national legal systems from the point of view of national law and national political debate and inquire into the actions that have been taken. What did the government of the country say about the UDHR in the General Assembly of the United Nations, domestically at the time of the adoption of the UDHR and at a later stage, when the implementation of human rights started? Was the UDHR ever referred to in any piece of law, such as the constitution, and if so, when and in which law? What do the preparatory documents to legislation or the parliamentary debates say about the UDHR? Did the political parties use the UDHR, for example, in their charters or argumentation? Has the UDHR been referred to in any court case? If so, when was the first time the UDHR was mentioned and what kind of cases has it been used in since? What was said in the press after the adoption of the UDHR and how has the press treated the UDHR since? In which ways has the UDHR influenced thinking in a country? Did the NGOs pay attention to the UDHR?

This publication, born out of the co-operation between 41 universities within the framework of the European Master's Programme in Human Rights and Democratisation in the 27 EU countries, is a commentary and a narrative from the national perspective concerning the reception and understanding of the UDHR in the legal and political order of each country. In addition, the three European international organisations (the Council of Europe, the European Union, and the Organisation for Security and Cooperation in Europe) contribute to the book from their respective perspectives.

The volume is unique from the point of view of human rights and democratisation in Europe, because it illustrates the national position of different European countries on human rights and also democratisation with a view to historical development during the past 60 years, that is, the formative years of what Europe is right now. The experience of the original West European countries that created the Council of Europe and later became the European Union is in many ways intriguing but did not by any means exhaust the range of options concerning reception of the UDHR. The experience of countries which have been under dictatorship (such as Greece, Portugal and Spain) and managed to rid themselves of the yoke of authoritarian rule opened up new paths for the reception of the UDHR. The experiences of the Central and East European countries that remained so long behind the 'Iron Curtain' certainly re-instated the value of the UDHR as a standard of achievement and went in some respects even beyond the South European countries in enforcing the substance of the UDHR at the national level. There is also the experience of a number of countries (such as Austria and Finland) which were placed in a particular historical context in 1948 and which display a varying response to the standard of achievement set by the UN. The articles in this volume illustrate the steps that the various European countries originally set out to take and since have taken towards human rights and democratisation under the inspiration of the UDHR.

This book is unique also from the point of view that for the comparative reader, it actually compiles a pool of normatively relevant empirical information which is of interest both from the perspective of international law and comparative law. However, it should be underlined that the point of departure in the book and in the articles it contains is not only legal, but incorporates also historical and political perspectives. Therefore, all countries and international organisations involved were able to find, from this multi-disciplinary perspective, a suitable methodological approach to the issues raised.

One perspective that can be assumed to be relevant from the point of view of history and international politics is reflected in the table of contents and its grouping of the different states in the chronological order according to the time the state first came into contact with the UDHR. In the first part, those European states are included which were members of the drafting bodies of the UDHR between 1946 and 1948, while at the same time being members of the UN (Belgium, France and the United Kingdom). These countries can be regarded as being in the vanguard with respect to framing the contents of the UDHR. The countries in the second part (Denmark, Greece, Luxembourg, the Netherlands, Poland and Sweden) were also important in proposing ideas for the UDHR and influenced in many ways the contents of the declaration, and this group also contains one state, Poland, which abstained from voting on the UDHR together with seven other states primarily of the Socialist bloc.

The third part contains countries many of which were associated with Germany in the Second World War and which for this reason (or for some other reason) were not members of the UN by the time of the adoption of the UDHR (Austria, Bulgaria, Finland, Hungary, Ireland, Italy, Portugal, Romania and Spain). The fourth part brings in the special experience of Germany and of the two colonial countries in Europe, those of Cyprus and Malta. None of these countries were really independent in 1948, but emerged as independent states later on. Part five deals with the situation in the newly independent states of Central and Eastern Europe (the Czech Republic, Estonia, Latvia, Lithuania, the Slovak Republic, and Slovenia), some of which were members of the UN early on through their predecessor states Czechoslovakia and Yugoslavia, but which chose to pursue separation into independent states, perhaps in part for reasons that can at least remotely be linked to human rights issues. Part six recognizes the impact of the three European organisations (the Council of Europe, the European Union and the Organisation for Security and Cooperation in Europe): the Council of Europe was seminal in making human rights binding in the European space, while the observance of human rights in the European Union is important because the EU actually functions as a state in exercising legislative and also executive and judicial powers over the individuals in the member states of the European Union. In this context of European organisations, the role of the OSCE cannot be underestimated, because the collapse of the authoritarian regimes of Central and Eastern Europe may at least partly be attributed to the influence that the OSCE had in the area of human rights.

Finally, part seven looks at the European human rights experience from two different angles. On the one hand there is a look at Europe with respect to the UDHR from an exogenous, non-European perspective, assessing the profile of the European states from a more global point of view. On the other hand, there is a look from a comparative perspective that identifies at least some of the most salient features that characterise the reception of the UDHR in the various states and international organisations.

The contributors were deliberately not asked to follow any strict template when authoring the national contributions. Instead, they were presented with the above-mentioned questions relating to the reception of the UDHR and allowed certain latitude of freedom in choosing the methodological approach to the topic. Some of the articles are therefore clearly more legal in nature, and some more political or historical, but in most cases the contributions are a mix of all these approaches. While the focus of each article is on the reception and understanding of the UDHR in a particular country or international organisation, the contributions are, in a number of instances, complemented with an explanation of the incorporation of human rights covenants through different legislative mechanisms and with information on particular substantive provisions in the UDHR.

What is a windfall, beyond the original conception of the idea to undertake this research, is the amount of new material unearthed by the respective researchers in dealing with the reception of the UDHR in both its narrow and broad contexts in their respective countries. That is an impressive facet when writing about a document which is regarded as the most translated one in the world, and one which has existed for 60 years.

PART I

EUROPEAN STATES IN THE DRAFTING BODIES OF THE UDHR

2. BELGIUM: A REFERENCE INSTRUMENT, BUT WITHOUT BINDING FORCE

Paul Lemmens
Ludovic Hennebel
Arnaud Van Waeyenberge
Evelien Vandeven

1. HISTORY

After the creation of the United Nations in 1945, the Economic and Social Council (ECOSOC) established in 1946 the Commission on Human Rights.[1] The Commission was explicitly directed to submit proposals, recommendations and reports to the Council regarding, among other things, "an international bill of rights". Belgium had the opportunity to make its mark, as it was a member of this Commission since its early stages. At that time, the Commission consisted of only a small number of members,[2] which made the influence of the original members all the more important.[3]

The Belgian delegation[4] distinguished itself for its work in a number of crucial areas which can be classified into three distinct categories. The first category consists of questions related to the Universal Declaration of Human Rights (UDHR) itself, its title and legal value, the second is concerned with questions of a more substantive nature (stateless peoples' status, women's rights, and the work force's rights), whereas the third category revolves around a particularly sensitive issue in Belgium: the rights of minorities.

---

[1] ECOSOC Resolution 5 (I) of 16 February 1946.

[2] Apart from a 'nucleus' Commission of nine members (individuals) in the first months, the Commission was composed of 18 members (States) until 1961.

[3] J. ORAÁ ORAÁ, 'The Universal Declaration of Human Rights', in F. GÓMEZ ISA and K. DE FEYTER (eds), *International Protection of Human Rights: Achievements and Challenges* (Publicaciones de la Universidad de Deusto, Bilbao, 2006) pp. 73–134.

[4] The Belgian representatives within this Commission were Prof. Fernand Dehousse (later member of parliament and minister) and Mr. Roland Lebeau. At the Third Committee of the General Assembly Belgium was represented by Count Henri Carton de Wiart (at that time an elder statesman), with Messrs. Dehousse and Pierre Ryckmans as his substitutes.

The Belgian position concerning the Declaration's title supported the French view. In fact, the Declaration was initially referred to as the '*International* Declaration of Human Rights'. The title '*Universal* Declaration of Human Rights' was first suggested by René Cassin (France), seconded by Count Henri Carton de Wiart (Belgium), and finally adopted by the General Assembly. Even though this modification was purely symbolic, it emphasised the human and global nature of this document, rather than merely treating it as part of international law.

The second sphere of Belgian influence demonstrated the strength of Belgium's support for the UDHR, though Belgium was not as successful in this endeavour as in the first one. This second sphere involved questions relating to the interpretation and the legal value of the UDHR. The Belgian delegation wanted the International Court of Justice to pass judgment on the interpretation of the UDHR's disputed terminology basing its judgment on the preparatory work of the Commission on Human Rights. Undoubtedly, this request was a result of the Belgian delegation's desire to endow the Declaration with a certain legal force.[5] This particular position, a minority one, considered the international bill of rights as a complete, coherent and indivisible whole. Therefore, the UDHR had to be of the same legal nature as the covenant on human rights, which was also to be drafted. Moreover, it had to be viewed as "a tool for authentic interpretation" which developed and supplemented the United Nations Charter while also introducing human rights into the realm of positive international law.[6]

Similarly, the Belgian delegation made its mark through its staunch support of the rights and freedoms of the stateless (Article 15 of the UDHR[7]), women (Articles 16[8] and 23[9]) and the work force (Article 23[10]). The position of Belgium on each of these issues can be explained by the fact that its own legal system contained a series of protective laws for the said marginalised

---

5 R. NGOY LUMBU, *L'instauration du mécanisme de communications individuelles devant le Comité des droits économiques, sociaux et culturels: une contribution à l'étude des voies et moyens additionnels pour une mise en oeuvre efficiente du Pacte international relatif à ces droits,* The theses library of the Catholic University of Louvain, Louvain-la-Neuve, 2007, pp. 28-29.

6 *Ibid.*

7 A. VERDOODT, *Naissance et signification de la Déclaration universelle des droits de l'homme* (Éditions Nauwelaers, Louvain-Paris, 1964) p. 158.

8 *Ibid.*, pp. 162–167.

9 *Ibid.*, p. 222.

10 *Ibid.*, pp. 226–228.

groups, making it easier for the Belgian delegation to suggest an international system of rights that ran parallel to its national one.

Finally, taking into consideration the sociological composition of Belgium,[11] it was no wonder that the Belgian delegation proved particularly sensitive to minority rights. It made numerous efforts to ask for serious consideration of minority rights such as respect for language, culture and education.[12]

Belgium was clearly a dedicated proponent of the UDHR. Its support of the UDHR gave it a highly privileged position in the world, allowing it to incorporate its beliefs into the UDHR itself. Given this reality, it is surprising that Belgium took a long time to adhere to the two covenants emanating from the UDHR. The Covenant on Civil and Political Rights (CCPR) and the Covenant on Economic, Social and Cultural Rights (CESCR), which could not be adopted before 1966 because of international political tensions caused by the Cold War, were ratified by Belgium only in 1983.

2. REFERENCES TO THE UDHR IN LEGISLATION

The UDHR was published in the *Moniteur belge* (Belgian official gazette) of 31 March 1949. This is remarkable, as resolutions adopted by international organisations are normally not published in the *Moniteur*.

There are not many explicit references to the UDHR in legislative acts, including the statutes and the government decrees, both at the federal and the community or regional levels. References to the UDHR are typically to be found when the rule maker imposes a number of obligations on private entities, as conditions for official recognition or public funding. In such cases, it is not uncommon to place upon these entities an obligation to respect human rights as they are proclaimed in the UDHR, sometimes in combination with the European Convention on Human Rights (ECHR). Relatively recent examples include a decree of the French Community relating to the recognition of youth houses and other youth centres and a decree of the Flemish Government relating to the recognition of institutions for persons with a handicap.[13] Another category of legislative acts with references to the

---

11 There are three official languages spoken in Belgium (French, Dutch and German). Belgium counts two sensitive minority groups (the French speaking community at the national level, and the Dutch speaking community at the Brussels level).

12 VERDOODT, *supra* note 7, pp. 287–299.

13 Decree of the French Community of 20 July 2000 establishing the conditions for recognition and funding of youth homes, encounter and accommodation centres, information centres for

UDHR are those relating to the field of education. Educational institutions are sometimes directed to respect the human rights of pupils and their parents, or to teach in a spirit of respect for human rights, and here again the UDHR can serve as a reference document.[14]

It is also worth mentioning that the UDHR, by virtue of its legitimacy as well as its symbolic significance, is sometimes referred to in bills tabled by individual members of parliament, more precisely in the justification of the text.[15] This seems to illustrate that the UDHR forms, in the mind of at least a number of lawmakers, a basic foundation of the national legal system and a source of inspiration for its further development.

In conclusion, it seems that the UDHR is more a political concept than a legal one. It serves as the written expression of universally accepted values and principles. Rather than to refer to an abstract notion such as 'universally accepted human rights', drafters of legal texts sometimes prefer to refer to the more tangible UDHR. When this happens in a binding legal text, such as a statute or a government decree, the UDHR nevertheless is indirectly given a binding force, albeit only in the specific area that is the object of the said legal text.

3. THE UDHR IN BELGIAN CASE LAW

For the past 60 years, Belgian case law has emphasised the non-binding nature of the UDHR. The result is that, although violations of the UDHR have occasionally been reported within the Belgian judiciary (in a wide variety of areas[16]), the UDHR's influence on judgments has remained extremely modest through the decades.

---

young people, and their federations (Article 1, §1); decree of the Flemish Government of 15 December 2000 on the quality of institutions for the social integration of persons with a handicap (Article 1, 9°).

14 *See, e.g.*, decree of the French Community of 17 December 2003 organising the neutrality of the subsidised official education and containing various measures relating to education (Article 3); decree of the German speaking Community of 27 June 2005 establishing an autonomous school of higher learning (Article 2.1).

15 A recent and speaking example is a bill submitted in the federal Senate by Madame Durant and others, aiming at the recognition of conscientious objection against the military purposes of spending of tax income as well as at the creation of a peace tax fund (*Parliamentary Documents, Senate*, 2007–2008, No. 4–258/1).

16 Mention of the UDHR has been made in cases of criminal law, as well as in cases of labour law, migration law, town planning, copyright law and education law.

The tone has been set in 1965, when the Court of Cassation (*Cour de cassation*)[17] held that the Declaration could not constitute a 'law', susceptible of being invoked in support of an argument that a judicial decision had violated the law, as the Declaration had been adopted by the General Assembly of the United Nations and had not been introduced into Belgian law. A possible violation of the UDHR could therefore not lead to the annulment of the judgment challenged before the Court.[18] The Court's case law has remained unchanged since then.[19]

For applicants before the Court of Cassation, claiming that their human rights have been violated, it will thus be necessary to invoke other instruments, in particular international human rights treaties. Among these treaties the ECHR is by far the most popular one. Other treaties, such as the two UN Covenants or the European Social Charter, are much less invoked. Of course, since these major treaties are at least indirectly based on the UDHR, one can say that there is an indirect influence of the UDHR in the case law of the Court of Cassation.

The case law of the Court of Cassation has been applied without any notable exceptions by all of the Belgian ordinary courts and tribunals. A decision of the Labour Court of appeal (*Cour du travail*) of Liège of 24 May 1983 is an excellent example. In this case, a female unemployed person had refused an offer to work in a restaurant with very early working hours, claiming that the day care centre for her child did not open until 6 a.m. The Labour Court of appeal held that the family situation invoked by the appellant did not constitute a serious obstacle to the convenient character of the work offered. It further refused to remedy the situation on the basis of Article 23 of the UDHR (right to work, in particular right to just and favourable conditions of work), as the UDHR did not have "a normative character in the Belgian internal legal order". The court thus concluded that the unemployment office had legally imposed a sanction on the appellant for

---

17 The Court of Cassation, or Supreme Court, has as its mission to supervise the correct application of the law by the Belgian courts and tribunals. To this end, it does not decide on the facts of the case, but on the law and the forms, or more generally, on the legality and the regularity of the decisions handed down by the lower courts.

18 Court of Cassation, 15 March 1965, *Pasicrisie 1965*, I, p. 734.

19 *See*, amongst others: Court of Cassation, 30 November 1976, *Pasicrisie 1977*, I, p. 356; Court of Cassation, 10 March 1980, *Pasicrisie 1980*, I, p. 844; Court of Cassation, 1 December 1983, *Pasicrisie 1984*, I, No. 185; Court of Cassation, 6 January 1993, *Pasicrisie 1993*, I, No. 9; Court of Cassation, 21 June 2000, *Pasicrisie 2000*, No. 389; Court of Cassation, 6 November 2001, *Pasicrisie 2001*, No. 603; Court of Cassation, 4 December 2001, *Pasicrisie 2001*, No. 664; Court of Cassation, 25 September 2003, *Pasicrisie 2003*, No. 454.

her unjustified refusal of a job offer.[20] It should be noted that the consequences of the lack of binding force of the UDHR were serious here, as neither the CESCR nor the European Social Charter had been introduced into Belgian law at the time of the dispute.

Turning to the administrative courts, the Council of State (*Conseil d'Etat*)[21] has also adjudicated on the legal value of the UDHR. It did so for the first time in 1966. Like the Court of Cassation, the Council of State held that the UDHR had only the value of a statement of principles which as such did not generate legal effects and which therefore could not be invoked as a ground for annulment by the Council of State.[22] This case law has not changed. The UDHR until now remains an instrument without any legally binding force.[23]

The Constitutional Court (initially called Arbitration Court, *Cour d'arbitrage*) is the last court created in Belgium. It has followed the case law of the other courts, and also considers that the UDHR has no binding force in the Belgian legal order.[24] Furthermore, it is interesting to note that the Court holds that the provisions of the Belgian Constitution have to be interpreted in the light of corresponding provisions of international human rights treaties. This has led to interpretations of the Constitution in the light of the ECHR. Until now, the Court has not referred to the UDHR for guidance.

Generally speaking, it results from the case law that parties occasionally invoke the UDHR. However, by comparison to other, binding norms of the international law of human rights, the UDHR is generally invoked as a subsidiary tool in the parties' arguments rather than as the primary basis.

As such, the position of Belgian judges with regard to the non-binding nature of the text, whose 60th birthday is being celebrated in 2008, has not changed at all. Moreover, it is only exceptionally that the UDHR is used as an interpretative tool for other human rights norms invoked before the courts, even though the UDHR forms the very foundation of the rights and

---

[20] Labour Court of appeal Liège, 24 May 1983, *Journal des tribunaux du travail* (1984), p. 330.

[21] The Council of State is the supreme administrative court. Its main task is to examine requests for annulment of acts of administrative authorities.

[22] Council of State, 9 February 1966, de Meyer, No. 11.634. *See also*, in the same period, Council of State, 16 May 1967, Van Dijck, No. 12.394; Council of State, 13 October 1967, Association 'Soeurs de la Charité de J.M.', No. 12.590.

[23] *See, e.g.*, Council of State, 1 December 1983, Baziou, No. 23.734; Council of State, 29 March 2005, X, No. 142.691; Council of State, 21 December 2005, X, No. 153.073; Council of State, 4 January 2006, X, No. 153.232.

[24] Constitutional Court, 1 December 1983, No. 82/93. In the same sense: Constitutional Court, 24 April 2008, No. 73/2008.

freedoms. The reasons for this 'non-use' of the UDHR are most likely the fact that there is an abundant case law of the European Court of Human Rights on the ECHR and, to a lesser extent, of the Human Rights Committee on the CCPR. These sources, together with the legal doctrine available, make it generally superfluous to have recourse to the UDHR in order to determine the scope of the human rights invoked before Belgian courts — they can base their interpretations on other instruments available to them.[25]

In this context, it should not come as a surprise that Belgian courts have not relied on the UDHR to establish the existence of a human rights rule of customary international law.[26]

4. RECEPTION OF THE UDHR BY THE MEDIA, POLITICAL PARTIES AND LEGAL DOCTRINE

While the UN meeting at the Palais de Chaillot was front-page news, the adoption of the UDHR at this meeting was not. Especially the Flemish press only mentioned the adoption briefly, if at all. It did not comment on the contents of the UDHR or the possible meaning thereof, only the abstentions

---

25 Among the exceptions, one must note that in several cases relating to welfare aid for aliens, Belgian courts and tribunals referred to Frédéric Sudre, who considers that poverty and social exclusion infringe human dignity, "a fundamental value solemnly proclaimed by the UDHR in its preamble and article 1" (F. SUDRE, 'La première décision "quart-monde" de la Commission européenne des droits de l'homme: une 'bavure' dans une jurisprudence dynamique. L'affaire Van Volsem c. Belgique', *RUDH* (1990) p. 349, and particularly p. 352; translated by the authors). *See, e.g.*, Labour Court of appeal Brussels, 8 June 2000, *Chroniques de droit social* (2000) p. 397.

26 Reliance on the UDHR or any other UN General Assembly resolution to establish the existence of an *opinio juris* (essential constitutive element of any rule of customary international law) must not be excluded. The International Court of Justice itself has accepted to deduce an *opinio juris* relating to the prohibition of the use of force from, among other elements, the attitude of States towards Resolution 2625 (XXV) of the General Assembly, entitled Declaration on Principles of International Law concerning Friendly Relations and Co-operation among States in accordance with the Charter of the United Nations. *See Case concerning Military and Paramilitary Activities in and against Nicaragua (Nicaragua* v. *United States)*, 27 June 1986, ICJ, Merits, *I.C.J. Reports* 1986, pp. 98–100, para. 188. For more details on that subject, *see* separate opinion of judge Lauterpacht in *South-West Africa-Voting Procedure*, 7 June 1955, ICJ, Advisory Opinion, *I.C.J. Reports 1955*, pp. 118–119; *see also* J.A. CARILLO SALCEDO, 'Les valeurs juridiques de la Déclaration dans l'ordre national', in *La Déclaration universelle des droits de l'homme — 1948–1998, Avenir d'un idéal commun*, Actes du colloque des 14–15–16 septembre 1998 à la Sorbonne (Paris) (La Documentation française, Paris, 1999) pp. 283 *et seq.*

of the Soviet bloc were pointed out.[27] The French speaking press generally covered the UN meeting more extensively, and also paid more attention to the adoption of the UDHR. It did not only mention the position of the Soviet bloc, but also elaborated on the position taken by Belgium at the General Assembly, which had emphasised the importance of this declaration.[28]

Over the years the media, in all their forms, have shown a growing interest in the UDHR. The extensive coverage of the 50th and now of the 60th anniversary of the UDHR is a good example of this growing interest. There are articles, sometimes even series, radio and television programmes devoted just to the UDHR.[29] While the media definitely point out the immense impact of the UDHR, they do remain critical. Questions about the existing violations of human rights and the universality of the UDHR are not avoided.[30]

Most political parties in Belgium state in their bye-laws that they will uphold the rights and freedoms guaranteed by the ECHR. Only the Flemish liberal party explicitly refers to the UDHR, by stating that they will not collaborate with parties or groupings that have goals contrary to the UDHR.

It should be noted that the legislation on public financial aid for political parties makes the right to receive a donation also dependent on respect for the ECHR. There is no reference to the UDHR.[31]

It took a couple of years before there was legal doctrine about the UDHR, and even then the commentary was limited. The main question discussed in the beginning concerned, not surprisingly, the legal value of the UDHR.[32]

---

27 'Het doek gevallen te Parijs', *De Nieuwe Gids*, 12 December 1948, p. 1; 'De laatste dag in het Palais de Chaillot', *Het Nieuwsblad*, 12 December 1948, p. 3; 'Liquidatie wegens bankroet', *Het Volk*, 12 December 1948, p. 3.

28 'A l'O.N.U.', *La Libre Belgique*, 11 December 1948, p. 3; 'Les dernières heures de l'O.N.U. à Paris', *La Libre Belgique*, 12 December 1948, p. 3.

29 *See, e.g.*, 'Série: Anniversaire de la Déclaration universelle des droits de l'homme', *Le Soir*, 2008; Radio 1, 10 December 1998; '50e anniversaire de la Déclaration universelle des droits de l'homme, 10 December 1998', *La Une*.

30 *E.g.*, Y. DESMET, 'Feestje', *De Morgen*, 10 December 1998, p. 2; LDV, 'Wereldleiders komen beloftes uit 1948 niet na' [World leaders do not live up to promises of 1948], *De Tijd*, 28 May 2008, p. 9.

31 *See, e.g.*, Act of 4 July 1989 on the limitation and the control of expenses for the elections of the federal assemblies, the financing and the open accounting of political parties (Articles 15*bis* and 15*ter*).

32 E. VAN BOGAERT, 'Het verwezenlijken van de rechten van de mens in het volkenrecht', *Rechtskundig Weekblad* (1950–1951) cols. 1592–1594; J. BACALU, 'Het verdragsrecht betreffende de rechten van de mens', *Rechtskundig Weekblad* (1957–1958) cols. 1327–1330.

One had to wait until 1964 for the first book dedicated to the UDHR. Verdoodt's *Naissance et signification de la Déclaration universelle des droits de l'homme* discusses in detail the preparatory work for each article of the UDHR.[33] It remains one of the most valuable tools for the interpretation of the UDHR.

Generally speaking, the legal doctrine focuses on the ECHR. Belgian key works on human rights only discuss the ECHR and refer just briefly to the UDHR, as another source of fundamental rights.[34]

5. INFLUENCE OF THE UDHR

5.1. INFLUENCE FROM A SUBSTANTIVE POINT OF VIEW

5.1.1. Completion of the List of Constitutionally Guaranteed Rights: The Case of Economic and Social Rights

Perhaps the most important and most manifest influence of the UDHR in Belgium is at the constitutional level. In fact, although the Belgian Constitution of 1831 provided for numerous fundamental rights, socio-economic rights remained unaddressed. It was not until 1988 that a proposal to incorporate socio-economic rights into the Constitution was introduced in the Senate. The author of the proposal explicitly referred to the UDHR.[35] In 1994 the proposal was adopted (after amendment) and the economic and social rights are now effectively the object of Article 23 of the Constitution. According to that provision, economic and social rights are to be guaranteed by the respective legislators, taking into account the corresponding duties. The text also contains a non-exhaustive list of these rights.

The process by which these rights were ultimately recognised was a difficult one, given the extremely divergent opinions on this issue. The idea

---

33 VERDOODT, *supra* note 7.

34 *See*, in particular, J. VELU and R. ERGEC, *La Convention européenne des droits de l'homme* (Bruylant, Brussels, 1990) No. 6; J. VANDE LANOTTE and Y. HAECK, *Handboek EVRM, Deel 1 Algemene beginselen* (Intersentia, Antwerp, 2005) pp. 4–6.

35 M. Stroobant, Proposal to revise Title II of the Constitution by the insertion of an article 24*bis* relating to the economic and social rights, *Parliamentary Documents, Senate* (1988–1989), No. 100–10/2, p. 1.

that economic, social and cultural rights were fundamentally complementary to civil and political rights, did not convince all the parties involved.[36]

From a more textual perspective, it is clear that the economic and social rights listed in the Belgian Constitution are almost identical to those contained in the UDHR and the subsequent international texts seeking to reinforce economic and social rights. Rights in the socio-economic sphere that are not recognised at the international level, such as the right to economic democracy, are not mentioned in Article 23 of the Belgian Constitution or in any other article of the Constitution.[37] The same is true for the right to international solidarity and the right to a national as well as an international social order, both of which can be considered to be essential to the effective implementation of human rights.[38]

It should perhaps be noted that Article 23 of the Constitution refers not only to the economic and social rights, but also to the corresponding duties. According to the author of the bill, the Belgian constitutional legislator thus has expressly adopted the principle of horizontal application of the said provision, thereby making not only governmental authorities responsible, but also the fellow citizens.[39]

5.1.2. Are There Still Gaps?

When one compares the rights guaranteed in the UDHR to the constitutional and legal system of protection of fundamental rights in Belgium, including the international human rights treaties to which Belgium is a party, there seem to be two areas where Belgian law has not completely implemented the principles of the UDHR.

The first area is that of asylum. Article 14 of the UDHR recognises the "right to seek and to enjoy in other countries asylum from persecution". This right is not included in any of the other lists of fundamental rights. It is true that Belgium is a party to the 1951 Convention Relating to the Status of Refugees. Like in many other Western States, however, for reasons relating to

---

36 M. STROOBANT, 'De sociale grondrechten naar Belgisch recht. Een analyse van de parlementaire werkzaamheden bij art. 23 G.W.', in M. STROOBANT (ed.), *Sociale grondrechten* (Maklu, Antwerp-Apeldoorn, 1995) pp. 64 *et seq.*

37 M. STROOBANT, 'La Déclaration universelle et les droits matériels de l'homme', in *50e Anniversaire de la Déclaration universelle des droits de l'homme: Colloque du 28 octobre 1988 au Palais d'Egmont à Bruxelles, organise par le Ministère des Affaires étrangères et le Ministère de la Justice* (Brussels, 1999) p. 15, No. 13.

38 *Ibid.*, p. 15, No. 12.

39 *Ibid.*, p. 15, No. 13.

the migration phenomenon, the Convention receives a rather timid application by the Belgian authorities.

The second area is that of fundamental duties. Article 29(1) of the UDHR states that "everyone has duties to the community in which alone the free and full development of his personality is possible". Apart from a reference to individual duties with respect to economic and social rights (see *supra*, point 5.1.1.), there is no mention of fundamental duties and responsibilities in the Constitution or elsewhere. Whether this will ever be the case, is difficult to predict. The feeling that it is not appropriate to place fundamental duties at the same level as fundamental rights, seems to be widespread.[40]

5.2. INFLUENCE FROM AN INSTITUTIONAL POINT OF VIEW

The adoption of the UDHR did not immediately inspire citizens to create NGOs in Belgium. It was only in the years 1960–1970 that most NGOs were founded. This does not mean that there is no link between the UDHR and NGOs. Major human rights NGOs in Belgium, like Amnesty International (Flemish and francophone sections), *Ligue des Droits de l'Homme* and *Liga voor Mensenrechten*, all refer to the UDHR as one of the reference instruments, on which they base themselves to take a stand.

On the public side, one has to regret that there is no Belgian national human rights institution that fulfils the criteria mentioned in the so-called Paris Principles. In April 2006, however, several NGOs submitted an elaborated proposal for the creation of a Belgian Commission for Fundamental Rights. The UDHR again served as a reference instrument: the draft stated that the Commission's mission would be to protect and promote fundamental rights, as defined in the UDHR and the international instruments arising from this.[41] Unfortunately, things do not seem to have changed since then. The complicated institutional structure of the country, with various entities having competences in the field of human rights, probably explains the difficulty in setting up a national human rights institution.

---

40 For a critical view on fundamental duties, consult, among others, G. HAARSCHER, 'La limitation des droits de l'homme ou les "devoirs de l'homme": boîte de Pandore ?', in *50e Anniversaire de la Déclaration universelle des droits de l'homme*, *supra* note 37, pp. 21–25.

41 <mensenrechten.be/word/Belgische_Commissie_Grondrechten-ontwerp.doc>, p. 7.

6. CONCLUDING REMARKS

The UDHR has been a significant milestone in the development of human rights. It has been the starting point for the internationalisation of human rights: universal and regional instruments have followed the UDHR, and they often explicitly refer to the UDHR as their main source of inspiration. Supranational control mechanisms have been created, in order to make it possible to hold States accountable. These developments at the international level have in turn influenced the creation of standards at the national level and — although not in Belgium — the setting up of domestic control institutions.

It is fair to say that Belgium, an active member of the assemblies that produced the text of the UDHR, is a country where human rights are generally respected. However, international concern over what happens in Belgium shows that the situation is not on all points as it could be, and that at least the spirit, if not even the text, of the UDHR is sometimes lost out of sight. It may suffice to refer to some of the recurring themes that can be found in the concluding observations of the UN treaty bodies, released after an examination of a periodic report submitted by Belgium: the treatment of asylum seekers and, more generally, migrants;[42] a refusal to officially recognise minorities within its territory;[43] prison conditions and treatment of prisoners;[44] various forms of discrimination, in particular racial discrimination[45] and discrimination of women on the labour market.[46]

So, the work is never finished. Threats to human rights can come from all corners, and may require a swift response. The UDHR continues to have as strong a message as it had in 1948.

---

[42] Committee against Torture, Conclusions and recommendations (2003), UN Doc. CAT/C/CR/30/6, para. 5(c) to (f); Human Rights Committee, Concluding observations (2004), UN Doc. CCPR/CO/81/BEL, paras. 14, 17 and 22; Committee on the Elimination of Racial Discrimination, Concluding observations (2008), UN Doc. CERD/C/BEL/CO/15, paras. 17 and 18.

[43] Committee on Economic, Social and Cultural Rights, Concluding observations (2008), UN Doc. E/C.12/BEL/CO/3, para. 23; Committee on the Elimination of Racial Discrimination, *supra* note 42, para. 19.

[44] Committee against Torture, *supra* note 42, para. 5(i) and (j); Human Rights Committee, *supra* note 42, paras. 16 and 19.

[45] Human Rights Committee, *supra* note 42, para. 27; Committee on Economic, Social and Cultural Rights, *supra* note 43, para. 14; Committee on the Elimination of Racial Discrimination, *supra* note 42, paras. 11, 13, 14 and 16.

[46] Committee on the Elimination of Discrimination against Women, Concluding comments (2002), UN Doc. A/57/39, para. 161; Committee on Economic, Social and Cultural Rights, *supra* note 43, para. 15.

3. FRANCE: THE ORIGINS, WITH THE PROSPECT OF INCREASING EFFECT

Florence Benoît-Rohmer

1. INTRODUCTION

The French like to remind people that it was in Paris, at the Palais Chaillot, that the Universal Declaration of Human Rights was voted on and adopted on 10 December 1948 and they recall with pride the role played by René Cassin alongside Eleanor Roosevelt in drafting what he called the new *Table de la loi humaine*. Cassin brought a universalist vision of human rights to the Universal Declaration, one rooted in the Enlightenment and enshrined by the French Declaration of the Rights of Man and the Citizen of 1789.

Yet the impact of the Universal Declaration is rather limited in France. Lip-service is paid to it by diplomats to justify French foreign policy, even if hard-nosed commercial realism often carries the day over humanist ideals. It is also often invoked by NGOs working to advance human rights. But at a national level, France prefers to make reference to the French Declaration of the Rights of Man and the Preamble to the 1946 Constitution which adds a great many economic and social rights to the earlier declaration. These two seminal documents in the French history of human rights are today fully integrated into positive law through the jurisprudence of the Constitutional Council and constitute a catalogue of rights whose content matches in large part the rights guaranteed by the Universal Declaration. This is also the reason why French courts are reluctant to consider the Universal Declaration a customary source of law and apply it as such.

2. RENÉ CASSIN'S INFLUENCE ON THE UNIVERSAL DECLARATION OF HUMAN RIGHTS

Reaching a consensus on the text of the Declaration was no mean feat. Indeed, the West and the Socialist bloc had to agree upon a common declaration, and the resulting text was one of synthesis and compromise. Amongst those who influenced the drafting of the Declaration was Frenchman René Cassin, a French government advisor to the Human Rights Commission, who was made vice-chairman at the request of chairwoman

Eleanor Roosevelt.[1] While it was Roosevelt who insisted upon the inclusion of the principle of men and women's equality in the Declaration and who gave it its clarity and strength, Cassin also contributed greatly to its drafting, even if the ideas — sometimes utopian, it must be admitted — he put forth did not all make it into the final text.

Eleanor Roosevelt entrusted Cassin with the task of drawing up a draft declaration, which he undertook based upon the documents prepared by the United Nations secretariat under the Canadian, professor Humphrey. This draft declaration was to be the basis for discussion until a final version could be adopted.

René Cassin was awarded the Nobel Peace Prize not only for his contribution to drafting the Universal Declaration but also for his qualities as a diplomat. He had to be a master strategist — not least when dealing with his own countrymen — to reach the compromises necessary to make the Declaration acceptable to all UN member states. Cassin put it this way: "It was essential to consider both the aim, to be sought without concession nor capitulation in the interest of mankind, and the need to move step by step, taking into account present or future resistance". The greatest debt we owe him is for his success in gaining acceptance for the idea of the universality of human rights, which consisted in recognising rights common to all human beings. To Cassin's mind, it was not a question of imposing a one-size-fits-all model and a uniform vision of the rights asserted but simply to make visible, beyond any cultural differences, rights that all could recognise as universal. What must be emphasised, said Cassin with respect to the Declaration, "is the worldwide nature of the principles laid out for the first time in the history of the world by an international organisation". René Cassin also managed to ensure that at the end of the negotiations the title of the Declaration was changed to 'universal' from 'international', a title favoured by the Anglo-Saxons who would appear to have been trying to limit its scope.

Although it was more difficult — and against Mrs. Roosevelt's wishes — Cassin also pushed through the idea of the indivisibility of human rights thanks to strong support from Socialist countries which considered traditional rights and freedoms to be tainted by abstract formalism. Only after long and animated debate did economic and social rights come to be considered as fundamental ones. But Cassin took care to keep the concessions made to states

---

1 AGI M., *René Cassin, Prix Nobel de la Paix, 1887–1975: père de la Déclaration universelle des droits de l'homme*, Ed. Perrin, 1998, and E. PATEYRON, *La contribution française à la rédaction de la Déclaration universelle des droits de l'homme: René Cassin et la Commission consultative des droits de l'homme*, la Documentation française, 1998.

demanding mainly proclamations of economic and social rights for obviously ideological reasons to a minimum. He sought to emphasise that by proclaiming them in the same declaration as civil and political rights, economic and social ones would be irrevocably linked to them.

Cassin's great regret was to have failed to convince the UN member states to create a means to collectively guarantee the human rights proclaimed in the Universal Declaration. He would have wanted the Declaration to be more than a simple moral document and for it to include commitments on the part of its signatory states, most of all to subscribe to a control process or even the creation of an international court. To him it appeared difficult to speak of the universality of human rights while leaving their protection as the sole responsibility of sovereign states. This objective has now been reached at a regional level through the framework of the European Convention on Human Rights.

However, at the United Nations the states defended the principle of sovereignty in their affairs tooth-and-nail and refused. Not even France shared its illustrious representative's point of view. France planned on retaining its sovereignty and was mistrustful of the international oversight that would have allowed the UN to get involved in its domestic affairs. Furthermore, did France, which considered itself the home of human rights, need to be told how to behave on this subject?

This attitude towards international control bodies lasted quite some time. For instance, it was only in 1974 that France ratified the European Convention on Human Rights (despite having signed it in 1950) and in 1981 that the right to individual complaint was recognized. This suspicion was found at the national level, as the Constitution at the time did not allow for any challenge to the constitutionality of laws, not even as to whether they infringed upon fundamental rights. In a broader sense, the colonial powers feared the Declaration might lead to demands from colonised or decolonizing countries and that too broad an application of the Universal Declaration of Human Rights might put them in a difficult position with regard to the anti-colonialist majority of the UN and be turned against them. In addition to the difficulty related to decolonisation, the Cold War was already well underway and the liberal powers feared falling victim to hostile campaigns and being challenged before the UN whereas the Communist dictatorships had the means of propaganda and action at their disposal that allowed them to better defend themselves.

3. IDEAS BORROWED FROM THE FRENCH CONCEPT OF HUMAN RIGHTS

The Universal Declaration of 1948 only raises principles proclaimed at a national level to a higher one and extends a broad historical movement that started with the Virginia Bill of Rights and the American Declaration of Independence of 1776 but also with the French Declaration of the Rights of Man and the Citizen of 1789. With regard to the question of universalism, the Universal Declaration follows the same path as the French Declaration of the Rights of Man and the Citizen and openly draws from it. The idea of the universality of human rights grew and spread in France during the Enlightenment and was reflected in the French Declaration of the Rights of Man and the Citizen of 1789 which by its abstract nature espoused a universalist vision from the beginning. In this, it differs from both the English declarations of the 17th century and the American Declaration of Independence of 1776 whose primary aim was to affirm the independence of British colonies and to create the United States of America. Their similar wording attests to the French Declaration's obvious influence on the Universal Declaration. Where Article 1 of the French Declaration states that "all men are born free and equal in rights", the first article of the 1948 text echoes this phrase with: "All human beings are born free and equal in dignity and rights. They are endowed with reason and conscience and should act towards one another in a spirit of brotherhood".

The influence of the French Declaration does not stop there. The French Declaration states in its Preamble that "ignorance, neglect, or contempt of the rights of man are the sole cause of public calamities and of the corruption of governments". This founding principle appears almost verbatim in the 1948 text which states that "disregard and contempt for human rights have resulted in barbarous acts which have outraged the conscience of mankind". The Universal Declaration's list of civil and political rights bears a strong resemblance to that of the French Declaration, even if some of these rights were formulated differently as a compromise between liberal and Marxist states.

Finally, if Cassin took care to extend human rights to encompass economic and social ones, it also reflects the evolution of French thinking as laid out by the Council of Resistance during the Second World War and in the Preamble of the 1946 Constitution. The latter document, influenced by the ruling Socialists, completes the list of civil and political rights from the Declaration of the Rights of Man with a series of economic and social ones.

4. FADING MORAL AUTHORITY

At the time it was adopted, the Universal Declaration garnered a great deal of attention in France. The press picked up the story and a great many articles were devoted to it, all the more so as it was adopted during a session of the UN General Assembly held in Paris. Some saw this as a tribute to France as the country of human rights.

The UDHR was even published in the Official Journal of the French Republic, something normally reserved for treaties. But its scope is foremost a moral one and is based on the authority granted by the signature of the great majority of states in the world.

It underlies French diplomacy even if state interest, trade and security concerns often take precedence. Furthermore, France has gone on to sign many UN conventions based on the Universal Declaration of Human Rights and human rights in the world remain a constant political concern. The Declaration drives French diplomacy. Today, social rights are emphasised such as the right to freedom from hunger and the right to exist. The Declaration is often cited by NGOs advocating human rights in condemning violation of these rights in France and abroad.

Still, it plays a minor role in France, if only because it is not legally binding and because the substance of the rights set out therein had already been broadly integrated into French positive law. This is why the current French Constitution makes absolutely no reference to the Universal Declaration of Human Rights. The authors of the current French Constitution of 1958 did debate whether its Preamble should refer to the Universal Declaration of 1948 but René Cassin himself, vice-president of the *Conseil d'Etat* at the time, opposed such a move. He won his colleagues over by pointing to the fact the Declaration did not meet the requirement of being legally binding and that its discrepancies with the Declaration of the Rights of Man and the Preamble of the 1946 Constitution that the current Constitution refers to ran the risk of muddying Council of State jurisprudence.

The Constitution's authors thus chose to make reference to the Declaration of the Rights of Man and the Citizen of 1789 which enshrined civil and political rights and to the Preamble of the 1946 Constitution which added "economic, political and social principles", "especially necessary in our time". The 1958 Constitution fully assumes the mantle of this legacy which was honoured by the Constitutional Council and given its scope through the interpretation of these two documents and by strengthening the effectiveness of the rights they enshrine. French positive law thus includes a large body of law that very closely matches the Universal Declaration of Human Rights. But it is more precise and better suited to French specificities and thus simpler to apply.

Moreover, the Universal Declaration is now overshadowed by the European Convention on Human Rights which has pride of place in France by virtue of its implementation of a legal framework for imposing sanctions upon states which do not fulfil their obligations. No state appreciates the bad publicity of having the European Court of Human Rights rule against it, and France is no exception to this rule. If the Convention is frequently invoked in France, one must not forget that it was drawn up with the aim of rendering effective in Europe the rights and principles laid out in the Universal Declaration of Human Rights. The Convention's Preamble — referring to the Universal Declaration from its first paragraph — states that the signatories are "resolved ... to take the first steps for the collective enforcement of certain of the Rights stated in the Universal Declaration".

5. A DISPUTED LEGAL SCOPE

The Declaration is not considered to be an international treaty concluded by France and its legal value is not considered any differently from any of the other declarative resolutions of the United Nations General Assembly. Yet this does not mean that the Declaration's provisions are inapplicable in domestic law. Everything depends on the courts in question. For some, the provisions have no legal value and cannot be invoked before them, for others they sometimes have value as a customary rule or as a general legal principle recognised by civilised nations or as a general principle of international law or as rules of public international law. The bevy of legal definitions used by judges is due to the fact that even when a national judge accepts the application of a customary norm, he is reluctant to expressly recognise it as such.

The practice of administrative courts is well established however: the Declaration cannot be invoked before an administrative judge. This conclusion comes from the Council of State judgment under the regime of the 1946 Constitution.[2] The Council of State was ruling on whether, in order to annul an election, the petitioner could invoke the violation of the Universal Declaration of Human Rights through the ordinance of 21 April 1944 which declared certain individuals ineligible by reason of their acts of collaboration with the enemy during the war. The High Court confirmed that the Declaration is not legally binding because it is not genuinely an international

---

2 *Nolay elections*, 18 April 1951, dig. p. 189.

treaty. The Council of State thus rejected the use of the Universal Declaration of Human Rights as a source of customary law.

The Council of State's thinking remains unchanged under the current Constitution and the phrase that justifies this is now well worn: "the UDHR's publication in the Official Journal dated February 1949 does not in itself confer upon the Declaration the same status as that of treaties or international accords which have, being ratified and approved regularly by virtue of article 55 of the Constitution, an authority greater than national laws".[3] In other judgments, the Council of State has simply stated that it will not discuss the Universal Declaration.

To temper this harsh reasoning, the Council of State occasionally mentions the Declaration in its rulings,[4] but this practice does not affect the Council's position with regard to the principle that the Declaration has no legal value.

The position of the other courts is much less clear. Generally speaking, the Declaration is deemed applicable by the Court of Cassation. While the social chamber ruled on 22 January 1998 that "the UDHR proclaims general objectives towards which States must strive … it does not create rights that may be invoked before national courts",[5] the criminal chamber recognises the inalienable nature of certain rights, as in the *Gallien* judgment of 29 January 1997 where it recognised the applicability of Article 22 of the Declaration concerning the right to benefit from social security.[6] The commercial chamber shares this attitude.[7] The Court of Cassation has started a journey down the path of progressively integrating the principles of the Universal Declaration into French positive law by first transforming them into customary norms.

---

3 CE 3 décembre 2003, M. X, req. No. 250140.

4 As in the aforementioned judgment of 2003; CE 21 December 1990, *Confédération nationale des associations familiales catholiques et autres*, rec. p. 369; CE Ass. 5 November 2004, *Union des organisations de fonctionnaires et assimilés*.

5 *M/X. c. Caisse d'allocations familiales de la Seine Saint Denis et autres*, Bull. soc. 1998 No. 31 p. 23.

6 Bull. crim. 1997, No. 40, p. 115.

7 Judgment of 26 May 1998, *Société anonyme du château de la Douve*, Bull. civ. No. 168 p. 136.

6. CONCLUSIONS

The legal value of the Universal Declaration is questioned because it only states general aims which are not precise enough to have judicial effects before national courts. However, the UDHR is well known in France and it is frequently invoked by NGOs in order to denounce international as well as national human rights violations. France also feels proud because of the influence exercised by the French Declaration of the Rights of Man and the Citizen adopted in 1789 on the content of the Universal Declaration. The latter has in France an unquestionable symbolic value, as is shown by the public reading that occurred at the French national celebration of 14 July 2008.

4. THE UNITED KINGDOM: DEVELOPING A HUMAN RIGHTS CULTURE

Rory O'Connell
Tom Obokata

1. GENESIS

The United Kingdom's involvement with the Universal Declaration of Human Rights (UDHR) goes back to the discussions during the war against the Axis powers.[1] Human rights were discussed by popular writers[2] and Cambridge professor Hersch Lauterpacht published the first legal discussion on an international bill of rights.[3] In January 1942, Prime Minister Churchill agreed with President Roosevelt a "Declaration by United Nations", undertaking to "preserve human rights and justice in their own lands as well as in other lands".[4]

With the creation of the United Nations, the UK participated in the debates about the drafting of the UDHR. The UK representatives often did not obtain what they wanted in the negotiations. The initial UK position was that the UN should adopt a detailed convention instead of or alongside the Declaration, which would spell out exact legal obligations for states.[5] This position did not prevail. In other ways, the British view was not successfully pursued. The UK at one point proposed a draft Declaration of Rights, very different from the one we have: it set out only nine rights, all classic civil and political rights. It did not provide for social, economic, cultural or minority rights. As Simpson notes, this proposal would have merely packaged for export the civil and political liberties traditionally professed in the UK.[6] The draft did not find favour with the other state representatives. Throughout the

---

1 B. SIMPSON, *Human Rights and the End of Empire* (Oxford University Press, Oxford, 2001) Ch. 4.

2 H.G. WELLS, *The Rights of Man* (Penguin, Harmondsworth, 1940).

3 H. LAUTERPACHT, *An International Bill of the Rights of Man* (Columbia UP, New York, 1945).

4 SIMPSON, *supra* note 1, p. 183.

5 J. MORSINK, *The Universal Declaration of Human Rights: Origins, Drafting and Intent* (University of Pennsylvania Press, Philadelphia, 2000) p. 8.

6 SIMPSON, *supra* note 1, pp. 399, 417.

negotiations the UK representatives tried to limit the scope of the 'new' social and economic rights.[7] Ironically these were the representatives of the same British government that was constructing the Welfare State within the UK. The UK representatives were more successful in arguing against a clause on minority rights, whilst constructively playing a role in inserting the term 'rule of law' in the Preamble and in stressing the importance of education in spreading the values of the UDHR.[8]

The discussions on the Declaration do not seem to have ignited public debate within the United Kingdom. The archives of the main newspaper for the years 1948–1950 record only twelve mentions of the UDHR, two of which were letters from individuals about the 'closed shop' and freedom of association. Meanwhile in Parliament, Prime Minister Clement Attlee stressed the difference between a non-binding declaration and a legally binding convention: whilst the UK subscribed "generally to the ideal embodied in the Declaration", there was no obligation to enact legislation for either the UK or the colonies. Indeed the Prime Minister believed that human rights were better respected in the UK and the Commonwealth than elsewhere.[9] When pressed about Article 24's mention of "equal pay", the Prime Minister stressed that one always had to consider duties along with rights and that no state could realise these rights immediately.[10]

If there are any themes emerging from this early history of Britain's involvement with the UDHR, then it is the disfavour generally shown to social, economic, cultural and minority rights, and a preference for legally binding mechanisms. In many ways, the 1950 European Convention on Human Rights (ECHR) is more in tune with these sentiments than is the Declaration.[11]

2. THE DECLARATION IN THE POLITICAL AND ADMINISTRATIVE WORLD

The United Kingdom's political architecture has become more complicated in recent years, with the arrival of devolution in 1998. The central Parliament and Executive based in Westminster, are now complemented by devolved

---

7 MORSINK, *supra* note 5, pp. 192, 225.

8 *Ibid.*, pp. 312, 323.

9 Hansard, 18 January 1949, Column 17.

10 *Ibid.*

11 On the role of the UK during the drafting of the ECHR, *see* SIMPSON, *supra* note 1.

assemblies with varying competences in Wales, Scotland and Northern Ireland. The UK later described the devolution process (carried through in the year marking the fiftieth anniversary of the UDHR) as implementing the right to self-determination as recognised in the common Article 1 of the International Covenant on Civil and Political Rights 1966 and the International Covenant on Economic, Social and Cultural Rights 1966.[12]

Though none of the major political parties reference the UDHR in their formal constitutions, politicians do refer to it. Members of Parliament have referred to the UDHR when addressing such diverse topics as the slave trade,[13] forced marriage,[14] the death penalty in Singapore,[15] and other matters. Outside of Parliament too, politicians have invoked human rights. In relation to anti-terror measures implemented since 11 September 2001, David Blunkett, then the Secretary of State for the Home Department, was reported as stating that:

> "The universal declaration of human rights ... recognises that the most fundamental human rights are those of life, liberty and security of person. This implies for me that people who are killed or maimed, bereaved or put in fear by terrorists are stripped, cruelly and arbitrarily, of their rights and that security and safety is the underpinning raison d'etre of government."[16]

These examples show that politicians refer to the UDHR to highlight pertinent policy issues in the United Kingdom.[17] It is ironic, or even hypocritical, that the UK Government is often blamed for its failure to abide by the UDHR and other human rights instruments,[18] and yet it is using the

---

[12] 999 UNTS 171, 993 UNTS 3. UK, *State Party Report*, UN Doc. CCPR/C/UK/99/5, 11 April 2000, paras. 9–17.

[13] Baroness Verma, Hansard 28 June 2007: Column 787, <www.publications.parliament.uk/pa/ld200607/ldhansrd/text/70628-0014.htm>, visited on 11 May 2008.

[14] Lord Sheikh, Hansard, 26 January 2007: Column 1331, <www.publications.parliament.uk/pa/ld200607/ldhansrd/text/70126-0002.htm>, visited on 11 May 2008.

[15] Margaret Beckett, 18 January 2007: Column 1333W, <www.parliament.the-stationery-office.co.uk/pa/cm200607/cmhansrd/cm070118/text/70118w0022.htm>, visited on 11 May 2008.

[16] 'Blunkett Seeks New Debate on Anti-Terrorism', *The Guardian*, 8 March 2004.

[17] *See also* the speeches given by Tony Blair, the former Prime Minister on security in the UK: 'Blair Calls for New Law to Tackle Rouge States', *The Times*, 5 March 2004, and by Lord Goldsmith, the former Attorney-General of the United Kingdom in relation to UK's approach to terrorism: 'Attorney General's Speech in Full', *The Times*, 10 May 2006.

[18] In December 2004, the House of Lords ruled that a significant aspect of the UK's anti-terrorism strategy was incompatible with the ECHR: *A* v. *Secretary of State for the Home Department* [2004] UKHL 56, referring also to Articles 1 and 2 UDHR in para. 58.

rhetoric of the UDHR to justify some of the measures, particularly in relation to terrorism and asylum, which have enormous impact on the protection and promotion of human rights.

The UDHR receives little direct reference in legislation. According to the official Statute Law Database, the term does not appear in any legislation.[19] However, arguably, the spirit of the UDHR animates much of legislative policy, even if there are few references. The fiftieth anniversary of the Declaration coincided with an impressive array of national and international measures: the UK ratified the Council of Europe Framework Convention on National Minorities, the Statute of the International Criminal Court, and Additional Protocols I and II to the Geneva Conventions, while the Good Friday/Belfast Agreement seemed to offer an end to the Northern Ireland conflict.

Most significantly the UK incorporated the ECHR into domestic law via the Human Rights Act (HRA) 1998. Given the dualist nature of the UK legal system, this was necessary to give effect to the Convention rights in domestic law. In some ways the HRA indicates the UK preference for the ECHR over the UDHR: the Government White Paper introducing the Human Rights Bill makes no mention of the UDHR.[20] Understandably the failure to incorporate other human rights treaties means that for UK public authorities 'human rights' may be limited to 'Convention rights'. The Human Rights section in the Ministry of Justice concentrates on the ECHR,[21] as does the Human Rights Unit within the Northern Ireland public service.[22] One struggles to find any reference to the UDHR on the official Government information website, DirectGov.

However there is more to this story. A leading academic, Francesca Klug, has suggested the HRA must be seen as a bill of rights which takes seriously Article 29 of the UDHR.[23] Article 29 introduces a 'communitarian' theme in the protection of human rights, referring to the duties owed to the

---

19 *See* <www.statutelaw.gov.uk>, visited on 10 May 2008.

20 UK Government, *Rights Brought Home: The Human Rights Bill* (London: Stationary Office, 1997) Cm 3782, <www.archive.official-documents.co.uk/document/hoffice/rights/contents.htm>, visited on 12 May 2008.

21 *See* <www.justice.gov.uk/whatwedo/humanrights.htm>, visited on 15 May 2008.

22 *See* <www.ofmdfmni.gov.uk/index/equality/human-rights.htm>, visited on 15 May 2008. The heading "Where your rights come from" leads to the answer: statute law, common law created by judges and EU law; there is *no* mention of the Universal Declaration or the treaties sponsored by the United Nations.

23 F. KLUG, 'The Human Rights Act — A "Third Way" or "Third Wave" Bill of Rights', 4 *E.H.R.L.R.* (2001) p. 361.

community, and the need to allow rights to be restricted to meet certain "just requirements" in a "democratic society". Klug believes that the HRA represents a distinctive way of respecting that communitarian dimension. Klug believes the HRA may foster what some call a culture of human rights, a culture which is neatly encapsulated in Article 28 of the UDHR: "Everyone is entitled to a social and international order in which the rights and freedoms set forth in this Declaration can be fully realized."

This idea of a human rights culture has other bases in the UK. The devolution legislation does not refer to the UDHR, but the legislation makes it clear the devolved authorities must not act against the UK's "international obligations",[24] which presumably includes human rights obligations in unincorporated treaties and international customary law.[25] There is strong institutional support within Parliament for a human rights culture in the form of the specialist Joint Select Committee on Human Rights.[26] Its remit includes all issues of human rights within the UK (though it cannot look at individual cases), and is not limited to the ECHR rights. The Committee has addressed a much wider range of rights than those found in the ECHR and regularly references the UDHR and major human rights treaties.[27] Other Parliamentary Committees occasionally make use of the UDHR: the Select Committee on International Development has urged the Government to promote the right to food as found in Article 25 of the UDHR.[28]

Further, the period since 1998 has seen a plethora of statutory scrutiny bodies, including several human rights institutions. As part of the Northern Ireland peace process, the Northern Ireland Act 1998 created the UK's first Human Rights Commission (NIHRC). Since then, many scrutiny bodies or

---

24 Scotland Act, 1998, section 35; Government of Wales Act, 1998, section 108; Northern Ireland Act, 1998, section 26.

25 S. LIVINGSTONE, 'The Northern Ireland Human Rights Commission', 22 *Fordham International Law Journal* (1999) p. 1465.

26 The Committee's home page is found at <www.parliament.uk/parliamentary_committees/joint_committee_on_human_rights.cfm>, visited on 13 May 2008.

27 Joint Committee on Human Rights, Sixth Report: The case for a Human Rights Commission (UK: Parliament, 2002–2003) HL 67 / HC489, <www.publications.parliament.uk/pa/jt200203/jtselect/jtrights/67/6702.htm>, visited on 12 May 2008; Joint Committee on Human Rights, Twenty-first Report: The International Covenant on Economic, Social and Cultural Rights (UK: Parliament, 2003–2004) HL 183/HC 1188, <www.parliament.the-stationery-office.com/pa/jt200304/jtselect/jtrights/183/183.pdf>, visited on 13 May 2008.

28 Select Committee on International Development, *International Development — Third Report of 2002–2003*, para. 169. <www.publications.parliament.uk/pa/cm200203/cmselect/cmintdev/116/11611.htm#a62>, visited on 15 May 2008.

'champions'[29] for particular groups have been created. Britain now has an Equality and Human Rights Commission (EHRC),[30] while Scotland has a Scottish Commission for Human Rights.[31] Importantly all these commissions are charged with protecting and promoting human rights beyond those in the ECHR, thus offering the possibility that all the human rights in the international Bill of Rights will be promoted.[32]

This is an appropriate point at which to note the significance of the UDHR in the context of Northern Ireland. Northern Ireland enjoyed a period of devolution in the United Kingdom from 1921 to 1972, an experiment which ended with three decades of violent conflict. At several points during the first experience of devolution, a minority member of the Northern Ireland Parliament (in 1964 and 1968) submitted a motion to introduce a Human Rights Bill in Northern Ireland, presciently believing this was necessary to deal with human rights violations and discrimination in Northern Ireland. These proposals came to naught, and today human rights are seen as central to any political settlement in Northern Ireland.[33] The NIHRC's predecessor proposed a Bill of Rights for Britain, or failing that for Northern Ireland.[34] The 1998 Good Friday/Belfast Agreement refers to an idiosyncratic list of rights, not based on the UDHR and not treating social and economic rights as rights,[35] while both the Agreement and the Northern Ireland Act 1998 envisage a possible Bill of Rights for Northern Ireland. Under the 2006 St. Andrew's Agreement, the UK Government established a consultative forum on this Bill of Rights.[36] This Forum has now produced recommendations embracing many rights beyond the ECHR, and put those

---

29 Examples include the Children's Commissioners found in Wales, Northern Ireland, England and Scotland. Wales has a Commissioner for Older People, while Northern Ireland plans to introduce one.

30 Created by the Equality Act, 2006, its website is at <www.equalityhumanrights.com>, visited on 12 May 2008.

31 Scottish Commission for Human Rights Act 2006.

32 Scottish Commission for Human Rights Act 2006, Section 2; Equality Act, 2006, section 8; Northern Ireland Act, 1998, sections 68, 69. *See* their website <www.nihrc.org>, visited on 13 May 2008.

33 B. DICKSON, 'The Protection of Human Rights: Lessons from Northern Ireland', 3 *E.H.R.L.R.* (2000) pp. 213–226.

34 SACHR: Standing Advisory Committee on Human Rights, *The Protection of Human Rights by Law in Northern Ireland* (HMSO, Belfast, 1977) Cmd. 7009, <cain.ulst.ac.uk/hmso/cmd7009.htm>, visited on 15 May 2008.

35 Agreement Reached in the Multi-Party Talks 1998, <www.nio.gov.uk/agreement.pdf>, visited on 15 May 2008.

36 *See* the website <www.billofrightsforum.org/>, visited on 15 May 2008.

recommendations to the NIHRC.[37] The NIHRC will present its own recommendations to the relevant minister and is expected to do so on the symbolic date of 10 December 2008, the sixtieth anniversary of the UDHR.

Ironically this development occurs as the rest of the United Kingdom has begun its own debate on a "British statement of values" and a possible "British (or UK) Bill of Rights".[38] The Leader of the Opposition called for such a debate in 2006, though his speech seemed to imply the ECHR went too far in protecting human rights.[39] The early Government contributions to this debate do not base themselves on the UDHR, but on more local concerns, and place a particular emphasis on civic responsibilities alongside rights.[40]

3. THE DECLARATION IN THE LEGAL WORLD

In the United Kingdom, the key instrument for protection and promotion of human rights is the ECHR. The HRA gave this instrument further effect and has allowed victims of human rights violations to assert their rights before domestic courts and tribunals. As a result, the ECHR has become more important in the UK as noted above. However, it is fair to state simultaneously that the UDHR has played, and continues to play an important role in the legal field in the United Kingdom. This may be evidenced in, among others, references made to the UDHR before the UK domestic courts and tribunals. A non-exhaustive list of references to the UDHR include Article 2,[41] Article 3,[42] Article 5,[43] Article 7,[44] Article 11,[45]

---

37 Bill of Rights Forum, *Final Report* (Bill of Rights Forum, Belfast, 2008), <www.billofrightsforum.org/borf_final_report.pdf>, visited on 15 May 2008.

38 Secretary of State for Justice and the Lord Chancellor, *Governance of Britain* (London: TSO, 2007) CM 7170, <governance.justice.gov.uk/>, visited on 12 May 2008.

39 D. CAMERON, 'Balancing freedom and security — A modern British Bill of Rights', 26 June 2006, <www.conservatives.com/tile.do?def=webcameron.story.page&obj_id=130572&speeches=1>, last visited on 19 May 2008.

40 J. STRAW, 'Modernising the Magna Carta' (2008) 2008/02/13, <www.justice.gov.uk/news/sp130208a.htm>, visited on 13 May 2008.

41 *Derbyshire and others* v. *St Helens Metropolitan Borough Council (Equal Opportunities Commission and others intervening)*, [2007] UKHL 16 (House of Lords), and *Islam* v. *Secretary of State for the Home Department*, [1999] 2 A.C. 629 (House of Lords).

42 *The Queen on the Application of Corner House Research and Campaign Against Arms Trade* v. *The Director of the Serious Fraud Office, BAE Systems Plc*, [2008] EWHC 714 (High Court).

43 *Regina* v. *Bow Street Metropolitan Stipendiary Magistrate And Others, Ex Parte Pinochet (No. 3)*, [2000] 1 A.C. 147 (House of Lords).

Article 12,[46] Article 16,[47] Article 17,[48] Article 23,[49] Article 27[50] and Article 29.[51] Of particular relevance is Article 14, which touches upon the right to seek asylum.[52] The UK is a popular destination for many refugees and asylum seekers from various parts of the world, and immigration has consistently been a priority for the UK Government. This is reflected in the abundance of case law on refugee and asylum issues, and lawyers and judges have made occasional references to Article 14. This is particularly important as the right to seek asylum is not enshrined in the ECHR.

UK courts and tribunals have acknowledged that the UDHR does not create any legal obligations. Thus, in *Alexander* v *Halifax Plc (Statement of Claim)*,[53] when Alexander appealed against an order striking out his claim that the Halifax Plc had, by constant harassment, breached the Article 25 UDHR right to earn living, the court held that the UDHR was not legally enforceable. Other cases have confirmed this,[54] in line with the accepted legal nature of the UDHR within the United Nations and Member States. This does not mean, however, that the UDHR is irrelevant within the UK legal system. For one, despite the fact that the UDHR has no legal force in the UK, not only

---

44 *Akbarali Appellant* v. *Brent London Borough Council Respondents*, [1983] 2 A.C. 309 (House of Lords).

45 *Waddington* v. *Miah Alias Ullah*, [1974] 1 W.L.R. 683 (House of Lords).

46 *Douglas* v. *Hello! Ltd*, [2001] F.S.R. 40 (Court of Appeal), and *Kay* v. *London Borough of Lambeth*, [2006] L. & T.R. 8 (House of Lords).

47 *J. and Another Appellants* v. *C. and Others Respondents*, [1970] A.C. 668 (House of Lords).

48 *Harrow LBC* v. *Qazi*, [2004] 1 P. & C.R. 19 (House of Lords).

49 *Krayem* v. *Secretary of State for the Home Department*, [2003] EWCA Civ 649 (Court of Appeal), *Langston* v. *Amalgamated Union of Engineering Workers and Another (No. 2) (National Industrial Relations Court)*, [1974] I.C.R. 510 (National Industrial Relations Court).

50 *Whaley* v. *Lord Advocate* 2004 S.C. 78 (Court of Sessions, Scotland).

51 *Brown* v. *Procurator Fiscal, Dunfermline*, [2001] R.T.R. 11 (Privy Council, Scotland).

52 *Regina (European Roma Rights Centre and Others)* v. *Immigration Officer at Prague Airport and Another (United Nations High Commissioner for Refugees intervening)*, [2005] 2 A.C. 1 (House of Lords), *The Queen on the Application of Yusif Adam* v. *Secretary of State for the Home Department* (High Court), [2004] EWHC 354 (High Court), *R. (on the application of Q)* v. *Secretary of State for the Home Department*, [2003] H.L.R. 57 (Court of Appeal), *Regina (Yogathas)* v. *Secretary of State for the Home Department*, [2003] 1 A.C. 920 (House of Lords), and *Revenko* v. *Secretary of State for the Home Department*, [2001] QB 601 (Court of Appeal).

53 1999 WL 33232675 (High Court).

54 *Carlos Caeiro (Amexa De Carril)* v. *The Commissioners for Her Majesty's Revenue*, 2008 WL 371136 (VAT and Duties Tribunal), *Januzi* v. *Secretary of State for the Home Department*, [2006] 2 A.C. 426 (House of Lords), *R (On the Application of European Roma Rights Centre)* v. *Immigration Officer, Prague Airport*, *supra* note 52, and *Boyce and Another* v. *The Queen*, [2004] 3 W.L.R. 786 (Privy Council).

judges of the lower courts, but also senior judges in the Court of Appeal, the House of Lords and the Privy Council continue to refer to this instrument.[55] Further, the courts and tribunals have acknowledged that the UDHR was the forerunner of the ECHR.[56] All of these seem to show that the UDHR serves as a guiding principle when the UK courts and tribunals examine human rights related cases.

Another interesting point is that while the UDHR itself has no legal effect in domestic law, some aspects of it may be regarded as legally binding. For instance, the prohibition on torture under the Convention against Torture and Other Cruel, Inhuman or Degrading Treatment or Punishments 1984[57] was incorporated into UK domestic law through the Criminal Justice Act 1988.[58] Therefore, Article 5 of the UDHR can be regarded as binding in the UK. In addition, other norms are regarded as binding by virtue of their status as constituting customary international law or *jus cogens*. In accordance with Article 53 of the *Vienna Convention on the Law of Treaties 1969*,[59] *jus cogens* is a peremptory norm of general international law "accepted and recognized by the international community of States as a whole as a norm from which no derogation is permitted and which can be modified only by a subsequent norm of general international law having the same character". This suggests that the *jus cogens* norms have a higher status in international law. Some of these *jus cogens* norms which are pertinent to human rights include, but are not limited to, the right to life, prohibition on racial discrimination, torture, slavery and other international crimes[60] and all of these are enshrined in the UDHR. One of the influential scholars of international law in the UK, professor Ian Brownlie, sums up the legal nature of the UDHR in the following terms:

---

55 *See* various cases in footnotes.

56 *R. (on the application of Uttley)* v. *Secretary of State for the Home Department*, [2004] UKHL 38 (House of Lords), *Harrow LBC* v. *Qazi*, [2003] UKHL 43 (House of Lords), *R.* v. *Lambert*, [2001] H.R.L.R. 55 (House of Lords), *Judicial Committee of the Privy Council*, [2001] H.R.L.R. 9, *John Junior Higgs and Another. Appellants* v. *Minister of National Security and Others*, [2000] 2 A.C. 228 (Privy Council), and *Attorney-General and Another Appellants* v. *Antigua Times Ltd. Respondent*, [1976] A.C. 16 (Privy Council).

57 1465 UNTS 85.

58 Section 134.

59 1155 UNTS 331.

60 A. ORAKHELASHVILI, *Peremptory Norms in International Law* (Oxford University Press, Oxford, 2006) p. 54. In relation to torture, the House of Lords stipulated that Member States (of the Torture Convention) are *required* to do more than eschewing the practice. One example given was to reject "fruits of torture inflicted (e.g. confessions) in breach of international law" *A and Others* v. *Secretary of State for the Home Department*, [2005] UKHL 71, para. 34.

> "The Declaration is not a legal instrument, and some of its provisions ... could hardly be said to represent legal rules. On the other hand, some of its provisions either constitute general principles of law or represent elementary considerations of humanity ... No doubt there is an area of ambiguity, but the indirect legal effect of the Declaration is not to be underestimated, and it is frequently regarded as a part of the 'law of the United Nations'."[61]

While most of these norms relate to civil and political rights, this does not exclude the possibility of economic and social rights acquiring the *jus cogens* status.[62] It is worth noting in this regard that in *M, A, MM* v *Her Majesty's Treasury*,[63] the Administrative Court held that "peremptory provisions of jus cogens include Article 17(2) of the UDHR which provides that 'no one shall be arbitrarily deprived of his property'". This is an innovative interpretation of non-binding instruments such as the UDHR, and this practice should be encouraged by the judiciary to provide protection of economic and social rights in the UK. Protection of economic and social rights is not rigorously pursued in the UK partly because the ECHR itself does not touch upon these rights,[64] and the UK is not a party to the Revised European Social Charter 1996.[65] In order to facilitate the protection of economic and social rights, then, reference to the International Covenant on Economic, Social and Cultural Rights 1966[66] as well as the UDHR has at least a symbolic significance.

In addition to the judiciary, lawyers (hence clients they represent) in the UK use the UDHR to develop their legal arguments. For instance, in *EB (Ethiopia)* v *Secretary of State for the Home Department*,[67] the lawyers for the applicant argued that the deprivation of nationality of the applicant was contrary to Article 15 of the UDHR.[68] In *Regina* v *F*,[69] it was argued on behalf

---

61 I. BROWNLIE, *Principles of Public International Law* (6th ed.) (Oxford University Press, Oxford, 2003) pp. 534–535.

62 ORAKHELASHVILI, *supra* note 60, p. 60.

63 2006 WL 2929334 (High Court).

64 Except for protection of property and the right to education under Protocol No. 1 to the ECHR, ETS No. 9.

65 ETS No. 163.

66 *Supra*, note 12.

67 [2007] EWCA Civ 809 (Court of Appeal).

68 Para. 29. See also *Huang* v. *Secretary of State for the Home Department*, [2007] 2 A.C. 167 (House of Lords), in which the lawyers referred to Article 16(3) of the UDHR in talking about private and family life.

69 [2007] Q.B. 960 (Court of Appeal).

of a client that Article 21 of the UDHR recognised the right of every citizen to take part in the conduct of public affairs through freely chosen representatives.[70] What is evident here is that the alleged victims of human rights violations are relying on the UDHR to rectify their situations. In summary, it seems reasonable to argue that the value of the UDHR has been widely recognised within the UK legal world.

4. THE DECLARATION AND CIVIL SOCIETY

As noted above, while the UDHR is recognised in the administrative, political and legal world in the UK, in order for its value to be realised, the UDHR must be communicated effectively to the UK general public. The role of the media becomes important in this regard, and the UDHR has been referred to by the UK media on numerous occasions. To begin with, the UDHR is often referred to when the UK media report on foreign human rights issues. For instance, when an Afghan national faced the death penalty because of his conversion to Christianity, a reference was made to Article 18 of the UDHR.[71] In October 2007, the *Guardian* newspaper reported on the plight of a young Palestinian trapped in Gaza who could not continue his education, which is a breach of a provision of the UDHR.[72] However, the UDHR is also mentioned in the UK context. In August 2008, a Catholic bishop, in referring to the right to life under the UDHR, was reported to have left the Amnesty International over its change of policy on abortion.[73] In reporting on poverty in various parts of the UK, the *Guardian* newspaper mentioned Article 27 on the right to an adequate standard of living.[74] The UK media do not refer to the UDHR in every single human rights related case they report. Therefore, their occasional references to it suggest that the media is aware of its existence and uses it as guidance to elucidate human rights law and disseminate information to the general public.

Similar to the media, the role played by NGOs has been crucial in raising awareness of the UDHR in the UK. NGOs use the UDHR when campaigning for protection and promotion of various human rights, and many of them

---

70 *See also Huang* v. *Secretary of State for the Home Department, supra* note 68.

71 'Afghan Faces Death Penalty for Christian Faith', *The Times*, 20 March 2006.

72 'Palestinian Students Trapped in Gaza', *The Guardian*, 5 October 2007.

73 'Second Catholic Bishop Leaves Amnesty over its Backing for Abortion', *The Times*, 28 August 2007.

74 'Abolish Slums', *The Guardian*, 15 February 2006.

have the actual document on their website. Some organisations have a special relationship with the UDHR. A good example is the well known human rights organisation, Amnesty International. It was established as a result of a campaign launched by a British lawyer Peter Benenson who instituted 'Appeal for Amnesty 1961'. As a symbolic gesture, the first Amnesty candle was lit in the church of St-Martin-in-the-Fields in London on 10 December 1961, commonly known as the Human Rights Day held annually to honour the adoption of the UDHR. According to its vision statement, Amnesty International strives to help everyone to enjoy all human rights enshrined in the UDHR.[75] Another prominent NGO, Article 19, takes its name from Article 19 of the UDHR and is devoted to the protection of the freedom of expression.[76] Other UK based NGOs including Anti-Slavery International, Committee on the Administration of Justice, Islamic Human Rights Commission, Oxfam, Refugee Council, Save the Children UK, and Youth for Human Rights UK make reference to the UDHR to implement their mandates of activities. It may be argued, then, that the UDHR serves as an inspiration for many of these organisations.

However, the extent to which the UDHR is recognised by the general public in reality is difficult to measure.[77] In theory at least, public authorities should have some familiarity with the Declaration as they are under international law duties to protect and promote human rights. There is some doubt, however, whether or not information is reaching out to the wider general public. Human rights abuses occur on a daily basis in various parts of the UK, and this perhaps shows a lack of awareness or education on the part of the general public and a failure of the UK government to promote and protect human rights in accordance with the UDHR and other relevant human right instruments. However, it is simultaneously important to recognise that the topic of human rights has become an important component of education, and this is particularly evident at the university level. Many of the leading universities now offer specialised modules on human rights, and this certainly helps raise awareness of the UDHR. Another important point to note is the existence of student clubs and societies which focus on human rights, including the student sections of Amnesty International and other human rights related organisations. They play an important part in educating

---

75 Amnesty International Annual Report 2007.

76 <www.article19.org/about/index.html>, visited on 19 May 2008.

77 The Anglican churches have endorsed the Universal Declaration at their 1998 Lambeth Conference: Affirmation and Adoption of the United Nations Universal Declaration of Human Rights.

fellow students and reaching out to their local communities. If the human rights education can start earlier, then this will help the UK general public to become aware of the UDHR and the importance of human rights.

5. UK AND THE WIDER WORLD

Finally we turn to the role of the UK and the UDHR in the wider world. This external dimension is critical: the Declaration is of universal rights, and several provisions in the Declaration recognise this: the Preamble, Article 2 (second sentence), Article 22, and Article 28. Unsurprisingly the UK officials were wary of the Declaration's implications for the colonies, even to the extent of querying the suitability of the use of the secret ballot in certain colonies.[78]

The UK largely withdrew from its colonies in the decades following the Second World War. As part of this process, many colonies drafted their own constitutional documents and bills of rights. In other cases though, UK officials and experts wielded significant influence in the drafting and formal approval of constitutional documents.[79] The advice from these officials and experts was rarely based on the UDHR, and tended to be based on perceptions about local needs or the British experience of rights. Across many colonies, this resulted in Bills of Rights that focused on civil and political rights to the exclusion of social and economic rights, a situation some ex-colonies have now seen fit to rectify.[80]

Post decolonisation, the UK plays a role in promoting human rights throughout the world. The Department for International Development (DFID) supports human rights initiatives across the globe,[81] whilst the Foreign and Commonwealth Office (FCO) adopted an 'ethical' foreign policy in 1997. According to its website the FCO bases itself on the UDHR,[82] and every year produces an Annual Report on Human Rights which makes

---

78 MORSINK, *supra* note 5, pp. 59, 99–101.

79 Though a formality, the 1982 Canadian Charter of Rights and Freedoms had to be passed as an Act of the UK Parliament: Canada Act, 1982.

80 C. PARKINSON, *Bills of Rights and Decolonization: The Emergence of Domestic Human Rights Instruments in Britain's Overseas Territories* (Oxford University Press, Oxford, 2007).

81 *See* <www.dfid.gov.uk/>, visited on 15 May 2008.

82 *See* <www.fco.gov.uk/en/fco-in-action/conflict/human-rights/>, visited on 15 May 2008.

copious reference to the UDHR.[83] These reports are subject to scrutiny by the Parliamentary Foreign Affairs Committee.[84] There is an unsettling aspect to the ethical foreign policy, with human rights language being used, in varying degrees, and sometimes retrospectively, to justify UK military intervention in Kosovo, Sierra Leone, Afghanistan and Iraq.[85]

6. CONCLUSION: FROM 1948 TO 2008

In 1948, the UK had a world wide empire, no domestic bill of rights, and a rapidly developing Welfare State. On the sixtieth anniversary of the Declaration, ironically, its armed forces are deployed in at least two countries formerly occupied during the days of Empire (Afghanistan, Iraq). The UK's story of the Declaration goes beyond this: it has taken important steps to make human rights legally enforceable domestically, and to promote human rights abroad.

Yet there remains a reluctance to treat social and economic concerns as rights rather than interests, thus undermining the interdependence and indivisibility of all human rights. Further, public policy in relation to national security and immigration frequently seems to undermine human rights. As the UK's human rights culture continues to develop, with new institutions and possibly new Bills of Rights, it will be fascinating to see how they cope with these challenges.

---

83 *See* <www.fco.gov.uk/en/about-the-fco/publications/annual-reports/human-rights-report/>, visited on 15 May 2008.

84 *See* <www.parliament.uk/facom/>, visited on 15 May 2008.

85 *See* Prime Minister's speech: 'Doctrine of the International Community', at the Economic Club, Chicago, <www.number-10.gov.uk/output/Page1297.asp>, visited on 15 May 2008; The Iraq Dossier of 24 September 2002, <www.number-10.gov.uk/output/Page271.asp>, visited on 15 May 2008.

PART II

EUROPEAN STATES THAT WERE MEMBERS OF THE UN BY THE TIME OF THE ADOPTION OF THE UDHR

5. DENMARK: A DOCUMENT OF IDEOLOGICAL IMPORTANCE

Eva Maria Lassen[1]

1. INTRODUCTION

When one evaluates the contribution of Demark to the development of the Universal Declaration, one would have to begin with acknowledging its largest contribution in the domain of the rights of women, driven by the tenacity and energy of its representative. The reception of the document in society was originally modest when the some politicians had reservations but those who were most affected welcomed the progress after World War II. The newspapers carried information that was selective and newsworthy to a society who initially believed that there was little new in the Declaration. I also examine the role the Declaration has played in the courts and legislature and end with a few concluding remarks.

2. BRINGING HUMAN RIGHTS TO THE WOMEN OF THE WORLD

> "Unforgettable was a conversation I had with the prince of Yemen … I asked him if the women of his country were taught to read and write. He looked at me arrogantly and replied with an air of surprise: 'Who on earth would they write to?'"[2]

This incident, as recollected by Bodil Begtrup, the Danish Chairman of the UN Commission on the Status of Women, took place at a dinner in connection with one of the numerous UN meetings in 1946. It was not the only time she was to find in the UN such ambiance which ridiculed the rights of women. But the women of the world had found in Bodil Begtrup someone

---

1 I am grateful for comments from Mu'ayyad Mehyar and Joergen Lassen. Translations from Danish are mine.

2 B. BEGTRUP, *Kvinde i et verdenssamfund: Erindringer af Bodil Begtrup* [Woman in the International Community: The memoirs of Bodil Begtrup] (Centrum, Denmark, 1986) p. 68.

who did not take lightly to women's equal rights being scorned, and who fought for these rights with defiant dedication.

From 1938 until the outbreak of the War, Begtrup had been part of the Danish delegation to the League of Nations. In Denmark she had contributed significantly to the improvement of the social and economic conditions of women and children, not least children's health, in her capacity of vice-president of the Danish National Council of Women from 1931 (she became its president in 1946). Begtrup served as advisory member of the Danish delegation to the United Nations General Assembly from 1946 to 1953. In 1946, she was personally appointed by the UN to the Sub-Commission on the Status of Women, where she served as chair. In the autumn of 1948, she was elected to and became the vice-president of the UN General Assembly's Third Committee, which was given the task of scrutinizing the draft Declaration prior to its presentation to the General Assembly.

She was to be extraordinarily successful in advancing the incorporation of women's rights in the Universal Declaration. The words of Johannes Morsink, one of the leading experts of the history of the United Nations summarise her role best:

> "From the point of view of the rights of women the Declaration is a remarkably progressive document. The credit for this goes to the effective women's lobby, made up of the representatives of the Commission on the Status of Women and the delegates from communist countries. I would single out Mrs. Bodil Begtrup, the Danish representative and the chair of the Commission, as the single most important individual in this respect."[3]

Thus, it is an often overlooked fact that as far as women's rights in the Universal Declaration are concerned, Begtrup was more progressive than Eleanor Roosevelt, who according to Morsink had a "blind spot" when it came to women's equal rights.[4]

The Women's Sub-Commission prepared the United Nations' work with the equality of men and women, and presented a report to the Human Rights Commission in 1946. In Begtrup's view, the Human Rights Commission "discussed it in a way which to us was rather unsatisfactory ... It was a strange and bitter experience to see the report being scorned in the eyes of the public. It was, after all, created by a group which represented half of the

---

3 J. MORSINK, 'Women's Rights in the Universal Declaration', 13:2 *Human Rights Quarterly* (May 1991) pp. 229–256, at p. 255.

4 *Ibid.*, p. 256.

world's population".[5] Discontent with this reception, Begtrup managed to bypass the Human Rights Commission, ensuring that the Women's Sub-Commission obtained direct access to the Economic and Social Council. Accordingly, the report was presented to the Council in the spring of 1946. The report emphasised political rights (including equal voting rights), civil rights (including women's equal marital rights), social and economic rights, and equal right to education.[6] In addition, the report suggested guidelines for implementation — the result of which eventually was a UN Secretariat for women's rights. In October 1946, and as a result of Begtrup's efforts, the Women's Sub-Commission became an independent Commission.[7] As Chair of the Commission and later as vice-chair of the Third Committee, Begtrup aimed at having the above-mentioned rights for women reflected in the Universal Declaration; among the issues which turned out particularly controversial can be mentioned the question of the abolition of polygamy and the right to equal pay.[8]

Begtrup also fought successfully to make the Universal Declaration gender neutral. This came across very strongly in her intense attempts at making Article 1 inclusive of women. Again, in the words of Morsink, "[i]t seems that the absence of sexism in the Universal Declaration is primarily due to the aggressive lobbying of Mrs. Begtrup and the steady pressure of the Soviet delegation".[9] One of the founding fathers of the Universal Declaration, John Humphrey, said with some admiration of the Women's Commission: "More perhaps than any other United Nations body the delegates to the Commission on the Status of Women were personally committed to its objectives ... they acted as a kind of lobby for the women of the world".[10] However, Humphrey did not feel quite at ease with Begtrup and describes her as somewhat "formidable and unbending".[11] He also did not like the rather unorthodox way in which she sidestepped the Human Rights Commission, and was less

---

5 BEGTRUP, *supra* note 2, pp. 62–63.

6 *Ibid.*, pp. 64–65.

7 *Ibid.*, p. 66.

8 *See* MORSINK, *supra* note 3, pp. 244–250.

9 *Ibid.*, p. 231.

10 J. HUMPHREY, *Human Rights and the United Nations: A Great Adventure* (Translantic Publishers, USA, 1984) p. 30.

11 *Ibid.*, p. 31.

than pleased when she was elected to the Third Committee and became the vice-chair.[12]

Begtrup took part in the First General Assembly in Paris in 1946 as advisory member of the Danish delegation. Working with the Women's Report, she had conceived the idea that the Danish delegation propose that UN member states must grant women the same political rights as men. As a result, the First General Assembly passed a resolution which asked member states to "adopt measures necessary to fulfil the purposes and aims of the Charter by granting women the same political rights as men".[13] It is the only time that Denmark alone, and successfully at that, has made a proposal to the United Nations General Assembly. In addition, Begtrup proposed that future applicant states would be considered disqualified as members of the United Nations if they did not comply with these rights. This more radical proposal was not accepted.[14]

Denmark attempted to leave its mark on other areas as well. It was in favour of a covenant which provided a right of petition to individuals and groups.[15] Denmark was also active in endeavours to include specific social and economic rights in the Declaration, for instance related to the right to work, an issue where Denmark joined forces with the Soviet bloc and several Latin American countries.[16] Finally, it should be mentioned that Denmark pushed for the protection of minority rights, including educational rights of national minorities, an issue spurred by problems related to Danish and German minorities living at either side of the Danish-German border.[17]

Meanwhile, on 11 December 1948, the Danish Foreign Minister arrived back in Copenhagen after having attended the United Nations General Assembly in Paris. He was met by a number of journalists, to whom he expressed a certain disappointment with the General Assembly sessions as a whole. However, he continued: "One of the positive achievements is the great Declaration of human rights. The Declaration has developed the ideas of

---

12 He confided his disapproval of this election to his diary. *On the Edge of Greatness: The Diaries of John Humphrey, First Director of the United Nations Division of Human Rights*, Vol. 1, 1948–1949, edited by A.J. HOBBINS (McGill University Libraries, Montreal, 1994) pp. 49-50, 57-58.

13 MORSINK, *supra* note 3, p. 230.

14 BEGTRUP, *supra* note 2, p. 67.

15 M.A. GLENDON, *A World Made New: Eleanor Roosevelt and the Universal Declaration of Human Rights* (Random House Trade Paperback Edition, New York, 2001) p. 197.

16 *Ibid.*, p. 158.

17 *Ibid.*, p. 160, and J. MORSINK, 'Cultural Genocide, the Universal Declaration, and Minority Rights', 21:2 *Human Rights Quarterly* (1999) pp. 1009–1060, at p. 1045.

1789, and it has established a set of standards which all countries of the World must strive to realise".[18]

When meeting the press on her arrival to Denmark a few days later, Begtrup proclaimed the Universal Declaration of Human Rights "one of the greatest social documents of its time", and expressed the hope that an international tribunal would be established with a mandate to monitor the implementation of the Declaration.[19]

3. THE DECLARATION'S RECEPTION AMONG THE DANES

3.1. THE DECLARATION IN DANISH NEWSPAPERS

Denmark's adoption of the Universal Declaration of Human Rights in 1948 took place without much prior or subsequent debate in Denmark. Substantial parts of the limited debate that did take place were carried out in the national newspapers, which quite diligently followed the sessions of the UN General Assembly in Paris. In what follows, some of the leading national newspapers' coverage of the debates on the Universal Declaration in the General Assembly will be discussed.

The correspondent Erhardt Larsen of the national newspaper *Berlingske Tidende*, an organ of the Conservative Party, was not attracted by the idea of a Universal Declaration of Human Rights. Wondering how such a document could ever become common to the entire world, he went on:

> "Should a piece of paper really have the power to obtain for the individual who lives in the East the freedoms enjoyed by individuals in the West? Or is it conceivable that we in the West would be content with the freedoms and rights enjoyed by individuals in the East? With the broad text and the nice list of the many rights so much desired by human beings, there will be ample opportunity for numerous transgressions and disappointments. One should have been satisfied with the short biblical commandment about loving your neighbour as a guideline for interaction amongst human beings and amongst nations."[20]

---

18 *Politiken*, 'Gustav Rasmussen om UNO's Samling', 12 December 1948.

19 *E.g.*, *Nationaltidende*, 15 December 1948.

20 *Berlingske Tidende*, 'Tegn paa voksende Respekt i Kreml for Vestens Styrke', 2 December 1948.

Other newspapers had a more positive — albeit still cautious — attitude to the Declaration. An editorial in *Politiken*, an organ of *Det Radikale Venstre,* a liberal central party, aired the following view:

> "The Declaration of Human Rights and the Convention on Genocide were adopted within the last few days. It is all very well that this big Assembly, representing virtually the entire world, has agreed on these truly noble principles that are embodied in the Declaration and the Convention respectively. There is no reason to underestimate this achievement. But it would have done no harm had we been able to transmit a little of this noble agreement to the more practical matters of the day's work."[21]

The editorial has a strongly critical attitude to the Soviet Union and ends with the following pragmatic wish: "Let us rejoice in these human rights and let us hope that they will be interpreted in the right way".[22] As this editorial shows, the newspaper, although in favour of human rights, was sceptical towards the process leading to the creation of the Declaration as well as its future implementation. This is also expressed in the following article, referring to General Assembly debates on the Universal Declaration: "Of course it is bound to turn out a strangely inanimate affair when 58 nations, each with their cultural, social and ideological backgrounds toil to reach a common result".[23]

The most unconditional support of the Universal Declaration can be found in *Information*, a newspaper started by the Resistance during the Second World War. The newspaper dedicated a series of articles to the background and progress of the General Assembly in Paris. The foreign correspondent Erling Bjoel considered the Universal Declaration "an important tool to promote human rights",[24] and he expressed the following view:

> "Cynics may claim that this Declaration contains but empty phrases of propaganda which a majority of the members of the United Nations will not observe ... But this is a narrow-minded and Western European view point. The great majority of the World's population lacks even the most basic notions of

21 *Politiken*, 'Editorial', 13 December 1948.

22 *Ibid.*

23 *Politiken*, 'Hitlers myrderier skal ikke gentages', 10 December 1948.

24 *Information*, 'Kronikken', 13 December 1948.

> what democracy is and of the political objectives they may have to make life more tolerable for themselves."[25]

The fact that the human rights debates in the UN were coloured by the emerging Cold War is strongly reflected in the Danish newspapers, which emphasised the different approaches to human rights of the Western democracies and the Soviet Union respectively. The newspapers made no attempts at being neutral in the conflict: with the exception of the Communist newspaper *Land og Folk*, the organ of the Danish Communist Party, they were clearly on the side of the Western countries, to which Denmark belonged. Illustrative is *Politiken*'s coverage of a speech by the Russian Foreign Minister delivered in the General Assembly. The speech was, in the newspaper's opinion, illustrative of a "propaganda, which is as monotone as that of Goebbels".[26] The dichotomy between the East and the West comes across particularly strongly in the two newspapers *Socialdemokraten* — the newspaper of the Social Democratic Party, the then largest party in Denmark — and *Land og Folk*, the former representing the most fierce opponent to the Soviet regime, the latter officially endorsing the politics of the Soviet Union. Significantly, the different newspapers only pay little attention to the fact that the Soviet Union and Denmark were fighting side by side on several occasions in UN debates on the Universal Declaration.

It is to a certain extent characteristic of the Danish media's coverage of the Universal Declaration that the importance of human rights to the individual and the world's population — in other words the Declaration's substance — is played down in favour of the exposure of the confrontation between the Soviet and the Western blocs.

Moreover, it is characteristic that the Danish newspapers mostly perceived the values, the legal order and the guarantees of the individual underpinning human rights as something which other nations rather than Denmark were in need of (not least nations under the domination of the Soviet Union).[27] This idea is undoubtedly linked to the fact that the creation of human rights as international law first and foremost was a response to massive human rights violations — violations of which Denmark largely had been spared. In addition the idea prevailed in Danish society that the existing democracy in Denmark was sound and already included what many countries still lacked, including human rights.

---

25 *Information*, 'UN vedtager sit Magna Carta', 11 December 1948.

26 *Politiken*, 'Editorial', 13 December 1948.

27 *See, e.g., idem.*

3.2. THE IMPACT OF THE DECLARATION ON DANISH SOCIETY IN THE POST-WAR YEARS

Within the Kingdom of Denmark, an immediate and concrete outcome of Begtrup's accomplishments in the United Nations was that Greenland's women, who did not have voting rights at the time, by her interference and insistence were granted equal voting rights in April 1948 (Greenland was a Danish colony until 1953).[28] In this way, Denmark was complying with its own proposal to the UN, namely the requirement of women's equal political rights.

Mainly through the channels of the Danish National Council of Women, Begtrup made sure that Danish women were kept up-to-date about the developments related to women taking place at the international scene, and a few initiatives to improve women's equality in Denmark in the late 1940s were influenced by the work carried out by the UN.[29]

Generally speaking, however, the view that the Universal Declaration is something that is particularly relevant to *the rest of the world* can be observed among Danish politicians and lawyers of the time. Thus many Danish lawyers in the immediate post-war years were of the opinion that human rights, on the one hand, were something that came "from the outside" and, on the other hand, were "obvious" in Denmark: the Universal Declaration of Human Rights proclaimed a legal system and values that already existed in Denmark.[30] In addition, a number of Danish lawyers were far from impressed by the Declaration as a legal document and referred to it in less than flattering terms. In a textbook aimed at law students, a professor of constitutional law called the Declaration a "peculiar mishmash".[31]

There was one group of Danes, however, who looked at the Declaration with interest and acclaim: the Jewish community. In comparison with other countries occupied by Nazi Germany, the majority of the Danish population had not suffered greatly during the Second World War, and after the war the general perception, as mentioned above, was that the existing Danish democracy was not in desperate need of a universal human rights declaration. But the Danish Jews, who had felt the evils of Nazism more deeply than the

---

28 BEGTRUP, *supra* note 2, p. 69. D. BENTZON GOLDSCHMIDT, *Oprindelige folks rettigheder i Norden* (Det Danske Center for Menneskerettigheder, Copenhagen, 1994) p. 117.

29 J. LARSEN, 'Snapshot of Danish State Feminism 1947', <www.kvinfo.dk>.

30 M. NOERREGAARD, *Menneskerettighedskonventionens anvendelse mellem private* (Forlaget Thomson Copenhagen, 2004) pp. 79 *et seq.*

31 P. ANDERSEN, *Dansk Statsforfatningsret* (Gyldendal, Copenhagen, 1954) p. 596.

Danish population at large, welcomed human rights and the Universal Declaration with open arms.

Historically, anti-Semitism existed in Denmark at a much smaller scale than in most other European countries, and in 1943 the majority of the Danish Jews managed to flee to Sweden, thus escaping the Holocaust. Even so — and closely linked to loyalty with world Jewry — human rights found a more whole-hearted support in the small Jewish community, *Mosaisk Troessamfund*, than in Danish society at large. The Danish-Jewish community's enthusiasm for human rights is reflected in a series of articles in *Mosaisk Troessamfund*'s monthly community magazine, in the second half of the 1940s. It is interesting that, in contrast to articles in the Danish newspapers, human rights are mostly looked upon *independently* of the Cold War: in articles found in this magazine, *Joedisk samfund* (Jewish Society), focus is on the substance of human rights and on their importance to individuals, in particular Jews, around the world.[32]

As early as 1946 — shortly after the Jewish magazine was re-established after the war — the Chief Rabbi underlined the importance of human rights to the peaceful development of the world.[33] In an article from June 1949, the Universal Declaration is hailed as "the first attempt in history to introduce a moral constitution of all countries". The article stresses human rights as being of "incalculable importance to Jews, now and in the future", and notices with pride Jewish efforts to create legally binding human rights.[34] The positive Jewish attitude to international human rights can also be traced in an article from December 1948, where World Jewish Congress, WJC, is commended for its work for the development of international law, including human rights.[35] In the following decades, the Jewish community conveyed its public support of human rights in different ways, not least in connection with the protection of refugees and their reception in Danish society. For instance, *Mosaisk Troessamfund* was co-founder of the Danish Refugee Council in 1957, and several prominent members of the community has since then played significant roles in this organisation.

Today, *Mosaisk Troessamfund* still regularly expresses its support of human rights, but it is noteworthy that it is not the Universal Declaration but

32 The monthly magazine of the Jewish community, *Joedisk Familieblad*, had been closed down during the German occupation to be re-established as *Joedisk Samfund* shortly after the war.

33 M. FRIEDIGER, 'Verdenskonferencen af 'The Coucil of Christians and Jews'", *Joedisk Samfund*, 15 September 1946, pp. 1–2.

34 'Mrs. Roosevelt og "Menneskerettighederne"', by TM. *Joedisk Samfund*, June 1950, pp. 4–5.

35 E. HILB, 'Hvad er WJC?', *Joedisk Samfund*, December 1948, pp. 8–9.

the European Convention on Human Rights which is referred to in the Statutes of the religious community: "The community supports the principles of the protection of human rights and fundamental freedoms, as enshrined in the European Human Rights Convention, striving for tolerance and understanding between people and combating xenophobia, racism and anti-Semitism".

This shift from the Universal Declaration to the European Convention on Human Rights is in accordance with the development in Danish society at large, where the European Convention came to play a major role. In 1953, Denmark ratified the European Convention on Human Rights, which was incorporated into Danish law in 1992. Denmark played an active part in the creation of the European Convention (and Court), and since its early days politicians as well as lawyers have focused on this convention — and eventually on other international conventions — rather than on the Universal Declaration as far as human rights in Denmark are concerned.

4. THE DECLARATION AND THE DANISH CONSTITUTION

In the immediate post-war years, the Danish politicians prepared a revision of the Danish Constitution, and it is evident from the debates carried out in parliamentary committees that the lawmakers did not think of the Universal Declaration as relevant in this context. Accordingly, the amended Constitution of 1953 does not reflect the Universal Declaration and contains only a few more human rights than the old constitution, which primarily included the classical civil and political rights.

One 'new' right which found its way into the amended constitution was the right to work (§75). Further more, §71 of the amended constitution states that: "[P]ersonal liberty shall be inviolable. No Danish subject shall, in any manner whatsoever, be deprived of his liberty because of his political or religious convictions or because of his descent". This paragraph was new, but as it had already been suggested in 1939, when an amendment of the constitution was unsuccessfully proposed, it was de-linked from the Universal Declaration. The same applies to §70 of the amended constitution. The text of this paragraph was part of the old constitution, but the amended constitution added 'descent' to the paragraph, which now reads: "No person shall by reason of his creed or descent be deprived of access to the full enjoyment of civic and political rights, nor shall he escape compliance with any common civic duty for such reasons". The reference to descent was the result of the persecution of the Danish Jews during the war.[36]

These and a few other prominent novelties notwithstanding the predominant attitude among politicians at the time was that *historical continuity* held the key to a successful development of Danish democracy, and hence they faithfully remained within the rather narrow framework of the constitutional tradition going back to 1849.[37] The Danish constitution has not been amended since 1953. With regular intervals, it is being debated, inside as well as outside of Parliament, whether there is a need for a constitutional revision. In these debates, it is often being argued that the constitution needs to reflect the whole human rights catalogue. Most recently, the director of the EU Agency for Fundamental Rights, Morten Kjaerum, advocated this view.[38] However, there are no signs in the present political climate that the very complicated process of revising the constitution will be initiated in the foreseeable future.

5. IN COURT

Judgments of the Danish courts rarely refer to the Universal Declaration. In recent years the Declaration is mentioned in two court cases. It is not a coincidence that both relate to the question of freedom of association: the Universal Declaration contains something that the European Convention on Human Rights lacks, namely an absolute prohibition of forced membership of an association in Article 20(2).[39] The first case concerned the question of compulsory payment to the relief fund of the Danish Bar Association, *Advokatsamfundet*. The Bar Association brought the case before the High Court. The defendant stated that Danish law "must be interpreted in light of the Universal Declaration of Human Rights ... which in Article 20.2 contains

---

36 S. LAGOUTTE and E.M. LASSEN, 'Menneskerettigheder i forfatningen. Billeder af fransk og dansk forfatningshistorie', in M. KJÆRUM et al. (eds), *Grundloven og menneskerettigheder i et dansk og europæisk perspektiv* (Jurist- og Økonomiforbundets Forlag, Copenhagen 1997) pp. 88-89.

37 For a more developed discussion of the limited expansion of the rights catalogue in the amended constitution of 1953, see *ibid.*, pp. 86–90.

38 Interview with M. Kjaerum in *Jyllandsposten* on the Danish Constitution Day, 5 June 2008.

39 In comparison, the European Convention on Human Rights states that "Everyone has the right to freedom of peaceful assembly and to freedom of association with others, including the right to form and to join trade unions for the protection of his interests" (Article 11(1)).

an absolute prohibition on forced membership of the associations. Rule 20.2 is a statement of intent, and must weigh heavily in the interpretation of the law". However, in its judgment the High Court did not mention the Universal Declaration among the relevant international legal sources, and sustained the claim of the Bar Association. The defendant appealed the case to the Supreme Court, which upheld the judgment of the High Court.[40]

In the second case, a case concerning compulsory membership of a trade union was brought before the City Court. The plaintiff had unsuccessfully attempted to resign his membership of a trade union and brought an action against the union. The claim of the plaintiff was not sustained by the City Court. He appealed the case to the High Court, which referred to Article 20 of the Declaration in a judgment that sustained the claim of the plaintiff.[41]

6. THE DECLARATION IN THE DANISH PARLIAMENT

Only one Danish law refers explicitly to the Universal Declaration, namely the Founding Law of the Danish Center for International Studies and Human Rights of 2002. The law refers to the mandate of the Danish Institute for Human Rights as a national human rights institution, and this mandate not surprisingly refers to the Universal Declaration.[42]

Explanatory remarks to Bills sometimes refer to the Universal Declaration. In recent years, this has, for instance, been the case with the Minister of Justice's explanatory remarks accompanying a proposal to amend, amongst others, the Danish Penal Code (as part of the effort to strengthen the combat against terrorism).[43] The Universal Declaration is regularly referred to in parliamentary debates and in accounts to Parliament. To give an example, in 2001 the Foreign Minister, explaining ways in which Danish foreign policy aims at promoting religious freedom in the world, stated that the Declaration

---

[40] 'Advokat pålagt at betale medlemsbidrag m.v. til Advokatsamfundet. Søgsmålskompetencen vedrørende bidrag til samfundets erstatningsfond'. *UfR ONLINE, U.2003,380H (Oestre Landsrets dom den 17. april 2000 (15. afd); H.D. 26 November 2002 i sag 206/2000 (2.afd.).*

[41] 'Klausul om manglende adgang til udmeldelse af fagforening tilsidesat efter aftalelovens §36', *UfR ONLINE, U.2005.16770 (Oe.L.D. 25 Februar 2005 i anke 9, afd. nr B–1255–04; Københavns Byrets dom 5. april 2004).*

[42] 'Lov 2002–06–06 No 411 om etablering af Dansk Center for Internationale Studier og Menneskerettigheder', *WESTLAW DANMARK L20002411.*

[43] 'Betænkning over Forslag til lov om ændring af straffeloven, retsplejeloven og forskellige andre love (Styrkelse af indsatsen for at bekæmpe terrorisme m.v.)'. *WESTLAW DANMARK LFB2005–2006.1.217.*

is a document which enjoys exceptional authority, the validity of which no one will dispute.[44]

Equally, the Universal Declaration comes up in questions raised by members of Parliament and addressed to Cabinet Ministers. An example is a question raised 14 May 2003 to the Minister of Interior and Health concerning legislation which discriminates non-Danes *vis-à-vis* Danes. As part of his reply, the minister stated: "It is in accordance with the Universal Declaration of Human Rights that Danish nationality is a precondition for the right to vote at elections to the Danish Parliament".[45]

Another question was raised by a member of the opposition and addressed to the Prime Minister on the understanding of humane treatment of prisoners by the U.S. Government.[46] The reply stated that the common understanding of such treatment was derived from the Universal Declaration and the five international human rights conventions of the UN.[47]

It is characteristic of the parliamentary questions and debates, examples of which are mentioned above, that when the Universal Declaration is mentioned, the debate often has an ideological twist, expressing conflicting and value-based views of Government and opposition respectively.

---

44 'Redegoerelse af 17/1 01 om fremme af religionsfriheden', *Folketinget.dk/Samling/20001/redegoerelse/R10.* Another example is found in a report to the Parliamentary Standing Committee on Nationality, *Folketinget.dk/1998–99, 1. samling — Indfødsretsudvalget, Alm. del bilag 36: 'Besvarelse af spørgsmål nr. 1 og 2 fra Folketingets Indfødsretsudvalg (Alm. Del — bilag 18 og 19)'.* See also a proposal for a parliamentary decision on the incorporation of the UN conventions on human rights in Danish law. In the explanatory report to the proposal, it is stated that the international covenants together with the Universal Declaration provide the backbone of the protection of global human rights. *Folketinget.dk/Samling/2003–4 — B 134 (som fremsat): 'Forslag til folketingsbeslutning om inkorporering af FN-menneskerettighedskonventioner i dansk ret. Fremsat 25. februar 2004 af Margrete Auken (SF), Anne Baastrup (SF), Kamal Qureshi (SF) og Aage Frandsen (SF)'.*

45 *Folketinget.dk/doc/samling 2002–03 — Svar på § 20-spørgsmål: Om forskelsbehandling af danskere og ikke danskere som følge af lovgivning. Spm. nr. S 3319.*

46 "Can the Prime Minister provide information as to whether the Government has at any time investigated or requested the U.S. Government to provide information related to that government's promise of 7 February 2002 to treat prisoners 'humanely'. Furthermore, has the Prime Minister's Office offered its own interpretation of the concept 'humanely', and, if so, how and on what basis did the Ministry interpret it?".

47 "I base my answer on the following information provided by the Ministry of Foreign Affairs and the Ministry of Defense in preparation of the reply to the question. Denmark and the United States have to a large extent common grounds for defining the concept of 'humane treatment', not least based on the Universal Declaration of Human Rights and five of the UN's core human rights conventions, which both countries are parties to". <www.folketinget.dk/samling/20061/spoergsmaal/s2058/svar/endeligt20070123>.

7. BRINGING THE DECLARATION TO THE TOP OF THE WORLD: THE DECLARATION AS A BEARER OF VALUES

In today's public debates concerned with *concrete and specific* human rights, it is Danish law together with the European Convention on Human Rights and other internationally binding conventions rather than the Universal Declaration which are referred to.

The Declaration nonetheless enjoys a high degree of visibility in Denmark as a document of ideological importance. That this will continue to be the case is indicated by a recent initiative by the Ministry of Education. A Committee under the auspices of the Ministry was asked by the Minister to come up with a proposal for a so-called History Canon, the purpose of which is to ensure that all Danish school children are made familiar with a number of significant events from antiquity to the present, nationally and globally. The Universal Declaration has been singled out as one of the 29 historical episodes or sources making up the History Canon as part of the collection which have become accepted as the best of its kind. In the explanatory remarks accompanying the Canon, the Committee explained that the Declaration can be seen as the pivotal point for peoples' basic needs for freedom and justice.[48]

The presumed high visibility of the Universal Declaration of Human Rights as a bearer of values in Danish society now and then gives birth to imaginative activities. Most recently, a group of Danish men decided to celebrate the 60th anniversary of the Declaration by climbing Mount Everest and hoisting a Tibetan flag with imprints of the Declaration on top of the mountain. They hope to reach their destination in the spring of 2009. In their own words, their goal is to bring the Universal Declaration to the highest mountain in the world as a symbol that human rights are for everybody and hence should be at the top of the agenda of the world. If the expedition succeeds, it will be the first time in the history of the Declaration that it has reached such heights.[49]

In conclusion there is little doubt that the Universal Declaration of Human Rights has proved to be a document of ideological importance to Denmark. At the same time it has contributed to the benchmarking of the rights of women which has since been accepted as a common feature of most

---

48 <www.emu.dk.gsk/fag/his/historie-kanon>.

49 *See* the homepage of the expedition: <www.everest2009.dk>. *See also Berlingske Tidende*, 'Danskere bringer menneskeret til tops på Mount Everest', 31 May 2008.

states in the world. For that Denmark needs to be grateful to its indefatigable representative.

6. GREECE: MORE VERBALISM, LESS EFFECTIVENESS?

Stelios Perrakis[1]

1. INTRODUCTION

The Universal Declaration of Human Rights (hereinafter UDHR) has had a major impact on international human rights law. Many international instruments on human rights explicitly aspire to implement the UDHR as well as the two United Nations covenants on human rights and the regional conventions, namely the European Convention on Human Rights (hereinafter ECHR), the American Convention on Human Rights, the Banjul African Charter of Human and Peoples' Rights, even the recent Arab Charter on Human Rights. Also the UDHR has had a significant impact on national constitutions and legislation, in particular for the third world countries.

The global influence of the UDHR is explained by the fact that substantively, it is not a mere 'lowest common denominator' but, on the contrary, it solemnly proclaims the 'common ideal to be attained'. Several features corroborate this influence and reveal the modern-day importance of the historic 1948 text. The UDHR is:

– a complete text: it comprises all individual and collective rights, the principles of universality, indivisibility and interdependence of rights and the concept of individual duties;

– an important text: it is ideological and progressive and enshrines rights which are still not recognized today, such as the right of asylum;

– an ambitious and surprisingly topical text aimed at establishing an international/universal order guaranteeing human values, rights and freedoms.

1 The author expresses his acknowledgements to Vasiliki Saranti, Ph.D. Candidate in International Law, for her precious contribution in the research of the Greek case law and practice.

Sixty years after the adoption of the UDHR, the wording of its Article 28 reminds us that the authors of the document did indeed have in mind the idea of an international public order. "Everyone is entitled to a social and international order in which the rights and freedoms set forth in this Declaration can be fully realized".

This politico-legal aspiration has blossomed particularly in Europe, where human rights as a political discourse and binding legal action have, over the years, become the foundation of a European public order.[2]

The adoption of the UDHR, with Greece voting in favour, was perceived in Athens with mixed feelings about the importance of the instrument and its impact on the national legal order. This was probably due to the very difficult political momentum; the country was experiencing a devastating civil war (1946–1949), which was destroying it just after the end of the Second World War and the triple occupation by Germany, Italy and Bulgaria.

Two examples of the press, reporting the adoption of the UDHR, are significant: the newspaper *To Vima* (12 December 1948, p. 6), in the context of a general information given on the conclusions of the Paris United Nations General Assembly, preferred to give more details on the session (numbers of meetings, delegates, visitors, interpreters, press releases, cost and so on). Rather short was the reference to the "adoption of the first universal declaration of human rights", without any legal or political evaluation and with few words about the result of the vote and the rights/freedoms included in the instrument.

On the other hand the newspaper *Ta Nea* (14 December 1948, p. 1) chose an indirect way to report on the adoption of the UDHR. Quite peculiar was the fact that the interesting legal and political comments were included in the correspondence from the USA, "The American Echo" entitled "Between serious and non-serious". The journalist E. Tzamouranis from New York wrote: "the most important instrument of all times, the UDHR, was adopted by the UN". With a surprisingly dynamic language qualifying the declaration as "the great light" and "the invisible force" of history he expressed "the duty of all free peoples believing in human values to become crusaders of the UDHR". With good reason he stressed that the question of freedom was a right and a duty for all and that "we have to work to promote and build a better happy world, even if the declaration is just an instrument with

---

2 *See* S. PERRAKIS, 'La Déclaration Universelle des droits de l'homme et l'instauration d'un ordre public européen dans le domaine des droits de l'homme', Allocution, in L'effectivité de la protection des droits de l'homme 50 ans après la Déclaration universelle, Actes du Colloque, Strasbourg, 2–4 septembre 1998, Conseil de l'Europe, pp. 47–56.

idealistic promises and truths and the immediate implementation of the rights and freedoms incorporated therein is impossible".

It is just after the civil war when the first debate on human rights and the UDHR opened in Greece and the first legal analyses of the universal instrument were published. In the meantime Greece had been admitted to the Council of Europe (1949), while the new Constitution was promulgated in 1952. But this new legal situation had no real impact on the legal and administrative framework of the Greek society, living, until the 1960s, under emergency legislation, political prisoners, deportations and violations of human rights of the defeated part of the civil war.

2. THE STATUS OF THE UDHR IN THE INTERNATIONAL AND NATIONAL LEGAL ORDERS

Despite the historical, moral and political value of the UDHR and the repeated references to it by several international instruments of universal application (most human rights treaties of general or specific application, such as the 1966 Covenants on human rights, but also several other legal instruments as the Declaration of the World Conference on Human Rights in Vienna in 1993, the Final Document of the 2005 UN Summit), the status of the UDHR in international law remains still an open question. The discussion in the legal theory of this very particular legal instrument is still controversial. Binding for the United Nations (hereinafter UN) organs, with political and moral force and value for the rest of the world, it has received an important legal impetus from the International Court of Justice judgments on *Hostages* (1980)[3] and *Nicaragua* (1986)[4] through references to some of its articles as expression of customary law.

In light of the views of international lawyers, the legal standing of the UDHR has been evaluated on a range between legal value and the binding character of the instrument.[5] It is accepted, on the one hand, as incorporating general principles of international law, or as a reflection of customary law

---

3 Para. 91, *Case Concerning United States Diplomatic and Consular Staff In Tehran (United States of America v. Iran)*, Judgment of 24 May 1980, Reports of Judgments, Advisory Opinions and Orders (1980) pp. 3 *et seq.*

4 *Case Concerning Military and Paramilitary Activities in and against Nicaragua (Nicaragua v. United States of America)*, judgment of 27 June 1986, Reports 1986, pp. 14 *et seq.*

5 *See* in the early years after the adoption of the UDHR the discussion from H. LAUTERPACHT, *International Law and Human Rights* (1950) pp. 406 *et seq.*; S. TCHIRKOVITCH, 'La Déclaration Universelle des droits de l'homme et sa portée internationale', *RGDIP* (1949), pp. 378 *et seq.*

and, on the other hand, just as a recommendation without creating obligations for states and without being a direct source of law.[6]

Thus, the question of the legal force and effect of the UDHR in the domestic legal orders has, in a universal regard, raised plenty of discussions, while it remains — even today — a topic of great controversy.[7]

3. THE UDHR AND THE HELLENIC LEGAL ORDER

3.1. GENERAL REMARKS

Insofar as the Hellenic legal order is concerned, in spite of the fact that Greece is among the adopting states, there is no national legal instrument (law, presidential decree, ministerial decision and so on) that ratifies the UDHR, thereby incorporating it formally in national law with binding effect. Nevertheless, the UDHR became in several occasions an important and significant reference through the ratification of different international treaties and agreements, including European community agreements with references to the UDHR. Also, several introductory reports of legislative instruments refer to the UDHR, such as for instance the Law 3304/2005 for the elimination of all kinds of discrimination (national, racial, religious, due to disabilities, age, sexual orientation and so on) in matters of labour and employment. In this case the legislator underlines that "the equality before the law and the protection of all persons against discrimination is a right recognized by the UDHR".[8]

---

6 For a recent position, *see* F. SUDRE, *Droit européen et international des droits de l'homme* (7th ed., PUF, 2005) p. 174.

7 *See* indicatively M. KDHIR, 'Quelques réflexions sur la nature juridique de la Déclaration universelle des droits de l'homme', *Revue de Droit International et de Droit Comparé* (1999) p. 333 *et seq.*; J.-A. CARRILLO-SALCEDO, 'Les valeurs juridiques de la Déclaration dans l'ordre national', in Commission Nationale Consultative des Droits de l'Homme, La Déclaration universelle des droits de l'homme (1948–1998), Actes du colloque 14–16.9.1998 à Sorbonne (La Documentation française, Paris, 1999) pp. 283 *et seq.*; J. ORAA, 'The UDHR', in F. GOMEZ and K. DE FEYTER (eds), *International Protection of Human Rights: Achievements and Challenges* (Bilbao, 2006) pp. 73–133; P. TAVERNIER, 'Heurs et malheurs de la Déclaration universelle des droits de l'homme: La crise de l'universalité des droits de l'homme en 1998', in G. CHIANEA and J.-L. CHABOT (texts presented by), *Les droits de l'homme et le suffrage universelle* (L'Harmattan, Paris, 2000) pp. 380–381.

8 Law No. 3304/27.1.2005, accessible through the website of the Athens Bar Association <www.dsanet.gr>.

Several times members of the government have referred to the UDHR during relevant debates in the national Parliament. For instance, the Minister of Interior, when recently answering a question of the opposition regarding the minimum standards for procedures for granting and withdrawing refugee status (Council Directive 2005/85/EC, 1 December 2005), stated that "law enforcement organs totally respect the human rights of asylum seekers in Greece according to the rules laid down by the UDHR".[9] Generally, however, the legal value of the UDHR is raised only occasionally in political and legal debates, within political and legal institutions, the civil society, and so on.

3.2. THE VIEWS OF THE HELLENIC LEGAL THEORY

Nonetheless, in the first decades after the adoption of the UDHR, the prevailing view among Greek legal scholars was that the UDHR lacked legal effect but that it encompassed, partially at least, general principles of international law.[10] Its high moral value was of course undisputed. In particular, according to the constitutionalists Svolos and Vlachos just after the adoption of the Constitution of 1952, "without incorporation in national law,

[9] Question No. 7084/25.2.2008 of the Member of the Parliament M. Damanaki, Answer No. 7017/4/7995/18.3.2008 of the Deputy Minister of Interior P. Chinofotis (website of the Greek Parliament <www.parliament.gr>).

[10] On the UDHR, *see* G. DASKALAKIS, 'The UDHR' (Athens, 1953); A. SVOLOS and G. VLACHOS, 'The Constitution of Greece' (vol. I, 1954, Athens) pp. 157 *et seq.*; A.-B. PAPAKOSTAS, 'The UDHR' (PhD Thesis, Athens, 1956); The impact of the UDHR in the modern Constitution (10 years), *Review of Public Law* (1959) pp. 278 *et seq.*; N. LOLIS, 'The UN adopted UDHR and positive law' (ND 1968) pp. 561 *et seq.*; G. VLACHOS, 'The sociology of human rights' (1976); C. EUSTATHIADES, 'La Déclaration universelle des droits de l'homme' (Études de Droit International IV, Athènes, 1977) pp. 123 *et seq.*; G. KASSIMATIS, 'The UDHR', *Nomiko Vima* (1979) pp. 705 *et seq.*; N. ANTONOPOULOS, 'The UDHR: 30 years' (Athens, 1981); A. MANESIS, 'Individual freedoms' (Sakkoulas Publ., 1982) pp. 7 *et seq.*; D. TSATSOS, 'Constitutional law', vol. 3 (1987) pp. 127 *et seq.*; N. ANTONOPOULOS, 'The UDHR of the UN: 40 years of application' (Athens, 1989); K. KAKOURIS, 'The universality of human rights – The right to particularity – Some observations', 20 *The Constitution* (Review) pp. 6 *et seq.*; N. KALTSOGIA-TOURNAVITI, 'Era crisis – institutional crisis – state crisis', in *Essays in honour of F. Vegleris*, vol. II, pp. 398–399; L.-A. SICILIANOS, 'The UDHR fifty years later', 46 *Nomiko Vima* (1998) pp. 1545–1556; L.-A. SICILIANOS, 'The Universal Declaration, the principle of democratic legitimacy and the recent practice of the UN', in 50 years of UDHR, colloquium, Thessaloniki 15–16 May 1998; C. ARGYROPOULOS, 'The Principle of Fair Trial in the UN Universal Declaration of Human Rights', 46 *Nomiko Vima* (1998) pp. 1557-1571; A. YOTOPOULOU-MARANGOPOULOU, 'UDHR and real equality', *Nomiko Vima* (1998) pp. 1572–1578; K. KOUFA (ed.), *50 Years of the Universal Declaration of Human Rights (1948–1998)* (Sakkoulas ed., Athens-Thessaloniki, 1999); P. PARARAS, 'The Legal Character of the UDHR', *Revue Hellénique des droits de l'homme* (2004/II) pp. 283–303. All these contributions are in Greek.

a direct legal effect of the Declaration ... is most uncertain".[11] Likewise Sgouritsas expressed reservations as to the legal value of the UDHR,[12] while Vlachos maintained that it is a text of political significance solely.

Furthermore, it is interesting to mention that just after the dictatorship, there was a debate in the Parliament during the drafting of the 1975 Constitution and particularly its Article 19 (regarding the confidentiality of correspondence). While the Member of the Parliament G.A. Mangakis referred to the value of the UDHR, the Minister of Justice Stefanakis clarified that the UDHR did not have any binding self-executive character and that it did not form part of the domestic law.[13]

However, there are notable exceptions from this restrictive approach. In one of the first studies on the UDHR, published just five years after its adoption, Daskalakis held that "as legal text (the UDHR) is imperfect ... as many other international instruments" and that "it is compulsory but not self-executive" and further on that "one cannot deny the legal character and obligatory content of the UDHR ... it forms part of national law, even if it is not technically therein incorporated by a typical act of the legislature".[14] The same author stated that the UDHR "has the validity of constitutional rules since it is based on the generally accepted rules of international law", while "constitutional provisions that are contrary to the UDHR are ipso facto void".[15] In addition, Konstantopoulos and Antonopoulos[16] are of the same opinion, namely that the UDHR is the written expression of general principles accepted by all civilized nations.[17] The view that the UDHR codifies general principles of law was also stressed by Vallindas[18] and Zotiadis.[19]

In the current legal theory, Tsatsos pointed out that "the UDHR constitutes an important moment for the protection of human rights, since it

---

11 'The Constitution of Greece' (vol. I, 1954, Athens) p. 157 (in Greek).

12 'Constitutional Law' (vol. II, Athens, 1966) pp. 12 *et seq.* (in Greek).

13 Hellenic Parliament, Minutes of the meetings on the debate of the Constitution of 1975, Athens, August 1975, pp. 589–590.

14 DASKALAKIS, *supra* note 10, pp. 96, 103–104.

15 *Ibid.*

16 ANTONOPOULOS (1981), *supra* note 10, p. 51.

17 For the Greek scholarly views on the legal value of the UDHR, *see* S. PERRAKIS, 'Dimensions of the international protection of human rights' (2nd ed., Ant. N. Sakkoulas, Athens-Komotini, 2004) pp. 55–56 (in Greek); PARARAS, *supra* note 10, pp. 289–291.

18 Public International Law, Sakkoulas Publ., Athens-Thessaloniki, 1974; 'UDHR and the general principles of law', in review *Aktines* (1957) p. 100 (in Greek).

19 Public International Law, I, Athens (1973) p. 281 (in Greek).

expresses the common denominator of opposing ideological concepts on the same ideal, the human rights".[20] Dagtoglou considers that the UDHR has no direct legally binding effect, even if it is logical to support the conclusion that it expresses general rules of international law in the light of Article 28 of the Constitution.[21] From his side Roucounas states that a list of UDHR provisions incorporate principles of customary law.[22]

Based on the importance and extent of the protection that the UDHR offers, another opinion holds that the majority of its provisions reflect customary international law.[23] Finally, another legal opinion observes that the UDHR "contains generally accepted rules of international law which are integrated and form part of the national legal order under article 28 § 1 of the Constitution".[24] These positions have re-evaluated the legal standing of the UDHR within the national legal order, taking into account the global evolution of international human rights law.

3.3. THE UDHR UNDER ARTICLE 28 §1 OF THE CONSTITUTION AS AN EXPRESSION OF GENERALLY ACCEPTED RULES OF INTERNATIONAL LAW

It seems that in Greece, the UDHR has not been duly considered during the drafting of the Constitutions of 1952 and 1975.[25] However and given the negative experience of the country during the seven-year military junta (1967–1974),[26] due attention was paid by the members of the Parliament to the importance of the general principles of law and the necessity of their integration in the new Constitution. The result of this debate was Article 28 §1 of the Constitution of 1975/1986/2001,[27] according to which the generally accepted rules of public international law[28] form an integral part of Greek

---

20 'Constitutional Law. Vol. II: Fundamental rights' (Ant. N. Sakkoulas Publ., Athens-Komotini, 1988) p. 129.

21 'Constitutional Law. Human rights', vol. I (2nd ed., Ant. N. Sakkoulas Publ., Athens, 2005) p. 33.

22 E. ROUCOUNAS, 'International protection of human rights' (Estia, 1995) p. 71 (in Greek).

23 PERRAKIS, *supra* note 2; SICILIANOS, *supra* note 10, p. 1556.

24 ARGYROPOULOS, *supra* note 10, p. 1557.

25 ANTONOPOULOS (1981), *supra* note 10, p. 106.

26 *See* S. PERRAKIS, 'The "Greek case" before the international organisations' (Ant. N. Sakkoulas Publ., Athens-Komotini, 1997) (in Greek).

27 This article establishes the supremacy of international over national law.

28 These encompass the general principles of international law as recognized by the civilized nations and the customary rules of international law (Article 38 of the ICJ Statute).

national law and prevail over any other conflicting national provision. Consequently, the UDHR, as long as it incorporates or reflects general principles or customary rules of public international law — and this is true at least as to the civil and political rights — its provisions are binding for the Greek judge, superior to any contrary provision of national law, and should be applied accordingly, despite the fact that the international instrument has not been ratified by a national law.[29]

In the subsequent amendments to the Constitution of 1975 (in 1986 and 2001 respectively), the legal standing of the UDHR did not seem to be of particular concern. This is probably due to the fact that human rights were deemed to be properly incorporated in the domestic legal order after the ratification of the ECHR,[30] the International Covenant on Civil and Political Rights (hereinafter ICCPR)[31] and of course several other human rights treaties whether of general or special character.[32]

3.4. THE UDHR IN THE HELLENIC CASE LAW

The rather progressive view that the UDHR reflects generally accepted rules of international law has not been in general supported by the Greek judiciary. On the one hand and in general terms, the initial and clear position is that the UDHR has no legal effect in the Greek legal order, because there is no incorporation or ratification of it. On the other hand, it is interesting to note that in many cases, the legal value of the UDHR was raised before the Greek judges. A common finding is that the judge refers to the UDHR mostly without specifying, positively or negatively, its legal value. He or she prefers just a reference without further comments.

However, the references to declaratory texts of general acceptance, such as the UDHR, are not unusual. In judgment No. 1618/2006 of the Council of State (High Administrative Court), the applicant contended that the age limit imposed by the law for the employment in a bank is contrary, *inter alia*, to the UDHR because of incompatibility with the principle of equality. The Court rejected the application without further comments on the particular argument.

---

[29] *See* K. IOANNOU, 'The application of generally accepted rules of international law in the Greek legal order', 29 *Armenopoulos* (1975) pp. 2 *et seq.* (in Greek).

[30] Legislative Decree No. 53/1974, Official Gazette A, vol. 256.

[31] Law No. 2462/1997, Official Gazette A, vol. 25.

[32] *See* S. PERRAKIS, 'International protection of human rights', Instruments of International Practice, vol. 4 (ed. Ant. N. Sakkoulas, Athens-Komotini, 2000) (in Greek).

The Supreme Court (*Areios Pagos*) may refer to the UDHR, in the majority of the cases just to conclude that the relevant provision of the declaration has not been infringed upon, albeit without specifying its legal value in the domestic legal order. In one of its early cases, regarding the prohibition of proselytism, the Court concluded that Articles 18 and 19 of the UDHR (freedom of thought, conscience and religion) had not been violated, since the scope of the national law was not to punish the religious beliefs of the person that proselytized the victim but actually it was to protect the freedom of religion of the person that was being proselytized.[33] This view has been confirmed in subsequent judgments.[34]

Nonetheless, one can witness an interesting application of the provisions of the UDHR in Order No. 1540/1996 of the Supreme Court (Penal Chamber).[35] The case concerned the imminent extradition to Egypt of a person having been condemned of issuing a dud cheque. This offense is punished, according to the Penal Code of Egypt, by forced labour. The Court concluded that the Greek authorities could not extradite the person to Egypt, since the offense he had committed was punished by a heavier penalty in that country. Furthermore, it emphasised that according to the Greek Constitution "which is harmonized with the Universal Declaration of Human Rights of 1948 as well as the European Convention of Human Rights", any form of forced labour is prohibited.

As far as the Council of State (High Administrative Court) is concerned, it has in its case law systematically overruled the argument that the national law in question is contrary to the UDHR by stating that "since the Universal Declaration of Human Rights has not been ratified by the legislature, it does not form part of the domestic law".[36]

This case law of the Council of State has been confirmed recently by judgment No. 1207/2007,[37] whereby the High Administrative Court after having made extensive references to international case law,[38] concluded that

---

33 *See Areios Pagos,* judgment No. 840/86, *Penal Annals* (1986) pp. 767–768 (in Greek).

34 *See,* for instance, *Areios Pagos,* judgment No. 1266/1993, *Penal Annals* (1993) pp. 1017–1020 (in Greek). Also in 42 *Nomiko Vima* (1994) p. 247. The High Court used the expression that the national dispositions "went along with the UDHR".

35 45 *Nomiko Vima* (1997) pp. 644–646 (in Greek).

36 *See* judgments No. 4039, 4040/88, 933/91, 2183, 2184/91, 2905/99, 761/2000.

37 56 *Nomiko Vima* (2008) pp. 229–232 (in Greek).

38 *Nottebohm case (Lichtenstein v. Guatemala),* 6 April 1955, ICJ; *Slivenko* v *Lithuania,* 23 January 2002 ECtHR; *case Yeah and Bosico,* 8 September 2005, IACtHR; *Amendment of the naturalization provisions of the Constitution of Costa Rica,* 19 January 1984, IACtHR, Advisory Opinion; Human Rights Committee, comm. No. 1136/2002, views 25 August 2004.

the naturalisation of a foreign citizen was a sovereign right of each state, that there was no international regulation of the criteria that each state should apply (with the exception of its obligations under human rights law[39]), and rejected the argument that denial of naturalization was contrary to Article 22 of the UDHR.[40]

However, it is worth mentioning the wording of another judgment according to which "article 23 of the UDHR has to be interpreted in the light of the international treaties that protect the right to work of every individual".[41] Materially, the Council of State has thus granted increasing legal value to the UDHR.

In a more recent judgment, the Council of State seems to upgrade the legal value of the UDHR. The case concerns the request of review of a judicial decision which has rejected the initial application due to lack of legitimisation of the attorney at law. The applicants contended that their right to effective judicial protection (Article 6 of the ECHR and Article 10 of the UDHR) had been infringed upon. The Court rejected their appeal by stating that the relevant domestic provision was not contrary to article 6 ECHR or to Article 10 of the UDHR. However, as to Article 10 of the UDHR, the Court underlined that "the right of effective judicial protection contained in Article 10 of the UDHR is covered by the provision of Article 6 of the ECHR, which is not infringed upon by the relevant domestic legal regulation".[42] Bearing in mind that in previous cases of a similar kind, the Court had just confined itself to saying that the UDHR "has not been legislatively ratified by Greece", this is a very positive development, not as to the final outcome, which is the same, that is, rejection of the application, but as to the legal standing of the declaration within the Greek legal order.[43]

Moreover, other lower courts and tribunals refer quite frequently to the provisions of the UDHR, albeit without specific references as to its legal value. In a case regarding the proper limitations of the freedom of expression and information (defamation of the former Governor of a Greek bank

---

39 For instance protection of the private and family life of the individual, Article 8 of the ECHR.

40 *See in general* Z. PAPASIOPI-PASIA, 'Article 15 of the UDHR and Greek nationality law', in K. KOUFA (ed.), *50 Years of the Universal Declaration of Human Rights (1948–1998)* (ed. Sakkoulas, Athens-Thessaloniki, 1999) pp. 81 *et seq.* (in Greek).

41 Council of State, judgment No. 3265/90.

42 Council of State, judgment No. 239/2003, reproduced in *Hellenic Review of Human Rights,* special edition (2004/II) pp. 298–303 (301) (in Greek).

43 *See,* for instance, Council of State, judgment No. 2184/1991, *The Constitution* (1991) pp. 608–610 (in Greek).

through the publishing in a newspaper of false accusations against him) the Court of Assizes made reference to the general limitation clause of Article 29 of the UDHR and characterised it as "the clause of the democratic society".[44]

In another case regarding the protection of a lawyer's speeches made in the course of the exercise of his profession or in the court, the Judges' Board for Misdemeanours (*symvoulio plimelleiodikon*) referred generally to the UDHR as an instrument that encompasses the proper protection (for instance, of freedom of speech) for the functions of the lawyer.[45]

3.5. THE UDHR AND THE INDEPENDENT AUTHORITIES IN GREECE

In the 1990s, Greece witnessed a major boost in the establishment of independent authorities entrusted with the task of assisting the public sector in matters of human rights protection. The National Commission on Human Rights,[46] the Data Protection Authority[47] and the Greek Ombudsman (*Synigoros tou Politi*),[48] are some of these. These institutions introduced in a dynamic way the culture of human rights protection in the everyday life of the Greek citizens.

As far as the application of the UDHR is concerned, the practice of the National Commission on Human Rights is worth mentioning. In its 2003 annual report it referred steadily to the Declaration. Following the ratification by Greece of the International Treaty to Ban Landmines (Ottawa Treaty) on 25 September 2003, the Commission declared that "the existence of landmines in the frontier region of Evros, which is a basic entrance area of refugees and asylum seekers, prevents in practice, in the worst possible way, the access of asylum seekers to our country, contrary to the provisions of article 14 UDHR".[49]

In another reference regarding a Muslim wedding by proxy, the National Commission noted that this practice is contrary to the Greek public order and rules of international law pursuant to Article 16 sub-section 2 of the UDHR

---

[44] Court of Assizes (Trimeles Efeteio Kakourgimaton), Athens, judgment No. 4054/1992, 40 *Nomiko Vima* (1992) p. 923 (in Greek).

[45] Judges Board for Misdemeanours, Thessaloniki, Decision No. 1006/1999, *Armenopoulos* (2000) p. 555 (in Greek).

[46] Law No. 2667/1998, Official Gazette A, vol. 281, 18.12.1998.

[47] Law No. 2472/1997, which integrates in the national law the directive 95/46/EC.

[48] Law No. 2477/97.

[49] NCHR, Annual Report 2003, p. 41.

which spelt out that "[M]arriage shall be entered into only with the free and full consent of the intending spouses".[50]

The references to the UDHR go further on. In the proposals formulated by the Commission concerning the Constitution of the European Union, due attention was paid to the value of peace. In particular, the Commission proposed the addition of this notion to Article 2 of the draft European Constitution "since the states have already declared their commitment to the preservation of peace in the Charter of the UN, whereby it is recognized as a fundamental aim of the Organization, as well as in the Universal Declaration of Human Rights".[51] Furthermore, in its observations as to the legal value of cultural rights in the domestic legal order and the protection of the culture of Roma, it used as guidance Article 27 sub-section 1 of the UDHR according to which "[e]veryone has the right freely to participate in the cultural life of the community, to enjoy the arts and to share in scientific advancement and its benefits".[52]

Finally as to the registration of the religious adherence in the national identity cards, the Commission underlined that such an action was contrary to the Constitution and the international obligations of the state emanating, *inter alia*, from Article 18 of the UDHR which protects the freedom of belief, conscience and religion.[53]

In a more recent report, the Commission referred to article 12 of the UDHR in its observations on the draft law for the protection of personal data and the private life in the field of electronic communications, incorporating directive 2002/85/EC.[54]

4. CONCLUSIONS

Even if the present legal theory in Greece has a positive interpretation as to the legal value of the UDHR and despite the high moral and political authority of the instrument, the implementation of the UDHR by Greek judges remains uncertain.

On the other hand, the invocation of the UDHR before Greek judges by lawyers tends to become more usual. As Greek advocates become increasingly

---

[50] *Ibid.*, p. 62.

[51] *Ibid.*, p. 67.

[52] *Ibid.*, p. 104.

[53] *Ibid.*, pp. 150–151.

[54] NCHR, Annual report 2005, p. 127.

acquainted with international law, especially with international protection of human rights, they resort to the international instruments to sustain their views. Of course the instrument that is more often used by the solicitors is the ECHR, due to the fact that it has been legislatively incorporated in the domestic legal order. Many times the reference to the UDHR is 'absorbed' by a reference to the ECHR or the International Covenant on Civil and Political Rights. But as a matter of fact, the interpretation given under Article 28 §1 of the Constitution that the UDHR is part of the national legal order and exists at a supra-legislative level, may reconcile their position.

As to the UDHR, in this first period of the 21st century of the Hellenic society, despite the existing reservations from the judiciary, it remains an important and precious reference and source of inspiration, but also a platform for legal action.

7. LUXEMBOURG: CONTENT WITHOUT REFERENCE?

Jean-Paul Lehners
Fabienne Rossler[1]

1. INTRODUCTION

From 10 May 1940 until its liberation by the Allies on 10 September 1944, the Grand Duchy of Luxembourg was occupied by the German troops. The Government in exile in the United States and London was in close contact with the Allies during that time. So, it was quite normal that after the liberation, and already during the Second World War, Luxembourg invested all its efforts in the reorganisation of the international community.

The Grand Duchy of Luxembourg is one of the 51 founding member countries of the United Nations (hereinafter UN). When it joined the organisation on 24 October 1945, the day on which the UN Charter was ratified, the Grand Duchy was the smallest member state in this new world organisation. With the 191 current member states, the Grand Duchy sat in one of the six main bodies of the UN, the General Assembly. It is worth pointing out in this context that in 1974 Gaston Thorn, Luxembourg's then Prime Minister, took on the role of President of the 30th session of the General Assembly. He is the only Luxembourg politician ever to have been elected to that office.

It was only in 1958 that Luxembourg decided to establish a Permanent Representation to the UN in New York. Today Luxembourg has a permanent representation in various UN institutions in Geneva (since 1968), Paris (1966) and Rome (1990). Luxembourg has announced its application for a non-permanent membership in the UN Security Council for the period 2013-2014.

On 30 September 1988 the Luxembourg Government donated the sculpture "The Knotted Gun" by Fredrik Reuterswärd, a Swedish artist, to the UN as a symbol of non-violence. The unveiling of the sculpture took place in

---

[1] We would like to thank Jean Feyder (Permanent Representative at the UN in Geneva), Olivier Baldauff, Olivier Maes and Nadine Feyder (Ministry of Foreign Affairs), Pierre Mores (former President of the Council of State), ALNU for their valuable contributions, and also Linda Gieres, Tim Reuter and Cathy Nelson for helping with the translation.

front of the UN Conference Centre in New York in the presence of Mr. Pérez de Cuellar, Secretary General of the UN and Mr. Robert Goebbels, Luxembourg's Secretary of State for Foreign Affairs, who declared that "the human being needs symbols that inspire, guide and express his/her actions".[2]

Within the framework of the ongoing work of the UN, Luxembourg has been involved very actively in the transformation of the Human Rights Commission into the Human Rights Council.[3] Explicit references to the Universal Declaration of Human Rights (hereinafter UDHR) are in general rather rare. A fundamental but not a legally binding instrument, the UDHR has been a source of inspiration to many other legally binding instruments, among which are the International Covenant on Civil and Political Rights (hereinafter ICCPR), the International Covenant on Economic, Social and Cultural Rights (hereinafter ICESCR) and the European Convention on Human Rights (hereinafter ECHR) of 1950. It seems therefore evident that references to these texts would be more frequent.

In order to get a more precise idea on this topic, we will take a closer look at the different areas where reference is made to the UDHR in the context of Luxembourg.[4]

2. THE UDHR AND THE CONSTITUTION

In May of 1948, the Parliament or Chamber of Deputies (*Chambre des Députés*) as Constituent Assembly, influenced by the preparations of the UDHR adopted on 10 December 1948, wished to complete the list of individual rights protecting the individual against abuses of political power by the addition of new social rights. The traditional rights, also called 'rights of', were then completed by the 'rights to', as for instance the rights to education, culture, social protection, and so on.[5] In the article-by-article comment on the Luxembourg Constitution written by members of the Council of State,

---

[2] Comité national pour la coopération avec les Nations Unies (ed.), *Le Luxembourg et l'ONU (1945–1995), 50e anniversaire de l'Organisation des Nations Unies*, Luxembourg, October 1995.

[3] Webpage of the Ministry of Foreign Affairs, Le Luxembourg dans les organisations internationales (<www.mae.lu>).

[4] We do not touch upon the human rights dimension in the different European institutions in Luxembourg such as the European Court of Justice, the European Investment Bank or the Court of Auditors.

[5] Le Conseil d'Etat, gardien de la Constitution et des Droits et Libertés fondamentaux. Luxembourg 2006, pp. 58–59. However, the Council of State considered the reference to the UDHR to be inappropriate (*Ibid.*, p. 59).

reference is made to historical documents, such as the Declaration of the Rights of Man and of the Citizen of 1789[6] and 1793,[7] but not the UDHR. It is worth mentioning that the thematic index developed by the same authors include the categories Rights and Freedoms, Citizens, Justice and General Principles of Law and it provides valuable information on the different types of rights.[8]

In a very interesting reflection on the revision of the Constitution, the authors made the following proposal: "Considering the growing importance of the European Union in our daily legal order, one should decide whether it would not be better to distinguish between our obligations to the EU and the obligations to other international organisations".[9] Hence, there is a clear priority for the European instruments. In this same context, it is said that the Constitution does not have references to a certain number of other rights[10] and one could ask if the Constitution should not "formally reaffirm the rights deriving from international human rights obligations",[11] following the example of the Spanish Constitution that refers notably to the UDHR.

A model for a structure for a new Constitution, as submitted by the authors but not accepted by the Council of State as an institution, contained new rights such as environmental protection and sustainable development.[12]

3. THE UDHR AND THE COUNCIL OF STATE

When making reference to international documents, the Luxembourg Council of State, an advisory body on legislative matters (that, among other things, issues compulsory opinions on all bills of law), mainly refers to European texts. However, in its opinion of 22 May 2007 on the revision of Article 16 on the right to own property of the Constitution, the Council of State refers to Article 17 of the UDHR.[13]

---

6 *Ibid.*, pp. 50, 11, 118.

7 *Ibid.*, p. 115.

8 *Ibid.*, pp. 413–440; *see also* 'Renvoi aux pages des articles. Chapitre "II – Des libertés publiques et des droits fondamentaux"', pp. 441–442.

9 *Ibid.*, p. 691.

10 *Ibid.*, pp. 693–694.

11 *Ibid.*, p. 694.

12 *Ibid.*, p. 732.

13 Council of State, No. 47.355, Proposition de révision de l'article 16 de la Constitution, 22 May 2007.

Moreover, the Council of State touched on the ECHR, the ICCPR, the Treaty on the European Union and the Charter of Fundamental Rights of the European Union in the framework of the legislation concerning freedom of expression in the media (opinion of 3 June 2003).[14] In its opinion of 8 December 1970 on the draft bill on the rights and duties of the spouses and reforming marriage settlements, the Council mentions the UDHR as well as the UN Charter while concluding that Luxembourg "is lagging a bit behind the others",[15] although it admitted that this delay could also have advantages by using "the experiences done by other countries".[16] A comparative study on the opinions of the Benelux Councils of State concerning fundamental rights and freedoms once more pointed out, in the list of international instruments, the predominant role of references to the UN Charter, the ICCPR as well as the European texts.[17] In this context it is mentioned however that the Covenant "refers in its preamble to the UDHR and the UN Charter".[18] In a synopsis of the international and national texts on fundamental rights and freedoms the UDHR was missing, whereas the ICCPR is mentioned.[19]

4. THE UDHR AT GOVERNMENTAL AND MINISTERIAL LEVEL

4.1. INTRODUCTION

The commitment in favour of democracy and good governance, rule of law, human rights and fundamental freedoms has always been part of the efforts of the Luxembourg diplomacy to denounce human rights violations all over the world.[20]

---

14 Le Conseil d'Etat face à l'évolution de la société luxembourgeoise. Luxembourg 2006, pp. 141 *et seq.*

15 *Ibid.*, p. 383.

16 *Ibid.*

17 Le Conseil d'Etat gardien (*supra* note 5), Miroirs et reflets de droits et libertés fondamentaux dans les avis des Conseils d'Etat des pays du Benelux, pp. 529–678. One chapter concerns the "Place occupée par la CEDH dans l'ordre juridique interne des pays du Benelux", pp. 580–586.

18 *Ibid.*, p. 536.

19 *Ibid.*, pp. 663–668.

20 Examples, *see* <www.mae.lu> (webpage of the Ministry of Foreign Affairs: Luxembourg in the international institutions).

The anniversaries of the UDHR are opportunities to recall the existence of this fundamental document. That is why the government created an organising committee composed of representatives of several ministries, as well as representatives of civil society and human rights experts placed under the High Patronage of his Royal Highness the Grand Duke of Luxembourg on the 50th anniversary.[21] This committee developed a whole programme of awareness-raising activities on human rights for the general public and especially for young people. Among those awareness-raising activities, one can mention human rights days in schools, a colloquium on human rights organised by the *Centre Universitaire* of Luxembourg in cooperation with the Ministry of Foreign Affairs and the inauguration of a human rights documentation centre of the ALNU. Moreover, a 'human rights bus' visited several secondary schools during the first semester of 1998/1999 and offered young people the necessary tools and elements for an interactive human rights approach.

In order to give a sustainable impact to these actions, a working group was created. This group had the mission to examine the different possibilities to improve human rights education by incorporating them systematically into the curricula.[22] In addition to these activities, a certain number of Luxembourg NGOs organised theatre performances, concerts and other human rights events.[23]

4.2. FOREIGN AFFAIRS

On several occasions, the Ministers of Foreign Affairs have made reference to the UDHR in their declarations on foreign policies or in their speeches at the international organisations, to insist on the importance of the moral and legal commitments of the country as well as the very often alarming situation concerning the most basic rights of millions of human beings worldwide

In December 1988 for example, on the 40th anniversary of the UDHR, the Minister of Foreign Affairs declared at the Chamber of Deputies that "the integral application of the UDHR of 1948 is an essential criterion for the quality of Luxembourg's relations with other States".[24] In this same context, in reply to the question of whether it was not frustrating for a small nation to

---

21 List of activities on the occasion of the 50th anniversary of the UDHR, 23 November 1998, Ministry of Foreign Affairs.

22 *Ibid.*

23 *Ibid.*

24 Compte-rendu de la 18e séance publique de la Chambre des Députés, 6 December 1988.

play the role of mediator but not being able to sustain this elsewhere, Ms. Lydie Err, Secretary of State, said that "if we were looking for publicity, we would be finished with our mediator role very fast. In the end, it is not important who is following a specific position, but who can impose his or her position".[25]

During his speech at the seventh session of the UN Human Rights Council in Geneva in March 2008, Mr. Jean Asselborn, the Minister of Foreign Affairs, declared in the context of the 60th anniversary of the UDHR that "it will be the opportunity to recall the historical meaning of this document, to evaluate the progresses and failures made and to establish a new roadmap for the upcoming years".[26]

4.3. DEVELOPMENT COOPERATION

Luxembourg has always shown solidarity towards the developing countries. The primary objective of Luxembourg's development cooperation is the eradication of poverty, notably in least developed countries. Its actions and interventions are conceived in the spirit of sustainable development, which is reflected in its social, economic and environmental dimensions — placing men, women and children in their centre. These actions are primarily seen as part of the implementation of the Millennium Development Goals until 2015. As concerns Official Development Assistance (ODA), since 2000 Luxembourg has been among the group of (currently five) industrialised countries which allocate more than 0.7 per cent of their gross national income (GNI) to development cooperation.[27]

4.4. NATIONAL EDUCATION

The Ministry of National Education has published an edition in Luxembourgish language of the UDHR, thus bringing it closer to the biggest part of the population. In December 2008, the Ministry published a special edition of the *Courrier de l'Education nationale* on human rights. This special edition includes written contributions of representatives of the civil society, independent institutions and teachers. It also recalls in different languages the

---

[25] 'Menschenrechte in der Luxemburger Außenpolitik. Ein *forum*-Gespräch mit Staatssekretärin Lydie Err', *Forum*, October 1998, pp. 8–13.

[26] Discours du ministre des Affaires étrangères devant le Conseil des droits de l'Homme, Geneva, March 2008.

[27] 0.92% in 2007, Ministry of Development Cooperation, Annual Report 2007, p. 8.

main documents on human rights, such as the UDHR and the Convention on the Rights of the Child.

4.5. EQUAL OPPORTUNITIES

In its preamble, the National Action Plan on Equal Opportunities for women and men, elaborated in 2006 by the Ministry for Equal Opportunities, refers to the UDHR principle of non-discrimination and announces that "all human beings are born free and equal in dignity and rights" and that "everyone is entitled to all the rights and freedoms set forth in this Declaration, without distinction of … sex".[28]

4.6. INDEPENDENT INSTITUTIONS FOR THE PROMOTION AND PROTECTION OF HUMAN RIGHTS

The *Association luxembourgeoise pour les Nations Unies* (Luxembourg UN Association; ALNU) was founded on 11 July 1946 under the guidance of Minister Pierre Frieden, who became the chair of the Association. The aim of the ALNU is to offer an insight into the UN system and to contribute to peacekeeping and the respect of human rights.[29]

Other institutions have been created in the course of the last years, most notably the National Advisory Human Rights Commission (2000), the Ombuds-Committee on the Rights of the Child (2002), the Office of the Ombudsman (2003) and the Centre for Equal Treatment (2006) The Luxembourg Human Rights Institute (*Institut luxembourgeois des Droits de l'Homme*), founded in 1992, edits the *Bulletin des Droits de l'Homme.*

Since its creation in 2000, the Advisory Human Rights Commission has written about 20 opinions on the human rights situation in Luxembourg.[30] On several occasions it has made reference to the UDHR, notably in the context of asylum law,[31] the right to education[32] and women's rights.[33] None of the

---

28 Plan national d'égalité des femmes et des hommes, Ministère de l'Egalité des chances, February 2006.

29 Comité national pour la coopération avec les Nations Unies, *supra* note 2.

30 <www.ccdh.lu>.

31 Avis de la CCDH sur le projet de loi 5437 relatif au droit d'asile et à des formes complémentaires de protection (April 2005); Avis de la CCDH sur le projet de loi N°5572 visant à transposer quatre directives européennes et à modifier la loi du 28 mars 1972 sur l'entrée et le séjour des étrangers (October 2006); Communiqué de la CCDH: "Le projet de loi no. 5737 portant modification de la loi du 5 mai 2006 relative au droit d'asile et à des formes complémentaires de protection et le projet de règlement grand-ducal du 18 avril 2007 fixant une liste de pays

other above-mentioned institutions has a direct reference to the UDHR. However, the creation itself of these 'third type actors' shows that Luxembourg is keen on respecting its commitments in human rights matters.

5. THE UDHR AND THE CHAMBER OF DEPUTIES

The UDHR is a source of inspiration for the elaboration of the national legislation. Thus, the parliamentary debates, the opinions of the parliamentary and other commissions (Advisory Human Rights Commission and the *Chambres professionnelles* for example) refer rather often and in different contexts to the UDHR. At each anniversary of the UDHR, the members of the Chamber of Deputies recall the fundamental principles of the UDHR. During a solemn session at the Chamber of Deputies, on the 50th anniversary of the UDHR, the President of the Chamber encouraged Members of Parliament to face up their responsibilities and to ensure that the Luxembourg legislation be elaborated in accordance with the UDHR.[34]

In a parliamentary question on the creation of an advisory human rights commission, submitted in September 1998, the MP Jean Huss (Green Party) put the creation of such a commission into the context of the 50th anniversary.[35]

As concerns asylum policy, in November 1999 the Green Party submitted a motion, in which it refers to Article 5 of the UDHR on the prohibition of torture, inviting the government to respect human rights and particularly children's rights while implementing asylum policy.[36] Moreover, a Green Party resolution on the question of housing refers to Article 25(1) of the UDHR on the right for everyone to a standard of living adequate for the health and well-being of himself or herself and of his or her family, including food, clothing, housing for example, in order to recommend the insertion of a

---

d'origine sûrs" (6 July 2007); Communiqué de la Commission au sujet de "quelques principes majeurs de droit international des réfugiés" (19 April 2006).

32 Avis de la CCDH sur l'intégration des enfants à besoins spéciaux (December 2005). Avis sur l'èducation aux droits de l'homme (July 2001).

33 Communiqué de la Commission: "Les droits de la femme sont des droits humains" (8 March 2008).

34 Compte-rendu de la 10e séance publique de la Chambre des Députés, 3 December 1998.

35 Chambre des Députés, Question parlementaire No. 110, 4 December 1998.

36 Chambre des Députés, Motion I–1999–O–M–1185–01 d'Alex Bodry: Politique d'asile et respect des droits de l'homme notamment des droits de l'enfant, modalités de transfert de personnes.

provision regarding the right to housing into the Luxembourg Constitution (1 February 2007).[37]

6. THE UDHR AND LUXEMBOURG TRIBUNALS

Luxembourg courts and other adjudicatory bodies refer to the UDHR on very few occasions, in particular because of the non-binding character of the declaration. The Court of Appeal for instance referred in one of its decisions to the prohibition of arbitrary interference with privacy, family, home or correspondence as set down in Article 12 of the UDHR.[38] In another decision, the Court of Appeal referred indirectly to the UDHR stating that, although the UDHR has not been incorporated into national law, its principles were developed in the International Covenant on Civil and Political Rights which has been transposed into national law in June 1983.[39] The District Tribunal of Luxembourg referred to Article 7 (equality in law) and Article 16 (right to marry and to found a family) of the UDHR in a decision concerning a case of divorce.[40]

7. THE UDHR IN POLITICAL PARTY PROGRAMMES

While browsing through the programmes of the different political parties in Luxembourg, one notices that only two of them refer to the UDHR and, more generally to human rights. The Democratic Party is based on the fundamental principles of liberalism: "as concerns philosophy: tolerance, individual freedom, humanism and the respect of all philosophical and religious concepts in accordance with the Universal Declaration on Human Rights".[41] For the Green Party, human rights are part of its fundamental programme.[42]

In general, and from what has just been said, one can see that the statements of the ministers and members of Parliament on the UDHR underline the importance of this fundamental document merely in an

---

[37] Chambre de Députés, Résolution I–2006–O–M–0242–01 de Claude Adam: Inscription du droit au logement dans la Constitution.

[38] Cour d'appel, Arrêt No. 414/96 V du 29 octobre 1996.

[39] Cour d'appel, 99833645 du 5 décembre 2002.

[40] Tribunal d'Arrondissement du Luxembourg, 98913413 du 13 juillet 1989.

[41] Fondements du Parti Démocratique, Chapitre I, article 1er, 21 November 2006.

[42] "Déi Gréng", Grundsatzerklärung, Kapitel 2. Grundwerte, 14 February 2008.

abstract way. But how does this play out in practice? For quite some time, Luxembourg has been facing new challenges, such as the question of asylum seekers and the increasing number of foreigners who represent 40 per cent of the total population, with the risks of a declining economic situation. It is clear that the economic situation has so far spared Luxembourg from many problems and failures. Nevertheless, as this welfare is not safe for ever and even if there are no gross human rights violations, the situation could be improved.

8. THE UDHR AND CIVIL SOCIETY

In a publication of the *Centre Universitaire de Luxembourg*, edited in collaboration with the Luxembourgish National UNESCO Commission and the *Cellule de Recherche sur la Résolution de Conflits*,[43] representatives from very different social, political, cultural and religious backgrounds evaluate fundamental freedoms as well as political, economic, social, cultural, individual and collective rights in Luxembourg from their respective point of view. This publication picks up some general questions, such as asylum law, racism, education, rights of women, children and elderly persons. These contributions indicate that the human rights situation in Luxembourg is not really a major issue, but quite unsatisfying in regard to certain aspects. This has also been underlined by the numerous recommendations and reports by the regional and international human rights bodies and organisations, such as the Council of Europe and the UN treaty bodies.

The UDHR has always played a crucial role for civil society. Many organisations indeed refer to the UDHR in their statutes or in the elaboration of their projects, whether they deal with education, asylum, health or food, to mention only a few. In a global society, the importance of economic and social rights is increasing. Civil society defends these rights through different projects concerning development aid, education, solidarity, the fight for the respect of the basic human rights and it is doing its utmost to raise awareness among the population.

On the 40th anniversary of the UDHR in March 1988, Amnesty International launched a campaign inviting citizens all over the world to associate themselves, through their signature, to the noble declaration and to require respect for human rights from the governments of all States. On 9

---

43 Enquête sur les Droits de l'Homme, La situation au Luxembourg, Fascicule II.1, Luxembourg 1998.

December 1988, a delegation of Amnesty International Luxembourg was received by the government with some 9000 signatures in support of the campaign. At the same occasion the Ministry of Education authorised Amnesty International to organise activities meant to inform about human rights related questions in secondary schools on 10 December.[44] For two years now, Amnesty International Luxembourg has carried out investigations on human rights violations at national level.

9. THE UDHR AND THE MEDIA

It is clear that the anniversaries of the declaration are opportune moments to talk about the UDHR. Yet, the picture that is portrayed is far from being perfect. Poverty is rising, the unemployment rate, although much lower than in other European Union countries is increasing and the gap between the rich and the poor is getting bigger. There is a lot of criticism towards the general indifference to the problem.[45] One newspaper states:

> "It seems that human rights, one of the favourite topics of politicians, represent today an idea that works and that can be sold in press columns ... Equality in law for everyone is very often only symbolic — the gap between the industrial world and the developing countries is so large that one can hardly speak about economic and social equality. In our country, a new 'race' of poor people is about to emerge. In addition to the Third World, there is a Fourth World, excluding all kinds of people. Forty years after the UDHR, there is still a lot to be done. The concept of human rights remains, for the younger generations, a new idea ... As well as the fight for peace, the idea of human rights requires a daily vigilance."[46]

---

44 '40 années des droits de l'Homme, La campagne d'Amnesty International', *Luxemburger Wort*, 5 December 1988.

45 E. ROSSLER, '40 Jahre Menschenrechte', *Luxemburger Wort*, 10 December 1988.

46 "Sujet de prédilection des hommes politiques, les droits de l'Homme semblent représenter aujourd'hui une idée qui marche et qui se vend bien à travers les colonnes de la presse ... L'égalité de tous devant la loi est souvent symbolique, le fossé entre le monde industriel et le monde en développement est tel qu'on ne saurait décemment parler d'égalité économique et sociale. Chez nous, une nouvelle race de pauvres fait son apparition. Au Tiers-Monde s'est ajouté le Quart-Monde constitué d'exclus de tous bords. Quarante ans après la DUDH, bien du travail reste à faire. Au point que pour les jeunes générations, le concept des droits de l'Homme reste une idée neuve ... Comme la défense de la paix, celle des droits de l'Homme requiert une vigilance quotidienne". Danielle Fonck, 'Les droits de l'Homme, une idée neuve', *Tageblatt*, 12 October 1988.

Another continues:

> "There is a lot to do to eliminate the Babel of incapability to mutual understanding. This applies as well to our own welfare state, where the individual is not as protected as one could think … We should first of all work on the respect of human rights in our country, before we point the finger at developments that are taking place far away from us."[47]

10. FINAL REMARKS

This article is an initial analysis of a topic that certainly deserves more exhaustive research. It is as important to underline the references to the UDHR as it is to notice the absence of any reference. This is a conclusion based on our first approach.

One notices that the UDHR is mainly mentioned at the occasions of its anniversary. The 60th anniversary is not an exception. The Advisory Human Rights Commission managed to coordinate the activities planned by about 20 associations that stem from civil society. Another anniversary is coming: the 60th anniversary of the ECHR, the reference text. That might be the occasion for a new consideration of human rights.

[47] "Es fehlt noch viel, um das Babel der Unfähigkeit zum gegenseitigen Verständnis auszumerzen. Auch bei uns, wo das Individuum keineswegs immer so geschützt ist, wie es im Wohlstandsstaat als gegeben angesehen wird … Wir sollten zunächst bestrebt sein, die Menschenrechte bei uns selbst zu respektieren, bevor wir mit dem Finger auf Entwicklungen im fernen Ausland zeigen". R. ROEMEN, 'Ein weiter Weg', *Journal*, 10 December 1988.

8. THE NETHERLANDS: RELIGIOUS INSPIRATION, BUT LITTLE DOMESTIC IMPACT

Fons Coomans
Willemijn Noordhoek

1. INTRODUCTION

This contribution will focus on two issues, namely the role of the Netherlands during the process of drafting the Universal Declaration on Human Rights (hereinafter UDHR) and the reception of the UDHR in the Netherlands. With respect to the former, the role of the Netherlands government was quite remarkable. The government showed a strong desire to include in the UDHR a reference to the divine origin of human rights. The present chapter will discuss this proposal, its background and its reception during the negotiations, as well as the role played by the Dutch representatives. It will also consider whether the proposal had backing in Parliament at that time. These efforts show that the role of religion in post-Second World War Dutch politics was important.

Once the UDHR was adopted, interest in Dutch society for its meaning waned. The UDHR had little impact on the domestic level. In political and legal circles, the press and in case law its significance has been quite limited. The present contribution will discuss a number of these developments.

2. RELIGIOUS INSPIRATION FOR THE UDHR

2.1. THE DUTCH CONTRIBUTION TO THE DISCUSSIONS IN THE THIRD COMMITTEE OF THE GENERAL ASSEMBLY

The Netherlands was not a member of the United Nations (hereinafter UN) Commission on Human Rights when the UDHR was drafted. Consequently, one occasion to express the Dutch view on the draft Declaration was the seventh meeting of the Economic and Social Council in Geneva in the summer of 1948. At this meeting, the Dutch delegate Van der Mandele supported an amendment proposed by the Lebanese delegate Malik during the second session of the Commission on Human Rights. At that session, Mr. Malik had suggested to formulate the article on the protection of the family[1] as follows: "[t]he family deriving from marriage is the natural and fundamental group unit of society. It is endowed by the Creator with inalienable rights antecedent to all positive law".[2] The first sentence of this amendment was accepted; however the second sentence was rejected by the vast majority of the Commission on Human Rights. In ECOSOC, Mr. Van der Mandele declared that it was regrettable that the Commission had not accepted this proposal, and that he wished the topic to be discussed again at a later stage of the debate on the UDHR. In response, Mr. Malik assured him that the Lebanese delegation would return to the proposal during the discussions in the Third Committee of the General Assembly.[3]

The Third Committee had received two amendments that aimed at introducing a reference to God in the Declaration. The first one was proposed by the Brazilian delegation that wished to add a reference to God in draft Article 1.[4] The Dutch delegation was very much in favour of this idea; however the plan received severe criticism from many of the other delegations. The main reason was that Article 1, which was to become the cornerstone and foundation of the whole of the UDHR, should neither assert nor imply that the system of human rights is based on any conception of Human Nature, Nature or God.[5] Eventually, after discussing the matter with their Dutch colleagues, the Brazilian delegation decided to wait for the discussion on the (then unknown) Dutch amendment regarding the Preamble

---

1 Current Article 16.

2 J. MORSINK, *The Universal Declaration of Human Rights: Origins, Drafting, and Intent* (University of Pennsylvania Press, Philadelphia, 1999) p. 284, referring to UN Doc. E/CN.4/SR.37, p. 11.

3 Ministerie van Buitenlandse Zaken, *Universele Verklaring van de rechten van de mens*, (Ministerie van Buitenlandse Zaken, Publicatie nr. 16, 's-Gravenhage, 1949) pp. 34–35.

4 Draft Article 1: "All men are born free and equal in dignity and rights. They are endowed by nature with reason and conscience, and should act towards one another like brothers". The Brazilian delegate proposed the following amendment: "Created in the image and likeness of God, they are endowed with reason and conscience, and should act towards another in a spirit of brotherhood".

5 T. LINDHOLM, 'Article 1', in A. EIDE, G. ALFREDSSON et al. (eds), *The Universal Declaration of Human Rights: A Commentary* (Scandinavian University Press, Oslo, 1992) p. 47.

and withdrew the article.[6] The debate on the Preamble was held after the debates on the separate articles.

The spokesman for the Dutch delegation was professor L.J.C. Beaufort (1890–1965).[7] He was a priest and a Friar Minor. He had been a member of the Lower House for the Roman Catholic Party (KVP) between 1937 and 1946, and since August 1948 a member of the Upper House for that party. In addition, he was extraordinary professor of international law at the Catholic University in Nijmegen. He later became the first Dutch member of the European Commission for Human Rights. At that time it was quite common that Members of Parliament participated in governmental delegations to important international meetings or conferences.[8] During his speech before the Third Committee, Beaufort introduced a proposal containing a controversial religious stance suggesting a reference to the divine origin of human rights in the Preamble.[9]

The first sentence of the Preamble as proposed by the Commission on Human Rights ran as follows: "Whereas recognition of the inherent dignity and of the equal and alienable rights of all members of the human family is the foundation of freedom, justice and peace in the world". To this sentence, Beaufort proposed an amendment which added the words "based on man's divine origin and immortal destiny" after the words 'human family'.[10] Beaufort was aware of the fact that similar amendments by the Lebanese and Brazilian delegations[11] had been disapproved of by many of the other

---

6 MORSINK, *supra* note 2, p. 287; and Ministerie van Buitenlandse Zaken, *supra* note 3, pp. 43-44.

7 J.W.H.C.M. SCHNEIDER, 'Beaufort, Leo Josephus Cornelis (1890–1965)', in J. CHARITE and I. SCHÖFFER (eds), *Biografisch Woordenboek van Nederland* (Martinus Nijhoff, The Hague, 1979) part III, p. 36.

8 It was, however, quite exceptional that Beaufort was a member of the Netherlands delegation to the UN General Assembly for 14 years (1948–1962).

9 This was not the only proposal that Beaufort and the Dutch delegation submitted; they also submitted proposals that were devoted to articles concerning the rights to political asylum, the family being the cornerstone of society, and the rights for parents to choose the education for their children that they thought would be best. *See also* Ministerie van Buitenlandse Zaken, *supra* note 3, pp. 39–77; M.C. CASTERMANS-HOLLEMAN, *Het Nederlands mensenrechtenbeleid in de Verenigde Naties* (T.M.C. Asser Instituut, 's Gravenhage, 1992) pp. 174–177; MORSINK, *supra* note 2, pp. 124 and 266.

10 UN Doc. A/C.3/2191. *See also* Ministerie van Buitenlandse Zaken, *supra* note 3, p. 39; and M. KOSKENNIEMI, 'The Preamble of the Universal Declaration of Human Rights', in G. ALFREDSSON and A. EIDE (eds), *The Universal Declaration of Human Rights* (Martinus Nijhoff Publishers, The Hague, 1999) p. 31.

11 As was discussed before, the Lebanese wished to add the divine origin of men to (the current) Article 16 and the Brazilians wished to do the same to (the current) Article 1.

delegations, for two main reasons: firstly, these kinds of amendments were unacceptable to countries that did not adhere to the divine origin of man at all, and secondly many delegations asserted that a universal declaration was simply not the place for metaphysical discussions. Because of these negative attitudes towards adding anything like a divine origin to the UDHR, Beaufort started his argument by paying attention to these objections. He asserted that the state of mind of people that did not believe in the divine origin would not be affected by the amendment, since "[t]o all those I just mentioned, the Netherlands proposal is just meaningless, it has no sense to them, but certainly it cannot hurt them, it cannot offend their conscience, because they do not believe in a Supreme Being".[12]

Subsequently, he turned to the positive aspects of his proposal by stating that the majority of all peoples would welcome this addition, whereas they would "be hurt in their deepest convictions" when a reference to the divine origin of man would be omitted. According to Beaufort, the earlier omission of the divine origin of man in the Preamble to the Charter of the United Nations was still felt "by hundreds of millions as a deplorable shortcoming", and therefore inserting a reference to God would be a relief to them.[13] Secondly, by not adding the relationship between man and his Creator, Beaufort believed that a fundamental dimension of the human being was not mentioned in the Declaration, and therefore the conception of the human person would be "distorted" and "mutilated". As a third argument, he asserted that it was of great practical importance to add the divine origin of human rights to the Preamble, "more particularly in those cases where the human rights are in need of protection against violation, where the adherents of the omnipotence of the State proclaim, that the rights of State are always of higher order than those of the individuals".[14] This was a reference to the lack of freedom of religion in Communist states at that time.

The reactions in the Third Committee were mixed and the subsequent debate was fierce. Only the delegations of Argentina, Bolivia, Brazil, Lebanon, Luxembourg and New Zealand gave their consent, while the delegations from, amongst others, India, China, France, Ecuador, and all countries in Eastern Europe, were very much opposed to it and requested the amendment to be withdrawn immediately. This mixed group of opponents based the request for withdrawal on several grounds, for example, they stated that a political document was not apt for metaphysical discussions, these

---

12 Speech of 29 November 1948. Ministerie van Buitenlandse Zaken, *supra* note 3, p. 96.

13 *Ibid.*, pp. 96–97.

14 *Ibid.*, p. 98.

kinds of questions were already dealt with during the French revolution, and one should look at these topics only from a scientific point of view.[15]

However, there was also a large group of countries (amongst others: Belgium, United Kingdom and Canada) that did support the views of Beaufort, but that still did not want to include his proposal in the UDHR, because they wanted the UDHR to have a more neutral stance in these matters. Mr. Davies of the UK explained this position by pointing at the fact that delegations representing "more than half of the world's populations" objected to a reference to God, and that since "the Declaration was to be of universal character the views of those delegations should be respected".[16] Also, many of the Christian delegations did not approve of the idea to vote on a delicate topic like the origin of man. Beaufort was disappointed and all in a flutter, he said that he "did not share the opinion that controversial questions should be eliminated in order to attain unanimity. Was agreement really impossible between those who believed that human rights were inalienable and those who affirmed that man was only a means and that the State was an end in itself?"[17] What he overlooked in the remainder of his speech was the fact that not only the Communist and other non-Christian delegations opposed his proposal, but also that other Christian countries had disapproved of it. Finally, he decided to withdraw the proposal, because he realised that he did not have enough support.

In a publication in a Dutch Catholic magazine in 1949, Beaufort expressed his disappointment on the course of events. He explained that the Dutch delegation did expect some difficulties, but not as many as were manifested during the discussions. In addition, he rejected the idea that by the omission of the origin of man, the United Nations could be considered being a non-religious organisation, and he also stressed that despite its shortcomings, the document was an important milestone in human rights discussions.[18] In an article on the European Convention on Human Rights (hereinafter ECHR) that he wrote in 1959, Beaufort reflected again on the UDHR and concluded once again that the main flaws of this document were the disagreement on the origin of human rights and its non-binding nature.[19]

---

15 MORSINK, *supra* note 2, pp. 288–289.

16 *Ibid.*, p. 289.

17 *Ibid.*

18 L.J.C. BEAUFORT, 'Universele Verklaring van de Rechten van de Mens', 1 *Katholiek Staatkundig Maandschrift* (1949) pp. 488–490.

19 L.J.C. BEAUFORT, 'Some Remarks about the European Convention for the Protection of Human Rights and Fundamental Freedoms', in R.J. ALFARO et al. (eds), *Varia juris gentium: vraagstukken van international recht* (Sijthoff, Leiden, 1959) p. 42.

Beaufort was not the only one who regretted the amendment being withdrawn; also the other members of the Dutch delegation thought the withdrawal to be a serious defeat. This can be inferred from the fact that the Dutch Ambassador Van Roijen returned to the amendment in his speech in the General Assembly on 9 December 1948: "The fact that man's rights and freedoms are based on his divine origin and immortal destiny, the fact that there is a Supreme Being who is the fount of these rights, increases their value and their importance. To ignore this relation would mean the same thing as breaking a plant from its roots or building a house and forgetting its foundations".[20] The Ambassador emphasised that the belief in the divine origin of man and his immortal destiny had constituted the basis for Dutch resistance in the Second World War.

2.2. THE ROLE OF THE DUTCH GOVERNMENT AND PARLIAMENT

At that time (late 1940s), the government of the Netherlands did not show much interest in drafting human rights documents within the framework of the UN. Its main concern was the relationship with the overseas territories in Asia (East Indies) which was quite tense. This created room for the members of the Netherlands delegation, Beaufort in particular, to come up with their own ideas.[21] The amendment proposed by Beaufort was not suggested by the Dutch Government, and also the government did not exactly know the strategy of the Dutch delegation. However, the delegation had informed the government of Beaufort's plans to deliver a speech in which he would plead for the religious aspect of human rights.[22] According to one of the Dutch delegates, Ms. Klompé (KVP), the inspiration for the Dutch delegation to introduce the amendment came from the general instruction that they had received from the Dutch Government, which said that the delegation had to motivate in the Third Committee why human rights were so important. Hence, the delegation decided that the best way to stress this value was by referring to the divine origin of human rights in the Preamble.[23]

Most likely, this instruction by the Government and the way the delegation decided to deal with it, stem from some discussions that arose in

---

20 Ministerie van Buitenlandse Zaken, *supra* note 3, p. 111.

21 CASTERMANS-HOLLEMAN, *supra* note 9, pp. 180–182.

22 I. JUNGSCHLEGER and C. BIERLAAGH, *Marga Klompé. Een gedreven politica haar tijd vooruit* (Veen uitgevers, Utrecht/Antwerpen, 1990) p. 62.

23 F. OBBEMA and T. DUIN, 'Je blijft afhankelijk van de goede wil van iedere staat afzonderlijk', 10 *Wordt Vervolgd* (1983) pp. 1–4.

the Dutch Parliament in the course of the year 1948. From the beginning of the drafting process of the UDHR, this human rights document had not been an important topic on the agenda of the Government and Parliament. Several reasons can be given for that, of which the ongoing troubles in the overseas territories can be said to be one of the most important. Secondly, the Dutch had lost their key interest in the UDHR when it became clear that a binding instrument on human rights would not be developed in the near future.[24] Thirdly, legally speaking Parliament also did not have an important role in policies regarding international relations, as can be inferred from Article 58 of the Dutch Constitution of 1948: "The King shall have the supreme discretion of foreign relations".[25]

Hence, not many meetings of Parliament were dedicated to discussions on the UDHR. However in the course of the year 1948, when the drafting process of the UDHR was already in an advanced stage, both the Lower and the Upper House did refer to the drafting of the UDHR. First, during a discussion on the Brussels Treaty Organisation[26] in the Lower House in April 1948, Member of Parliament Mr. Serrarens (KVP) commented on the fact that in the ECOSOC meeting in Geneva, the Lebanese proposal to include the Creator in the Declaration on Human Rights had not received much support. Mr. Serrarens said that this rejection disappointed him very much, especially because several Christian countries had also rejected it. He therefore asked the Minister to make sure such an omission would not be acceptable with respect to the Brussels Treaty Organisation.[27] Secondly, in a meeting of the Upper House on the same topic on 23 June 1948, Member of Parliament Mr. Schneider (KVP) also referred to the dismissal of the proposal of Lebanon, and he emphasised that he had large difficulties with the fact that many so-called Christian states had rejected the proposal. Many of the other Members shared his concerns, which eventually led to a motion by Mr. Van Voorst tot Voorst (KVP) in which the Upper Chamber stated that in treaties and international agreements concerning human rights, recognising the notion of Christianity was necessary, and that it therefore asked the Government to seriously seek for incorporation of this notion in future treaties and

---

24 P. MALCONTENT and F. BAUDET, 'The Dutchman's Burden?', in B. DE GRAAFF et al. (eds), *De Nederlandse buitenlandse politiek in de twintigste eeuw* (Boom, Amsterdam, 2003) pp. 79–80.

25 'The King' in this context is the Government.

26 Established on 17 March 1948 by the United Kingdom, France, Belgium, the Netherlands and Luxembourg. It was aimed to be an organisation for collective self-defence. In 1949, it was succeeded by NATO.

27 Kamerstukken II 1947/48, 774, p. 1629.

agreements.[28] One day later, the Dutch Minister of Foreign Affairs, Mr. Boetzelaer van Oosterhout (without party affiliation), asserted that he completely supported this idea, but that one had to recognise the fact that many countries that were involved in the drafting and signing of these treaties and agreements definitely did not support this idea, and that therefore it was not always possible to refer to Christian values in universal treaties and/or agreements. However, he was not successful in convincing the majority of the Upper House, and the motion of Van Voorst tot Voorst was accepted with 26 against 3 votes (1 Member was absent).[29] Legally speaking, the Government could simply ignore this motion by pointing to Article 58 of the Constitution.[30] However, it probably realised that it would be difficult not to take into account the Parliament's opinion on a fundamental issue like this. Moreover, the Government was composed of members of the Roman Catholic Party (KVP), the Socialist Labour Party (PvdA) and some members that were not affiliated with a political party.[31] The KVP was the biggest group in parliament. Since the motion was initiated by a member of the KVP and was also supported by all members of the PvdA, it is very likely that the Ministers of these parties were also in favour of the motion. Thus, the amendment proposed by Beaufort certainly had the backing from his political friends in Parliament.

With hindsight, the Dutch proposal to include a reference to the divine origin of human rights in the Preamble of the UDHR was characterised by weakness for two reasons. First, the Netherlands held a quite isolated position when it proposed the amendment. It was not seconded by other countries and the delegation was quite passive in searching for support from other countries. Secondly, the Dutch proposal reflected traditional Christian values that indeed had backing in Dutch society, but not necessarily at the international level among other countries with different world visions.[32] Indeed, the role of religion in post-war Dutch politics was important.

---

28 Kamerstukken I 1947/48, 774, p. 673: "De Kamer, van oordeel, dat in verdragen en internationale overeenkomsten, welke beogen den grondslag te vormen van bescherming van de rechten van den mens, de erkenning van de Christelijke gedachte noodzakelijk is, nodigt de Regering uit, bij het sluiten van verdragen en het aangaan van overeenkomsten, als vorenbedoeld, met ernst daarnaar te streven, en gaat over tot de orde van den dag."

29 Kamerstukken I 1947/48, *supra* note 28, p. 684. The three Members of Parliament that voted against the motion were members of the Communist Party.

30 *See* the previous page.

31 When the motion was tabled, the Government consisted of 14 Ministers, 7 of which were a member of the KVP, 5 were a member of the PvdA and 2 without party affiliation.

32 CASTERMANS-HOLLEMAN, *supra* note 9, pp. 177–178, 182–183.

According to Voorhoeve, who wrote a key study on Dutch foreign policy, "many observers have commented on Calvinist features in the Dutch analysis of national and international politics: a strong tendency to make sharp divisions between good and bad, formulate elevated targets, and subordinate daily life to a gradual, methodical movement towards moral goals, with much forthrightness, but little tact and diplomacy, in an effort to set an example for the rest of the world".[33] This emphasis on Christian values in Dutch foreign policy vanished in the 1960s and 1970s, but moral issues remained an important factor in Dutch human rights policy and development cooperation. Although the interventions by Beaufort may be characterised as incidents, they also show to some extent the willingness of politicians to bear witness of Christian ideas and inheritance at the international level.[34]

3. THE RECEPTION OF THE UDHR IN THE DUTCH PRESS

The Dutch press[35] dedicated some lines to the adoption of the UDHR but only a few daily papers and journals really published an opinion on the format and content of the UDHR. All newspapers informed their readers about the underlying idea of the UDHR and the fact that Mrs. Roosevelt had put a lot of work in its drafting. In addition, all newspapers discussed the Russian position in the Assembly and they explicitly expressed their condemnation of this stance; only the socialist newspaper *Het Vrije Volk*

---

33 J.J.C. VOORHOEVE, *Peace, Profits and Principles: A Study of Dutch Foreign Policy* (Martinus Nijhoff, The Hague, 1979) p. 17. See also CASTERMANS-HOLLEMAN, *supra* note 9, p. 183, holding the same view. In an address to the UN in 1955, the then Foreign Minister of the Netherlands, Mr. Luns (Roman Catholic) made the following observation: 'The *civitas mundi* cannot exist unless it has caught some reflection of the *civitas dei*'. Quoted by VOORHOEVE, p. 197.

34 On 4 October 2003, the 28 Heads of State and Government of the Member States, of acceding countries and candidates to the European Union, met in Rome for the opening of the Inter-Governmental Conference (IGC) 2003–2004. The aim of this Conference was to develop a definite text for the European Constitutional Treaty. During the opening session, several Heads of State/Government expressed their view on how to proceed and what they thought were the most important issues to be incorporated in the Treaty. Some countries indicated that they would like to have an explicit reference to the Judeo-Christian inheritance in the Preamble. During his speech, the Dutch Prime Minister Balkenende (CDA) also asked to add such a reference to the Preamble. See, Ministerie van Buitenlandse Zaken, *Verslag Europese Raad Brussel 16–17 oktober 2003* (Doc. DIE/598/03) p. 8.

35 The newspapers that have been investigated are: *Nieuwe Rotterdamsche Courant*, *De Volkskrant*, *Trouw*, *Het Parool*, *Het Vrije Volk*, *Nieuwe Courant*, *Haagsche Courant*, *De Tijd* and the weekly magazine *Vrij Nederland*.

remained silent with respect to this topic.[36] The Liberal newspaper *Nieuwe Rotterdamsche Courant* claimed that the UDHR could have an important moral influence in the states adopting it. However it also stressed that it would be very likely that the theory of the UDHR will not become widespread practice. Secondly, this newspaper informed its readers about the Dutch efforts to adopt the divine origin of man in the UDHR. The author of the piece shared the view of the states that did not want to incorporate this divine origin and he emphasised that the UDHR should be appealing to all, not only to Christians.[37]

The Catholic newspaper *De Tijd* also touched upon the divine origin of man: obviously, the (Catholic) author was not pleased with the fact that the origin of man was not incorporated. However, he still believed that the UDHR could be an important document. Similar to his colleague of the *Nieuwe Rotterdamsche Courant*, he doubted if the theory of the UDHR would be ever put into practice, and he stated that it would be very difficult for all participating states to change their legislation in accordance with the UDHR.[38] The opinion of the Socialist paper *Het Vrije Volk* did not differ that much from its Liberal and Catholic counterparts; the author did not mention the origin of man issue, but he did point at the theory versus practice problem. In his opinion, the UDHR had little practical relevance at the time of its adoption and he believed that a binding convention would lead to better results. However, he doubted if such a convention would ever get into practice.[39] The most critical position can be found in the independent weekly journal *Vrij Nederland*: the author specifically questioned if any government would put any effort in making the UDHR work, since "during the meetings of the Third Committee, all the large states have fought to formulate the Universal Declaration of Human Rights in a way that it will not affect them in their actual political activities".[40]

Overall, the newspapers did not give much attention to the UDHR, and when they did, their position was quite critical about its practical importance. The fact that the UDHR did not receive that much attention can probably also be attributed to the fact that in the week after its adoption, the Netherlands experienced major troubles in their overseas colonies in Asia, and all papers completely devoted their attention to these developments. This

---

36 'Mensenrechten', *Het Vrije Volk*, 10 December 1948, p. 5.

37 'De Rechten van de Mens', *Nieuwe Rotterdamsche Courant*, 3 December 1948, p. 3.

38 'De UNO-vergadering in beeld', *De Tijd*, 11 December 1948, p. 1.

39 'Mensenrechten', *Het Vrije Volk*, 10 December 1948, p. 5.

40 L. DE JONG, 'Uno-vergadering verdaagd', *Vrij Nederland*, 18 December 1948, p. 2.

might also be the reason why in January 1949 *Het Parool* eventually published the complete text of the Declaration, and stated in its commentary that it was a milestone in the journey of mankind.[41] However, this positive reaction was not very surprising, taking into account the fact that the editor-in-chief of this newspaper was a member of the National Advisory Committee on Human Rights.[42]

4. THE RECEPTION OF THE UDHR IN DUTCH LEGAL AND POLITICAL CIRCLES

Already in November 1948, the leading Netherlands Lawyers Weekly Journal (*Nederlands Juristenblad*) presented a brief overview of the draft text of the UDHR. The author argued that the UDHR would contain the idealistic slogan of human rights which was of a high moral value. It would certainly have its impact on national law and international law. However, more was to be expected from a really legally binding covenant.[43] In 1949, the same journal published the complete text of the UDHR with the following comment: "Whether the impact of this document for world history will be as large as object and content would suggest remains to be seen. However, a lawyer should know the text and be able to consult it easily".[44]

One leading constitutional lawyer, professor A.M. Donner, objected to a separation between the declaration and covenant. He was of the view that proclaiming human rights by means of 'half poetic' clauses was not enough. A legally non-binding UDHR might perhaps be seen as a grand gesture. However, it lacked teeth and was of cheap quality.[45] The most important Dutch manual on international law published in the post-war period by professor François, when addressing the question whether individuals were subjects of rights under international law, observed about the UDHR that it lacked legally binding force. In his view, its vague orders do not have

41 'Universele Verklaring voor de Rechten van de Mens', *Het Parool*, 22 January 1949, p. 5.

42 M.C. CASTERMANS-HOLLEMAN, 'Nederland en de totstandkoming van de universele verklaring van de rechten van de mens', 23:8 *NJCM-Bulletin* (1998) p. 967.

43 VAN DULLEMEN, 'Een internationale verklaring van mensenrechten', *Nederlands Juristenblad*, 13 November 1948, pp. 661–665.

44 *Nederlands Juristenblad*, 5 March 1949, p. 184.

45 A.M. DONNER, 'Een internationale "Declaration on Human Rights"?', *Opstellen op het gebied van recht, staat en maatschappij* (S.J.P. Bakker, Amsterdam, 1949) pp. 208, 219.

practical significance.[46] In 1953, the Netherlands Lawyers Association held its annual meeting on the question whether social rights as included in the UDHR should also be incorporated into the Netherlands Constitution. After discussing two expert reports, the large majority of those who were present voted against such incorporation. One of the main objections was that these rights were slogans rather than real rights and too complex and diverse to be included in a key legal document like the Constitution.[47]

The reaction of the Dutch Government and Parliament to the adoption of the UDHR can be found in the debates on the national budget for 1949. One of the agenda items was the functioning of the United Nations. In general, Parliament and the Government were not very pleased with the way the UN was functioning at that time, and with respect to the UDHR, several Members of Parliament again criticised the omission of a reference to God in the Declaration.[48] The reply of the Government was similar to the reply that Minister Boetzelaer van Oosterhout gave on the motion of Van Voorst tot Voorst; it explained that it was impossible for a universal organisation like the UN, in which so many different countries were involved, to have a basis in the Christian faith.[49]

Several political parties again referred to the UDHR when the approval of the European Convention on Human Rights (hereinafter ECHR) was discussed in Parliament. Spokesmen from a number of political groups regretted that the ECHR did not contain a reference to the divine origin of man. This was very similar to the opinion of political parties during the drafting process of the UDHR. Political parties emphasised that the ECHR was more important than the UDHR because it was legally binding and contained an individual complaints mechanism. However, some members also stressed that in a way the UDHR was a more comprehensive document than the ECHR, because it included social, economic and cultural rights.[50]

In 1959, the Socialist Labour Party incorporated the text of the UDHR as an annex to its Programme of Basic Principles, thus indicating the close relationship between the realisation of social welfare for all and the

---

46 J.P.A. FRANÇOIS, *Grondlijnen van het Volkenrecht*, 2nd ed. (W.E.J. Tjeenk Willink, Zwolle, 1957) p. 232.

47 *Handelingen der Nederlandse Juristen Vereniging 1953*, vol. 83 (W.E.J. Tjeenk Willink, Zwolle, 1953). Only in 1983 were social rights included in the Netherlands Constitution.

48 Kamerstukken II 1948/49, 1000, III, No. 10, p. 3.

49 Kamerstukken II 1948/49, 1000, I, No. 5–7, p. 3; Kamerstukken II 1948/49, 1000, III, No. 10, p. 3; Kamerstukken II 1948/49, 1000, III, No. 12–13, p. 7.

50 Kamerstukken II 1953/54, 3043, No. 6, p. 3; Handelingen II, 4 March 1954, p. 827; Handelingen I, 27 July 1954, p. 615, 619.

implementation of human rights. Neither the Netherlands Constitution nor any other law refer to the UDHR.

5. THE ROLE OF THE UDHR IN DUTCH CASE LAW

The role and impact of the UDHR in Dutch case law has been very modest. The reason for this is the status given to rules of international law in the Netherlands legal order. The Netherlands is a country with a monist system regarding the relationship between international and national law. Since the revision of the Netherlands Constitution in 1956, the following two provisions characterise this relationship:

> "Article 93:
> Provisions of treaties and of resolutions by international institutions which may be binding on all persons by virtue of their contents shall become binding after they have been published."

> "Article 94:
> Statutory regulations in force within the Kingdom shall not be applicable if such application is in conflict with provisions of treaties that are binding on all persons or of resolutions by international institutions."

These provisions concern the internal effect of provisions of treaties (and resolutions by international organisations) that are self-executing (Article 93) and the prevalence of such provisions over rules of domestic law (Article 94). The courts decide whether such provisions are self-executing. Resolutions of international institutions refer to decisions of bodies of international organisations to which legislative, executive and judicial powers have been conferred, such as the UN Security Council and institutions of the European Communities.[51]

An early mention of the UDHR can be found in a judgment which refers to the objective of the ECHR, laid down in its Preamble, to enforce collectively certain rights stated in the UDHR.[52] Since the late 1960s there have been occasional examples of cases in which defendants or complainants have invoked provisions of the UDHR in order to strengthen their argument. In a case which came before the Supreme Court (*Hoge Raad*) in 1969, the

---

[51] *Compare* Article 92 Netherlands Constitution.

[52] Hoge Raad, 5 May 1959, *Nederlandse Jurisprudentie* 1959, Nr. 361, quoting a paragraph from a judgment of the Regional Court in Maastricht, 27 January 1959.

Advocate-General argued that the UDHR has a superior legal status.[53] However, without exception courts have refused to qualify articles of the UDHR as provisions in the sense of Article 93 of the Constitution. The reason for this is that in the view of the courts, the UDHR is based on the power of the General Assembly under chapter IV of the Charter of the UN to make non-binding recommendations. The UDHR is not based on a conferred power to adopt resolutions which may be binding on all persons. Consequently, provisions of the UDHR cannot be invoked directly before a court of law; they lack direct effect in the Netherlands legal order. Its influence, therefore, is very limited. This interpretation is shared by the highest courts in civil, criminal and administrative matters, namely the Supreme Court, the Council of State and the Central Court of Appeal.[54] Over the years, courts have not changed their position.[55] Generally speaking, the courts only need a few words to strike down any claim that is based on the UDHR.

In the view of the courts almost all provisions of the ECHR and the International Covenant on Civil and Political Rights do have direct effect in the Netherlands legal order. Invoking similar provisions from the UDHR therefore does not have much of an added value. However, the courts have refused to accept the self-executing nature of provisions included in the International Covenant on Economic, Social and Cultural Rights and the European Social Charter.[56] Social and economic rights included in the UDHR cannot help citizens in such cases, because of its weak status in the Netherlands legal order.

6. CONCLUDING REMARKS

This chapter has shown that in general the Dutch did not attach very much importance to the UDHR. During the drafting process, the focus of the Dutch representatives was quite different from that of many of the other countries involved. The Dutch delegation to the Third Committee was primarily preoccupied with including a reference to the divine origin of human rights

---

[53] Hoge Raad, 7 January 1969, *Nederlandse Jurisprudentie* 1969, Nr. 259.

[54] *Compare* Hoge Raad, 23 November 1984, *Nederlandse Jurisprudentie*, 1985, Nr. 604; Judicial Branch of the Council of State, 16 March 1978, *Administratiefrechtelijke Beslissingen*, 1979, Nr. 198; Central Court of Appeal, 5 December 2003, *LJN* AO2554.

[55] *See*, for example, Council of State, Judicial Branch, 12 September 2007, *LJN* BB3416.

[56] With one exception, namely Article 6(4) European Social Charter (the right to strike) has been given direct effect by the Supreme Court; *see* Hoge Raad 30 May 1986, *Nederlandse Jurisprudentie* 1986, Nr. 688.

in the UDHR, while other countries — even the Christian ones — thought this was not a good idea, because the UDHR as a universal document should be neutral. During the drafting process, the Dutch Government and Parliament did not spend much time on the UDHR. The few debates that were devoted to the UDHR also focused on the need to incorporate a reference to the divine origin of human rights in the text and on the fact that the UDHR was not legally binding. The main reason for this lack of interest was the troubles the Dutch experienced in their overseas colonies which required full attention of key players in politics and society.

The reception of the UDHR in the press and legal circles was rather lukewarm. The press was much more occupied with the overseas colonies, but when it did discuss the UDHR, absence of the divine origin and the non-binding nature of the text were the main issues. The weak legal status of the UDHR was also the principal concern of several Dutch lawyers: since the UDHR was not binding, they thought it to have little practical relevance. In addition, because of the Dutch monist legal system, it was (and still is) impossible to successfully invoke provisions of the UDHR before the courts. Consequently, the UDHR has not been a milestone or signpost for the development of human rights in the Netherlands. One might have expected otherwise in a country which often sees itself as strong advocate of human rights protection worldwide.

9. POLAND: FROM OBLIVION TO LEGAL USE

Roman Wieruszewski[1]

1. INTRODUCTORY COMMENTS

When discussing the reception of the Universal Declaration of Human Rights (hereinafter UDHR) in a given country, one has to base the analysis in the historical context. In case of Poland, until the end of the so-called Socialist/Communist era, in the second half of the year 1989, the influence of the UDHR, in particular, and the international system of protection of human rights, in general, was very minimal as far as the legal position of an individual was concerned. In fact, one may justifiably claim that it was non-existent. The reason was very obvious. After the Second World War, the people of Poland had not been able to freely decide about their political system. As we know, the Communist regime, which has been imposed on Poland, effectively deprived it of sovereign decisions about its legal system as well as about methods and forms of participation in the international cooperation. Human rights belonged to the very sensitive areas of competition between the Communist and the Western countries. The Communist doctrine was not prepared to accept the concept of universally binding human values. At the same time those countries, including the Polish Peoples Republic (hereinafter PPR), during the debate on the draft of the UDHR, promoted the so-called collective right of peoples to democracy. As it is known, the PPR together with seven other countries abstained from voting on the UDHR during the General Assembly vote in 1948. It is therefore irrelevant to recall what the government of the PPR said about the UDHR at the time of adoption. It could not be referred to as "our" government in the way of a government representing the will of the people. The same is true for the media of those times.

---

[1] Author would like to express gratitude to Ms Aleksandra Gliszczynska and Ms Katarzyna Sękowska–Kozłowska, assistants at the Poznan Human Rights Centre, for valuable help in preparing this article.

The PPR had ratified both international covenants and a number of other United Nations (hereinafter UN) human rights treaties. However, when reporting to the Human Rights Committee, the PPR informed that provisions of those treaties could not be directly applied. This meant that during the whole period of the existence of the PPR until the end of 1989, neither the UDHR nor any other international human rights provision played any role in the domestic legal system.

However, the democratic opposition was frequently invoking the UDHR while opposing violations of human rights in Poland. In 1976, in particular, when further anti-democratic amendments were made to the PPR Constitution, the opposition used provisions of the UDHR to protest against those changes. Of course, those protests were ignored.

One should not overlook the fact that also during that period, in particular at the second half of the 1980s, judicial bodies started to quote the UDHR and, in some cases also the international Covenants. For example, before the transition into the democratic system, the Constitutional Tribunal and the Supreme Administrative Court cited the UDHR as a persuasive argument, but not as a binding legal norm.[2]

The situation changed when a new political system was created in Poland after the collapse of the Communist regime. Poland belonged to the category of countries that changed its political and legal system while not formally replacing its Constitution at the same time. However, in the years 1989/1990 several substantial amendments to the 1952 Constitution were adopted, thus eliminating almost all of the remaining normative elements of the previous political system. A new Constitution was adopted only in 1997. However, based on provisions of the so-called Small Constitution and on the interpretation of the clause 'democratic state ruled by law', provided by the Constitutional Tribunal, a new concept of the position of international human rights law, including the UDHR, was adopted. Poland decided to fully adhere to the international system of human rights protection, including its control mechanisms. It meant, for example, the ratification of the First Optional Protocol to the International Covenant on Civil and Political Rights.

At the beginning of the 1990s, Poland was not accepted into the Council of Europe pending the holding of the first fully democratic elections. Therefore the United Nations system of international protection of human rights was for Poland the only binding international system at that time until

---

2 R. WIERUSZEWSKI, 'National Implementation of Human Rights', in A. ROSAS and J. HELGESEN (eds), *Human Rights in a Changing East–West Perspective* (Pinter Publishers, London and New York, 1990) p. 272.

1993. During that period of time, both the Constitutional Tribunal and ordinary courts, including the Supreme Court, started to quote the UDHR more frequently.

In the debate leading to the adoption of the new Constitution the provisions of the UDHR and both Covenants were used as models for new constitutional formulas for human rights provisions. Also the new Constitution contained in Article 9 the rule that "the Republic of Poland respects binding international law". On the basis of judgments of the Constitutional Tribunal and other courts, presented below, it is clear that the UDHR has been considered as part of binding international law.

This article concentrates on the presentation of judicial decisions in which the UDHR has been quoted. However, international human rights law, including the UDHR, played an important role in the legislative process This was so in particular at the beginning of 1990s, when many new laws were adopted in order to replace the old laws of the Communist times. For example, the preamble of the statute concerning the educational system proclaims that education in Poland is guided, *inter alia*, by principles embodied in the UDHR.[3]

2. THE CONSTITUTIONAL TRIBUNAL

The Constitutional Tribunal (hereinafter CT) played a very important role as a guardian of the constitutional system for protection of human rights in Poland. One should remember that the CT had been established already in December 1985, and it passed its first judgment on 28 May 1986. The CT jurisprudence, already under the former legal system, had exerted a significant impact on the creation of a new legal system based on the principle of the rule of law. However, only after transformation of the political system was the CT able to fully use its powers. Of particular interest from the human rights point of view is the CT jurisprudence that emerged upon the adoption of the 1997 Constitution and that was based on the mechanism of the individual constitutional complaint. Judgments passed upon those complaints considerably increased the understanding of the system for the protection of human rights and freedoms. Below, all 11 CT decisions, in which provisions of the UDHR have been quoted, are presented.

For the first time after the transition into the democratic system, the CT invoked provisions of the UDHR in a case dealing with the constitutionality

---

3 Law of 7 September 1991, Dz.U. 1996 nr 67 poz. 329.

of a law allowing the teaching of religion in a public school. The CT quoted, *inter alia*, Article 18 of the UDHR and ruled that a law which will prohibit or impose the teaching of religion against the will of the parents will contradict international standards.[4] That argument was also used in the next CT decision concerning the same subject matter, and Article 18 of the UDHR was again invoked.[5]

In another decision concerning the right to unemployment benefits the CT, while defending that right, invoked Article 23 paragraph 1 of the UDHR.[6] The CT had the following occasion to quote the UDHR in its decision concerning the new law on taxation when it based its rejection of that law as violating right to privacy, *inter alia*, on the wording of Article 12 of the UDHR.[7]

General reference to the UDHR was made in the CT judgment concerning the law which regulated the method of shaping employment salaries in the mining industry. The CT explained that the law at hand is of discriminatory nature and violates as such rights embodied in the UDHR and relevant ILO conventions.[8] In the decision concerning the permissible regulation of the right to perform certain professional activities, the CT based its rejection of such rules, *inter alia*, on Article 23 paragraph 1 of the UDHR.[9]

A very important statement which explained the position of the CT as far as the role of the UDHR and other international instruments in the domestic legal system are concerned, can be found in the next CT judgment where it ruled that the "expression 'constitutional freedoms and rights' used in Article 79 paragraph 1 of the Constitution covered also human and citizens rights as regulated in basic documents of international law, that is, the Universal Declaration of Human Rights".[10]

In another judgment concerning the regulation of right to education, the CT, while reconstructing the international standard of that right, quoted Article 26 of the UDHR.[11] The same approach was used in a judgment concerning the right to property. The CT quoted Article 17 of the UDHR.[12]

---

4 K. 11/90, 30 January 1991, Constitutional Tribunal, OTK 1991 poz. 2.

5 U. 12/92, 20 April 1993, Constitutional Tribunal, OTK 1993/I poz. 9.

6 P. 2/92, 1 June 1993, Constitutional Tribunal, OTK 1993/II poz. 20.

7 K. 21/96, 24 June 1997, Constitutional Tribunal, OTK ZU 1997/2 poz. 23.

8 K. 6/99, 7 December 1999, Constitutional Tribunal, OTK ZU 1999/7 poz. 160.

9 K. 33/98, 26 April 1999, Constitutional Tribunal, OTK ZU 1999/4 poz. 71.

10 SK 21/99, 10 July 2000, Constitutional Tribunal, OTK ZU 2000/5 poz. 144.

11 SK 18/99, 8 November 2000, Constitutional Tribunal, OTK ZU 2000/7 poz. 258.

12 P. 4/99, 31 January 2001, Constitutional Tribunal, OTK ZU 2001/1 poz. 5

One recent judgment, in which the CT once again confirmed that norms specified in the UDHR have a binding effect in Poland, merits a longer reflection. The judgment deals with the relationship between the freedom of speech and the protection from interference with privacy, honour and reputation. The CT recalled that human dignity should be considered as a fundamental principle governing the whole system of human rights protection and supported that statement by the preamble of the UDHR. Later it quoted Article 12 of the UDHR and stated that "[t]hose norms of international law — without prejudice to the assessment of the legal value of the Universal Declaration of Human Rights — are binding in the Republic of Poland (Article 9 of the Constitution)".[13] In the last case so far, the CT quoted the UDHR and Article 10 therein in its judgment concerning the freedom of speech.[14]

To sum up the above-described jurisprudence of the CT in which provisions of the UDHR have been quoted, one may argue that the CT was using the provisions of the UDHR as customary norms of international law of human rights. According to the CT, the UDHR constitutes part of the domestically binding international human rights law in Poland.

3. THE SUPREME COURT

The Supreme Court (hereinafter SC) has generally speaking followed the above-presented line of the CT with regard to the position of the UDHR in the Polish legal system. The SC, unlike the CT, has, however, been dealing only with individual cases. While during the period of the PPR it was rather reluctant to use international law in general, and human rights law in particular, as part of its judgments, that attitude has drastically changed after transformation. The SC has opened itself up for international law, and at present, the SC treats it as a set of binding norms directly applicable. In this section, only a handful of selected judgments are presented in order to illustrate that tendency. Altogether, there are 11 SC decisions of different kinds in which provisions of the UDHR have been mentioned. The first one dates back to 1992.

As a matter of interest I would like to point out that the SC judgments in which reference was made to the UDHR have dealt with two rights, the freedom of speech (Article 19) and the access to court (Article 11). For the

---

13 P 10/06, 30 October 2006, Constitutional Tribunal, Dz. U. Nr 202, poz. 1492.

14 P 1/06, 20 February 2007, Constitutional Tribunal, Dz. U. Nr 36, poz. 234.

first time, the SC unequivocally made reference to the UDHR as binding law in the ruling of the Administrative, Labour and Social Security Chamber of the SC in July 1992. The SC stated that "to the Covenants and treaties, either directly ratified by Poland or having a binding effect in Poland due to our accession to the Council of Europe, belongs the UDHR".[15] That ruling dealt with the right to access to court in case of an administrative decision concerning the reassignment of a judge. In a couple of other decisions concerning that problem, reference was made to the UDHR as a source of binding international law.[16] Some years ago that ruling was again confirmed in a decision concerning the principle of *nullum crimen sine lege*.[17] In those decisions the UDHR has been treated as having the same binding effect as international treaties, such as the International Covenant of Civil and Political Rights or the European Convention on Human Rights.

A series of SC judgments and rulings have dealt with the freedom of speech, the rights and obligations of journalists, the prohibition of censorship, and so on. In all those decisions, reference was made to the UDHR.[18] In that context one could quote a recent decision of the SC according to which "[a]t the international level, the freedom of the press has been guarded by acts of public international law of the UN system, among them in particular the International Covenant on Civil and Political Rights and the Universal Declaration of Human Rights".[19]

4. APPELLATE COURTS

Lower courts in Poland, including appellate courts, are by far more reluctant to base their decisions on provisions of international law. However, in some cases they do. I have been able to identify two judgments of two different appellate courts in which reference was made to the provisions of the UDHR.

---

15 III AZP 9/92, 23 July 1992, Supreme Court, OSNCP 1994/7–8 poz. 147.

16 III AZP 20/93, 21 December 1993, Supreme Court, OSNCP 1994/6 poz. 119. The SC stated that principle of an universal access to courts derives from Polish obligation embodied in international Covenants and treaties in particular in the UDHR".

17 V KKN 511/99,14 January 2000, Supreme Court – Criminal Law Chamber.

18 III CZP 53/2004, 18 February 2005, Supreme Court – Civil Law Chamber – the ruling of seven judges, OSP 2005/9 poz. 110; II CKN 1095/99, 5 April 2002, Supreme Court – Civil Law Chamber, judgment, OSNC 2003/3 poz. 42; III ZP 32/2000, 13 June 2001, Supreme Court – a ruling of Administrative, Labour and Social Security Chamber, OSNAPiUS 2002/7 poz. 165.

19 III KK 243/06 7 February 2007, Supreme Court – decision, OSNKW 2007/5/43.

In its judgments concerning some aspects of unlawful threats made by a certain individual, the Appellate Court in Lublin based its acquittal decision, *inter alia*, on provisions of the UDHR.[20] In a very controversial and interesting case concerning anti-strike actions undertaken by the military regime in Poland during the martial law in 1982, the Appellate Court in Warsaw ruled that those actions constituted so-called Communist crimes since they violated fundamental human rights, more specifically the right to life and the right to strike as formulated, *inter alia*, in the UDHR.[21] These decisions prove that also those courts treat the UDHR as a source of binding international standards.

5. ADMINISTRATIVE COURTS

Until the reform of the administrative judiciary, which took place in 2002, the Supreme Administrative Court (hereinafter SAC) was the only administrative court handling cases of an administrative nature. In its jurisprudence, it invoked provisions of the UDHR on three occasions.

As early as in 1991, the SAC quoted the UDHR and its Article 10 for the first time in a case concerning the dismissal of a police officer from service and his right to appeal against that decision before the court. The SAC ruled that the right to access to court should also be guaranteed in such a case since Article 11 of the UDHR provides for such a right. However, the SAC did not claim that the UDHR had a directly applicable effect in the Polish legal system, but was of the opinion that it should serve as an interpretative indicator while implementing Polish law.[22]

The next time the SAC made a reference to the UDHR was in its decision concerning the right to refugee status in the year 2000. In that judgment, however, the SAC hinted that the UDHR does not have an unequivocally binding character in Poland. The SAC stated that the "prohibition of arbitrary arrest or detention derives not only from Article 9 of the invoked in the preamble of the Geneva Convention and UDHR, but is also directly binding under Polish law — due to Article 87 paragraph 1 and Article 90 paragraph 1 of the Constitution — norms of Article 9 paragraph 1 of International

20 II AKa 338/2003, 27 November 2003, Appellate Court in Lublin, OSA 2005/6 poz. 39 p. 30.

21 II AKa 440/2004, 10 February 2005, Appellate Court in Warsaw, judgment, OSA 2005/9 poz. 67, p. 41.

22 I SA 35/91, 5 May 1991, Supreme Administrative Court, judgment, ONSA 1991 3–4 poz. 64.

Covenant of Civil and Political Rights".[23] In the most recent of its judgments in this field, the SAC, also in a case concerning refugee status, quoted the UDHR as formulating binding standards.[24]

After the reform of the administrative courts, when a first instance was created, the Wojewodship Administrative Courts (hereinafter WAC) also made references to provisions of the UDHR. In a series of cases, the same Warsaw WAC ruled that, based on the concept of human dignity as formulated, *inter alia*, in the UDHR, the right to access to court should be granted to everybody regardless of his or her financial situation.[25] In a refugee case, Article 14 of the UDHR was invoked.[26]

6. THE UDHR IN MEDIA AND PUBLIC OPINION

The UDHR as such has not been a subject of extensive publication in Polish media. When it has been quoted, it has taken place only in a broader context of different human rights related topics.

One can trace references to the UDHR in particular in two daily newspapers, the *Gazeta Wyborcza* and the *Rzeczpospolita*. In the first one the reference to the UDHR had been made on a regular basis during the first stage of transition period, in years 1990–1998. The second mentioned paper devoted more regular attention to the human rights issues, including the UDHR also at present times. Both papers published articles to commemorate the 50th anniversary of the UDHR in 1998. Quite often the UDHR has been quoted in the context of serious human rights violations, for example, in the cases of Darfur, Somalia, Kosovo, Rwanda, and Chechnya. The two newspapers have also been publishing information about different projects conducted by NGOs, for example, campaign of letters written to authorities of countries where human rights are violated, organised by Amnesty International in the context of anniversaries of the proclamation of the UDHR.

In some other papers with very strong ideological affiliations, such as the *Nowy Dziennik*, a right-wing Catholic-populist paper, the UDHR has been quoted in the context of the campaign against abortion and in support of the

---

23 V SA 1781/99, 24 August 2000, Supreme Administrative Court, ONSA 2001/4 poz. 176.

24 V SA 2211/2001, 27 March 2002, Supreme Administrative Court, ONSA 2003/2 poz. 76.

25 III SA/Wa 426/08, 31 March 2008 – WAC; III SA/Wa 86/08, 15 January 2008 – WAC; III SA/Wa 87/08, 15 January 2008 – WAC; III SA/Wa 188/08, 22 February 2008 – WAC.

26 V SA/Wa 2289/07, 29 January 2008, WAC.

right to life. In the post-Communist *Trybuna*, the UDHR has been mentioned a couple of times among other human rights related documents.

As far as weeklies are concerned, the situation is even worse. The most popular one, the *Polityka* has sometimes mentioned the name of the UDHR but never published an article dealing with the meaning and role of it. An interesting article was published in 1998 in another weekly, the *Wprost*, written by a human rights expert, former Prime Minister of Poland and at present Ambassador to the Holy See, Ms. Hanna Suchocka, in which the author analysed the importance of the UDHR in the context of the efficiency of systems for protection of human rights.

One has to stress that overall, in the Polish media, there is a lack not only of analytical publications concerning the UDHR and the UN system of human rights protection but also informative articles presenting elementary facts in this area. That situation has an obvious impact on the way in which the Polish population views the international system of human rights protection.

A sociological survey concerning the knowledge about human rights conducted in Poland in connection with the 50th anniversary of the UDHR showed that only 4 per cent of the respondents were aware that Poland, in fact, had abstained during the voting on the UDHR in the General Assembly. It is interesting to learn that when asked which rights listed in the UDHR are the most important, 54 per cent opted for the right to privacy, 47 per cent for the freedom of thought and religion, 34 per cent for the right to health and 33 per cent for the equality between men and women in family life. When asked to whom they would address complaints about human rights violations, 75 per cent mentioned the Ombudsman, 55 per cent the courts and 54 per cent international organisations. However, in that last category, priority is given to the European institutions, in particular to the European Court of Human Rights.[27] The UN machinery is neither known nor used.

7. CONCLUSIONS

The Polish political elite as well as members of the legal profession were determined to prove that the decision of the Communist rulers of Poland to abstain from voting during the adoption by the General Assembly of the UDHR was against the will of the Polish people. Poland's first democratic Minister of Foreign Affairs, professor Krzysztof Skubiszewski, made it clear,

---

27 OBOB, Warsaw December 1998.

during his speeches at the General Assembly of the UN, that protection of human rights belongs to the priority of the Polish government.[28] One of his successors, Dariusz Rosati, speaking at the General Assembly meeting in September 1997 pointed out: "1998 will be a special year for human rights. Half a century ago the General Assembly adopted the [UDHR], a catalogue of the individual's rights and duties ... [A]s we emphasized in Warsaw this January when inaugurating the celebration of the fiftieth anniversary of the [UDHR], it is worth considering how to use this variety to build a universal concept of human rights, just as the Declaration initially assumed. At the same time, we oppose any attempt at the so-called revision of the Universal Declaration, which must remain a common minimal standard for all humanity".[29]

From the above it is clear that the UDHR plays an important role in the Polish legal system. It is considered an indispensable part of the international law on human rights. Its role was particularly important at the beginning of the transformation process, before the European regional system took precedence over the universal one. When the new democratic, human rights oriented legal system in Poland was created, the letter of the UDHR, as well as its spirit, served as model for new laws, including the Constitution.

---

[28] *See* A. BIEŃCZYK-MISSALA, *Human Rights in Polish Foreign Policy after 1989* (Warsaw, 2006) p. 70.

[29] UN Doc. A/52/PV.13.

10. SWEDEN: UNDERESTIMATION OF RIGHTS

Jonas Grimheden[1]

1. INTRODUCTION

Sweden was not part of the narrow drafting group of eight when the Universal Declaration of Human Rights (hereinafter UDHR) was being formulated. Neither was Sweden among the then 18 members of the United Nations (hereinafter UN) Commission on Human Rights.[2] Being one of the then 56 members of the United Nations, Sweden did vote in favour of the adoption of UDHR on 10 December 1948. The role of Sweden in the process of adoption could, however, have been much greater. The work of the Commission drew remarkably little attention in Sweden. Even though Sweden has since been a promoter of human rights and indeed of the UDHR, the role of the Declaration in Swedish law and politics was and remains surprisingly small. Other events and other focuses seemed to have occupied Sweden in the aftermath of the World War. This situation has continued and, arguably, it reflects an underestimation of the significance of the document and of rights more generally.

In the following pages I will elaborate on how the UDHR was — and continues to be — received in Sweden by looking at three main aspects: coverage around the time of adoption in Swedish media, references from 1948 and onwards in political and academic contexts, and the role of the UDHR in Swedish constitutional and other developments.

---

1 I am grateful for comments from, in addition to the editors, Gudmundur Alfredsson, Uta Bindreiter, Catarina Carlsson, Hans Corell, Andreas Føllesdal, Vreni Hockenjos, Timothy Maldoon, Otto Malmgren, Katarina Månsson, Joakim Nergelius, Gregor Noll, Lena Olsson, Vilhelm Persson, Rolf Ring, Charlotta Schlyter, and Carl Söderbergh. Translations from Swedish are my own unless otherwise noted.

2 J. MORSINK, *The Universal Declaration of Human Rights: Origins, Drafting, and Intent* (University of Pennsylvania Press, Philadelphia, 1999) p. 10.

2. MEDIA COVERAGE

The media coverage of the time is an indicator of where the focus of attention was in Sweden around the time of adoption of the UDHR. Neither of the two major dailies carried any headline or even article on the adoption on or around 10 December. Swedish media appears to have been absorbed by other matters. Then as now, on what has become the global Human Rights Day, 10 December, Sweden focuses on the Nobel Prize Awards.[3] Actually, Sweden was one of the five countries that did not vote in favour of the resolution establishing the Human Rights Day in 1950 in commemoration of the UDHR.[4] In 1948, the focus was also on the peace proposal related to Palestine made by the, at that time already-assassinated Swede, Count Bernadotte. On Sunday 12 December 1948, one of the main dailies covered on page six in a brief section that the concluding session of the third United Nations General Assembly (hereinafter GA) did not even refer to the Bernadotte-proposal in the resolution on Palestine. The peace plan is, as a result, concluded to have been given the 'mortal stab' by the GA.[5]

Other coverage of the work of the United Nations in that issue is fascinating — sad and maybe even a tad bit amusing. International news covered the civil war in China extensively. The front-page was basically only on domestic matters with some brief views in the neighbouring countries. With the smallest of the notes on the front-page, using a mere 60 words, the conclusion of the work of the UN was nevertheless dealt with under the caption "UN's results — 50 million words". The brief text deserves being quoted in full: "During the 12 weeks of the UNGA sessions the 2,000 delegates from 58 countries have uttered 50 million words". A second paragraph adds: "The three months in Palais de Chaillot have amounted to expenditures for the governments of over 5 million dollars. The US has been represented by 200 delegates and the small state of Yemen by nine".[6] A slightly longer piece on the work of the Assembly was to be found on page 15 the same day. From a press conference the main achievements from the meeting included prominently, nevertheless, the UDHR and the Genocide

---

3 Proposed to the UN General Assembly by US in 1950, A/1559, res. III.

4 The resolution was adopted with 47 votes in favour and 5 abstentions. *Aktstycken utgivna av Kungl. Utrikesdepartementet, Ny Serie I: A: 1, FN:s Generalförsamlings femte ordinarie möte, New York 1950–1951* (Stockholm: Norstedts, 1951) p. 128.

5 *Svenska Dagbladet*, 12 December 1948, p. A6.

6 Actually, the British newspaper *The Times* reportedly also referred to the wordiness of the UN sessions. On the 13th an editorial was to be captioned "Too Many Words", according to *Svenska Dagbladet*, 13 December 1948.

Convention. The piece paraphrased Dr. Evatt (the Australian Foreign Minister and UNGA President), stating that, "for the first time in the history, the world in its entirety has collectively expressed themselves regarding the human freedoms and rights, for which single nations have fought, suffered, and died during centuries".

The following day the Swedish newspaper formulated a significantly more analytical piece. On page six quite a lengthy article appeared that mainly drew on an interview with the Swedish Ambassador to the UN Sven Grafström (during 1948–1952), the Swedish envoy during the sessions in Paris in 1948. The initial passage of the article captioned "The Working Methods of the UN Need to be Radically Effectual", articulated in bold two main ambitions: that the tensions between various groups of member states will be reduced, and that the Scandinavian proposal for effective working methods would be accepted. After a long passage on how this, according to Grafström, could be achieved the analysis moves on to the benefits of the UN, not the least in its efforts towards creating peace. An adjacent piece, referring to an editorial in *The Times*, criticised the results of the sessions. The tasks given were close to impossible to solve and the East-West divide made actual outcomes diluted. Among the meagre results were mentioned a resolution on human rights, "adopted by those states that believe in such".

The more conservative daily, *Svenska Dagbladet*, was in its coverage of the adoption of the UDHR more limited than its main competitor, *Dagens Nyheter*, a more Left-oriented newspaper. Still, as the negotiations in Paris were coming to a halt on 10 December 1948, the front-page of *Dagens Nyheter* carried nothing on the United Nations. Among the main headlines were that the Swedish King (Gustaf V) was back after a period of illness, back hunting hare (*sic*) even though he was still too weak to award the Nobel Prizes later that week. With time to ponder, write and dispatch an article to Stockholm from Paris, the daily covered on 12 December the conclusions of the Assembly.[7] Even though the many shortcomings of the UN were mentioned, a bit more of a positive view was offered. Nevertheless, the extensive bureaucracy was blamed for much and the decision to make Spanish the organisation's third working language added to this. This led to proposals to also add Russian and Chinese, which according to the Paris correspondent would make the UN "the world's, and in the history of mankind, greatest red-tape".

---

7 *Ibid.*, p. 10.

Apart from an extended description of the failed proposal by Bernadotte and references to the very time-consuming, wordy, and "procedural-ridden" sessions, two issues were noted as positive: the Genocide Convention and the UDHR. The journalist stressed that also on these matters, however, the divide between East and West had dominated, even though "other directions" had also been problematic. The following day, Monday 13 December, carried another piece on the conclusions in Paris. The UDHR was described in very negative terms, as one of a set of "ideological rockets, nicely shining, but totally without effect". The same was said about the Genocide Convention with a reference to the lack of an implementation mechanism that would have allowed at least some form of scrutiny behind the Iron Curtain. Much blame was put on the USSR.[8]

A final article is included in the same issue.[9] The work of the Swedish delegation that was preparing to return to Sweden is described. The Swedish "gentlemen" (even though the delegation included not only men) of the delegation are praised for taking stronger stances than during previous sessions but nonetheless "by accident" ended up on the side of the majority and the Western powers on most issues. On a few issues the Swedes were actually in minority but then still with the Western group! The Swedish representatives are ascribed the noble skill of only speaking when needed, and as an example of such, commented with the majority on the atomic issue "fearlessly" against the USSR and the Eastern bloc. This was indeed important given the neutral stance of Sweden, it was stated. Again, the Palestine issue was highlighted as an area where this would have been solved, had the other states only supported the Swedish Bernadotte-proposal! And again the Swedish proposal to make the operations of the UN more effective was stressed.

The Swedish delegation was said to have participated diligently in all the committees. Maybe the greatest of these inputs was made by the delegate Mrs. Ulla Lindström (member of the Swedish Parliament and a Social Democrat), on the debate of human rights. Her contribution was to force a time limit onto the speakers to limit "the unbelievable eloquence that was flowing day after day". Actually, and here lies the main contribution by Sweden to the UDHR (apparently, without which there would have been no declaration), it was "exclusively thanks to the limitations on the speakers" that the UDHR was eventually adopted. The only substantial input on the

---

8 *Ibid.*, p. 4. A lengthy elaboration on the negative perspective of the USSR was published a few days later, *Dagens Nyheter*, 15 December 1948, p. 10.

9 *Ibid.*, p. 9.

Declaration that is mentioned is a Swedish initiative to include the right to strike, but this failed mainly due to "the poorly considered proposal", according to the journalist.

Thus far, I have considered the coverage of the two main Swedish dailies of the events surrounding the adoption of the UDHR. There is clear focus on the Swedish proposals, on the 'Swedish' perspectives on the organisation and on what the worries in Sweden were at the time. Little, indeed very little, attention was given to the more visionary idea of the global constitutional development of human rights. Even so, in the view of Swedish media, without Sweden's intervention there would have been no UDHR!

3. POLITICAL AND ACADEMIC DISCUSSIONS

3.1. POLITICS

The coverage in the daily press is surely one side of the story but there are others. The Swedish diplomats involved in the process of negotiating the Declaration and the minister of government in charge ought to have more to say than what the media offered. The Minister for Foreign Affairs at the time of the adoption of the UDHR, Östen Undén, very prominent in Sweden, was professor of and indeed an authority on international law.[10] He was, however, a strong advocate of Sweden's policy of non-alliance and neutrality. His position towards international organisations and human rights seemed to have been strongly influenced by this, in seeking to avoid supra-national institutions that would jeopardise the stated neutrality.[11] Undén's notes from his days as foreign minister are published.[12] In November 1948, he had meetings in Paris but left late that month. His notes made no references to the development of the UDHR then or around its adoption. On 10 December 1948 his entry reads: "Nobel Prize festivities and dinner at the City Hall." His notes at the time were focused on the thoughts of a Scandinavian neutrality pact.[13]

---

10 1886–1976, Minister of Foreign Affairs 1945–1962 (and earlier also 1924–1926).

11 *See, e.g.,* the biography on Undén, Y. MÖLLER, *Östen Undén: en biografi* (Norstedts, Stockholm, 1986) pp. 301, 339. Nothing in the biography covers the UDHR. Undén's meetings in Paris in late November 1948 seemed to have focused on the neutrality.

12 *Östen Undén: anteckningar 1918–1952* (Kungl. Samfundet, Stockholm, 2002).

13 pp. 262 *et seq.* Undén's own memoirs, *Minnesanteckningar* (Bonniers, Stockholm, 1996), makes no reference to the UDHR either.

The notes of the ambassador heading the Swedish delegation in Paris in the late autumn of 1948, the above-mentioned Grafström, were similarly published.[14] The entry closest to the date of adoption, on 12 December, mentioned that the Assembly was over and that he must admit that none of the issues on its agenda had actually been solved.[15] No mention is made of the UDHR. He prides himself a few days earlier with having gotten the Danes and Norwegians to agree on a proposal that had been accepted, aimed at improving the working methods of the Assembly. His main concern seems to be the lengthy orations. He even recites jokes along the lines of the need for this reform. Hector McNeil (from the British Foreign Office) suggested that the UN needed what the House of Lords had, the possibility of stopping a speaker by exclaiming "The Lord is not heard". Earlier that fall, Grafström also made reference to a feature proposed by Sir Alexander (Cadogan, British Chairman of the Security Council at the time) over dinner: the button by which one by magic could control what language that would be heard in the earpiece at the UN should be supplemented with one that would by majority call slowly lower the speaker under the floor, beyond sight — and sound.[16]

Apparently there was a general sense of too much lengthy talk in the debating, and even seen as a delaying tactic used by the Soviet bloc. Charles Malik, the Lebanese ambassador to the UN and core member of the group of UDHR drafters, was in the autumn of 1948 as chair of the sessions forced to introduce night sessions as well as a merciless stopwatch. It was at this occasion, as we know also from the media, where Sweden contributed, motioning successfully to limit interventions to three minutes.[17]

Sweden's input to the UDHR was also found in other areas. Even though Sweden was outside of the Commission itself, other UN members were given the opportunity to offer suggestions. On four occasions governments were invited to comment. As the drafting of the UDHR was commencing, John Humphrey, the Canadian Director of the UN Human Rights Division, solicited examples of constitutional rights from governments around the world. Sweden is not on record as having done so nor to have submitted any draft proposal when this was requested.[18] At the third opportunity to engage

---

14 *Sven Grafström: anteckningar 1945–1954* (Kungl. Samfundet, Stockholm, 1989).

15 *Ibid.*, pp. 910 *et seq.*

16 *Ibid.*, pp. 896–897.

17 M.A. GLENDON, *A World Made New: Eleanor Roosevelt and the Universal Declaration of Human Rights* (Random House, New York, 2001) pp. 152–153. 108th meeting, 20 October 1948, pp. 199–200.

18 *The United Nations Yearbook, 1948–49* (Hutchinson, London, 1950) p. 525. *See also* MORSINK, *supra* note 2, p. 10. GLENDON, *supra* note 17, p. 49. K. MÅNSSON, 'Reviving the "Spirit of

for non-Commission members, Sweden was one of the 13 who commented. Sweden was worried about the non-compatibility of aspects of their legislation with the draft UDHR. The details of Sweden's concerns suggest that other, maybe more fundamental aspects, were considered to be compliant. Sweden asked about mandatory blood tests in paternity and drunk-driving cases. Another problem was with freedom of religion where the law at the time prescribed that members of the state church could only change religion but not simply to relinquish the membership.[19]

As the final voting in the General Assembly got started late in the evening of 10 December, Sweden made no intervention and voted consistently with the majority on the final four suggestions.[20] As we have seen, however, the event left few traces in the notes and memoirs of Swedish key actors and the media coverage was focusing on other matters. It seems from these accounts that Sweden was not taking human rights all that seriously.

Sweden's position remained hesitant as the work on a binding instrument continued after the adoption of the UDHR. Sweden argued against giving the monitoring body of the convention power to request interpretative opinions from the International Court of Justice and that its powers should be advisory rather than legally binding.[21] Sweden voted against, together with 15 others, a proposal to take measures on guaranteeing the right to self-determination.[22] Sweden voted against, together with 16 others, the inclusion of economic, social, and cultural rights, supposedly on the grounds that this important topic needed further consideration. Sweden also argued that they should be included in a separate convention.[23] Sweden voted against, with 10 others, a resolution for a provision making the rights equally applicable in a state as in the state's non-self-governing territories, colonies, and areas of trusteeship.[24]

It is noteworthy that Sweden positioned itself against making the rights justiciable by the supervising mechanism given that, as will be explored, a main official argument against the UDHR and rights catalogues in Sweden

---

San Francisco": The Lost Proposals on Human Rights, Justice and International Law to the UN Charter', 76 *Nordic Journal of International Law* (2007) p. 222. Her article also shows that Sweden was not participating in the drafting of the UN Charter with its elaborated discussions on the role of human rights, including a rights catalogue forming part of the Charter.

19 GLENDON, *supra* note 17, p. 107. The relevant document, E/CN.4/82, 16 April 1948, however, does not make mention of the Swedish contribution, only five telegrams received are included.

20 183rd meeting, 10 December 1948, pp. 930–935.

21 *Aktstycken utgivna av Kungl. Utrikesdepartementet*, *supra* note 4, p. 125.

22 *Ibid.*, p. 126.

23 *Ibid.*, p. 127.

24 *Ibid.*, pp. 127–128.

that has remained pervasive was that they were not legally binding. It is also interesting to note that Sweden argued that economic, social, and cultural rights just needed separate preparation and that they in fact were not sceptical of the inclusion of such rights given, again as will be discussed later, the unwillingness of including such rights in the domestic catalogue of rights. Sweden nevertheless argued that alleged violations against the convention should also be able to be brought forward by organisations and individuals. However, some kind of screening mechanism would be needed to exclude anonymous and obviously ill-founded complaints.[25]

3.2. ACADEMIA

The leading legal journal in Sweden throughout the 20th century, *Svensk Juristtidning* (the *Swedish Jurist Journal*) remains since its commencement in 1916 a leading forum. Articles are published by academicians and practitioners under various headings, corresponding to classical divisions of law. Under international law, however, there was nothing to be found on the UDHR in the years following the adoption. The first major mentioning even of the United Nations is not until 1952, and then again the focus is on the working methods of the United Nations.[26] Human rights are only dealt with to some extent ten years later, and then related to the Council of Europe.[27] The UDHR is not mentioned until 1968, and then only as a result of the recent adoption of the two UN covenants.[28]

The situation is similar with the Nordic *Tidskrift for Rettsvitenskap* (*Journal for Legal Science*) based in Norway. No article covered the UDHR at the time of its drafting. Not until 1967, and again in relation to the Council of Europe, are human rights referred to.[29] In 1969, the UDHR is mentioned in an

---

25 *Ibid.*, p. 125.

26 Å. HOLMBÄCK, 'Arbetssättet i Förenta Nationernas Generalförsamling', *Svensk Juristtidning* (1952).

27 L. KELLBERG, 'Sverige och Europarådets konvention om de mänskliga rättigheterna', *Svensk Juristtidning* (1961) p. 503.

28 H. DANELIUS, 'De nya FN-konventionerna om de mänskliga rättigheterna — backgrund och innehåll', *Svensk Juristtidning* (1968) p. 154. *E.g.*, *Nordisk Kriminalistisk Årsbok 1954* contains, however, a discussion under the heading of human rights but without references to the UDHR (by the Finnish Professor Bruno A. Salmiala, talking about various forms of inhuman treatment of detainees) pp. 93 *et seq.*

29 Also here it is by Danelius: H. DANELIUS, 'Mänskliga rättigheter i Europeisk praxis', *Tidskrift for Rettsvitenskap* (1967) p. 201.

article about theory and practice of human rights,[30] and in 1971 another reference is made to the UDHR.[31] Already in 1965 however, a piece appeared on ILO standards.[32]

The previously mentioned Minister Undén writes in a book on foreign policy that the UDHR was at the time "still not a legally binding document. It is rather an expression of opinions. But the [European Convention on Human Rights, hereinafter ECHR] is an international agreement, for which respect is guaranteed by specialised institutions".[33] Nonetheless, Undén was not a strong advocate of this kind of international monitoring of rights.[34] In an article from 1963 on the courts of the UN and the Council of Europe he referred to the ongoing constitutional developments in Sweden (see further below) with a reference to catalogues of rights and that the ECHR was a model in this regard. He noted, however, that the ECHR had been drafted in too much detail, enabling risks of diverging interpretations (*sic*).[35] In the same paragraph he elaborated that jurists in Sweden indicated that the usage in Sweden of various committees rather than courts taking decisions on some matters might come into conflict with the requirements of the ECHR. Undén writes: "One can of course say that the risk that an international court-case would come about in such matters is minimal. What government [*sic*][36] would come up with the idea of for example suing Sweden before the court of the Council of Europe for alleged violations of the [ECHR]?"[37]

Undén developed his argumentation against the Court. He suggested in the interests of simplicity and costs that perfectionism should not be sought

---

30 A. EIDE, 'Menneskerettighetene i teori og praksis', *Tidskrift for Rettsvitenskap* (1969) p. 117. Eide also published a piece a couple of years later on the first international human rights institute being established in Strasbourg, making references to the two 1966 Covenants: 'Det første internasjonale institutt for menneskerettigheter opprettet i Strasbourg', *Tidskrift for Rettsvitenskap* (1971) p. 197.

31 A review by H. Olsson on a commentary to CERD, *Tidskrift for Rettsvitenskap* (1971) p. 651. That issue also featured another review by M. Sørenssen, p. 663, of Frede Castberg's book on the European Convention: *Den europeiske konvensjon om menneskerettighetene* (Universitetsförlaget, Oslo, 1971).

32 K. NANDRUP DAHL, 'Kontrollen med gjennomføringen av ILO-Standarder', *Tidsskrift for Rettsvitenskap* (1965) p. 480.

33 Ö. UNDÉN, *Tankar om utrikespolitik* (Stockholm: Rabén & Sjögren, 1963) pp. 13–14.

34 Undén has even been described as very negative to the outside world, J.W.F. SUNDBERG, *Human Rights in Sweden: the Annual Report 1985* (Fred B. Rothman & Co, Littleton, 1987) p. 105.

35 Ö. UNDÉN, 'Om FN:s och Europarådets domstolar', *Svensk Juristtidning* (1963), p. 657.

36 *See*, however, below on Sweden's recognition of the Courts jurisdiction only in 1966.

37 UNDÉN, *supra* note 33, p. 659.

and focus ought to remain on conventional international law dispute settlement (between states). "The more subtle problems [as those that may come before the Court] hardly require the large machinery [of the Council of Europe]. Sweden has maybe gone too far in the contribution to the details of the [ECHR]", he concluded. There was no real need for the Court. A response from the President of the Norwegian Supreme Court, Terje Wold, criticises heavily the position towards the ECHR of Undén and Sweden. To have politicians rather than courts determining violations was according to Wold not appropriate: "Human rights are not 'internal matters'. In our times only dictatorships seriously argue this".[38]

A new generation and new perspectives also in Sweden could be represented by an article in the same journal as the dispute between Undén and Wold played out. In 1968, Hans Danelius (then serving at the legal secretariat of the Swedish Foreign Ministry, subsequently member of the European Commission of Human Rights, and Justice of the Swedish Supreme Court), introduced the two 1966 Covenants. Danelius stressed the advantages of the ECHR in relation to the UDHR in terms of its level of detail, but acknowledged also the wider scope of the UDHR and the two Covenants in terms of rights included.[39]

3.3. UDHR v ECHR

It becomes clear that to further understand how the international cooperation on human rights was perceived in Sweden after the adoption of the UDHR, it is more telling to look at the engagement with the work of the Council of Europe. Of course, the ECHR does in its very first preambular paragraph acknowledge the UDHR as the source. That a treaty was concluded less than two years after the UDHR was adopted was a feat. The economic, social, and cultural rights in the UDHR had by all means also been taken out. Being one of the ten founding members of the Council of Europe from May of the year following the adoption of the UDHR, Sweden ratified the ECHR on 4 February 1952 without any reservations. In the examination preceding ratification, it was concluded that there were no contradictions between the rights of the Convention and Swedish law.[40] Contrary to the other member

---

38 T. WOLD, 'Om FN's og Europarådets domstoler', *Svensk Juristtidning* (1964) p. 541.

39 DANELIUS, *supra* note 28, p. 155.

40 *See* H. CORELL, 'The European Convention on Human Rights: Swedish Experiences — Thoughts for the Future', in J. RAMBERG et al. (eds), *Studies in International Law* (Norstedts, Stockholm, 1990) p. 103.

states, however, Sweden did for a long time not accept the jurisdiction of the Court, only that of the Commission.[41]

The number of applications against Sweden as well as — once it was possible — judgments were, to begin with, very few.[42] The first couple of judgments came in 1976 but without finding Sweden in breach of the Convention. In 1982, in the third judgment, Sweden lost for the first time.[43] To date, Sweden has been found to be in breach of the Convention in about half of the some 80 judgments. The number of cases pertaining to Sweden were during the 1980s 13, a figure that was doubled in the following decade and set to be doubled again during the first decade of the 21st century. Only when Sweden 'lost' its first case, in 1982, was the reaction at home to human rights strong. *Dagens Nyheter* reported the following day on the front page: "Unique verdict, Sweden found guilty".[44] Until then, the Swedish government had apparently perceived itself as above the reach of the Court and beyond the possibility of violations.

Even though Sweden ought to finally have realised that there might be human rights problems also in Sweden, the then Swedish Prime Minister Olof Palme, when visiting Strasbourg in the 1980s, referred to the Court as a "kindergarten".[45] The status of the Court, the ECHR and of international human rights was also hotly debated in the Swedish Parliament. Sessions from 1988, in "the most extensive and most revealing of the debates relating to the European Convention which ha[d] taken place so far in [the Parliament]", are indicative of the positions of the political parties.[46] A representative of the government party admitted that upon ratification "we considered that the provisions of Article 6 [on fair trial] were fully met by our Code of Judicial Procedure". He continued: "I cannot envisage incorporating

---

41 Prior to the unified Court in 1998, under former Article 46(1), states had to make a declaration to accept the jurisdiction. Sweden made this declaration only on 13 May 1966. For a chart over these declarations, *see* <conventions.coe.int/treaty/en/Treaties/Html/005-1.htm>. *See also* mentioning in KELLBERG, *supra* note 27, p. 503.

42 In 1981, there were 7 and the following few years between 30 and 50 annually. SUNDBERG, *supra* note 34.

43 *Sporrong-Lönnroth*, Judgment 23 September 1982.

44 *Dagens Nyheter*, 24 September 1982, p. A1.

45 Actually he referred to it as Gustaf Petrén's kindergarten. Petrén, who was active for civil rights and had been working for the Parliament, was assumed to be positive towards the ECHR. He was at the time Justice of the Swedish Supreme Administrative Court. J.W.F. SUNDBERG, *Human Rights in Sweden: the Annual Report 1988* (Fred B. Rothman & Co, Littleton, 1991) p. 11, referring to *Svenska Dagbladet*, 29 September 1983.

46 Deliberations on 13 April 1988 on a report by the Constitutional Committee on the ECHR and the right to legal review. Proceedings offered in English by SUNDBERG, *supra* note 45, p. 31.

into Swedish law something that is so vague (not *pregnant*), and this Convention can never be particularly precise (*pregnant*). It would not mean any improvement".[47]

A leading politician for the main opposition party stated: "Now Swedes do have an inclination to judge the outer world according to what things look like back home. Our internationalism, so much spoken of and bragged about, is a rather thin veneer. What has happened in Strasbourg has been a useful reminder for many self-satisfied Swedes".[48] A member of the Communist Party, typically in cooperation with the Socialist government opined: "I do not think that it is a reasonable order of things that we should have a European Court ... dealing with this kind of matter".[49] Another opposition party member argued: "I would like that the various Court decisions had been already now more extensively implemented so that they could be used today already when courts and administrative authorities decide, thereby establishing themselves in our own case law".[50]

This distinction between parties certainly relates to who was in government and who was in opposition. There is also the traditional fear of the Socialists to trump the parliamentary system with courts, either national or international.[51] The long political dominance of the Swedish Socialist Democratic Party, in government over 60 years out of the last 75, has institutionalised the parliamentary dominance and shaped the view on sovereignty and international concerns.[52] The view on the ECHR as already stated above, supports this claim. The status of the ECHR since these debates has changed. As from 1995 the ECHR has been made part of Swedish law by way of incorporation, occupying in theory a position between the

---

47 *Ibid.*, pp. 22–23, 25, Olle Svensson (Social Democratic Party).

48 *Ibid.*, p. 10, Anders Björck (Moderate Party), regarding the *Sporrong Lönnroth* case.

49 *Ibid.*, p. 22, Bo Hammar (Leftist Party of Communists), referring to the *Sporrong Lönnroth* case (*see* above) and other cases where Sweden had lost (treatment of children).

50 *Ibid.*, p. 31, Birgit Friggebo (People's Party).

51 *See, e.g.*, H. CORELL, 'Swedish Cases Before the European Court of Human Rights: Are the Findings Acceptable to Swedish Politicians?', in L.A. REHOF and C. GULMANN (eds), *Human Rights in Domestic Law and Development Assistance Policies of the Nordic Countries* (Martinus Nijhoff, Dordrecht, 1989).

52 Years in government: 1932–1976, 1982–1991, 1994–2006. *See generally* S. HADENIUS, *Swedish Politics During the 20th Century: Conflict and Consensus*, 3rd ed. (Swedish Institute, Stockholm, 1990) pp. 60 *et seq.* *See also* K-G. ALGOTSSON, *Sveriges författning efter EU-anslutningen* (SNS, Stockholm, 2000) p. 339.

constitutional documents and ordinary statutes, but to a large extent serving as the rights catalogue for Sweden.[53]

As for publications, when searching the Swedish national library catalogue, LIBRIS,[54] the first book on human rights is from 1951, dealing with the ECHR.[55] The Nordic Information Office of the UN published an introduction to the UDHR in 1963.[56] From then on, during the 1960s, an additional four volumes came out, dealing with human rights from the Ten Commandments and onwards,[57] with human rights and poetry,[58] human rights explained for youth,[59] and for the analphabetic issued by the Swedish UNESCO Council to commemorate the International Year for Human Rights in 1968.[60] In the middle of the 1970s, the number of publications grew. The UDHR was given as a theatrical staging for children,[61] Amnesty International started its contributions,[62] and the first classical textbook on human rights was published.[63] The annual production in the 1970s averaged that of the whole 1960s in terms of published items on human rights. By the mid-1980s the annual number was at 15, a figure that had doubled ten years later. Around the turn of the century the number reached eighty but has since remained slightly lower than that.

The UDHR has not had a large direct impact on Sweden. Through the ECHR, some of the rights of the UDHR and indeed the concept of international human rights law have made their way into Sweden — against many obstacles for sure — but nevertheless. Before coming to a conclusion,

---

53 Reference to the ECHR in the Instrument of Government (one of four constitutional documents), Chapter 2, §23, to ECHR as Swedish Law, Swedish Code of Statutes, SFS 1994:1468.

54 <libris.kb.se/form_extended.jsp?language=en>.

55 T. SALÉN, *Europarådets konvention om mänskliga rättigheter och friheter* (Stockholm, 1951).

56 *Den allmänna förklaringen om de mänskliga rättigheterna: vad betyder den?* (FN:s informationskontor för de nordiska länderna, Köpenhamn, 1963).

57 H. SCHREIBER, *Från Sinai till FN: en bok om de mänskliga rättigheterna* (Gummesson, Stockholm, 1964), translation from German.

58 K. LAGRUP, *Mänskliga rättigheter: dikter* (Bonnier, Stockholm, 1966).

59 E. SUNDSTRÖM, *Våra mänskliga rättigheter: en presentation för ungdom* (Gummesson, Göteborg, 1968).

60 *Analfabetism och mänskliga rättigheter: utg. med anledning av det internationella året för de mänskliga rättigheterna 1968* (Svenska Unescorådet, Stockholm, 1968), translation from English.

61 G. WERSÉN, *Du är fri: Förenta Nationernas förklaring om de mänskliga rättigheterna utformad som teaterscener för barn* (Gummessons läromedel, Göteborg, 1971).

62 *Paraguay och de mänskliga rättigheterna* (Svenska sektionen, Amnesty International, Stockholm, 1974).

63 H. DANELIUS, *Mänskliga rättigheter* (Norstedt, Stockholm, 1975).

the possible traces of the UDHR on the constitutional reform that Sweden underwent in the early 1970s should be considered.

4. CONSTITUTIONAL AND OTHER DEVELOPMENTS

4.1. CONSTITUTIONAL RIGHTS

In Sweden, the ECHR is better known than the main constitutional document containing rights, *Regeringsformen* (the Instrument of Government).[64] The previous Instrument dated from 1809 and the need for reform was apparent. The Constitution was surprisingly unaffected by the developments on the continent, including the lack of a catalogue of rights.[65] Only as late as in the end of the 1930s were voices raised for a catalogue: this was done by members of a right-wing party in response to dictatorial inroads on the continent.[66] Minister Undén, again, was not a strong believer in declarations of rights:

> "The value of having declarations on human rights incorporated into a country's constitution should not be exaggerated. A tyrant that usurps power through a coup has many possibilities to reinterpret these concepts. Not the least can we in the constitutions of Communist states find examples of declarations of rights that seemingly contain democratic formulas but in its implementation appear as either empty words or the direct opposite to what the concepts mean in democratic states."[67]

This basis was not very sound for the development of a declaration of rights. Various inquiries were nevertheless commissioned on constitutional reform, in 1941, 1954, 1966, and 1973, respectively, but a new Constitution was not

---

64 SUNDBERG, *supra* note 45, p. 55. *See also*, on the very rare usage of the constitution in Swedish practice, B. ROTHSTEIN, 'Grundlagen i det mångkulturella samhället', in K. BLÜCKERT and E. ÖSTERBERG (eds), *Gränslöst — forskning i Sverige och i världen* (Natur och kultur, Stockholm, 2006).

65 J. NERGELIUS, *Konstitutionellt rättighetsskydd: Svensk rätt i ett komparativt perspektiv* (Fritzes, Stockholm, 1996) p. 545. There was, however, a long tradition in the area of freedom of the press, with a constitutional document originating from 1766.

66 K-G. ALGOTSSON, *Medborgarrätten och regeringsformen: debatten om grundläggande fri- och rättigheter i regeringsformen under 1970-talet* (Norstedt, Stockholm, 1987) pp. 22–23. *See also* NERGELIUS, *supra* note 65, p. 601.

67 UNDÉN, *supra* note 33, p. 13.

adopted until 1974.[68] The inquiry behind the 1974 constitutional reform dealt with the rights catalogue in three pages out of several hundred.[69] The Minister of Justice at the time (Herman Kling, minister 1959–1969) pronounced in the process of that inquiry that constitutional rights should be limited to the most important of rights. He rejected declarations of rights since "the intention is not [that such] should have a legally binding effect".[70] The inquiry concluded that constitutional rights would restrain societal change too much, not the least given the inherent ideological nature of rights.[71]

In the constitutional reform, rights were among the issues the most difficult to agree upon.[72] As a result a compromise was reached through subsequently including some rights while at the same time enabling limitation through ordinary law — indeed living up to the expectations of not being meant to be legally binding.[73] The Constitution that entered into force in 1975 was immediately seen as in need of revision and an amendment expanding the list of rights was adopted, entering into force in 1977.[74] Inquiries in preparation for the amendment included a study on the ECHR as well as the European Social Charter and a comparative study of six other countries.[75]

The inquiry of the European rights made references to the UDHR already in the introductory paragraphs, along with the two UN Covenants of 1966.[76] The UDHR was also included as an appendix. The comparative study looked for some reason only into the constitutional rights in Norway, Denmark,

---

68 Government Proposal, Prop. 1975/76:209, 18. *See generally* O. NYHOLM, 'Some Basic Features of Swedish Constitutional Law', in S. STRÖMHOLM (ed.), *An Introduction to Swedish Law*, 2nd ed. (Norstedts, Stockholm, 1991) p. 58. *See also* J. NERGELIUS, 'Constitutional Law', in M. BOGDAN (ed.), *Swedish Law in the New Millennium* (Norstedts, Stockholm, 2000) pp. 68 *et seq.*

69 Swedish Government Official Reports, SOU 1972:15, pp. 106–109.

70 *Ibid.*, p. 72.

71 *Ibid.*, pp. 72, 107.

72 O. NYMAN, 'The New Swedish Constitution', 26 *Scandinavian Studies in Law* (1982) p. 190.

73 Swedish Government Official Reports, SOU 1972:15, p. 107. Eventually a protection was achieved giving a political minority of at least one sixths of the members of parliament can force a 12 month delay in the adoption of the law. Government Proposal, Prop.1978/79:195, p. 135. This was a political compromise between left and right, where the former did not want any restrictions in law-making. *See* J. NERGELIUS, *Svensk statsrätt* (Studentlitteratur, Lund, 2006) p. 144.

74 Government Proposal, Prop.1975/76:209 (references to ECHR at, *e.g.*, 75 and 84). Swedish Code of Statutes, SFS 1976:871.

75 Many of the provisions reflect the articles of the ECHR, *see* CORELL, *supra* note 40, p. 104.

76 Swedish Government Official Reports, SOU 1974:88.

Finland, Great Britain, Germany, and Austria.[77] Several references were made to the ECHR and even one to the UDHR.[78] The draft proposal on the basis of the inquiries discussed the possibility of including a rights catalogue based on international conventions.[79] This was discarded, however, since it was argued that the conventions were difficult to access and overly complex often concluded with a terminology that was not consistent with Swedish drafting techniques. A majority of the entities that were asked to comment on the proposal supposedly agreed. The proposal even argued that on some points the protection in Sweden was stronger than the international instruments.[80]

The rights that were deemed essential for inclusion were those seen as central for a democratic form of government. Some rights considered were excluded since they were not even conceived as possible to uphold.[81] The presumption of innocence for instance, was seemingly not even up for discussion. However, the UDHR was mentioned specifically in relation to racial discrimination.[82] Another detailed reference was made to "the UN Convention", Article 15.[83] Given the context it should have been the International Covenant on Civil and Political Rights that was referred to. Additional changes in the Constitution related to rights were also made in 1979 and 1994, dealing with, for instance, procedural guarantees guarding against changing constitutional rights, rights of minorities, and rights of the Sámi people (right to reindeer husbandry).[84] The landmark change, however, was the mentioned incorporation of the ECHR into the Swedish domestic legal order, entering into force in 1995.[85]

In 2004, a new commission was appointed to again look into constitutional matters.[86] The focus for the inquiry was clearly stated to be the election process for the Parliament but also the relationship between the executive and the Parliament. Other aspects within the mandate were the need for a constitutional court, the status of the courts in the constitutional

---

77 Swedish Government Official Reports, SOU 1975:29, pp. 11–234.

78 *Ibid.*, p. 238.

79 Government Proposal, Prop. 1975/76:209, p. 85.

80 *Ibid.*, p. 85. Several entities did, however, suggest an expanded list of rights.

81 *Ibid.*, pp. 124–128.

82 *Ibid.*, p. 157.

83 *Ibid.*, p. 125.

84 Swedish Code of Statutes, SFS 1979:933, 1994:1468, *see also* 1988:1439, 1988:1443, 1991:1471, 1998:1437, 2002:903.

85 Swedish Code of Statutes, SFS 1994:1219.

86 Government Directive, Dir 2004:96.

system and judicial review of legislation also post-adoption. Many fundamental questions were thus being considered. The directives for the inquiry, however, while not ruling out any area other than fundamental structures of the state, did not mention the catalogue of rights or the incorporation of any additional human rights treaty.[87] The debate surrounding the constitutional reform this time around has not dealt with such issues either. However, the long-debated issue of the need for a constitutional court in Sweden, should there be an agreement, would surely bring the catalogue of rights to the centre of attention. The government at the time, now in opposition, also issued a document stressing the link between human rights and democracy, a possible indication of a shift in attitude opening up for greater opportunities for agreement across party lines.[88]

4.2. COURT CASES AND OTHER REFERENCES TO THE UDHR

What the constitutional reforms of the 1970s did not manage was to stimulate rights-thinking, something that the increasing role of the ECHR and the Strasbourg Court in Sweden of the 1990s actually had been able at least to initiate.[89] Earlier on, courts had refused to cite the Strasbourg Court, but this had become quite common practice.[90] In a study of cases from Swedish courts 1995 to 2002, almost 30 per cent of cases that dealt with rights referred to the case law from the Strasbourg court.[91] The actual number of cases was, however, less than 40, seemingly quite a low figure. The number of constitutional rights-related cases was during the period in single digit figures, while the reference to the ECHR started off in 1995 with six cases but grew thereafter and has remained between 15 and 20.[92] The number of these

87 Norway has for instance not only made the ECHR into national law but also UN conventions.

88 Government Communication, Skr. 2003/04:110 (*Demokratipolitik* / Policies for Democracy), available in English at <www.sweden.gov.se/sb/d/574/a/47013>.

89 M. SCHEININ, 'Constitutionalism and Approaches to Rights in the Nordic Countries', in J. NERGELIUS (ed.), *Constitutionalism — New Challenges: European Law from a Nordic Perspective* (Martinus Nijhoff, Leiden, 2008) p. 141.

90 *Ibid.*, pp. 140–141.

91 K. ÅHMAN, *Kartläggning av i vilka fall svenska domstolar tillämpat bestämmelserna i 2 kap. regeringsformen och i Europakonventionen*, Report to the Ministry of Justice, 31 May 2003.

92 *Ibid.*, composed of the data available in chart 2. A quick search of the published cases from the Swedish Supreme Court (HD, published in NJA) reveals some 20 cases out of 340 (17 per cent) from 2007 that have made reference to the ECHR.

cases in relation to the entire caseload of the courts is a fraction, over the period about half a percent.

When reverting to the UDHR, the direct impact has been much less. Still, the UDHR has been referred to on some occasions. Searching a database[93] with cases from the appeals courts and the two supreme courts, five cases appeared. The first one was from 1973 and concerns gender equality. The UDHR was among other instruments referred to by the complainant. The Supreme Court was, however, not willing to apply directly the UDHR or the international treaties that Sweden had ratified.[94] The second case was from 1982 and dealt with negative freedom of association. Members of a trade union wanting to renounce their membership were refused to do so by the union. The members argued before the courts that they should be free to leave. A dissent in the appeal court argued on the basis of the clarity of the UDHR, among other sources, that when it came to the negative freedom of association, it should be applicable in the situation. The Supreme Court sided with the minority from the appeal court, but without actually citing the UDHR.[95]

A third case, from 1984, concerned travel restrictions outside of the national borders on suspects in a tax-evasion case. An appeals court referred to the rights guaranteed in the constitutional documents with clear reference, firstly, to the UDHR, but also to UN and Council of Europe conventions. On this basis the court lifted the restrictions in place.[96]

A fourth case from 1988 centred on punishment for violating competition law. The appeals court interpreted principles of criminal procedures in the light of international instruments, including the UDHR.[97] The most recent case where the UDHR has been referred to was a rather well-known one related to positive discrimination at a Swedish faculty of law. The Supreme Court started its reasoning by referring to the UDHR as a basis for non-discrimination, along with other relevant documents.[98] On human rights more generally, some 25 cases in 2007 alone make reference to 'human rights', most commonly, however, concerning extraditions.

93 *Rättsbanken*. Also *Zeteo* gives the same results, save an additional case from the Labor Court, AD 1972:5, where the court gave no weight to the claims based on the UDHR.

94 NJA 1973:75.

95 NJA 1982:130.

96 RH 1984:26.

97 RH 1988:134.

98 NJA 2006:84.

Not only the courts made reference to the UDHR. The most recent Swedish National Human Rights Action Plan starts off by recognising the UDHR as fundamental.[99] The Speaker of Parliament commemorated the 50th anniversary of the UDHR by elaborating on the importance of the document agreed upon in Palais de Chaillot.[100] Also other inquiries than those on constitutional matters refer to the UDHR on diverse topics such as food safety,[101] hunting and fishing rights of indigenous peoples,[102] migration,[103] court counsels for victims of crime,[104] and gender equality (actually related to the Instrument of Government).[105] In addition, Members of Parliament also make references to the UDHR in their motions.[106] Actual legislation referring to the UDHR does not seem to exist, other than, of course, the second preambular paragraph of the ECHR. In 2007, five Acts of Parliament refer to the concept of human rights. Of these, three relate to cross-border issues and development cooperation.

Searching on UDHR or to some extent also ECHR in Swedish is problematic and highlights the problem of socialising concepts. When studying different formats in which 'the Universal Declaration of Human Rights' appear and in which it is possible to write the term given the possibilities of the language and the various forms of translations from English, I listed for search purposes altogether 70 different versions. In common usage, one would at least find a handful of different versions. The official version (*allmän förklaring om de mänskliga rättigheterna*)[107] is quite far from the English terminology. Therefore, it is often referred to in more

---

99 Government Communication, Skr. 2005/06:95, summary in English at <www.sweden.gov.se/content/1/c6/08/34/74/36e631ca.pdf>. *See*, however, also the evaluation of the first action plan, stressing the need for the government to clearly acknowledge the legal implications of ratified treaties in Sweden as well as the whole spectrum of rights. T. HAMMARBERG, *Bra början, men bara en början* (2005), available at <www.manskligarattigheter.gov.se>.

100 Parliament Protocol 1998/99:33 of 10 December 1998.

101 Swedish Government Official Reports, SOU 2002:75.

102 Swedish Government Official Reports, SOU 2005:79.

103 Swedish Government Official Reports, SOU 2006:37.

104 Swedish Government Official Reports, SOU 2007:6.

105 Swedish Government Official Reports, SOU 2007:67.

106 *See, e.g.*, Motion 1990/91:U631 (Maria Leissner et al., People's Party), on various aspects of human rights; Motion 1990/91:U638 (Claes Roxbergh et al., Green Party), on pesticides; Motion 2004/05:U315 (Holger Gustafsson et al., Christian Democrats), on shortcomings in Sweden related to human rights, such as explanations of non-ratification of human rights treaties.

107 *See* <www.unhchr.ch/udhr/lang/swd.htm> but note also that, *e.g.*, the human rights site of the government is not even consistent with this, (*FN:s allmänna)* <www.manskligarattigheter.gov.se/extra/pod/?module_instance=7>.

modern language (*universella deklarationen*). Not even the Swedish national encyclopaedia has the correct name listed.[108] This confusion adds to the many challenges the UDHR has faced in Sweden.

5. CONCLUSIONS

The UDHR — and indeed rights — have had to fight an uphill battle in Sweden. Media reports from the time of adoption show where the interests were, at least as perceived to be among the readers. Domestic issues, Swedish neutrality, and fear of the USSR were the headlines. To the extent that the work going on in the UN was at all noteworthy, it was because Sweden took pride in trying to restrain the UN bureaucracy and even 'rescuing' the UDHR from unduly talkative diplomats stalling the process. Records of leading diplomats and politicians of the time support this perspective. The Minister of Foreign Affairs, Undén, insisted then on the supremacy of the Parliament and voiced his scepticism towards rights. These positions have remained a heritage for decades and are still to some extent part of the Swedish debate abroad and at home — on for example justiciability of economic, social, and cultural rights internationally and at home and on constitutional rights catalogues more broadly.[109] Still, a quick search in the two Swedish major dailies that were discussed early on in this article, produced only a few references to the UDHR. However, in the years available for searches, since 2002, 'human rights' average in each of the newspapers at a rate of more than one reference daily.[110] A recent comment in one of these articles on a domestic rights-issue suggested that the positioning of the Swedish political parties on human rights was negative, irrespective of location on the Left-Right scale.[111]

An overview of the academic discourse shows a few attempts at discussing the ECHR early on, but even the mentioning of the UDHR was indeed rare. The ECHR and its institutions in Strasbourg fared poorly in Sweden, at least

---

[108] UDHR is briefly references under 'the UN' as well as 'the human rights declaration' (*deklaration* not *förklaring*) and the main description under 'human rights' but then incorrectly labelled (*den allmänna förklaring om de ...* ought to be *förklaringen* when written in that format). *Nationalencyklopedin*, Band 13 (1994).

[109] *See, e.g.*, the contribution to this volume on the UK for a parallel perspective.

[110] About two thirds are however concerned with non-domestic matters.

[111] M. ZAREMBA, 'Ska läkaren bli bödel?', *Dagens Nyheter*, 11 May 2008. *See also* his comment on the constitutional debate: <www.grundlagsutredningen.se/templates/pages/ StandardPage____259.aspx>.

to begin with. The binding nature of the ECHR and the fact that it was European made it more likely to be noted. However, academics, politicians, media, and citizens alike, all paid little attention until the Swedish government in 1982 was found in violation of the ECHR for the first time. Since then, the ECHR and human rights have grown in importance. The constitutional reform of the 1970s had taken on some of the continental influences through a very limited — but still — catalogue of rights. It was not until the increased attention to a possible Swedish EU-membership was on the agenda in the early 1990s that a strong discussion on human rights took place. The incorporation of the ECHR at a quasi-constitutional level was a milestone. With the European Constitution and the Treaty of Lisbon as well as the EU Charter of Fundamental Rights which refers in its very first article being based on the UDHR, the UDHR is again coming into the Swedish realm.[112]

A piece that appeared in 1961 in the *Swedish Jurist Journal*, concluded with an aspiration that Sweden should join the developments on the continent with a lively interaction at all levels with the ECHR, "not only with the legal scholars but with legislators and those charged with adjudication of justice". This piece ended with a statement that this interaction is of "utmost importance for the continued development of the democratic ideals in an ever more integrated Europe".[113] A current op-ed by leading lawyers refers to the Swedish constitutional rights as "dead material" and urges the ongoing constitutional reform process to consider expanding the rights catalogue and make the rights in the Constitution alive and truly justiciable.[114] A recent commentator, again in the *Swedish Jurist Journal*, holds that given the customary status that the UDHR has achieved, it is central for human rights law and a role model for constitutional rights.[115]

Courts and other entities of authority in Sweden are increasingly using the ECHR and at times making references also to UN conventions and even the UDHR. Swedish history, which very much shapes the contemporary, suffers from a politicisation of the debate on rights. The causes include the long, almost uninterrupted rule by one political party, patriotism, exaggerated self-perception, and a tradition of human rights as symbolic. Sweden's success

---

112 On sources of the respective articles, *see* <ec.europa.eu/justice_home/unit/charte/en/charter02.html>.

113 KELLBERG, *supra* note 27, p. 506.

114 A. RAMBERG et al., 'Stärk våra fri- och rättigheter', *Svenska Dagbladet*, 5 May 2008.

115 H. CORELL, 'Rättspositivismen i folkrätten i ett praktiskt perpektiv', *Svensk Juristtidning* (2008) p. 35.

in staying neutral during World War II reinforced a perception of continuity in contrast to our neighbouring countries — as exemplified earlier with the debate between Wold and Undén. The pervading dualistic view on international law should certainly be added to this. On a more abstract or legal-theoretical level, the school of Scandinavian Legal Realism was not conducive to human rights.[116]

In 1948, Dag Hammarskjöld had just joined the Swedish Foreign Service but became a representative to the General Assembly only in 1951, and elected Secretary General in 1953. Hammarskjöld held that the UDHR was the most extensive effort thus far that crystallizes the beliefs in the dignity of the human being, and that it was among the most central of a government's tasks to ensure peace — peace through human rights. Human rights, Hammarskjöld argued, should be the laws of each nation in the future.[117] The view Hammarskjöld expressed was quite distinct from that prevailing within the Swedish government.[118]

A hesitant view on human rights remains at times in Swedish politics. As the UN Declaration on the Rights of Indigenous Peoples was adopted in 2007, while commending the adoption, Sweden nevertheless expressed scepticism towards collective rights, stating that collective rights did not form part of international law.[119]

Reform ought not to be limited in order to maintain traditional structures and contents of a constitution, as is often held by Swedish politicians. A constitution's legitimacy does not rest alone upon continuity of historical formulations and labels. Sweden has long underestimated the value of human rights, be it those in the UDHR or indeed in its own Constitution. With a stronger standing of human rights — as exemplified here with the UDHR — a more dynamic form of governance would have been achieved and with focus not only on the ECHR, a wider spectrum of rights, from civil and

---

[116] *See* A. PECZENIK, *On Law and Reason* (Kluwer Academic, Dordrecht, 1989) pp. 260 *et seq.* Also, *e.g.*, J. BJARUP, 'The Philosophy of Scandinavian Legal Realism', 18:1 *Ratio Juris* (2005). *See also* A. FØLLESDAL, 'Rawls in the Nordic Countries', I *European Journal of Political Theory* (2002). *See also* a critique by F. CASTBERG, 'Menneskerettighetene, grunnloven og domstolene', *Tidskrift for Rettsvitenskap* (1965) p. 385.

[117] These statements are paraphrased from the collection of Hammarskjöld's speeches, *Dag Hammarskjöld: Tal 1953–61* (Norstedts, Stockholm, 1962) pp. 115, 144, 147.

[118] On Hammarskjöld and human rights, *see, e.g.*, K. MÅNSSON, 'Dag Hammarskjöld — vördnad för livet genom internationell tjänst', 23:3 *Nordisk Tidsskrift for Menneskerettigheter* (2005) p. 441.

[119] <www.un.org/News/Press/docs/2007/ga10612.doc.htm>.

political to economic, social, and cultural rights, would have been at hand. Rights should apply equally at home and abroad.[120]

[120] Sweden's most recent foreign policy document on human rights does indeed start off referencing the UDHR. Government Communication, Skr 2007/08:109 (Mänskliga rättigheter i svensk utrikespolitik).

PART III

EUROPEAN STATES THAT BECAME MEMBERS OF THE UN IN THE DEAL OF 1955

11. AUSTRIA: KEEPING A LOW PROFILE

Wolfgang Benedek
Manfred Nowak[1]

1. INTRODUCTION

Austria became independent on 27 July 1955 after ten years of occupation by the allied powers as a result of World War II. Accordingly, Austria was not in a position to participate in the elaboration and adoption of the Universal Declaration of Human Rights (hereinafter UDHR) in 1948 and had to wait until 14 December 1955 to join the United Nations (hereinafter UN).

This partly explains why the UDHR has not played a major role in Austria, which has rather kept a low profile in using this fundamental instrument of human rights. This contribution will first explore how Austria has implemented the two UN international covenants, which have been adopted to translate the rights enshrined in the UDHR into legally binding obligations. Then, it will enquire into the role of the UDHR in the political discourse in Austria on the national but also on the local level. As an innovative good practice of living the obligations and values of the UDHR on the local level, the example of the human rights city of Graz, a process that draws inspiration from the UDHR, will be presented. Finally, after a short investigation of the role of the UDHR before Austrian courts, some general conclusions are drawn.

As there does not exist much specific literature on the UDHR in Austria, the focus of this contribution has been enlarged to cover essential human rights instruments based on the UDHR, such as the two international covenants and their relationship with the regional human rights instruments.

---

[1] The authors would like to thank Lisa Heschl, Matthias Kettemann and Julia Kozma for their assistance in producing this contribution.

2. THE UDHR IN THE AUSTRIAN LEGAL ORDER

Austria gained its independence under the Austrian State Treaty of 15 May 1955, which also contains human rights obligations in Article 6 and obligations with regard to minority protection in Article 7. Whether there is a direct relationship between the UDHR and the general obligation to respect human rights in Article 6 could not be ascertained. In practice, though, Article 7, containing minority protection for Slovenes and Croats in Austria, has been of larger significance although it has never been fully implemented. There are no references to the UDHR in the Austrian Federal Constitution, the core provisions of which date from 1920. However, the UDHR is referred to in the Preamble of the European Convention on Human Rights and Fundamental Freedoms (hereinafter ECHR) of 1950, which has been ratified by Austria on 3 September 1958 and which has been given constitutional rank by the Federal Constitutional Law Amendment of 1964.[2] The ECHR is thus directly applicable under Austrian domestic law. Austria has also ratified all protocols to the ECHR except Protocol No. 12.

When Austria acceded to the United Nations, no references were made to the UDHR specifically. On 10 September 1978, Austria ratified the two international Covenants based on the UDHR, namely the International Covenant on Civil and Political Rights (ICCPR) and the International Covenant on Economic, Social and Cultural Rights (ICESCR). Both Covenants were discussed in Parliament for years before being ratified. The explanatory report by the government and the report of the Foreign Affairs Committee followed the Preamble of the international Covenants in arguing that the purpose of the Covenants was to bring the essential principles of the UDHR into a legally binding form. Austria had signed both Covenants in December 1973 and the government presented the project of ratification in 1976 just after the Covenants had entered into force.

Unlike with the ECHR, however, Parliament, at the instigation of the conservative People's Party did not give the Covenants or any provision thereof constitutional rank — notwithstanding that the government had proposed to treat the Covenants as constitutional amendments and Parliament was aware that certain provisions in Austrian laws needed to be amended. The explanatory report to the ratification clearly spells out a number of provisions in the ICCPR which go beyond the legal obligations derived from the ECHR, including, for example, the prohibition of war

---

[2] Article II Z 7 Federal Constitutional Law Amendment 1964, Federal Register 1964/59. *Cf.* Constitutional Court Decisions VfSlg 4706/1964, 5100/1965.

propaganda and incitement to national, racist or religious hatred (Article 20) or the rights of members of minorities (Article 27). Another particularity was that the act of ratification by Parliament stipulated that both Covenants did not directly become part of Austrian law but needed to be implemented by the adoption of pertinent legislation.

This also means that no subjective rights of private persons are created by the State Treaty and that authorities have only the obligation to interpret domestic law in conformity with the treaty, in particular the legislation eventually adopted in order to implement it.[3] However, Austria consequently took the position that the obligations contained in the Covenants were already sufficiently implemented by existing Austrian law, in particular by the ECHR and its protocols. This is largely but not fully the case for civil and political rights, but not correct as regards economic, social and cultural rights. In addition, the latter are usually only to be found in legislation without constitutional rank.[4] Austria has also made a number of reservations to the ICCPR, but not to the ICESCR. Together with the lack of national legislation on the implementation, this has made the Covenants practically inapplicable in daily practice.[5]

It took a long time, until 20 December 1987, for Austria to ratify the Optional Protocol to the ICCPR providing for individual complaints to the Human Rights Committee. On this ground individuals can base their claims on the UN ICCPR as an 'international subjective right'.[6] There have been

---

3 T. ÖHLINGER, *Verfassungsrecht* [Constitutional Law], 7th ed. (facultas.wuv Universitätsverlag, Vienna, 2007) pp. 81 *et seq. See*, for the principle of interpretation in conformity with international law guarantees of human rights, W. BERKA, *Die Grundrechte: Grundfreiheiten und Menschenrechte in Österreich* [Fundamental Rights: Fundamental Freedoms and Human Rights in Austria] (Springer, Vienna, 1999) p. 76. *See also* the Collection of Constitutional Judgements, VfSlg. 11.500/1987, and, further, H. FLORETTA and T. ÖHLINGER, *Die Menschenrechtspakte der Vereinten Nationen: Ein Beitrag zur Struktur der Grundrechte in Österreich, insbesondere zu den sozialen Grundrechten* [The Human Rights Covenants of the United Nations. A contribution to the Structure of Basic Rights in Austria, with Special Emphasis on Social Rights] (Manz, Vienna, 1978).

4 *See* BERKA, *supra* note 3, p. 40, and J. CERNY, 'Die Bedeutung der UNO-Menschenrechtspakte für die österreichische Sozialpolitik' [The Relevance of the UN Human Rights Covenants for Austrian Social Policy], *Das Recht der Arbeit* (1983) pp. 65 *et seq.*

5 *See* M. NOWAK, 'Die Durchsetzung der UNO-Menschenrechtskonventionen in Österreich' [The Implementation of the UN Human Rights Conventions in Austria], in R. MACHACEK et al. (eds), *70 Jahre Republik, Grund- und Menschenrechte in Österreich* [70 Years Republic, Fundamental and Human Rights in Austria] (Engel, Kehl, 1991) pp. 703 *et seq.*

6 *Cf.* already F. ERMACORA, 'Die UN-Menschenrechtspakte als Bestandteil der österreichischen Rechtsordnung' [The UN Human Rights Covenants as Part of the Austrian Legal Order], *Juristische Blätter* (1979) pp. 191 *et seq.*

several decisions in which the Human Rights Committee found that Austria had violated certain provisions of the Covenant, such as the right to equality in Article 26 or the right to a fair trial before an independent tribunal in Article 14.[7] Unfortunately, in several cases Austria did not comply with the respective recommendations of the Committee. For instance, in *Perterer* v *Austria* the Human Rights Committee on 20 July 2004 found that the applicant had been dismissed from civil service in violation of Article 14 of the ICCPR. In accordance with Article 2(3) of the ICCPR, the Committee held that Austria was under an obligation to provide the complainant with an effective remedy, including payment of adequate compensation.[8] Rather than providing him with an adequate compensation *ex officio* the government again referred him to pursue his compensation claims before domestic civil courts, which so far has been unsuccessful.[9] In conclusion, the declared purpose of the ratification, that is, to translate the essential principles of the UDHR into legally binding obligations under domestic law has not been achieved.

While most provisions of the ICCPR have legal counterparts in the ECHR, which is directly applicable at the level of constitutional law, an Austrian 'Bill of Rights' still does not contain economic, social and cultural rights, which form an essential part of the UDHR (Articles 22–27). Austria is not living up to its commitment to the equality, interdependence and indivisibility of all human rights under the Vienna Declaration and Programme of Action (hereinafter VDPA) of the Vienna World Conference on Human Rights of 1993. Despite several attempts by the Social Democrats and other parties to incorporate economic, social and cultural rights into an Austrian 'Bill of Rights' since 1919, the conservative People's Party so far blocked these attempts and economic, social and cultural rights play no role in the Austrian human rights law.

---

7 *See* M. NOWAK, *UN Covenant on Civil and Political Rights, CCPR Commentary*, 2nd rev. ed. (Engel, Kehl, 2005).

8 *Perterer* v *Austria*, Communication No. 1015/2001, Decision of 20 August 2004.

9 Other examples include the cases of *Pauger* v *Austria*, Communication No. 415/1990, Decision of 26 March 1992, and Communication No. 716/1996, Decision of 25 March 1999; *Weiss* v *Austria*, Communication No. 1086/2002, Decision of 3 April 2003; *Lederbauer* v *Austria*, Communication No. 1454/2006, Decision of 13 July 2007.

3. THE UDHR IN THE AUSTRIAN POLITICAL DISCOURSE

A review of pertinent practice has shown that references to the UDHR are made only rarely, as in particular on the occasion of the 50th anniversary of the Austrian membership in the United Nations on 14 December 2005,[10] or on the occasion of a pertinent symposium on fundamental rights by Federal President Heinz Fischer,[11] or, again, with regard to the 50th anniversary of the UDHR in a press release by former Federal President Thomas Klestil on 10 December 1998.[12]

The Austrian Federal Minister for Foreign Affairs (now called Federal Minister for European and International Affairs) occasionally refers to human dignity and the universal character of human rights, which are supposed to be at the centre of Austrian foreign policy. Such reference was included, for example, in a speech on the International Day of Human Rights on 10 December 2007.[13]

The Austrian Parliament has a Committee on Human Rights which deals with human rights issues. In 2008, for example, three members of this committee asked the Parliament to adopt a resolution requesting the government to provide the Parliament with a national action plan on the protection and promotion of human rights in Austria within a year.[14] However, an analysis of the practice of the Parliamentary Committee on Human Rights has not turned up any specific references to the UDHR.

---

[10] H. FISCHER, Federal President of the Republic of Austria, *50. Jahrestag der Mitgliedschaft Österreichs bei den Vereinten Nationen* [50th Anniversary of the Austrian Membership to the United Nations] 14 December 2005, <www.hofburg.at/show_content2.php?s2id=400>.

[11] H. FISCHER, Federal President of the Republic of Austria, *Grundrechte im Wandel?* Rede beim 16. Juristentag in Graz [Fundamental Rights in Flux? Speech at the 16th Conference of Austrian Legal Professionals, Graz] 8 October 2006, <www.hofburg.at/show_content2.php?s2id=657>.

[12] T. KLESTIL, former Federal President of the Republic of Austria, *Rede zum Jubiläums-Festakt für Menschenrechte* [Speech at the Ceremonial Act for Human Rights, Vienna], Press Release of the APA (Austrian Press Agency) 10 December 1998.

[13] U. PLASSNIK, Federal Minister of European and International Affairs, *Menschenwürde und universaler Charakter der Menschenrechte im Zentrum der österreichischen Außenpolitik* [Human Dignity an the Universal Character of Human Rights in the Centre of the Austrian Foreign Policy], Speech on the occasion of the International Day on Human Rights, 10 December 2007, <www.bmeia.gv.at/aussenministerium/aktuelles/presseaussendungen/2007/plassnik-menschenwuerde-und-universaler-charakter-der-menschenrechte-im-zentrum-der-oesterreichischen-aussenpolitik.html?no_cache=1&sword_list%5B%5D=dezember>.

[14] Parliamentary Committee on Human Rights, Motion for a Resolution, *Maßnahmen für eine aktive Menschenrechtspolitik in Österreich* (Provisions for an active human rights policy in Austria), 11 March 2008, <www.parlament.gv.at/PG/DE/XXIII/A/A_00628/pmh.shtml>.

A review of drafts of pertinent laws and commentaries thereon confirms a general absence of references to the UDHR, while there are a number of references to the ECHR and other relevant human rights conventions. In 1998, on the occasion of the 50th anniversary of the UDHR, human rights coordinators where established in all ministries, but in fact this cannot be seen as a direct response to it.

There are also no references to the UDHR in charters of political parties, which rarely address it in the political discourse.

Outside of the realm of politics, however, the UDHR has gained some significance in Austria. A case in point is Graz, Austria's second largest town, whose city council, on 8 February 2001, unanimously passed a declaration making Graz the first European Human Rights City. The process is based on this specific human rights declaration according to which Graz, in particular the members of the city council and of the city government will be guided in all their activities by international human rights standards. The objective is that human rights shall be respected in the daily (and the political) life of the city. In this way it may become engrained in the population and thus become more effective. Deficits in the field of human rights at all levels of society can thus be effectively countered. With the Human Rights City process, Graz has committed itself to ensuring that human rights serve as guidelines for all decisions in relation to the city's future development.[15]

Without mentioning the UDHR specifically, the declaration has guided the efforts of the city of Graz in practice. In April 2007, the Human Rights Advisory Council was established by the mayor of Graz with the task to advise him on human rights aspects and to manage the further development of the Human Rights City of Graz. The basic rules of this body, dated 6 June 2007, explicitly refer to the UDHR as one foundation of the concept of human rights employed.[16]

When the Human Rights Advisory Council was entrusted with monitoring the elections for the city council, which took place in January 2008, the main yardstick for the assessment of the election campaign was, again, the UDHR. Furthermore, the Human Rights Advisory Council drafts an annual 'Human Rights Report', which is structured according to the articles of the UDHR. The UDHR is also visible in a particular way in public as one winner of the human rights prize of the province of Styria used his

---

15 *Grazer Menschenrechtserklärung* [Graz Declaration on Human Rights], 8 February 2001, <www.menschenrechtsstadt.at/index.php?option=com_content&task=view&id=63&Itemid=1>.

16 By laws of the Human Rights Advsisory Council of the city of Graz, 6 June 2007 (on file with the authors), para. 2.4.

prize money to produce an installation of the text of the UDHR along one of the most popular public trails, where strollers can walk from display to display that provide details of the thirty articles of the UDHR.

The UDHR also forms an integral part of human rights education in Austrian schools. Teachers are assisted by the Centre for Political Learning in Schools (Polis) operated by the Ludwig Boltzmann Institute of Human Rights (hereinafter BIM) with funding from the Federal Ministry for Education, the Arts and Culture.[17] The same ministry also supported the German edition of the Manual on Human Rights Education, Understanding Human Rights.[18] The Manual's pedagogic concept is based on the UDHR and it has been made available to all secondary schools and the pedagogical academies. There are also a number of UNESCO schools in Austria, which have a particular focus on UDHR-based human rights education in the curriculum.[19]

Human Rights Day, the date of the adoption of the UDHR on 10 December is usually celebrated in various ways by a special week with a number of human rights-related activities in the main cities of Austria. In Graz, this is usually also the date when the human rights prize of the city of Graz, which has been established in 2007, is awarded to persons or institutions with an outstanding human rights record. A similar prize has already existed for a longer time at the provincial level. Accordingly, 10 December is commemorated every year. Larger activities will take place on the occasion of the Declaration's 60th anniversary in 2008.

For the same reason, the Austrian Ministry for European and International Affairs, in cooperation with the BIM and the European Training and Research Centre for Democracy and Human Rights (hereinafter ETC Graz), has organised an international expert conference in August 2008. The year 2008 also marks the 15th anniversary of the adoption of the Vienna Declaration and Programme of Action at the World Conference on Human Rights which took place from 14 to 25 June 1993 in Vienna. Drawing from and developing the human rights guarantees of the UDHR, the VDPA contains the solemn commitment by the international community to the universality and interdependence of all human rights, and to the legitimacy of effective international action in case of serious violations of human rights. One of the most important recommendations of the VDPA, namely the

---

17 *See* Centre for Political Learning in Schools (Polis), <www.politik-lernen.at/goto/polis>.

18 *See* W. BENEDEK (ed.), *Understanding Human Rights, Manual on Human Rights Education*, 2nd ed. (Neuer Wissenschaftlicher Verlag, Vienna and Antwerp, 2006).

19 *See*, for the different UNESCO schools and their curricula in Austria, *UNESCO-Schulen in Österreich* [UNESCO Schools in Austria], <www.unesco-schulen.at>.

creation of the function of an United Nations High Commissioner for Human Rights, was fulfilled by the General Assembly soon after. A specific focus was also put on questions of human rights education as well as various other human rights issues, such as the rights of women, the prohibition of torture and enforced disappearance as well as racism.[20]

Since the adoption of the UDHR in 1948 and the VDPA in 1993, the international community has established a comprehensive body of universal standards, institutions and mechanisms for the promotion and protection of human rights. The main human rights challenges the world faces today stem from imperfect implementation of these standards and mechanisms on the ground. The Vienna conference in August 2008 has brought together high-level representatives of the United Nations system, regional human rights institutions, human rights defenders, experts from civil society and academia, representatives of national human rights institutions and select government representatives. It was aimed at assessing the progress in the implementation of the commitments made by all states in relation to the promotion and protection of human rights in the VDPA, and to reaffirm the key accomplishments of the VDPA, such as the universality of all human rights. The conference generated practical recommendations to be presented to the UN Human Rights Council and the UN General Assembly as a contribution to the Human Rights Year 2008.

4. THE UDHR IN COURTS

With regard to the judiciary, the main institution for the protection of human rights in Austria is the Constitutional Court (*Verfassungsgerichtshof*), which reviews decisions of the executive branch and tribunals with regard to the standards contained in the ECHR and other human rights provisions in the Austrian Constitution. However, no judgments of the Constitutional Court could be found, that mention the UDHR explicitly.

The Federal Administrative Court (*Verwaltungsgerichtshof*), the highest body for administrative disputes, only refers to the UDHR in relation to its lack of binding character. This is exemplified by a decision of 16 December 1966.[21] The Supreme Court (*Oberste Gerichtshof*), the highest court in civil and criminal matters, has not expressly referred to the UDHR, nor the

---

[20] World Conference on Human Rights, *Vienna Declaration and Programme of Action*, UN Doc. A/CONF.157/23, 12 July 1993.

[21] *See* the Collection of Judgments of the Federal Administrative Court, VwSlg 7045 A/1966.

Independent Federal Asylum Senate, until 1 July 2008 the highest body in asylum procedures.

One reason why references to the UDHR are so rare in Austrian practice is that the ECHR is directly applicable under domestic law and in 1964 was even given constitutional rank. Therefore, courts and other public institutions or representatives as well as national laws usually refer to the ECHR. Its provisions are more specific and are part of the Federal Constitution of Austria, which does not have its own catalogue of human and fundamental rights except those contained in the Basic State Law (*Staatsgrundgesetz*) of 1867, which dates back to monarchical times.

5. CONCLUSIONS

The fact that the ECHR, which is differently treated in most European countries, has been given constitutional rank in Austria and that the ECHR is also an accepted standard in the law of the European Union explains why this instrument is most usually referred to in the Austrian political and judicial discourse. Civil and political rights in the UDHR are thus well taken care of. However, the same level of protection and application is not ensured for economic, social and cultural rights.

While the relevance of the UDHR for the further development of human rights is generally recognized, it seems — not least because of the late entry of Austria into the United Nations — that the UDHR has had little relevance for Austrian politics. Only indirectly, the UDHR has found its way into the Austrian 'Bill of Rights' via the ratification and direct application of the ECHR, which, in its preamble makes explicit reference to the UDHR. Accordingly, a survey of the relationship of Austria and the UDHR has to come to the conclusion that Austria has been keeping a low profile.

12. BULGARIA: EVOLVING INTO DEMOCRACY UNDER THE UDHR TEMPLATE

Maria Mandova

1. INTRODUCTION

The concept of human rights in Bulgaria has gone through periods of evolution and devolution since 1948. It has been defined, blurred and re-defined by two distinct political models of governance: socialism and pluralist democracy. The real impact of the Universal Declaration of Human Rights (hereinafter UDHR) on the values, principles and limitations of governance in Bulgaria could be clearly seen with the adoption of the current Constitution of 1991 after the fall of the Berlin wall. It is the achievement in 1991 which cemented a substantive catalogue of human rights into the country's fundamental law practically incorporating, and in places directly quoting the UDHR. It is also worth noting that the priority of social, economic and cultural rights ardently defended during the socialist times has contributed greatly to the contemporary understanding of human rights in Bulgaria and to the acceptance of the essential indivisibility and interconnectedness of all human rights originally spelled out in the UDHR.

This article attempts to contextualise the understanding of human rights in Bulgaria in the post World War II period comparing it to the norms laid out in the UDHR. It traces the concept of rights in the three Constitutions that Bulgaria has had between 1947 and 1991 and briefly discusses the media and public attention to the human rights debates.

2. HUMAN RIGHTS AS A DEMAND AFTER THE SECOND WORLD WAR

The Treaty of Paris from 10 February 1947, which mandated the relations and duties of the losing sides in the Second World War, made references to specific rights guarantees on the territories of the Axis allies prior to the adoption of the UDHR in 1948. The Treaty is an important document for contextualising the concrete human rights norms that were being contemplated during the time of the drafting and adoption of the UDHR.

Bulgaria's responsibilities towards its citizens and the Allied Powers, as a country which supported the Axis Powers, were also detailed. In addition to reparations and scaling down the military, specific human rights clauses such as equality and non-discrimination and a commitment to minority rights made the checklist of duties against which Bulgaria had to build its new image as a republic, as a 'peaceful state',[1] and to carve its place internationally as a member of the United Nations (hereinafter UN). These norms initially mentioned in the Treaty, and more importantly universalised and expanded in the UDHR, were idly, or less so, incorporated into the Constitutions of Bulgaria in the coming years.

At the time of the adoption of the UDHR the acceptance of new members into the UN was a significant battleground for the preservation of the delicate geo-political balance of the Cold War. A lack of respect and implementation of the rights and disarmament related clauses of the Treaty of Paris had been an argument of the United States and Britain to block Bulgaria's entry into the UN until 1955.[2] Accusations about violations of specific rights such as prohibition of racial discrimination, right to education in a minority language, freedom of the press and free speech, freedom of association, freedom of conscience and religion were at the centre of Bulgaria's negotiations for UN membership. Their importance becomes clear in the two notes of response sent on 21 April and 27 July 1949[3] in which the Bulgarian government discussed and rejected the accusations of the United States for violations of the right-clauses in the Paris Treaty citing provisions of the newly adopted Constitution of 1947.

A demand for the protection of a core group of rights had an impact on the political image of Bulgaria and naturally on the Constitution which it voted for on 4 December 1947, just ten months after the peace treaty had been signed. Filled with contradictions, claw-back clauses and vagueness, the 1947 Constitution was a leap forward in the incorporation of rights into the law in comparison with Bulgaria's nineteenth century *Tarnovska* Constitution (1879) which spelled out only mandatory military service (Article 71) and payment of taxes (Article 69) under the rubric of citizens'

---

1 'Писмо на Г. Димитров до Генералния секретар на ООН Тригве Ли', *Работническо дело*, 26 July 1947.

2 И. Гарвалов, 'Приемането на България в ООН', V *Български дипломатически преглед* (2005) pp. 16–18.

3 Bulgarian News Agency Archive. БТА Бюлетин, *Дипломатически архив: Борбата за приемането на НР България в ООН*, 1975, Из N 4, 'Меморандум на българското правителство до правителството на САЩ по повод приемането на НР България за член на ООН', p. 149.

responsibilities. Concrete responsibilities contained in the Treaty of Paris and the experience of the war itself have carved a place, as small as it may be, for a novel understanding of rights in Bulgaria after 1947, namely, the inclusion of specific political, social, economic and cultural rights for the citizens into the fundamental law and the conception of rights as a public good that the State needed to protect. The next and most problematic measure was creating a system of guarantees for those rights, a step which Bulgaria had not seriously thrust its energy into until the next millennium.

3. HUMAN RIGHTS IN SOCIALIST BULGARIA

3.1. A NEW CONCEPT OF HUMAN RIGHTS AND DEMOCRACY

Bulgaria was not a member of the UN when the UDHR was drafted and adopted. Emerging from a devastating war on the side of Nazi Germany with the only pride of saving its Jews from annihilation, on 9 September 1944 a 'socialist revolution' took place after which Bulgaria chose to change its previous monarchic model with a referendum in 1946 and become a republic. The new model was a one-party 'socialist democracy',[4] where the Bulgarian Communist Party defined itself as the embodiment of the will of the people,[5] that is, representing the sovereignty of the people. Later on this concept of people's or socialist democracy was gradually refined along the lines of international human rights norms underlying Bulgaria's commitment to the socialist conception of human rights which was to guarantee the indivisibility of all human rights. In an article from 1980 entitled *Bulgaria and International Cooperation in the Field of Human Rights*,[6] the need for explicit clarification of the relationship between socialism and human rights in Bulgaria received due attention under ideological camouflage:

> "[t]he socialist model creates the best conditions for the flourishing of human personality, for the respect of human dignity, for the reinforcement and

---

[4] *Constitution of People's Republic of Bulgaria* (1947), *see* Article 1 and *Constitution of People's Republic of Bulgaria* (1971) *see* Article 1, <www.www.constcourt.bg>, visited on 29 August 2008. Original text without amendments of the 1947 Constitution published in *Държавен вестник*, бр. 284, 6 December 1947.

[5] Preamble and Article 2, original text without amendments of the 1971 Constitution published in *Държавен вестник*, бр. 39, 1971.

[6] Original title in Bulgarian: "*НР България и международното сътрудничество в областта на правата на човека*".

> guaranteeing not only of the civil and political but also of the economic, social and cultural rights. Socialism and democracy are indivisible."[7]

Promotion of the fundamental premise of the UDHR, namely the indivisibility of human rights, ideologically undermined during the Cold War by both sides of the Iron Curtain, was a significant element in the debate about human rights and socialism which had been at the core of the democratic changes in Bulgaria in the late 1980s.

3.2. A PEOPLE'S REPUBLIC: CONSTITUTION OF 1947

During the drafting of the Constitution of 1947 at least three main 'external demands' occupied the law-makers and politicians: firstly, an aspiration to become a member of the UN, therefore creating a fundamental law that did not go against its Charter, secondly, reinforcement of the alliance with fellow Socialist countries, most notably the Union of Soviet Socialist Republics (USSR) and thirdly, payment of the reparations and respect for the Treaty of Paris provisions and its concrete responsibilities. During the forty-five years of socialist rule (1944–1989), the 'rights of the citizens' were understood as a public good *given* and *defined* by the government in a largely collective fashion. Among the many documents by the Party which displayed heightened political emotion, the interpretation of the 'common good', ultimately the 'good of socialism' itself, is justified in the *Encyclopaedia of Bulgaria* because: "collective ownership of the means of production destroys the possibility of exploitation of a human by another human … [and] generates the unity of public interest".[8]

At the time of the drafting and adoption of the fundamental law the UDHR was in its making. Therefore, any comparison of specific articles and principles need to bear in mind the approximately one year time lapse from the adoption of the 1947 Constitution and the UDHR in 1948. The 1947 Constitution was written in a revolutionary spirit announcing the break away with the "fascist-monarchy dictatorship" (Article 1) and outlining a new system of primarily collective ownership of land, natural resources and the means of production (Articles 6, 7, 8, 11). The concept of rights during the socialist regime was that they were a means to an end, the end being the

---

7 Л. Кулишев, 'НР България и международното сътрудничество в областта на правата на човека', 1 *Международни отношения* (1980), p. 15. Translation from Bulgarian by the author.

8 *Енциклопедия "България", том 6* (Българска академия на науките, София, 1988) p. 326. Translation from Bulgarian by the author.

creation of a people's democracy as "a new type of political organisation, a form of proletarian dictatorship"[9] and a "preliminary phase to communism — a highly organised society of free and conscious workers".[10] In contrast, the genius of UDHR is its fundamental assertion that the protection of human dignity, inherent to everyone, by way of guaranteeing her or his economic, social, cultural, civil and political rights is both the means to and the end itself of a peaceful, humane and just system.

The individual good in socialist Bulgaria was conceived as an extension of the collective good. This fundamental idea explains the lack of discussion in official documents and in the media of human rights as individual rights. Plural forms such as 'the citizens' and 'the people' in the Constitution of 1947 replace 'everyone' as the right-bearer in the UDHR.[11] Such vague formulations, exclusive to citizens, were the hallmark of Bulgaria's post-war Constitution and as problematic as they are, they also serve as a point of contemplation and a reminder of the absence of collective rights in the UDHR.

The chapter *Fundamental Rights and Responsibilities of the Citizens* in the Constitution referred to a list of rights also contained in the UDHR, those include: equality before the law[12] (Articles 56 and 71), special care for the woman-mother such as paid maternity leave and free medical care, right to paid vacation (Article 74), right to social security (Article 75), protection of family life (Article 76), right to work (Article 73). Among the limited number of progressive articles in the Constitution were Article 79 which granted the right to education in their mother tongue and development of their culture to the national minorities,[13] and Article 72 which recognised gender equality in all spheres of life and equal social and economic benefits for women and men, a norm mentioned only in the Preamble of the UDHR. Internationally a non-

9 Г. Димитров, *Съчинения, том 14* (Издателство на Българската Комунистическа Партия, София, 1955).

10 X Congress of the Bulgarian Communist Party, Sofia 1971. *See* БКП, Конгрес, X, София, 1971, *Доклади. Решения* (Партиздат, София, 1973). *Also see Енциклопедия „България", том 2* (Българска академия на науките, София, 1981) pp. 280–281. Translation from Bulgarian by the author.

11 The April Meeting (*Пленум*) of the Central Committee of the Bulgarian Communist Party 2–6 April 1956 rejected the cult of personality and reinforced the collective method as the highest principle of party leadership. *See* Йордан Василев Зарчев, Марин Илиев Цуцов (eds), *Априлският пленум на ЦК на БКП 1956: Пълен стенографски Протокол* (Атлас прес, София, 2002).Translation from Bulgarian by the author.

12 Notably, political views were omitted from the prohibited basis for discrimination in Article 3 and as illegitimate reasons for privilege in Article 71.

13 Nevertheless, studying Bulgarian language was mandatory for all minority groups.

derogable right, the freedom from torture, degrading and inhumane treatment along with the right to freedom of movement were absent in the Constitution and the basis for terrifying violations over the years.

The limited number of rights in the Constitution of 1947 was not the largest drawback because formally for a country emerging from a devastating war and plunging into an incomprehensibly new system, the attempt to create a catalogue of rights was respectable. A lack of a system that guaranteed those rights, however, and legal stratagems such as claw-back clauses (for example, right to property, freedom of assembly, freedom to elect and be elected) are what made the Constitution of 1947 a half-hearted attempt at placing the rights and freedoms in the centre of the governance model. Moreover, the Constitution allowed for merging of executive, legislative and judicial powers (for example, Article 25, Article 35, Article 65) making it impossible for independent monitoring of violations. Perhaps a comparison of the 1947 Constitution to the UDHR is a rather abstract exercise given the different points of departure of the two documents and their chronology. On the other hand, the Constitution adopted in 1971 had evidence of external and internal pressure on Bulgaria to expand the catalogue of rights with definitions closer to those in the international human rights instruments, naturally including those contained in the UDHR.

3.3. BULGARIA BECOMES A MEMBER OF THE UN

Membership in the UN had been a much expected event and the United Nations Association of Bulgaria was founded in 1948 to support this endeavour. After long negotiations and a last-minute package deal between the powerful of the day with the help of Canadian diplomacy, Bulgaria's entry materialised on 14 December 1955. The interest of the government-controlled media was steady on reporting daily about the sessions of the General Assembly in 1955. Coverage of the issues, however, was very selective. The mass media and academic journals remained silent about the adoption of the UDHR and the discussions on international level about the protection and promotion of human rights. Instead, the priorities for Bulgaria at that time included the General Assembly debates on disarmament, decolonisation and the use of nuclear energy for peaceful purposes.[14]

The protection of human rights was not mentioned as a goal of the UN in international statements by the Bulgarian government during the time of the

---

[14] *See* the daily newspaper *Работническо дело* from 1955 and 1956.

country's application for membership.[15] Instead, the focus was on its role to promote peaceful cooperation referring mostly to military deterrence. Bulgaria was accepted a member of the UN on 14 December 1955 together with fourteen other 'undivided' states among them Albania, Romania, Jordan, Cambodia, Italy, Finland, Austria and Spain.[16] Difficult logistics at the time allowed for Bulgaria's Minister Dimitar Halov to travel to New York a week later to deliver a declaration about the new membership restating the country's readiness to contribute to international peace and cooperation and committing to the responsibilities of the Charter.[17] The principles and ideals of the UDHR as an integral element of the mission of the organisation were not mentioned this time either.

The reference to violations of certain rights by Western powers found a place in Bulgaria's official statements later on. In the 1960s and 1970s, Bulgaria sent multiple letters to UN Secretary General condemning the racist regime in South Rhodesia (Zimbabwe)[18] and apartheid in South Africa[19] and made statements in support of the decolonisation of Algiers, Laos and Vietnam. A call to stop the "cruel repressions in Chile" was made by Bulgaria's Chairman of the State Council, that is, the head of government Todor Jivkov, in an urgent letter sent to Secretary General Kurt Waldheim in 1978.[20]

In the 1960s and 1970s, Bulgaria began to participate more actively in the organs and agencies of the UN.[21] It became a party to both international

---

15 *Supra* note 1. *See also* 'Писмо на Председателя на Министерски съвет и Министър на външните работи Васил Коларов до ГС на ООН за приемане на НР България в ООН, 22 септ., 1948г', 3 *Международи отношения* (1975).

16 A day after the vote in the General Assembly, the UN Secretary General Dag Hammarskjöld sends a note of congratulation to Bulgaria's Minister of Foreign Affairs published in a main daily newspaper. *See* 'Министъра на външните работи', *Работническо дело*, 16 December 1955, p. 1.

17 The Declaration is published in a main daily newspaper. *See* 'Декларация по повод приемането на България в ООН', *Труд*, 22 December 1955.

18 Bulgarian News Agency Archive. БТА Бюлетин, *МИНФ*, 1967, N 82, 'Писмо представено от НРБ в ООН до У Тан'.

19 'Енергичен протест против покровителите на расизма и апартейда', *Работническо дело*, 5 October 1974.

20 'До негово превъзходителство господин Курт Валхайм генерален секретар на ООН', *Работническо дело*, 7 October 1978.

21 For a history of Bulgaria's acceptance as a member of the United Nations and a history of its activities, *see* the memoirs of the prominent Bulgarian diplomat and current Chairman of UNA Bulgaria Ivan Garvalov. И. Гарвалов, *Средище на възможните мисии: ООН в спомените на един български дипломат* (ГорексПрес, София, 2005).

Covenants and a member of a number of international organisations including the ILO (since 1920), UNESCO (since 1956) and WHO (since 1948). Bulgaria was elected three times as a non-permanent member of the Security Council (1966–1967, 1986–1987, 2002–2003). Human rights arose as a concern in the 1970s and the country began to be more active in seeking and receiving chairmanships[22] in deliberative and monitoring organs (First Committee, Third Committee, Human Rights Commission, CAT, ECOSOC, CEDAW, Commission on the Status of Women).[23] After the ratification of the International Covenant on Civil and Political Rights (hereinafter ICCPR), a Human Rights Committee was set up in Bulgaria in 1976.

Specific issues such as the rights of the child and the rights of women had been more or less 'safe areas', in which the otherwise strict political control and censorship of information grew lax and permitted their public promotion. An example of an international event of large magnitude was the celebration of the International Year of the Child. In August 1979, Bulgaria hosted the *First International Children Assembly "A Flag for Peace"* (*"Знаме на мира"*) whose Honorary Patron was UNESCO's Director-General Amadou-Mahtar M'Bow. A second Assembly took place in 1982 significantly increasing the number of represented countries from 76 in 1979 to 102 in 1982.[24]

Despite the efforts to voice opinion on issues related to human rights internationally, domestically Bulgaria took no substantial measures to create a system that guaranteed human rights. Formally, however, the new Constitution of 1971 expanded the catalogue of rights and for the first time included a reference to State's responsibility to protect *human dignity* which is an indirect acknowledgement of the core objective of the UDHR.

3.4. "DESTROYING THE POSSIBILITY FOR EXPLOITATION OF A HUMAN BY ANOTHER HUMAN":[25] CONSTITUTION OF 1971

The Constitution of 1971 attempted to expand the guiding principles of governance and the formal catalogue of rights in Bulgaria. It appeared contradictory when it also made explicit that "[t]he leading power in the

[22] Literally, there were no women with representative functions on behalf of Bulgaria at the UN at the time.

[23] Гарвалов, *supra* note 21.

[24] *Енциклопедия „България", том 4* (Българска академия на науките, София, 1984) pp. 153–155.

[25] Preamble of Constitution (1971). Original text, *supra* note 5.

society and in the State is the Bulgarian Communist Party".[26] In 1990, in a feeble attempt to put a band-aid on this fundamentally contradictory document, Article 5 was amended to mention political pluralism and the separation of power as a fundamental principle of the political system in Bulgaria. Less than a year after, a new Constitution was adopted which sweepingly changed Bulgaria's principles and form of governance.

The Preamble of the 1971 Constitution declared that one of the main goals of the State, therefore the Party, was to create "ever more favourable conditions for the all-round flourishing of the free human personality".[27] For the first time a Constitution proclaimed that the State served the people by guaranteeing the free development of the person, by guaranteeing his or her[28] rights and by protecting his or her dignity (Article 3.1). Although nowhere did the Constitution call the rights it granted to its subjects 'human rights', the reference to *dignity* inevitably recalled the UDHR. Furthermore, the use of more general terms in addition to "rights of the citizens" to describe its subjects (for example, human personality) was evidence of the influence of international norms and human rights documents on the concept of rights in Bulgaria. New and significantly expanded rights in the Constitution included prohibition of hate speech and discrimination (Article 35), right to free education at all levels (Article 45), universal free medical care (Article 47), prohibition of retroactivity of law and extrajudicial sentences (Article 136), right to legal aid (Article 138), and special protection for vulnerable groups such as minors, the disabled and elderly (Article 44). Legal detention without permission from a judge was lowered to twenty-four hours from forty-eight hours in the 1947 Constitution.

A human rights regime is strong when it creates a system that guarantees these rights. Both Constitutions of 1947 and 1971 have been influenced by the UDHR and include an array of rights some of which were progressive for their time. However, both documents leave out a clear system of guarantees through an independent legal system with an oversight mandate. The majority of power was centred in the hands of the National Assembly and therefore in the Party functionaries. The lack of procedural clarity of the oversight institutions and limitations of the power of the government made a large number of rights granted by the Constitutions short of substantial. The

---

26 Article 1.2, Constitution (1971). Original text, *supra* note 5.

27 Preamble of Constitution (1971). Original text, *supra* note 5. Translation from Bulgarian by the author.

28 In Bulgarian language 'person' (*човек*) is neutral; therefore the use of masculine/feminine possessive pronouns is the choice of the author by way of giving a more accurate translation.

abundance of claw-back clauses using vague qualifications such as "unless not contrary to public interest"[29] gave leeway for political interpretation of rights.

As the world started to change, disillusionment matured and extreme policies such as the attempt to forcefully assimilate the Turkish minority, ethnic Bulgarians of Muslim faith (*pomaks*) and Muslim Romas (*Възродителния процес*[30]) fired back, more critical voices appeared. In a statement to commemorate the 40th anniversary of the adoption of the UDHR, the Chairman of the Human Rights Committee in Bulgaria, Konstantin Tellalov, reminded Bulgaria that the Declaration was a living document which continued to embarrass the political division over human rights of the socialist and capitalist regimes. "In an era of global interconnectedness of countries and peoples and an attempt of survival in times of nuclear weapons", Tellalov continued, "the national interests now are measured by *universal human criteria*".[31]

4. END OF SOCIALISM AND THE UDHR: A REDEFINITION OF THE 'COMMON GOOD'

The values and principles laid down in the UDHR have had a prominent place in Bulgaria's most recent constitutional history. The UDHR has been a "guiding light"[32] for the drafting of the Constitution of 1991, which marked the end of socialism and the transition to pluralist democracy. In 1991, the new Constitution incorporated the values of the UDHR as the core principles of the country by reformulating in detail the relationship between the governed and the government and articulating the rights and freedoms of the individual. From a terminological point of view, it is important to note that in the spirit of the UDHR the Constitution used the phrase "the rights of the individual" (*права на личността*) going beyond "the rights of citizens" or

---

[29] *See* Article 9.2, Constitution (1971). Original text, *supra* note 5. Translation from Bulgarian by the author.

[30] *See* V. DIMITROV, 'In Search of a Homogeneous Nation: The Assimilation of Bulgaria's Turkish Minority 1984–1985', *Journal on Ethnopolitics and Minority Issues in Europe* (December 2000), <www.ecmi.de>, visited on 1 September 2008. *Also see* M. NEUBURGER, *The Orient Within: Muslim Minorities and the Negotiation of Nationhood in Modern Bulgaria* (Cornell University Press, New York, 2004).

[31] Bulgarian News Agency Archive. БТА Бюлетин, *ВИНФ*, 1988, N 208, pp. 10–11. Translation and emphasis by the author.

[32] Г. Близнашки, 'Всеобща декларация за правата на човека и Конституцията на Република България от 1991 година', *Демократически преглед* (зима 1998/99), p. 32.

"the rights of the people" used in the previous Constitutions. As Bliznashki observes, the rights catalogue of the UDHR had been "more or less well recreated in the formulation of rights in the new Constitution".[33] Acknowledgement of the significance of the UDHR as the primary inspiration for the domestic human rights system of protection comes directly from the government. The official website of Bulgaria's Ministry of Foreign Affairs states:

> "The protection of human rights and fundamental freedoms and the observance of the commonly accepted international standards in this field is a major priority of the domestic and foreign policy of the Republic of Bulgaria. The Constitution of the Republic of Bulgaria adopted in 1991, through a literal reproduction, incorporates the standards contained in the UN Universal Declaration of Human Rights."[34]

As a *lex superior*, Bulgaria's Constitution of 1991 corrected the vagueness of its predecessors and not only described the rights and freedoms of persons under its jurisdiction but also their limitations leaving fewer grey zones for legislative mischief. Guaranteeing a nucleus of non-derogable rights in a state of emergency (Article 57.3) added significant legitimacy to a substantive system of protection. Non-derogable rights under the current Constitution of Bulgaria are the right to life (Article 28), prohibition of torture, degrading treatment and medical experiments without written consent (Article 29), right to a fair trial (Article 31 paragraphs 1, 2, 3), right to private and family life (Article 32.1) and freedom of religion and conscience (Article 37). Guaranteeing freedom of religion and conscience under any circumstances is an important peculiarity of the regime which paid due attention to the past socialist policies of 'secular assimilation' as well as to the delicate ethnic and religious balance on the Balkans.

In its decisions, the Constitutional Court indirectly referred to the principles contained in the UDHR by referring to the Constitution itself. Case law about human rights violations most frequently evoke the European Convention on Human Rights (ECHR) and the International Covenant on Civil and Political Rights in cases such as violations of religious freedom,[35] *ex*

33 *Ibid.*, p. 33. Translation from Bulgarian by the author.

34 Министерство на външните работи, *България и правата на човека*, <www.mfa.bg>, visited on 20 August 2008.

35 Decision No. 12 from 15 July 2003 (Case No. 3 from 2003), Bulgarian Constitutional Court, <www.constcourt.bg>, visited on 18 August 2008.

post facto sentences,[36] rights of foreigners,[37] the right to information and classified dossiers,[38] intelligence methods[39] and minority rights.[40] Nowadays, Bulgaria is a party to all core human rights treaties and has withdrawn its reservations related to the complaint procedures. Officially, the country rejects the cultural relativism approach to human rights.[41]

The significance of the UDHR for Bulgaria's contemporary legal development is highlighted by the Chairman of the Parliament in 1998 in connection with the abolition of the death penalty. At a special session of the Parliament honouring the 50th anniversary of the adoption of the UDHR, the Chairman stated that "the ideals of the UDHR have inspired the development of contemporary and democratic Bulgaria … They have [also] inspired the important decision yesterday of the Parliament to abolish the death penalty, by way of which we reinforced the sacred right to life written in Article 3 of the declaration".[42]

5. CONCLUSION

Bulgaria has come a long way and still has further to stride, in order to create a system which not only formally acknowledges, but also guarantees human rights. The discrepancy between paper and substantial rights has haunted Bulgaria since the creation of the UDHR. Not a member of the UN at the time of the adoption of the UDHR, Bulgaria without explicitly acknowledging the

---

[36] Decision No. 1 from 13 February 2007 (Case No. 9 from 2006), Bulgarian Constitutional Court, <www.constcourt.bg>, visited on 18 August 2008.

[37] Decision No. 4 from 23 February 2001 (Case No. 15 from 2000), Bulgarian Constitutional Court, < www.constcourt.bg>, visited on 18 August 2008.

[38] Decision No. 3 from 25 September 2002 (Case No. 11 from 2002), Bulgarian Constitutional Court, <www.constcourt.bg>, visited on 18 August 2008. *See also* Decision No. 14 from 30 May 2001 (Case No. 7 from 2001), Bulgarian Constitutional Court, <www.constcourt.bg>, visited on 18 August 2008.

[39] Decision No. 1 from 10 February 1998 (Case No. 17 from 1997), Bulgarian Constitutional Court, <www.constcourt.bg>, visited on 18 August 2008.

[40] Decision No. 2 from 18 February 1998 (Case No. 15 from 1997), Bulgarian Constitutional Court, <www.constcourt.bg>, visited on 18 August 2008.

[41] В. Сотиров, 'Всеобщата декларация за правата на човека и съвременността', XXVI *Международни отношения* (1997) p. 69.

[42] Нар.събрание, XXXVIII, Сес. V, 1988. Стенографски дневници: Кн. 72. Заседания 208-210, 32–33 извънредни и тържествено честване на 50-годишнината от приемането на Всеобщата декларация за правата на човека от 8–11 декември (София, 2000), pp. 172–175. Translation by the author.

legal and political value of the UDHR has slowly incorporated its principles into the law. Most notably, the UDHR became the central reference point for the drafting of the Constitution in 1991 which marked the country's transition from a socialist state to a pluralist democracy. Despite the ideological divisions of the past or perhaps because of them, Bulgaria vigorously strives to put into practice the fundamental principle of the Declaration that of the indivisibility, interrelatedness and interconnectedness of all human rights.

13. FINLAND: POLITICAL, NOT LEGAL

Markku Suksi[1]

1. INTRODUCTION

By the time of the establishment of the United Nations (hereinafter UN) in 1945, Finland found itself in a group of states which was not invited to San Francisco and with which Finland actually did not want to be associated. After developing a reasonably viable parliamentary rule between the two world wars[2] and with a wish to maintain a peaceful neutrality policy in relation to the neighbouring countries, Finland ended up on the losing side in the Second World War: as a co-belligerent with Germany against the Soviet Union in the so-called Continuation War between 1941 and 1944,[3] Finland

---

[1] I wish to thank Ms. Ilona Nieminen for invaluable assistance in collecting the materials and commenting on the draft. I also extend my sincere gratitude to Mr. Holger Rotkirch, former Director of the Department of International Law of the Finnish Ministry of Foreign Affairs, for ideas at the early stages of the research related to this article.

[2] As a fairly new state, independent since 1917, Finland nonetheless did not follow the pattern of many European states in the post-World War I situation that led to authoritarian rule, as was the case in, for instance, Estonia, Latvia and Lithuania as well as in older states, such as Germany, Italy and Spain. Instead, the semi-presidential form of government with parliamentary accountability and a regularly elected parliament was able to resist the calls for authoritarian rule. Even during the war, the Parliament of Finland continued to function. In addition, during the Second World War, Finland did not become a Fascist country and, it should be added, Finland did not become a Socialist country or a so-called People's Democratic Republic in the aftermath of the Second World War.

[3] As a letter to the editor by Mr. Antti Alanen in the main Finnish daily newspaper, *Helsingin Sanomat*, formulated on 15 March 2005, Finland was between Stalin and Hitler, and nobody has ever had to make such an unpleasant choice. In the so-called Continuation War of 1941–1944, in which Finland was co-belligerent with Germany, Finland aimed at re-taking the areas in the eastern and northern parts of Finland that were lost to the Soviet Union in the Winter War but was probably not really sharing the political aims of the German war campaign so as to make Finland a true ally of Germany in the Axis. In the two wars against the Soviet Union, Finland lost areas in the east and in the north, but the country was never occupied by the Soviet Union, and one could say that the two wars actually ended in a tie of some sort. One positive detail in the maelstrom of events during the Second World War is that the Jewish population of Finland was not subjected to the holocaust, although Germany made a few attempts to press Finland on the point. Instead, the Jewish citizens were treated on an equal basis with other citizens of the

unwillingly[4] became a member of a group of states that was not part of the creation of the United Nations and not part of the drafting and approval of the Universal Declaration of Human Rights (hereinafter UDHR).

Sidelined as Finland was in the 1940s and much of the 1950s from the international community, it could be assumed at the outset that the emergence of international human rights and their evolution would not have much impact in Finland. Yet at the same time, the internal development of the Finnish society cannot have been entirely disconnected from the general idea of human rights or individual rights. The Form of Government (Constitution) Act of 1919 established constitutional rights for the individuals in a manner that ensured at an early stage a compatibility with the human rights established in the UDHR. In comparative terms, it seems that Finland has since fared relatively well in the implementation of, *inter alia*, the freedom of the press, equality between the sexes, participation of women in politics and the right to education.[5]

2. OUTSIDE OF THE UN (BUT INSIDE OF THE HUMAN RIGHTS DISCOURSE?)[6]

Early on, one of the aims of the UN and the UDHR was to introduce human rights norms at the international level as a part of public international law so as to compel states to respect individual rights in the domestic legal orders. When it became evident that a domestic guarantee of constitutional rights or individual rights was not sufficient for the protection of human beings, the Charter of the UN introduced in 1945 the concept of human rights in several of its provisions. The UN did not define the material contents of the concept until 1948, when the UDHR was adopted.

---

country, although some Jewish refugees were returned from Finland to Germany and a ship with Jewish refugees were refused entry to port.

4 It is still a matter of some controversy whether the decision to join the German attack to the East in 1941 was a decision that Finland could have opted out from. For one of the most recent accounts on, *inter alia*, this matter, *see* H. YLIKANGAS, *Romahtaako rintama?* (Otava, Helsinki, 2007), *passim*.

5 *See* <en.wikipedia.org/wiki/Lists_of_countries>, visited on 14 October 2008, with lists of rankings at the end of the page.

6 *See* M. SCHEININ, *Ihmisoikeudet Suomen oikeudessa* (Suomalainen Lakimiesyhdistys, Helsinki, 1991) for an analysis of the legal position of human rights in the legal order of Finland and M. HALME, *Human Rights in Action* (Helsinki University Printing House, Helsinki, 2008) pp. 31–62, for a general account of the Finnish human rights discourse.

Because Finland was on the losing side in the Second World War, the concept of human rights and even some material contents of it were made binding upon Finland already in 1947 through the Peace Treaty of Paris,[7] incorporated in the domestic legal order in the manner prescribed by the 1928 Parliament (Constitution) Act for constitutionally relevant treaties.[8] In Article 6 of the Peace Treaty, some of the core substance of human rights is identified in a binding form in relation to Finland one year before the adoption of the General Assembly resolution containing the UDHR:

> "Finland shall take all measures necessary to secure to all persons under Finnish jurisdiction, without distinction as to race, sex, language or religion, the enjoyment of human rights and of the fundamental freedoms, including freedom of worship, of political opinion and of public meeting."

The concept of human rights and fundamental freedoms thus became binding upon Finland as a State, on the one hand, and inside Finland in the domestic jurisdiction, on the other hand, at least with respect to non-discrimination, freedom of worship, freedom of political opinion, and freedom of public meeting.[9] The list of material human rights was non-exclusive, and therefore, the enjoyment of human rights and of fundamental freedoms could also encompass other individual rights. However, as pointed out above, many of these individual rights were already a part of the Finnish legal order, for instance, on the basis of the 1919 Form of Government (Constitution) Act.[10]

---

7 As explained in K. TÖRNUDD, *Finland and the International Norms of Human Rights* (Martinus Nijhoff Publishers, Dordrecht, 1986) pp. 19–20, the inclusion of such contents in an individual peace treaty (not only in relation to Finland, but also in relation to Bulgaria, Hungary, Italy and Romania as well as Austria in 1955) as in Article 6 was initiated by the United States and recommended by the so-called Nuclear Commission on Human Rights in April–May 1946 and by the UN Economic and Social Council during its second session on 21 June 1946. For more analysis, *see also* T. SUONTAUSTA, 'Rauhansopimus ja Suomen kansalaisten yleiset oikeudet sekä oikeusturva', 47 *Lakimies* (1949) pp. 617–619. As pointed out by Castrén, the previous practice with extensive freedoms became legally binding. *See* E. CASTRÉN, *Suomen kansainvälinen oikeus* (Werner Söderström Osakeyhtiö, Porvoo, 1959) p. 20.

8 Lag om godkännande av fredsfördraget mellan Finland och Socialistiska Rådsrepublikernas Förbund, Förenade Konungariket, Australien, Sydafrikanska Unionen, Indien, Kanada, Tjeckoslovakien, Ukrainska Socialistiska Rådsrepubliken, Nya Zeeland samt Vitryska Socialistiska Rådsrepubliken (Statutes of Finland nr 690/1947, with a supplementing Decree No. 691/1947).

9 *See also* Article 7 of the Peace Treaty. Whereas Article 6 had a root in a US initiative and in UN recommendations (*see supra* note 7), Article 7 is evidently based on an initiative of the Soviet Union.

10 *See* SUONTAUSTA, *supra* note 7, p. 626 (esp. fn. 17), and K. WESTERHOLM, 'Förenta Nationerna och de mänskliga rättigheterna', 88 *Tidskrift, utgiven av Juridiska Föreningen i Finland* (1952) p. 3, fn. 9, where the point is made that the existence and application of constitutional rights in

Consequently, for the average Finn, this article was probably devoid of all practical meaning. The general perception was that these rights of the individual already existed in Finland. It is, nonetheless, possible to emphasise the concept of 'all persons' in the context of political opinion and public meetings, because in the 1930s, legislation was adopted which aimed at circumscribing extremist activities, especially those of the Communists, who advocated revolution and were closely associated with the Komintern, the Soviet-led international organisation for the worldwide promotion of Communism. Hence already on the basis of this article alone, the extreme Left would have been able to resume its subversive activities.[11]

On the top of Article 6, the Peace Treaty contained in Article 8 language that sustained this conclusion and further specified the aim of the human rights.[12] The general impression on the basis of the Peace Treaty should have been that human rights were intended for the protection of those persons who were in favour of the Soviet Union and who were working for a swift transition of Finland into a Socialist country. Conclusive and definite development into this direction did not take place, but it seems clear that such a development would have jeopardized the free society that already existed in Finland. It is important in the context that human rights became

---

Finland was emphasised from the Finnish side during the Peace Conference of Paris. Suontausta explains that the human rights provisions in the Peace Treaty could be understood as a sign of distrust concerning the democratic system that was in effect in Finland, but that upon ratification of the Peace Treaty, the Finnish state organs did not have to amend in any way the fundamentals of the democratic state order of Finland. Some evidence for the understanding in Finland that the legal order already reflected human rights can also be found in the Government Bill to the Parliament concerning the ratification of ILO Convention 87 concerning Freedom of Association and Protection of the Right to Organise, RP 58/1949, according to which the Finnish provisions of relevance for the Convention are mainly to be found in the Form of Government (Constitution) Act of 1919, the Act on Associations of 1919 and the Act on Labour Contracts of 1922. The point was that the requirements of the Convention had already been realised in Finland and that there were, therefore, good reasons for Finland to ratify the Convention. *See also* J-M. JANSSON, 'Finland och de mänskliga rättigheterna', in *Vår syn III: Liberala debattinläggningar.* Nyliberala skriftserien N:o 16 (Söderström & Co, Helsingfors, 1957) pp. 63-92.

[11] For a comment in this direction, *see also* SUONTAUSTA, *supra* note 7, pp. 620 *et seq.*

[12] "Finland, which in accordance with the Armistice Agreement has taken measures for dissolving all organisations of a Fascist type on Finnish territory, whether political, military or paramilitary, as well as other organisations conducting propaganda hostile to the Soviet Union or to any of the other United Nations, shall not permit in future the existence and activities of organizations of that nature which have as their aim denial to the people of their democratic rights". Whereas Article 6 had a root in a US initiative and in UN recommendations (*see supra* note 7), Article 8 is evidently based on an initiative of the Soviet Union.

formally binding on Finland at a moment when the UDHR itself was still in the making.

Paradoxically, the obligation was created in the Peace Treaty for Finland and not for the Soviet Union, where human rights really would have been needed. The implicit 'monopolisation' of Finland by the Soviet Union after the Second World War was formally established in the 1948 Treaty on Friendship, Co-operation and Assistance between the two countries, but this treaty was considerably less intrusive than the corresponding treaties concluded with the so-called satellite states of the Soviet Union in Central and Eastern Europe. The particular relationship with the Soviet Union nonetheless prevented Finland from full participation in the West European structures, including the Council of Europe and the European Convention on Human Rights (hereinafter ECHR), and affected, *inter alia*, the freedom of the press through a self-censorship that took into consideration the anticipated opinions of the Soviet Union on different political issues.[13] However, in spite of the uncertainties of the times, it was possible for Finland to preserve its parliamentary form of government.[14]

By the time of the adoption of the UDHR, the reaction of the press was not very enthusiastic. The major Finnish-language daily, *Helsingin Sanomat*, did not devote any space for the issue, but the main Swedish-language daily, *Hufvudstadsbladet*, included a short article about the UDHR and the UN in its issue of 12 December 1948 under the title "Charter of Human Rights Adopted — only morally binding". The point was made that the UDHR covered more than the Magna Carta, the American Declaration of Independence and the French Declaration of the Rights of Man and that it guaranteed for all men and women equal dignity and up to 31 different rights irrespective of race, colour, sex or political opinion. The newspaper also

---

[13] Finland became member of the Council of Europe only in 1989 and ratified the ECHR in 1990 (*see* below).

[14] In his speech concluding the parliamentary session of 1948, Mr. Paasikivi, President of Finland, alluded to this by saying, when commenting the extraordinary elections in July 1948 and the subsequent new government, that in a free parliamentary democracy, which Finland had been from the beginning of independence through the Second World War, the issue of the government is bound to lead to difficulties if there exists, as was the case in Finland (and still is), several parties none of which has absolute majority in the Parliament. In the situation it was necessary to justify the existence of a minority government, acting until the Parliament decides to refuse the Government its trust. *See Riksdagen 1948, Protokoll i sammandrag* (Statsrådets tryckeri, Helsingfors, 1952) p. 301. There was probably a message not only to the Soviet Union in the speech, but also to the wider international community, at the same time as the domestic audience, riddled by the confrontation between the (revolutionary) Left and the non-leftist parties, was reminded of the constitutional rules of the parliamentary game.

informed the readers of the fact that some countries did not support the UDHR, such as the Soviet Union. The newspaper *Uusi Suomi*, a more conservative Finnish-language daily, also covered the UDHR on the same day and with the same contents. This daily also devoted on 14 December 1948 a section of its report on the UN General Assembly of 1948 to the UDHR and added that the UDHR was likely to have no practical or immediate effect, but that it presented instead the ideals and objectives which the majority of the peoples consider worthy to aim at. The text of the Declaration was published already in 1949 both in Finnish and in Swedish by the Finnish Federation of Peace–UN Association in its series of publications,[15] and the UDHR has since been used as a reference document by different NGOs.

In the professional journals, mainly the legal ones in articles written by academics,[16] the UDHR was dealt with on a number of occasions after 1948. An early comment is included in 1949 in an article by Tauno Suontausta dealing with the Peace Treaty and the general rights and legal protection of Finnish citizens. Suontausta made the point that each war has its own political ideology and that the political ideology of the Second World War was that of human rights, which originated in the Atlantic Charter of 1941. He concluded that the UDHR does not have any legal relevance, but that its value as a guideline should not be under-estimated.[17] In 1951, Jan-Magnus Jansson wrote a piece illustrating the contents of the UDHR and making the point that it does not have any real legal importance, while its real value would be at the pedagogical and ideological level, demonstrating the great shift in thinking about the obligations of the state for ensuring fair conditions of life for its citizens.[18] In 1952, Kurt Westerholm analysed the contents of the UN Charter and of the UDHR.[19] In 1950, Erik Castrén concluded that the human being must be respected and protected, if need be even against his or her own home-state, a principle that he understood to be established in the UDHR.[20] In 1953, he explained the origins and drafting of the UDHR and the

---

15 *Suomen lainopillinen kirjallisuus II* (1949–1958) (Suomalainen lakimiesyhdistys, Helsinki, 1959) pp. 361 *et seq.* The Finnish UN-Association is still today, 60 years later, an active organisation in the civil society and promotes the UDHR. *See* <www.ykliitto.fi/ihmisoikeusjulistus/etusivu>.

16 For other sources, *see also Suomen lainopillinen kirjallisuus II*, *supra* note 15, pp. 361 *et seq.*

17 SUONTAUSTA, *supra* note 7, pp. 621–623, 627.

18 J-M. JANSSON, 'En deklaration om de mänskliga rättigheterna', 44 *Nya Argus* (1951) pp. 255-258.

19 *See* WESTERHOLM, *supra* note 10, *passim.*

20 *See* E. CASTRÉN, 'Kansainvälinen oikeus', 48 *Lakimies* (1950) p. 681 and fn. 1 in particular.

contents of the document,[21] which he in 1956 characterised as a document with programmatic value.[22] Knowledge about human rights in general and about the UDHR in more specific terms was hence fairly widely distributed at least in the legal community, but also in a wider circle of individuals. Interestingly, at least Westerholm and Castrén indicated that human rights were no longer the internal matter of a sovereign state, but the concern of the international community. The former of the two authors even suggested that intervention on the basis a Security Council decision may be justified for the defence of human rights, provided that a threat to peace existed.[23]

3. INSIDE OF THE UN BUT OUTSIDE OF THE COUNCIL OF EUROPE

Finland became a member of the UN only in 1955. Although there was general consensus in the UN on the Finnish membership already by 1947, the decision was delayed because the Soviet Union only wanted to accept new members if at the same time a number of somewhat controversial member candidates were accepted.[24]

In this context, it is interesting to note that the Parliament of Finland gave its consent to Finnish UN membership already in June 1947. In the Government Bill to the Parliament proposing the consent,[25] the Government, *inter alia*, mentioned as one of the aims of the UN the promotion of the

---

21 *See* E. CASTRÉN, 'Yhdistyneiden Kansakuntien ihmisoikeuksien ohjelma', *Defensor Legis* (1953) pp. 215–224.

22 E. CASTRÉN, 'Viimeaikaisia virtauksia kansainvälisessä oikeudessa', 54 *Lakimies* (1956) p. 731. The same point was made by Castrén in his book *Suomen kansainvälinen oikeus*, *supra* note 7, p. 144. *See also* K. SIPPONEN, 'Yksilö kansainvälisten oikeuksien subjektina', 55 *Lakimies* (1957) pp. 670–672, for a presentation of the UDHR and problems of implementation of the non-binding document.

23 *See* WESTERHOLM, *supra* note 10, pp. 8, 12; CASTRÉN, *supra* note 21, p. 217.

24 *See* V. SAARIO, 'Suomi Yhdistyneissä Kansakunnissa', 55 *Lakimies* (1957) pp. 507–508. The controversy in 1947 in the Security Council over the membership of, *inter alia*, Bulgaria, Hungary and Romania caused the General Assembly to conclude that Austria, Finland, and Italy fulfilled the membership conditions, after which the controversy was submitted to the International Court of Justice, which ultimately gave an Advisory Opinion on the procedural points of the matter. *See Conditions of Admission of a State to Membership in the United Nations (Article 4 of the Charter)*, decision of 28 May 1948. A membership which at the time was regarded at least as important as membership in the UN was membership in the Nordic Council, which was effectuated in 1956.

25 Regeringens proposition till Riksdagen angående medgivande till Finlands upptagande som medlem i Förenta Nationerna, RP 51/1947.

respect of human rights and fundamental freedoms for all. There was no need to deal with the matter in the Parliament again in 1955, when the UN finally made the admission decision. After the membership, Finland also ratified the Genocide Convention, but no reference to human rights was made in the preparatory documents.[26] Twenty years later, in 1976, there was a Question to the Government by an MP concerning the prevention of human rights violations in Cambodia,[27] but a little bit more activity in the Parliament can be noted only towards the end of the 1980s, when there was a Question about the position of a Finnish ambassador towards violations of human rights[28] and a Question about the Finnish position concerning a conference on human rights in Moscow.[29] It is plausible that these questions were at least in part made against the background of human rights awareness derived from the UDHR.

The political position of Finland between the West and the East during the so-called Cold War placed it in a unique spot with a view of framing the co-operation that later on became the OSCE. In the Final Act of Helsinki on 1 August 1975, the participating States declared their common adherence to the principles which are set forth in the Final Act and which are in conformity with the Charter of the UN. In Section 1 (a) VII of the Declaration on principles guiding relations between participating States, the states pledge that "[i]n the field of human rights and fundamental freedoms, the participating States will act in conformity with the purposes of the Charter of the United Nations and with the Universal Declaration of Human Rights".[30] The reference to the UDHR in the Final Act may or may not have a root in Finnish proposals to the preparatory work preceding the Helsinki meeting, but against the background of what was said above about the early reception of the UDHR in Finland, the language of the Helsinki Final Act concerning the UDHR is certainly not out of line in respect of the attitude towards the

---

26 Regeringens proposition till Riksdagen om godkännande av vissa stadganden i konventionen om förebyggande och bestraffning av brottet folkmord, RP 49/1958.

27 Muntligt spörsmål 173/1976 rd (rdm. Kortesalmi) om förhindrande av att de mänskliga rättigheterna kränks i Kambodja (utr.min. Sorsas svar 1623).

28 Muntligt spörsmål 259/1986 rd (rdm. Turpeinen) om ambassadör Keijo Korhonens ställningstagande till kränkningar av de mänskliga rättigheterna (utr.min. Väyrynens svar 1742).

29 Muntligt spörsmål 194/1988rd (rdm. Laine) om Finlands ställningstagande till en konferens om de mänskliga rättigheterna i Moskva (utr.min. Sorsas svar 3522).

30 *See* A. BLOED (ed.), *The Conference on Security and Co-operation in Europe* (Kluwer Academic Publishers, Dordrecht, 1993) p. 147 (with reproduction of the text of the Helsinki Final Act).

UDHR. Therefore, it is not entirely wrong to point at the linkage between the UDHR and the Helsinki Final Act.[31]

In the Cold War context, Finland had, out of concerns related to the special relationship with the Soviet Union, not sought membership in the Council of Europe, but remained outside this major human rights structure. The political transformations in the East bloc at the end of the 1980s created a new situation in Europe and made it possible for Finland to apply for membership. In relation to the approval of Finnish membership, the Government of Finland submitted in 1989 a Bill to the Parliament concerning Finnish membership in the Council of Europe which alluded to the states which founded the Council of Europe and concluded that they greatly facilitated the approval of the UDHR in 1948. The Government also pointed out that the aim of the European Convention on Human Rights (hereinafter ECHR) was to implement the UDHR at a regional level.[32] This characterisation was repeated in 1990 in the Government Bill to the Parliament concerning the approval of certain provisions in the ECHR.[33] A link to the UDHR was hence maintained.

4. DRAFTING LEGISLATION WITH A HUMAN RIGHTS CONTENT AND RAISING POLITICAL ARGUMENTS IN PARLIAMENT

Between 1989 and 2008, the Parliament of Finland dealt with issues which have been described by reference to human rights on some 250 occasions, and a reference to the UDHR can also be found in a fairly great number of parliamentary documents. It is not possible to analyse all of these instances in detail, but some examples may be presented.

There was an interesting mention in support of the particular recognition of the rights of the child in the Government Bill for the amendment of the provisions on constitutional rights in the 1919 Form of Government

[31] The linkage was strengthened in the Helsinki Document of 1992, when the Human Dimension of the CSCE was strengthened by means of an enhanced role of the ODIHR and the creation of the High Commissioner on National Minorities. *See* BLOED, *supra* note 30, pp. 715-721, 743–757.

[32] Regeringens proposition till Riksdagen om Finlands anslutning till Europarådet, RP 17/1989, p. 5.

[33] Regeringens proposition till Riksdagen om godkännande av vissa bestämmelser i konventionen om skydd för de mänskliga rättigheterna och de grundläggande friheterna samt i tilläggsprotokollen till konventionen, RP 22/1990, p. 2.

(Constitution) Act in 1993. The point was made that Article 25 of the UDHR emphasised already in 1948 the right of the child to special care and assistance and the right of children, whether born in or out of wedlock, to the same social protection.[34] However, it seems that this was the only instance at which a reference to the UDHR was made in the process of reforming the constitutional rights in 1995, currently part of the Constitution of Finland that entered into force in the year 2000.

The Government Bill concerning the rights of the patient contains several references to the UDHR, such as the respect of thought and conscience in Article 18, protection from arbitrary interference with his privacy in Article 12, prohibition of inhuman or degrading treatment in Article 5 and the guarantee of personal liberty in Article 3.[35] In the area of social services, a Government Bill made the point that relevant declarations adopted by the UN, such as the UDHR, were binding upon Finland in a political and moral way. In addition, the Government concluded that the UDHR contained different freedoms and also a couple of economic, social and cultural rights, and continued that according to Article 1, all human beings were born free and equal in dignity and rights. Each individual had the right to life, liberty and personal security under Article 3, and in Article 19, it is established that each individual has the freedom of opinion and expression. Against this background, the Government concluded that the principles of the UDHR were important for the position and the rights of the client of social services.[36] In the context of proposing provisions to the criminal code on rape, the Government started its review of international recommendations by mentioning that the UDHR departed from the understanding of equality between human beings.[37]

The influx of asylum seekers from the disintegrating Yugoslavia in the beginning of the 1990s caused the Government to submit a Bill to the Parliament with a proposal of an extraordinary treatment of asylum applications in which the Government concluded on the basis of Article 14 of the UDHR that there was a right to asylum but that the UDHR was not a

---

[34] Hallituksen esitys Eduskunnalle perustuslakien perusoikeussäännösten muuttamisesta, HE 309/1993.

[35] Hallituksen esitys Eduskunnalle laiksi potilaan asemasta ja oikeuksista, HE 185/1991 vp.

[36] Hallituksen esitys Eduskunnalle laeiksi sosiaalihuollon asiakkaan asemasta ja oikeuksista sekä sosiaalihuoltolain muuttamisesta ja eräiksi niihin liittyviksi laeiksi, HE 137/1999 vp.

[37] Hallituksen esitys Eduskunnalle laiksi rikoslain väkisinmakaamista ja vapautta loukkaavaa haureutta koskevien säännösten muuttamisesta, HE 365/1992 vp.

legally binding document.[38] When proposing a new Act on Immigrants, the Government made reference to Article 14 of the UDHR when it concluded that everyone had the right to seek and enjoy in other countries asylum from persecution.[39] In the context, the Government noted that the Refugee Convention did not use the word asylum, but that the UDHR did. When the legislation concerning the Discrimination Ombudsman was drafted, the Government mentioned in its Bill that there was a non-discrimination provision in Article 2 of the UDHR.[40]

There is no direct mention of the concept of human rights in the Basic Education Act (628/1998), and the Government Bill leading to its adoption did not explicitly refer to the UDHR,[41] but Article 2 of the implementing Decree (1435/2001) that contains the national objectives of instruction issued by the Government specified the contents of the Act by making, *inter alia*, the respect of human rights a point of departure for instruction in schools. The same is the case with the Government Decree (955/2002) containing the national objectives of instruction in high schools. While municipalities, individual schools and their teachers have a relatively wide latitude and independence in determining the exact curriculum and what the children are taught, including the choice of textbooks, the basic features of the curriculum, established by the National Board of Education, contain many references to the concept of human rights, but without explicit mentioning of the UDHR.[42] In actual instruction in schools, the UDHR is, however, in practice relatively often used as the reference document concerning the contents of human rights.

In addition to regular law-making, the UDHR has also been referred to in the context of Finnish accession to international treaties. The above-mentioned non-discrimination principle of the UDHR was brought up when Finland ratified and incorporated the Statute of the International Criminal

---

38 Hallituksen esitys Eduskunnalle laiksi eräiden entisen Jugoslavian kansalaisten tekemien turvapaikkahakemusten poikkeuskäsittelystä, HE 294/1992 vp.

39 Hallituksen esitys eduskunnalle ulkomaalaislaiksi ja eräiksi siihen liittyviksi laeiksi, HE 265/2002 vp. A similar reference was included in Bill HE 15/2000.

40 Hallituksen esitys Eduskunnalle syrjintäasiain valtuutettua koskevaksi lainsäädännöksi, HE 39/2001 vp.

41 Hallituksen esitys Eduskunnalle koulutusta koskevaksi lainsäädännöksi, HE 86/1997 vp.

42 *See* Grunderna för läroplanen för den grundläggande utbildningen 2004, Helsingfors: Utbildningsstyrelsen, 2004, at <www.oph.fi/svenska/ops/grundskola/LPgrundl.pdf>, visited on 19 October 2008.

Court.[43] The Government Bill to Parliament concerning the approval of the Optional Protocol to the CEDAW contained a reference to non-discrimination in Article 2, in particular with regard to the prohibition of discrimination based on sex.[44] A reference to the UDHR and its principle of non-discrimination in Article 2 was also included in the Government Bill to the Parliament proposing the ratification and incorporation of Protocol No. 12 to the ECHR.[45] In proposing ratification and incorporation of the European Union Treaty in 2006, the Government mentioned in the Bill that one of the sources of the European Charter of Fundamental Rights was the UDHR at the same time as the Government referred to the universal human rights values.[46] There are also other international treaties the incorporation and ratification of which have involved references to the UDHR, such as the ILO Conventions and many of the external treaties of the EU that the Finnish Parliament has dealt with.

Human rights nowadays have a role in the foreign policy of Finland. For instance, in its 2004 Report to the Parliament on the human rights policy of Finland, the Government referred to universal human rights on many occasions, but specifically in relation to the right to work, the Government concluded that this right is established as a human right in the UDHR.[47] In a reply to a Question to the Government concerning the human rights situation in Myanmar in 1991, the Minister representing the Government explained the actions that the Government of Finland had taken during the years, amongst which there was the preparation of and the support for the GA Resolution concerning the situation in Myanmar of 29 November 1991. The Government told the Parliament that in the context, reference was made in the GA Resolution to the provision in the UDHR according to which the will of the people shall be the basis of authority of government and that the Government of Myanmar had been urged to fulfill the political rights of the

---

[43] Hallituksen esitys Eduskunnalle Kansainvälisen rikostuomioistuimen perussäännön hyväksymisestä sekä laeiksi sen lainsäädännön alaan kuuluvien määräysten voimaansaattamisesta ja rikoslain muuttamisesta, HE 161/2000 vp.

[44] Hallituksen esitys eduskunnalle Yhdistyneiden Kansakuntien kaikkinaisen naisten syrjinnän poistamista koskevan yleissopimuksen valinnaisen pöytäkirjan hyväksymisestä ja laiksi pöytäkirjan lainsäädännön alaan kuuluvien määräysten voimaansaattamisesta, HE 135/2000 vp.

[45] Hallituksen esitys Eduskunnalle ihmisoikeuksien ja perusvapauksien suojaamiseksi tehdyn yleissopimuksen kahdennentoista pöytäkirjan hyväksymisestä ja laiksi pöytäkirjan lainsäädännön alaan kuuluvien määräysten voimaansaattamisesta, HE 121/2004.

[46] Hallituksen esitys Eduskunnalle Euroopan perustuslaista tehdyn sopimuksen hyväksymisestä ja laiksi sen lainsäädännön alaan kuuluvien määräysten voimaansaattamisesta, HE 67/2006.

[47] Valtioneuvoston selonteko Suomen ihmisoikeuspolitiikasta, VNS 2/2004 vp.

people.[48] The human rights of women and girls in Afghanistan resulted in a Question in the Parliament, making the point that the then Taliban Government was not abiding by the UDHR.[49] The appalling human rights situation in Afghanistan caused the then opposition to file a written Question in 2006. The Question mentioned that the new Constitution of Afghanistan had been approved in January 2004 and that as one part of that Constitution, the fundamental rights of the UDHR have been implemented, *inter alia*, in the equal position of women and the freedom of religion. The problem was the conservative Islamic interpretation of law. More specifically, the reported death penalty of Mr. Abdul Rahman, who had converted from Islam to Christianity, was referred to as an appalling violation of human rights, contrary to Article 18 of the UDHR.[50]

The conclusion that can be drawn from the references in parliamentary documents is that the UDHR has been used as a reference on numerous occasions, but its legal effect was weak. In most cases, there is no reflection of the effect of the UDHR on the matter that is being dealt with, but when there is a reflection, the UDHR is clearly positioned among non-binding documents or perhaps mentioned as a document that creates political and moral obligations for Finland so as to give direction to legislative work.[51] The encouraging dimension from the point of view of the UDHR is that the Government and the Parliament of Finland are clearly aware of the UDHR and are willing to use the document and the rights it contains as a reference.[52]

It is evident on the basis of the review that the UDHR is in many cases used as an entry point for opening up a human rights discussion on the basis of binding human rights treaties. On other occasions, the UDHR is also used to justify some legislative choices. This is the case, for instance, in respect of the ratification and incorporation of treaties. In a number of cases, the UDHR has also provided some substantive backing to law-making, and finally, the

48 KK 378/1991 vp - Haavisto /Vihr ym.

49 KVN 17/1998 vp - Krohn, Irina /Vihr ym.

50 KK 221/2006 vp - Sari Essayah /kd ym.

51 It is interesting in this context to note that none of the charters of the currently nine political parties represented in the Parliament refer to the UDHR, and only one, the charter of the Centre Party, refers to the concept of human rights. However, in their political materials, most of the parties seem to refer to the concept of human rights.

52 For instance, the programme of the current Government contains references to human rights (mainly in the area of foreign policy and law-drafting), although it does not mention any specific human rights documents. *See Pääministeri Matti Vanhasen II hallituksen ohjelma* (Edita, Helsinki, 2007).

UDHR has, from time to time, had the role of a springboard for criticism. The role of the UDHR should not, however, be over-estimated.

5. RELEVANCE IN COURTS

The text of the UDHR was for the first time included in the collection of statutes entitled *Suomen Laki II* in 1960,[53] a book published by a private publisher listing most of the normative enactments in their annotated form, and it has since remained part and parcel of the normative information in the daily use of Finnish lawyers. Therefore, in principle, the UDHR could have had an impact as a source of argumentation, even as a source of customary law, because the text of the Declaration was found in the same collection of statutes as the regular Acts of Parliament and lower normative enactments. It should be emphasised, however, that the UDHR has not been officially promulgated in the Statutes of Finland or in its treaty section, because the UDHR is not a Finnish normative enactment or a treaty ratified by Finland. Hence from the point of view of the categories of reception of international law that can be identified,[54] the UDHR has never been incorporated. Against the background of what was said above in section 4 about the role of the UDHR in the political process, it should be emphasised that there is no single Act of Parliament in Finland that would make reference to the UDHR (although *travaux preparatoires* may do so), but there are many Acts of Parliament that make reference to the concept of human rights, *inter alia*, the immigration legislation, the criminal code, and the legislation that covers administrative detention or imprisonment. To the extent the UDHR has established itself in the domestic legal order of Finland, it has done so by way of transcription and especially by way of transformation. The fact that the UDHR is not formally speaking a norm in the Finnish legal order would require a judge in a court of law to take a quantum leap of some sort into the unchartered terrains of customary law if a provision included in the document were to be applied in an individual judgment.

Therefore, a search for the UDHR in the Finnish legal database yields just a few results. In two of the cases, the declaration has been invoked by one of

---

[53] The text of the UDHR was not found in the issues of 1956 or 1958. However, even in these issues, the keyword 'ihmisoikeudet', that is, human rights, was included in the subject index of *Suomen Laki*, with a reference to Article 1 of the UN Charter.

[54] *See* SCHEININ, *supra* note 6, pp. 19–20, in which the following methods are mentioned: adoption, reference, incorporation, transcription and transformation.

the parties without the courts in question, the Supreme Court and Supreme Administrative Court, taking a stand on the matter.[55] Instead of using the UDHR, the courts based their decisions on domestic legislation. In the other two cases, found at lower instances, the appeal judgments included the UDHR in the list of relevant legal provisions. Both of these appeal judgments are Finnish in style, that is, brief. Therefore, it is not really possible to say that they would dwell on the theoretical notions concerning the legal status of the UDHR.[56]

In both of these judgments, the courts based their decisions not only on the UDHR as such but also on fundamental rights provided by Constitutional Acts and provisions of international conventions, namely the ECHR and the two International Covenants. Hence the UDHR is included in a mix of provisions of international human rights and domestic constitutional rights. However, in the larger scheme of things, reliance on the UDHR in courts is extremely rare.

In spite of the inclusion of the UDHR in the collection of statutes used by lawyers and courts in practical work and a clear increase of direct application of international legal materials, especially human rights norms, in Finnish

---

55 In the Supreme Court case 1996:17, the defendant, who was a lawyer, had written a text on behalf of his client which contained materials that the prosecutor felt was defamatory. The defence lawyer was sued by the prosecutor, and in the trial, the respondent lawyer referred to Articles 11 and 30 of the UDHR, claiming that the domestic norms that the prosecutor was referring to could not be applied because of the provisions in the UDHR. In the Supreme Administrative Court case 2003:58, the applicant asylum-seeker grounded his appeal, *inter alia*, on the understanding that the family enjoys a certain protection as a fundamental human right and derived this understanding from the UDHR, the ICCPR, the ICESCR, and the ECHR.

56 In a case from the Court of Appeals of Vaasa (26.5.1993/1031), the matter dealt with an experiment with community service as a punishment, applied only in some parts of the country. The point raised before the court was that such an experiment is discriminatory, because in most parts of the country, the community service was not possible as a punishment. The Court of Appeals was of the opinion that the equality principle guaranteed by the UDHR and the ICCPR is not violated in such a manner that the experiment with the community service should be applied also in other courts. A case from the Administrative Court of Central Finland (26.3.1997/227) dealt with the application of social benefits for housing expenses in a situation where the applicant had been granted a payment schedule for loans deriving from the apartment by a civil court. The social authorities of local government had denied the application of housing benefits and the appeal referred, *inter alia*, to the UDHR, the ICESCR, and domestic legislation. The Administrative Court revoked the decision that was appealed and returned the matter to the social authorities of the local government for renewed determination. In the grounds for its decisions, the Administrative Court made the point that the basic income referred to by the applicant in relation with the UDHR and the ICESCR is an issue that the domestic Act on Social Care makes provisions of when presenting the opinion that the applicant had the right to the housing benefit. The Administrative Court referred to, *inter alia*, Article 25 of the UDHR. Hence in the latter case, the court invoked the argument of transformation as a means of reception.

courts, the legal culture can still generally be described as fairly "positivist or legalistic",[57] and incorporation of treaties is seen by Finnish judges more or less as a precondition for their applicability. It has not, however, on some occasions debarred courts from applying also customary international law.[58] References to customary international law remain, however, rare.

All this does not, as we have seen from the few court decisions, completely preclude the possibility of reference to the UDHR, which can sometimes be the most familiar or suitable human rights instrument to a person feeling that human rights have been violated. This was the case in a complaint brought before the Parliamentary Ombudsman in 2004 in which the complainant argued solely on the basis of the UDHR that the admission procedure for new students was not in conformity with human rights provisions.[59] Although the Ombudsman discussed the case on the basis of domestic legislation, the attempt should not go unnoticed.

6. CONCLUDING REMARKS

All the way from 1948 until 2008, it has been clear that the UDHR is not legally binding, but places a political and a moral obligation on Finland. In terms of discussions related to the UDHR, the first decade seems to have been very lively, while the 1960s and the 1970s can be characterised as a low period. More attention has again been paid to the UDHR after the end of the 1980s, but mainly in the area of political discussion and in the *travaux preparatoires* of legislation as an argument to initiate a human rights dimension to the legislation proposed by the Government. With regard to the usage of the UDHR in the courts, there is nothing much to be reported, probably because the courts would, in cases where international norms have been referred to, use the binding treaties of international law as ratified by Finland and incorporated as Act of Parliament or Governmental Decree in

---

57 M. SCHEININ, 'Incorporation and Implementation of Human Rights in Finland', in M. SCHEININ (ed.), *International Human Rights Norms in the Nordic and Baltic Countries* (Martinus Nijhoff Publishers, The Hague, 1996) pp. 258, 270. *See also* J. KLABBERS, 'Coming in from the Cold? Treaties in Finland's Legal Order', in T. KOIVUROVA (ed.), *Kansainvälistyvä oikeus: Juhlakirja professori Kari Hakapää* (Lapin yliopisto, Rovaniemi, 2005) p. 148.

58 *See* the Supreme Court case 1993:120. *See also* SCHEININ, *supra* note 57, pp. 270–271.

59 Ombudsman (as decided by vice-ombudsman Petri Jääskeläinen) EOAK 2839/4/03 of 31 December 2004 at <217.71.145.20/TRIPviewer/show.asp?tunniste=eoak+2839/2003&base=ereoapaa&f=WORD&kieli=su&ylapalkki=eoaratk/eoartripview&palvelin=www.eduskunta.fi&triptemp=eoa>, visited 14 June 2008.

the Finnish legal order. Hence the courts may feel they do not need the UDHR. Having said all this, it should be added that it is possible that the development looks more rational in retrospect than it has been in reality. It is, nonetheless, possible to defend the conclusion that in the Finnish society in general and also in the state institutions of Finland, there is awareness of the existence and of the contents of the UDHR.

14. HUNGARY: THE IMPACT ON THE FREEDOM OF EXPRESSION

Gábor Halmai
Eszter Polgári

1. INTRODUCTION

In the last 60 years of Hungary's legal history one cannot find too many references to the Universal Declaration of Human Rights (hereinafter UDHR). There were almost none made until the democratic transition in 1989, and relatively few since then. The very reason of the lack of references in the time of the adoption is that Hungary was not then member of the United Nations. Interestingly two days before the adoption of the Declaration the General Assembly discussed the possible admission of some of the so-called socialist countries, including Hungary's, and the main concern raised by the Western member states was the alleged violations of human rights in these countries.[1]

In the contemporary legal literature the UDHR was treated controversially. The leading Hungarian legal philosopher, the director of the Legal Institute of the Hungarian Academy of Sciences at the time, Imre Szabó argued that there were three reasons why at that time the six socialist member states abstained during the voting in the General Assembly. The first argument against the support of the UDHR was the lack of certain rights, and the total lack of the citizens' duties. Second, they criticised the declarative, non-binding character of the Declaration. Their third objection was based on the fact that the Western countries did not want to expressly concemn fascism.[2] Particularly Article 19 of the UDHR was the subject of criticism: this provision guarantees the freedom of opinion and expression without any

---

1 *See* I. SZABÓ, *Emberi jogok* [Human Rights.], (2nd ed., Akadémia Kiadó, Budapest, 1978) p. 80.

2 *See* I. SZABÓ, Egyetemes Nyilatkozat és emberi jogok mai problémái [The Universal Declaration and the Current Problems of Human Rights], 2 *Állam- és Jogtudomány* (1968) p. 196.

special limitations of fascist ideology.[3] This is one of the most important reasons for choosing Article 19 for more detailed analysis. The other one is, that the jurisprudence of the only institution, which after the transition regularly mentions the UDHR, the Constitutional Court, established in 1989 is very rich and also the subject of public debates concerning freedom of expression. As we will see, the jurisprudence of the Court on free speech is not only extensive, but also varied. The court has shown a predilection to apply beside the various measures developed both by the corresponding courts of large countries, like the US and Germany, also the patterns of international and regional human rights instruments, like the UDHR, as well as the European Convention on Human Rights.

2. THE UDHR IN THE HUNGARIAN LAW AND JURISPRUDENCE

Hungary joined the United Nations only in 1955, almost seven years after the adoption of the Universal Declaration of Human Rights. However, after World War II in the transitory period before the Communist Party took over power, and the 1949 Constitution established the Hungarian People's Republic, Act I of 1946 introduced the republican form of state, defining the powers of the head of the state and declaring the fundamental rights of the citizens, including the right to life with dignity. The Act X of 1946 on the "more efficient protection" of human rights considered it a crime, punishable by a five-year imprisonment, for any official authority to unlawfully violate someone else's natural and inalienable right. Also in the Paris Peace Treaty concluded on 10 February 1947,[4] reference was made to the protection of human rights and fundamental freedoms: Article 2 explicitly formulates an obligation to "secure all persons under the jurisdiction of Hungary, without distinction as to race, sex, language or religion, the enjoyment of human rights and of fundamental freedoms, including freedom of expression, of press and publication, of religious worship, of political opinion and of public meeting". Furthermore, Article 4 of the same treaty reinforces the prohibition of Fascist-like organisations already declared in the Armistice Agreement

---

3 *See* H. BOKORNÉ SZEGŐ, 'Az állampolgári jogok nemzetközi vonatkozásai: Az emberi jogok kérdése és a nemzetközi jog. [The International Law Perspectives of Citizens Rights: The Issue of Human Rights and the International Law], in J. HALÁSZ, I. KOVÁCS and I. SZABÓ (eds), *Az állampolgárok alapjogai és kötelességei* [The Fundamental Rights and Duties of the Citizens] (Akadémiai Kiadó, Budapest, 1965) p. 586.

4 Incorporated into the Hungarian law by Act No. XVIII of 1947.

signed in 1945.[5] By this provision Hungary undertook the obligation to prohibit and ban the existence and activities of "organisations of that nature which have as their aim the denial of the people of their democratic rights". The above rule was challenged before the Constitutional Court in 1992 the petitioner claimed that the prohibition is in violation of Article 3 of the Constitution declaring that parties may be founded freely and of Article 63(1) granting the freedom of association. The Court in 1993 upheld Article 15 of the Armistice Agreement, emphasising that the Constitution itself contains the most important limitation on founding parties freely — without making explicit reference to political views or ideas — when it makes the founding conditional on the respect of the Constitution and laws enacted in accordance with that. In the implementation of the challenged article this constitutional requirement must be observed, thus only parties aiming at the destruction of the Constitution are prohibited. Similarly, the freedom of association may be exercised in accordance with the law.[6]

Despite the early references to human rights, after the Communist Party took over the power and enacted the 1949 Stalinist Constitution, the Universal Declaration has failed to have a significant impact on the Hungarian legal system. This is not surprising, when considering the fact that the original text of the 1949 Constitution regulated the rights of the working class, and stated the leading role of 'the' party as vanguard of this working class. According to the paragraph on civil rights — which was literally taken from the 1936 Soviet Constitution — these must be practiced in accordance with the interests of the socialist society, and the exercise of the rights was inseparable from the fulfilment of civil obligations. This meant that civil rights, like freedom of assembly or association were mostly limited to politically neutral programmes, festival marches, or to the possibility of setting up associations (for instance, sport or stamp collecting), but excluding the freedom to conduct anti-government demonstrations, to establish parties, to create independent trade unions, which was only developed in the late 1980s.[7]

Although from the second half of the 1970s onwards other human rights documents — such as the two most important follow up instruments of the UDHR, namely the International Convention on the Elimination of All Forms of Racial Discrimination (1965), incorporated into the Hungarian legal

---

5 Incorporated by Act No. V of 1945.

6 Constitutional Court Decision 810/B/1992 (02/11/1993).

7 *See* G. HALMAI, 'Regeneration of Civil Society in Hungary: The Recodification of the Right of Assembly and Association', *Law and Policy*, April (1991) pp. 135–147.

system in 1969 or the International Covenant on Civil and Political Rights (1966), incorporated by Hungary in 1976 — are occasionally referred to, we cannot find a genuine reference to the UDHR in any piece of legislation; it is only mentioned when the incorporated treaty or agreement mentions it in its Preamble. It has not become a reference point for human rights issues; it retained its declaratory character.

It is not surprising that ordinary courts do not have recourse to the human rights catalogue of the UDHR. Empirical studies show that judges have considerable difficulty in applying the European Convention on Human Rights (hereinafter ECHR), which by its incorporation became part of the Hungarian law and thus it is — at least in principle — directly enforceable.[8] Against this background the lack of reference to the UDHR by ordinary courts is not a surprising finding. There is no single judgment available that mentions the UDHR in any context, not even when the relevant international human rights documents are summarized.

In comparison to ordinary courts the Constitutional Court seems to be more receptive to international law, various decisions that concern basic rights include a broad overview of the relevant international human rights documents. Although there is a significant overlap between the basic rights catalogue of the Hungarian Constitution and the UDHR, the latter is not widely referred to in the jurisprudence of the Constitutional Court either. Until today seven decisions quoted the provisions of the UDHR, four of which are in support of the limitation or narrow interpretation of constitutional rights. The following examples show the different approaches and references to the UDHR among other international human rights documents.

In the first abortion decision[9] of 1991 the Court struck down the then valid regulations by the Minister of Health and the Government on formal grounds — according to Article 8(2) of the Constitution fundamental rights shall be regulated exclusively by an Act of Parliament. Since some petitioners challenged the regulations on the basis of being in violation of Article 54(1) of the Constitution guaranteeing the right to life and human dignity, the Constitutional Court addressed the question whether the foetus is a legal subject. The reasoning provides a thorough overview of the relevant

8 *See* a recent study by G. HALMAI, K. ENYEDI, A. NÉMETH, E. POLGÁRI, P. SÓLYOM and B.D. TÓTH, *Alkotmányos és nemzetközi emberi jogi követelmények a rendes bíróságok gyakorlatában* [Constitutional and International Human Rights Requirements in the Jurisprudence of the Hungarian Ordinary Courts] (Legal Institute of the Hungarian Academy of Sciences, Budapest, 2008).

9 Constitutional Court Decision 64/1991 (XII. 17.).

international human rights norms, including Article 6 of the Universal Declaration which guarantees everyone's right to recognition everywhere as a person before the law. By the recognition of every person's legal capacity, a human being — in the view of the Court — "has become a normative concept". There are two substantive fundamental rights that supplement a human being's legal status, that give content to the formal requirements of the right to legal capacity — as enshrined in the UDHR — and express a person's human quality: the right to life and human dignity. The Court was mindful of the changes that had occurred in the second half of the 20th century, but it took a very deferential role by concluding that the answer for the question presented cannot be derived from the Constitution, therefore only the Parliament is entitled to take a position of the legal status of the foetus.

The UDHR was used as a supporting argument in favour of the restrictive interpretation of a constitutional provision on marriage in the similarly controversial case concerning the legal equality of same-sex partnerships in 1995.[10] On the basis of the equal protection clause, the Constitutional Court called on the Parliament to eliminate the distinction between heterosexual and homosexual couples living together in domestic partnerships, but it did not accept the petitioner's arguments that the definition of marriage in the Act on Marriage, Family and Guardianship is unconstitutional as it encompasses only the union of a man and a woman. From the wording of the most important international human rights documents the Court derived that the family is conceived as the relationship of a man and a woman: also the International Covenant on Civil and Political Rights, the ECHR, Article 16 of the UDHR contain similar formulation. In addition to the Hungarian cultural and legal tradition, the recalled international norms supported the traditional understanding of marriage. Although the Constitutional Court offered various options for the legislature to acknowledge and integrate same-sex partners into the society and did not explicitly rule out gay marriage, it failed to recognize discrimination in this regard. In 2007, the Court reiterated the same reasoning, but on the basis of the very same line of arguments arrived at an even more restrictive interpretation: a referendum for same-sex marriage would call for the amendment of the Constitution.[11]

In the decision on local government apartments in 1993 the Constitutional Court reinterpreted the right to property and extended the protection beyond the civil law notion of ownership to rights and

---

10 Constitutional Court Decision 14/1995 (III. 13.).

11 Constitutional Court Decision 65/2007 (X. 18.).

entitlements of economic value.[12] The Court afforded constitutional protection for property in its capacity as the traditional means of securing the economic basis for the autonomy of individual action. Therefore, the protection might extend to public law entitlements — such as social insurance — when individual autonomy is at stake. However, it made this extended protection relative by recognizing the restriction of property for the sake of public interest, in certain cases even without compensation. The Court emphasised that this broad notion of property corresponds to Article 17 of the UDHR, and to the case law of the European Court of Human Rights on Article 1 of Protocol No. 1. Unlike in the above described decision, the reference in the present case to the UDHR served more as a supporting argument for the activist interpretation of the Constitution.[13]

In 2000, the Constitutional Court examined the alleged inequality of men and women under the acts regulating military duties, pensions, restitution life annuity and rent allowances.[14] The Court reviewed the evolution of international norms guaranteeing the equality of sexes: among other human rights treaties, Article 2 and Article 7 of the Universal Declaration are mentioned. The decision also summarized the relevant case-law of the European Court of Human Rights and the European Court of Justice in the field of positive discrimination, and recalled the practice of the Constitutional Court on this issue, and concluded as follows: the prohibition of discrimination does not exclude all sorts of distinctions, it requires that everyone shall be treated equally before the law and with equal dignity. A social aim or constitutional right may be implemented by affirmative action, but the positive discrimination of a group cannot outweigh the individual basic rights. The case was mainly decided on the basis of the earlier case law of the Constitutional Court, so the historical overview of the evolution of the equality of women did not play a conclusive role in the decision.

Reference was made to the UDHR in the decision on hate speech as well which is analysed below.[15]

---

12 Constitutional Court Decision 64/1993 (XII. 22.).

13 The reasoning was repeated in the Constitutional Court Decision 33/2002 (VII. 4.).

14 Constitutional Court Decision 28/2000 (IX. 8.).

15 Constitutional Court Decision 18/2004 (V. 25.).

3. THE FREEDOM OF EXPRESSION IN THE JURISPRUDENCE OF THE CONSTITUTIONAL COURT WITH REFLECTIONS ON THE CONTENTS OF ARTICLE 19

In the following we try to highlight the jurisprudence of the court in two key issues of freedom of expression, namely constitutional limitations of hate speech, and criticism of public officials.

3.1. CONSTITUTIONAL LIMITATIONS ON EXPRESSIONS OF HATRED

The most striking fact in this area of the freedom of expression is the divide in the standards applied in American jurisprudence, which rejects all limitations, and those of a (Western) Europe inclined toward more resolute limitation based on the "concept of militant democracy".[16] The Hungarian Constitutional Court first encountered the problem in examining the constitutionality of the provision in the nation's Criminal Code concerning public incitement. Article 269 of the Criminal Code had regulated the facts defining two readily distinguishable forms of incitement whose only common element was their being committed in public. While the facts of the more serious (criminal) offence under paragraph 1 included incitement of hatred against "the Hungarian nation, any other nationality, people, religion, race or certain groups among the general population", paragraph 2 provided for the prosecution of those who use an offensive or disparaging expression against "the Hungarian nation, any other nationality, people, religion, or race", or of those who commit similar acts. As is apparent, the facts of the two paragraphs differ not only in respect of the protected legal subjects (that is, individual groups within the general population do not figure in paragraph 2) but also in the behaviour inherent to the act committed. Indeed, while incitement to hatred has the potential to disturb the public peace, in that it embodies the danger of violence or the making of threats of violence, this cannot be said of the reasons stated in the Criminal Code for the milder form of incitement to hatred, that of defamation.

---

[16] The term, first used by Karl Loewenstein ('Militant Democracy and Fundamental Rights', 31 *American Political Science Review* (1937) p. 417) alludes to the self-defence of political life and especially the means to protect the state governed by rule of law against their enemies. The most important decision of the European Court of Human Rights using this concept is the Refah Partisi (*The Welfare Party and Others* v *Turkey*, 13 February 2003, Application numbers 41340/98, 41342/98, 41343/98, 41344/98).

In Decision 30/1992, the Constitutional Court found the facts of the crime of incitement of hatred as spelled out in Article 269(1) of the Criminal Code to be constitutional and annulled the form of defamation laid down in paragraph 2 of the same article. Its reasoning was based on the notion that the freedom of expression has a distinguished role among other fundamental rights guaranteed by the Constitution; that in fact it was a sort of a "mother right" of the so-called rights to "communication".[17] According to the Court justices, the right to free expression of opinion protected opinion without regard to its content in terms of value and truth, for this condition alone lived up to the ideological neutrality of the Constitution.[18] In confirming the constitutionality of the facts of the crime of incitement, the justices apparently reasoned on grounds similar to U.S. Supreme Court Chief Justice Oliver Wendell Holmes's famous test of 'clear and present danger'. At the same time, it must be said that the 'danger' attached by the Hungarian Constitutional Court justices as a condition of constitutionality is more distant and contingent than the sort their erstwhile American peers had in mind. Presumably this was why the Constitutional Court elaborated on its decision by explaining that the "unavoidable social tensions of system-change" (that is, the post-1989 political-economic transition) notably increased the danger of incitement, before large public audiences, to hatred against certain groups.

In contrast to U.S. jurisprudence, the Hungarian Constitutional Court did not address the problem of the 'scope' of the facts, that is, whether the incitement provision can be applied even in the absence of a real possibility that hatred would develop. In other words, the Hungarian justices did not set a constitutional standard that requires incitement to hatred to actually *cause* 'clear and present danger'. This approach, along with the citing of the historical circumstances of the change of system, recalls not so much the American concept of justice in this respect, but that of Germany's Federal Constitutional Court, which likewise cited historical reasons in reacting to militant threats to democracy by limiting the freedom of expression — namely, Germany's interest in avoiding a repeat of the scenario that followed the collapse of the Weimar Republic.

---

[17] One of the Constitutional Court justices who presided in this case, Court President László Sólyom, explained this special role accorded freedom of expression among fundamental rights by observing that this right forms the basis of the individual's relationships to society. *See* L. SÓLYOM, 'Az emberi jogok az Alkotmánybíróság újabb gyakorlatában' [Human Rights as Reflected in the Recent Jurisprudence of the Constitutional Court], 1 *Világosság* (1993) p. 23.

[18] The justices expanded this interpretation in a later decision, that on freedom of religion, declaring that the laws restricting this right must be interpreted with rigor similar to those that limit freedom of expression. *See also* Constitutional Court Decision 4/1993 (II. 12.).

The main reason for declaring defamation unconstitutional was, however, that in this case the Hungarian Parliament had in fact made its qualification on the basis of the value content of the opinion expressed, in other words, with the violation of public peace attached to this only on the basis of presumption and statistical probability. Moreover, the Constitutional Court pointed out, not even the public peace is independent of the degree of the freedom of expression that prevails in society. Indeed, in countries where people can encounter numerous different opinions, public opinion becomes more tolerant, whereas in closed societies particular instances in which people express opinions out of the norm have far more potential to disturb the public peace. Further, the needless and disproportionate limitation of the freedom of expression has a detrimental effect on an open society. Indeed, in such a society those who use abusive language only mark themselves as 'slanderers' in the arena of public opinion. Criticism was the appropriate response to slander, not criminal prosecution, argued the Constitutional Court justices. At the same time they added that the need to protect the 'dignity of communities' may constitute a valid constitutional limitation on the freedom of expression. Thus the Court decision did not rule out the possibility that Hungary's lawmakers might establish such protection under criminal law even beyond the scope of incitement to hatred. In the assessment of the justices, however, the expansion of other legal instruments, for example non-pecuniary compensation, was also suitable for the effective protection of the 'dignity of communities'. In other words, in deciding on the constitutionality of this particular element of fact in the statutory provision on incitement, the justices looked to an American standard still being applied in the present day.

At the same time, the uncertainty caused by the application of varying standards is reflected in László Sólyom's later remark, in which he rejected the idea of adopting certain consequences of U.S. Supreme Court jurisprudence. "[I]f here in Hungary we follow the simple logic that would see us adopt the decision on flag-burning brought in *New York Times* v. *Sullivan*, why then, in the name of unlimited freedom of expression must we consequently also adopt the test applied in the *Skokie* case and allow neo-Nazis to hold a threatening procession in a Jewish district?"[19] However, if the justices had consistently upheld the principle of guaranteeing special protection to the freedom of expression without regard to truth or value

[19] *See* Attila Gábor Tóth's interview with László Sólyom, 'A "nehéz eseteknél" a bíró erkölcsi felfogása jut szerephez' [A Judge's Individual Moral Perspective Comes into Play in 'Difficult' Cases], 1 *Fundamentum* (1997) p. 42.

content in determining the crime of defamation to be unconstitutional, then this principle should have been applied with respect to the constitutionality of the crime of incitement as well.

In 1996, the Penal Division of Budapest City Court acquitted an infamous neo-fascist party leader and his associates on charges of public incitement and of another crime that had meanwhile been added to the Criminal Code, the public display of symbols of autocratic rule. The reasoning of the decision was more or less in line with that of the Constitutional Court's 1992 decision: "[P]ublic incitement is realized only when someone incites passions to a degree capable of summoning hatred and of leading to the disturbance of the public peace". Until which time such danger prevails, "the free expression of opinion also embraces thoughts and views that are offensive, shocking, or that cause distress". The Parliament amended the legal provision against public incitement, supplementing the crime of incitement to hatred with that of "another action capable of inciting hatred". Indeed, this revising of the provisions on public incitement called into question whether it met the criteria set down in the Constitutional Court's 1992 decision.

The answer was that the Constitutional Court in its Decision 12/1999 annulled the new text that had been introduced in the law, with the reasoning that the criminalisation of 'other acts' suitable to incite hatred was unconstitutional because it is indeterminate and lowers the threshold of limitation.

In December 2003, the Government again initiated the modification of the hate-speech provision of the Criminal Code for three reasons. First, the modification of the hate speech provision was partly a reaction to the acquittal of priest Loránt Hegedűs, the Vice President of the Hungarian Truth and Justice Party (MIÉP) and Member of Parliament, who published an article in ÉBRESZTŐ, in the journal of the party's 16th District organisation, under the title "Christian Hungarian State". Appearing on the front page of the journal, which was delivered to letterboxes throughout the district, the article included statements such as, "SHUT THEM OUT! IF YOU DON'T DO IT TO THEM, THEY'LL DO IT TO YOU! This we know from a thousand years of torture, from the remaining legacy 'on high' of our country that has been stolen and looted thousands of times, and not in the least by the stone-throwing sons of Ramallah". Second, according to the Government's reasoning, the application of Article 269 of the Criminal Court by the ordinary courts[20] was so divergent that it raised legal certainty

[20] I mean 'ordinary courts' as opposed to the Constitutional Court. Some experts contend that ordinary courts do not take into consideration the Constitutional Court's 1992 ruling (Decision

concerns.[21] Third, the Government also referred to the constitutional duty of Hungary to harmonise its domestic laws with its international obligations.[22] It was the Government's view that Parliament had not yet fulfilled its obligation in the area of hate speech.

On 8 December 2003, the Hungarian Parliament voted with a slight majority (184 to 180) for the modification of the Criminal Code. According to the Bill, hate speech criminalisation would have become stricter. Any incitement of hatred against any nation, national, ethnic, racial or religious minority, or calling for violent acts before the general public would have been a felony offence punishable by imprisonment of up to three years. Violating other people's human dignity by disparaging or humiliating them because of their national, ethnic, racial or religious origin would have been a misdemeanour punishable by imprisonment of up to two years.

The adopted bill prescribed publicity for the incitement of hatred. The word 'nation' was a new element. Before the amendment, one could commit this crime against the Hungarian nation, while, according to the new bill, the crime could have been committed with regard to any nation. The legislator argued that in order to avoid the trap of being restrictive on content-based consideration, it is not the speech itself but the degree of fierceness created by it that should be the decisive factor in punishment.

Because the President of the Republic considered the already adopted but not yet signed Act on amending the hate speech provisions of the Criminal Code to be unconstitutional, he submitted it to the Constitution Court for *ex ante* constitutional review on 22 December 2003.

The Constitutional Court in its Decision 18/2004 ruled that the adopted but not yet enacted amendment to the Criminal Code was unconstitutional. The Constitutional Court among other international human rights agreements explicitly referring to Article 19 of the UDHR applied its 1992 precedent in deciding the constitutionality of the amendment. The Court emphasised again that it would not accept content-based restriction of communication. According to the Constitutional Court, communication can only be punished if it directly and foreseeably threatens individual (constitutional) rights. Since the amendment would have punished certain communications the effects of which on their audiences would fall below this

30/1992. (V.26.)) in the course of interpretation and application of Section 269 of the Criminal Code.

21 *See* the reasoning of Bill No. T/5179 (a T/5179. számú törvényjavaslat indokolása).

22 The reasoning of the Bill explicitly referred to Article 4 of the International Convention on the Elimination of All Forms of Racial Discrimination and the ECRI.

threshold, the amendment would restrict free speech unnecessarily, disproportionately and, thus, unconstitutionally.

The most recent developments concerning the limitation of hate speech are represented by two new attempts of the Parliament, which were decided by the Constitutional Court. Following the swearing in ceremony of the anti-Semitic Hungarian Guard, a uniformed paramilitary brigade set up by the extreme right-wing party Jobbik in the end of August 2008, the Parliament in October approved an amendment to the Civil Code. Persons who felt they were the target of discriminatory remarks could have taken legal measures to defend themselves on the basis of this law. The modification would have meant that not only people who are explicitly named, but also any member of a minority or a group representing one, as well as civil rights NGOs could have taken legal action against anyone who denigrates their minority identity in a public speech. The President of Hungary László Sólyom, the former head of the Constitutional Court challenged the adopted law before the Constitutional Court. The Court in its Decision 96/2008 declared the law unconstitutional, because of the disproportional limitation on free speech.[23] In the reasoning of the decision the judges argued that the rejection of the law does not mean that the Court refuses the necessity of protection of the members different communities, so the Parliament should find another, constitutionally acceptable solution to this problem.

The other law, also sent to the Court by the President was another amendment of the Criminal Code initiated by six MPs of the Socialist Party and adopted by the Parliament in March 2008. The new provision put in another chapter of the Code, as the previous annulled ones, criminalises disparaging expressions or even body movements towards the Hungarian nation, any other ethnic, national racial, religious groups, which can violate the honour and dignity of the persons. The President's argument against the law in this case was also that it unconstitutionally limits freedom of expression. The Court in Decision 95/2008 declared this law as being unconstitutional as well.[24] The argument of the majority of the judges was similar to the previous ones that the activity the law seeks to punish does not need to fulfil the requirement of 'clear and present danger'. A new element in this decision is however that three of the judges expressed their concerns about the new circumstances of social hatred, which should have been taken into account by the Court, when deciding the constitutionality of the

[23] Constitutional Court Decison 96/2008. (VII. 3.)

[24] Constitutional Court Decison 95/2008. (VII. 3.)

challenged law.[25] One of the justices also referred to the international obligations of the Republic of Hungary to use legal tools, including criminal sanctions to eliminate all forms of racism and xenophobia, with special regard to the principles of the UDHR.[26]

On 19 April 2007, the Council of the European Union — pending the lifting of some parliamentary reservations — reached a general approach on its Framework Decision about racism and xenophobia; it is possible that a conflict with the constitutional interpretation of freedom of expression and freedom of assembly will arise. The Council emphasised that the Framework Decision will not have the effect of modifying the obligation to respect fundamental rights and fundamental legal principles after adoption, including freedom of expression and association, as enshrined in Article 6 of the Treaty of the EU. The Council also stated that member states will not have to modify their constitutional rules and fundamental principles relating to freedom of association, freedom of the press and the freedom of expression. Member States will have two years to comply with the Framework Decision. For the moment, it is not possible to predict for certain what the position of the Hungarian constitutional judges will be on the constitutionality of Hungarian legislation drafted in the wake of the EU Framework Decision on combating racism and xenophobia.[27]

The question of the Constitutional Court's jurisdiction in matters of Community law, in the absence of regulation in either the Constitution or in the Constitutional Court Act, which requires the two-third majority of the votes of the MPs present, shall be essentially settled by that body's own interpretation of its jurisdiction. Such new powers can arise even when the Constitutional Court, by an interpretation of the Act setting it up, extends its jurisdiction to retrospective constitutional review of international treaties (Decision 4/1997). Some opinions view the Constitutional Court Decision 30/1998 as presaging a similar danger of jurisdiction-determination related to the review of Community law. Here, the Constitutional Court reviewed the constitutionality of Article 62 of the European Agreement signed with the EU (then still the EC) and ratified by Act I of 1994. Although it did not find

[25] *See* the dissenting opinion of Judge László Kiss, as well as the concurring opinions of Judges Miklós Lévay and Péter Kovács.

[26] *See* the concurring opinion of Judge Kovács.

[27] Article 34(2) of the Treaty of Union states, "the Council may adopt framework decisions for the purpose of approximation of the laws and regulations of the Member States. Framework Decisions shall be binding upon the Member States as to the result to be achieved but shall leave to the national authorities the choice of form and methods. They shall not entail direct effect".

unconstitutionality, it drew up constitutional requirements regarding its application.

This single decision does not, in our opinion, provide sufficient grounds to presume that the Constitutional Court will arrogate the right to review or even set aside community law. The judges clearly emphasised in the decision that the opportunity for review derived from Hungary not being an EU member at that time, and so the principle of primacy of community law could not yet be applied to the Hungarian legal system. It is beyond doubt, however, that in particular the Italian and the German constitutional courts — the latter serving as the model of the Hungarian body in many respects — have in several decisions called into question the primacy of community law over the catalogue of basic rights set into the national constitution and the level of basic right protection it represents.[28]

In consideration of the Constitutional Court's position, the government's stance was that a special amendment to the Constitution is needed in order to avoid the review of community law's conformity with the Hungarian Constitution by the Hungarian Constitutional Court. The amendment was not adopted and the above outlined possibility continues to exist in principle. Certainly, the 1998 position of the Hungarian Court is not decisive. After all, with similar rhetoric of national supremacy of constitutional law other constitutional courts have managed to find ways to avoid confrontation with EU law. (The conflicts are mostly emerging in the context of new EU powers, though undeniably these may result from the interpretation of the ECJ.)

For the moment, it is not possible to predict for certain what the position of the Hungarian constitutional judges will be on the constitutionality of Hungarian legislation drafted in the wake of the EU Framework Decision on hate speech, if passed, but the question as to whether they will express their opinion at all, and if so in what form, also depends on the practice they formulate in the matter of reviewing the constitutionality of Community law.

---

[28] In their famous *Fragd* judgment of 21 April 1989, the Italian constitutional judge reserved the right to review certain rules of community law and their consistency with articles of the Italian constitution related to human rights. The German Federal Constitutional Court's *Solange I* judgment (BVerfGE 37, 271) stipulates that the German Constitutional Court will not renounce the power to judge the consistency of Community provisions with German constitutional basic rights, until European law offers suitable basic rights guarantees. This formula was reversed by *Solange II* (BVerfGE 73, 339), saying that as long as the ECJ provides effective protection of basic rights, intervention by the Federal Constitutional Court is not necessary. These decisions still retain the possibility of intervention in principle.

3.2. CRITICISING THOSE IN HIGH PUBLIC OFFICE — THE DISPUTABLE NATURE OF PUBLIC AFFAIRS

One of the key conditions of the new, open society occasioned by Hungary's change of system was the dismantling of the earlier inviolability of state authority and public officials and representatives — that is to say, the ban on criticising them. The Parliament resolved this dilemma by acting in spring 1993 — when beefing up the content of a provision addressing offences against authority and persons holding state offices — to extend the scope of those state officials specifically protected under this statutory provision to include the President of the Republic and the Prime Minister. At the same time, virtually the entire range of state officialdom fell within the scope of 'inviolable' persons: political state secretaries, constitutional court justices, ombudsmen, notaries public (who in Hungary are, technically, state employees), and, indeed, the staff of the Constitutional Court, the State Audit Office, the Office of the President, and Parliament.

With Decision 36/1994 the Constitutional Court annulled, with immediate effect, the provision of the Criminal Code referring to "the defamation of state authority or a person in public office". This was the statutory provision based on which courts had condemned politicians and social scientists who had criticised heads of government ministries. Although this 1994 decision of the Court made it clear that the protection under criminal law of state authority or of the honour or reputation of persons holding public office was theoretically not contrary to the Constitution, it gave more constitutional leeway to express opinions about persons in positions of public authority, including politicians — this, notwithstanding that the Criminal Code had imposed stricter guarantees to protect those in public office from disparagement. With the annulment of this provision, the protection of those in public office now fell under the provision of the Criminal Code protecting all citizens from defamation and libel. Yet the Constitutional Court had articulated not one, but several directives for the use of courts applying the law. According to one of these, the scope of expression protected, or unpunishable, under the freedom of expression, must be broader in the case of public officials than in respect to other individuals. The Constitutional Court's other theoretical holding completely prohibits prosecution for expressions of opinion that convey a judgment of value, however much such criticism may violate the honour of a public official. Statements of fact that are capable of degrading another's honour are considered constitutional only if the individual who made the accusation knew that the essential content of what he said was untrue or instead did not know whether it was true or not because, for example, as a journalist he neglected to devote a degree of attention that, based on his profession, he would have been expected to devote to it.

This Constitutional Court decision effectively gave free reign not only to journalists and in particular commentators who tended towards bold expressions of opinion, but to investigative journalism, even in cases where facts unearthed in public affairs reporting carried the potential to violate the honour of public officials. It did so knowing that if the sword of Damocles in the form of criminal law were ever waving about above the head of every investigative journalist in Hungary, this would render a true debate on public affairs impossible. On the other hand, the decision of the Court does not allow for the making of public assertions that are knowingly false and reflect a serious disregard of the basic rules of the journalistic profession. Even in nineteenth century Hungary, however, the great statesman Ferenc Deák had articulated this maxim when he observed that the single necessary provision of his own era's law on the media was the one that prohibited lying.

The number of criminal cases initiated by those in high public office fell dramatically in the wake of this Constitutional Court decision. This is explained by the fact that if a leading state official can no longer count on his superior to initiate proceedings aimed at protecting his honour, but that he must personally do so, he will obviously think twice before assuming the risk of failure. While the number of petitions submitted by individuals after 1994 fell notably, those that did come in were mostly from public figures to whom the abrogated provision of law did not pertain (that is, not public officials), but who on account of their work in the public arena, be that political or otherwise, are nonetheless participants in public life. But changing jurisprudence also contributed to the steady decline in the number of such cases brought on the basis of private prosecutions. In recent years the bulk of criminal cases centred on defamation, libel, and profanation have seen acquittals citing the freedom of expression.[29]

As for the patterns that served as the basis for this decision, one is by all means the famous 1964 U.S. Supreme Court decision in the case of *New York Times* v *Sullivan*.[30] The other pattern followed by Hungary's Constitutional

---

29 *See* G. HALMAI, 'A sajtónyilvánosság határainak módosulásai' [Modifications in the Limits of Media Openness], in M. VÁSÁRHELYI and G. HALMAI (eds), *A nyilvánosság rendszerváltása* [The Change of System *vis-à-vis* Societal Openness] (Új Mandátum, Budapest, 1998) pp. 95–112.

30 *New York Times* v *Sullivan*, 376 U.S. 254 (1964). The following words from this decision were to reverberate in several other decisions: "[W]e consider this case against the background of a profound national commitment to the principle that debate on public issues should be uninhibited, robust, and wide-open, and that it may well include vehement, caustic, and sometimes unpleasantly sharp attacks on government and public officials". *See also Watts* v *United States*, 394 U.S. 705 (1971). *See* these cases in detail on pp. 144–149 of G. HALMAI, *A véleményszabadság határai* [The Limits of Freedom of Expression] (Atlantisz, Budapest, 1994).

Court justices was the consistent jurisprudence of the European Court of Human Rights, whose most important decisions are indeed cited in the reasoning of the Hungarian decision, as the most well known among these *Lingens* v *Austria* (1986).

The Hungarian Constitutional Court's 1994 decision thus follows not only the jurisprudence of the U.S. Supreme Court but especially also that of Strasbourg in setting a lower threshold of allowable criticism in the case of politicians than private individuals, arguing that the reputation of such public figures must be balanced with society's interest in ensuring the free and open debate of public affairs. Indeed, the Hungarian justices determined, even greater tolerance is necessary when it comes to criticism of the government as a whole or of public authorities. Although this standard of criticism of public officials and the disputable nature of public affairs was not explicitly expressed in the UDHR, but the 'right of criticism' could be connected to the term of 'genuine elections' in Article 21 of the UDHR at least as concerns elected members of public authorities. The requirement of genuine elections definitely presumes the existence of certain political freedoms, most importantly freedom of expression of political opinions under Article 19.

4. CONCLUDING REMARKS

In sum, it may be concluded that freedom of expression as enshrined in Article 19 of the UDHR and as well as in the Hungarian constitution is a right, generally taking precedence over other rights in the event where such fundamental rights come into conflict with one another. The Hungarian Constitutional Court developed this approach by following the patterns elaborated especially by the U.S. Supreme Court, and international courts (most notably, the European Court of Human Rights), and enshrined in both national and international human rights documents, including the UDHR. The main critique of this jurisprudence is that it does not take into account the social changes in the last years in Hungary, where racist and homophobic hatred has never been present to such an extent in the public life after the transition as today. Because of the interpretation and partly misinterpretation of the praxis of the Constitutional Court the ordinary judiciary does not provide neither criminal nor civil law protection against hate speech to people belonging to Roma, Jewish, gay or other minorities. Therefore the Parliament has to find a constitutional solution to limit hate speech. One possible solution can be the implementation of the mentioned EU Framework Decision, if enacted. In this option the Constitutional Court would be able to keep its standing interpretation of the preference of freedom of expression in the Hungarian constitutional system, and at the same time take into account the international obligations of the country to protect the dignity of the members of communities.

So, paradoxically enough in the country, which officially criticised the UDHR for not providing enough protection against racial, especially fascist hate speech, now almost twenty years after the democratic transition mostly because of an almost absolutist concept of freedom of expression by its Constitutional Court, seems to be unable to provide protection against neo-fascist hate speech. This situation, in which the rights and sometimes even the existence of national, ethnic, religious, linguistic and other minorities is threatened by illegal discrimination, prejudice and incitement to hatred, was already acknowledged by the parliamentary resolution issued on the occasion of the 50th anniversary of the UDHR.[31]

---

31 Parliamentary Resolution No. 1/1998 (XI. 16.). Cited by one of the most liberal constitutional justices, who delivered one of the mentioned leading cases of the Court (18/2004. AB), declaring the unconstitutionality of the special defamation provision of the Criminal Code *See* I. KUKORELLI, 'Az Emberi Jogok Egyetemes Nyilatkozatának jelentősége, mai üzenete' [The Importance and Todays Message of the UDHR], 34 *Acta Humana* (1999) pp. 4–10.

15. IRELAND: FROM DOMESTIC PRE-OCCUPATIONS TO WIDER RECEPTION

Attracta Ingram
Vinodh Jaichand[1]

1. INTRODUCTION

Like so many of the other countries in this book, the historical context played a large role in the reception of human rights in Ireland. Irish history is replete with various efforts to gain the right to self-determination, although not referred to in such language, from the United Kingdom of Great Britain from the seventeenth century onwards. After 1922 the twenty-six counties in the south of Ireland seceded from the United Kingdom as the independent Irish Free State. But at the time the Universal Declaration of Human Rights (hereinafter UDHR) came before the plenary session of United Nations General Assembly in 1948 for approval, Ireland was not then a member of the United Nations.[2]

Ireland's membership had been vetoed in 1946 by the Union of Soviet Socialist Republics[3] which precipitated the first advisory opinion of the International Court of Justice.[4] It held that a Member State could not make its

---

1 The authors would like to acknowledge the research assistance of Marc Gionet and Aisling O'Sullivan. Our thanks also go to Niamh Hardiman and Mark Kelly for their comments on an earlier draft.

2 The United Nations comprised of 58 states in 1948. In 1949, Israel was admitted and in 1950 Indonesia. Only in 1955 was Ireland admitted together with 15 additional states of which Albania, Austria, Bulgaria, Finland, Hungary, Italy, Portugal, Romania and Spain were from Europe.

3 *See generally* J.M. SKELLY, *Irish Diplomacy at the United Nations 1945–1965: National Interests and International Order* (Irish Academic Press, Dublin, 1997). *See also* ongoing research by the Irish Centre for Human Rights, *Ireland's Participation in International Human Rights Law and Institutions*, Funded by Irish Research Council for Humanities and Social Sciences <www.nuigalway.ie/human_rights/Projects/ireland_project/UN.html>.

4 *Conditions of Admission of a State to Membership in the United Nations* (Article 4 of the Charter) 12 December 1947. Sales Number 11. *See* <www.icj-cji.org/docket/index.php?p1=38p2=48k=2e&case=38cpde=asun83p=6>.

consent for the admission of a state contingent on the simultaneous admission of other states. In these circumstances, Ireland could make no major contribution to the development of the UDHR, nor did it participate actively as it tried to assert itself and promote its cause for recognition in the international domain.

There was another domestic issue which focused the attention of the nation on 22 December 1948, namely, the signing of the Republic of Ireland Bill which created the Republic of Ireland in 1949.[5] The latter over-shadowed the international developments in human rights law.

2. REALISING THE ADVOCACY ROLE

In 1949, John Humphrey, one of major contributors to the development of the UDHR, encountered Eamonn de Valera in Strasbourg during the inaugural meeting of the Council of Europe which gives us an early view about some of the preoccupations of Ireland.[6] In his diaries Humphrey observed on 16 August 1949 that the debates in Strasbourg were featured by an attack of the Irish delegate on Britain "for preventing the union of Ireland".[7] On hearing de Valera speak on 17 August 1949 he noted that he was "so full of Irish nationalism that he has no vision of European unity".[8] The domestic pre-occupations continued, when Sean MacEntee spoke about Article 21 of the UDHR on the principle of elections "it soon became apparent that this was a pretext to attack British policy in regard to Ireland".[9]

John Humphrey's meeting with Eamonn de Valera, who was then leader of the opposition in the Dáil Éireann, was most revealing. De Valera said that Ireland would never accept Article 16 which recognised equal rights for men and women during the marriage and at its dissolution because Ireland did not believe in divorce. Humphrey pointed out that marriage could be dissolved for other reasons, such as death, and that the Vatican had not raised an objection to this article. Apparently, de Valera rejected this, stating that marriages were made in heaven and continued there. Humphrey observed

---

5 *The Irish Times*, President Signs Republic Bill, 22 December 1948, p. 1.

6 J.P. HUMPHREY, *Human Rights and the UN* (Baxter Publishing Company, 1963) p. 93.

7 J.P. HUMPHREY, *On the Edge of Greatness*, Vol. 1 (McGill, 1996) p. 200.

8 *Ibid.*, p. 201.

9 *Ibid.*, p. 204.

disapprovingly of de Valera: "He apparently subsists in a strait-jacket of Catholicism and Irish nationalism".[10]

De Valera's attitude was reflective of a powerful strand of conservative thinking in Ireland that sought normative standards in the catholic natural law tradition strictly construed in accordance with Vatican teaching. From that perspective, a central concern about the very idea of human rights was its association with the protection of individual liberties, including the right to challenge tradition, authority, and social institutions. These were subversive 'liberal' notions for a country set on building an identity on communitarian values, promulgated and guarded by a partnership of church and state.

Fundamental rights were protected in the 1937 Constitution but their embeddedness in a constitutional frame of religious belief, family, and the common good, distinguished their social implications from the unfettered individual rights deriving from John Locke's Second Treatise on Government. This difference between rights in context and full liberal rights was at the heart of the debates that dominated the Irish political agenda on denominational education, health, reproduction and divorce until the 2000s when the third referendum on abortion (2002) backfired badly for the government's proposal to remove the threat of suicide as a ground for legal abortion.[11] But these debates had not then begun in 1948, and the international development of the UDHR took backstage to Ireland's need for recognition and position in the post–World War II order. Nevertheless, Ireland had a committed actor in the emergent human rights regime, in the form of Sean McBride.

McBride's credentials as a human rights advocate and institution builder were exemplary.[12] Indeed his initial attempts to establish the Office of the High Commissioner for Human Rights were so forceful that John Humphrey, the first Director of the UN Division of Human Rights from 1946 to 1966 was troubled. As Hobbins reports, "McBride's advocacy for the concept … was so strong that Humphrey became progressively uneasy about the former's

---

10 HUMPHREY, *supra* note 6, p. 93.

11 There are no laws providing for abortion in Ireland. No hospital would perform one.

12 President of Ireland (1963–1970), member of Dáil Éireann (1947–1958). Minister of Foreign Affairs (1948–1951), founding Chairman of the International Board of Amnesty International (1961–1975). In 1974, he was awarded the Nobel Prize for Peace for his efforts to establish international mechanisms for protecting human rights.

role".[13] Later, as the relationship matured, he spoke of the great respect he had for McBride.[14]

McBride, as Minister for External Affairs for Ireland, played a significant role in Ireland's contribution to the development of the European Convention on Human Rights (ECHR), which was largely modelled on the UDHR.[15] It would be unfair to judge Ireland's total contribution to the statute of the Council of Europe by reference to unsuccessful proposals, but it is worth drawing attention to a few features of Ireland's strategy as revealing its domestic and British-Irish concerns. The first proposal was that the ECHR should contain a reference to 'Christian civilisation' which might resonate with the Netherlands proposal to do the same with the UDHR; the second that 'national right to self-determination' be included in the Preamble; and the third, for the Council to establish mechanisms for the peaceful settlement of disputes and for the resolution of boundary problems.[16] The intention behind the latter two was to continue the pressure on Britain. Despite the absence of Ireland from the UN process of the UDHR, the Department of External Affairs was aware that not all the rights listed in the UDHR were included in the European Consultative Assembly resolution.[17] Ireland was a strong supporter of individual petitions to the European Commission of Human Rights where MacBride was reported to have said that a "convention on human rights which did not grant any right of redress to individuals was not worth the paper it was written on".[18]

While the United Kingdom was an adherent of the UDHR, it had grave concerns about their potential application in the British colonies and territories contained in the UDHR, some of which surfaced quickly.[19] This opened up opportunities for criticism that were not missed in Ireland. On the first anniversary of the UDHR the then recent history with Britain and the

---

13 A.J. HOBBINS, 'Humphrey and the High Commissioner: The Genesis of the Office of the UN High Commissioner for Human Rights', 3 *Journal of the History of International Law* (2001) pp. 38–74, at p. 58.

14 *Ibid.*, p. 61.

15 W.A. SCHABAS, 'Ireland, the European Convention on Human Rights and the Personal Contribution of Sean MacBride', in J. MORISON, K. MCEVOY and G. ANTHONY (eds), *Human Rights, Democracy and Transition* (Oxford University Press, Oxford, 2007) p. 252.

16 *Ibid.*, p. 256.

17 *Ibid.*, p. 257.

18 *Ibid.*, p. 259.

19 *See* the reference to the secret meeting with France and Belgium in 1949 which is referred to in this book by Kalliope Agapiou-Josephides in 'Cyprus: From an Interesting Colonial Legacy to Post-conflict Contextualisation'.

Soviet Union was resuscitated in a radio broadcast by the Ministry for External Affairs[20] which referred sarcastically to the record of both countries on human rights. The efficacy of the UDHR as a document for advocacy was acknowledged in this broadcast where, after protests from the Irish delegates at the Council of Europe meeting in Strasbourg in August 1948, many intended regulations that went counter to the principles of the UDHR were revoked in Northern Ireland.[21]

Ireland continued its internationalisation efforts by positioning itself with the non-aligned nations, for example, and pursued its national interests through skilful manoeuvring and agenda-shaping in the emergent EEC negotiations in the late 1950s. But neither the ECHR nor the UDHR became a focus for Irish domestic activity in those early days. We found no reference to the UDHR in the Dáil before 1963 and substantive debates and references came as late as the new millennium. This, despite the fact that human rights normative standards were growing in importance with Ireland's membership of the European Economic Community (subsequently the European Community, and then the European Union) in 1972. In the period from the late 1960s to the Belfast (or Good Friday) Agreement of 1998, the single and most successful, appeal to international human rights standards was the 1978 case brought by the Irish Government to the then European Commission of Human Rights, and the European Court of Human Rights at Strasbourg, citing Britain for breach of human rights under the Convention's Article 3 for the use of internment without trial and robust interrogation techniques on IRA suspects.

The conflict in Northern Ireland is an important element in the explanation of the silence on human rights standards within the Republic in that period. The Republic had an Offences Against the State Act in force since 1939. The Act's sweeping powers allowed for introduction of internment without trial by government order, used in 1952 to suppress the IRA Border Campaign, and for limitations on broadcasting, for establishment of special courts, and a reduced standard of evidence. In the perceived conflict between

---

20 "Indeed, we know to our own cost that many of the principles [in the UDHR] are in some measure violated by those who have what is generally regarded as a clean record. Britain is proud, and justly proud, of her liberties and we know that many of the principles laid down in the Declaration were first formulated by Englishmen. Yet under British rule in our country several of the human rights set forth in the Declaration have been infringed. Not, indeed, not barbarously violated as they are in the countries of the Iron Curtain but yet seriously and deliberately infringed". Transcript from Radio Eireann broadcast, 10 December 1949.

21 "The fact that they were driven to do this is a good illustration of the practical use of what may appear at first sight purely academic discussions and declarations such as the UDHR". Transcript from Radio Eireann broadcast, 10 December 1949.

liberty and security in the thirty years of the euphemistically named 'The Troubles' in Northern Ireland, it did not suit either the Irish or the British governments to foster human rights sensibilities among citizens. Ireland was under tremendous pressure to defend nationalists in Northern Ireland, at the same time as delegitimising the Irish Republican Army (IRA), and keeping acceptable relations with the British government. The discourse of rights was largely latent and the potential of the UDHR to serve as a rallying point for political opposition to government policy on the IRA was not unleashed.

Official reticence in the use of the discourse of human rights changed dramatically when the Belfast Agreement finally signalled the end of the Northern Ireland conflict. The Agreement's reference point in relation to its strong human rights provisions was not the UDHR, but the ECHR which was, of course, inspired by the UDHR. The clear role of human rights in the peace-making and the establishment of human rights commissions, North and South, contributed significantly to human rights establishment in the Republic. Surprisingly, this went hand in hand with increased references to the principles of the UDHR (rather than the ECHR, though that was taken into Irish law in 2003[22]). This is a feature of a number of colonial settlements where the need for international human rights standards was stressed as independent governance structures were put in place as the colonial power was due to withdraw. Arguably, this reflected a perception of the reality of the UDHR as ideological and political, while regional instruments like the ECHR were more legal and binding with respect to concrete obligations. As elsewhere, the appeal of the UDHR in the Irish political arena had typically been for the persuasive force of its principles in arguments for new legislative policies or criticism of the government of the day.

3. DEBATING THE NORMATIVE VALUE OF THE UDHR

Since 2000 the UDHR has been cited frequently in the debates in both houses of the parliament. Members of the Oireachtas have used the normative standards of the UDHR as a guide to better legislative practice by the government and the opposition have often used them to expose the government's initiative of the day. In these instances, inevitably the government's replies have been defensive and often the record of

22 The European Convention on Human Rights Act, Number 20 of 2003.

achievement was cited as a counter-response.[23] Without labelling these debates as brinkmanship, they do illustrate how the UDHR is regarded as a useful tool for advancing human rights normative standards into law. A brief perusal of a few debates indicated the utility and value of arguments related to the normative values of the UDHR.

Sometimes the language of a rights-based approach was used to force government's hand to legislate in that way.[24] The right to health has been referred to as being a fundamental right.[25] The legitimate claims to asylum by an asylum seeker who did not possess adequate travel documentation arising from Article 14 of the UDHR and Articles 31 and 33 of the Convention Relating to the Status of Refugees have been raised.[26] When the Human Rights Commission was being established in Ireland the UDHR was cited, as has been noted earlier, in support of the creation of the national institution.[27] In a debate on overseas development aid reference was made to the right to water as part of the right to health in the UDHR.[28] Again, in the debate on human rights issues it was stated that it was most appropriate to evaluate these human rights issues in the light of the UDHR because as "a basic statement of human rights the declaration has never been improved on".[29]

The debates have been precipitated by concerns not only of a domestic nature but about international issues also through linkage with Ireland's involvement in them. The issue of 'extraordinary renditions' was raised when it was said that the United States' attempts to redefine torture were a violation of the ECHR and the UDHR and that Ireland was colluding with this behaviour when it permitted these aeroplanes to refuel at Shannon

---

23 Article 23 of the UDHR was cited in the failure of the state to give adequate priority and focus to labour affairs especially the right to be free from exploitation, the right to fair remuneration, the right to join trade unions, the right to safe working conditions, the right to access lifelong learning opportunities and vocational training. The government spokesperson responded by asking whether there were inadequate legal frameworks to protect these rights when so much was already done. Dáil Éireann, Volume 615, 22 February 2006.

24 In the debate on the Disability Bill the government was attacked for failing to deliver a rights–based approach. It was pointed out that the rights identified, like equality and human rights, were not arbitrary or optional but were reflected in international agreements and international instruments like the UDHR. Dáil Éireann, Volume 596, 2 February 2006.

25 Dáil Éireann, Volume 571, 1 October 2003.

26 Dáil Éireann, Volume 570, 2 July 2003.

27 In a similar vein, Mr. Howlin supported the establishment of the Human Rights Commission because the commitment to the rights in the UDHR had to be "recognised in deeds and not words alone". Dáil Éireann, Volume 540, 5 July 2001.

28 Dáil Éireann, Volume 628, 23 November 2006.

29 Dáil Éireann, Volume 506, 3 June 1999.

Airport.[30] The government's belief in the fundamental principles of the UDHR was invoked in its condemnation of what was happening in Guantanamo Bay to support the campaign for its immediate closure.[31]

Anniversaries of the UDHR have presented politicians with the occasion to laud it "as a common standard of achievement for all peoples and all nations"[32] and to recall the positive contribution of individuals and organisations in Ireland to its values. It also provided an opportunity to reflect on democracy in Europe when it was noted by one speaker that only three European states have had a longer period of continuous democracy in this century than Ireland. They were Sweden, Switzerland and the United Kingdom.[33] All other European states have had their democracy interrupted either by invasion or by civil war. A reference to the following revealed some honest appraisal:

> "Let us remember, however, that civilised Christian Western Europe — which we claim as the source of enlightenment, the centre of the French Revolution with a vision of liberty, equality and fraternity — has still managed to slaughter more of its citizens per capita than anywhere else on the planet."[34]

The focus on parliamentary debates on the human rights issues appeal to the highest normative values found only in the UDHR and, sometimes, a reminder that the task of implementation is not concluded.

4. JUDGING THE RIGHTS

Reference is made almost exclusively to the ECHR on human rights matters in cases before the Irish courts in the positivist mould of most European states. There have been occasions when reference was made to the UDHR on a more limited scale. The cases that have come before the Irish courts have been set out chronologically so that the development of the law can be noted. Although Ireland became a member of the UN in 1955, it was as early as 1952, in a case that began in 1950, that the UDHR was cited in the High

---

30 Seanad Éireann, Volume 183, 8 June 2006.

31 Dáil Éireann, Volume 621, 13 June 2006.

32 Dáil Éireann, Volume 497, 1 December 1998.

33 To be more accurate, Norway should be included in this number.

34 Seanad Debates Official Reports, 10 December 1998. Found at: <www. irlgov.ie/debates-98/s10dec98/sect2.htm>.

Court in Ireland. In an extradition case, it was held that the UDHR did not purport to be an existing law of nations.[35]

In other cases the norms of the UDHR were used illustratively. A right cannot be claimed in a way that excludes the rights of others, as is pointed out in Article 29(2) of UDHR, in a case of an appeal against the admissibility of evidence.[36] Another case held that Article 4(1) of the UDHR on the prohibition against slavery and servitude did not apply even though the UDHR was accepted by the government of Ireland, because it was not part of the domestic law of Ireland.[37] Here the UDHR has been used as a declaratory text of general acceptance.

It is a fairly common experience in most jurisdictions that judges sometimes look for a co-incidence in a particular constitutional norm with an international human rights norm through comparison. It was held that the need for public hearings as part of the administration of justice was a requirement[38] because this fundamental principle was contained in the Constitution of 1937. It was observed that more than a decade later this was incorporated in certain international instruments dealing with human rights like Article 10 of the UDHR in 1948 and Article 26 of the American Declaration of the Rights and Duties of Man, also of 1948, each of which required public hearings for the administration of justice. Similarly, the principle of the presumption of innocence was evaluated as being widespread and enjoying universal recognition by referring to Article 11 of the UDHR, Article 6(2) of the European Convention on Human Rights and Fundamental Freedoms, Article 8(2) of the American Convention on Human Rights, and Article 7 of the African Charter on Human and Peoples' Rights.[39]

---

35 *The State (Duggan)* v *Tapley* [1952] 62 1 IR, "The Declaration, therefore, though of great importance and significance in many ways, is not a guide to discover the existing principles of international law", at p. 83.

36 *The People (at the Suit of the Director of Public Prosecutions)* v *Shaw* [S.C. No.129 of 1979].

37 *The Application of Woods* [S.C No. 162 of 1970] at pp. 161–162. The later case of *Director of Public Prosecutions* v *Murphy* [High Court] 2001 1 I.R. 171 distinguished the *Woods* case in the light of section 11(5) of the Criminal Law Act of 1997.

38 *In re R. Limited* [1988 No. 8775P]. However, the dissent was of the view that discretion was given to judges in certain cases to depart from this fundamental principle. These observations on the international instruments were cited with approval in *The People (Director of Public Prosecutions)* v *W.M.* [High Court]1995 I I.R. 226 at 231 in an incest case calling for an in camera hearing.

39 *O'Leary* v *The Attorney General* [1989 No. 8949P]. This judgment was cited with approval in *The People (Director of Public Prosecutions)* v *D. O'T* [Court of criminal Appeal] [2003] 4 I.R. 286.

In another case the applicant drew the attention of the Court to the provisions of the UDHR and the European Convention for the Protection of Human Rights and Fundamental Freedoms which provided for compensation for victims of miscarriage of justice.[40] The right to education of handicapped children was brought by the Cope Foundation in Cork where the right to dignity and the right to education from the UDHR was referred to. The relevant provisions of the Declaration on the Rights of Disabled Persons were also cited in a successful action against the state.[41] To what extent the court was persuaded by the UDHR norms as being legal norms under Irish law is unclear.

There are a number of cases that use the UDHR for illustrating universal and specific constitutional norms as a declaratory text. The UDHR was utilised to define a family and the rights inherent to the family.[42] A reference was made to the UDHR in a summary of international progress towards judicial review.[43] The UDHR norms on the status of marriage and the family were referenced to complement the Irish constitutional provisions.[44] Similarly the Irish constitutional values that limit the intervention of the state in parental matters were compared to UDHR norms.[45] The UDHR's norms that proclaim fundamental rights and fair procedure were referred to in the necessity of judicial review in the safeguarding of human rights.[46]

In these cases the citations of the UDHR were undertaken for different purposes starting from a reference to it but acknowledging that it has no legal binding power on the court, in its earlier judgments. Later there is a more pragmatic approach taken. Some courts used the occasion to illustrate that the Irish Constitution was a far-sighted document that afforded protection of human rights at least a decade before the UDHR. To the extent there is consonance with this, the norms are further validated. Another feature is that a reference to the UDHR is often occasioned by reference to the ECHR and the UN Charter. Most recently, there is a general acknowledgement of the UDHR as a common standard for all nations without any caveats about its

---

40 *The People (Director of Public Prosecutions)* v *Meleady* [1995] 2.I.R.517, *In The People (Director of Public Prosecutions)* v *Pringle* (No. 2) 2 I.R. 547. *The People* v *Meleady* was cited with approval by O'Flaherty J.

41 In *The People (Director of Public Prosecutions)* v *Pringle* (No. 2) 2 I.R. 547.

42 *North West Health Board* v *H. W* [High Court and Supreme Court] [2001] 3 I.R.662.

43 *Maguire* v *Ardagh* [High Court; Supreme Court] [2002] 1 I.R. 385.

44 *D.T* v *C.T* [High Court; Supreme Court] [2002] 3 I.R. 334.

45 *A.O & D.L* v *Minister of Justice* [Supreme Court] [2003] 1 I.R 1.

46 *A* v *Governor of Arbour Hill Prison* [High Court; Supreme Court] [2006] 4 I.R.88.

binding nature. This last development is facilitated by a wider claim that, over the past 60 years, the standards set out in the UDHR have come to acquire many of the characteristics of customary law or general principles of international law, an approach that fits generally with the Irish approach to customary law. Thus, the UDHR's contested customary law status may now assist it to trump its unincorporated status in Irish law.

5. LEGISLATING WITH THE UDHR IN MIND

With regard to legislation, generally a reference to UDHR is made where the legislation involves the adoption of treaties as part of the dualist system in Ireland. International law does not become part of the domestic law unless explicitly made so by an Act of the Oireachtas, which is not the case as far as the UDHR is concerned. This may be seen as acting as a break on the reception of the UDHR by the Oireachtas and the judiciary. However, without being exhaustive, or indicating the UDHR's larger influence on other pieces of legislation in Ireland, we found 16 pieces of legislation that mention the UDHR.[47]

One of the examples of this type of legislation is the European Convention on Human Rights Act of 2003 which refers to the UDHR in the schedule of the act which makes it possible to prosecute one's European Convention rights before the Irish courts. In the remedies, Ireland ironically imitated the British solution where the court may issue a declaration of incompatibility against the offending legislation with a limited award of damages to the successful litigant. Another example is the Refugee Act of 1996 which referred to the UDHR in the third schedule. The Act seeks to provide for the rights and remedies of applicants for refugee status in Ireland, in keeping with its international obligations, through the creation of formal mechanisms. The role of the UDHR appears to be relegated to the schedules of legislation.

A third example illustrates that political expediency was the driving force for the legislation. When the Prohibition of Incitement to Racial, Religious or

[47] Criminal Justice (Terrorist Offences) Act 2005, Schedule 1; Maritime Security Act 2004, Schedule 1; European Convention on Human Rights Act 2003, Schedule 1; S.I. No. 334/2002 — European Communities (Personal Insolvency) Regulations 2002; S.I. No. 333/2002 — European Communities (Corporate Insolvency) Regulations 2002; S.I. No. 173/2002 — Extradition Act 1965 (Application of Part II) (Amendment) Order 2002, Finance Act 2001, Section 45; S.I. No. 474/2000 — Extradition Act 1965 (Application of Part II) Order, 2000; Criminal Justice (United Nations Convention Against Torture) Act 2000; Taxes Consolidation Act 1997, Section 209; Taxes Consolidation Act 1997; Refugee Act 1996; Finance Act 1973, Section 20.

National Hatred Bill was being debated the Minister for Justice said that this legislation was necessary to enable the ratification of the United Nations Covenant on Civil and Political Rights. The Minister noted that Ireland in 1989 had few instances of incitement to hatred cases because it did not have a large multi-racial population like other parts of Europe and the government did not want to create problems where none previously existed. He then traced the genesis of the Covenant from the UDHR before presenting the bill to the house. This perfunctory approach characterised the Act which has since been overtaken by rapid immigration into the country in the next decade and half.

If one has regard to legislation that has been influenced through a positive reception of the UDHR in Ireland, they are few and far between.

6. RECALLING THE INFLUENCE OF THE UDHR IN THE PRESS

In Ireland there was limited general press cover on the adoption of the UDHR in 1948 for reasons already stated, namely, its pre-occupation with domestic matters.[48] However, the advisory opinion of the International Court of Justice was reported by the *Irish Times* under the heading "World Court Says Russia is Wrong"[49] as this was a matter of national concern. Surprisingly, since then the Irish press has been very active in disseminating information on events that have shaped the world, and the birth of the UDHR has been counted amongst them.

At each anniversary the Irish press has, over the years, evaluated the role and effect of the UDHR. Every decade appears to be covered with a greater sense of direction and purpose. After the expiry of the first ten years of the UDHR, messages from Eleanor Roosevelt, Rene Cassin and Charles Malik were published exhorting us, respectively, to look to the future in the ratification of the UN covenants, pointing to the gathering momentum of human rights since the Declaration, and reminding us of the challenge to live up to the standards of the those natural rights of the people.[50]

The *Irish Times* carried the text of a lecture given by Sean McBride in Athlone on 13 February 1960 on the European Convention on Human

48 *The Irish Independent* on 22 December 1948 announced the adoption of the UDHR in a brief statement under the heading "Human Rights".

49 *The Irish Times*, Saturday, 29 May 1948.

50 *The Irish Times*, Tuesday, 30 December 1958 "Messages on Human Rights", p. 4.

Rights[51] which recognised the impact the UDHR had made on legal and political thought around the world and that many states had regarded it as part of international law. In his introduction of the ECHR he spoke of the impetus of the UDHR which led to the formulation of the ECHR.

In the year of the twentieth anniversary of the UDHR the *Irish Times* noted that many international lawyers regarded some of the provisions of the UDHR as part of the substantive part of customary international law. However, in practice there was a great deal to accomplish with regard to human rights around the world.[52]

On the fortieth anniversary of the UDHR the *Meath Cronicle* reported that the members of the Kells and Navan groups of Amnesty International called for the Irish ratification of the two UN covenants.[53]

On the fiftieth anniversary the *Irish Times* noted that as the Cold War was over, mankind would have the opportunity to rekindle the spirit which led to the Declaration.[54] The *Irish Times* also marked this anniversary with a report on a real example of a human rights issue: a Tajik child exiled from home. The reporter contextualised the human rights obligations of Ireland at this time by addressing migration issues:

> "Irish hypocrisies about refugees, asylum seekers and migrant workers are powerfully exposed in such a framework [of international obligations arising from conventions]. We are making the transition from an emigrant to an immigrant society belatedly and unevenly, the last of the EU member-states to do so. The process lays bare raw experiences of exclusion and inclusion built up over centuries of colonialism and migration."[55]

---

[51] *The Irish Times*, Friday, 12 February 1960, "The Convention of Human Rights-1", p. 7.

[52] *The Irish Times*, Friday, 5 January 1968, "Free by Right", p. 11.

[53] *Meath Chronicle*, 13 December 1986, "Human Rights". *The Irish Times*, Saturday 10 December 1998 also carried an article titled "The Seed Germinates after 40 Years", p. 6. *The Irish Times*, Saturday 10 December 1988, p. 11, published "Forty Years On" in which it makes a poignant observation: "If the world was perfect there would be no need of a Declaration of Human Rights: thus the idealists who conceived its aspirations were realists in so far as they defined what was missing, and what ends must be sought to reduce the incidence of imperfection".

[54] *The Irish Times*, Wednesday, 9 December 1998, "Mankind has the Chance to Rekindle the Spirit of '48". *See also The Irish Times*, Tuesday, 8 December 1998, "Rights Declaration Celebrated Amid Dismay at Violations of Principles", where Lara Marlowe reported from Paris.

[55] *The Irish Times*, Wednesday, 4 November 1998, p. 46. On 9 December, *the Irish Times* carried an article called "A Challenging Declaration" in which it examined the role of Ireland in both international and domestic human rights developments.

The *Irish Times* has already begun the sixtieth anniversary celebrations by publishing each week an article by a famous Irish writer on one article of the UDHR together with Amnesty International. To mark the 60th anniversary the full book of illustrative stories has been published. The role and contribution of all NGOs in popularising the UDHR has been immense.

7. CONCLUSION

It would be too large a claim to conclude that the UDHR was part of the laws of Ireland. However, it would be no exaggeration to say that it has come to have an important role as the standard to be achieved. After 60 years, this may seem too little by way of accomplishment, especially from the perspective of the developing world which looks to the developed countries to deliver on their human rights universalism.

From its initial domestic concerns with the trappings of independence, Ireland learned quickly how to utilise the UDHR for its own national interests and international standing, which itself is an exemplary human rights achievement. Even though the UDHR does not have an uncontested place in customary international law, politicians have welcomed it as a new source of political argument for reform and criticism of the government of the day. Creative lawyers have cited the UDHR in persuasive arguments on behalf of their clients in courts of law. And citizens have embraced its principles to expand their rights through available European and national instruments.

Of late, Ireland has shed its poor-country image and become an economic powerhouse internationally. As a result people from around the world have converged on Ireland for its employment opportunities. But Ireland remains ambivalent between national assimilation and multicultural accommodation of its new immigrants. Much as the principles of the UDHR have been taken as standard-setting in recent times, its efficacy in the development of economic, social, and cultural rights has been curtailed by a consistent genuflexion to the directive principles of the Irish Constitution which are said to bar it from making economic, social and cultural rights cognisable in a forum for dispute resolution such as a court.[56]

This is an area in which the debate over the legal status of the UDHR really matters. It is the only document that protects all human rights which

[56] The Indian Constitution was modelled on the Irish and also contains similar directive principles which do not prevent economic, social and cultural rights from being justiciable.

was the original intention of all States who were members of the UN at that time. The bifurcation between civil and political rights and economic, social and cultural rights was the result of political concerns in the so-called Cold War. Under international law it is not possible to avoid legal obligations by raising domestic obstacles.[57] In the 60 years, Ireland has moved from its domestic concerns to receiving the UDHR in a wider sphere but it has yet to explore, accept and implement its full national and international commitments in terms of all the promises in the document and subsequent conventions.

57 Articles 27 and 46 of the Vienna Convention on the Law of Treaties. As Ireland has ratified the International Covenant on Economic, Social and Cultural Rights, these obligations would apply.

16. ITALY: A LEGAL PUZZLE, BUT THE CIVIL SOCIETY HAS TAKEN THE BALL AND RUNS WITH IT

Paolo De Stefani

1. INTRODUCTION: THE UDHR AND THE ITALIAN POST-WORLD WAR II POLITICAL LANDSCAPE

When the Universal Declaration on Human Rights (hereinafter UDHR) was adopted in Paris by the United Nations General Assembly, Italy was not a member of the organisation — it joined it only in 1955. At the time when the UDHR was being drafted, the country was recovering from one of the hardest moments of its history, the worst since the unitary State was established in 1861. The Fascist regime had collapsed on 25 July 1943, and the kingdom's interim government had signed an armistice with the Allies on 8 September of the same year, while most of the territory was under the *de facto* military occupation of the Nazis. A liberation war started soon in Italy against the German troops, but also against the pro-Nazi 'republic' that Mussolini had created in the North.

The civil war, whose brutality is hard for the Italian people to admit even today, lasted until April 1945, but its aftermath of revenge and widespread violence endured for years. The post-war internal political scenario, from the liberation until 1948, was marked by the confrontation in the new-born republic (a referendum revoked the monarchy on 2 June 1946) between the Left, largely represented by the Socialist and Communist parties, and the Centre-Right, grouped around the Christian-Democrats. The year 1948 marked a turning point in the Italian history: the first general elections were held (in 1946 the country had voted for an interim Constituent Assembly). The campaign was extremely intense and somehow dramatic, because Italy was a key domino in the Cold War scenario. The vote of 18 April gave a strong majority in the Parliament to the Christian-Democratic party, and showed the relative collapse, inside the leftist Popular Front of the Socialist party, overwhelmed by the Communists. In summer of the same year, an attempt to the life of the Communist leader, Palmiro Togliatti, shocked the whole nation. Once again the prospect of a civil war was haunting the country.

All in all, it is not surprising that the promulgation of the UDHR was not the top story in Italian newspapers in those days of December 1948. Nonetheless, the importance of the UDHR was immediately perceived in Italy by some leading figures of culture. Giuseppe Sperduti, an outstanding international lawyer, who later on was the Italian representative at the United Nations (hereinafter UN) Human Rights Commission and member of the European Human Rights Commission, in his inaugural address at the opening of the 1949–1950 academic year of the University of Sassari, clearly identified the two major challenges that the UDHR was posing to international law: the status of the individuals as 'subjects' of the international legal order, and the need to move from a sovereign state-based international community towards a human being-based one, where states and intergovernmental institutions are functional to the realisation of universal human rights, as required by Article 28 of the UDHR.[1]

Giuseppe Capograssi, a prominent, far-sighted legal philosopher, welcomed very soon the UDHR. His Introduction to the Italian translation of the UDHR, published in 1950, stressed the moral and political significance of the text. The UDHR embodied a lesson peoples had learnt during the recent history, and especially through the tragedy of the Second World War, namely that between impersonal, 'collective' values, such as the 'nation', the 'class', the 'race', the 'state', on the one hand, and the 'natural' values of the human person, on the other hand, the UN had chosen the latter and rejected the former ones.[2] The same choice — in spite of the non-binding nature of the instrument — became mandatory for both the governments and the citizens.

Another philosopher, Norberto Bobbio, adopted a similar stance. According to Bobbio, with the UDHR, the international community — represented by the UN — assumed the legal responsibility to protect individuals *vis-à-vis* their own state; the UDHR marked the beginning of a 'second phase' of the historic struggle of the individual against the modern state — the first phase being the affirmation of the moral and legal autonomy of the individual based on natural law doctrines.[3]

---

1 The speech was published as G. SPERDUTI, 'La Dichiarazione universale dei diritti dell'uomo', 5 *La Comunità Internazionale* (1950) pp. 216–235.

2 G. CAPOGRASSI, *La dichiarazione universale dei diritti dell'uomo e il suo significato* (Cedam, Padova, 1950) pp. 9–19.

3 N. BOBBIO, 'La dichiarazione universale dei diritti dell'uomo', in N. BOBBIO et al., *La dichiarazione universale dei diritti dell'uomo* (Torino, 1951) pp. 53–70. Bobbio, one of the leading law theorists of the 20th century (he died in 2004), has constantly addressed the issue of universal human rights; particularly relevant is *The Age of Rights* (Policy Press, Cambridge, 1996).

So philosophers and inspired international lawyers were the first estimators of the UDHR. According to their vision, it was a watershed in modern history, an epochal achievement of human civilisation. But it would be difficult to find in their seminal works some more concrete consideration concerning the direct effects the UDHR could produce on the international socio-political arenas, and even less on the national legal and political system.

The political implications of the UDHR were overshadowed, in the perception of columnists, political analysts and policy-makers, by other issues: the developments of the Cold War, the Peace Treaty, the fate of the Italian colonies, and the internal tough confrontation between the Leftist and the Centre-Right parties. In particular, the impact of the UDHR on the legal and institutional fabric of the young republic was weakened by the almost contemporary debate carried out in the Constituent Assembly on the new Italian Constitution.

2. THE UDHR AND THE ITALIAN CONSTITUTION

In the crucial post-war years of 1945–1948, the political fight within the unified anti-Fascist front that was governing the country (a forced cohabitation of Catholic Democrats, Socialists, Communists, and liberal moderates) was harsh, but loyal. The most important achievement of the time, from a legal perspective, was the adoption on 22 December 1947 and the entry into force on 1 January 1948, of the Italian Constitution. This 'rigid' and 'long' supreme charter was successful in integrating harmoniously the many diverse political and cultural traditions and experiences in a single compact that has governed, almost unchanged, the national social and political life for more than 60 years.

The Constitution echoed the debate on human rights that was characterising the post-World War II era at the national and international levels.[4] A first reference to Italy's obligations concerning human rights set forth in an international instrument was included in the 1947 Peace Treaty. Its Article 15 provided that measures must be taken in order to ensure to all individuals under Italian jurisdiction, without discrimination, their human rights and fundamental freedoms, namely freedom of expression, press and publication, freedom of religious worship, of political opinion and public

4 In the Constituent Assembly, particularly keen of the fundamental rights' issue were the Christian-Democrat delegates adhering to the Jacquest Maritain's personalist philosophy.

meeting (the same obligation rests under Article 19 on the states having jurisdiction over the territories transferred to them by Italy).[5]

A detailed and comprehensive list of rights and freedoms was, nonetheless, provided in the Constitution, namely in its Fundamental Principles (Articles 1–12) and Part I (Rights and Duties of the Citizen, Articles 13–54). The Constitution's bill of rights clearly reflected the contemporary international debate and it is a widespread opinion among Italian scholars that there is a substantial convergence between the inviolable rights granted to everyone by the Constitution and especially referred to in its Article 2, on the one hand, and the human rights enshrined in the UDHR on the other.

As a matter of fact, the national legal and political debate about the constitutional rights widely absorbed the one on the UDHR. The Constitution preceded by almost one year the UN UDHR, so that it can be said that in Italy, the impact of the latter was somehow softened. By the same token, the UDHR has been consistently conceived of as a single compact covering the whole range of human rights. As seen above, it attracted the interest of philosophers, legal theorists and international lawyers, but for a long time, it had a modest influence as such on domestic legal scholars, practitioners and the courts. When national laws or court decisions were mentioning the UDHR, it was generally because the UDHR encapsulated the general ideal of universal human rights, and sometimes because it epitomised, without providing details, the subsequent set of treaties, covenants and international standards elaborated by international law (mainly in the UN system, as the European Convention on Human Rights (hereinafter ECHR) is generally referred to separately).

It is therefore extremely difficult to distinguish, in a piece of law or in a court judgment, between a reference made to the UDHR as a specific international instrument and a mention of it merely as a synonym of the whole range of international norms (binding and non-binding, universal and regional) on human rights that Italy has agreed upon. The way the Italian Constitutional Court and more generally the national courts have applied international human rights norms may illustrate the point.

---

5 Treaty of Peace with Italy, signed at Paris, on 10 February 1947, entered into force on 15 September 1947; States Parties: USA, France, the United Kingdom, USSR, Yugoslavia, Italy, India, Pakistan, Canada, Byelorussia, Ukraine (UNTS, Vols. 49 and 50, Registration No. 747).

3. THE ADAPTATION TO THE INTERNATIONAL LAW OF HUMAN RIGHTS

It is mainly through an interpretation of Article 2 of the Italian Constitution[6] that conventional international law on human rights is incorporated into the Italian legal order. Its status of constitutional or sub-constitutional disposition is in accordance with the formal status of the domestic act that endorsed the treaty (an ordinary or a constitutional law; it should be remembered however that, to my knowledge, in only one case, the ratification of the Convention on Genocide, the incorporation involved the enactment of a constitutional law[7]). Article 10.1 of the Constitution provides instead for the automatic adaptation of the Italian legal system to customary international law,[8] the legal status of which is therefore that of supreme law.[9] Finally, the provisions of Article 11 have been consistently regarded as granting a special status of supremacy to European Union (hereinafter EU) law.[10]

According to an interpretative trend that emerged during the 1980s in the case-law of the Constitutional Court, the 'inviolable rights' granted to any individual by Article 2 are not only those detailed in Articles 13–54 of the Italian Constitution, but they also include some non-specified rights, the recognition of which is, nevertheless, required by the evolving notion of human dignity.[11] In other words, Article 2 contains an 'open clause', allowing for the protection of (relatively) 'new' rights by reference to international sources that already have recognised them as human rights. However, this

---

6 "The Republic recognizes and guarantees the inviolable rights of man, as an individual, and in the social groups where he expresses his personality, and demands the fulfilment of the intransgressible duties of political, economic, and social solidarity".

7 Constitutional Law 21 June 1967, No. 1, "Extradition for crimes of genocide", <www.italgiure.giustizia.it/nir/1967/lexs_39639.html>, visited on 1 August 2008.

8 "Italian laws conform to the generally recognized tenets of international law".

9 It is worth mentioning that, according to an *obiter dictum* in the Constitutional Court Judgment No. 10/1993, all international treaties (the case concerned the European Convention on Human Rights) belong to an 'atypical' kind of law source, below the Constitution, but above ordinary laws, with the result that norms of international treaties, although incorporated in the domestic order through an ordinary law, cannot be repealed or amended by a successive ordinary law covering the same subject. This jurisprudence has remained isolated.

10 "Italy … agrees, on conditions of equality with other states, to the limitations of sovereignty necessary for an order that ensures peace and justice among Nations; it promotes and encourages international organizations having such ends in view".

11 For an example of a court decision rejecting the 'open' nature of Article 2, *see*, among others, Constitutional Court Judgment No. 188/1980; for an opposite approach, *see* Constitutional Court Judgment No. 161/1985.

position has not helped in clarifying the effective status of the UDHR and other human rights in international instruments — especially the ECHR, the International Covenant on Civil and Political Rights (hereinafter ICCPR) and, more recently, the Convention on the Rights of the Child. The Italian Constitutional Court has, in fact, consistently used the reference to the "international human rights Charters" essentially to reinforce the expansive interpretation of the 'inviolable rights' enshrined in the 'open list' of Article 2, and not as independent standards of constitutionality. Accordingly, the international norms have hardly been the subject of thorough examination; the legal authority of the different sources (UN resolutions, treaties, customary law) has rarely been investigated in detail. As regards the content of the UDHR, for instance, there is no explicit recognition of it being part of international custom, which would facilitate the integration of it in the constitutional setting via the automatic adaptation process of Article 10.1. It is sufficient for the Court to ascertain that a given interpretation, widening the scope of the provisions of Article 2 of the Constitution, is supported by international human rights law, and to use international norms to integrate and better explain the meaning of domestic legislation, including constitutional norms.

The implicit assumption is that Italian law recognises virtually all rights covered by the international instruments, and safeguards them with at least an equivalent level of protection. Hence, there are somewhat rhapsodic references to the UDHR, the international Covenants, the ECHR, and the general principles of human rights protection, while little attention is paid — at least until recently — to the actual case law of the international bodies providing for the application of the same instruments, in particular to the case law of the European Court of Human Rights.[12]

This situation, however, has slowly changed, also due to the new Article 117.1 of the Italian Constitution, introduced by the Constitutional Law 3/2001 that amended the entire balance of central and regional competences and introduced a quasi-federal rule.[13] The provision, without intentionally modifying the established paradigm of the hierarchy of norms, mandated the legislative assemblies of the country to abide by European Union legislation and obligations of international law. In a judgment of October 2007, the

---

[12] However, the last cited judgment provides an exception to this rule, by corroborating the recognition of the right to the individual's sexual identity with reference both to Article 8 of the European Convention and to the case law of the Strasbourg Court.

[13] "Legislative powers shall be vested in the State and the Regions in compliance with the Constitution and with the constraints deriving from EU-legislation and international obligations".

Constitutional Court clearly stated that the radical incompatibility of a provision in a domestic law with an article of the ECHR — indisputably an international agreement creating legal obligations for the ratifying country — involved a violation of Article 117.1 of the Italian Constitution. Most importantly, the judges added that the meaning of the norm in the ECHR shall be determined by the Italian Constitutional Court in accordance with the jurisprudence of the Strasbourg Court.[14]

The Constitutional Court has consistently endorsed a moderate opening of the Italian Basic Law to international values. In this vein, the use of the UDHR and other international instruments on human rights has been a key factor. The internationalisation of the Italian Constitution has been operated to a large extent by emphasising the role of human rights standards, that is, by expanding the mechanism of Article 2. This has not led the Court to vest international legal standards on human rights with formal constitutional relevance. The Court has rather used them as interposed parameters of constitutional legitimacy integrating the basic Charter provisions. Some human rights regimes though, namely the one created by the Council of Europe with the 1950 convention, seem close to enjoying the same treatment reserved to European Union law, grounded on Article 11, and allowing for direct applicability in courts, and an almost full autonomy from domestic constitutional scrutiny.

4. THE UDHR AND THE HUMAN RIGHTS IN GENERAL BEFORE THE ORDINARY COURTS

What is said above with reference to the Constitutional Court may be extended also to the entire Italian judicial system. The lip service paid to the universal principle of human rights protection has covered for a long time a substantial indifference to the actual content of human rights instruments, including the UDHR. Human rights treaties were considered as merely declaratory, carrying almost exclusively 'programmatic' norms, incapable of giving rise to any rights for individuals, because they were essentially addressed to the states (the government, the legislature) and were thus 'non-self-executing'.

A major shift occurred around 1990, when in some judgments, the Court of Cassation (the Supreme Court) for the first time, using the ECHR as a

[14] Constitutional Court Judgment No. 349/2007, especially paragraphs 6.1 and 6.2. *See also* Constitutional Court Judgments No. 120/2004 and 154/2004.

parameter for the interpretation of an internal norm, affirmed in principle the direct applicability of the provisions of the ECHR and suggested that the national courts should abide by the relevant case law of the Strasbourg Court.[15] The judicial applicability of the human rights provisions of international treaties (provided they are *in concreto* self-executing) has been later confirmed by the Supreme Court[16] as well as by the regular courts. In a recent case the Court of Cassation went even further, disposing the reopening of a penal trial because the Strasbourg Commission had found a violation of the rights of the accused, even though no national legal provision permitted the reopening of a case in those circumstances.[17] With the last decision, the Court virtually extended to the regime established by the ECHR the same treatment which is governing the relationship between domestic legislation and EU law (interpretation in conformity or inapplicability of internal law inconsistent with the EU law, with the European Court of Justice as the single authoritative interpreter of EU law).[18]

It is evident that Italian courts have showed a variety of positions *vis-à-vis* the relevance of human rights norms. The fluctuations in the attitude of the Supreme Court are reflected and magnified in the jurisprudence of lower courts.[19] Unfortunately, the outcome of this judicial activism is, at all levels, a

15 *Polo Castro*, 23 November 1988, judgment, Cassation Court, united sections; *Medrano*, 10 July 1993, Judgment, Cassation Court, penal section I.

16 *See*, for instance, the judgments 26 January 2004, No. 1338, 1339, 1340, 1341, Cassation Court, united civil sections.

17 Dorigo, 1 December 2006 - "5 January 2007, Cassation Court, penal section I. For the Strasbourg jurisprudence see Dorigo v Italy, 9 September 1998, No. 33286/96, Report, ECommissionHR, <cmiskp.echr.coe.int/tkp197/view.asp?item=11&portal=hbkm&action=html&highlight=DORIGO&sessionid=12245928&skin=hudoc-en>, visited on 1 August 2008.

18 The legitimacy of this line of reasoning was rejected by the Constitutional Court in the judgment 349/2007, *supra* note 14.

19 It is not possible here to summarise such a huge and various case law. In one case the (hidden) interplay between constitutional and international law norms on human rights is particularly striking. In January 1991, near Verona, some demonstrators concurred to stop for a while a train carrying to Pisa military tanks to be embarked for the Persian Gulf, where Italian troops were operating in the anti-Iraq coalition. The pacifists were acquitted by the tribunal of Verona (the appeals court confirmed), on the ground that to demonstrate against the war was an exercise of the freedom of thought and expression "with reference to the rejecting of the war as a means for settling international controversies", especially considering the "conformist views" trumpeted by the Government and the media that the war as an "operation of international police". The point, although quoting only Article 11 of the Italian Constitution, seems to interpret the norm in the light of Article 20 ICCPR: "any propaganda for war shall be prohibited by law". (Criminal Tribunal, Verona, judgment, 27 January 1997).

persistent uncertainty about the real relevance of the human rights instruments.

Undoubtedly, human rights claims are now more frequently occurring in the Italian judicial practice. One could measure through them the openness of the Italian legal order to international and global legal values. The two main 'doors' that the Constitution provided for the internationalisation of the domestic system (incorporation of international custom in Article 10.1–2 and sovereignty limitations for the sake of promoting peace and justice in Article 11), are both closely related to the human rights discourse. In fact, the more 'international' the legal and political discourses have become, the more have the human rights found place in the courts.

Lawyers and judges have grown familiar over the past two decades with human rights sources and they have been using them professionally and skilfully. The UDHR is no longer a purely political or philosophical manifesto, but is recognised as a component of the international bill of rights, as 'positive' international law, likely to have some practical impact on real world, in the field, for example, of family rights, detainees' condition, children's rights, women's empowerment, the fight against discrimination, and so forth. The shift from a mere rhetoric of human rights to a practical use of human rights occurred roughly 40 years after the adoption of the UDHR. It was not the result of some official political event (the ratification of a treaty, the entry into an international organisation, the enactment of a human rights act), but rather a response to a pressure from below, from a national public opinion and organised civil society that 'discovered' the potential of the human rights discourse well before the state institutions.

5. THE ADVANCEMENT OF UDHR KNOWLEDGE IN ITALY AND THE ROLE OF THE CIVIL SOCIETY

It took several decades for the UDHR to acquire a real relevance in the social and political life of the nation. The interest for the international human rights discourse remained for long time confined to some specialists in the field of international law, legal theory and moral philosophy. Domestic constitutional law theorists and practitioners, as well as law-makers and political leaders, preferred to focus on the parallel system of inviolable rights established by the republican Constitution. It was generally accepted that the international standards largely tallied with Italian legal provisions, to the effect that the UDHR and international human rights law in general was regarded as virtually irrelevant. Apart from a few cases, the legislature did not find it necessary to enact any adaptation laws when entering into new international treaties on human rights, on the assumption that their 'full and entire execution' in Italy did not require any change in the domestic legislation. In the unlikely event a treaty was actually introducing a 'new' right, with no equivalent in the municipal law, the Constitution would provide for its 'domestication'. This approach may explain also the relatively few reservations Italy has entered to the human rights instruments. Thus, no need has been felt to change the law, and even less to establish new institutions specifically designed to promote and implement human rights as such.[20]

The first body bestowed with a specific mandate of supporting human rights education was the Advisory Committee on Human Rights — later the Human Rights Committee — established in 1961 within the Italian Society for International Organisations (*Società italiana per l'organizzazione internazionale* — SIOI, a public law entity supervised by the Ministry of Foreign Affairs). The Committee was created on the basis of input from the Italian government, following a UN recommendation. The Committee is still active. Its status, however, is that of a group of experts (academics, diplomats, politicians), and in no way can it be regarded as a National Institution for Human Rights according to international standards. Later on, a National Human Rights Commission[21] and an Inter-Ministry Committee on Human Rights[22] were established as governmental bodies. The Commission, with the mandate of providing advice to the Prime Minister mainly on international relations issues has been convened only occasionally and has been *de facto* dismissed since 2001. The Committee, in its turn, is the "organ coordinating the government action in the field of promotion and protection of human rights". It coordinates, in particular, the drafting of the periodic reports to the human rights treaty bodies. A Committee of Ministers for Direction and Strategic Guidance in the Field of Human Rights was established in 2007, with the objective of coordinating at ministerial level the policies of the

---

20 Within the Senate of the Italian Parliament, during several legislatures has operated an Extraordinary Commission on Human Rights. Its outcome in law-making has been modest. During the XIV legislature (2001–2006) though, it conducted an extensive survey on international levels and mechanisms of human rights protection: materials and trascripts of the hearings are collected in: Commissione straordinaria diritti umani, *Il Senato e la tutela dei diritti umani. XIV Legislatura, Indagini conoscitive. Raccolta di atti e documenti* (Roma, May 2003); a complete documentation is also available online: <www.senato.it/commissioni/4530/3758/commelencoindagini.htm>, visited on 1 August 2008.

21 DPCM [Prime Minister Decree] 31 October 1984.

22 The Committee, established in 1978, is currently regulated by DPCM 11 May 2007 (<www.retepariopportunita.it/Rete_Pari_Opportunita/UserFiles/Normativa/Novita/Commissione_Pari_Opportunita.pdf>, visited on 1 August 2008).

Italian executive on human rights.[23] As explained below, any effort to establish a proper system of national institutions for human rights according to the Paris Principles has so far been unsuccessful.

A look at the celebrations that were organised every 10 December — and most solemnly every decade from 1958 on — to honour the UDHR shows that for the first 20 years, the interest was essentially attracted by the doctrinal aspect of the document, that is, by the concept of universal human rights, their precedents in the American and French Declarations, and the philosophical foundations of the human rights discourse. In the second phase, roughly between 1968 and 1978, the commemoration of the UDHR gave the opportunity to present the evolution of the international human rights law and machinery. In the newspapers, intellectuals, scholars and opinion leaders emphasised the link between the human rights norms and the development of the international organisation — namely the UN. It was in this period, however, and especially during the following decade, that columnists and opinion leaders begun to raise the issue of the effectiveness of human rights. To celebrate the UDHR meant indeed to become aware of how much and for how long human rights have been violated. The 10 of December appointment was no longer the gathering of a restricted circle of international law experts, diplomats and politicians, mainly interested in the developments of the human rights cause in the agenda of the international institutions. Increasingly, during the 1980s and especially the 1990s, the date of 10th of December attracted the interest of a large audience of human rights activists — members of Amnesty International (first settled in Italy in 1975), volunteers of development cooperation NGOs, affiliates of political parties and social movements — in particular pacifist and anti-war movements, including a significant component of non-violent, 'gandhian' groups and conscientious objectors to the military service.

There is no space to sketch a reconstruction of the role played by Italian social movements and civil society groups for the promotion of peace and human rights. The merging of the two issues — the claim for peace or disarmament and the claim for human rights or justice — marked the development of the civil society initiatives during the late 1980s and all along the following decade. The combination in a single strategic platform of the

---

[23] DPCM [Prime Minister Decree] 13 April 2007, <www.cortedicassazione.it/Notizie/Avvisi/Nazionale/SchedaAvvisi.asp?ID=584>, visited on 1 August 2008. On the Italian human rights institution framework, *see* A. PAPISCA, 'Infrastruttura nazionale per i diritti umani: l'Italia è in ritardo', 4:2 *Pace diritti umani / Peace human rights* (2007) pp. 7–18. More generally, on the Italian attitude, *see also* S. MARCHISIO and F. RASPADORI (eds), *L'Italia e i diritti umani* (CEDAM, Padova, 1995).

two dimensions of the progressive global social fronts that have characterised the second half of the 20th century, namely the 'peace' and the 'civil rights' movements, has become the hallmark and a distinctive feature of the Italian experience. From this perspective, Italy has followed and somehow anticipated the global mainstream that took place in the second half of the 1990s and beyond. The peace-through-law programme (conceptualised by Hans Kelsen and supported in Italy by thinkers like Norberto Bobbio) has merged with the peace-through-(non-violent) revolution approach of radical pacifism, and both have found a point of convergence in the UDHR, especially in the general clauses of Articles 28 and 29.

Two factors have greatly contributed to give the UDHR (and the human rights law and policy programmes it symbolises) a central role. On the one hand, the dramatic conflicts of the post-Cold War era (particularly the 1991 war in Iraq, the Balkans conflicts, including the 1999 NATO Kosovo campaign, the African wars, including the Rwanda genocide), conveyed the idea that neglect and patent violation of human rights is the direct cause of wars and that a 'positive' anti-war action cannot avoid tackling the legal dimensions of the individuals' and peoples' condition.[24] On the other hand, the human rights ideal and strategy received a decisive boost by the *magisterium* of Pope John-Paul II (1978–2005). Karol Wojtyla re-actualised the seminal documents of the Catholic Church of its 2nd Vatican Council (1962–1965), especially the *Gaudium et Spes* Pastoral Constitution,[25] promoting through his pastoral and political activity a consistent human rights approach. His very first Encyclical, *Redemptor Hominis*,[26] denounced vigorously the persistent gap between a verbal consensus on human rights standards and a reality of blatant violation of human dignity. The promotion and protection of the internationally recognised human rights is assumed as a

[24] The Norwegian social scientist Johan Galtung has profoundly influenced (also) the Italian peace research groups as well as the social action of many other actors. The human rights discourse has increasingly encountered his theories: *see*, for instance, *Human Rights in Another Key* (Polity Press, Cambridge, 1994, Italian translation: *I diritti umani in un'altra chiave*, Esperia, Milano, 1997).

[25] *Pastoral Constitution on the Church in the Modern World* "Gaudium et Spes", promulgated by His Holiness, Pope Paul VI, on 7 December 1965 (available online: <www.vatican.va/archive/hist_councils/ii_vatican_council/documents/vat-ii_cons_19651207_gaudium-et-spes_en.html>, last visited May 2008). Another more direct source of the Catholic Church position on human rights is the pope John XXIII Encyclical letter *Pacem in Terris* (<www.vatican.va/holy_father/john_xxiii/encyclicals/documents/hf_j-xxiii_enc_11041963_pacem_en.html>, visited on 1 August 2008), the first papal document to quote the UDHR.

[26] Iohannes Paulus II, *Redemptor Hominis*, 4 marzo 1979 (<www.vatican.va/edocs/ENG0218/_INDEX.HTM>, visited on 1 August 2008).

pastoral objective for the Catholic Church.[27] The impact of such a position among Italian Catholics could hardly be overestimated.

6. THREE EXAMPLES

The 40th anniversary of the UDHR represented a fresh start for the dissemination of the human rights charter in Italy. All the necessary elements for a mature assessment of its relevance were there: a general awareness of the new perspective that the UDHR has introduced in the theory and practice of international law and international relations; the consciousness of the need to fulfil its promises by opposing worldwide human rights violations, including war; an understanding of the multi-level (global, international, transnational, domestic, local) dimensions of human rights policies, requiring any country to set suitable monitoring devices to monitor its own performance.[28] It is indisputable that, since the end of the 1980s, Italy has enhanced, both in quantity and quality, human rights oriented initiatives and policies. Most importantly, the human rights awareness in the general public and the young people has progressed. This is, however, not to say that Italy has not experienced some serious drawback in its human rights engagements. In recent years Italy has not excelled internationally for its human rights performance. There is evidence to the fact that perhaps the opposite has occurred. Nonetheless, human rights of citizens, migrants, minority groups, including children, persons with disabilities, and gender issues — in brief, the full breadth of the current human rights discourse — have become a regular component of the national and local agendas, both of governmental and other public agencies and of NGOs and civil society organisations. Three experiences can illustrate this positive trend.

---

[27] Compare for instance the following sentence: "The first objective of the pastoral promotion of human rights is therefore to see that the acceptance of the 'letter' of universal rights also entails their practical application in 'spirit', everywhere and in the most effective way, starting with the truth about man and the equal dignity of every person, man or woman" (Address of the Holy Father Pope John Paul II to the Participants in the World Congress on the Pastoral Promotion of Human Rights, 4 July 1998, <www.vatican.va/holy_father/john_paul_ii/speeches/1998/july/documents/hf_jp-ii_spe_19980704_pastoral_en.html>, visited on 1 August 2008).

[28] A fortunate slogan, launched on the eve of the 1995 Perugia-Assisi Peace March and the first Assembly of Peoples' UN, read: "human rights from the neighbourhood to the UN" (diritti umani, dal quartiere all'Onu): it anticipated the current debate of several years on multi-level human rights protection.

The first one pertains to the development of human rights studies within the Italian educational and university system. The first human rights centre, fully integrated in an academic institution although open to extra-university cooperation, was established at the University of Padua in 1982.[29] Its founder Antonio Papisca, professor of international relations, designed the mission of the centre in fully consistence with the relevant recommendations issued by the UN, the UNESCO and the Council of Europe. The ties between international human rights and the academic institution were later acknowledged, in 1995, in Article 1 of the Statute of Padua University. The Padua Centre's activity has gradually expanded from the area of academic research and formation (among others, it set up in the academic year 1988-1989 a three-year post-graduate School on human rights, the first in Italy, and established in 1997, in partnership with other European universities and the European Commission, the European Master's degree in human rights and democratisation),[30] to the areas of human rights education,[31] collaboration with NGOs and civil society organisations,[32] and cooperation with domestic human rights structures.[33] The Centre of Padua University is a good example of how, around the 40th anniversary of the

---

[29] Interdepartmental Centre of Research and Services on Human Rights and the Rights of Peoples, <www.centrodirittiumani.unipd.it>. This was not the only research centre created in the same years on human rights issues. Worth mentioning is also the International Institute for Human Rights Studies (1986), based in Trieste (<www.istitutodirittiuomo.net>). A European Human Rights Justice Council, specifically addressed to law practitioners, was set in Rome in 1986 (Consulta per la Giustizia Europea dei Diritti dell'Uomo, <www.dirittiuomo.it/>). A special mention deserves the Forensic Union for the Protection of Human Rights (<unionedirittiumani.it>), established in 1968, on the 20th anniversary of the UDHR, with the mission of enhancing information, networking, and research on human rights, especially on legal and judicial issues, and advocating for their effective protection. It edits the journal *Diritti umani – Cronache e battaglie* (since 1990).

[30] It must be added that the University of Padua was among the first ones in Italy to establish regular courses on international human rights law, curricula on human rights (in the Faculty of Political Sciences), and degrees on human rights institutions and policies. In recent years many other Italian universities have started similar courses as well as some PhD programmes. The Padua Centre edits the journal *Pace Diritti Umani / Peace Human Rights* (since 1987).

[31] From its inception, the Centre started an intense programme of education and training for teachers, mainly at the level of the Padua's region, the Veneto, but more recently also in other parts of Italy.

[32] A deep relationship has been established with the Peace Table — on which, *see* below.

[33] Apart from a pioneer role in promoting the local and regional ombudsmanship since 1990, and in advocating (unsuccessfully so far) for the creation of national institutions for human rights, the Centre has run regular cooperation programmes with the ombudsperson and the children commissioner of the Veneto Region (both based in Venice) since 1995.

UDHR,[34] an interdisciplinary scientific interest has begun to spread into the Italian academia, thanks to the top-down and bottom-up input of international bodies, on the one hand, and individuals, schools,[35] NGOs and grassroots groups, on the other. The non-governmental sector was indeed keen to adopt a human rights-based political and cultural agenda.

The second example of the new course of the human rights discourse in Italy after the end of the Cold War era regards the progressive involvement of Italian local governments (regions, municipalities, and provincial administrations) in the politics of human rights. This refers not only to their formal policies in those traditional fields of welfare (social cohesion, health, environment, and so on) that relate to human rights protection, but also to some specific human rights oriented political initiatives, including incorporation of international law standards. The Region of Veneto passed in 1988 a law on the culture of peace, on the basis of which it has financed regional actions and projects of local associations aimed at promoting human rights awareness and protection from violations. Article 1 of that law mentioned, as source of inspiration for the statutory provisions, besides the Italian Constitution, also the international law of human rights. Many other Regional Councils followed the example set by the Venice assembly. The new basic laws of some Region, when setting the institution's goals, associate the national Constitution and the UDHR.[36] The 'peace and human rights' provision has been subsequently inserted in the norms of thousands of local government entities. Moreover, specialised 'human rights structures', which Italy has not yet established at the national level, have been created (with unfortunately the limitations deriving from operating within a normative and administrative system still highly centralised) at the level of Regions and Autonomous Provinces: 16 of them, out of 21, have a functioning

---

34 In 1988, the official national event celebrating the UDHR was held at the University of Padua. On that occasion were introduced both the presidential decree establishing the Post-graduate school on human rights and the draft regional law on the culture of peace.

35 Human rights education is not compulsory in the Italian school system. However, a large number of significant experiences have been developed in this field, mainly in connection with programmes of intercultural education. A survey on the teaching of human rights in the Italian university and school system was published in 1993 — Accademia Nazionale dei Lincei, *Inchiesta sull'insegnamento e l'informazione relativi ai diritti umani in Italia* (Roma, Presidenza del Consiglio dei Ministri, 1993); no up-to-date survey has been produced at national level, although the Ministry of Education and some of its regional delegations are actively promoting and monitoring the process.

36 This is spelt explicitly, for example, in the basic law (*statuto regionale*) of Umbria (Regional law 16 April 2005, No. 21): "The Region works … for the full realisation of the principles of the Constitution and of the UDHR".

ombudsperson, and five have a commissioner for children's rights. Since 1991, hundreds of Italian municipalities — including all the biggest cities — have established autonomously, on the basis of a national statute, local ombudspersons and more rarely a peace/human rights commission. The trend here described can be considered as evidence of a widespread appreciation, shared by a huge number of local and regional administrations, of the importance of human rights focused institutions. National laws only allow for specialised advisory bodies, at the various levels of public governance, on women's rights, immigration policies, children's rights, and so on, but generally little attention is paid to their fitting the international standards of a proper national human rights structure (for example, the 1990 Paris Standards). In this scenario, the regional ad local administrations in Italy are filling a gap — although only partially.

A final story that can illustrate the way the UDHR, and more generally the international law of human rights, has been received and 'used' in Italy in the past 10–20 years concerns the work of the Peace Table,[37] a coalition of hundreds of NGOs, non-profit organisations, social movements and local administrations.[38] The Table's establishment in 1996 was one of the major outcomes of the 1995 Peace March and the first UN Peoples' Assembly, celebrated in Perugia and Assisi in 1995, the 50th anniversary of the San Francisco Charter.[39] Since then, the Table, acting collectively or through its members, has been the most effective and coherent promoter of a human rights oriented political platform, addressing its proposals to the Italian government and the Parliament, as well as to the international institutions, including the EU. In recent years, the Table has been the major coordinating unit of the public events and political actions that institutions, schools, universities, civil society groups and NGOs organise on the eve of 10 December.

---

37 On the web: <www.tavoladellapace.it>, visited on 1 August 2008.

38 In particular, in the governing body of the Table is represented the 'Coalition of local governments for peace and human rights'. The Coalition was established in 1986 as "Coalition of local governments for peace" — the reference to human rights dates to 1991; formerly, it was known as the 'Association of denuclearized municipalities'. *See* the website: <www.entilocalipace.it>.

39 Remarkably, the idea of the UN Peoples' Assembly was suggested by the Padua human rights centre. To my knowledge, it was the 1995 Assembly that coined the slogan "another world is possible", which lately would become the logo (but the word does not suit ...) of the World Global Forum. The Perugia and Assisi Assemblies raised also their claim for a stronger and more democratic UN.

7. CONCLUSIONS

The UDHR has found in Italy a rather fertile ground, especially among the myriads of associations, groups and NGOs that compose the civil society landscape. The state agencies have not met the expectations of such a vibrant and creative movement. This is reflected in the generally low profile of the Italian government's representatives in the international human rights institutions (with some exception though: for instance, the leading role that the Italian government has taken within the UN in the anti-death penalty and pro-moratorium campaign). In the domestic sphere, the absence of any functioning national human rights structure at the state level, modelled on the standards recommended by the international organisations, reflects the tepid interest of the Executive and the Parliament in implementing far-reaching human rights based reforms inspired to the UDHR. The adaptation of the domestic legal order to the ratified international human rights instruments — apart from the problem of the status of international law norms in the hierarchy of legal sources — is quite frequently slow, fragmentary, or inaccurate.[40] The normative puzzle can explain the similarly puzzling case law of Italian courts, where some very innovative attitudes towards the inclusion of international values in the domestic system stand side by side with other approaches, far more conservative and conformist.

The civil society organisations, with the support of a significant segment of the academic world, the school, many local governments and administrations, and — but only in recent years and selectively — the media, have been the most effective actors in the challenging process of making human rights work.

40 An astonishing example is the lack of a law on the crime of torture and inhuman treatment, after more than two decades from the ratification and the entry into force of the UN convention.

17. PORTUGAL: HUMAN RIGHTS GUIDELINES FROM THE CONSTITUTION TO SUGAR BAGS

Tereza Pizarro Beleza
Helena Pereira de Melo

1. INTRODUCTION

Portugal was admitted to the United Nations (hereinafter UN) in December 1955. The Portuguese State first applied in 1946, but membership was refused since it did not promote the right of all peoples to self-determination in its African colonies. After becoming a member of the UN and until 1974 (when the dictatorship ended), Portugal always argued it was acting in accordance with the principles proclaimed in the Charter of the United Nations, since it viewed the African territories under Portuguese administration as a part of the Portuguese Nation that was considered to be a unitary state. Several resolutions were adopted by the UN's General Assembly in order to make the Portuguese State respect the right of all peoples to freely determine their political status. In 1961, an armed struggle for independence began in the Portuguese Colonies, and the Portuguese Government was several times called upon by the General Assembly to respect the right to self-determination.

Although Portugal as a member of the UN had the obligation to promote and publicize the text of the Universal Declaration of Human Rights (hereinafter UDHR), this only really happened after 25 April 1974, when Portugal was liberated from dictatorship by a revolution that started as a *coup d'état* staged by discontent military officers who had fought in the long colonial wars. Before that, the Portuguese Government disliked the ideas both of a 'universal declaration' (since it defended the principle of political nationalism), and that the State could not engage in any activity that aimed at the destruction of any of the rights set forth in the Declaration.[1] Nevertheless, many lawyers, amongst whom it is possible to find some professors who fought against the dictatorship, invoked the UDHR as a way of rebelling

---

1 J. MIRANDA, 'A Declaração Universal e os Pactos Internacionais de Direitos do Homem', *Escritos Vários sobre Direitos Fundamentais* (Principia Editora, Estoril, 2006) p. 112.

against the existing political oppression and the acts violating the human rights in the country, and as a way for promoting the full realisation of these rights in the national legal order.[2]

Only on 9 March 1978 was the text of the Declaration published in the official journal of the Portuguese Republic in its Portuguese version. But already before that, the new Constitution of the Portuguese Republic (hereinafter CPR), approved by the Constituent Assembly on 2 April 1976, explicitly referred to the UDHR in Article 16 ("Fundamental Rights: Scope and Interpretation"). The new Constitution represented — as stated in its Preamble — "a revolutionary change and an historic new beginning in Portuguese society".

2. THE UDHR PROVISION IN THE CONSTITUTION

Article 16 is inserted in the first section ("General Principles") of Part I ("Fundamental Rights and Duties") of the Constitution. It establishes that:

> "1. The fundamental rights contained in this constitution shall not exclude any other fundamental rights provided for in the laws or resulting from applicable rules of international law.
>
> 2. The provisions of this Constitution and of laws relating to fundamental rights shall be constructed and interpreted in harmony with the Universal Declaration of Human Rights."

When one considers the UDHR, two main principles are stated here: the principle that the human rights and fundamental freedoms recognized by the Portuguese Constitution should not exclude other rights proclaimed by the UDHR, and the principle of the interpretation of the provisions of the Constitution and of law in accordance with the provisions of the UDHR.

Since all rights and freedoms proclaimed in the UDHR are also recognised in the Constitution of the Portuguese Republic, the first principle has no relevant application as concerns the UDHR. The correspondence between the two texts can be represented as follows:

---

2 *See*, for instance, F.M. PEREIRA COELHO, *Curso de Direito da Família*, vol. I, t. 2, 2nd ed. (Cooperativa Académica de Consumo, Coimbra, 1973) pp. 10–11; B. DE MAGALHÃES, *Os Direitos Fundamentais do Homem sob o Ponto de Vista Internacional* (Seara Nova, Lisboa, 1951); F. DE SÁ CARNEIRO et al., *Os Direitos do Homem em Portugal* (Telos, Porto, 1974); S. CARDIA, *Os Direitos do Homem* (Lisboa, 1968); F. DE ABRANCHES-FERRÃO and F. SALGADO ZENHA, *O Direito de Defesa e a Defesa do Direito* (Ordem dos Advogados, Lisboa, 1971).

Box I
(Articles 1 to 20 of the UDHR)

Content	UDHR	CPR
Dignity of the human person	Art. 1	Art. 1
Principle of universality	Art. 2	Art. 12
Principle of equality	Art. 2 and 7	Art. 13
Right to life	Art. 3	Art. 24
Right to liberty	Art. 3	Art. 27
Right to security	Art. 3	Art. 27
Right not to be held in slavery or servitude	Art. 3	Art. 27t[3]
Right to personal integrity	Art. 5	Art. 25
Right to civil capacity	Art. 6	Art. 26(1)
Right to equal protection of the law	Art. 7	Art. 26(1)
Right to an effective remedy by the competent national tribunals	Art. 8	Art. 20
Right not to be subjected to arbitrary arrest, detention or exile	Art. 9	Art. 27(2)
Right to a fair and public hearing	Art. 10	Art. 20(4)

3 *See*, as well, Article 7 of the Rome Statute of the International Criminal Court, adopted on 17 July 1998. It was ratified by Portuguese Parliament's Resolution No. 3/2002, of 18 January. Portugal is also a State Party to the Geneva Convention on Slavery, of 25 September 1926, and to the Supplementary Convention on the Abolition of Slavery, the Slave Trade, and Institutions and Practices Similar to Slavery, adopted by a conference of plenipotentiaries convened by the Economic and Social Council Resolution 608(XXI) of 30 April 1956 and done at Geneva on 7 September 1956. Portugal has also signed and ratified the International Covenant on Civil and Political Rights, by Law No. 29/78, of 12 June.

Right to be presumed innocent until proved guilty	Art. 11(1)	Art. 32(2)
Right not to be held guilty of any penal offence on account of any act or omission which did not constitute a penal offence	Art. 11(2)	Art. 29(1)
Right to protection of privacy, good name and reputation	Art. 12	Art. 26(1)
Right to freedom of movement and residence	Art. 13(1)	Art. 44(1)
Right to leave any country and to return to each one's country	Art. 13(2)	Art. 44(2)
Right to seek asylum	Art. 14	Art. 33(7)
Right to a nationality	Art. 15	Art. 15[4]
Right to marry and to found a family	Art. 16	Art. 36
Right to private property	Art. 17	Art. 62
Right to freedom of thought, conscience and religion	Art. 18	Art. 41
Right to freedom of opinion and expression	Art. 19	Art. 37
Right to assemble peacefully	Art. 20	Art. 45
Freedom of association	Art. 20	Art. 46

[4] This article states in §1 that "aliens and stateless persons temporarily or habitually resident in Portugal shall enjoy the same rights and be subject to the same duties as Portuguese citizens". This paragraph does not apply, according to §2 of the same article to "political rights, to the performance of public functions that are not predominantly technical or to rights and duties that, under this Constitution or the law, are restricted to Portuguese citizens". The attribution, acquisition and loss of Portuguese nationality is ruled by Decree-Law No. 237–A/2006, of 14 December.

Box II
(Articles 21 to 27 of the UDHR)

Content	UDHR	CPR
Right to take part in the government of the country	Art. 21(1)	Art. 48
Right of equal access to public service	Art. 21(2)	Art. 50
Right to vote	Art. 21(3)	Art. 49
Right to social security	Art. 22	Art. 63(1)
Right to work	Art. 23(1)	Art. 58(1)
Right to free choice of employment	Art. 23(1)	Art. 58(2)
Right to just and favourable conditions of work	Art. 23(1)	Art. 59
Right to protection against unemployment	Art. 23(1)	Art. 53
Right to equal pay for equal work	Art. 23(2)	Art. 59(1)
Right to just remuneration	Art. 23(3)	Art. 59(1)
Right to form and join trade unions	Art. 23(4)	Art. 55
Right to rest and leisure	Art. 24	Art. 59(1)
Right to an adequate standard of living	Art. 25(1)	Art. 9, 59, 63, 64 65 and 81[5]

[5] One of the basic responsibilities of the Portuguese State is, according to Article 9, "to promote the welfare and quality of life of the people". Article 59 recognises to all workers, the right to remuneration for their work "so as to guarantee to them an appropriate livelihood". Article 63 determines that the social security system organised by the State "provides protection for citizens in sickness or old age or when disabled, widowed, orphaned or unemployed, and in

Motherhood's right to special care and assistance	Art. 25(2)	Art. 68
Childhood's right to special care and assistance	Art. 25(2)	Art. 69
Children's right to same social protection whether born in or out of wedlock	Art. 25(2)	Art. 36(4)
Right to education	Art. 26(1)	Art. 74(1)
Parents' right to choose the kind of education given to their children	Art. 26(3)	Art. 77(2)[6]
Right to participate in the cultural life of the community	Art. 27(1)	Art. 78
Right to share in scientific advancement and its benefits	Art. 27(1)	Art. 73(4)[7]
Right to the protection of interests resulting from scientific, literary or artistic production	Art. 27(2)	Art. 42(2)

all other situations in which the means of subsistence or the capacity to work have been lost or impaired". Article 64 states that "everyone has the right to have his or her health safeguarded" and that this right shall be met by the creation of "a national health service available to all and free of charge to the extent that the economic and social conditions of citizens require". Article 65 states that "everyone has the right, both personally and for his or her family, to a dwelling of adequate size that meets satisfactory standards of hygiene and preserves personal and family privacy". Article 81 determines that one of the primary duties of the State is "to promote an increase in the social and economic well-being and quality of life of the people, in particular of those most underprivileged, in the context of a strategy of sustainable development".

[6] According to this paragraph "the law shall regulate the manner of participation of associations of teachers, students and parents and of the scientific community and institutions in the determination of the policy for education". Law No. 45/78, of 11 July, ratified the International Covenant on Economic, Social and Cultural Rights (hereinafter ICESCR), that is an integral part of Portuguese law, and recognizes the liberty of parents and legal guardians to choose for their children schools, other than those established by the public authorities.

[7] According to this paragraph, the Portuguese State shall encourage and support scientific creativity, research and technological innovation. The right of everyone to enjoy the benefits of scientific progress and of its applications is also recognised in Article 15(1) of the ICESCR.

As concerns the second principle, it is worth noting that several professors of public law wrote about the principle of the interpretation of the rules relating to the fundamental rights in accordance with the UDHR. For instance, Jorge Miranda, who teaches public law at the Faculty of Law of the University of Lisbon, considered that this principle has three main functions: "To enlarge and clarify the content of the constitutional rules on fundamental rights, to strengthen their protection and to open a universalistic perspective larger than the closed and narrow horizons" that may appear at a national level. As a consequence, the fundamental rights recognised by the CPR "are not created but only declared by the State, finding their roots in man's and a people's juridical conscience".[8] The importance of the UDHR in the interpretation of the CPR is also referred to by other professors of public law in Lisbon and in Coimbra, such as Joaquim Gomes Canotilho, Jorge Bacelar Gouveia and Vital Moreira. They all consider that the interpretation of the constitutional rules in accordance with the UDHR is a very useful tool, especially when the rule has several possible meanings or when it appeals to concepts that are vague and indeterminate.[9]

3. THE UDHR IN THE PRAXIS OF THE CONSTITUTIONAL COURT

This principle has also been reaffirmed by the jurisprudence of the Portuguese Constitutional Court. In several of its decisions, the Court has considered that the UDHR is of the greatest importance for the full respect of fundamental rights and freedoms in Portugal. For instance, in *Acórdão no.*

8 *Vid.* J. MIRANDA, 'A Declaração Universal dos Direitos do Homem e a Constituição', in *Estudos sobre a Constituição*, vol. 2 (Livraria Petrony, Lisboa, 1977) pp. 53 and 58; J. MIRANDA, 'A Declaração Universal e a Constituição Portuguesa', in *Repensar a Cidadania, Nos 50 Anos da Declaração Universal dos Direitos Humanos* (Editorial Notícias, Lisboa, 1998) p. 193; J. MIRANDA, 'A Declaração Universal e a Constituição Portuguesa', *Finisterra, Revista de Reflexão e Crítica*, No. 30 (1999) p. 88; and J. MIRANDA, 'Artigo 16', in J. MIRANDA (ed.), *Constituição Portuguesa Anotada*, vol. I (Coimbra Editora, Coinbra, 2005) pp. 137–142. A similar position is defended by P. OTERO, 'Declaração Universal dos Direitos do Homem e a Constituição: a Inconstitucionalidade de Normas Constitucionais?', *O Direito* (July–December 1990) pp. 605–608.

9 J.J. GOMES CANOTILHO and V. MOREIRA, *Constituição da República Anotada*, vol. I, 4th ed. (Coimbra Editora, Coimbra, 2007) p. 367, and J. BACELAR GOUVEIA, 'A Declaração Universal dos Direitos do Homem e a Constituição Portuguesa', *Estudos de Direito Público*, vol. I (Principia, Cascais, 2000) pp. 72–73.

6/84, of 18 January 1984.[10] Before the CPR clearly proclaimed the right to the full development of one's personality (which only happened with its fourth amendment in 1997), the Court stated that the constitutional text already recognised it. The argument used was, mainly, that the UDHR referred to "the full development of personality" in §2 of Article 26, and that everyone was entitled, as a member of society, to the realisation "of the economic, social and cultural rights indispensable for his dignity and the free development of his personality".[11]

The Constitutional Court has referred to the UDHR in other decisions. For instance, in *Acórdão no. 522/00*, of 29 November 2000[12] the Court considered that the principle of counter-pleading recognised by Article 34 of the Convention on Jurisdiction and the Enforcement of Judgments in Civil and Commercial Matters of September 1968, had constitutional dignity directly through Articles 2 ("Democratic state based on the rule of law") and 20 ("Access to law and effective judicial protection") of the Portuguese Constitution, or indirectly through Article 16. It reached the conclusion that the principle of pleading and counter-pleading was directly recognised in the constitutional text.

Even if Article 16 of the CPR did not exist, the UDHR would be an integral part of Portuguese law according to Article 8 ("International Law") of the Constitution. According to §1 of the provision, "the rules and principles of general or customary international law are an integral part of Portuguese law", and under §3 of the same article "rules made by the competent organs of international organisations to which Portugal belongs apply directly in national law to the extent that the constitutive treaty so provides". Since the rules of the UDHR can be considered as rules of *ius cogens*[13] and the Declaration was adopted by a resolution of United Nations' General Assembly, its contents would apply in national law as a result of the referred paragraphs.

---

10 This decision was published in Tribunal Constitucional, *Acórdãos do Tribunal Constitucional*, vol. 2 (1984) (Tribunal Constitucional, Lisboa, 1986) pp. 259–261.

11 Article 22 of the UDHR.

12 This decision was published in Tribunal Constitucional, *Acórdãos do Tribunal Constitucional*, vol. 48 (2000) (Coimbra Editora, Coimbra, 2002) pp. 535–540.

13 MIRANDA (1999), *supra* note 8, p. 87.

4. CONCLUSIONS

Several books were published when the UDHR turned fifty years,[14] and almost every year, a new article on the Declaration appears in Portuguese law reviews.[15] A special Commission was set up for the anniversary commemorations, and its work spawned all sorts of events and publications for a few years.

A recent popular version of the public presence of the UDHR in Portuguese society can be seen in the little sugar bags of the kind that are provided with cups of coffee or tea in cafeterias or tea rooms all over the country. A commercial brand started recently to issue a series of bags with the articles of the Universal Declaration printed on the packaging. It is mentioned on the bags that the project is based on a protocol that was signed with an NGO (Humana Global). One can say that, at a symbolic level, such *advertising* is a sure sign that the UDHR has come of age in this country.

The UDHR has in many ways been essential in Portugal for the last sixty years. First it was important to keep faith in human rights in the face of adversity, when they were often seriously disrespected by the existing dictatorship. When political democracy was finally restored, it was important to reaffirm that faith in order to build a society founded on freedom and justice, where the fundamental rights and the dignity of the human person would be respected, as it is proclaimed both in the UDHR and in the Constitution of the Portuguese Republic.

---

14 For instance *Finisterra, Revista de Reflexão Crítica*, a Portuguese journal, published in 1999 a special number (No. 30) on the UDHR. A book – *Repensar a Cidadania, Nos 50 Anos da Declaração Universal dos Direitos Humanos* – with articles by several authors, was published in Lisbon, by Editorial Notícias, in 1998. Another book was published in the same year, edited by José Menéres Pimentel, *A Provedoria de Justiça na Salvaguarda dos Direitos do Homem* , Lisboa, Edição da Comissão Nacional para as Comemorações do 50º Aniversário da Declaração Universal dos Direitos do Homem. Two editions of the UDHR were published in 1998: Comissão Nacional para as Comemorações do 50º Aniversàrio, *Declaração Universal dos Direitos do Homem: 50 Anos*, Lisboa: Assembleia da República, and Comissão Nacional para as Comemorações do 50º Aniversàrio, *Declaração Universal dos Direitos do Homem*, Lisboa: Imprensa Nacional – Casa da Moeda.

15 For instance, J. BACELAR GOUVEIA, 'A Declaração Universal dos Direitos do Homem e a Constituição da República Portuguesa', *Perspectivas de Direito*, Macau (1999) pp. 23–60, and P. OTERO, 'Declaração Universal dos Direitos do Homem e Constituição: a Inconstitucionalidade de Normas Constitucionais?', *O Direito*, 122, No. 3–4 (1990) pp. 603–619.

18. ROMANIA: SIDELINED TO THE MARGINS OF LEGAL PLURALISM

Iulia Voina-Motoc[1]

1. INTRODUCTION

Legal pluralism was actually born in Romania through the work of Ehrlich, who discovered that in Bukovina, the official law was not applied. Instead the law enforced was customary.[2] The account by Ehrlich is a very complicated theoretical legal construction which caused not only a sophisticated legal dispute with Kelsen,[3] but can also be found in most studies of legal theories concerning international law.

It is submitted here that the Communist law is (or was) one of the best examples in this regard, especially in the years after the signature of the Helsinki Final Act. The publications from that period show us that the Polish dissident movement was constantly related to law. Suddenly, there was a consensus that revolved around legal values. Prior to that, in the beginning of the 1970s, during the heyday of the Leftist movements, everything was politics; law itself was a form of war. Once the social movements in Eastern Europe started to grow, the population began slowly to understand that the reference to law had to coexist with all forms of democracy.

This type of speech had relatively little space in the Romanian dissident movement, although one must recall the contribution of Monica Lovinescu in her broadcasts from Radio Free Europe, a radio station banned in the Communist world. Monica Lovinescu was the one who tried to inform and pass on comments to the Romanian public about dissident movements in

---

1 Some of these ideas were presented in I. VOINA-MOTOC, 'European Tradition and European Society of International Law: Some Remarks about the Totalitarian Legacy', *Baltic Yearbook of International Law* (2006) pp. 85–109.

2 E. EHRLICH, *Fundamental Principles of the Sociology of Law* (Harvard University Press, Cambridge, 1934).

3 H. KELSEN, 'Eine Grundlegung der Rechtssoziologie', in H. KELSEN and E. EHRLICH, *Rechtssoziologie und Rechtswissenschaft: Eine Kontroverse (1915/1917)* (Nomos Verlagsgesellschaft, Baden-Baden, 2003) pp. 3–54.

other countries in her literary radio programmes.[4] Taking into account that the dissidents of these Central European movements placed human rights in the centre of their discourse, the Universal Declaration of Human Rights (UDHR) became known in Romania.

In this sense, as Vladimir Tismaneanu pointed out, Monica Lovinescu was the first political scientist of Romania, but she was at the same time a person who gave us a good human rights education.[5] In the same vein, H.R. Patapievici made a parallel with another important Romanian intellectual and victim of the Communist regime, Nicolae Steinhardt, who was a constitutional lawyer by training.[6] He spoke extensively about human rights during the years of the Communist regime and remained keen about his fundamental freedoms despite his religious beliefs.

The years that followed were devoted to — following the terminology of Althusser — the interpellation of force in the name of law; the Left enthusiastically adopted this practice, as well. Thus, the Soviet intervention in Afghanistan was denounced in the name of the rights of peoples; in other times, we would have probably assisted the Soviet Union with a harsh critique of imperialism followed by references to a philosophy of history that promoted the perspective of a Socialist future. At the same time, the interpellation of force in the name of law moved to the reports presented by smaller groups, such as Amnesty International or Medicines sans Frontiers.[7]

After the fall of Communism, the attention paid to the UDHR faced the same fate in Romania as in some other Eastern European countries: it did not last. The UN was forgotten very quickly in favour of the Council of Europe, the European Union and the NATO. The international human rights regime was abandoned for the regional human rights one.

---

4 Why does Monica Lovinescu matter? by Vladimir Tismaneanu, 30 April 2008, <www.romanianewswatch.com/2008/04/why-does-monica-lovinescu-matter.html>, visited on 18 November 2008.

5 *Ibid.*

6 H.R. PATAPIEVICI, 'Despre Monica Lovinescu, cu dragoste si recunstinta', *Evenimentul zilei*, 24 April 2008, p. 6.

7 A. RENAUT and L. SOSOE, *Philosophie du droit* (Harvard University Press, Cambridge, 1936) p. 27.

2. DOMESTIC IMPLICATIONS

An important human rights provision was included in the Romanian Constitution, comparable with some other constitutions, when it was adopted in 1991. According to Article 20 of the Constitution:

> "Constitutional provisions concerning the citizens' rights and liberties shall be interpreted and enforced in conformity with the Universal Declaration of Human Rights, with the covenants and other treaties Romania is a party to.
>
> Where any inconsistencies exist between the covenants and treaties on the fundamental human rights Romania is a party to, and the national laws, the international regulations shall take precedence, unless the Constitution or national laws comprise more favourable provisions."

This is indeed a very important provision of the Romanian Constitution. It gives priority to the human rights and mentions the UDHR in its first sub-section as a guiding principle. Unfortunately the UDHR remained more in the letter of the Constitution once Romania had joined the Council of Europe, and it did not become a part of the provisions used in legislation or practice.

The application of the constitutional provision was promoted by the Romanian Institute for Human Rights (IRDO), which is an independent national institution, "invested under its constitutive law with powers of research, training, dissemination of information and consultancy. The law also guarantees independence and equidistance, in conformity with the criteria established for this type of institutions by the United Nations and the Council of Europe, which recommend that all democratic countries should establish such institutions".[8]

After the creation of the Institute in 1990, the United Nations Center for Human Rights in Geneva and the Romanian Government signed an agreement on the implementation of a Technical Assistance Programme for several years. On the conclusion of the Programme, in the final evaluation, it was appreciated as "the first comprehensive country programme of advisory services and technical assistance in the field of human rights" that had been conducted by the Human Rights Center. The efforts of the Institute were seen in terms of training and dissemination, but not in concrete terms. For

8 <www.irdo.ro/index.php?txt_id=DespreNoi&lang=en>, visited on 18 November 2008.

instance, it was found that the UDHR had not been quoted in any of the important judgments of Romanian courts.[9]

With regard to human rights, it is mainly the decisions of the Constitutional Court that have dealt with human rights, and in that context, reference has been made to the European Convention on Human Rights (ECHR), but almost never to the UDHR. There are very few cases where the UDHR is quoted by Romanian courts. One of them is a decision regarding the right to property stipulated in Article 17 of the UDHR, connecting this article of the UDHR to the other relevant articles of the Romanian Constitution. The Court just mentioned the right to property without further references to the UDHR.[10]

The relationship between the rule of law and human rights was stated in a very clear manner in a decision adopted in 2005. In the decision, the Constitutional Court stated that Romania was a state governed by the rule of law in which human dignity represents the main value.[11] This conclusion is certainly relevant from the point of view of Article 1 of the UDHR.

Many of the decisions of the Constitutional Court made reference to human rights, and the ECHR has been quoted quite often during the recent years, but already in the first years of its activities, the Court had many opportunities to take into account the fundamental human rights. In a decision adopted in 1994, the Constitutional Court concluded that a tax for passing the frontier with a view to constitute some resources that could be credited towards social protection was unconstitutional because it was a restriction of the freedom of movement provided by Article 25 of the Constitution and because its restriction was not justified in relation to Article 49 of the Constitution.[12]

One of the most important decisions was adopted by the Constitutional Court in 1996 concerning the constitutionality of the law concerning the political parties. The Court stated that the "public mission" as expressed by the law concerning the political parties was not the same as the mission of the state; on the contrary, as far as the parties were concerned, the public mission reflected a pluralist mission. At the same time, the Constitutional Court stated that political parties could not propose the revision of the Constitution. By the same decision the Court stated that the freedom of expression of the parties had to be corroborated by Article 11 of the ECHR and the restrictions

---

9 *Ibid.*

10 Official Gazette of Romania No. 1027/18 November 2005.

11 Official Gazette of Romania No. 664 of 26 July 2005.

12 Decision No. 337/2004, in Official Gazette No. 11–12/2004, p. 91.

have to be justified. Also, in respecting the principle of pluralism, the Court, while referring to members of national minorities, concluded that the political parties could be constituted by citizens with the same nationality. In essence, this meant that so-called minority parties could not be prohibited.[13]

3. CONCLUSIONS

It seems that the history of the UDHR experienced the strange history of what Ehrlich described by his reference to the development from the denial of pluralism with contradictory sources to a plurality of sources: it marginalised the UDHR in favour of regional instruments.

[13] Decision No. 437/2006, in Official Gazette 15–16/2006.

19. SPAIN: FROM TOTALITARIANISM TO FULFILMENT

Felipe Gómez Isa
Carmen Márquez Carrasco[1]

1. INTRODUCTION

The absence of a true culture of human rights has been one of the defining features of Spanish constitutional history.[2] Only during the Second Republic (1931–1936), and, especially, during the democratic transition after General Franco's dictatorship (1939–1975), human rights became one of the central pillars of the attempts to democratise the State and society.

The aim of this chapter is to shed some light on the very limited impact of the adoption of the Universal Declaration of Human Rights (UDHR) in a country that was suffering from a harsh dictatorship and was not a member of the United Nations (UN) in 1948, that is, at the time of the adoption of the UDHR by the UN General Assembly. Additionally, we will carefully examine the process of incorporation of the UDHR into the text of the Spanish Constitution of 1978, and some relevant jurisprudential references to the UDHR by the Spanish Constitutional Court.

2. HUMAN RIGHTS UNDER THE SECOND REPUBLIC (1931–1936)

The adoption of the republican Constitution on 9 December 1931, under the clear influence of the Mexican (1917) and the Weimar (1919) constitutions, opened the door for a strong recognition of human rights in our political

1 A long and fruitful conversation with Professor Juan Antonio Carrillo Salcedo (University of Seville) was very helpful for the development of this paper.

2 J.A. MARTÍN PALLÍN, 'Treinta años de lucha', in Asociación Pro Derechos Humanos de España (eds), *Treinta años de derechos humanos en España* (Icaria, Barcelona, 2008) p. 11.

system.[3] Both civil and political rights,[4] and, above all, economic, social and cultural rights[5] were proclaimed, and it was the first time in history that Spanish women had access to the right to vote.[6] As far as public international law is concerned, the Constitution of 1931 was very progressive, since it stipulated in Article 7 that "[t]he Spanish State shall observe universal norms of International Law, incorporating them into its legal order".

Unfortunately, due to great political and social turmoil in the early 1930s and an increasing radicalisation of political forces, the system of fundamental rights established in the Constitution could not develop and consolidate. After the elections of February 1936, in which the so-called *Popular Front* (a coalition of left wing parties) won, the political atmosphere became more and more difficult, thus paving the way for the *coup d'état* by General Franco on 18 July 1936 and the coming of the Spanish Civil War (1936–1939).[7] After a tragic civil war with thousands of victims, including many civilians,[8] in April 1939 General Franco established a dictatorial regime that lasted for almost 40 years during which human rights, in particular civil and political rights, were absolutely absent, as most of the literature has adequately shown.[9]

3. FRANCOISM AFTER THE SECOND WORLD WAR

Due to the Franco regime's political support and the substantial aid to Hitler's Nazi Germany and Mussolini's Fascist Italy during the Second World War,

---

3 A global overview of the Second Republic can be found in J. HERNÁNDEZ ALIQUES and J. TUSELL GÓMEZ, *La Segunda República: de la Segunda República a la Guerra Civil* (Espasa-Calpe, Madrid, 1997).

4 *See* Articles 25–42 of the Constitution, Chapter I ("Individual and political guarantees") under Title III ("Rights and duties of Spaniards").

5 *See* Articles 43–50, Chapter II ("Family, economy, and culture"), under the same Title III.

6 *See* Article 36 of the Constitution.

7 P. PRESTON, *The Coming of the Spanish Civil War: Reform, Reaction and Revolution in the Second Republic* (Routledge, London, 1994).

8 S. JULIÁ (coord.), *Víctimas de la Guerra Civil* (Temas de Hoy, Madrid, 1999).

9 M. RICHARDS, *A Time of Silence: Civil War and the Culture of Repression in Franco's Spain, 1936–1945* (Cambridge University Press, Cambridge, 1996), S. PAYNE, *The Franco Regime, 1936-1975* (University of Wisconsin Press, Madison, 1987), M. GALLO, *Histoire de l'Espagne Franquiste* (Laffon, Paris, 1969). On the legal framework that allowed Francoist Repression of civil liberties, *see also* M. CARRILLO, 'El marco legal de la represión en la Dictadura franquista durante el periodo 1939–1959', in F. GÓMEZ ISA (dir.), *El derecho a la memoria* (Institute of Human Rights-Alberdania, Zarautz, 2006) pp. 501–527.

the victorious powers initially expressed a hostile attitude towards it.[10] The political situation in Spain was discussed at the San Francisco Conference (March–June 1945) when drafting the Charter of the United Nations.[11] In the end, the Conference adopted an interpretative resolution according to which paragraph 2 of Article 4 of the UN Charter[12] "cannot apply to States whose regimes have been installed with the help of armed forces of countries which have fought against the United Nations so long as these regimes are in power".[13] During the debate on this resolution, the Mexican delegate, Mr. Quintanilla, made an explicit reference to Spain, stating that "the thousands of heroes that have fought and died in Spain for the cause of democracy were actually the first combatants for the United Nations".[14] It is obvious that this official position by Mexico, followed by some other countries, posed a significant obstacle to the future entry of Francoist Spain into the UN.[15] In the same vein, at the Potsdam Conference (17 July–2 August 1945) the Governments of the United Kingdom, the United States of America and the Soviet Union stated that they would not support a request for admission to the UN from the Spanish Government because it was "founded with the support of the Axis powers". In light of "its origins, its nature, its record and its close association with the aggressor States", they considered that Spain "does not possess the necessary qualifications to justify its admission".

Once the UN started its activities, the so-called *Spanish question* was always on its agenda. During its very first session, on 9 February 1946, the General Assembly (GA) discussed the attitude to be taken, and adopted a resolution in which it endorsed both the interpretative resolution of the San Francisco Conference and the Final Declaration of the Potsdam Conference, mentioned above, and recommended the Members of the UN to "act in accordance with the letter and spirit of these statements in the conduct of

---

10 D.J. DUNTHORN, *Britain and the Spanish Anti-Franco Opposition, 1940–1950* (Palgrave, London, 2000) p. 73.

11 An excellent overview of the difficult relations between Spain and the UN during this crucial period can be found in R. SANDERS, *Spain and the United Nations, 1945–1950* (Vantage Press, New York, 1966).

12 Article 4(2) of the UN Charter reads as follows: "[t]he admission of any such state to membership in the United Nations will be effected by a decision of the General Assembly upon the recommendation of the Security Council".

13 UN Doc. UNCIO, I/10.

14 UN Doc. UNCIO, T. I, pp. 615–616.

15 J.F. GONZÁLEZ CAMPOS, 'La admisión de España como miembro de la ONU: unas páginas de historia', in ANUE (ed.) *España y la ONU: 50 Aniversario* (Icaria, Barcelona, 2005) p. 27.

their future relations with Spain".[16] Some States, including France and the countries of the Soviet bloc, exerted firm pressure to adopt stronger measures against Franco's Government.[17] Against this background, Poland, using the prerogative established in Article 35 of the UN Charter, brought the Spanish question to the attention of the Security Council. As we can imagine, it was a very delicate issue, since some countries advocated not only diplomatic and economic sanctions, but also some kind of military measures.[18] In the end, the Security Council, after expressing a "unanimous moral condemnation of the Franco regime", decided "to make further studies in order to determine whether the situation in Spain has led to international friction and does endanger international peace and security". To this end, the Security Council appointed a "subcommittee of five of its members … to conduct such inquiries as it may deem necessary, and to report to the Security Council".[19] The subcommittee worked intensively between 29 April and 31 May 1946, and sent its report[20] to the Security Council. The Council declared that the report "fully confirmed the facts which led to the condemnation of the Franco regime", but did not take further action. On this matter, the Security Council expressed its intention "to keep the situation in Spain under continuous observation and maintain it upon the list of matters of which it is seized".[21] Taking into consideration that the Franco regime was totally

---

16 UN Doc. Resolution 32(I), 9 February 1946, Relations of Members of the United Nations with Spain, para. 3.

17 J.L. NEILA HERNÁNDEZ, 'The Foreign Policy Administration of Franco's Spain: From Isolation to International Realignment (1945–1957)', in C. LEITZ and D.J. DUNTHORN (eds), *Spain in an International Context, 1936–1959* (Berghahn Books, New York, 1999) pp. 279 *et seq.*

18 *See* the different positions expressed within the discussions of the Security Council in F. PORTERO, *Franco aislado: La cuestión española (1945–1950)* (Aguilar, Madrid, 1989) pp. 157 *et seq.*

19 UN Doc. Resolution 4 (1946), 29 April 1946, The Spanish Question. It is interesting to observe that this resolution was adopted by 10 votes to none, with the abstention of the Soviet Union which claimed for stronger sanctions against Franco's Spain motivated by the pressure coming from anti-Franco communist opposition. *See* in this respect G. SWAIN, 'Stalin and Spain, 1944–1948', in LEITZ and DUNTHORN, *supra* note 17, pp. 237 *et seq.*

20 UN Docs. S/75 and S/76. The subcommittee found unanimously that: "a) in origin, nature, structure and general conduct, the Franco regime is a fascist regime patterned on, and established largely as a result of aid received from Hitler's Nazi Germany and Mussolini's Fascist Italy; b) during the long struggle of the United Nations against Hitler and Mussolini, Franco, despite continued Allied protests, gave very substantial aid to the enemy powers … ; c) Incontrovertible documentary evidence establishes that Franco was a guilty party with Hitler and Mussolini in the conspiracy to wage war against those countries which eventually in the course of the world war became banded together as the United Nations".

21 UN Doc. Resolution 7 (1946), 26 June 1946.

immune to international criticism, the General Assembly passed a much harsher resolution on December 1946. First of all, the GA declared that it was convinced that the Franco Fascist Government, "which was imposed by force upon the Spanish people with the aid of the Axis Powers … does not represent the Spanish people".[22] As a result, the GA recommended the following sanctions:

> 1) "that the Franco Government … be debarred from membership in international agencies … and from participation in conferences or other activities … until a new and acceptable government is formed in Spain";
>
> 2) "if, within a reasonable time, there is not established a government which derives its authority from the consent of the governed, committed to respect freedom of speech, religion and assembly and to the prompt holding of an election … the Security Council consider the adequate measures to be taken"; and
>
> 3) "that all Members of the United Nations immediately recall from Madrid their Ambassadors", something that most of them effectively did.

Very much in line with this international criticism, the President of the United States of America, Harry S. Truman, explicitly excluded Spain in April 1948[23] from the *Marshall Plan* for the recovery of a Europe devastated by the Second World War. One of the arguments used by Truman was the lack of human rights protection under the Franco regime, in particular the protection of religious freedom.[24] This exclusion greatly contributed to the economic blockade of the Franco regime and to its political ostracism.[25]

---

22 UN Doc. Resolution 39(I), 12 December 1946, Relations of Members of the United Nations with Spain.

23 On 3 April 1948, President Truman signed the *Foreign Assistance Act*, the legislation that established the so-called Marshall Plan. As we know, the original idea of this Plan is due to a speech given by George Marshall at Harvard University on 5 June 1947.

24 R. MARTÍNEZ DE CODES, 'La libertad religiosa en la época de Castiella: una visión pionera (1957–1969)', in M. OREJA AGUIRRE and R. SÁNCHEZ MANTERO (coords.), *Entre la historia y la memoria. Fernando María Castiella y la política exterior de España (1957–1969)* (Real Academia de Ciencias Morales y Políticas, Madrid, 2007) p. 424.

25 B. POLLACK and G. HUNTER, *The Paradox of Spanish Foreign Policy: Spain's International Relations from Franco to Democracy* (Pinter Publishers, London, 1987) p. 18.

Despite the efforts to force some political changes, the reality is that the debate on the Spanish question at international level during the period 1945-1950 internally strengthened the increasingly isolated Franco Dictatorship.[26] The mass media, fully controlled by the Government, denounced the foreign intervention into Spanish domestic affairs as induced by what the regime referred to as "international communism and Soviet propaganda".[27] As a result, the UN as such received bad press in Spain, not only within the political spectrum but also within a significant part of the academic community.[28]

Against all this background, the adoption of the UDHR on 10 December 1948 went totally unnoticed in Spain, with a very limited impact in the mass media,[29] the public opinion and, surprisingly, in academic circles.[30] The truth is that the role played by Francoist Spain in the development of the international system for the protection of human rights was, for obvious reasons, virtually insignificant.[31]

---

26 R. CARR and J.P. FUSI, *España, de la Dictadura a la Democracia* (Planeta, Barcelona, 1979) pp. 31–32.

27 It is very interesting to see the official position of the Franco regime as expressed by the Ministry of Foreign Affairs in a speech addressed to the Spanish Congress, A. MARTÍN ARTAJO, *La política de aislamiento de España seguida por las naciones aliadas durante el quinquenio 1945-1950* (Oficina de Información Diplomática, Madrid, 1950).

28 A.J. LLEONART AMSÉLEM, 'La admisión de España a la luz de los documentos oficiales de las Naciones Unidas', in ANUE, *supra* note 15, p. 45.

29 It is quite interesting to observe the critical attitude of the Spanish press on the UN achievements and the very succinct information about the adoption of the UDHR. In this sense, *see* 'El triste balance de la ONU', *La Gaceta del Norte*, 10 December 1948, p. 1; 'La Asamblea de la ONU aprueba la Declaración de los Derechos del Hombre', *Madrid. Diario de la Noche*, 11 December 1948, p.1; 'El fracaso de la ONU puede abrir las puertas a una nueva actitud respecto a España', *El Correo Español-El Pueblo Vasco*, 14 December 1948; 'La Asamblea General de la ONU ha finalizado su labor en París. El balance no puede ser más deplorable', *La Gaceta del Norte*, 12 December 1948, p. 1.

30 In fact, the most important Spanish journal of international law, the *Revista Española de Derecho Internacional*, did not pay any attention neither to the adoption of the UDHR nor to relevant issues of international protection of human rights for many years. This is probably due to the fact that Academia was under full political control, censorship being common practice of the Franco regime.

31 F. VILLAR, 'España y las Naciones Unidas', *Revista de la Facultad de Derecho de la Universidad Complutense* (1987) p. 255.

4. A NEW GEOPOLITICAL SCENARIO: THE ADMISSION OF SPAIN IN THE UN

By the end of the 1940s, the Cold War started to influence international relations to a great extent. In this new emerging context, General Franco's anti-communist discourse and the strategic situation of the Iberian Peninsula motivated a more flexible approach of the foreign policy of both the United States and Western European powers *vis-à-vis* Spain.[32] The first step of this new attitude was to revoke the sanctions imposed by the General Assembly in December 1946. On 4 November 1950, the GA adopted a resolution in which it resolved "[t]o revoke the recommendation for the withdrawal of Ambassadors and Ministers from Madrid ... and the recommendation intended to debar Spain from membership in international agencies".[33] As a consequence of this new policy which, to a certain extent, contributed towards legitimising the Franco regime both internally and internationally,[34] many Ambassadors came back to Madrid, and Spain joined some relevant international organisations. Accordingly, Spain entered into the FAO and the WHO in 1951, and the UNESCO in 1952.[35]

The crucial year in the Spanish Government's attempt to be internationally accepted was 1953. In August 1953, Spain signed the Concordat with the Vatican which established the identification between Church and State and Catholicism as the *official* religion of the country, and, shortly thereafter, in September 1953, it signed the military and economic

---

32 F. ALDECOA, 'Las constantes de la política exterior española', 2 *Política y Sociedad* (1989) pp. 64 *et seq.*

33 UN Doc. Resolution 386 (V), 4 November 1950, Relations of States Members and specialised agencies with Spain.

34 This reorientation of the position of the UN caused much frustration in the anti-Franco opposition, as illustrated by an official letter sent by the Government of the Spanish Republic in exile to the President of the UN General Assembly. In this letter, after criticising the revocation of sanctions by the GA in November 1950, it expressed its hope that Spain will not be admitted to an organisation created "to promote human rights and fundamental freedoms for all", in 'El Gobierno de la República Española se dirige a las Naciones Unidas', Paris, 22 November 1952, quoted in P. PAGÈS I BLANCH, 'España en la ONU: un largo debate', in ANUE, *supra* note 15, pp. 60-62.

35 The debate over the entrance of Spain in the UNESCO was much more intense, with many intellectuals, especially from Catalonia, firmly opposing it. In fact, there was an international campaign to denounce the repression of culture and minority languages by the Franco regime led by some relevant Catalonian academics in exile. *See* the Manifesto 'Cataluña se dirige a la UNESCO. Memorial de los catalanes a los delegados de las naciones representadas en la séptima sesión de la UNESCO', 1952, quoted in PAGÈS I BLANCH, *supra* note 34, pp. 62–66.

agreements with the United States, which "marked the welcoming of Franco's regime into the international community".[36]

Fully aware of the more favourable new scenario, Spain applied for admission to the UN in September 1955. The question of admission of new members was very controversial within the UN because of political considerations in the framework of the East-West divide.[37] In the end, like many other times, the admission of 16 States on 14 December 1955,[38] including Spain, was the result of a *package deal* between the Great Powers, a "diplomatic *do ut des*".[39] As we can clearly see, the Spanish foreign policy of *wait and see* was, on the one hand, a success. In the view of the historian Florentino Portero, Franco's international success was due to "a correct evaluation of the strategic value of the Iberian Peninsula, the Western interests, the communist expansionism, the evolution of international relations, and his firm determination".[40] On the other hand, the entrance of Spain into the UN generated an enormous sense of frustration within the different anti-Franco movements; for them, the UN represented a democratic and a human rights reference, and the last hope to exert international pressure on Francoist Spain.[41]

During the 1960s Spain actively participated in the international community, entering into international organisations such as the OECD, the World Bank, and the IMF, and concluding a number of international treaties. But it is important to emphasise that Spain did not ask for admission in political international organisations such as the Council of Europe (with the most advanced system for the protection of human rights), and did not ratify the relevant UN human rights treaties.

---

[36] B.N. LIEDTKE, 'Compromising with the Dictatorship: US-Spanish Relations in the Late 1940s and early 1950s', in LEITZ and DUNTHORN, *supra* note 17, p. 265.

[37] This controversy motivated two Advisory Opinions by the International Court of Justice in 1948 and 1950 on the political considerations to be taken into account for admission and on the competence of the relevant bodies of the UN thereon, respectively. On this issue, *see* N. FEINBERG, 'L'admission de nouveaux membres à la Societé des Nations et à l'ONU', 80:I *Recueil des Cours* (1952), pp. 293 *et seq.*

[38] *See* the proposal by the Security Council, UN Doc. Resolution 109 (1955), 14 December 1955, and the resolution of admission by the GA, UN Doc. Resolution 995 (X), 14 December 1955, Admission of new Members to the United Nations. According to this resolution, the GA decided to admit to membership in the UN the following countries: Albania, Jordan, Ireland, Portugal, Hungary, Italy, Austria, Romania, Bulgaria, Finland, Ceylon, Nepal, Libya, Cambodia, Laos and Spain.

[39] LLEONART AMSÉLEM, *supra* note 28, p. 37.

[40] PORTERO, *supra* note 18, p. 403.

[41] M. BRU and X. PONS RAFOLS, 'Presentation', in ANUE, *supra* note 15, p. 15.

This new period in Spain also created windows of opportunity for the civil society. In this sense, the creation of the Spanish Association of the United Nations[42] in 1963 in Barcelona was a great step forward, since it opened the door for the discussion of the UN values and democratic principles within the Spanish civil society. The Association, together with other social movements, extensively contributed to the generation of a human rights culture in a Spain that was still under a cruel dictatorship.[43]

5. THE END OF FRANCOISM: HUMAN RIGHTS AS A PILLAR OF THE NEW POLITICAL SYSTEM

The death of General Franco in November 1975 constituted a decisive turning point in the history of human rights and democracy in Spain. As the Minister of Foreign Affairs of the new Spanish Government, Mr. Oreja Aguirre, in a speech addressing the UN General Assembly during the general debate on 27 September 1976, stated: "The Spanish Government wants to express its firm intention towards respecting human rights and fundamental freedoms as a key part of its domestic and foreign policies".[44] Consequently, on 27 April 1977 Spain ratified both the International Covenant on Civil and Political Rights (CCPR), and the International Covenant on Economic, Social and Cultural Rights (CESCR).[45]

The ratification of the UN Covenants was a first step that was followed by Spain's admission into the Council of Europe on 24 November 1977. That very same day, as a clear symbol of the Spanish commitment to human rights, Spain signed the European Convention on Human Rights.[46] As Juan A. Carrillo Salcedo has rightly pointed out, "Spain's acceptance of international

---

42 *Asociación para las Naciones Unidas en España*, ANUE, *see* <www.anue.org>.

43 F.L. CARDONA CASTRO, 'La Asociación para las Naciones Unidas en España', in ANUE *supra* note 15, pp. 79–94.

44 *Discursos y Declaraciones del Ministro de Asuntos Exteriores* (Oficina de Información Diplomática, Madrid, 1978) p. 18.

45 *Boletín Oficial del Estado (Official Gazette)*, No. 103, 30 April 1977.

46 This link between accession to the Council of Europe and the acceptance of its basic human rights instrument has become common practice after the Spanish admission. Spain ratified the ECHR on 26 September 1979, *Boletín Oficial del Estado (Official Gazette)*, No. 243, 10 October 1979.

obligations in human rights is one of the key steps of the democratisation process during the first moment of political transition".[47]

6. RECEPTION OF THE UNIVERSAL DECLARATION OF HUMAN RIGHTS IN THE SPANISH CONSTITUTION

6.1. THE FUNDAMENTAL PROVISION

Very much in line with the new position of the Spanish Government in the field of human rights and democratic principles, the Constitution (hereinafter CE) adopted in December 1978[48] explicitly incorporated the UDHR into the Spanish legal order. The reception of the UDHR in the domestic legal order is set out in Article 10, paragraph 2, of the Spanish Constitution, which reads as follows:

> "The principles relating to the fundamental rights and liberties recognised by the Constitution shall be interpreted in conformity with the *Universal Declaration of Human Rights* and the international treaties and agreements thereon ratified by Spain." (emphasis added)

An indirect reference to the UDHR can also be found in the first paragraph of Article 10 CE, which states that "[t]he human dignity, the inviolable and inherent rights, the free development of the personality, the respect for the law and for the rights of others are the foundation of political order and social peace". The text of this provision was included in the pre-draft of the Spanish Constitution, published on 5 January 1978.

The idea of human dignity as the basis of the political and social order is taken from the 1949 German *Grundgesetz*, and is ultimately anchored in the Universal Declaration of Human Rights. The Universal Declaration, in its Preamble, refers to the inherent dignity of all members of the human

---

47 J.A. CARRILLO SALCEDO, 'The International Dimension of Human Rights during the Political Transition in Spain', 1 *Spanish Yearbook of International Law* (1991) p. 6.

48 Passed by the *Cortes Generales* (Spanish Parliament) in a plenary session of the Congress and the Senate held on 31 October 1978, it was ratified by referendum of the Spanish people on 6 December 1978 and sanctioned by His Majesty the King before the *Cortes Generales* on 27 December 1978.

family.[49] For the human dignity of the individual to be respected, all his or her rights must be respected.

We will first examine the drafting process of Article 10.2 CE, followed by the analysis of the rights and fundamental freedoms that "shall be interpreted" in accordance with the UDHR.

6.2. THE GENESIS OF ARTICLE 10.2 CE

The origins of Article 10.2 CE are not to be found in the first draft of the Spanish Constitution but in two amendments to that text submitted with distinct goals.[50] On the one hand, the Member of Parliament (MP) for UCD (*Union de Centro Democrático*/Union of Democratic Centre), Mr. Rafael Arias Salgado, submitted an amendment aimed at replacing the actual constitutional rights by the direct reference to international instruments that enjoyed a great of political legitimisation (the UDHR, the CCPR, the CESCR, the ECHR, and the European Social Charter).[51]

On the other hand, the MP for *Unió Democrática de Cataluña* (the Catalonian Minority parliamentary group), Mr. Antón Cañellas Balcells, a very important person in the political opposition against Francoism and an activist in the international movement for human rights, submitted an amendment proposing a reference to the UN human rights covenants as an interpretative parameter of the rights and fundamental freedoms recognised in the Spanish Constitution.[52]

Both amendments were rejected by the Lower House (*Congreso de los Diputados*) because it was thought that they did not add any value to Article 96, paragraph 1, of the Constitution. Most parliamentary groups considered

---

49 *See* N. BLÁZQUEZ, 'El recurso a la *dignidad humana* en la Declaración Universal de Derechos Humanos de las Naciones Unidas', in *Dignidad de la Persona y Derechos Humanos* (Instituto Pontificio de Filosofía, Madrid, 1982) p. 110.

50 A. SAIZ ARNAIZ, *La apertura constitucional al Derecho internacional y europeo de los derechos humanos: El artículo 10, 2 de la Constitución española* (Consejo General del Poder Judicial, Madrid, 1998). *See also* M. RIVAS ARJONA, *Génesis del Título I de la Constitución española de 1978 en el seno de la ponencia* (Publicaciones del Congreso de los Diputados, Madrid, 2001).

51 Amendment No. 777 to Article 13 of the first draft of the Spanish Constitution, in <www.congreso.es/constitucion/ficheros/enmiendas/enmcongreso.pdf>, p. 362, visited on 5 May 2008. "La Constitución incorpora y reconoce solemnemente los derechos y libertades definidos en los siguientes textos internacionales ... a) La Declaración Universal de los Derechos del Hombre, de 10 de diciembre de 1948".

52 Amendment No. 246 to Article 152 of the first draft of the Spanish Constitution, in <www.congreso.es/constitucion/ficheros/enmiendas/enmcongreso.pdf>, p. 126, visited on 5 May 2008. Añadir al apartado b) lo siguiente: "Para interpretar las normas a que se refieren dichos derechos se tomarán en consideración los Pactos Internacionales sobre Derechos Humanos"

the new provision pointless, while the UCD abstained. Paragraph 1 of that provision read:

> "Validly concluded international treaties, once officially published in Spain, shall form part of the internal legal order. Their provisions may only be repealed, amended or suspended in the manner provided in the treaties themselves or in accordance with the general rules of international law."

Nonetheless, the UCD parliamentary group re-submitted the issue in the Senate, including Mr. Cañella's reading, but not Mr. Arias Salgado's amendment proposal. The Socialist parliamentary group opposed the amendment; they believed that it aimed at providing constitutional status to the right to private education, thus allowing such entities to receive public subsidies. The Socialists interpreted Article 13, paragraph 3, of the CESCR in such a way. Finally, the amendment was accepted, albeit with some minor changes, and led to the present text of Article 10, paragraph 2, of the Spanish Constitution.

Other sources for the Spanish text included the then recent 1976 Portuguese Constitution with an almost identical wording in its Article 16, paragraph 2, according to which,

> "[T]he provisions of this Constitution and of laws relating to fundamental rights shall be construed and interpreted in harmony with the Universal Declaration of Human Rights."

During the debates on the draft of the Spanish constitutional text, the Portuguese Constitution was frequently mentioned as a precedent in the regulation of fundamental rights and freedoms.

6.3. RIGHTS AND FUNDAMENTAL FREEDOMS THAT SHALL BE INTERPRETED IN CONFORMITY WITH THE UNIVERSAL DECLARATION OF HUMAN RIGHTS

Although there is disagreement regarding the exact constitutional meaning of the term 'fundamental rights' due of the semantic confusion generated by the incoherent terminology used in Title I of the CE, the relevant doctrine defines those rights as the ones included in Articles 14 to 38. Some scholars expand the notion to all those listed in Title I.

The Spanish Constitutional Court interprets as fundamental rights those which are regulated through an organic law, and which are protected by the *recurso de amparo* (a judicial remedy before the Constitutional Court). On the rights listed in Articles 14 to 29 CE, there is no unanimity within the Constitutional Court.

Article 10, paragraph 2 of the CE sets out the obligation to interpret the fundamental rights and liberties recognised by the Constitution "in conformity with the Universal Declaration of Human Rights and the international treaties and agreements thereon ratified by Spain". The commitment expressed in the provision has had an echo in the Spanish constitutional jurisprudence, as will be shown below.

6.4. THE UNIVERSAL DECLARATION OF HUMAN RIGHTS AS AN EXPRESSION OF GENERAL INTERNATIONAL LAW

The discussion about the legal nature and binding effect of the UDHR has been reproduced several times over among Spanish scholars:[53] it is a moral statement, an ideal to be fulfilled, customary international law, expression of general principles of international law, and so on.

Certain international scholars have voiced concerns over the incoherence and the lack of technical quality of the provisions of the Spanish Constitution as regards the relationship between international law and national law. Article 10, paragraph 2 of the CE, by its reference *expressis verbis* to the Universal Declaration of Human Rights, has been widely interpreted in Spanish doctrine as evidence of the automatic reception of general international law into Spanish law. Hence, an assumption is made that the Universal Declaration is an expression of general international law.

7. REFERENCES TO THE UNIVERSAL DECLARATION OF HUMAN RIGHTS IN THE SPANISH CONSTITUTIONAL JURISPRUDENCE

Doctrinal analysis of the constitutional jurisprudence correctly notes the different ways in which the Universal Declaration of Human Rights has been taken into consideration by the Spanish Constitutional Court in numerous cases.[54] The jurisprudential practice may then be summarised as follows:

---

[53] J.A. CARRILLO SALCEDO, 'Algunas Reflexiones sobre el Valor Jurídico de la Declaración Universal de los Derechos Humanos', in *Hacia un Nuevo Orden Internacional y Europeo: Homenaje al Profesor Manuel Díez de Velasco* (Tecnos, Madrid, 1993). *See also* J. ORAÁ, 'The Universal Declaration of Human Rights', in F. GÓMEZ ISA and K. DE FEYTER (eds), *International Protection of Human Rights: Achievements and Challenges* (University of Deusto-EIUC, Bilbao-Venice, 2006) pp. 117 *et seq.*

[54] L. MARTÍN-RETORTILLO, 'La efectiva aplicabilidad de la Declaración Universal de Derechos Humanos en el sistema jurídico español', *Revista de Administración Pública* (september-

a) The Universal Declaration of Human Rights is frequently quoted in the decisions of the Constitutional Court as an interpretative parameter, either by direct referral or quoting Article 10, paragraph 2, CE.[55]

b) In other cases the Constitutional Court has grounded its reasoning on the contents of specific provisions of the UDHR.[56]

c) The Constitutional Court refers to the UDHR in its Orders (Autos),[57] also contributing to the elaboration of constitutional doctrine.

Therefore it can be said that the UDHR is not merely a decorative part of the jurisprudential landscape. The Constitutional Court has invoked its contents to support its decisions in several cases, thus providing the Universal

---

december 2000) pp. 41–52. The author selects 25 decisions, research ends back in 2000; a current search into the data base of the Spanish Constitutional Court shows a result of 120 entries.

55 Judgment of the Spanish Constitutional Court (SCC) 25/2/2008, in <www.boe.es/boe/dias/2008/03/28/pdfs/T00019-00026.pdf>; judgment SCC 19/12/2007 in <www.boe.es/boe/dias/2008/01/22/pdfs/T00050-00058.pdf>; judgment SCC 7/11/2007, in <www.boe.es/boe/dias/2007/12/10/pdfs/T00059-00083.pdf>; judgment SCC 2/7/2007, in <www.boe.es/boe/dias/2007/08/03/pdfs/T00041-00045.pdf>; judgment SCC 10/5/2007, in <www.boe.es/boe/dias/2007/06/08/pdfs/T00078-00106.pdf>; judgment SCC 9/5/205, in <www.boe.es/boe/ dias/2005/06/08/pdfs/T00022-00029.pdf>; judgment SCC 31/3/2005 in <www.boe.es/boe/ dias/2005/04/19/pdfs/T00095-00112.pdf>; judgment 9/2/2004, in <www.boe.es/boe/dias/ 2004/03/10/pdfs/T00003-00014.pdf>.

56 Judgment SCC 5/11/2007 (referring to Article 11, 2 UDHR), in <www.boe.es/boe/dias/2007/12/10/pdfs/T00038-00042.pdf>; judgment SCC 30/1/2006, in <www.boe.es/boe/dias/2006/03/01/pdfs/T00064-00069.pdf> (invokes Article 9 UDHR to support limits to extradition); judgment SCC 10/11/2005, in <www.boe.es/boe/dias/2005/12/13/pdfs/T00095-00104.pdf> (same); judgment SCC 4/4/2005, in <www.boe.es/boe/dias/2005/05/10/pdfs/T00017-00023.pdf> (invokes Article 13 UDHR); judgment 16/1/2004 SCC, in <www.boe.es/boe/dias/2004/02/12/pdfs/T00063-00068.pdf> (invokes Article 20 UDHR). For instance, in the judgment 22/1981, of 2 July, the problem arose in relation to the right to work and the limitations to continue working after fulfilling certain age. For the Constitutional Court, the right to work can be subject to limitations in order to protect other legal values. The Court invoked Article 29 paragraph 2 of the UDHR, that states that "in the exercise of his rights and freedoms, everyone shall be subject only to such limitations as are determined by law solely for the purpose of securing due recognition and respect for the rights and freedoms of others and of meeting the just requirements of morality, public order and the general welfare in a democratic society". According to the Court's view, this kind of limitations could be applied to the right to work. As we can clearly see, the UDHR is invoked to determine the scope of the right to work.

57 Order SCC 147/1983, 13 April; Order SCC 238/1985, 10 April. In this case, the applicant considered that the right to be judged by a jury was part of the judicial guarantees included in the right to due process set forth in Article 24.2 of the CE. The Constitutional Court established that the jury as a guarantee has not been recognised neither by the UDHR nor by the Rome Convention of 4 November 1950 and the CCPR.

Declaration in the domestic legal order of Spain with indisputable importance.

8. CONCLUSION

Spain cannot be proud of its history as regards human rights, especially during the relevant moment of the adoption of the Universal Declaration of Human Rights in 1948. In spite of the very limited legal, political and social influence of the UDHR at the time of its adoption, it became a political reference for democrats in the opposition to Francoism after Spain's entry into the UN in 1955 and, especially, during the period of transition to democracy after the death of General Franco. The explicit inclusion of a reference to the UDHR in our *Magna Carta* in 1978 marks a significant milestone in the long and difficult process of incorporating a culture of human rights in our country, as does the role played by the Spanish Constitutional Court.

PART IV

EUROPEAN STATES THAT BECAME MEMBERS OF THE UN BETWEEN 1955 AND 1989

20. CYPRUS: FROM AN INTERESTING COLONIAL LEGACY TO POST-CONFLICT CONTEXTUALISATION

Kalliope Agapiou-Josephides[1]

1. INTRODUCTION

The Universal Declaration of Human Rights (hereinafter UDHR) was quoted as being one of the ten texts that have shaped the world.[2] Translated into 335 languages, the UDHR obviously transcends individual regimes, cultures and customs.[3] Few documents in humanity's history can indeed claim to be so successful as a constant source of inspiration in so many countries, so frequently enshrined in various international treaties and covenants and so universal in their appeal. In reflecting on the impact of such a prominent document on a specific country, in this case Cyprus, one needs to place one's analysis within a historical perspective and within a local and a global context. Admittedly, no major event is free from the historical context in which it occurs, and the proclamation of the UDHR and its reception in the Member States are no exceptions.

At the *local level* and from a *historical perspective*, Cyprus was a British colony at the time the UDHR was proclaimed. Therefore, it was not part of the group of states that participated in the drafting of the Declaration. The country became an independent state in 1960. *Context wise*, two issues attracted significant attention in political discourse, leaving little space for international issues to gain important publicity or popular attention. The first was the discourse over the future of the country and people's aspiration for self-determination as a means to a better and more promising future. The second pertained to the general social and political context and discourse,

---

1 The author is particularly thankful to Demetrakis Stylianides, former President of the High Court and Andreas Mavrommatis, former United Nations Special Rapporteur on the situation of Human Rights in Iraq for their insightful comments on human rights in Cyprus at the initial stage of this research.

2 I. SERAGELDIN, 'Ten books that shaped the world. A Discussion', Shangai, China, 12/9/2007. Available online: <www.serageldin.com/ListSpeeches.aspx>.

3 Translations available on-line: <www.unhchr.ch/udhr/navigate/alpha.htm>.

namely upcoming municipal and church elections and social unrest, with strikes taking place all over Cyprus.

At the *global level*, from a *historical perspective*, one should bear in mind that human rights, as proclaimed in the UDHR adopted by the United Nations (hereinafter UN) General Assembly on 10 December 1948, are the outcome of a struggle that has been going on since the dawn of history. The scope of the Declaration's 30 articles cannot therefore be properly understood without reference to peoples' aspiration for a better life and the great efforts and sacrifices by many people in many countries.[4] *Context wise*, four important factors deserve to be mentioned, of which the most prominent one was undoubtedly the post-World War II trauma, which awakened a whole generation from its mood of complacency and led them to undertake their historic responsibilities. At the time, two overarching issues transcended political discourse worldwide; the struggle between communism and liberal democracies and the problem of race relations. Last, but not least, is the wind of decolonisation that started blowing through many parts of the world after World War II. Every single national story of the UDHR has been influenced fully or partially by this key set of factors. Cyprus is no exception.

The reception of the UDHR in Cyprus is part of a completely unexplored research agenda. This study constitutes the very first piece of academic work on this interesting and original topic. It builds on archival evidence located both in Cyprus and in the United Kingdom (hereinafter UK) and upon public sources. As the most interesting findings of the research on the national story of the UDHR pertain to its colonial legacy, this aspect is given a special focus. As a matter of fact, other international instruments of human rights, became prominent, for example, the legally binding European Convention on Human Rights (hereinafter ECHR), partly overshadowed the far-reaching impact of the UDHR. Nevertheless, the UDHR continues to be a constant source of inspiration and it is still referred to and celebrated as a source of high moral strength.

---

[4] Namely: the struggles for the abolition of slavery, the abolition of inhuman treatment, the protection against arbitrary arrest, equality before the law, the protection of family life and property, the dignity of labour and social security, the freedom of movement, the emancipation of women, the freedom of thought and opinion, the freedom of religion, the right to education, the right to participate in government, the right to participation in cultural life for example.

2. THE UDHR IN THE BRITISH COLONIAL CONTEXT

At the time of its proclamation, the UDHR received limited public attention in Cyprus. This is to be attributed, at least in part, to the concerns of the local Cypriot political scene of that time, but predominately, because of the in general carefully designed colonial dissemination policy. Therefore, the way the UDHR was received in Cyprus cannot be understood without reference to the overall United Kingdom of Britain strategy with regard to the UDHR and its application in the colonies. Official records reveal a fascinating colonial legacy of the UDHR and Cyprus. A careful study of official records sheds light on a number of interesting issues.

Firstly, it is worth noting that the UK acted as a global actor. Its representatives to the General Assembly of the United Nations expressly declared that the UK was acting just as much on behalf of Colonial Governments as on behalf of the UK, and that in voting for the UDHR it did so without reservation on behalf of the Colonies. In this respect, a consultation process was set up between the Colonial Office and the Colonial Governments.

Secondly, London not only supported, but also played an active role in the preparation and adoption of the UDHR, although with its own agenda, namely as to social and economic rights.[5] It did so despite the fact that it recognised that the UDHR could potentially constitute a source of embarrassment for Colonial Governments. In order to dispel any doubt about its willingness to apply the UDHR in the Colonies, the British Government referred to its active role in the abolition of slavery, which was considered by many as a mission impossible, as a dream that could never be realised because of its far-reaching socio-economic implications in both the short and long run.

Thirdly, the way the Colonial Office handled the issue of the dissemination of the UDHR, namely by informing the Colonies through simultaneous non-secret and secret dispatches, in fact, confirmed the politically sensitive character of the UDHR. In the non-secret dispatch, the Colonial Office commented briefly on some of the more important aspects of the UDHR. It underlined the efforts of the UK representatives to try to ensure that the UDHR should be framed as a sincere statement of ideals whose adoption might be of some genuine universal significance. The most

---

[5] On the issue of the British agenda with reference to the adoption of the UDHR, *see* J. MORSINK, *The Universal Declaration of Human Rights: Origins, Drafting and Intent* (University of Pennsylvania Press, Philadelphia, 2000).

interesting part, though, was to be found in the secret dispatch, namely the secret circular dated 28 March 1949.[6]

There were three major issues preoccupying the Colonial Office at the time, which were emphasised in the secret dispatch.

The first referred to the struggle for global influence. It is obvious from the content of the above-mentioned Secret Circular that the UK feared the likelihood of "Communist propaganda", which would "endeavour to make particular use of it [the UDHR] in regard to Colonies".[7] Their task was thought to be made easier by the fact that the countries of the communist countries abstained, on the ground that the text was not satisfactory. The British Government, by opting to adopt the UDHR unreservedly, just as much on behalf of Colonial Governments as on behalf of the UK, in fact, tried to avoid any special mention of non-self-governing territories with regard to the application of the UDHR:

> "Had there be any suspicion that the United Kingdom was not prepared to do so a majority of members would certainly have supported some Article on the lines of the Yugoslav proposal … making special reference to the application of the Declaration to non-self-governing territories, with all undesirable implications of such special mention."[8]

The second was the possible political impact that the UDHR could have on the various territories under British rule throughout the world and on the difficulties that they could face in the application of the UDHR. It is on the basis of this worry that so much stress was put on the non-legally binding character of the UDHR. The concerns and fears of the Colonial Office were crystal-clear:

> "I fully recognise the potentialities of the Declaration as a source of embarrassment to Colonial Governments ... I am, of course, aware that in certain territories it may be extremely difficult to reconcile one or two Articles in the Declaration, even as a statement of ultimate ideals, with lines of policy which are intended to govern developments well into the future. Again, however, it would undoubtedly have been most unwise for the United Kingdom Delegation to have tried to secure exemptions from the Declaration on behalf of any individual Colony, since such a course would only have served to turn the spotlight of international criticism upon the territory to a

---

6 National Archives, UK, CO/537/458D/Circular 25102/2/49/Secret.

7 *Ibid.*

8 *Ibid.*

disproportionate and quite unnecessary extent, with possibly embarrassing repercussions in the territory concerned as well."[9]

In the Cypriot context, in the context of the Cold War and as the winds of decolonisation began to blow, Article 19 (freedom of opinion and expression) and Article 20(1) (freedom of peaceful assembly and association) of the UDHR acquired a sensitive character and were possible causes of controversy as to the feasibility of their application. Archival evidence suggests that the liberty of the press and the freedom of association were strictly regulated and drastically controlled.[10] In the wider colonial context, other articles were considered as potentially problematic.[11] Thus, the formulation of a specific policy aiming to keep the process under control, whilst avoiding international criticism, was absolutely necessary. Fully supporting the adoption of the UDHR and presenting it as *a set of ideals to which all mankind should aspire* was the easiest way out, as it could be presented as a win-win situation.

Last but not least was the publicity obligation contained in Resolution D adopted by the General Assembly of the United Nations at the same time as the UDHR. In fact, Resolution D (Publicity) had been identified by the Colonial Office as likely to cause many difficulties to Colonial Governments and thus most careful thought was to be given as to what measures might be possible and feasible in giving effect to the Resolution in the Colonial territories. This preoccupation is to be understood in relation to the first concern mentioned above. This constituted the rationale behind the adoption of guidelines for the Colonial Governments concerning their publicity obligations under Resolution D. In fact, it seems that Resolution D caused the UK more problems than the UDHR itself.

Since the UDHR was bound to attract a good deal of publicity in one form or another, all Colonial Governments were urged, unless they had special reasons to the contrary in which case they should consult the Colonial Office, to arrange for the UDHR to be published in their Official Gazette. In this respect the archives search revealed interesting pieces of the puzzle. Colonial Governments were advised by the Colonial Office that there was no need to publish the relevant Resolutions adopted at the same time as the UDHR. The colonial government of Cyprus followed the guidelines provided by the

---

9 *Ibid.*

10 *See* Files SA1/965/1948 and SA1/988/1948 respectively, State Archives of the Republic of Cyprus.

11 Articles 26 (right to free and compulsory elementary education), 23(1) (right to work, to free choice of employment, to just and favorable conditions of work, to protection against unemployment) and 23(2) (right to equal pay for equal work, without any discrimination).

Colonial Office and the UDHR was published on 5 May 1949, without the Resolutions. Apart from this measure, which was to be taken at a date soon after the adoption of the Declaration, the Colonial Office did not press Colonial Governments to go any further in giving effect to the Resolution than they would consider to be desirable or appropriate, having regard to all the factors involved and especially to local conditions in each territory. This was the case particularly with regards to the recommendation, which was deemed very difficult to fulfil, that the UDHR be expounded to schools.

The Colonial Office was aware though that if a majority of members of the United Nations were to decide to take more far-reaching action in their own countries, it would be damaging for Colonial Governments to appear to be lagging too far behind. This is the reason why London tried to convince the French and Belgian Governments, as early as January 1949, to consult and to agree, if possible, upon a uniform policy on the question of the implementation of the Resolution regarding publicity. The aim, therefore, was to avoid any marked discrepancies between what was to be implemented in different territories and regions.

3. PUBLICITY UNDER THE CONTROL OF THE COLONIAL GOVERNMENT AND LIMITED REACTION BY CYPRIOTS

Generally speaking, media coverage is a good indicator for identifying salient issues and priorities of the social and political agenda, and equally insightful, in terms of what and how it addresses and what is ignored in silence. In the case of the UDHR in the British colonial context of Cyprus, one can pinpoint two interesting points in time to look at the media coverage pertaining to the UDHR: a) the adoption of the UDHR in December 1948; and b) its publication in the Official Gazette five months later, in May 1949.

a) Media coverage at the moment of the adoption of the UDHR: positive reception in a partisan mood. The adoption of the UDHR gained the attention of the people of Cyprus, who were aspiring for freedom from colonial rule, in the form of self-government, and renewed their hopes for a better and more promising future. The East-West divide, reflected locally in the left-wing/right-wing discourse and interspersed with national and local partisan goals, were the main features of the political discourse of the press pertaining to the UDHR at the time of its adoption.

In their reporting, right-wing newspapers were rather descriptive in their approach and rather laconic as to the content. The newspaper *Ethnos* (The Nation) in its edition of 12 December 1948, reported impressive details such as: that 2000 delegates met for 12 weeks in Paris, the cost of more than five million dollars, partly covered by the UN's own resources, that 230 policemen were in charge of the building, the size of the delegations and so on. There was no reference whatsoever to the content of the UDHR. Another newspaper exercised criticism towards the Eastern block, for example. "[I]n those countries, human rights are being infringed by fake elections whose result is being pre-judged".[12] Left-wing newspapers covered the issue of the proclamation of the UDHR more extensively. They focused more on the content, in a rather critical tone and thus, confirmed the concerns of the Colonial Office.[13] In fact, they saw in the UDHR 'a new', 'a powerful weapon' against colonial ruler of Cyprus: "[t]he implementation in Cyprus of a self-governance status, so that the will of the people forms the basis of the authority of government, is for the Cypriot people an inalienable *right*, protected by decisions and acts of the United Nations Organisation, whereas for Britain it is an *obligation*, undertaken from the moment its representatives signed the Declaration of Human Rights".

The East-West and left-right divides were more than obvious and interwoven with the 'national cause', that is to say the future of the country and the way the colonial rule should come to an end. Despite an apparently unanimous position, in fact, there were two conflicting approaches determining the different attitudes *vis-à-vis* the UDHR and which guided the way the Declaration was interpreted. The Right, headed by Nicosia's mayor Themistoclès Dervis, was a fervent supporter of unification with Greece, but was not eager to oppose the colonial ruler. Newspapers such as *Ethnos* (The Nation) and *Neos Kypriakos Phylax* (The New Cypriot Guardian), both leaning to the Right, suggested that the UDHR should be used for the promotion of unification with Greece and not for any other reason: 'Unification and only Unification' (*Enosis ke mono Enosis*). The second approach, as expressed by the Left, was also supportive of unification with Greece but adopted a step-by-step approach and a more critical stance *vis-à-vis* the colonial power. For right-wing newspapers the adoption of the UDHR was a significant achievement by the camp of democratic nations and they criticised the communist camp for not voting in favour of the Declaration. Left-wing ones were putting emphasis on the fundamental rights and freedoms set out by the Declaration and tried to highlight the violations of those principles in the countries that adopted the Declaration. In brief, every side tried to use arguments related to the UDHR with the purpose of attacking its political adversaries.

12 *See* newspaper *Neos Kypriakos Phylax* (The New Cypriot Guardian), 8 December 1948

13 *Ibid.*, p. 5.

Political discourse, as reflected in the media, revealed that the Declaration received relatively little substantial attention and its far-reaching implications were either not really understood or passed by in silence. It seems that the UDHR was primarily viewed as an instrument through which each side would attempt to promote its own interests and goals. The tone was more about the controversies and divides in the global and local context rather than about the UDHR's content and prospects.

b) Media coverage at the moment of publication: a publicity process under full-colonial control. In Cyprus, the UDHR was published in the Official Gazette on 5 May 1949, almost five months after its adoption. As provided by the UK general policy guidelines, the Resolutions were indeed not published with the text of the UDHR. A fully controlled information process was in place. On the day following the publication of the UDHR an article written by the Public Information Officer, under the pseudonym of Roy Fenton, "was issued to such newspapers' editors as were prepared to accept it".[14] In any event it was published in full by seven papers, namely: the *Cyprus Mail*, *Cypriot*, *Neos Kypriakos Phylax*, *Ethnos*, *Eleftheria*, *Phoni-tis-Kyprou* (all right wing), and *Hur Soz* (Turkish). In the communist newspaper *Democratis* (The Democrat) a version appeared in abbreviated form.[15] It is worth noting that, at that time, there were no radio or television broadcasts.[16] Archival evidence suggests that the article was written with the assistance of the material contained in the dispatches of the Secretary of State for the Colonies.

There were three highlights in this article. The non-legally binding character was mentioned first. It read: "[i]t is a Declaration only: that is to say, it is not a legally binding agreement: nor is it a statement of measures all of which are capable of immediate implementation in all territories".

The British Consultation with the colonies was mentioned second. By quoting Mr. Ernest Davies, the British delegate to the Assembly, the author underlined the fact that the UK accepted this Declaration "not only on its

---

14 *See* The Acting Governor's Telegram No. 58, dated 11 June 1949 to the Secretary of State for the Colonies.

15 An impressive number of newspapers were being published in the island during the 1940s. What is more impressive is the great interest all newspapers expressed in international affairs. Even weekly newspapers of a local character had regular columns on foreign issues. More important and bigger newspapers had daily external news columns and correspondents from all over the world. Undoubtedly, special emphasis was given on the British foreign policy and on the situation in other British colonies.

16 The Cyprus Broadcasting Service began life only in 1953, transmitting on one radio channel. Television broadcasts began in 1957 with three-hour transmissions, twice a week. *See* <www.kypros.org/CYBC/cybc.htm>, visited on 25 June 2008.

own behalf but on behalf of every one of the non-self-governing territories for which it is responsible".

The third highlight concerned the abstention of the Slav States, including Russia. Emphasis was put on the fact that the UDHR was voted for by 48 votes to nil with eight abstentions. It also gave details about individual articles of the UDHR for which the Russians voted against.[17]

Over all, the article explained the merits of this historic document encompassing *a set of ideals towards which humanity should aspire* on the one hand, and on the other, it praised the role of the British Government for being one of the signatories to the Declaration, which would be of great benefit to the people of the colonies.

The Acting Governor of Cyprus, contrary to many of his colleagues, was neither very explicit in his report to the Colonial Office on the UDHR nor proactive in his approach.[18] He adopted a rather prosaic and reactive method of reporting to the Colonial Office. In his above-mentioned correspondence, he confirmed that the Declaration attracted little attention:

> "2. The Reaction to the Declaration in the Greek and Turkish press … was insignificant, and the District Commissioner report no signs of local interest in it."

> "4. Unless new considerations arise from the conference referred to in paragraph 6 of your secret dispatch, it would be my advice that, as far as Cyprus is concerned, the Declaration should not be further publicised, but that should any interest in it develop in future further publicity and explanation along the lines already given should be considered."[19]

---

[17] Namely, Article 1 (equality of rights for all human beings), Article 13 (freedom of movement), Article 18 (freedom of thought and religion), Article 19 (freedom of opinion and expression), Article 26 (right to education) and Article 28 (right to social and international order).

[18] *E.g.*, the case of the Sierra Leone. *See* Correspondence Government House, Sierra Leone to Colonial Office, dated 12 May 1949/Secret.

[19] Paragraph 6 of the Secret Circular dated 28 March 1949 reads as follows: "6. I take this opportunity of informing Colonial Governors that a conference held at the Colonial Office from the 3rd to 5th January with representatives of the French and Belgian Colonial and Foreign Ministers, the main object of which was to consider the Agenda for the fourth session of the Trusteeship Council, the opportunity was taken of bringing this Resolution to the attention of the French and Belgian Representatives. They indicated that they had not previously been aware of the terms of the Declaration, and particularly not of the Declaration D (although it was proposed by the Representative of France in the Third Committee of the United Nations) and were anxious that a further conference should be held at a later date to enable the three governments to agree, if possible, upon a uniform policy on the question of the implementation on their Colonial territories of the Resolution regarding publicity. I am sure that, once I have

A study of the reports sent by the Governors and Acting Governors of the different Colonies to the Colonial Office reveals a common trend in their appreciation of the situation in their respective colonies. They referred to a 'comparative political immaturity' and inadequate 'standard of education' as counter arguments for the full implementation of Resolution D, and mainly for the full exposition of the UDHR in schools in the colonies. The main fear was that if they were to widely publicise the Declaration at that stage, "the admirable ideals of rights and freedoms laid down in the Declaration may well lay the foundations of a serious future discontent and even prepare the way to Communist propaganda".[20] Some of them even adopted a proactive position by suggesting "that there would not appear to be any serious objection to the expounding in schools and elsewhere such of the Articles in the Declaration which cover only those rights and freedoms which are most likely to be embodied in the Covenant on Human Rights and which have to be given the fullest publicity".[21]

4. THE UDHR AND THE CYPRIOT CONSTITUTIONAL ORDER

The Republic of Cyprus was established in 1960, after twelve and ten years of the adoption of the UDHR and the European Convention on Human Rights, respectively. Its constitutional order had greatly benefited from both instruments. The moral strength and the universal appeal of the first and the legally binding character of the second offered the new Republic a good legal and political framework for the protection of human rights.

Part II of the Constitution (Articles 6–35) is entirely devoted to Fundamental Rights and Liberties. It is generally admitted that the Rome Convention and the Protocol, as the most advanced legally binding international instruments, served as the prototype in drafting the relevant provisions in the Constitution of the Republic of Cyprus. The latter not only defines the fundamental rights and liberties in a clear legal language but also provides methods for their implementation and remedies for their contravention. Under Article 35, the legislative, executive and judicial

---

received the views of the Colonial Governors on the line of action they think it would be feasible to take, such a conference would be most useful".

20 *See, e.g.*, the report by the Acting Governor of St Helena/Secret/ 28 July 1949 (25102/2J/49, doc. No. 33).

21 *Ibid.*

authorities of the Republic are "bound to secure, within their respective competence, the efficient application of the provisions relating to this Part [the fundamental rights and liberties]".

For a number of reasons, the country experienced a hazardous state-building process. Rival geo-political and geo-strategic claims by implicated external powers (UK, Greece and Turkey) prevailed throughout the process, which was supposed to provide the country with a genuine constitutional framework and a functional political system to serve the interests of its citizens. The young Republic was created against a background of ethnic fragmentation and political segregation of its two communities and a duality had always tainted the situation in the country, whose prospects proved to be rather ominous and difficult.[22] The complexity on the political terrain was translated into constitutional complexity. The British constitutional lawyer S.A. de Smith observed that, "the Constitution of Cyprus is probably the most rigid in the world. It is certainly the most detailed and (with the exception of Kenya's new Constitution) the most complicated".[23] Therefore, it is not surprising that "[n]o constitutional and legal order is more difficult to describe than the one of Cyprus".[24] Problems appeared as early as 1963, when a major constitutional crisis occurred. The situation became even more critical in 1974 when, after a coup perpetrated by the military junta in Greece, Turkey invaded the island. The official reason was to re-establish the constitutional order. The latter has not been re-established, and Turkey still occupies more than one third of the island's territory. Ever since, Cyprus has remained a divided county. The Government of Cyprus did not declare a state of emergency after the events of 1974. In spite of the difficulties encountered,

---

22 Cyprus's Constitution was elaborated as an integrative part of a complex set of interrelated international treaties providing for the transfer of sovereignty from the UK to the newly established state (Appendix D), rather than a genuine constitutional text. No proper constitutional process was enacted, and the 1960 Constitution entered into force upon signing, with no popular ratification-process taking place. This constitutes the first irregularity of Cyprus's state-building process. The second one consists of the guarantor status that the three implicated foreign powers (United Kingdom, Greece and Turkey) orchestrated for themselves. Furthermore, unstable democratic regimes both in Greece and Turkey rendered the situation even more complicated. It is against such a background, namely ethnic fragmentation, political segregation of the two communities and foreign interventions, that the Republic of Cyprus was established. *See* K.-D. GROTHUSEN, W. STEFFANI and P. ZERVAKIS, *Zypern*, Südosteuropa-Handbuch (Vandenhoeck & Ruprecht, Göttingen, Zürich, 1998) 967 p. K. AGAPIOU-JOSEPHIDES, 'Chypre', in J.-M. DE WAELE and P. MAGNETTE (eds), *European Democracies* (Armand Colin, Paris, 2008) pp. 87–102.

23 S.A. DE SMITH, *The Commonwealth and Its Constitutions* (Stevens and Sons, London, 1964) p. 285.

24 CHR. RUMPF, 'Verfassung und Recht', in GROTHUSEN et al., *supra* note 22, p. 155.

it was considered more appropriate not to take any measures, which would in any way affect the enjoyment of human rights.

The division of the country has and continues to pose a number of challenges for human rights protection.[25] Most of the cases brought to the European Court of Human Rights (hereinafter ECtHR) refer mainly, but not exclusively, to allegations of human rights violations as a result of the conflict on the island. As a result, the ECtHR and some human rights protected by the European Convention, for example, the right to property are better known in Cyprus than the relevant articles of its own Constitution. This can be explained by the fact that, as they are in one way or another related to the country's main political problem, which is the de facto division of the country and foreign occupation of its territory, they receive important media coverage and public exposure.[26] The bulk of complaints in the ECtHR are lodged against Turkey.

5. THE UDHR AND CYPRIOT CASE LAW

As a matter of fact, seldom do the Cypriot Courts refer to declaratory texts in their decisions, even those of general acceptance, such as the UDHR. In the database of Court decisions, only four judgments referring to the UDHR were found. All of them were issued in the 1980s.

In none of the cases was there a comment on the legal validity of the UDHR. Neither have the Courts stated whether the UDHR was referred to as a moral statement, as an ideal to be fulfilled, as an expression of general principles of international law or as customary international law, and so on. As a general observation, the Courts have mainly referred to the UDHR both as an interpretative parameter and as an interposed parameter of constitutional legitimacy. In all four cases, reference to the UDHR was meant to illustrate a universally accepted human rights code and/or to provide an interpretative parameter. Beyond the general reference, in two cases, the court decisions referred to specific articles of the UDHR.

In the first case, *Georgios Apostolides and Others* v *The Republic, through the Ministry of Labour and Social Insurance and Others (1982), (Case No. 383/81)*, the UDHR was referred to by the Court as source of legitimacy for

[25] *See* Document CCPR/C/1/Add. 6, 'Cyprus', Initial Report, and Document CCPR/C/1/Add. 28, Supplementary Report, United Nations, Yearbook of Human Rights Committee 1977–1978, International Covenant on Civil and Political Rights, Vol. II, Documents of the first to fifth sessions including the reports of the Committee to the General Assembly.

[26] *See* ECtHR cases: *Loizidou* v *Turkey*, *Xenides-Aresti* v *Turkey* and many others.

clearly reaffirming the equal status of social and political rights. Judge Pikis stated in his judgment that "Article 9 [of the Constitution] has the effect of placing social rights on equal footing with political rights, both fundamental under the Cyprus Constitution, as well as the Universal Declaration of Human Rights proclaimed by the General Assembly in 1948".

The second case, *Costakis P. Apostolou and Others* v *The Republic of Cyprus, Through the Director of Social Insurance Services (1984)*, referred to the UDHR not only generally, but also specifically, though again as an interpretative parameter: "[t]here have been further developments and the period after World War II seems to show the general acceptance of Social Rights as Human Rights. Articles 22–28 of the United Nations Universal Declaration on Human Rights of 1948 and the International Covenant on Economic, Social and Cultural Rights of 1966 — ratified by Cyprus by Law 14 of 1967 — prove this on the international level, and the European Social Charter signed in Turin in 1961 and ratified by Cyprus by Law 64 of 1967 on the European level".

The third case, *1. Charalambos Telemachou Psaras, 2. Ramez Metanos Licha* v *The Republic (1987) (Criminal Appeals Nos 4715 & 4718)*, concerned the right to privacy. The judgment referred to the UDHR as a purely interpretative parameter: "Art. 15.1 is modelled on the European Convention of Human Rights that proclaims that a right to privacy as such, in turn fashioned in the spirit of the Universal Declaration of Human Rights".

The fourth case is *Christos Levantis* v *The Republic, through 1. The Minister of Interior, 2. The Migration Officer (1988), (Case No. 854/85)* and concerned the power of a State to exclude aliens. The interest in this case is the fact that the Court, implicitly but clearly, places Article 18 of the UDHR on an equal footing with Article 18 of the Constitution and Article 9 of the ECHR: In fact, the judgment states that: "The sub-judice decision and/or refusal of the respondents offends Article 18 of the Constitution, Article 9 of the European Convention of Human Rights which has been ratified by Law No. 49 of 1972 and also Article 18 of the Universal Declaration of Human Rights of the United Nations".

Although there is no specific reference made to the UDHR, it is worth mentioning an interesting case relating to reasonable restrictions or limitations to which fundamental rights are subjected (Article 29(2) of the UDHR) on the grounds of public interest. As decided by the Supreme Constitutional Court, ambiguous provisions in "legislation involving interference with the Fundamental Rights and Liberties safeguarded under the Constitution" should be constructed according to the settled principle that such provisions should be constructed "in case of doubt in favour of the said Rights and Liberties".[27] Jurisprudence has confirmed the high degree of protection safeguarded by Cyprus' legal system.

6. CONCLUDING REMARKS

The study of the reception of the UDHR in Cyprus has revealed a number of interesting insights, the most prominent by far being its colonial legacy. The country, established as an independent state in 1960 after the proclamation of the UDHR, benefited greatly, though indirectly, from the Declaration, as it was the ECHR which was used as the prototype for drafting the relevant provisions in its Constitution. Despite the courts' general reluctance to refer to non-legally binding texts, the UDHR was indeed quoted in a few cases. The UDHR has seldom been used in the legislative work of the Parliament, and the conflict and post-conflict situation prevailing on the island led to prominence being given to legally binding documents. It is however, included in school curricula and the Parliamentary Committee on Education together with the National Organisation for Human Rights arrange visits to schools, in the framework of awareness-raising campaigns. Furthermore a number of academic and other social events are staged every year on the occasion of the anniversary of the UDHR keeping the spirit of the UDHR alive among civil society.

The UDHR has proved to be a powerful idea which has swept the world. It has provided us with a lens through which we see and analyse our actions and those of others elsewhere in the world. In other words, it has contributed a lot to changing our perceptions of ourselves and of our relationships to other human beings. This is a challenge, which is of particular relevance to Cyprus, as the country is still to move beyond the post-conflict situation and find its own way to reunification and sustainable peace. In the near future, Cypriots may be called upon to rediscover the relevance and the moral strength of the Universal Declaration.[28]

In the same way, the real impact of small steps that lead to great achievements is difficult to evaluate in the short term, the developments, all

---

[27] Case of *Fina Cyprus Ltd. Nicosia* v *The Republic* (4R.S.C.C. at p. 33).

[28] In terms of a future research agenda, it seems that a comparative study on the reception of the UDHR in the British colonies and, at a later stage, in other colonies would constitute, undoubtedly, a fascinating and completely unexplored research direction.

the way from the proclamation of the UDHR in 1948 to 2008 seem much more important in retrospect than at the time. Just like good wine maturing with time, the UDHR has kept astonishing us for six decades with its comprehensive forward-looking list of fundamental rights and freedoms, its moral strength and its attractiveness as a constant source of inspiration.

21. GERMANY: FROM IMPOSITION TO ADHERENCE

Anja Mihr

1. INTRODUCTION: THE UDHR IN THE TWO GERMANYS

After the Nürnberg Trials in 1945–1946 and the arguments over the destiny of post-war Germany, the disputes among the allied powers France, United Kingdom, USA and the Soviet Union became irresolvable. Consequently the allies opted for a two-state solution of Germany in 1949. In 1947, first efforts for constitutional designs and a draft for both Germanys were under way, and both made a clear reference to the Universal Declaration of Human Rights (UDHR).[1]

The first West-German constitutional draft presented in 1948, later called *Grundgesetz* or the federal basic law, was the first post World War II state constitution that applied the UDHR. Most of the articles of the basic law were formulated according to the articles of the UDHR. The UDHR, like the *Grundgesetz*, was written in the aftermath of the atrocities and human rights violations that Nazi-Germany had been responsible for until 1945. Bearing this responsibility in mind the members of the constitutional committee of the German basic law emphasised in the first articles (Articles 1–20) the importance of dignity and indivisibility of all human rights, the rule of law, democracy and the right to opposition against suppressive regimes.[2]

Since both drafting committees in the Western and in the Eastern Germany acted under the auspices of the different allied powers, they had to follow the different political interests. Because of the incompatibility of the two ideologies of the West and the East, the two constitutions of Germany opposed each others. Even so, the two constitutions nevertheless reflected Germany's past with different interpretations of the legacy of World War II. In the West, the founding fathers leaned on the UDHR, trying to avoid any anti-democratic laws. In the East, the new Communist leadership emphasised

---

1 H. WEBER, *Die DDR 1949–1990, Oldenburg Grundriss der* Geschichte (Oldenburg Verlag, München, 2000) pp. 28–29; C. KLEßMANN, *Die doppelte Staatsgründung, Deutsche Geschichte 1945–1955* (Vandehoek und Rupret, Göttingen, 1991).

2 D. HESSELBERGER, *Das Grundgesetz* (Luchterhand Verlag, Neuwied, 1995) pp. 42–48.

the importance of creating a Socialist society in order to establish peace and equality among all people. Although both constitutions highlighted the importance of civic and social rights as grounded in the UDHR, they nonetheless followed very different political and ideological aims. The only aspects they had in common was that both constitutions had to be superior, more humane, more civic (for the Western Allies) and more Socialist (for the Soviet Union) to all the constitutions Germany had had during the past decades, referring to the ones of the Weimar Republic and the Nazi-Regime.

In May and October of 1949 the two Germanys were established under the allied auspices. West Germany became a Federal Republic with the adoption of the Basic Law, and in the Soviet sector, the founders of East Germany declared the sector to be a Socialist state. East Germany titled itself as a people's republic with a Constitution based on Socialist and Communist norms and standards. The East German Constitution made no reference to the UDHR. It was a consequence after the abstention of the Soviet Union from voting for the UDHR in December 1948, the other one being that neither the Communist bloc nor East Germany approved the document then.

East Germany sought membership to the UN strongly since the 1960s, anticipating that this membership would finally manifest its statehood and independence. The highest governing body in East Germany, the *Politbüro*, passed the order to sign and support any international document whatsoever, including the UDHR, in order to show the international community the readiness of the state to become member of the UN and thus to manifest its status as an independent state. In this context, the right to self-determination — even though not pro-claimed by the UDHR — was highly emphasised by the East German government. Even though East Germany never was independent from the political will of the Soviet Union and thus from the Socialist-Communist party and the vigilance of Moscow, it succeeded in establishing a quasi-independent state with its membership in the UN.[3]

West Germany instead, which was not a fully sovereign state either but had more independent political power than East Germany, insisted on the one state solution and wanted to join the UN with East Germany as one state. This policy, the *Hallstein* doctrine, was dropped in 1972 and West Germany had to acknowledge the two state solution until its reunification in October 1990.

Even though the Western Allies supported the membership of West Germany in international organisations such as UNESCO and others, the

---

[3] I. MUTH, *Die DDR Außenpolitik 1949–1972 — Inhalte, Strukturen, Mechanismen* (Links Verlag, Berlin, 2, 2001).

membership to the UN was denied. The same was true for East Germany. Again, this was due to the fact that the allied powers on both sides of the political divide held a veto in the UN Security Council. The sole membership of only one German state without the other would have been vetoed by the other side. The Soviet Union vetoed West Germany's membership; the British, French and the US ambassadors did so in the case of East Germany. Only after the heated relationship between the East and West cooled down and West Germany reluctantly accepted the existence of East Germany as a separate state in 1972, the door opened for the membership to the UN. Due to the high political sensitivity of the matter in the Cold War, both states had to become members of the UN on the same day, on 18 September 1973, to avoid any unnecessary diplomatic disputes on which one of the two was the better state and who had the more humane political system and was thus more acceptable by the world community than the other side. With this membership they both formally agreed and adhered to the UDHR.

2. THE ROLE OF THE NGOs

With the formal membership in the UN in 1973, the rivalry between both countries became even stronger and this included competing in the fulfilment of human rights standards. Who was the more successful state? Who had the better ideology? Who adhered more to human rights principles and the UDHR? Both states claimed to comply and to be the freer or the more social and more equal state than the other. Both signed and ratified international treaties as soon as they were available on the international agenda. Nothing was left out, no exceptions made. International human rights norms, the UDHR as well as the two covenants on social and political rights, and the other main conventions served also political purposes. When reporting to the UN Committees in the 1980s on a periodic basis, both states wished to confront the other side with their failure in the field of human rights and violations not only of the covenants but also concerning the objectives of the UDHR in general.[4]

The Cold War had also led in Germany to the emergence of a number of peace movements, anti-war organisations and human rights NGOs. West German based human rights NGOs like the *Humanistische Union* or the *Internationale Gesellschaft für Menschenrechte* fought strongly against East

---

4 A. MIHR, *Amnesty International in der DDR, Der Einsatz für Menschenrechte im Visier der Stasi* (Ch. Links Verlag, Berlin, 2002).

German Communist dictatorship and accused it of severe human rights violations. Many of their activists were refugees from the German Democratic Republic. In the 1960s and 1970s, Amnesty International grew strongly in West Germany. It was there that the post World War II generation at the same time felt guilt and responsibility for the atrocities of the past, and this led to a large engagement of activists in human rights and humanitarian NGOs. Likewise, West Germany soon became the ground for many active national and international human rights NGOs, some using the UDHR in pointing precisely towards the other side of the Iron Curtain.[5] Most of the literature and publications on human rights and the UDHR in Germany were either by NGOs like Amnesty International or by lawyers teaching international human rights laws at the university level and in academic programmes.[6]

Despite the political manifestation on both sides to adhere to the UDHR, violations and abuses were not avoided. Human rights in both countries were partly violated due to the strong pressure of the Cold War. Laws such as the *Nostandsgesetze* (state of emergency laws) until 1968[7] and the law to 'ban someone from a profession' used against public officers in West Germany because of membership in the Communist party or contacts to organisations in East Germany (from 1951–1968)[8] were anti-democratic and against the spirit of the UDHR. On the other side of the Iron Curtain, the multitude of political imprisonments in East Germany, estimated up to 60,000 since 1949, of those who opposed the Socialist one-party regime when claiming the human right to leave one's own country, to assemble or speak freely, outnumbered by far the political imprisonments in West Germany.[9]

West Germany as a democratic country adhered much stronger and more sincerely to international human rights norms even though it failed in some aspects. This was so not only because it was a liberal state with a strong political will to be the more democratic state of the two, but also because it

---

5 L. WILDENTHAL, 'Human Rights Advocacy and National Identity in West Germany', 22 *Human Rights Quarterly* (2000) pp. 1051–1059.

6 Amnesty International, *Der Internationale Menschenrechtsschutz* (Fischer Verlag, Frankfurt, 1981); Amnesty International, *Politischer Mord durch Regierungen* (Fischer Verlag, Frankfurt, 1983).

7 C. KLEßMANN, *Zwei Staaten, eine Nation, Deutsche Geschichte 1955–1970* (Bundeszentrale für Politische Bildung, Bonn, 1997).

8 D. POSSER, 'Die feindlichen Schwestern: BRD und DDR. Politische Verfolgung im Kalten Krieg', in F-J. HUTTER and C. TESSMER (eds), *Die Menschenrechte in Deutschland, Geschichte und Gegenwart* (Becksche Reihe, München, 1996) pp. 222–252.

9 J. RASCHKA, *Zwischen Überwachung und Repressalien — Politische Verfolgung in der DDR 1971–1989* (Leske und Budrich, Opladen, 2001).

had mechanisms such as a constitutional court and federal administrative courts which adapted international human rights standards in their judgments as well as free elections and media which prevented the young state from falling back into authoritarian rule. This was particularly important in the early years of the country when it was not clear whether West Germany would fall back into an authoritarian regime. In contrast, the East German government since its foundation in 1949 claimed the dictatorship of the proletarian class and the one party ruler by the Socialist party. Therefore, violations of fundamental freedoms and rights were inherent in its dictatorial leadership and constitution and the reality constituted the opposite to the norms of the UDHR.

Forty years after the declaration of the UDHR in 1988–1989, the civil rights movement in East Germany and the members of the *Bürgerrechtsbewegung* followed the civil unrest in other Eastern bloc countries, went onto the streets of Leipzig, Dresden and Berlin, and 'lived the UDHR'. On their banners they wrote their claims against the one party system and the dictatorship and asked for more freedom and human rights, making a clear reference to the UDHR.[10] What followed was the fall of the Berlin Wall in November 1989, the negotiations between the two states and the reunification in October 1990 into one Federal Republic of Germany under the West German *Grundgesetz*.

3. DISSEMINATION AND MAINSTREAMING OF HUMAN RIGHTS

With the reunification of Germany, some of the human rights issues that had been politically and ideologically motivated over the past decades became irrelevant. Instead, other human rights issues became more prevalent and visible, such as racism, changing asylum laws in 1993, the rise of xenophobia, migration, anti-Semitism in the late 1990s and Islamophobia and the fight against terrorism after 2001.[11] Overall, migration and xenophobia as well as acts of ill-treatment in police custody were issues that were widely discussed and brought up to by NGOs and political parties over the past decade. The case of Daschner, the head of Frankfurt police department, who threatened a

[10] U. POPPE, R. ECKERT and I.S. KOWALCZUK (eds), *Zwischen Selbstbehauptung und Anpassung, Formen des Widerstandes und der Opposition in der DDR* (Chr. Links Verlag, Berlin, 1995).

[11] W. HEITMEYER, 'Feindselige Normalität, In Deutschland breitet sich die Bereitschaft aus, Mitmenschen zu verachten — wenn sie anders sind', *Die Zeit*, 11 December 2003, p. 19.

suspect in custody alleged to have abducted and hidden an 11-year-old boy (who later died) with torture was widely disputed among experts and the public and came only to an end by the verdict of the Frankfurt court in 2003 which sentenced Daschner. It was one of the most prominent human rights cases in Germany after the processes and imprisonment of members of the terrorist group Red Army Fraction (RAF) in the 1970s.[12]

Nevertheless, the world-wide human rights euphoria of the 1990s, the Vienna World Conference on Human Rights in 1993, the promotion of human rights awareness through the UN decades, the Council of Europe's years on human rights learning and education and the special engagement of the European Union for human rights and democracy left also its mark in Germany. With a strong reference to the UDHR, the initiatives made human rights more fashionable in German schools, media, universities and the non-formal education sector. Human rights managed to escape from the law faculties of universities and became more mainstreamed beyond the expertise of international lawyers and diplomats. In consequence, the awareness about human rights became slightly broader. The increase of human rights awareness was also a consequence of the 50th anniversary of the UDHR in 1998. It was the first anniversary of the UDHR after the Cold War in the reunified Germany and it was more widely received than previous anniversaries. The events for 10 December in 1988 were not visible except through a few statements of human rights NGOs and only one official publication by the Ministry of Foreign Affairs acknowledged the UDHR in 1988.[13] This changed a decade later.

In 1998, Amnesty International Germany had for the first time organised a main event to commemorate the UDHR. It took place in the *Frankfurter Paulskirche*, the historical venue of the first democratic national assembly in Germany 150 years earlier. It was also meant to commemorate the first democratic and 'human rights movement' in Germany in 1848–1849. During the event on 10 December 1998 human rights prizes were awarded and both the media and politicians emphasised the importance of the UDHR. The UN and UNESCO Associations, political parties and NGOs, schools, and governmental institutions highlighted the 10 December with publications,

[12] S. BAUMANN, 'Der Fall Daschner', in Deutsches Institut für Menschenrechte (ed.), *Jahrbuch Menschenrechte 2006: Freiheit in Gefahr, Strategien für Menschenrechte* (Suhrkamp Verlag, Frankfurt, 2006) pp. 323–324.

[13] Auswärtiges Amt, *Menschenrechte in der Welt, Konventionen, Erklärungen, Perspektiven* (Bonn, 1988).

exhibits, lecturers and press releases.[14] The first edition of the German-Austrian Yearbook for Human Rights, the *Jahrbuch Menschenrechte*, was published, supported later by the German Institute for Human Rights in Berlin and the Ludwig Boltzmann Institute of Human Rights in Vienna.[15] In addition, books and educational materials were published.[16] The 50th anniversary was used mainly by human rights activists and NGOs to disseminate the idea and the content of the UDHR as widely as possible and get further commitments by politics in Germany.[17] Consequently the Federal Ministry for Economic Cooperation emphasised the importance of the UDHR in 1998 in its development aid work and the Foreign Ministry underlined Germany's commitment to adhere to the principles of the UDHR.[18] But even though the UDHR was highly emphasised in the official documents, statements and publications, it was stated clearly that human rights were part of Germany's foreign policy and development policy abroad as they had been during the Cold War, too.[19]

The 1990s was the decade of human rights initiative in Germany, as it was elsewhere in the world. With the rise of human rights NGOs and after the Vienna World Conference on Human Rights in 1993 the first NGO Forum or Platform for Human Rights, the *Forum für Menschenrechte*, was established in 1994. In 1995, the Nürnberger Center for Human Rights, the *Nürnberger Menschenrechtszentrum*, constituted itself, partly as the legacy of the Nürnberg Trials 50 years earlier. Today the Forum consists of as many as 50 human rights NGOs and foundations in Germany. Furthermore, the lobbying efforts of the Forum and the demands by NGOs led to the establishment of the German Institute for Human Rights, the *Deutsches Institut für Menschenrechte*, in 2001 in Berlin. Although officially founded by the

14 Menschenrechtszentrum Potsdam (ed.), *50 Jahre Allgemeine Erklärung der Menschenrechte* (Themenheft, Menschenrechtsmagazin, Dezember 1997).

15 Deutsches Institut für Menschenrechte et al. (eds), *Jahrbuch Menschenrechte* (Suhrkamp Verlag, Frankfurt, 1999–2008).

16 Bundeszentrale für Politische Bildung (ed.), *Menschenrechte* (Informationen zur Politischen Bildung, Bonn, 1998).

17 H. BRUNKHORST, W.R. KÖHLER and M. LUTZ-BACHMANN (eds), *Recht auf Menschenrechte, Menschenrechte, Demokratie und internationale Politik* (Suhrkamp Taschenbuch Wissenschaft, Frankfurt, 1999).

18 Auswärtiges Amt (ed.), *4. Bericht der Bundesregierung über ihre Menschenrechtspolitik in den auswärtigen Beziehungen* (Bonn, 1998), and Bundesministerium für wirtschaftliche Zusammenarbeit (ed.), *Förderung der Menschenrechte, eine Aufgabe der Entwicklungszusammenarbeit* (Bonn, 1998).

19 U. SELCHOW and F.-J. HUTTER (eds), *Menschenrechte und Entwicklungszusammenarbeit, Anspruch und politische Wirklichkeit* (Verlag für Sozialwissenschaften, Wiesbaden, 2004).

German Bundestag and mainly financed by the German Foreign Ministry and the Ministry for Cooperation and Development, it would have not come into force without the pressure of NGOs and the Forum. In the same year the first UNESCO Chair for Human Rights Education was granted to the University of Magdeburg and many more initiatives for spreading the message of the UDHR followed. Numerous training seminars in human rights, NGO workshops and higher education learning programmes in particular outside the law faculties are becoming part of the academic life and more comprehensive learning programmes. A professorship for human rights in political sciences was recently established at the University of Erlangen. Today human rights education is a subject better known than ever before. However, the knowledge and the understanding regarding the UDHR are only slowly growing.

Surveys conducted by the University of Leipzig and Marburg among the general population in Germany in 2003 and 2004 have shown that 50 per cent of the people interviewed recalled that "there exists some sort of a human rights document" but only 4 per cent could name that it is somehow called "the UN human rights convention" or "the human rights Charter". What they meant was the UDHR but it was not known to the people under the correct title. Up to 30 per cent of the interviewees had never heard about any documents concerning human rights.[20] When again people were asked how they knew about these documents or human rights, the majority of the interviewees mentioned Amnesty International as the main source of information. Thus the few who knew something about the UDHR knew it from an NGO and not through the formal education sector, school or media, even though efforts were undertaken in the 1990s.[21]

Nevertheless, in the 60th year of the UDHR, Germany has more NGOs, institutions, training and educational programmes for human rights than ever before. Human rights awareness is increasing, but so is also scepticism and controversial debates over social and economic rights as well as over other freedoms and rights. As part of a promotional campaign, a big German publisher, Fischer Verlag, is promoting the UDHR by issuing a free copy of the UDHR in every one of its publications — a number that runs in the millions. A significant number of commemoration events and publications by

---

20 G. SOMMER, J. STELLMACHER and E. BRÄHLER, *Einstellung der Deutschen zu Menschenrechten* (Deutsches Institut für Menschenrechte, Berlin, Press Release, 10 December 2003).

21 G. SOMMER, J. STELLMACHER and E. BRÄHLER, *Menschenrechte in Deutschland: Wissen, Einstellungen und Handlungsbereitschaft, Zusammenfassung der Ergebnisse zweier repräsentativer Studien* (Deutsches Institut für Menschenrechte, Berlin, Press Release, 10 December 2004).

foundations, by the Federal Agency for Political Education and academic institutions are planned. The media as well as political institutions will report on and respond to it. In comparison to all previous decades, the 60th anniversary of the UDHR will be the most acknowledged and widely celebrated one.

4. INTERNATIONAL HUMAN RIGHTS LAW IN THE DOMESTIC LEGAL ORDER

Already before signing and ratifying international human rights treaties on the UN level, West Germany adhered to the principles of the European Convention on Human Rights (ECHR) since 1952. Until today, the ECHR has constituted a legal standard equal to legislation for the courts. Courts are assigned to interpret federal law according to the Convention and other international human rights treaties which relate directly to the UDHR. Before entering the UN in 1973, both Germanys had already undertaken efforts for signing international conventions and treaties. Of the eight major international human rights treaties with monitoring mechanisms, Germany has ratified six, signed an additional two and — seemingly in line with other European states — has neither considered nor signed the International Convention on the Protection of the Rights of All Migrant Workers and Members of Their Families.[22]

Most cases of conflict between international human rights standards and national legislation occur in the context of decisions by the European Court of Human Rights (ECtHR) in Strasbourg and other monitoring mechanism by the Council of Europe, for example, as concerns prison conditions or policy custody. Germany's legislation has so far mostly followed the decisions of Strasbourg except in the case of asylum and *non-refoulement*.

---

[22] For West Germany and the reunified Germany after 1990: International Convention on the Elimination of All Forms of Racial Discrimination (ICERD) ratified 1969; International Covenant on Economic, Social and Cultural Rights (ICESCR) ratified 1968; International Covenant on Civil and Political Right (ICCPR) ratified 1968; Convention on the Elimination of All Forms of Discrimination against Women (CEDAW) ratified 1985; Convention against Torture and Other Cruel, Inhuman or Degrading Treatment or Punishment (CAT) ratified 1990; Convention on the Rights of the Child (CRC) ratified 1992; International Convention for the Protection of All Persons from Enforced Disappearance (CPPED) signed 2007; Convention on the Rights of Persons with Disabilities (CRPD) signed 2007 (ratification expected in 2008); International Convention on the Protection of the Rights of All Migrant Workers and Members of Their Families (CPRMF) not signed.

Concerning the right to asylum, the right to be free from torture or ill-treatment and the issue of *refoulement* of refugees, Germany has been in conflict with international standards of the Convention against Torture and Other Cruel, Inhuman or Degrading Treatment or Punishment, the ECHR and the UDHR. Article 16 of the Basic Law guarantees the right to asylum, but with the exception of the UDHR, which declares the right to asylum as an objective, neither the ECHR nor other international treaties declare the right to asylum as legally binding or as hard law. The German Constitutional Court (*Bundesverfassungsgericht*) has emphasised this fact and has defined the domestic customary law as not being in contradiction to the ECHR. Today, due to the 'third-country regulation' in Europe, Germany is no longer accepting those asylum seekers, individuals and families alike, as refugees who come via so-called 'safe' third countries. These persons will be returned to their country where they arrived from or directly to their country of origin and citizenship upon arrival without double checking whether they would be subject to imprisonment, ill-treatment or torture when they return.[23] This asylum practice has caused a number of open disputes and conflicts in Germany involving representatives of the UNHCR and civil society. NGOs, activists and opposition parties have widely criticised this practice as an open violation of human rights and the UDHR since it has been repetitively proven that some persons who have been returned to their home country were subject to torture, ill-treatment and even death.[24] It was of particular interest for civil society activist to mention that due to Germany's recent history and the two dictatorships in the 20th century it should carry a particular responsibility to protect refugees and guarantee asylum to people regardless of whether they come from third countries or directly to Germany.

The ECtHR has raised certain concerns and asked for a revision of the procedures because they violate Article 3 of the ECHR. The human rights to life, freedom from torture and personal liberties have been abused by German authorities also in the context of *non-refoulement*, because according to Article 33 of the 1951 Refugee Convention, refugees should not be returned to the country of origin if they are persecuted there. Since 1953 German customary law and interpretation of Article 33 define that a refugee has to be persecuted by state authorities in the country of origin if she or he wants to receive the status of a refugee or asylum seeker. If this is not the case —

[23] According to the judgment of the Federal Administrative Court on *Asylverfahrensgesetz* referring to *Sichere Drittstaaten* (safe third countries) from 1992; revised, confirmed and published on 2 September 2008 §26a AsylVfG, <norm.bverwg.de/jur.php?asylvfg_1992,26a>, visited on 10 November 2008.

[24] For examples and individual cases, *see* <www.proasyl.de>, visited on 10 November 2008.

which indeed is often the case if persecution and violence is conducted by non-state actors — refugees can be returned to their country of origin.

The violations of standards and norms concerning refugees, asylum and *non-refoulement* have constituted bad examples and caused the human rights community in Germany to challenge national legislation and customary law by comparing it with international human rights standards and the UDHR. Due to higher awareness of human rights through public education institutions, media and politics, it can be anticipated that more controversial debates and discussion about the German customary law, its *Grundgesetz* and the objectives of international human rights standards will take place in the future.

5. CONCLUDING REMARKS

When, in 1949, human rights standards and the UDHR were seen as a rather formal exercise to be included in the German *Grundgesetz* under the auspices of the allied forces, a decade later and due to the developments of the Cold War, human rights turned to become important political and societal tools in the competition among the two Germanys. The UDHR was often used to confront the 'other side' of the Iron Curtain and to show the world community in general that one Germany was better then the other. Civil society movements in the West and opposition groups in the East took ownership of the proclaimed human rights adherence by their governments in the 1970s and 1980s and obliged the systems to comply with these norms. In the 1970s in East Germany, the UDHR played a key role for many opposition leaders when they were asking for changes of the Communist regime and guarantees for political freedoms and civil liberties. In West Germany the civil and human rights movement used it to ask for the unique responsibility of the government to include human rights standards in their foreign, asylum and refugee policies.

As of today, the legacy of World War II and the Nazi regime plays a key role in the political debates reflected in the national legislation and in the foreign policy. The government is constantly reminded that due to this specific responsibility it became a duty to include, adhere and comply with international human rights standards in its legislation and foreign policy. The asylum and refugee policies and thus customary laws have been one of the most liberal and open ones in Europe for most of the past decades. Due to Germany's compliance to EU asylum and migration policies and the high number of refugees and asylum seekers caused by the war on the Balkans in the 1990s, this has changed and has led to a number of confrontations and human rights debates among government authorities and the civil society movement in the country.

Nevertheless, the human rights community is more vital and larger than it has ever been in the past. The 60th anniversary of the UDHR with a record number of events and publications will once again increase the awareness and idea of human rights in Germany. It can therefore be expected that there will be a greater demand by civil society, lawyers, judges and politicians alike to dispute, challenge and at the same time implement human rights standards in and outside the country in the future.

22. MALTA: A TENUOUS LINK IN HUMAN RIGHTS PRACTICE AND PROCEDURE

Ian Refalo

1. INTRODUCTION

The Universal Declaration of Human Rights (hereinafter UDHR) has perhaps not been, in Malta, the primary instrument for the advancement of human rights. This is not to detract from its importance nor to deny that it had an effect on the Maltese system of law. But that effect, in so far as human rights law in Malta is concerned, was not immediate and direct but indirect through the adoption of other instruments which were mainly inspired by the UDHR itself. The UDHR eventually not only gave rise to international instruments protecting human rights to which Malta has become a party, but has also promoted on a regional basis the development of convention arrangements to protect human rights.

At the time that the UDHR was adopted Malta was a British colony under the sovereignty of the British Crown. It could not therefore participate directly in the adoption of the UDHR. However the UDHR itself, and the principles of the United Nations Charter, especially the idea of the rights to self-determination of peoples were relevant to Maltese constitutional development and must have in no mean way fuelled the adoption of policies aspiring to full independence for Malta from the United Kingdom.[1]

It is in this sense that the UDHR, as a declaration of the rights of people all over the world, is extremely relevant to Maltese development. In so far as human rights law is concerned the position in Malta is characterised both by the adoption of a fundamental rights charter within the Maltese Constitution of 1963 which, in a manner, owes its progeny also to the UDHR, as well as by the adoption and incorporation into Maltese law of the European Convention for the Protection of Human Rights and Fundamental Freedoms (hereinafter ECHR). Eventually also the United Nations conventions on human rights came to be incorporated into Maltese law.

1 *See* the chapters on Cyprus and Ireland for similarities in the result of the UDHR.

But human rights in Malta is very much the story of the incorporation into Maltese law of the ECHR and it is a story worth telling if one wants to assess the influence which the UDHR itself has had over Maltese affairs. Malta has also adhered to the International Covenant on Economic, Social and Cultural Rights, 1966 (hereinafter ICESCR), on 13 September 1990, to the International Covenant on Civil and Political Rights, 1966 (hereinafter ICCPR), on 13 September 1990, the Optional Protocol to the ICCPR, on 13 September 1990, and to the Second Optional Protocol to the ICCPR, on 29 December 1994.

2. DESCRIPTION OF THE LEGAL ORDER AND ITS RELATIONSHIP TO HUMAN RIGHTS

To properly understand the full effect in Maltese law of the ECHR one has to consider the matter not only from the perspective of the European Convention itself but also from that of Maltese law. In order to be able to do so, some basic facts of the Maltese legal system are necessary to mention and need to be understood. The Maltese legal system manifests in a number of points the cross cultural influences which run through the skeins of Maltese history. The main point to keep in mind in order to obtain a proper understanding is that prior to Malta becoming a British colony in 1814 the law applied in Malta was the *jus comunis* of Europe;[2] Malta was therefore in reality a civil law jurisdiction, with its laws very similar to those obtaining in Italy and France. Its civil law was heavily influenced by French civil law and when Malta came to codify its civil law in the 18th century the French Civil Code served as a model for the codification.[3] On the other hand, on issues of public law the model adopted in Malta was the common law in Great Britain, and it is possible to find a number of judgments of the Maltese Courts which hold that as a matter of Maltese law where, in the area of public law, there is no specific provision of Maltese law, recourse has to be made to the English common law.[4] This in reality has meant that Malta has developed a hybridised system of law with a marked continental bias where the civil law is concerned but heavily influenced by the common law in the areas of

---

2 *See*, for example, the so-called Code de Rohan promulgated by the Order of the Knights of Malta in 1784.

3 *See* the private notes of Sir Adriano Dingli on the codification.

4 Most notably *Lowell* v *Caruana* decided by Judge Maurice Caruana Curran sitting in the First Hall of the Civil Court in 1969.

Constitutional Law, Administrative Law, Criminal Law and Private International Law.

The main point to make for the purpose of this chapter is that Maltese Constitutional Law has been heavily influenced both by British principles of parliamentary government[5] and by English common law. Maltese law adopted the dualist approach to public international law, and this has remained so at least until recent constitutional amendments on the entry of Malta into the European Union.[6] The relevance of this to our subject is that in relation to the adoption of the ECHR by Malta one has to consider on two separate planes the coming into force of the ECHR in relation to Malta both as a matter of Public International Law and the incorporation of the ECHR into the Maltese legal system.

Another point which arises in relation to the ECHR is the acceptance by Malta of the right of individual petition which gave access to persons having complaints relating to breach of human rights by Malta to the Strasbourg authorities. This of course meant that although the ECHR rights may not have been enforceable rights within the local system, still the individual might obtain a remedy by having access to an international forum. The adoption of the ECHR by Malta has therefore to be considered in three separate stages, that is the adherence by Malta to the ECHR, the acceptance by Malta of the optional clause under the former Article 26 of the ECHR (the acceptance of the right of individual petition) and the incorporation of the ECHR into Maltese law.

Before considering these matters directly, some further background information is needed in relation to the protection of human rights in Malta independently of the ECHR. Naturally the history of Malta, like the history of most other nations, is filled with claims of rights and their respect and observance by the sovereign authority. Even at as an early a date as the early 1500s when the islands were enfeoffed by Charles V to the Order of the Knights of Malta the Maltese claimed respect for their rights and privileges. In taking office the Grandmaster of the Order would swear to uphold the rights and privileges of the Maltese. In the early 1800s the Maltese, in the fashion of the French declarations of the rights of man, had adopted a declaration of rights. But these were not judicially enforceable rights as we now understand human rights to be.

---

5 *See* the Malta Independence Constitution of 1963 which was granted to Malta by the United Kingdom and was modelled on other ex colonial constitutions.

6 Act V of 2003.

More to the point is that on Malta becoming a colony under the British Empire the Governor had declared that the government of Malta had to be conducted in accordance with the rule of law with the judges being independent from the executive and legislative branches of government. Human rights as judicially enforceable rights contained in a charter of rights were first introduced to Malta in the Constitution granted to Malta by the United Kingdom in 1961, and then again in the Independence Constitution of 1963. Both constitutions contained a chapter of rights which were judicially enforceable and entrenched within the constitution.[7] Procedures were defined in both Constitutions providing for and giving access to the courts to individuals in order to obtain and secure protection of their fundamental rights. The fundamental rights entrenched in the 1963 Independence Constitution, were largely modelled on the rights contained in the ECHR.

There were, however, significant differences between the rights entrenched in the Constitution and the rights contained in the ECHR. The rights contained in the Constitution were restricted in the sense that a number of pre-existing laws, such as the Civil Code, the Commercial Code, the Criminal Code and the Code of Organization and Civil Procedure, were saved from the operation and application of the rights contained in the Constitution: this was a saving which operated to prevent a Court from declaring that any provision contained in these Codes was in breach of the fundamental human rights of the individual. Later this saving was removed from the Constitution.[8] The fundamental right to property was more closely defined in the Maltese Constitution than in the ECHR. Again this right remained largely a dead letter for pre-existing laws regarding the expropriation and taking of property by the government which were protected from the operation of this right.[9]

Lastly there were significant differences between the right to non-discrimination as contained in the Constitution and that as defined in the ECHR. There were two main differences here; the ECHR protected against discrimination in the enjoyment by the individual of his fundamental human rights independently of the motivation for such discrimination whereas the Maltese Constitution protected against discrimination motivated by a proscribed purpose such as political opinion, race, place of origin and so on.[10] Another difference between the Maltese position on discrimination and the

7 Chapter IV of the Malta Constitution 1963.

8 Act XIX of 1991.

9 Section 47(9) of the Malta Constitution.

10 Section 45(3) of the Malta Constitution.

ECHR lay in respect of discrimination on the basis of sex which was not initially prohibited until 1991.[11]

Despite these differences the position in relation to human rights under the Malta Constitution and the ECHR were largely similar. The identity of the wording adopted in the definition of these rights would have made it natural for the local courts to refer to the case law as developed in the European Court of Human Rights (hereinafter ECtHR) to define the Maltese position. Initially the Maltese courts were heavily influenced by case law developed on the subject within the British Commonwealth, and it was only after the incorporation of the ECHR into Maltese law that the case law of the ECtHR came to have a preponderant and determining influence on the interpretation of the fundamental human rights applicable in Malta.

3. INDIRECT INFLUENCE THROUGH THE ECHR

In reality the ECHR, inspired by the UDHR, was extended to the Maltese territory at a very early date even before Malta had become an independent nation. As already pointed out, Malta prior to 1963 was a British colony and only became independent of the United Kingdom with the grant to it of the Independence Constitution of 1963. The United Kingdom which had acceded to and ratified the ECHR had in the late 1950s extended the application of the ECHR to the Maltese territory, which at that time was a colony under the control of the United Kingdom.

In this sense the European Convention was applicable to the Maltese territory even before Malta became independent on 21 September 1963. With independence the applicability of the ECHR to the Maltese territory lapsed. The Malta Labour Party had alleged that the Maltese Government was in breach of its obligations under the ECHR; it argued that the Maltese Government was still bound by the ECHR as successor to the obligations assumed by the United Kingdom Government when it had extended the application of the ECHR to its Maltese territory. Though there is some academic opinion to the effect that in issues concerning human rights and similar conventions state succession would operate to ensure the continuance in force of such ECHR to territories to which they had been extended by the former sovereign, the prevailing opinion seems to be that state succession does not operate in such situations and that therefore Malta had to accede afresh to the ECHR after independence, as the obligations created by the

---

11 Act XIX of 1991.

extension of the convention obligations to the Maltese territory by the United Kingdom lapsed on independence.

Malta then acceded to the ECHR in 1966. The question of whether in the interim period, that is, between the date of independence and that of accession, Malta was still bound by the ECHR or not became therefore largely academic. Although accession to the ECHR was an important fact and bound Malta by the obligations imposed on it under public international law, Malta had not adhered to the right of individual petition available under the then Article 26 of the ECHR. So it was impossible for persons to bring individual complaints against Malta for violations of fundamental human rights. Also as Malta adhered at the time to the dualistic notion of law, accession by Malta to the ECHR did not mean that the convention became part of Maltese law or that persons present in Malta would enjoy any rights under the ECHR. In reality even though at this point Malta as a signatory to the ECHR was bound by the convention provisions under international law, the convention itself and the case law produced by the ECtHR was not necessarily given the relevance it deserved by the Maltese courts.

A considerable period of time had to pass before Malta decided to make the necessary optional declaration under the then Article 26 of the ECHR granting to individuals the right of individual petition. This declaration was made by Malta on 5 May 1987, nearly on the eve of the then general election. This declaration followed considerable public pressure in the media and in political circles, following the 1981 general election, to ensure adherence by Malta to the human rights values as enshrined in the ECHR. Although the making of this declaration opened up the possibility to individuals to bring forward claims concerning the violation of their fundamental rights by Malta, still it did not amount to the incorporation of the ECHR into Maltese law.

It is interesting to note that one of the very first cases brought against Malta under the ECHR was precisely brought in virtue of this fact. Proceedings had been commenced against a certain Mr. Demicoli in the Maltese House of Representatives for breach of privilege and contempt. Mr. Demicoli had brought action in the Maltese courts claiming that the proceedings in question were in breach of his fundamental right to a fair hearing, a right similar to that contained under Article 6 of the ECHR, but also protected under the Maltese Constitution.[12] The House of Representatives had proceeded with the hearing despite this judicial proceeding and found Mr. Demicoli guilty of contempt, but deferred the imposition of a penalty pending the conclusion of the judicial proceedings. In

12 Section 39 of the Malta Constitution.

October 1986, the Constitutional Court of Malta finally decided the matter holding that the proceedings did not breach of the right to a fair hearing. After that decision the House of Representatives resumed the contempt proceedings and on 9 December 1986 mulcted Mr. Demicoli for contempt.

The acceptance of the right of individual petition by Malta gave the opportunity to Mr. Demicoli to bring his complaint to the ECtHR for violation of his right to a fair hearing as protected under Article 6 of the ECHR. The ECtHR in its judgment was of the opinion that the six-month period had to run from 9 December 1986, the date on which the House of Representatives chose to mulct Mr. Demicoli for his contempt. Mr. Demicoli was successful in his complaint and the ECtHR made a declaration that his right to a fair hearing under Article 6 of the ECHR had been violated and granted him compensation.[13]

4. THE EFFECT OF THE ECHR ON NATIONAL LAW

After the election of a Nationalist government in May 1987, the government proceeded to set up a Commission to advise on the incorporation of the ECHR into Maltese law. The Commission drafted the necessary legislation which was subsequently adopted by the Maltese Parliament as the European Convention Act of 1987.[14] The Act provided for the incorporation of the ECHR into Maltese law; the granting of remedies under Maltese law for the violation of convention rights; the provision for the enforceability of judgments obtained from the Strasbourg Court in Malta and the entrenchment of the ECHR into the Maltese legal system.

Human rights and fundamental freedoms are defined by the Act as those rights and freedoms as set out in Articles 2 to 18 (inclusive) of the ECHR and Articles 1 to 3 (inclusive) of the First Protocol, Articles 1 to 4 (inclusive) of the Fourth Protocol, Articles 1 and 2 of the Sixth Protocol and Articles 1 to 5 (inclusive) of the Seventh Protocol to the Convention, which articles are reproduced in the First Schedule to the Act.

The Act also provides for the enforcement of these human rights and fundamental freedoms within the Maltese system and this independently of the remedy the individual may have at European level. In this respect the Maltese Constitution already provided a remedy for the violation of human rights as defined in the Constitution.

---

13 *Demicoli* v *Malta* 210 27 August 1991.

14 Now Chapter 319 of the Laws of Malta.

The position in Malta is rather different from that obtaining in the United Kingdom as there is a written Constitution in Malta of a rigid type, in so far as certain parts of the Constitution, among which the human rights as defined in the Constitution itself, need the approval of Parliament by a special majority, and that is two-thirds of the members thereof. To effectively make the position binding you need a constitutional amendment; but this was not the case when the Malta Convention Act was enacted as the parties failed to reach agreement between them to constitutionalise the ECHR rights and incorporated them by the enactment of an ordinary piece of legislation, which in its turn may be repealed by a similar Act of Parliament.[15]

The Constitutional Court has adopted the position that the ECHR enclosed superior values and that they will therefore prevail over ordinary legislation. In one particular case the Court went to hold that the human rights would also control parts of the Constitution which were found incompatible with the human rights. The provision in the 1987 Act which established that law in conflict with the ECHR would be deemed to be invalid and would not be any longer applied by the courts seems to have effectively achieved in Maltese case law the purpose it set out to achieve. It would still be possible, though unlikely, for a determined Maltese Parliament to repeal the 1987 European Convention Act. But as long as such repeal is not put into effect it must be understood that Parliament wants its legislation to be controlled by the European Convention Act.

In this sense to a certain extent the ECHR, inspired by the normative values of the UDHR, was given a superior standing to that of ordinary legislation. The 2003 amendment to the Constitution has brought about a fundamental change to the Maltese perspective of international law, and it is legitimate to question whether in the light of this amendment, the Maltese position is still a dualist position or has in some manner approached a monist position. In any event the amendment is obviously relevant to the position of the ECHR under Maltese law and to a large extent makes local legislation in conformity with Malta's international obligations, not least those assumed under the ECHR.

---

[15] This is stated subject to the amendments affected to the Constitution in 2003 when Malta joined the European Union, which change impinges also on the position of the European Convention Act.

5. THE UDHR IN THE CONSTITUTION

At the 1993 World Conference on Human Rights, Malta called on all states "to implement and enforce in a concrete manner the principles and purposes of the *UN Charter and the Universal Declaration of Human Rights*, thus implying equality between the two documents and the binding nature of both" (emphasis in original).[16] This was a statement made by Joseph M. Fenech, Minister of Justice, in June 1993, in which he proposed the creation of a World Court on Human Rights, which would protect the rights in the UDHR for nationals of those states which had accepted the jurisdiction of such a court.[17] Ten years later Malta may have to reflect upon its call on the Maltese domestic laws as a result of accession into the European Union.

The status of human rights has changed considerably as a result of amendments made to the Constitution of Malta in the light of its entry into the European Union in 2003. Section 65 of the Maltese Constitution empowered the Maltese Parliament to make laws for the order and good government of Malta. When Malta came to join the European Union it was necessary to provide for the supremacy of European law in relation to Maltese law.

The power of Parliament to make laws for Malta was made subject to European law and to international treaties entered into by Malta. The section now reads:

> "Subject to the provisions of this Constitution, Parliament may make laws for the peace, order and good government of Malta in conformity with full respect for human rights, generally accepted principles of international law and Malta's international and regional obligations in particular those assumed by the treaty of accession to the European Union signed in Athens on the 16th April, 2003."

It is interesting to note that as a result of the 2003 constitutional amendment the ICESCR, 1966, the ICCPR, 1966, the Optional Protocol to the ICCPR, 1966, and the Second Optional Protocol to the ICCPR, 1989, have now become an integral part of Maltese law. This is by virtue of section 65 of the Maltese Constitution which is quoted above. There is no direct reference to the UDHR except that the "generally accepted principles of international law" may be regarded as an obligation directed to the legislature.

---

16 H. HANNUM, 'The UDHR in National and International Law', 3:2 *Health and Human Rights* (1998), Fiftieth Anniversary of the Universal Declaration, pp. 144–158, at p. 148.

17 *Ibid.*, in footnote 30.

In reality the link with the UDHR in Malta is tenuous. In practice, the effect of the UDHR thus far has been more than inspirational because it has spawned real protection of human rights in Malta. In fact, since 2003, some attention has been paid in the Maltese Parliament to the existence of the UDHR in general or to specific rights in the UDHR when political issues have been debated.[18]

6. CONCLUSION

The history of human rights in Malta has been influenced strongly by the history of the country. The writer was not able to find any academic article that dealt with the future prospects of the UDHR as general principles of international law, as human rights or as constitutional law. Perhaps the strength of the practice of the ECHR has not, so far, required a backward glance into history.

It would be speculative to assess the status of the UDHR in the light of the 2003 constitutional amendment. However, creative lawyers may raise the fact that the UDHR is representative of the general principles of international law which articulate the yardstick by which the 'respect for human rights' is measured. It is an open question in Malta whether the future effect of the UDHR will be more tangible, for example, in the protection of economic, social and cultural rights. Some support for this can be found in the 1993 World Conference on Human Rights where Malta called on all states to implement and enforce the principles and purposes of the UN Charter and the UDHR.[19] The statement by the Minister of Justice, 15 years ago, together with the language of the new section 65(1) of the Constitution of Malta may provide further opportunities for recognition of all the norms of the UDHR as human rights.

---

18 *See* debate of 9 June 2003 (Sitting Number 007; general debate on, *inter alia*, human rights), Debate of 26 July 2004 (Sitting Number 161; application of the UDHR on the ageing) and Debate of 6 November 2007 (Sitting Number 585; right to housing), at: <www.parliament.gov.mt/aspstuff/listfilesPar.asp>, visited on 16 November 2008.

19 HANNUM, *supra* note 16, p. 148.

PART V

EUROPEAN STATES THAT BECAME MEMBERS OF THE UN AFTER 1989

23. THE CZECH REPUBLIC: FROM LIP SERVICE TO CONCRETE APPLICATION

Jan Holzer
Hubert Smekal

1. INTRODUCTION

Writing a study on 'The Universal Declaration of Human Rights in the Czech Republic' is a complicated matter for two reasons. First, the study involves not only the Czech Republic's adherence to the Universal Declaration of Human Rights (hereinafter UDHR), but that of its predecessor Czechoslovakia as well, which spent some 45 years under the UDHR, while the independent Czech Republic has only a recent history of 15 years with the UDHR. Secondly, there has been surprisingly little written about the topic on an academic level. This article was therefore created as an original synthetic study based on a number of sources such as literature on human rights movements in Czechoslovakia, newspaper articles, the texts of constitutions, and court judgments involving references to the UDHR.

The scope of the study is broad, encompassing both political and legal insights and trying to map out the impact of the UDHR in Czechoslovakia and in the Czech Republic, which offers a complex setting for the task. Accordingly, the text describes the role of Czechoslovakia in the process of drafting the UDHR, and examines the attitude of the official Communist press towards it in a way that may help to construct a general analysis of Czechoslovakia's approach to human rights. A human rights 'audit' of the constitutions of Czechoslovakia and the Czech Republic is provided as well. Further on, the significance of references to human rights, and to the UDHR in particular, in the activities of civic movements under the Communist rule is studied. The last chapter is devoted to the rulings of the high courts of the Czech Republic (the Constitutional Court, the Supreme Court and the Supreme Administrative Court) concerning references to the UDHR.

2. CZECHOSLOVAKIA AND ITS POSITION DURING THE DRAFTING PROCESS OF THE UNIVERSAL DECLARATION

After World War II, Czechoslovakia found itself in a turbulent position with uncertain prospects for the future. The Soviet Union had already exerted a considerable influence on the smaller countries of Central and Eastern Europe which were, moreover, grateful to the emerging superpower for their liberation from Nazi rule. The inclination to follow the course of the Soviet Union at the United Nations (hereinafter UN) is already evident in the Yearbook of the United Nations 1946–1947 when Soviet and Czechoslovak representatives shared the same opinions on the composition of the Sub–Commission on Freedom of Information and of the Press, and jointly criticised the uneven representation (four to one) of Western and Central European delegates in the Sub–Commission on Prevention of Discrimination and Protection of Minorities.[1]

Czechoslovakia played rather unremarkable a role in the first years of the UN human rights activities and during the drafting process of the UDHR. Czechoslovakia was not a member state of the UN Commission on Human Rights (hereinafter UNCHR), although Czechoslovak František Kraus acted as a chairman at the first and second sessions of the Drafting Committee on the Bill of Human Rights.[2]

During 1948, a crucial year for our region, Czechoslovakia along with other Central and East European countries signalled its proximity to the positions of the Soviet Union. It is necessary to take into account the February 1948 Communist upheaval in Czechoslovakia, which largely contributed to the gradual subordination of Czechoslovakia to the will of the Soviet Union, and a quick shift from inter-war democratic ideals to a Communist totalitarian setting. The new direction of Czechoslovakia was evident in the proceedings of the Third Committee of the UN General Assembly, where Czechoslovakia belonged to the camp of countries criticising the proposal of the UDHR. In particular, the Czechoslovak representative denounced the UDHR as "too abstract",[3] and the representative

1 *Yearbook of the United Nations 1946–1947* (Department of Public Information of the UN, Lake Success, 1947) pp. 526–528.

2 *Yearbook of the United Nations 1947–1948* (Department of Public Information of the UN, Lake Success, 1949) p. 701.

3 *Yearbook of the United Nations 1948–1949* (Department of Public Information of the UN, Lake Success, 1950) p. 529.

abstained when the Third Committee voted on the text of the UDHR as a whole in December 1948.[4] Czechoslovakia confirmed its tough course at the General Assembly plenary sessions on 9 and 10 December 1948, and its representative commented that the declaration lacked revolutionary spirit because the UDHR was "neither bold nor modern". Czechoslovakia further criticised the fact that fascism and aggression were not denounced publicly and formally, and that the right to work expressed only lofty ideals, but took no account of its practical aspects. Noticeably inspired by the Marxist critique of human rights, Czechoslovakia saw no point in proclaiming the right to leisure if man had no means of exercising that right.[5] Czechoslovakia was part of a group of eight countries (Byelorussian SSR, Czechoslovakia, Poland, Saudi Arabia, Ukrainian SSR, Union of South Africa, USSR, and Yugoslavia) that abstained in the UN General Assembly in the vote on the UDHR. Over the following years Czechoslovakia showed its indifference towards the UDHR. For example, the UDHR was translated into 19 languages by the end of 1949,[6] but Czech (or Slovak) was not among them.

3. A HISTORICAL OVERVIEW

3.1. THE CZECHOSLOVAK POSITION ON THE UDHR IN THE LIGHT OF PUBLIC DOCUMENTS

The following historical mosaic was assembled from articles in contemporary newspapers, legal texts and from articles and books about civic movements against the Communist repression.

Quite surprisingly, the Czechoslovak Communist media monitored the development of the negotiations in the UN quite closely, although much lesser space was devoted to human rights than to the power games between the Soviet Union and the United States in the UN. The main government newspaper *Rudé právo*, representing the party and state positions, reported on the approval of the "Charter of Human Rights" by the Third Committee of the UN General Assembly (Social, Humanitarian and Cultural Committee) despite the resistance and abstention of the Soviet Union and other "people's democratic" states, which criticised the document on the grounds that the Charter did not guarantee economic equality, and lacked an explicit

4 *Ibid.*, pp. 529–530.

5 *Ibid.*, p. 533.

6 *Ibid.*, p. 535.

statement of the necessary defence of democratic society against Fascism.[7] The Communist youth newspaper *Mladá fronta* added that the UDHR did not properly stress man as part of society, and over-emphasised freedom of speech.[8] The Czech delegate Hoffmeister characterised the text as a summary of human rights in civilised countries.[9]

After the UN General Assembly approved the UDHR, coverage in newspapers expanded. *Rudé právo* stated that the gravest objection to the UDHR was the fact that it did not set any state guarantees. The newspaper also reported that Czechoslovakia and the other Communist countries abstained but did not vote against the UDHR because the declaration even in that version provided for the development of several parts of the world, especially the colonial territories. *Rudé právo* characterised the UDHR as a "colourless proposal" backed by the Anglo-American bloc in pursuit of the interests of a "handful of imperialists".[10] The newspaper at that point was already playing its role as the mouthpiece of the Communist regime, and strongly supported the opinions of the Soviet delegation.

On 13 December 1948, at the end of the year when the Communists usurped power and just a few days after the adoption of the UDHR, *Rudé právo* published a commentary on the title page predicting that "the overwhelming majority of people in the capitalist states would not stop their fight until these rights become reality".[11] The Socialist camp including Czechoslovakia praised Articles 22–29 containing economic, social and cultural rights, duties to the community, and the entitlement to a favourable social and international order.[12] Manifestly, the Socialist countries had an entirely different conception of human rights than the Western democratic world, and the tough propaganda only reinforced the difference in opinions.

It is useful to examine the UDHR in the light of the first Czechoslovak post-war Constitution, enacted on 9 May 1948, seven months before the approval of the UDHR and two months after the Communist overthrow. The

---

7 'Valné shromáždění odhlasovalo Deklaraci lidských práv', *Rudé právo*, 12 December 1948, p. 2.

8 B.E. SVOBODA, 'Charta lidských práv', *Mladá fronta*, 10 December 1948, p. 2.

9 'Kulturní, sociální a humanitární výbor přijal konečné znění Charty lidských práv', *Rudé právo*, 9 December 1948, p. 2.

10 *Rudé právo*, *supra* note 7.

11 *Rudé právo*, 13 December 1948, p. 1.

12 UN General Assembly resolution 217 A (III) of 10 December 1948, *The Universal Declaration of Human Rights*, <www.un.org/Overview/rights.html>, visited on 3 March 2008.

Constitution of the Czechoslovak Republic[13] consisted of a Preamble, a Constitution, and Detailed Provisions of the Constitution. Article 3 of the Basic Articles enumerated only a limited number of rights, involving freedom of person and of expression, the right to education, work, leisure, and just remuneration, and provided for equal opportunity. Article III also contained a general duty to work for the benefit of the whole, and to participate in the defence of the state. Further articles provided for voting rights and an independent judiciary. Rights and duties were further particularised in the First Chapter of the Detailed Provisions which contained rights of the so-called first and the second generation, but omitted, for example the right to life, the prohibition of torture, and slavery.

The UDHR went almost unnoticed through the 1950s. As the regime toughened its stance towards opponents, there was no place for human rights in the 'witch-hunts' against 'traitors' to the Czechoslovak people. The malaise of the 1950s culminated in the enactment of the Constitution of Czechoslovakian Socialist Republic[14] of 1960, which declared that Socialism had been achieved in the country. The Constitution included a chapter entitled "Rights and Duties of Citizens". However, even political rights were distorted, for example by the provision guaranteeing the leading role of the Communist Party of Czechoslovakia, which undermined the principle of free elections.[15] The most telling was Article 19, which stated that the development and interests of citizens were part of the development and the interests of the whole society, and that these reinforce one another. Priority among rights was clearly given to the right to work and to social rights in general. However, the Constitution again included civil and political rights, and the rights of children, women, and minorities.

In the second half of the 1960s, the regime relaxed its heavy-handed policies to some extent in parallel with the overall positive atmosphere in society, which resulted in the fresh initiatives of the 'Prague Spring'. However, all attempts to change the system or to give it a more 'humane face' were definitively ended by the invasion of Soviet armies in August 1968.

The Constitutional Law of October 1968 on the Czechoslovak Federation[16] federalized the country and stressed in its Preamble the right to

---

[13] Ústavní zákon ze dne 9. května 1948, 150/1948 Sb., *Ústava Československé republiky*, <www.psp.cz/docs/texts/constitution_1948.html>, visited on 10 April 2008.

[14] Ústavní zákon ze dne 11. července 1960, 100/1960 Sb., *Ústava Československé socialistické republiky*, <www.psp.cz/docs/texts/constitution_1960.html>, visited on 10 April 2008.

[15] *See* Article 4.

[16] Ústavní zákon ze dne 27. července 1968, 143/1968 Sb., *o československé federaci*, <www.psp.cz/docs/texts/constitution_1968.html>, visited on 10 April 2008.

self-determination and equality of nations, retained the provisions on rights and duties, and moreover provided for the establishment of a Constitutional Court which, however, was never implemented under the Socialist rule.

Formally, none of the Czechoslovak constitutions from 1948 until 1989 referred explicitly to the UDHR, but they did include protection of both civil and political rights as well as economic, social and cultural rights, with great importance devoted to the implementation of social rights, especially to the right to work and to social security.

With regard to the two most important universal human rights pacts — the International Covenant on Civil and Political Rights (hereinafter ICCPR) and the International Covenant on Economic, Social and Cultural Rights (hereinafter ICESCR) — Czechoslovakia signed both on 7 October 1968, and submitted the instruments of ratification on 23 December 1975, which in the case of ICCPR meant that Czechoslovakia became the 35th state which ratified the Convention. This made it possible for the ICCPR to enter into force in 1976.[17]

The Czechoslovakian official press in 1968 commemorated, as in every other decennium, the anniversary of adoption of the UDHR. At that time newspaper articles truly reflected the atmosphere in society. For example in *Rudé právo* of 10 December 1968, still holding on to the remnants of hope and enthusiasm after the Prague Spring 1968, contained a long article which lacked the propagandistic features known from the late 1940s and 1950s. Instead, the text reported on and celebrated the responsible approach of Czechoslovakia towards human rights, stressing the upcoming reform of the country's administration and a constitutional judiciary that would have guaranteed the protection of human rights.[18]

If we can reflect once more to the 1968 Prague Spring, human rights played an important role in the objections presented by civic initiatives in Czechoslovakia during 1968 against the practices of the repressive Communist apparatus. For example, the *Klub angažovaných nestraníků* (the Club of Committed Non-Party Members) and *Společnost pro lidská práva* (the Association for Human Rights) demanded that the Constitution and the legal system as a whole be brought into conformity with the UDHR and other

---

[17] V. KOPAL, 'Současné mezinárodní právo a lidská práva', in *30 let Všeobecné deklarace lidských práv* (Horizont, Praha, 1979) p. 101; Vyhláška ministra zahraničních věcí 120/1976 ze dne 10. května 1976 o Mezinárodním paktu o občanských a politických právech a Mezinárodním paktu o hospodářských, sociálních a kulturních právech.

[18] J. CHALOUPEK, '20 let Všeobecné deklarace lidských práv', *Rudé právo*, 10 December 1968, p. 3. The author further states that the Declaration lacks legally binding form, but has markedly influenced the legal orders of many countries and the character of many international treaties.

international treaties on human rights. The regime responded quickly and dissolved the Association in 1969.[19] In 1969, a group of intellectuals including playwright Václav Havel, political scientist Václav Kohout, and writer Ludvík Vaculík presented the courageous "Ten-Point Declaration on the First Anniversary of the Occupation",[20] which contained a defence of the Prague Spring of 1968 and criticism of the presence of the Soviet occupation forces, the bad economic situation, repression of civic organisations, breaches of democratic principles, and the existence of censorship, and requested more freedom and democracy. For the first time, calls for the protection of human rights were heard loudly in Czechoslovakia, unfortunately without success.

The process of so-called normalization in the 1970s gradually brought a desperate and indifferent mood into society, but this unfortunate period also produced the most famous Czechoslovak movement against Communist repression. *Charta 77* (Charter 77)[21] dealt mainly with observance of human rights on the basis of the UN Covenants and the Helsinki Final Act, signed by Czechoslovakia in 1975. Charter 77 denounced human rights violations committed by the state, and provided many examples of these violations. Like the earlier Association for Human Rights, Charter 77, personified by its spokesmen philosopher Jan Patočka, former minister of foreign affairs Jiří Hájek, and Václav Havel, soon encountered repression of their activities by regime officials, and the Charter's sympathizers were branded as traitors and persecuted. The harsh reaction by the regime led to the establishment of the *Výbor na obranu nespravedlivě stíhaných* (Committee for Defence of the Unjustly Prosecuted) in April 1978, which monitored the trials of the unjustly prosecuted and issued annual lists of prisoners of conscience.[22] Despite the official constraints, Charter 77 continued to exist, and issued important reports and documents.[23]

---

[19] P. ORT, 'Postavení jednotlivce v právu ES', in *50 let Všeobecné deklarace lidských práv* (VŠE, Praha, 1998) p. 117; Anonym, 'Historie vzniku a zániku Klubu angažovaných nestraníků (KAN)', 12:45 *Svědectví* (1973) pp. 152–154.

[20] 'A Ten-Point Declaration on the First Anniversary of the Occupation', in H.-P. RIESE (ed.), *Since the Prague Spring: The Continuing Struggle for Human Rights in Czechoslovakia* (Vintage Books, New York, 1979) pp. 3–8.

[21] 'Charter 77', in H.-P. RIESE (ed.), *Since the Prague Spring: The Continuing Struggle for Human Rights in Czechoslovakia* (Vintage Books, New York, 1979) pp. 11–14.

[22] L. PLAČKOVÁ, 'Československý helsinský výbor', in *50 let Všeobecné deklarace lidských práv* (VŠE, Praha, 1998) pp. 145–153.

[23] Before the beginning of the Human Rights Experts Meeting in Ottawa in May 1985, when Charter 77 demanded legislative reforms to guarantee the right to freedom and personal security and to travel, and so forth – H.G. SKILLING, *Samizdat and an Independent Society in Central and Eastern Europe* (Ohio State University Press, Columbus, 1989) p. 56. In his book Skilling

With the regime's reputation newly blemished by a tiny island of resistance with an international voice, *Rudé právo* celebrated the 30th anniversary of the UDHR in December 1978 with the self-affirming title "Socialism Provides Guarantees of Real Humanism", which cited Czechoslovak delegate Luděk Handl emphasising that human rights must be understood in their complexity, encompassing both civil and political rights, as well as economic, social and cultural rights. Handl stressed that Socialist Czechoslovakia thoroughly saw to it that human rights were observed in practice, not only on paper, and called on the UN to accelerate its efforts to eliminate grave, systematic, and mass violations of human rights.[24] Surprisingly, Communist newspapers reported widely on a speech on human rights by UN Secretary General Kurt Waldheim in the General Assembly.[25] Coverage of the 30th anniversary of the UDHR was extensive, with articles on the front pages of newspapers. An editorial in *Rudé právo* linked the realisation of human rights with efforts towards the maintenance of peace. The right to life was perceived as the most fundamental right necessary to securing other rights, and rights were viewed in their indivisibility, involving civil freedoms and social securities, the realisation of which would be possible only under Socialism.[26] Moreover, an academic conference on the UDHR was held on the initiative of the Czechoslovak Association for United Nations.

In the second half of the 1980s, pressure by civic initiatives rose again. The Czechoslovak Helsinki Committee was established in November 1988 in order to report on the Helsinki Process, to monitor its fulfilment, and demand remedies in cases of the violation of the documents of the Conference on Security and Cooperation in Europe.[27]

Again, the significant shift in the atmosphere in society was clearly reflected in articles in official newspapers. The style of the editorial in *Rudé právo* on 10 December 1988 was free of strident rhetoric, more thoughtful, and above all anti-war. Wars were perceived as the gravest threat to human rights. A man had a right to live in a socially just society and was responsible in his duties. Protection and development of human rights were presented as

---

describes the typical means of dissemination of information among the dissident community through *samizdat*.

24 'Záruky skutečného humanismu poskytuje socialismus', *Rudé právo*, 12 December 1978, p. 7.

25 'Ke dni lidských práv', *Rudé právo*, 9 December 1978, p. 7; 'Ke dni lidských práv', *Svobodné slovo*, 9 December 1978, p. 2.

26 'Deklarace lidskosti', *Rudé právo*, 9 December 1978, p. 1.

27 PLAČKOVÁ, *supra* note 22, pp. 145–147.

the most pressing current political principle.[28] The overall coverage of human rights on the 40th anniversary of the UDHR again exceeded expectations — both *Rudé právo* and *Svobodné slovo* (the daily newspaper of Czechoslovak Socialist Party, a satellite of the Communist Party) devoted its first pages to developments in human rights during the days around 10 December. They reported especially on the *Fórum československé veřejnosti* (Czechoslovak Public Forum), which consisted of over 700 members, including politicians, academics, clerics, artists and also representatives of the civil society, especially the ecological initiatives. During the Forum's session, *Výbor pro lidská práva a humanitární spolupráci* (the Committee for Human Rights and Humanitarian Cooperation) was established with the objective of informing and mobilizing the public, and putting controls on the state administration.[29] The Committee was even prepared to receive complaints from citizens. Its chairman Zdeněk Dienstbier made a critical point that human rights were handled almost exclusively on the level of the state authorities, while the role of the public remained minimal. He therefore called for the establishment of expert groups and non-governmental independent organisations.[30] Nowadays, the objective of the Committee would be probably labelled as the 'mainstreaming' of human rights. Commentators shared their opinions about the great importance of the Committee and the Forum, and Secretary of Club of Social Democratic Parliamentarians Jiří Vyvadil even criticised the fact that the Czechoslovak legal system dealt more with the obligations of the individual than with his rights.[31] The gradual shift in the public mood could not have been better manifested.

Soon thereafter, the Communist regime was overthrown as the result of the 'Velvet Revolution' in November 1989 and the transition towards a market-oriented liberal democracy began, accompanied also by discussions on human rights and their role in state and society. As has been stressed many

---

28 'To nejzákladnější lidské právo', *Rudé právo*, 10 December 1988, p. 1. The editorial ended with the proclamation that human rights can be realised only when classes and states disappear and self-government is established.

29 It should be noted that the Forum did not try to question socialism; on the contrary, in its Declaration Forum it proclaimed that a socialist state creates conditions for fulfilment of human rights. At the same time the Forum pronounced full support for the UDHR – 'Prohlášení účastníků Fóra československé veřejnosti', *Svobodné slovo*, 12 December 1988, p. 3; 'Úctu a čest lidským právům', *Svobodné slovo*, 12 December 1988, pp. 1, 3 and 4.

30 M. Boudová et al., 'Ustaven Výbor pro lidská práva a humanitární spolupráci', *Rudé právo*, 12 December 1988, pp. 1 and 2; Z. Vávra and R. Valášek, 'Chceme aktivizovat veřejnost', *Rudé právo*, 12 December 1988, p. 2.

31 M. Boudová, 'Věc široké veřejnosti', *Rudé právo*, 13 December 1988, p. 2; J. Vyvadil, 'Den lidských práv', *Rudé právo*, 10 December 1988, pp. 1 and 4.

times, the strong influence of the 'Velvet Revolution' and its 'identification mark' of some sort were constituted by the human rights movement and the humanists, headed by Václav Havel.

The first post-1989 bill of rights was proclaimed as a Constitutional Law[32] on 9 January 1991, and was characterised by strong idealistic natural law rhetoric in its Preamble, acknowledging among other things the inviolability of the natural rights of man, and talking about generally shared values of humanity. It included a full range of rights of the so-called first and the second generation, and also rights of minorities and the right to a liveable environment. The Charter of Fundamental Rights and Freedoms was taken on by the Czech Republic after the dissolution of Czechoslovakia, made part of the constitutional order of the Czech Republic.[33]

The democratic constitutional order of the Czech Republic lacked an explicit reference to the UDHR, but its inspirational relevance was widely acknowledged.[34] Nevertheless, two important statutes — on rehabilitation of the unjustly convicted and on rectification of property injustices[35] — contain references to the UDHR. These statutes allowed for the vindication of persons convicted for acts directed towards the realisation of rights guaranteed in the Constitution and promulgated in the UDHR and in the UN international Covenants. The reference to the UDHR has played a major role in Czech case law, as will be stressed in below.

The year 1998 marked the 50th anniversary of the UDHR. The anniversary came, nine years after the 'Velvet Revolution' of 1989, and almost six years after the break-up of Czechoslovakia. News concerning human rights have become a common part of media coverage after the transition to democracy, and newspapers as well as radio and TV news have commemorated the UDHR on an annual basis. On 10 December 1998, all major newspapers in the country (for example, *MF Dnes*, *Lidové noviny* or *Hospodářské noviny*) reprinted the text of the UDHR, accompanied by

---

32 Ústavní zákon ze dne 23. ledna 1991, 23/1931 Sb., *kterým se uvozuje LISTINA ZÁKLADNÍCH PRÁV A SVOBOD jako ústavní zákon Federálního shromáždění České a Slovenské Federativní Republiky.*

33 *See* Article 3 of the Constitution of the Czech Republic (*Ústava České republiky* ze dne 16. prosince 1992, 1/1993 Sb.).

34 *See*, for example, a parliamentarian speech of the Chairwoman of one of two Czechoslovak Parliament Chambers before the adoption of the Czech Charter of Fundamental Rights and Freedoms (D. Burešová, 8 January 1991, <www.psp.cz/eknih/1990fs/slsn/stenprot/011schuz/s011003.htm>, visited on 7 March 2008).

35 Zákon č. 119/1990 Sb. ze dne 23. dubna 1990 *o soudní rehabilitaci*, as amended by later laws; Zákon č. 87/1991 Sb. ze dne 21. února 1991 *o mimosoudních rehabilitacích*, as amended.

historical overviews, comments and interviews. As on previous decennium anniversaries, an academic conference was held and a collection of papers published.

An analysis of media coverage on the UDHR or on human rights in general says much about the stance of the Czechoslovak administration and about the overall atmosphere in society. Propagandistic coverage in 1950s accompanied by strong oppression of anti-socialist elements was followed by a much more relaxed public mood in the late 1960s. The disillusionment and apathy of normalisation quickly replaced the Prague Spring enthusiasm in 1970s. Finally, just one year before the 1989 Velvet Revolution, a new impulse was felt in Czechoslovak society: under somewhat relaxed circumstances, new initiatives loomed and signalled deep changes. By 1998, the Czech Republic, as a member state of the Council of Europe or OECD with a prospect of membership in NATO and the European Union, was already a part of the developed world, with a solid human rights reputation, which was gained particularly because of the personality of President Václav Havel, who as a former dissident, quickly became a popular speaker in the international arena.

3.2. THE CONCEPT OF HUMAN RIGHTS IN SOCIALIST CZECHOSLOVAKIA

The most telling information on the way the concept of human rights was treated in the Socialist Czechoslovakia is provided by a presentation of main ideas of articles in the press, and from a collection of papers produced for an academic seminar held on the occasion of the 30th anniversary of the UDHR. The main paper of the seminar, written by Evžen Erban, introduced the intellectual sources of the Socialist approach towards human rights, citing for example Karl Marx, Friedrich Engels, and especially V.I. Lenin.[36]

The Socialist conception of human rights emphasised the indivisibility of rights. Economic, social, and cultural rights were considered of the same value as classical liberal civil and political rights. Human rights were perceived concretely and historically as dependent on the socio-economic conditions. Czechoslovakia protected the right to work, to rest, to cultural life, to health and social security, and to education, as well as the right to protection of disadvantaged groups like women and the disabled. The Socialist states called for a 'real' and not merely legal and formal equality; that

36 E. ERBAN, 'Hlavní referát', in *30 let Všeobecné deklarace lidských práv* (Horizont, Praha, 1979) pp. 11–41.

is, for a materially guaranteed equality in the realisation of rights, linked also to the idea of collective property.[37] The right to a dignified life was viewed as the supreme right, including the "right to peace, the right to work, and the right to revolution against all exploiting inhuman powers".[38] The Socialist conception included the idea derived from Lenin that people have not only the right to work, but also the duty to work,[39] thus explicitly recognizing not only human rights, but also human duties.

The Czechoslovakian press placed high value on the right to work, and frequently pointed to differences between the Socialist and capitalist states concerning unemployment. The UDHR was viewed as an instrument on the way towards development of a new world, towards the fraternity of nations and peoples, and towards winning their right to free creative work, dignity and happiness.[40] Among the ideals of Socialism was better protection of human rights (so-called first and second generation) than under capitalism.[41] Socialism and peace were viewed as fundamental conditions for the realisation of human rights and the happiness of man.[42] V. Kopal remarked in 1959 that the UDHR represented a necessary minimum number of human rights, which had already been far surpassed in Socialist states.[43]

The UDHR was criticised especially because of its legally non-binding character. However, the United Nations partly compensated for this deficiency by approving numerous binding human rights treaties (the two International Covenants on Civil and Political Rights and on Economic, Social and Cultural Rights, as well as treaties concerning genocide, racial discrimination, the rights of women, for example), which could be signed, according to official authors, thanks to "the growth of the powers of world Socialism, national liberation movements, and class-consciousness of the

---

37 Z. ČEŠKA, 'Úvodní projev', in *30 let Všeobecné deklarace lidských práv* (Horizont, Praha, 1979) pp. 9 and 24; M. MATOUŠ, 'Občanská práva a ideologický boj', in *30 let Všeobecné deklarace lidských práv* (Horizont, Praha, 1979) p. 46; J. BLAHOŽ, 'Ke kritice buržoazního pojetí občanských práv', in *30 let Všeobecné deklarace lidských práv* (Horizont, Praha, 1979) p. 59; S. ZDOBINSKÝ, 'Práva a svobody občanů v nové Ústavě SSSR', in *30 let Všeobecné deklarace lidských práv* (Horizont, Praha, 1979) pp. 71–72. M. SRNSKÁ, 'Lidská práva v kapitalistických a socialistických státech ve světle mezinárodního práva', 116:5–6 *Právník* (1977) p. 480

38 ERBAN, *supra* note 36, p. 11.

39 *Ibid.*, p. 16.

40 'Deklarace lidskosti', *Rudé právo*, 9 December 1978, p. 1; 'Socialismus je humanismus', *Rudé právo*, 9 December 1978, pp. 1 and 2.

41 J. SKODA, 'První je právo na život', *Svobodné slovo*, 12 December 1988, p. 3.

42 ERBAN, *supra* note 36, p. 18.

43 V. KOPAL, 'Deset let Všeobecné deklarace lidských práv', 3 *Časopis pro mezinárodní právo* (1959) p. 153.

exploited masses".[44] Czechoslovakia also supported nations fighting against colonialism and for their right of self-determination and for free determination of their political status and their right to natural wealth.[45] In other words, Czechoslovakia endorsed collective rights and rights of the so-called third generation as well. Respect for human rights was, nonetheless, not considered the most important issue in international relations; instead it was overshadowed by the principles of state sovereignty, self-determination, and non-intervention in internal affairs.[46] The human rights of individuals were useful especially for the development of interests towards society, for the distribution of material goods, and for the incorporation of a person into society.[47]

J. Blahož, a prominent official Czech constitutionalist of the 1980s, identified as the main difference between the constitutional provisions in Socialist and capitalist countries to be the setting of a positive purpose concerning civil rights and freedoms, which he thought was typical for Socialist constitutions.[48]

It seems obvious that Czechoslovakia's conception of human rights presented a classical example of a Socialist approach to human rights, clearly irreconcilable with the liberal democratic approach practised in Western countries. Czechoslovak officials, as well as those of other Socialist countries, were convinced that their handling of human rights was correct, while the capitalist states led by the United States consistently violated human rights, for example the right to work.

---

44 *Ibid.*, p. 14.

45 *Ibid.*, p. 15.

46 J. MRÁZEK, 'Mezinárodní dokumenty o lidských právech', in *30 let Všeobecné deklarace lidských práv* (Horizont, Praha, 1979) p. 125.

47 E. WAGNEROVÁ, 'Přetrvávající tendence z minulosti v činnosti soudů a obtížnost jejich odstraňování', in V. SIMÍČEK (ed.), *Role nejvyšších soudů v evropských ústavních systémech – čas pro změnu?* (MPÚ, Brno, 2007) p. 67.

48 BLAHOŽ, *supra* note 37, p. 59.

4. POLITICAL RELEVANCE OF THE UNIVERSAL DECLARATION IN CZECHOSLOVAKIA AND IN THE CZECH REPUBLIC

The 'usage' of the topic of human rights in political practice is clearly a crucial issue. The Czech situation as it evolved is fully represented and evidenced over the various political regimes: from the inter-war democratic model (1918–1938) through the pre-war authoritarian intermezzo (October 1938–March 1939) to the age of the Protectorate created by Hitler's Germany, to the pre-totalitarian period of years from 1945 till 1948 and then the changing faces of Communist totalitarianism, eventually to the final arrival of a long-desired form of governance — a consolidated democracy.

At the same time, the question of human rights and their guarantees has always presented itself as a topic to be used by the actors in contemporary political processes. Focusing on developments after 1948, one cannot avoid the following fact: at the heart of the Czech experience lays a warning about the tension, firstly, between formal and factual realisation of the list of human rights, and secondly, between activist and realist approaches to the dynamics and methods of their implementation.

It is necessary to recall and emphasise the fact that the Communist regime in Czechoslovakia, as well as other countries of the Socialist bloc including the Soviet Union, endorsed human rights in their own way. Moreover, Communism perceived itself as the historically necessary outcome of general social processes, superseding previous forms, especially capitalism. The regimes of the Socialist bloc thus considered themselves progressive, even exemplary, in the field of human rights as well. Hopefully, there is no need to widely enlighten the reader to the fact that daily political practice differed completely from proclamations and regime propaganda.

This aspect is crucial especially for an understanding of the role that the question of human rights played in the 1970s and the 1980s in shaping anti-regime opposition in Czechoslovak society. In fact it was precisely the full and real restoration of human rights guarantees that constituted the key justification for Charter 77. Charter 77 did not present any ambitious political programme; it 'merely' called for the observance of the principles of the Helsinki Process, which Czechoslovakia also signed. Meanwhile, conceptions of human rights among the different opposition movements encompassed many nuances and differences.

The fact that anti-regime movements and organisations perceived the issue of human rights as the crucial element of the whole process of removing Communism did not mean that this opinion was shared by the entire Czechoslovak society. This paper is not intended as a work on political transitions, but it nevertheless seems appropriate to remember that the theory of the collapse of Communism encompassed a wider range of factors, all of which played positive roles. The most frequently cited of these is a realistic perception of the predominantly economic and social expectations of the population, which the centrally-directed economies were not able to satisfy. The topic of restoration of human rights carries similar weight and importance as that of the main outside actors (USA and the Soviet Union) or the role of the Catholic Church.[49] An analysis of 'the loss of legitimacy of the Communist regime' might thus involve references to human rights aspects, but also to the overall power relations between the state (the Communist elite) and society; these relations were dominated by socio-economic factors. The conclusion on an ambiguous reflection of the role of human rights in the process of deconstruction of Communist power seems to be justified.

5. THE UNIVERSAL DECLARATION IN THE CASE LAW OF CZECH COURTS

From the legal point of view, the UDHR remained non-binding in Czechoslovakia, a recommendation without legal force. However, its impact as a historic, inspirational, and programmatic document was widely recognised.[50] The conception of the UDHR as a non-binding document with merely symbolic importance has also been passed down to the Czech Republic,[51] and for this reason it has not been made part of the legal code.

---

[49] *E.g.* Leslie Holmes, in his compendium of theories on the fall of Communism, acknowledged the role of the opposition and their acceptance of the concept of human rights, but at the same time added that various authors attached differing importance to human rights, including a view that marginalises their role. Z. Brzezinski, for example, rejected making heroes out of dissidents and opposition movements. *See* L. HOLMES, *Post-Communism: An Introduction* (Duke UP, 1997) pp. 23–27.

[50] *See, e.g.*, KOPAL, *supra* note 17, pp. 100–101; M. SRNSKÁ, 'ČSSR a kodifikace principu respektování lidských práv', in *30 let Všeobecné deklarace lidských práv* (Horizont, Praha, 1979) p. 116; O. KUNZ, 'Uskutečňování Všeobecné deklarace lidských práv a paktů o lidských právech v československém právním řádu', in *30 let Všeobecné deklarace lidských práv* (Horizont, Praha, 1979) p. 131.

[51] Leading legal experts pointed out that the UDHR does not establish binding legal norms. J. Malenovský, current judge of the European Court of Justice, criticised the Constitutional Court, which called the UDHR a part of general international law the principles of which the Czech Republic endorses, for a legal vagueness that leaves doubts about the legal effect of the UDHR. *See* J. MALENOVSKÝ, 'Ústavní soud České republiky a mezinárodní právo', 139:2 *Právník* (2000) p. 123. Similarly, K. ČERMÁK, 'Všeobecná deklarace lidských práv – 50 let', No. 1 *Bulletin advokacie* (1999) pp. 8–13.

However, especially at the turn of the millennium, the UDHR played a very interesting role in the case law of the Constitutional Court (hereinafter CC) and the Supreme Court. The CC in particular invoked the UDHR regularly in cases concerning the Communist past, especially property restitution cases and rehabilitation of unjustly persecuted individuals.

In *II.ÚS 14/04* and a range of other property restitution cases,[52] the CC labelled the UDHR as a model for the Czech Charter of Fundamental Rights and Freedoms. The CC also decided a number of cases concerning persons who between 1948 till 1990 refused to serve in the army because of their religious beliefs and conscience, and frequently referred to the UDHR in that context when applying for rehabilitation and reparation. The CC made an important step in invoking the UDHR in case *II.ÚS 285/97* of 7 October 1998 when it set the UDHR on the same level as to the European Convention on Human Rights, and acted *as if* the UDHR was legally binding. The position of the CC differed markedly from several decisions by the Supreme Court (hereinafter SC), and these two highest judicial institutions conducted 'legal warfare'. Interestingly enough, chambers within the SC diverged on issues containing human rights dimensions and respecting the pro-UDHR judgments of the CC.[53] Or more precisely, one chamber of the SC refused to follow the case law of the CC, but its judgment was subsequently cancelled by a decision of the CC of 11 March 2003 (*I. ÚS 671/01*)[54] which has been one of the most important cases concerning refusal to serve in the armed forces. The CC pointed to the law on judicial rehabilitation (see above), referring directly to the UDHR, which also included freedom of conscience (described as a fundamental freedom), and dismissed the judgment of the SC.

In the meantime, in October 2002 (case *15 Tz 47/2002*) the Grand Chamber of the SC held that cases from the 1950s should be adjudicated according to the facts and law of the period when the original decision was issued, that is, according to the laws of the early 1950s. The plenum of the CC then repealed the decision of the SC in the case *Pl.ÚS 42/02* (106/2003 Sb.)

---

52 *See, e.g.*, Pl. ÚS-st 21/05 (477/2005 Sb.). The practice of referring to international documents, including the UDHR, to point out that they also include the right in question is not by far exceptional (*see, e.g., III.ÚS 1103/07* of January 2008).

53 To illustrate the dramatic character of the situation — the Minister of Justice complained that the SC judges failed to conform to the case law of the CC, and that then-chairwoman of the SC Eliška Wagnerová threatened the judges with disciplinary measures (*see* (san), 'Právo na odmítnutí vojny uznal i Nejvyšší soud', *Mladá fronta Dnes*, 5 March 1999, p. 3).

54 E. WAGNEROVÁ, 'The Effects of the Decisions of the Constitutional Court in Relation to Other Jurisdictions', <www.concourt.am/hr/ccl/vestnik/2.24-2004/wagnerowa.htm>, visited on 30 June 2008.

of 26 March 2003, and disagreed with the interpretation of the SC. The CC stated that interpretation of laws from previous regime must be performed in the light of current constitutional values and principles of the democratic state and the rule of law. The CC argued explicitly as follows: "[T]he constitutional construction of freedom of conscience[55] after February 1948 differs legally and philosophically from the development of fundamental rights, which was initiated by the Nürnberg Tribunal and continued with the adoption of the *Universal Declaration of Human Rights*" (emphasis added).[56] The UDHR thus played a considerable role in substantiating the case, but the CC said nothing explicit about its legal effect. From an overall point of view, the influence of the UDHR on the legal review of the case is undeniable.

Similarly, the preamble of the UDHR was invoked by the CC in case *II. ÚS 243/05* of 8 March 2006 when judging on judicial rehabilitations, and using a teleological interpretation. Again, the UDHR played the role not as a direct source of law, but as a guideline.

The most concrete elaboration on the legal effect of the UDHR in current case law was provided by the CC in its decision *IV. ÚS 238/06* (a restitution case) from 10 July 2007, when the CC stated that the UDHR was a resolution of the UN General Assembly, and thus only a recommendation without legal effects. The UDHR was not legally binding for national courts, because it was not an international treaty. Consequently, one cannot invoke the UDHR before national courts.[57]

The basic features of the dispute between the Constitutional Court and the Supreme Court included a number of cases which have been already outlined. The senate of the SC, which refused to follow the judgments of the CC calling for a lenient approach towards persons who refused to serve in the Czechoslovak Socialist army because of their conscience, stated that it was not possible to conclude that Article 18 of the UDHR includes the freedom to refuse to serve in army (*5 Tz 149/2001*). The CC then overruled this judgment. However, it is interesting to take note of the fact that the SC also referred to the UDHR, but arrived at a different conclusion.

Like the CC, the SC also referred to the UDHR when it wanted to demonstrate that international instruments involved a right in question (*see, e.g., 11 Zp 7/98*). The SC also had the chance to rule on restitutions, in which

---

[55] The plenum of the CC reviewed this case not in terms of religious liberty as before, but for the first time in terms of the (stronger) liberty of conscience, calling it "an absolute fundamental right" (*see* WAGNEROVÁ, *supra* note 54).

[56] The grand chamber of the SC accepted this approach in judging *15 Tz 67/2003* of May 2003 in which, however, the UDHR was not a crucial element in the reasoning.

[57] The same reasoning can also be found in *IV. ÚS 553/06* of January 2007.

it used the law referring to the UDHR. The SC based its judgments on the possibility of a violation of the UDHR (Article 17 on the right to property), and sent cases back to lower courts to take this possibility into account.[58]

The Supreme Administrative Court (SAC) does not refer to the UDHR, even though applicants regularly try to invoke it. In one judgment, the SAC ruled that the UDHR is not an international treaty (*5 As 43/2006–36*).

Generally, the UDHR is considered a non-binding document, the importance of which is acknowledged, and which is perceived as a guideline in reasoning. However, in cases dealing with statutes that contain a direct reference to the UDHR, the UDHR has been a decisive element in judging the case.

6. CONCLUSION

The Czech Republic followed the path of full guarantees of human rights after the fall of Communism. Thus, the main issues of the opposition movements that confronted the ruling Communist powers before 1989 were satisfied. Experience with Communist totalitarianism and with its conception of human rights remains a significant element in Czech politics and society as a whole. However, we still lack unambiguous interpretations.

It is possible, from the viewpoint of human rights, to assess the nearly twenty years of development in the democratic Czech state in different ways. Our paper has tried to show the basic information and the formal aspects of the acceptance of human rights. However, a different level of analysis would also deal with the theme of the current conception of human rights, taking into account a wide array of the theoretical/academic and practical/strategic levels of the issue.

It would seem that a listing of the four main features of the current conception of human rights (universality, individuality, natural origin, and acceptance of human rights as claims) is not sufficient to conclude the debate.[59] On the contrary, we can also argue various other problems: the possibility/suitability of further expanding the list of rights; the potential extent of their cultural/social/religious/historic conditionality; the ideological contexts of their understanding and promotion; the role of the state and its control and enforcement function in their realisation, and so on. Admittedly,

58 *See 22 Cdo 456/2001* of April 2001.

59 *See* H. MAIER, 'Lidská práva – nárok na obecnou platnost a kulturní diferenciace', in J. HANUŠ (ed.), *Lidská práva: nárok na obecnou platnost a kulturní diferenciace* (CDK, Brno, 2001) pp. 8–9.

we can also hear sceptical opinions about the current dominant approaches to human rights, or some of their philosophical assumptions.

The present human rights situation in the Czech Republic, as well as in other places of the Western world, is characterised by a feeling that human rights are 'a matter of course', an automatic (historically inevitable?) feature of liberal society. However, the Czech experience, as well as the experiences of other so-called post-undemocratic states, suggests that human rights are anything but a matter of course. Therefore their active practical protection requires embedding in the individual steps of autonomous actors (citizens and their representatives).

In other words, comparison of the concept of human rights with the actual situation in the post-Communist countries realistically indicates the limits of the application of such concepts in the light of their proclaimed universality. Also, the current Czech experience, as a part of the post-Communist reality, shows that the concept of human rights has been a phenomenon always closely related to a concrete social reality, to a particular situation. The everyday implementation of human rights in diverse socio-cultural, economic, ethnic and confessional environments logically leads to a multi-dimensional set of concrete expressions, to a process of perpetual 'choices' by of actors affected by the problem. The expected universality of claims does not necessarily lead to a universality of result.

The idea of the inescapable and definite triumph of human rights, suggested by a certain conception of human nature, seems to be debatable. The Czech experience suggests that such a debate may well be useful.

24. ESTONIA: TRANSITION THROUGH HUMAN RIGHTS

Katre Luhamaa

1. INTRODUCTION

The Republic of Estonia is celebrating its 90th anniversary in 2008. Its history, however, is able to show only 35 years of substantive and full independence and development. When the Universal Declaration of Human Rights (hereinafter UDHR) was adopted in 1948, Estonia was occupied by the Soviet Union.[1] Although the Soviet Union was an important participant and supporter of the idea of the UDHR during the drafting process in Washington,[2] it is ironic that a mere four months later, on 25 March 1949 more than 20,700 persons, mainly children, women and the elderly, were deported from Estonia[3] to Siberia. This deportation was initiated by the USSR Council of Ministers and did not follow any legal procedure foreseen and prescribed in the UDHR.[4]

The 50 years of Soviet occupation and subordination of the Estonian legal system to the Soviet system was followed by rapid legal changes and transformation at the end of the 1980s. These changes culminated with the adoption of the Constitution of the Republic of Estonia in 1992. These historical developments are the reasons why it is difficult to analyse the

---

1 For history and legal analysis of the Soviet annexation, *see* I. MÄLKSOO, *Illegal Annexation and State Continuity: The Case of the Incorporation of the Baltic States by the USSR: A Study of the Tension between Normativity and Power in International Law* (Brill, Leiden, 2003) On Baltic history in the European context, *see* T. JUDT, *Postwar: A History of Europe Since 1945* (Penguin Press, New York, 2005). In particular, *see* pp. 668–671.

2 Estonia belonged into the Union of Soviet Socialist Republics and was thus not considered to be an independent legal subject of international law. In practice, this meant the existence of a two-level legal system where some of the legal acts were adopted on the USSR level and some on the level of the Estonian SSR; furthermore, the High Court of the Estonia SSR had an obligation to follow the practice of the USSR High Court etc.

3 Together with Latvia and Lithuania, the number of persons deported was over 90,000.

4 The secret decision No. 390–1388ss from 29 January 1949. L. MÄLKSOO, 'Soviet Genocide? Communist Mass Deportations in the Baltic States and International Law', 14 *Leiden Journal of International Law* (2001) pp. 757–787.

acceptance and application of the UDHR or the subsequent international Covenants in the era of the Estonian SSR[5] and the transition period.

The current article is only able to delineate some of the main historical developments in the application of international human rights during the Soviet era and it concentrates on the developments of the restoration period and on the period of time after the restoration of the Republic of Estonia. The analysis consists of three parts. The first part provides an overview of the position and application of the UDHR in the Estonian SSR (from 1948 until 1987). The second part concentrates on the transformation or pre-constitutional era (1987–1992), and the third part analyses the use of the UDHR in the Republic of Estonia (from 1992 onwards).

2. THE OCCUPATION YEARS (1948–1987)

2.1. BACKGROUND

The Estonian SSR was a part of the USSR first from June 1940 and then, after a short German occupation in 1941–1944, from September 1944, and it did not have a separate international legal personality or capacity. Therefore it did not have the possibility to participate in the drafting of the UDHR.[6] The USSR, however, participated in the drafting process of the UDHR[7] and signed both the International Covenant on Civil and Political Rights as well as the Covenant on Economic, Social and Cultural Rights on 18 March 1973 and ratified them on 16 October 1973.[8]

International law, international human rights law in particular, was neither a central research nor a study subject in the Estonian SSR. In one of the few books on the United Nations published in the Estonian SSR, Abner Uustal[9] discussed the Soviet position in regard to the United Nations system as a whole and concentrated on specific instruments adopted by the UN, explaining how the Soviet rhetoric saw the adoption of the Declaration as a

---

5 Estonia Soviet Socialist Republic.

6 For example, E. SARV, *Õiguse vastu ei saa ükski* (Greif, Tartu, 1997) <www.okupatsioon.ee/trykised/saateks.html>, visited on 31 May 2008.

7 Although the USSR supported and participated in the drafting of the UDHR, it (together with other Soviet block countries) abstained from voting in the General Assembly on the adoption of the UDHR.

8 Due to political reasons, the USSR did not ratify the Optional Protocol to ICCPR.

9 Lecturer of international law in Tartu University since 1945, professor of international law 1966–1985.

direct result of the Soviet initiative.[10] In addition, he expressed the views how civil and political rights and social rights in particular could never have been fully protected in the capitalist states as the position of a worker and a capitalist can never be equal. Therefore, civil and political rights as well as social and economic rights could be protected to the fullest extent only in a Socialist environment.[11]

Although the extent and variety of rights protected under the UDHR were praised, the weaknesses of the UDHR were identified as deficiencies in its legal status (it only enumerates rights and does not guarantee them),[12] in the lack of a sanctioning system (or lack of an obligation to enforce these rights in the national legal systems) and in the lack of a right to self-determination.[13] It was also stressed that the rights protected in the UDHR as well as in the successive covenants had been substantially and constitutionally protected in the Soviet system even before the adoption of these instruments, whereas in the capitalists systems these rights had remained formal to a great extent.[14]

2.2. THE CONSTITUTION OF 1941

Already in June 1940, the Soviet forces occupied Estonia which contentiously 'applied' for a membership to the USSR[15] and was formally annexed on 6 August 1940. The 1936 Constitution of the USSR[16] formed the basis for the new Soviet Constitution of the Estonian SSR of 1941 and from then onwards, the Estonian legal as well as institutional system closely followed that of the USSR.[17] The Constitution of the Estonian SSR was "unanimously adopted" on

---

10 A. UUSTALU, *Ühinenud Rahvaste Organisatsioon* (Eesti Raamat, Tallinn, 1970) p. 55.

11 *Ibid.*, pp. 83–84.

12 This statement contradicts the findings of Åshild Samnøy who states that "the representatives of the USSR were the most vocal supporters of a human rights document in the form of a declaration". Å. SAMNØY, 'The Origins of the Universal Declaration of Human Rights', in G. ALFREDSSON and A. EIDE (eds), *The Universal Declaration of Human Rights: A Common Standard of Achievement* (Kluwer Law International, The Hague, 1999) p. 10.

13 UUSTALU, *supra* note 10, p. 83.

14 *Ibid.*, pp. 85–87.

15 *Deklaratsioon Eesti astumise puhul Nõukogude Sotsialistlike Vabariikide Liituriigivõimust Eestis* State Gazette 1940, 76, 743.

16 Translation available <www.departments.bucknell.edu/russian/const/1936toc.html>, visited on 31 May 2008.

17 Most of the instruments referred to in the current and next chapter have recently been republished in the collection of documents E.-J. TRUUVÄLI, *Põhiseaduse teel* (Iloprint, Tallinn, 2008) and in H. SCHNEIDER (ed.), *Taasvabanenud Eesti Põhiseaduse eellugu* (Juura, Tartu, 1997).

25 August 1940.[18] This Constitution was re-enacted by the USSR in Estonia in 1944 after three years of German occupation.[19]

The 1941 Constitution included a chapter on citizens' rights: the right to work (Article 90), the right to rest (Article 91), the right to social security (Article 92) and the right to education (Article 93) as well as equal rights for men and women (Article 94). It also protected selected civil and political rights: the freedom of speech and consciousness (Articles 96 and 97). Some rights were worded vaguely in comparison with the Constitution of the Estonia of 1937.[20] The most notable example concerned the wide discretion of the prosecutor in connection to the right to liberty and security (Article 99 of the Constitution of the Estonian SSR).[21] The Constitution also enumerated the severest crimes and defined the obligation to protect one's fatherland.[22] It is notable that changing or amending the constitution was made very easy and required only the decision of the highest legislative authority.[23]

The Constitution did not mention any international legal instruments (nor was such a reference added later), international legal principles or international human rights law. This is, however, understandable as the Constitution was made before the UDHR was adopted. This could also be evidence of the claim that the international instruments were seen as declaratory aims of the states and that a concrete application of them was seen as being dependent on the national legal system.[24]

---

18 TRUUVÄLI, *supra* note 17, pp. 270–288.

19 *ENSV Ülemnõukogu Presiidiumi, ENSV Rahvakomissaride Nõukogu ja Eestimaa Kommunistliku Partei Keskkomitee määrus ENSV-s 1940–41.a. välja antud seaduste, määruste ja otsuste kehtestamise kohta* ESSR Gazette 1944, 1, 2.

20 State Gazette 1937, 71, 590.

21 Article 99 "Citizens of the Estonian SSR are guaranteed inviolability of the person. No person may be placed under arrest except by the decision of a court or with the sanction of a procurator".

22 Article 105: "To defend the fatherland is the sacred duty of every citizen of the Estonian SSR. Treason to the country — violation of the oath of allegiance, desertion to the enemy, impairing the military power of the state, espionage — is punishable with all the severity of the law as the most heinous of crimes".

23 Article 119 of the Constitution.

24 This is illustrated by the fact that the USSR proposed limitation clauses such as "in accordance with the law of state/country". SAMNØY, *supra* note 12, p. 16.

2.3. THE CONSTITUTION OF 1978

The new Constitution of the USSR was adopted in October 1977[25] and this forced through constitutional changes in the Soviet republics which in the Estonian SSR were adopted on 13 April 1978.[26]

From the perspective of international human rights law, this Constitution took a step forward on the extent of rights protected. All central civil and political rights as well as economic and social rights were enumerated but most of them had a 'social twist': the right to organise was connected with an obligation to build Communism (Article 49),[27] the freedom of speech had to guarantee the Socialist order (Article 48),[28] the right to work was protected in practice through an obligation to work (Article 38), and so on. The Constitution made no reference to the general principles of international law or to any particular international legal instrument.[29]

2.4. THE RESISTANCE MOVEMENT

Domestic resistance movements organised themselves and started international actions at the end of the 1960s when Stalin's actions were condemned and there was hope for changes.[30] The pro-independence movement in Estonia[31] signed a memorandum to the General Assembly of the

---

[25] *See, e.g.*, J. PENNAR, 'Reflections on Union Republics in the New Soviet Constitution', 25:1 *Lithuanian Quarterly of Arts and Sciences* (1979), <www.lituanus.org/1979/79_1_01.htm>, visited on 31 May 2008.

[26] TRUUVÄLI, *supra* note 17, pp. 303–336.

[27] Article 49: "In accordance with the aims of building communism, citizens of the Estonian SSR have the right to associate in public organisations that promote their political activity and initiative and satisfaction of their various interests".

[28] Article 48: "In accordance with the interests of the people and in order to strengthen and develop the socialist system, citizens of the Estonian SSR are guaranteed freedom of speech, of the press, and of assembly, meetings, street processions and demonstrations".

[29] Current research showed no reference to the basic rights in the practice of the High Court of the Estonian SSR. The position of the Court should, however, be looked at with caution. There were several political processes conducted in the High Court and it is questionable, whether contesting basic rights in the court would have been allowed. The position of the High Court would, however, need further research. *See, e.g.*, T. KÜMMEL 'Saladuslik Eesti NSV Ülemkohus', *Eesti Päevaleht*, 11 February 2003, <www.epl.ee/?artikkel=227450>, visited on 31 May 2008.

[30] M. KUKK, 'Political Opposition in Soviet Estonia 1940–1987', 24:4 *Journal of Baltic Studies* (1993) pp. 369–384.

[31] It included both the Democratic Movement of Estonia as well as the Estonian National Front.

UN on 24 October 1972. It reached Western societies only in 1974.[32] The memorandum described violations of human and civil rights protected by the UDHR and other international accords in the Soviet Union. It requested the UN's assistance to remove the Soviet troops and to organise free and democratic elections in Estonia. Furthermore, since Estonia had been a member of the League of Nations, the appeal reclaimed membership in the United Nations.[33] Notable is also the reference to Article 21, paragraph 3, of the UDHR.[34]

The memorandum was not personally signed. Nevertheless, the publication of the memorandum in international press was followed by arrests and a highly political process in the High Court of the Estonian SSR in which five of the persons who had participated in the drafting of the memorandum were accused and found guilty of treason.[35] This, however, did not stop the movement and one author of the memorandum, Tunne Kelam, while still under active investigation, prepared in June 1975 a document describing the repressive methods used against human rights activists in Estonia and sent it to the European leaders, who were meeting in Helsinki.[36]

Human rights argumentation was also used in 1980, in the "Letter of Forty" Estonian intellectuals, where attention was drawn on the deep internal problems and shortcomings of the Estonian SSR. Special attention was paid to the cultural conflict in Estonia and to the repression of native Estonians by the Soviet system.[37] All these actions led to severe repression of the participants. At the same time, it built a basis for future actions at the end of

---

32 Tunne Kelam, the main author of the memorandum states: "We based the memorandum on international law, being guided by the basic documents and covenants of the UN". T. KELAM, *Eluloointervjuu: Valik artikleid ja esinemisi* (SE&JS, Tallinn, 1999) p. 86.

33 *Eesti demokraatliku liikumise ja Eesti Rahvusrinde memorandum Ühinenud Rahvaste Organisatsiooni Peaassambleele,* 24 October 1972. Reproduced in KELAM, *supra* note 32, pp. 201-203.

34 "The will of the people should be the basis of the authority of government that should be expressed in periodic and genuine elections that guarantee free voting". Preamble of the memorandum, KELAM, *supra* note 32, p. 201.

35 KELAM, *supra* note 32, p. 88.

36 *Ibid.*, pp. 90–94.

37 The first publication of the letter of forty in Estonia took place in 1988. 'Avalik kiri Eesti NSV-st (Ajalehtedele 'Pravda', 'Rahva Hääl' ja 'Sovetskaja Estonia')', 7 *Vikerkaar* (1988) pp. 66-67. Translation <www.sirjekiin.net/40%20Letters.htm>, visited on 31 May 2008. For further analysis, *see* R. RUUTSOO, '40 kirja lugu', 7 *Vikerkaar* (1988) pp. 68–73; L. VALT, 'Rühma kultuuritegelaste avalikust kirjast ja selle tagamaadest', 7 *Vikerkaar* (1988) pp. 74–75; S. KIIN, R. RUUTSOO and A. TARAND, *40 kirja lugu* (Olion, Tallinn, 1990).

the 1980s and introduced the international human rights rhetoric that was later used in the pursuit of independence.

In the West, the Estonian diaspora worked with human rights organisations to free the prisoners of conscience, while simultaneously kept alive the idea of Estonia's independence.[38] Despite the rigid political control of the Soviet authorities, contacts on various levels were developed between Estonia and the outside world. Western broadcasts from, for example, BBC, Voice of America and Radio Free Europe gained a wide listening audience.

3. RESTORATION OF THE INDEPENDENCE (1987–1992)

3.1. PERESTROIKA AND THE FIRST STEPS

It is impossible to describe in detail all the historical as well as the rapid legal changes that took place from the beginning of the *Perestroika* until the adoption of the Constitution of the Republic of Estonian in 1992.[39] Although acceptance of international human rights was stressed from the beginning of the transformation, these rights did not gain full protection until the adoption of the Constitution in 1992. The transformation process meant that several rights such as the right of legitimate expectation did not apply. The reality was often such that laws were adopted without sufficient drafting time. This resulted in frequent changes in law and led to problems in application. The current section delineates the central constitutional changes and the drafting of the Constitution from the perspective of human rights and international law.

Michail Sergeyevich Gorbachev initiated *perestroika* (meaning 'reforms') and *glasnost* (meaning 'openness') in 1985, and it was very well received among Estonians.[40] The economic collapse of the USSR required action on all levels. *Glasnost* was of greatest importance, because it allowed previously forbidden topics to be discussed publicly. Estonia seized this opportunity and on the anniversary of the signing of the Molotov-Ribbentrop Pact (the

---

38 According to B. Meissner, occupation of Estonia was not accepted by the NATO states. B. MEISSNER, *Die Sowjetunion, die Baltischen Staaten und das Völkerrecht* (Verlag für Politik und Wirtschaft, Köln, 1956). On the position of the US, *see, e.g.*, 'Baltic States Investigation', Hearings Before the Select Committee to Investigate the Incorporation of the Baltic States into the USSR, Eighty-Third Congress, First Session, Under Authority of H. Res. 346, Part I (1954).

39 R. TAAGEPERA, *Estonia: Return to Independence* (Westview Press, New York, 1993).

40 On the topic of perestroika, *see* M. GORBACHEV, *Perestroika: New Thinking for Our Country and the World* (Harper & Row, New York, 1987).

MRP)[41] on 23 August 1987, there was a public rally in Tallinn, at which people demanded the condemnation of the secret protocols of the Pact.[42]

This rally triggered political, economic and legal changes. From the legal perspective, the constitutional changes of 1988 made the most difference. The motivation for the amendment came from the planned modifications to the Constitution of the USSR that would have limited the rights of the republics; in substance, the changes proposed would have created one unified Soviet state.[43] Over 800,000 Estonians voted 'no' to these changes and on 16 November 1988, the Supreme Soviet of the Estonian SSR passed three significant documents for the restoration of Estonia's sovereignty:

1. The Declaration of Sovereignty of the Estonian SSR.[44]
2. The Law amending the Constitution of the Estonian SSR.[45]
3. The Resolution on the Union Treaty.[46]

It is significant that the first two of these documents were based on international human rights instruments — the International Covenant on Civil and Political Rights (ICCPR) and the International Covenant on Economic, Social and Cultural Rights (ICESCR) — and that the preamble of the 1978 Constitution was supplemented with them.[47]

Civic movements in Estonia were considerably activated. The Committee of Estonian Citizens was created, parties opposing the Communist ideology were established[48] and political and legal decisions for the restoration of the

---

[41] 'The Molotov-Ribbentrop pact: the documents', 35:1 *Lithuaninan Quarterly Journal of Arts and Sciences* 1989, available online <www.lituainus.org>, visited on 31 May 2008. Estonian version of the MRP can be found in TRUUVÄLI, *supra* note 17, p. 246.

[42] Presidium of the USSR Supreme Council condemned the MRP on 24 December 1989.

[43] TRUUVÄLI, *supra* note 17, p. 346.

[44] ESSR Gazette 1988, 48, 685.

[45] ESSR Gazette 1988, 48, 684.

[46] ESSR Gazette 1988, 48, 686.

[47] Article 1 changed the last paragraph of the preamble of the Constitution and stated that an inseparable part of the Estonian legal system include "covenants that are generally accepted by the international community and ratified by the USSR, CESCR and CCPR and to other international treaties and declarations that protect civil and human rights." (translation by the author), KELAM, *supra* note 32. All three instruments were declared unconstitutional by the USSR Presidium of the Supreme Council on 26 November 1988.

[48] Estonian National Independence Party included in its programme a paragraph on the civil and political rights and stated that "the Universal Declaration on Human Rights as well as other generally accepted international law instruments is an integral part of the Estonian legal system".

Republic of Estonia were taken.[49] Changes in the legal system were rapid. As it was impossible to re-introduce the Constitution of 1938,[50] a process of creating a new democratic constitution (and of a legal system) started. In the meantime, Estonia functioned on the basis of the legal acts of the Estonian SSR that were appropriately revised.

3.2. RESTITUTIO IN INTEGRUM

Restoration started with the decision of the Estonian Supreme Council on 30 March 1990 with the aim of creating the constitutional and institutional system of the Republic of Estonia[51] which was followed by two acts establishing a minimal institutional and legal framework for transition. The Law on the Basis of Interim Government of Estonia had the objective of separating the Estonian legal and institutional systems (including the court system) from that of the USSR.[52] For legal certainty, all acts in force on the territory of Estonia at the time of the decision remained in force unless the Supreme Council annulled or changed them or new laws were adopted.[53] Following the general tradition of the transition time, the changes were rooted in international human rights as recognised by the international community.[54]

Estonia wanted to gain international recognition and membership in international organisations as soon as possible. This aim was included in the decision of the Plan of Action, which included, for example, international connections with the USSR and participation in international institutions.[55] It was deemed important to ask for diplomatic recognition from the international community and to participate, as soon as possible, as an observer in international institutions including the United Nations.[56]

Reproduced in J. ADAMS, 'Eelnõu sünd ja saatus', in E. PÄRNASTE (ed.), *Põhiseaduse tulek. Kogumik* (SE&JS, Tallinn, 2002) p. 142.

49 For a historical overview of the restoration, *see, e.g.*, SARV, *supra* note 6, chapter 8.

50 For the discussion of problems concerning the pre-war constitutions, *see* R. MARUSTE et al., *Taasvabanenud Eesti Põhiseaduse lugu* (Juura Õigusteabe AS, 1997) pp. 9–20; K. ARJAKAS, 'Eesti Vabariigi Põhiseadustest', in PÄRNASTE, *supra* note 48, pp. 17–39.

51 ESSR Gazette 1990, 12, 180.

52 ESSR Gazette 1990, 15, 247, para. 1, adopted on 16 May 1990.

53 *Ibid.*, para. 4.

54 *Ibid.*, para. 8 of the law makes reference to the "international law norms protecting economic, social and cultural rights as well as political rights" (translation by the author).

55 ESSR Gazette 1990, 15, 248, adopted on 16 May 1990.

56 *Ibid.*, part II of the decision.

These few examples show the general trend of the time when numerous decisions and laws made reference to international human rights instruments. Using arguments from international law and aiming at the acceptance of the international community were seen as important tools for guaranteeing the fulfilment of the ideal of independence. Nevertheless, it did not mean that Estonia was able, from the beginning, to fully guarantee all the rights provided in these instruments. It was rather an attempt to gain acceptance and support at the international level.[57] In practice, there were a number of deficiencies in the application of the international human rights standards, but there was no official body that could monitor or act upon these violations. For example, it was characteristic of the time that all legal acts were enforced from the moment of adoption thus already prior to their publication in the State Gazette.

Due to the politically complicated situation and the attempts in Moscow to restore the USSR, a general referendum on the question of independence was held on 3 March 1991. According to the official statement of the Supreme Council, the participation in the referendum was high and 77.83 per cent of the participants voted for the restoration of an independent Republic of Estonia.[58] In August 1991, the internal political tensions in the USSR were at their peak, and in order to prevent possible military or other hostile actions from the USSR and feeling that necessary preparations had been made, the Supreme Council adopted a Decision on the Independence of Estonia on 20 August 1991, whereby the statehood of the Republic of Estonia was restored *de iure* and *de facto*. It also established the Constitutional Assembly.[59]

At the same time, Estonia was looking for support from the international community. The General Assembly of the UN accepted Estonia as a member of the United Nations on 17 September 1991[60] and on 21 October 1991 Estonia signed the ICCPR and the ICESCR as well as numerous other UN human rights instruments. Estonia joined the Council of Europe in May 1993.[61]

---

57 TRUUVÄLI, *supra* note 17, pp. 359–360.

58 Statement of the Supreme Council on the 11 March 1991, State Gazette 1991, 8, 124.

59 State Gazette 1991, 25, 312.

60 General Assembly of the UN, Admission of the Republic of Estonia to membership in the United Nations, A/RES/46/4.

61 For a personal account on the accession to the Council of Europe, *see* L. MERI, 'Euroopa kui eesmärk', speech in the Council of Europe, Strasbourg on 26 November 1991. Published in Estonian in L. MERI, *Presidendi kõned* (Ilmamaa, Tartu 1996) pp. 268–270.

3.3. THE CONSTITUTIONAL ASSEMBLY

The Declaration of Independence foresaw the elaboration and adoption of the Constitution in 1992. Therefore, one of the first tasks of the Supreme Council was the establishment of the Constitutional Assembly. The Assembly had the task to draft a democratic constitution, taking into account the historical developments as well as the needs of a young democratic state.[62]

The more definite tasks of the Constitutional Assembly were defined two weeks later and the deadline for handing over the draft of the Constitution was set on 15 November 1991. This left the Constitutional Assembly approximately two months for carrying out the work.[63]

Juhan Kristjan Talve, a member of the Assembly's second working group on basic rights, wrote in his memoirs on the work of the Assembly that the UDHR and the European Convention on Human Rights were common tools of the working group and that all the rights in the draft constitution were analysed from a comparative point of view in order to guarantee that they were in conformity with the most important international human rights treaties.[64] It was even stated in the Constitutional Assembly that "when Estonia becomes a member of the Council of Europe, it is bound by the ECHR and this should be considered early on in the drafting of the basic rights".[65]

The work of the Constitutional Assembly received much publicity in the Estonian media. Although the debates in the media concentrated on the form of the parliament as well as on the determination of who is a citizen, there were some articles in the media that also discussed human rights issues. Rait Maruste analysed the importance of basic rights and freedoms and stated that the constitution would bring Estonia back among the democratic nations and that the international community was not interested in our problems of continuity and form of state, but it was important to show how and to which

62 *Supra* note 59, para. 2.

63 The decisions on the functions, working procedures and the composition of the Assembly were adopted on 3 September 1991, State Gazette 1991, 30, 357; State Gazette 1991, 30, 356. Full protocols of the Constitutional Assembly are reproduced in V. PEEP et al. (eds) *Põhiseadus ja Põhiseaduse Assamblee: Koguteos* (Juura, Tallinn, 1997). For an overview and personal accounts of the members of the Assembly, *see* PÄRNASTE, *supra* note 48.

64 J.K. TALVE, 'Nädalavahetustel Soomest Eestisse põhiseadust tegema', in PÄRNASTE, *supra* note 48, p. 212.

65 The statement of V. Rumessen, in PEEP, *supra* note 63, p. 172.

extent international human rights were protected in Estonia instead.[66] Professor Ilmar Rebane published an analysis of the draft constitution and concentrated on the systems of legal sources as well as on the substance of basic rights.[67]

The UDHR is not visibly present in the text of the Constitution; it is not mentioned. It was nevertheless an important comparative instrument used in the development of the second chapter of the Constitution on basic rights and freedoms. It was used as an example of the number of rights that should be protected by a democratic constitution.[68] On the 10th session of the Constitutional Assembly, international experts as well as representatives of the main international organisations had the possibility to comment on the draft constitution. Most of the experts stressed the importance of having a wide catalogue of rights in the constitution and the need for having clear limitation clauses (the example of the European Convention on Human Rights was frequently presented).[69] The Constitution was adopted on 28 June 1992.[70]

4. CONSTITUTIONAL DEVELOPMENTS AFTER 1992

4.1. BACKGROUND

The adoption of the Constitution created some stability in the Estonian legal system and the Constitution created institutional support for the protection of basic rights. The Supreme Court was given the task of conducting a constitutional review[71] and the Chancellor of Justice was allocated the task to

---

66 R. MARUSTE, 'Põhiseaduses ei tohi inimõigused jääda tahaplaanile', *Päevaleht,* 12 November 1991. For a more thorough analysis of the publicity of the work of the Assembly, *see* A. JARNE, 'Põhiseaduse assamblee ajakirjanduses 1991–1992', in PÄRNASTE, *supra* note 48, pp. 103–116.

67 I. REBANE, *Postimees,* 13 and 20 November 1991.

68 5th Session of the Constitutional Assembly, PEEP, *supra* note 63, p. 153.

69 10th session of the Constitutional Assembly, 28 October 1991, PEEP, *supra* note 63, pp. 313-335.

70 State Gazette, 1992, 26, 349. Unofficial translation: <www.legaltext.ee/et/andmebaas/tekst.asp?loc=text&dok=X0000K1&keel=en&pg=1&ptyyp=RT&tyyp=X&query=p%F5hiseadus>, visited on 31 May 2008. *See also* M. SUKSI, *On the Constitutional Features of Estonia* (Meddelanden från Ekonomisk-statsvetenskapliga fakulteten vid Åbo Akademi Ser. A:502, Åbo, 1999); C. TAUBE, *Constitutionalism in Estonia, Latvia and Lithuania: A Study in Comparative Constitutional Law* (Iustus Förlag, Uppsala, 2001) pp. 79–111 in particular; R. MARUSTE, *Konstitutsionalism ning põhiõiguste ja vabaduste kaitse* (Juura, 2004).

71 §149 of the Constitution.

review the legality of legal acts and to try individual complaints of a more general nature.[72]

The basic rights are enumerated in the second chapter of the Constitution and this list of the rights is not exhaustive (§10). Moreover, "the generally recognised principles and rules of international law are an inseparable part of the Estonian legal system".[73]

At the international level, Estonia aimed at signing all the major human rights instruments as quickly as possible. Central milestones were the joining of the Council of Europe on 14 May 1993, the ratification of the European Convention on Human Rights as well as its First Protocol on 16 June 1996 and the accession to the European Union on 1 May 2004. By 16 May 2008, Estonia has ratified 78 conventions of the Council of Europe.

4.2. LEGISLATIVE PRACTICE

It is peculiar how international human rights have not gained more prominent attention in the legislative process after the adoption of the Constitution. There are only a few examples of situations where the UDHR has been used in the political debate, and these cases have been highly political and sensitive.[74] The first mention of the Declaration is in the records of the *Riigikogu*, that is, the Parliament of Estonia, which was concerned with the discussion of the Collective Labour Dispute Resolution Act in 1994. Marju Lauristin, the Minister of Social Affairs at the time, reminded in her speech that the right to strike was a basic right and that this right had an important position in the Declaration.[75]

The UDHR has also been used in discussions concerning the position of the Russian minority in relation to the adoption of the Language Act, the Aliens Act[76] and the citizenship rules. Sergei Ivanov said that it was

---

[72] Chapter XII of the Constitution, §139 in particular.

[73] §3 of the Constitution. §123 of the Constitution established the hierarchy of international treaties in the domestic legal system: "The Republic of Estonia shall not conclude international treaties which are in conflict with the Constitution. If laws or other legislation of Estonia are in conflict with international treaties ratified by the Riigikogu, the provisions of the international treaty shall apply".

[74] An instrument that has received the widest attention among Estonia's international obligations is the ECHR.

[75] *VII Riigikogu stenogramm.* II session, item 11, 9 March 1993. <web.riigikogu.ee/ems/stenograms/1993/03/t93030907.htm>, visited on 31 May 2008.

[76] *VIII Riigikogu stenogramm.* VII session, 1 June 1998. <web.riigikogu.ee/ems/stenograms/1998/06/m98060116.html>, visited on 31 May 2008. S. Ivanov asked T.H. Ilves (who was at the time Minister of Foreign Affairs) a question on 'alien's passports' and their conformity with the

discriminatory to ask Russian-speaking Members of the Parliament as well as local government members to prove whether they mastered the Estonian language or not.[77] There were no further deliberations on these claims. The substance of his arguments was, however, accepted and the requirement of proof was repealed.[78]

As the quality of draft laws has improved tremendously over the last few years and substantive legal, economic and sociological analysis is made before submitting a draft for consideration in the *Riigikogu*, there seems to be a growing trend to analyse the conformity of the draft legislation with relevant international obligations.

In the practice of the Parliament during the last five years, references to the UDHR can only be found in connection to the gender equality and equal treatment issues. Using international human rights instruments seems to be particularly important when the legal act concerns some founding principles of human rights, such as the principle of non-discrimination.[79] This can lead to the conclusion that the Declaration is used only in the politically sensitive cases, where human rights arguments need to appear strongly and in a uniform manner. The use of the UDHR seems to stress the wide acceptance of these rights and to overrule controversial approaches of other international instruments or practices of the international institutions.

4.3. THE PRESIDENTS

The use of the UDHR by high state officials such as the President seems mostly to be dependent on the personal style of the person. President Lennart Meri did not have a tradition of referring to concrete international instruments when talking about human rights.[80] President Arnold Rüütel, however, has used the Declaration more frequently. For example, he refused to proclaim a Bill amending the Property Reform Act, basing his arguments partly on the UDHR because the proposed amendment did not protect the

right to move freely. In his response, T.H. Ilves did not concentrate on the UDHR but rather stated that there has been international approval on the legitimacy of this action.

77 *VIII Riigikogu stenogramm.* VI session, 19 November 1997.

78 State Gazette 1999, 1, 1.

79 *Võrdse kohtlemise seaduse eelnõu* (the Draft Act on Equal Treatment), 262 SE, Explanatory report. Submitted to the Riigikogu on 8 May 2008; *Soolise võrdõiguslikkuse seadus* (Gender Equality Act), draft act No. 227, 19 January 2004 <roller.riigikogu.ee/orb.aw/class=site_search_content_grp_fs/action=showdoc&op=roller/id=199/doc=3e650dbe7f993583cbf439df69b5cada/040200011.html>, visited on 31 May 2008.

80 For the collection of the speeches of Lennart Meri, *see* MERI, *supra* note 61.

right to housing to the extent required by international law and, therefore, he sent the law back to *Riigikogu* for further deliberation.[81]

The use of the Declaration has also been deemed necessary in the relations with non-European states. The best example is the mentioning of the Declaration in the Charter of Partnership signed between Estonia, United States, Latvia and Lithuania on 16 January 1998.[82]

4.4. THE SUPREME COURT

The Constitution of 1992 created a three-tier court system, at the top of which there is the Supreme Court with a double function: it acts as a court of cassation and also has the functions of the constitutional review court.[83] The Supreme Court and its Constitutional Review Chamber in particular uses international human rights arguments and instruments frequently. In all major cases of the Chamber, the need for interpretation of some basic right has arisen.

The European Convention on Human Rights, the International Covenants and the European Charter of Fundamental Rights and practice of the relevant supervisory bodies are, therefore, the Court's main instruments that help to substantiate and interpret basic rights. The UDHR has not received similar attention. The Declaration is considerably more popular in the argumentation of the parties than before the Court. The Court rather discusses the issues raised under domestic rules.[84]

---

81 *"Elamuseaduse ja Eesti Vabariigi omandireformi aluste seaduse §121 muutmise seaduse" väljakuulutamata jätmine*, No. 671, 30 June 2004, <vp2001-2006.vpk.ee/et/ametitegevus/otsused.php?gid=50748>, visited on 31 May 2008.

82 "The Partners will observe in good faith their commitment to promote and respect the standards for human rights embodied in the above-mentioned Organisation for Security and Cooperation in Europe (OSCE) documents and in the Universal Declaration on Human Rights. They will implement their legislation protecting such human rights fully and equitably". *A Charter of Partnership among the United States of America, the Republic of Estonia, the Republic of Latvia and the Republic of Lithuania*, 16 January 1998, <www.mfa.gov.lv/en/?id=4495>, visited on 31 May 2008.

83 Riigikohus, <www.riigikohus.ee>, visited on 31 May 2008. On constitutional review, *see* P. ROOSMA, 'Constitutional Review under 1992 Constitution', *Juridica International* (1998) pp. 35-42.

84 The research showed only one court-case where the Criminal Law Chamber noted that the parties have stressed the violation of Article 6 paragraph 3 of the ECHR and Article 11 of the UDHR. In the analysis, however, the Court based its argumentation solely on the ECHR. *Pello and Kangur* v *Estonia*, 16 October 2002, Criminal Law Chamber of the Supreme Court, case No. 3–1–1–98–02, <www.riigikohus.ee/?id=11&tekst=RK/3–1–1–98–02>, visited on 31 May 2008, p. 7.

The Administrative Law Chamber has clarified the position and use of international treaties among sources of law in its decision number 3–3–1–58–02, part of which concerned with the direct application of the ICESCR. The Court stated that international treaties usually have a supportive interpretative function. However, there may be cases where the international treaty is, in an individual matter, clearer than the Constitution. In such situations, international treaties can be directly applicable. Prerequisites for the direct application of a norm of international law are that, firstly, the norm regulates internal relations, and, secondly, that the norm is clear enough and does not need additional national regulation. International treaties that would have this potentiality should also have been ratified by the *Riigikogu*.[85]

Although the other Chambers of the Court have not clarified their position in relation to the application of international treaties, the practice of the Court (and of its Chambers) seems to follow the same line of argumentation. There are several cases where either the ICESCR or the ICCPR have been used and applied.[86]

5. CONCLUSION

The development of the Estonian legal order in times of occupation, transition and independence show the importance of international treaties during unwanted political regimes. During the transition to democracy, norms of international law give the feeling of stability and can therefore be used in the political or legal argumentation better than the rapidly changing domestic norms. The UDHR was of central importance in the pre-constitutional era also because the Estonian SSR was not a party to any international treaty *per se* and the use of such a declaratory instrument did not require any accession or other formal procedures.

The analysis of the legal practice shows that the emotional and practical values of the UDHR decreased when the Estonian legal order was stabilised after the adoption of the Constitution. Legal argumentation, whether in the legislative process or in the court practice, rather relies on more concrete and justiciable obligations that are internationally supervised. This is why the ECHR is the most used international legal instrument in the practice and

[85] *Martinson* v *Lihula Vallavalitus*, 20 December 2002, the Administrative Law Chamber of the Supreme Court, case No. 3–3–1–58–02, <www.riigikohus.ee/?id=11&tekst=RK/3–3–1–58–02>, visited on 31 May 2008, para. 11.

[86] *E.g.*, *Brusilov* v *Estonia*, 17 March 2003, Supreme Court *en banc*, case No. 3–1–3–10–02, <www.nc.ee/?id=419>, visited on 31 May 2008, para. 21.

argumentation in the Supreme Court of Estonia. It is probable that the additional value flowing from the ECHR enables the practice of the European Court of Human Rights to be used as supporting interpretative materials.

25. LATVIA: BINDING FORCE THROUGH COURT PRACTICE

Maris Burbergs
Arturs Kucs

1. INTRODUCTION

The anniversary of Universal Declaration of Human Rights (hereinafter UDHR) has a special tinge in Latvia and other countries that, for well known and tragic reasons, could not be there when the document was adopted.[1] In 1940, the USSR committed aggression against the Republic of Latvia, followed by illegitimate occupation, unlawful interference in the internal matters of the Republic of Latvia and illicit annexation of the Republic of Latvia. All this was done by completely ignoring international legal provisions and the fundamental national provisions of the Republic of Latvia.[2]

The legal and political evaluation of these historical facts became quintessential when in the 1990s — 50 years later — Latvia was on its way to regain national independence and became capable of assuming obligations in the human rights field. The first evaluation on behalf of the international society was given by the United States of America. On 23 July 1940, Sumner Welles, Under Secretary of State of the United States, announced to the press that the US would never acknowledge the violent occupation of Latvia and the other Baltic States.[3] This action by the United States created a precedent

[1] O. ESPERSEN, The Council of the Baltic Sea States, Commissioner on Democratic Institutions and Human Rights, including the Rights of Persons belonging to Minorities, The lecture of 11 December 1998 in the University of Latvia in honour of the 50th anniversary of the Universal Declaration of Human Rights, <www.humanrights.lv/pasak/esplat.htm>, visited on 2 April 2008.

[2] *See The Compliance of the Borderline Contract between Latvia and Russia with the Satversme*, 29 November 2007, Constitutional Court of the Republic of Latvia, No. 2007–10–0102, <www.satv.tiesa.gov.lv/upload/2007_10_0102_Robezligums.htm>, visited on 10 March 2008. *See also Ždanoka* v *Latvia*, 16 March 2006, ECHR Grand Chamber, No. 58278/00, <cmiskp.echr.coe.int////tkp197/viewhbkm.asp?action=open&table=F69A27FD8FB86142BF01C11 66DEA398649&key=4404&sessionId=8649936&skin=hudoc-en&attachment=true>, visited on 15 May 2008.

[3] R.G. VAITS, 'Amerikas Savienotās Valstis un padomju okupācija Latvijā. 1940.–1941. gads', *Latvijas Vēstnesis*, 20 June 2001, No. 95, <www.vestnesis.lv/index.php?menu=doc&id=25455>, visited on 20 March 2008.

for subsequent announcements and declarations from more than 50 nations[4] and several international organisations, including the Council of Europe, and the European Parliament, about the annexation of the Baltic States to the USSR. This attitude of the international society as well as the fact that Latvian diplomatic corps in the foreign countries that was created by the government of Latvia before the occupation kept existing during the years of occupation,[5] and were essential conditions that engaged the minds of the independence activists, while Latvia prepared to regain her independence. And the way Latvia regained her independence is of importance concerning the accession to international human rights documents.

Since 1989 two main options for regaining Latvia's independence were discussed.[6] One of the options proposed to form a second Republic of Latvia. In international law, such a solution would have meant that the LSSR (the Latvian Soviet Socialist Republic)[7] was to be separated from the USSR, thus becoming a new country. That way the provisions of *state succession* could have been applied. For example, Latvia would have had to face the obligations that derived from the international contracts of the USSR (including the human rights field). The other option, which was supported by the Latvian diplomatic corps,[8] suggested that, regardless of the 50 years of occupation,

---

4 The unlawful occupation of the Baltic states was not acknowledged not only by the USA, but also by Great Britain, Federal Republic of Germany, France, Italy, Canada, Japan and other countries (alltogether more than 50). *See The Compliance of the Borderline Contract between Latvia and Russia with the Satversme* case, *supra* note 2.

5 Considering the fact that the government of Latvia stopped its activity as a result of the aggression and occupation by the USSR, the envoys of Latvia distributed announcements about the unlawful actions of the USSR as well as about the continuance of their work as envoys of the Republic of Latvia. Based on these announcements, the envoys of Latvia continued their work throughout the years of occupation, and they never acknowledged the annexation of Latvia to the USSR. *See* A. LERHIS, *Latvijas Republikas ārlietu dienests. 1918–1941* (Latvijas Vēstures Fonds, Riga, 2006) pp. 224–286.

6 *See* E. LEVITS, '1990. gada 4. maija Deklarācija par Neatkarības atjaunošanu', in V. BLŪZMA, O. CELLE, T. JUNDZIS, D.A. LĒBERS, E. LEVITS un I. ZĪLE, *Latvijas valsts atjaunošana 1986–1993* (Fonds Latvijas Vēsture, Riga, 1998) p. 222; I. ZIEMELE, 'Latvijas prasība par valstiskuma turpināšanās atzīšanu 4. maija Deklarācijā un tās starptautiski tiesiskās sekas', in T. JUNDZIS (ed.), *4. maijs* (Fonds Latvijas Vēsture, Riga, 2000) p. 81.

7 The name of Latvia in the period when Latvia was one of the republics that made up the Soviet Union. *See* The Constitution of the Union of Soviet Socialist Republics, <www.departments. bucknell.edu/russian/const/77cons03.html>, visited on 15 May 2008.

8 The envoys of the last independent Latvian government made a fundamental investment in the discussion about the versions of the restoration of independence, by sustaining the claim about Latvia's existence *de jure*. *See* Latvijas sūtniecība Vašingtonā, Neatkarīgās Latvijas ārlietu dienesta apspriede Vašingtonā, Embassy Row Hotel, Washington, 14–15 April 1991 (Archive of the Ministry of Foreign Affairs of the Republic of Latvia); ZIEMELE, *supra* note 6, p. 81.

Latvia had not ceased to exist and that the independence of the Republic of Latvia had to be *restored*. In that case, the Latvian *state continuity* could be discussed under international law.[9] This choice was announced by the Supreme Soviet of the LSSR in the Declaration on the Restoration of Independence of the Republic of Latvia on 4 May 1990 (Declaration of Independence).[10] It stated that the restored Republic of Latvia is the same country the independence of which was unlawfully interrupted in 1940, and that the Republic of Latvia has existed *de jure* throughout all of the years of the occupation.[11] That means that regarding the international human rights documents, the restored Latvia was in the same state as in 1940 when Latvia lost its independence.

The *Satversme* (Constitution of the Republic of Latvia, established in 1922) was restored with the Declaration of Independence in 1990. However, this did not strengthen the guarantees of compliance with the human rights, because no human rights or constitutional rights section was included in the *Satversme* in 1922.[12] In 1990, some time before the restoration of the independence, the politicians felt the insecurity in a certain part of the society because of the upcoming vital events of the country and they wished to mark the independent Latvia's foundation in the principles of democracy, against the background of which human rights would be complied with:

> "In the formation of a new, free Republic of Latvia, we urgently need stability in the domestic policies and feeling of safety among the citizens. The matters of humanism and the human rights have to become the keystone of the country's political actions, and as soon as possible … We must not linger, we must come out with official guarantees in front of the whole world about the fact that the citizens of the USSR as well as their offspring who have come to Latvia after the

---

9 *Ibid.*

10 Latvijas Augstākās Padomes un Valdības Ziņotājs, No. 21, 24 May 1990; for full text in English, *see* <www.humanrights.lv/doc/latlik/neatkdek.htm>, visited on 6 May 2008.

11 The *continuity* of Latvia is also acknowledged by the international community. Initially it was shown by not acknowledging the unlawful annexation of Latvia to the USSR, but after the Declaration of Independence it turned into acknowledgement of the state continuity of the Republic of Latvia, meaning — the international community acknowledged that Latvia is the same country whose independence was unlawfully interrupted in 1940. *See The Compliance of the Borderline Contract between Latvia and Russia with the Satversme* case, *supra* note 2.

12 The section of the *Satversme* about citizen rights and obligations was worked out in 1922, but the draft law was turned down because it did not gather sufficient votes. But the deputies were not against the section as such. Sixty-two deputies abstained from voting, because their strives to obtain more rights in different fields did not get sufficient support. *See* V. BLŪZMA, '1922. gada Satversme', in D.A. LEBERS (ed.), *Latvijas tiesību vēsture (1914–2000)* (Fonds Latvijas Vēsture, Riga, 2000) pp. 165–175.

> war, should not be afraid about their future after the statehood of Latvia is restored."[13]

This situation was also understood by other deputies, and thus the guarantees of compliance with the human rights were added to the Declaration of Independence.[14] On the same day, right after the adoption of the Declaration of Independence, there was a plan to establish a Declaration of Compliance of Latvian Laws to the International Human Rights Provisions. The initial version of this declaration anticipated coordination of the Latvian laws so that they would comply with the international human rights provisions, but just before the document was accepted, the following proposition was made:

> "I have a proposition concerning the human rights documents — to do something better and longer-lasting here. I mean — to completely join these human rights bills. That would be politically a very strong act. We, the Supreme Council [of the Republic of Latvia – auth.], would ratify the international human rights documents for the first time ever."[15]

Accompanied by applauses, this proposition was supported and the Declaration on the Accession to International Instruments Relating to Human Rights was established by an affirmative vote,[16] thus declaring the accession of Latvia to 51 international human rights documents, the first one being the UDHR.[17]

---

[13] Deputy A. Gorbunovs, Supreme Soviet of the LSSR, stenogramme of the evening meeting, 3 May 1990, *see* <www.saeima.lv/steno/AP_steno/1990/st_900503v.htm>, visited in 29 April 2008.

[14] The 8th point of the Declaration of Independence: *"To guarantee citizens of the Republic of Latvia and those of other states permanently residing in Latvia social, economic and cultural rights, as well as those political rights and freedoms which comply with the universally recognized international human rights instruments. To apply these rights in full extent also to those citizens of the USSR who will express the desire to continue residing in the territory of Latvia without accepting its citizenship". See* <www.humanrights.lv/doc/latlik/neatkdek.htm>, visited on 6 May 2008.

[15] Deputy J. Bojars, Supreme Council of Republic of Latvia, stenogramme of the evening meeting, 4 May 1990, *see* <www.saeima.lv/steno/AP_steno/1990/st_900504v.htm>, visited on 29 April 2008.

[16] Supreme Council of Republic of Latvia, stenogramme of the evening meeting, 4 May 1990, *see* <www.saeima.lv/steno/AP_steno/1990/st_900504v.htm>, visited on 29 April 2008.

[17] Latvijas Augstākās Padomes un Valdības Ziņotājs, No. 21, 24 May 1990; for full text in English, *see* M. SCHEININ, *International Human Rights Norms in the Nordic and Baltic Countries* (Martinus Nijhoff Publishers, The Hague, 1996) pp. 94–96, or *see* <www.humanrights.lv/doc/latlik/ dokdekl.htm>, visited on 6 May 2008.

2. STATUS OF THE UDHR AT THE NATIONAL LEVEL — LEGAL DOCTRINE AND COURT PRACTICE

As mentioned above, the Supreme Council of the Latvian Republic adopted on 4 May 1990 a Declaration on the Accession of the Republic of Latvia to International Instruments Relating to Human Rights (Declaration on the Accession).[18] According to this document, the Republic of Latvia acceded to 51 UN and OSCE human rights instruments, the first one being the UDHR. This raises an interesting issue of whether by the Declaration on the Accession the deputies endowed the UDHR with legally binding effect at the national level, despite the fact that the UDHR as a source of international law is not legally binding, with the exception of those provisions of the UDHR which have acquired such status as norms of international customary law.

There are different views expressed on this issue in the Latvian legal doctrine. It is unlikely that deputies of the Supreme Council intended to give the UDHR binding effect at the national level. The Declaration on the Accession was rather a political step in order to illustrate the outside world the intention of the new government to transform the restrictive legal rules inherited from the authoritarian system and to promote democracy, the enjoyment of human rights and the rule of law. Furthermore, such a declaration facilitated the recognition of the restored independence of the country on the international arena, including the admission of the country to the United Nations.

However, despite the vague intentions of the drafters of the Declaration on the Accession, this document has created legal consequences as regards the status of the international human rights instruments at the national level. It should be mentioned that the Latvian legal system is monistic and international legal acts can be directly applied at the domestic level after they are adopted by the Parliament. Therefore some Latvian legal scholars argue that by the Declaration on the Accession, the Supreme Council of the Latvian Republic endowed the UDHR with legally binding effect at the national level. This view seems to be confirmed by the subsequent practice of the Latvian

---

[18] Deklarācija "Par Latvijas Republikas pievienošanos starptautisko tiesību dokumentiem cilvēktiesību jautājumos" [Declaration on the Accession of the Republic of Latvia to International Instruments Relating to Human Rights] Ziņotājs [Official Reporter], No. 21, 24 May 1990. English translation available in SCHEININ, *supra* note 17, pp. 94–96.

Constitutional Court.[19] In one of its first judgments, the Constitutional Court stated that:

> "On May 4, 1990 when adopting the Declaration 'On the Renewal of the Independence of the Republic of Latvia' the Supreme Council guaranteed to observe internationally recognized human rights in Latvia. On the same day, when passing the Declaration 'On the Accession to the International Legal Instruments Relating to Human Rights', Latvia joined to the Universal Declaration on Human Rights and the International Covenant on Civil and Political Rights. The Universal Declaration on Human Rights is the source of customary human rights law [as translated by author][20] that is acknowledged the world over. All the international instruments on human rights are based on it and the states willingly observe the Declaration."[21]

The Court has expressed its position on the status of the UDHR in the Latvian legal system also in subsequent case law. In a case on limitations to stand for election of those members of the Communist Party of Latvia and the Soviet Union who were active members of this organisation after 13 January 1991, when the *coup* against the new democratic state took place, the Court declared:

> "When adopting the Declaration 'On Accession of the Republic of Latvia to International Instruments Relating to Human Rights' on May 4, 1990, the Supreme Council proclaimed that it acknowledged as binding several international instruments relating to human rights, among them the Covenant and the … Universal Declaration of Human Rights, adopted in 1948."[22]

---

[19] The Constitutional Court was established in 1996. *See* more on the history and practice of the Constitutional Court at the home page of the Court: <www.satv.tiesa.gov.lv/ENG/STlikums.htm>, visited on 16 May 2008.

[20] On the home page of the Court one can find the following translation of this sentence: "The Universal Declaration on Human Rights is the source of practice of human rights that is acknowledged the world over". However, in Latvian version of the judgment the Court explicitly refers to the UDHR as the source of human rights customary law.

[21] *On Conformity of the Cabinet of Ministers 21 January, 1997 Regulations No. 46 "On Government Agreements" with the 20 November, 1998 "Information Accessibility Law"*, 6 July 1999, The Constitutional Court of the Republic of Latvia, Case No. 04–02–1999, paragraph 1, <www.satv.tiesa.gov.lv/?lang=2&mid=19>, visited on 25 May 2008.

[22] *On Compliance of Article 5 (Items 5 and 6) of the Saeima Election Law and Article 9 (Items 5 and 6) of the City Dome, Region Dome and Rural Council Election Law with Articles 89 and 101 of the Satversme (Constitution), Article 14 of the Convention for the Protection of Human Rights and Fundamental Freedoms and Article 25 of the International Covenant on Civil and Political Rights*, 30 August 2000, The Constitutional Court of the Republic of Latvia, Case No. 2000–03–01, paragraph 2. *Ibid.*

Furthermore, in the case on the minimum wage for the prison inmates, the Court stated that "[t]he responsibility to establish a minimum wage in the State is also provided by the international liabilities of Latvia. The third part of Article 23 of the UDHR provides that everyone who works has the right to just and favourable remuneration".[23] Lastly, in the case on the restrictions on persons in custody during pre-trial investigation procedure to participate in parliamentary elections, the Court made the following statement: "Legal issues relating to elections are regulated by several international legal acts, binding on Latvia. Thus Article 21 of the Universal Declaration of Human Rights (henceforth – the Declaration), adopted by the United Nations Organization … on December 10, 1948 establishes: '1. Everyone has the right to take part in the government of his country, directly or through freely chosen representatives'".[24] Then the Court followed this up with references to Article 25 of the International Covenant on Civil and Political Rights (hereinafter ICCPR) and Article 3 of First Protocol of the European Convention of Human Rights (hereinafter ECHR). Consequently, the Court placed the norms of the UDHR among the international legal acts binding on Latvia.[25]

Apart from integrating the UDHR in the Latvian legal system through the *Declaration on Accession* and case law of the Constitutional Court, the human rights contained in the UDHR were also established at the national level. On 10 December 1991, the Parliament adopted a Law 'On Rights and Duties of a Citizen and an Individual', which contained most of the rights which are included in the UDHR.[26] However, this law was hardly applied in court because at this period the prevailing attitude among legal practitioners

---

23 *On Compliance of the Second Part of Article 55 of the Code on the Execution of Sentences with Article 91 and 107 of the Satversme of the Republic of Latvia*, 14 June 2007, The Constitutional Court of the Republic of Latvia, Case No. 2006–31–01, paragraph 2, <www.satv.tiesa.gov.lv/upload/judg_2006-31-01.htm>, visited on 20 May 2008.

24 *On the Compliance of Article 2, Item 2 of the Saeima Election Law with Articles 6, 8 and 91 of the Republic of Latvia Satversme (Constitution)*, 5 March 2003, The Constitutional Court of the Republic of Latvia, Case No. 2002–18–01, paragraph 2, <www.satv.tiesa.gov.lv/?lang=2&mid=19>, visited on 25 May 2008.

25 The Court followed the same line of reasoning in case on the compatibility of the criminal penalty for the defamation of official persons with the right to the freedom of expression by making a reference to respective articles of the UDHR, the international Covenant and ECHR. *See* the judgment *On the Compliance of Article 271 of the Criminal Law with Articles 91 and 100 of the Republic of Latvia Satversme (Constitution)*, 29 October 2003, The Constitutional Court of the Republic of Latvia, Case No. 2003–05–01, paragraphs 2 and 2.2., 3 and 3.2. *Ibid.*

26 The English version of the law is accessible at: <www.oefre.unibe.ch/law/icl/lg__indx.html>, visited on 20 May 2008.

was to consider human rights as declaratory norms. This perception of human rights was inherited from the totalitarian past. For example, human rights norms were included in the Constitution of the Soviet Union and the LSSR, but most of the civil and political rights were never applied in practice. There was insufficient knowledge among judges about the sources of international law, about the methodology of its application and the scope and content of different human rights norms as interpreted by international supervisory bodies for human rights. Legal studies and training programmes for practitioners, the establishment of the Latvian Human Rights Office in 1995 and the Constitutional Court in 1996, and debates about the necessity to establish human rights in the Constitution were among the factors to increase the knowledge about human rights norms and to promote their application in legal practice.

The reason for the fundamental rights in Latvia not being granted in the Constitution, until 1998, lies in the fact that Latvia, contrary to other Baltic states, restored the pre-war Constitution (*Satversme*) of 1922, which, as mentioned above, did not contain a fundamental rights chapter. Some lawyers argued that fundamental rights might be derived from Article 1 of the Constitution which declares that "Latvia is an independent democratic republic".[27] The Constitutional Court has confirmed this view in a number of judgments. For example, in one of the first cases, the Court assessed how the right of the freedom of information is observed in government regulations restricting access to special agreements within government service that provide civil servants with additional remuneration. Despite the fact that the disputable government regulations were issued before the fundamental rights chapter of the Constitution entered into force the Court stated the following:

> "In compliance with Article 1 of the Satversme, the authority of which in Latvia was renewed on May 4, 1990, 'Latvia is an independent and democratic Republic'. One of the features of a democratic and law-based state is guaranteeing human rights and fundamental freedoms."[28]

Therefore, the catalogue of human rights protected at the constitutional level might have been developed through the jurisprudence of the Constitutional

---

[27] The Constitution of the Republic of Latvia, <www.saeima.lv/Likumdosana_eng/likumdosana_ satversme.html>, visited on 20 May 2008.

[28] *On Conformity of the Cabinet of Ministers 21 January, 1997 Regulations No. 46 "On Government Agreements" with the 20 November, 1998 "Information Accessibility Law"*, 6 July 1999, The Constitutional Court of the Republic of Latvia, Case No. 04–02–1999, paragraph 2, *supra* note 21.

Court and its interpretation of the notion of 'democracy'. However, such an approach would have left a lot of uncertainties about the scope of protected rights. Therefore, in order to define the catalogue of human rights protected at the constitutional level, the Parliament adopted on 15 October 1998 a Fundamental Rights Chapter for the Constitution. This chapter includes most of the rights granted by the UDHR, both civil and political rights and social, economic and cultural rights. The latter ones are still regarded in some countries as political aims and not legally enforceable individual rights.

The legal protection of social rights under the Constitution is not disputable. For instance in the case on exclusion of certain groups of population from access to the social insurance system, the Constitutional Court cited Article 22 of the UDHR,[29] which makes the implementation of the right to social security dependent on the amount of resources available to the state. Notwithstanding this fact the Court declared:

> "Not doubting the close connection of implementation of the social rights with the feasibility of every state, the following human rights' conclusion shall still be taken into consideration — if some social rights are included in the fundamental law, the State cannot relinquish them. These rights do not have just a declaratory nature."[30]

There is no direct reference in the fundamental rights chapter of the Constitution to the UDHR or any other international human rights instrument. However, the case law of the Constitutional Court, which is the major source of interpretation of the content of fundamental rights in the Constitution, illustrates the close link between the domestic legal order and the international norms of human rights law. In a number of judgments, the Constitutional Court emphasised that "[t]the aim of the legislator has not been to oppose norms of human rights, included in the *Satversme*, to the international ones. Quite contrary, the aim has been to achieve mutual

---

29 Article 22 of the UDHR states: "Everyone, as a member of society, has the right to social security and is entitled to realization, through national effort and international co-operation and in accordance with the organization and resources of each State, of the economic, social and cultural rights indispensable for his dignity and the free development of his personality". <www.un.org/Overview/rights.html>, visited on 21 May 2008.

30 *On Compliance of Item 1 of the Transitional Provisions of the Law "On Social Insurance" with Articles 1 and 109 of the Satversme (Constitution) of the Republic of Latvia and Articles 9 and 11 (the first Part) of the December 16, 1966 International Pact on Economic, Social and Cultural Rights*, 13 March 2001, The Constitutional Court of the Republic of Latvia, Case No. 2000–08–0109, <www.satv.tiesa.gov.lv/?lang=2&mid=19>, visited on 20 May 2008.

harmony of the norms".[31] Furthermore, the Court has stated that: "[t]he content of the human rights norms, incorporated in the *Satversme*, shall be interpreted as read together with the norms included in international human rights documents".[32]

The UDHR is certainly among these international human rights documents. This is confirmed by the fact that the Court has made reference to the UDHR in a number of its judgments, even though the applicants in their constitutional complaints often referred only to the norms of the Constitution and international human rights treaties, for instance the ICCPR and the ECHR. There have been different ways in which the Constitutional Court has applied the UDHR in its case law. In most cases the Court has quoted a particular article of the UDHR in line with articles of human rights treaties binding on Latvia in order to interpret the scope and the content of the provisions of the fundamental rights chapter of the Constitution. For example, in a case of unequal distribution of state funding to private educational institutions on the basis of the language of instruction at a particular school, the Court referred to Article 2, sub-section 1, of the UDHR in order to clarify, whether the right to equality in Article 91 of the Constitution[33] included the language criterion as the ground for non-discrimination.[34] Similarly in a case on the Latvian Civil Procedure Act, which determines that "in a matter adjudicated by a judge sitting alone, the removal application shall be adjudged by the judge himself/herself" the Court

---

31 *On Compliance of Article 5 (Items 5 and 6) of the Saeima Election Law and Article 9 (Items 5 and 6) of the City Dome, Region Dome and Rural Council Election Law with Articles 89 and 101 of the Satversme (Constitution), Article 14 of the Convention for the Protection of Human Rights and Fundamental Freedoms and Article 25 of the International Covenant on Civil and Political Rights*, 30 August 2000, The Constitutional Court of the Republic of Latvia, Case No. 2000–03–01, paragraph 5, *supra* note 22.

32 *On the Compliance of Section 21, Paragraph 3 of the Civil Procedure Law with Articles 1 and 92 of the Republic of Latvia Satversme*, 15 February 2005, The Constitutional Court of the Republic of Latvia, Case No. 2004–19–01, paragraph 6.2, <www.satv.tiesa.gov.lv/?lang=2&mid=19>, visited on 20 May 2008.

33 Article 91 of the Constitution: "All human beings in Latvia shall be equal before the law and the courts. Human rights shall be realised without discrimination of any kind". <www.saeima.lv/Likumdosana_eng/likumdosana_satversme.html>, visited on 25 May 2008.

34 *On the Compliance of Section 59 (Second Paragraph, Second Sentence in the Part on Participation in Financing of Private Educational Institutions if the Programs are Implemented in the Official language) of the Education Law with Article 91 of the Republic of Latvia Satversme (Constitution) and Article 14 of the European Convention for the Protection of Human Rights and Fundamental Freedoms (as Being Read in Conjunction with Article 2 of the First Protocol)*, 14 September 2005, The Constitutional Court of the Republic of Latvia, Case No. 2005–02–0106, paragraph 14, <www.satv.tiesa.gov.lv/?lang=2&mid=19>, visited on 25 May 2008.

discussed whether Article 92 of the *Satversme*, which provides for the right to fair trial, included also the right to an impartial court. To determine this issue, the Constitutional Court made reference to Article 6 of the ECHR, Article 14 of the ICCPR and Article 10 of the UDHR and came to the conclusion that there is no doubt that Article 92 of the *Satversme* included the right to an impartial court, because this right was guaranteed by all the above-mentioned documents.

The Court has also expressed its opinion on the UDHR as a source of international customary law in the area of human rights. In one of its first judgments, the Court stated that:

> "The Universal Declaration on Human Rights is the source of customary law in the area of human rights [as translated by authors][35] that is acknowledged the world over. All the international instruments on human rights are based on it and the states willingly observe the Declaration."[36]

Thus the Court demonstrated that it regards the UDHR as a source of the international customary law. At the same time, it is not certain whether the Court goes as far as to recognise that all norms of the UDHR have the status of international customary law. In a subsequent judgment concerning the interpretation of the right to a fair trial in Article 92 of the *Satversme*, the Constitutional Court emphasised that Article 10 of the UDHR contained norms which have a status of international customary law. Hence if the Court would recognise that all norms of the UDHR have the status of customary law, there would be no necessity to emphasise this in relation to one particular article of the UDHR. At the same time, this statement of the Court illustrates that the scope of norms to which the Court assigns the status of international customary law is not limited to the prohibition of torture or racial discrimination.

---

35 On the home page of the Court one can find the following translation of this sentence: "The Universal Declaration on Human Rights is the source of practice of human rights that is acknowledged the world over". However, in Latvian version of the judgment the Court clearly refers to the UDHR as the source of human rights customary law.

36 *On Conformity of the Cabinet of Ministers 21 January, 1997 Regulations No. 46 "On Government Agreements" with the 20 November, 1998 "Information Accessibility Law"*, 6 July 1999, The Constitutional Court of the Republic of Latvia, Case No. 04–02–1999, paragraph 1, *supra* note 21.

3. CONCLUSION

On 11 December 1998, in honour of the 50th anniversary of the UDHR, Ole Espersen, the former Commissioner on Democratic Institutions and Human Rights of the Council of the Baltic Sea States, gave a lecture at the University of Latvia on "How to make the Declaration a living reality?"[37] Today, ten years after this statement, one can say that the UDHR has become a living reality in Latvia. While the Republic of Latvia was occupied when the UDHR was adopted and the Latvian people were deprived of most rights proclaimed in the UDHR, it was the values and rights embedded in the UDHR, which ultimately helped to overthrow the totalitarian regime and to regain independence at the beginning of the 1990s. The rights established in the UDHR paved the way for the establishment of democratic institutions as well as for the promotion of human rights and the rule of law.

Certainly, the transition period did not go without problems as regards the implementation of human rights. It required not only the amending of restrictive legal acts inherited from the Soviet system, but also a change in those persons' minds who are applying the new laws. The collapse of the planning economy system resulted in the deterioration of the enjoyment of economic, social and cultural rights. The change in the composition of the population due to the deportation of local inhabitants in the early years of Soviet presence and immigration from what is now the Russian Federation and the other Soviet Union republics challenged the existence of Latvian as an official language, but also raised issues of minority rights.

However, individuals and groups have used the rights embedded in the UDHR in order voice their criticism of government decisions and to challenge in the Constitutional and ordinary Courts the laws on different issues, as mentioned above. The Constitutional Court has cited the UDHR among human rights instruments binding on Latvia on a number of occasions. The Court has referred to the UDHR both as a source of customary human rights law and as the source of interpretation of the human rights norms in the Constitution. While it is uncertain, whether the Supreme Council of Latvian Republic intended to give the UDHR legally binding force by adopting on 4 May 1990 the Declaration on Accession, the UDHR has acquired such status in the practice of the Latvian Constitutional Court. The active use of the UDHR in the Court's case law and debates about its status at

---

[37] *See* ESPERSEN, *supra* note 1.

the national level in legal doctrine has illustrated that also 60 years after its adoption, the UDHR is indeed a living reality in Latvia.

26. LITHUANIA: SUBTLE MATERIAL IMPACT

Vygantė Milašiūtė

1. INTRODUCTION

In the 20th century, the Republic of Lithuania experienced the establishment, loss and re-establishment of its independence. The independence of the Republic of Lithuania was proclaimed in 1918. In 1940, following the conclusion of the secret Protocols to the Ribbentrop-Molotov Pact, Lithuania was forcibly incorporated into the USSR. The legality of the incorporation was not recognised by the majority of European states and the USA. In 1990, the Supreme Council of the then Soviet Socialist Republic of Lithuania proclaimed re-establishment of the independent Republic of Lithuania, which was recognised by the international community of states in 1991. Hence the role of the Universal Declaration of Human Rights (hereinafter UDHR) in the history of Lithuania was changing as the times were changing.

2. THE UDHR AND ARMED RESISTANCE TO THE SOVIET OCCUPATION

When the UDHR was adopted, Lithuania was engaged in armed resistance against the Soviet occupation by a national liberation movement which, in this form, lasted from 1944 until 1953.[1] From the perspective of international law, the members of the resistance movement were combatants.[2] Up to 1946, while it was hoped that the International Peace Conference would restore the pre–war state borders, one of the major tasks of the resistance movement was to continuously remind the free countries of Lithuania's subjugation and inform them about Soviet terror in the country. Between 1946 and 1948,

---

1 A. ANUŠAUSKAS (ed.), *Lietuva 1940–1990: okupuotos Lietuvos istorija* (Lietuvos gyventojų genocido ir rezistencijos tyrimo centras, Vilnius, 2007, 2nd ed.) p. 320.

2 J. ŽILINSKAS, 'Lietuvos laisvės kovotojų statuso pagal tarptautinę teisę klausimai ir MGB agentų smogikų bylos', 2(16) *Genocidas ir rezistencija* (2004), <www.genocid.lt/Leidyba/16/zilinska.htm>, visited on 25 May 2008.

when the possibility of a new war seemed realistic, the Lithuanian resistance tried to slow down the process of collectivisation and the destruction of farmsteads. They also attempted to break the information blockade and to pass information on the Soviet-managed genocide in Lithuania to the West. After 1949, the Lithuanian liberation movement focussed its activities on ideological struggle.[3]

In 1949 the congress of the representatives of the military districts of the Lithuanian resistance formed the Movement of the Struggle for Freedom of Lithuania, and on 16 February 1949 (the anniversary of the Lithuanian independence declaration of 1918, which formed the legal basis for the establishment of the Republic of Lithuania), it adopted a political declaration stating that the Council of the Movement was the supreme political body of the nation to lead political and military struggle for the freedom of the nation and to re-establish an independent democratic republic.[4] The Declaration of 16 February 1949 specified the state system of Lithuania, and stated that the restored state of Lithuania should guarantee equal rights for all of Lithuanian citizens who had not committed any crimes against Lithuanian national interests, indicated necessary actions in dealing with social problems, and, joining in the efforts of other countries to create "constant peace founded on justice and freedom, drawing support from full implementation of true principles of democracy stemming from an understanding of Christian morality and declared in the Atlantic Charter, Four Freedoms, President Truman's Twelve Points, the Declaration of Human Rights and other declarations of justice and freedom", appealed to the entire democratic world for assistance in implementing its goals. Exactly 50 years later, in 1999, the *Seimas* (Parliament) of the Republic of Lithuania adopted an Act on the 16 February 1949 Declaration by the Council of the Movement of the Struggle for Freedom of Lithuania, in which it recognised that the said Council constituted the sole legal authority within the territory of occupied Lithuania, and granted the status of a legal act of the State of Lithuania to the abovementioned Declaration of 16 February 1949.[5]

---

3 N. GAŠKAITĖ-ŽEMAITIENĖ, 'Lietuvos laisvės kovos sąjūdžio strategija', 1(5) *Genocidas ir rezistencija* (1999), <www.genocid.lt/Leidyba/5/Nijole.htm>, visited on 25 May 2008.

4 A. STASIŠKIS, introductory comment in *Lietuvos Laisvės Kovos Sąjūdžio 1949 m. vasario 16 d. deklaracija. 50 metų. 50 Anniversary. February 16, 1949 Declaration of the Council of the Movement of the Struggle for Freedom of Lithuania* (Lietuvos Respublikos Seimas. Pasipriešinimo okupaciniams režimams dalyvių ir nuo okupacijų nukentėjusių asmenų teisių ir reikalų komisija, Vilnius, 1999).

5 Lietuvos Respublikos įstatymas dėl Lietuvos Laisvės Kovos Sąjūdžio Tarybos 1949 m. vasario 16 d. deklaracijos (Žin., 1999, Nr. 11–241). For an English text, *see Lietuvos Laisvės Kovos*

Thus, somewhat paradoxically, although the Republic of Lithuania was occupied between 1940 and 1990 and had substantial difficulty in exercising national sovereignty, only two months passed between the adoption of the UDHR on 10 December 1948 and the first reference to it in a legal act of the State of Lithuania on 16 February 1949.

3. THE UDHR AND THE HUMAN RIGHTS-ORIENTED DISSIDENT MOVEMENT

The human rights conception of the USSR and, consequently, of the Soviet Socialist Republic of Lithuania, focused on the implementation of the right to work and the notion of the unity of rights and duties. The use of human rights terms by the Soviet Union did not imply much freedom of choice for the rights beneficiaries in practice, which was felt as a difference between the Western and the Soviet bloc's idea of human rights in the process of elaboration of the UDHR[6] and which resulted in the abstention of the Soviet bloc in the vote for adoption of the UDHR.[7] However, the people of the USSR in general and of the occupied states in particular did not unanimously share the official Soviet vision of human rights.

When armed resistance in Lithuania became suppressed by 1953, the resistance continued in other forms both in Lithuania and abroad. Dissident movement based on the human rights ideology started in Russia in the mid-1960s. It started as a cultural opposition which demanded intellectual freedom and a free press. Contacts between Russian and Lithuanian dissidents developed in poetic circles and also in prisons where political prisoners were detained. The first public statements about human rights breaches in Lithuania were made by Catholic priests regarding the rights of believers (starting from 1968).[8] The underground periodical 'The Chronicle of the

---

Sąjūdžio 1949 m. vasario 16 d. deklaracija. 50 metų. 50 Anniversary. February 16, 1949 Declaration of the Council of the Movement of the struggle for Freedom of Lithuania (Lietuvos Respublikos Seimas. Pasipriešinimo okupaciniams režimams dalyvių ir nuo okupacijų nukentėjusių asmenų teisių ir reikalų komisija, Vilnius, 1999).

6 E. ROOSEVELT, *The Struggle For Human Rights. Speech delivered in Paris on 28 September 1948*, <www.americanrhetoric.com/speeches/eleanorroosevelt.htm>, visited on 25 May 2008.

7 United Nations Yearbook 1948, Chapter V, Social, Humanitarian and Cultural Questions; Section a., Human Rights, <www.udhr.org/history/yearbook.htm>, visited on 25 May 2008.

8 Ž. RAČKAUSKAITĖ, 'Pasipriešinimas sovietiniam režimui Lietuvoje aštuntajame dešimtmetyje', 2(6) *Genocidas ir rezistencija* (1999), <www.genocid.lt/Leidyba/6/Zivile6.htm>, visited on 25 May 2008.

Lithuanian Catholic Church' was started in 1972, modelled after the Russian underground periodical 'The Chronicle of the Current Time' which was first published in 1968. Both periodicals used the 'facts' language and published documentary materials regarding human rights breaches. In the case of the Lithuanian chronicle, breaches of believers' rights were highlighted. The Catholic Church stressed that it reacted against arbitrary restrictions by Soviet authorities of the freedom of thought which was guaranteed by Soviet laws. The Catholic Church also indicated that its demands were based on natural law and the UDHR.[9] The first statement regarding breaches of rights of everyone, not only of those of believers, was made in Lithuania in 1975 by the poet T. Venclova who alleged breaches of intellectual freedom and, relying on the UDHR, asked the Lithuanian Communist Party for a permission for him and his wife to emigrate from Lithuania.[10] Also, that same year, a famous anti-Soviet figure A. Terleckas wrote an open letter to the head of the KGB of the USSR, claiming on the basis of his own experience that persecution for political convictions was not an unusual phenomenon in the USSR.[11]

After the adoption of the Helsinki Final Act at the Conference on Security and Cooperation in Europe in 1975, Lithuanians abroad, in particular the Council of American Lithuanians, employed the policy of relying on the USSR human rights obligations under this Act when individual rights of Lithuanians residing in Lithuania were violated. The KGB of Lithuania reported internally that Western propaganda centres found some legal basis for interference with internal matters of the USSR. In the 1970s, human rights oriented dissident organisations came into existence in Lithuania. In 1976 a Lithuanian Helsinki Group whose aim was to observe how the USSR fulfilled its human rights obligations under the Helsinki Final Act was formed.[12] The Lithuanian Helsinki Group differed from analogous groups acting in other USSR republics in that it demanded implementation of peoples' rights in addition to individual rights.[13]

---

9 E. JASELIŪNAS, 'Periodinės savilaidos formavimasis: sovietinio disidentizmo reiškinys ir Lietuvos katalikiškasis judėjimas', 1(11) *Genocidas ir rezistencija* (2002), <www.genocid.lt/Leidyba/11/ egidijus.htm>, visited on 25 May 2008.

10 T. Venclova's letter is quoted from A. GAIGALAITĖ and J. SKIRIUS (eds), *Lietuvos istorijos chrestomatija (1861–1990.III.11)* (Šviesa, Kaunas, 1993) p. 347.

11 RAČKAUSKAITĖ, *supra* note 8.

12 J. BANIONIS, 'Helsinkio susitarimų įtaka Lietuvos laisvės bylai', 1(5) *Genocidas ir rezistencija* (1999), <www.genocid.lt/Leidyba/5/juozas2.htm>, visited on 25 May 2008.

13 RAČKAUSKAITĖ, *supra* note 8.

The Helsinki Final Act was not viewed positively by all. In the 15 June 1978 Declaration of the National Council of the League of Freedom of Lithuania, the Act was viewed as a hindrance to effective implementation of human rights because of the proclaimed fidelity of the participating States to the UN Charter and the UDHR. Since the USSR had not officially proclaimed the text of the UDHR by then (the UDHR had been published only in the underground press) and since the Western countries were aware of human rights breaches by the USSR, the tone of the Helsinki Act was felt to be too soft and was interpreted to mean acceptance by the West of further human rights breaches by the USSR and, in particular, further denial of the rights of the peoples. The belief was that "the notion of human rights should comprise not only a right to live behind the bars, but also a right to create a national state", the League of Freedom of Lithuania was formed and the aim of re-establishment of the independent Lithuania was proclaimed.[14]

Notwithstanding repressions against their members, the Catholic Church, the League of Freedom of Lithuania and Lithuanian Helsinki Group by means of highlighting human rights violations by the Soviet authorities in Lithuania in the underground press and in petitions to heads of foreign states and international organisations, succeeded in sensitising both the international community and the Lithuanian population with respect to repressions against dissidents, the wrongfulness of individual human rights violations and the link between human rights and the rights of the peoples.[15] In this process, the UDHR served in the role of a yardstick for assessment of human rights conditions in Lithuania from an international perspective.

4. THE UDHR AND HUMAN RIGHTS IN THE RE-ESTABLISHMENT OF THE REPUBLIC OF LITHUANIA

In the late 1980s, Mikhail Gorbachev's *perestroika* and *glasnost* resulted in greater actual freedom of expression in the Soviet society and in a higher tolerance level by the authorities concerning the criticism of the Soviet regime. One of visible signs of this freedom was the fact that human rights became a subject of a public debate and human rights oriented organisations

---

14 Lietuvos Laisvės Lygos deklaracija, in G. ŠIDLAUSKAS (ed.), *Lietuvos laisvės lyga: nuo "Laisvės šauklio" iki Nepriklausomybės. Dokumentai. Konferencijos medžiaga. Kalbos. Straipsniai. Biografija* (Naujoji matrica, Vilnius, 2004) pp. 119–121; originally published in an underground periodical 12(52) *Aušra* (1978).

15 *See generally* ANUŠAUSKAS, *supra* note 1, pp. 534–540, 603–606.

did not have to remain underground any longer. The concept of the sovereignty of the people was treated as related to human rights in general and individual freedom in particular. From the viewpoint of political science, the re-establishment of the independent State of Lithuania in 1990 was determined by the desire to achieve a greater level of protection of human rights.[16]

Notably, in May 1988 the Lithuanian Academy of Science formed a commission which was to prepare amendments to the Constitution of the Soviet Socialist Republic of Lithuania. Draft amendments envisaged, *inter alia*, the implementation of citizens' rights and freedoms according to the UDHR and the Helsinki Final Act. The right of access to courts for the purpose of protecting one's rights and freedoms was stressed.[17]

In June 1988, the Lithuanian Perestroika Movement, which later became merely Movement (*Sąjūdis*) and was a decisive force in fostering the process of the re-establishment of the Republic of Lithuania, was created. The General Programme of *Sąjūdis* approved by its Founding Congress in October 1988 had a chapter on human rights and indicated that the status of a citizen should be based on the UDHR, International Covenant on Civil and Political Rights and other international human rights acts.[18]

The same year a Lithuanian Initiative Group for the Protection of Human Rights was formed of well known scholars, lawyers, writers, dissidents. The group prepared and signed its Declaration on the Protection of Human Rights which stated the aim of protecting human rights in line with the UDHR and with the will of the people of Lithuania to re-establish economic and political independence of the Republic of Lithuania.[19] In 1989 the Group developed into a Lithuanian Association for the Protection of Human Rights.[20] One of the signatories of the abovementioned Declaration was Mr Kęstutis Lapinskas, the present Chairman of the Constitutional Court of the Republic of Lithuania.

On 14 May 1989, *Sąjūdis* together with analogous national independence movements of Estonia and Latvia adopted a Declaration of Baltic Peoples'

---

[16] E. ŠILEIKIS, *Alternatyvi konstitucinė teisė* (Teisinės informacijos centras, Vilnius, 2003) p. 244.

[17] J. ŽILYS, 'Konstitucija kaip laisvės raiškos teisinė politinė forma', 6 *Parlamento studijos* (2006), <www.parlamentostudijos.lt/Nr6/6_Teise_Zilys.htm#_ftn20>, visited on 25 May 2008.

[18] Lietuvos Persitvarkymo Sąjūdžio bendroji programa, in *Lietuvos Persitvarkymo Sąjūdis: Steigiamasis suvažiavimas 1988 m. spalio 22–23 d.* (Mintis, Vilnius, 1990) pp. 203–216.

[19] For an English text, *see* <www.lzta.lt/lt-02-deklaracija-en.php>, visited on 25 May 2008.

[20] *See* <www.lzta.lt/lt-01-istorija.php>, visited on 25 May 2008.

Rights in which they treated Baltic peoples' rights to regain their state sovereignty as derived from, *inter alia*, the UDHR.[21]

Amendments to the Constitution of Lithuanian SSR made on 18 May 1989 eliminated provisions stipulating that rights and freedoms of citizens were guaranteed by the Constitution of the USSR and USSR laws and inserted a provision to the effect that rights and freedoms of Lithuanian citizens, provided for in the Constitution of the Republic of Lithuania, were guaranteed by laws and universally recognised international legal instruments. The right of access to court for the purpose of protection of rights and freedoms was guaranteed.[22]

On 11 March 1990, the Supreme Council (Parliament) of the Republic of Lithuania adopted an Act on the Re-establishment of the State of Lithuania. In this Act, the State of Lithuania, *inter alia*, stressed its adherence to universally recognised principles of international law, recognised the principle of inviolability of borders as formulated in the Final Act of the Conference on Security and Co-operation in Europe in Helsinki in 1975, and stated that it guaranteed human and civil rights as well as rights of ethnic minorities.[23]

The authorities of the Soviet Union met the Lithuanian independence declaration of 11 March 1990 with ultimatums and sanctions. The 14 April 1990 demand by President M. Gorbachev and Prime Minister N. Ryzhkov to revoke the independence acts and to restore the state of 10 March 1990, declined by Lithuania, was followed by an economic blockade on the part of the USSR which lasted from April until June 1990.[24] The 11 January 1991 demand by President Gorbachev to re-establish the validity of the constitutions of the USSR and the Lithuanian SSR in order to safeguard the allegedly breached "political and social rights of citizens" threatened by "a policy which is aimed at re-establishing a bourgeois system and which is opposed to the interests of the people"[25] was declined by Lithuania's statement which assured that human rights in Lithuania were defended by

---

21 Baltijos tautų teisių deklaracija, in E. MANELIS and R. SAMAVIČIUS (eds), *Kovo 11-oji — Lietuvos Valstybės Nepriklausomybės atkūrimo diena* (Žaltvykslė, Vilnius, 2008) pp. 396–397.

22 J. ŽILYS, 'Some of the Legal Political Sources of the Constitution of the Republic of Lithuania', 50(42) *Jurisprudencija* (2004) pp. 96–106.

23 The text of the Act on the Re-establishment of the State of Lithuania in English and a description of its history is available on the Lithuanian Parliament website at <www3.lrs.lt/pls/inter/w5_show?p_r=281&p_d=3248&p_k=2>, visited on 25 May 2008.

24 *See ibid.*

25 K. SAJA et al. (eds), *Lithuania 1991.01.13. Documents. Testimonies. Comments* (State Publishing Centre, Vilnius, 1992) p. 23.

the Republic of Lithuania and its laws and that outside interference had no basis.[26] President Gorbachev's ultimatum was followed by a Soviet military attempt to overthrow the legitimate government of Lithuania, in which 14 unarmed Lithuanian persons lost their lives, the public press, radio, television and some buildings belonging to the State were forcibly occupied, and the Parliament of Lithuania was put under siege.[27]

Soviet military aggression was condemned by the international community of states and the public and the re-establishment of Lithuanian independence was formally recognised by Iceland on 11 February 1991, while Denmark declared it was ready to re-establish diplomatic relations with Lithuania.

In these circumstances, the Supreme Council (Parliament) of Lithuania on 12 March 1991 adopted a resolution to solemnly undertake obligations under the UDHR and to access to the International Covenant on Economic, Social and Cultural Rights (hereinafter ICESCR) and the International Covenant on Civil and Political Rights (hereinafter ICCPR).[28] Reiterating its fidelity to the UDHR and the two covenants, the Parliament also approached the UN Secretary General and the States Parties to the ICCPR with a request to discuss the situation in Lithuania in the UN, to condemn the aggression in January by the USSR against Lithuania, to mediate in order to start inter-state negotiations between the USSR and the Republic of Lithuania.[29] On the same day the parliamentary Commission of the Legal System was instructed to submit proposals on the best way how to carry out the compatibility check of existing Lithuanian laws and International Bill of Human Rights, that is, the UDHR and the two covenants.[30] Notwithstanding these efforts to employ international human rights law and even though the USSR aggression was

---

[26] *Ibid.*, p. 25.

[27] *See* the Lithuanian Parliament website at <www3.lrs.lt/pls/inter/w5_show?p_r=281&p_d=3248&p_k=2>, visited on 25 May 2008. For chronology of events, *see* SAJA et al., *supra* note 25, pp. 15–21. Historical and political background of January 1991 events in Lithuania is also described in *Kuolelis, Bartoševičius and Burokevičius* v *Lithuania*, 19 February 2008, ECHR, Nos. 74357/01, 26764/02 and 27434/02, paras. 7–25, <cmiskp.echr.coe.int/tkp197/view.asp?item=1&portal=hbkm&action=html&highlight=kuolelis&sessionid=11603886&skin=hudoc-en>, visited on 12 July 2008.

[28] Lietuvos Respublikos Aukščiausiosios Tarybos nutarimas "Dėl prisijungimo prie Tarptautinės žmogaus teisių chartijos dokumentų" (Žin., 1991, Nr. 9–244).

[29] Lietuvos Respublikos Aukščiausiosios Tarybos kreipimasis "Į Suvienytųjų Nacijų Organizacijos Generalinį Sekretorių ir į valstybes — Tarptautinio pilietinių ir politinių teisių pakto dalyves" (Žin., 1991, Nr. 9–245).

[30] *See* transcript of Parliamentary proceedings of 12 March 1991 at <www3.lrs.lt/pls/inter3/dokpaieska.showdoc_l?p_id=251432>, visited on 25 May 2008.

generally condemned, the Soviet military retreated from the occupied buildings only following the failed communist putsch in Moscow in August 1991, which effectively changed the balance of power in the USSR. Only then the re-establishment of independence of Lithuania was generally recognised and Lithuania was admitted to the UN.[31]

To summarise, the UDHR, together with other international human rights law instruments, played an important role in the process of the re-establishment of the independence of Lithuania. International human rights law standards were used to guide the development of domestic standards of human rights, that is, to improve domestic human rights protection. They were also used as an instrument of international politics to show that Lithuania was a trustworthy and a law-abiding actor in international relations.

5. THE UDHR IN THE CONTEMPORARY LEGAL AND POLITICAL DISCOURSE

5.1. INTRODUCTION

The trend of employing international human rights law standards to improve domestic human rights protection has continued in the independent Republic of Lithuania. Bringing domestic law and practice into line with European human rights standards was a condition *sine qua non* of European integration, notably of becoming a member of the Council of Europe and accessing EU. The strategic political focus of Lithuania on European integration resulted in greater attention of the legislative, executive and judicial power to the European Convention on Human Rights and Fundamental Freedoms (hereinafter ECHR) as compared to the UN human rights standards in general and the UDHR in particular. However, the UDHR features among those legal sources of human rights, which are referred to by lawyers, politicians and the public-at-large.

5.2. THE UDHR AS A SOURCE OF CONSTITUTIONAL LAW

Although the Constitution of the Republic of Lithuania adopted in 1992 did not contain any references to the UDHR, its perspective of human rights is

---

31 *See* the Lithuanian Parliament website at <www3.lrs.lt/pls/inter/w5_show?p_r=281&p_d=3248&p_k=2>, visited on 25 May 2008.

said to be modelled after the UDHR conception of inborn, natural rights.[32] Article 18 of the Constitution provides that "[t]he rights and freedoms of individuals shall be inborn".[33] The Constitutional Court of Lithuania confirmed that this Article, being the first one in the chapter devoted to the protection of the individual in the chapter "The Individual and the State", provides for a fundamental norm on the basis of which inborn human rights and freedoms are protected while other articles of the Constitution merely specify those rights and freedoms and provide for the ways of their protection. The Court also linked Article 18 of the Constitution to the UDHR by quoting in particular the 'inherent dignity' and 'equal and inalienable rights' from the Preamble of the UDHR to explain the notion of inborn rights.[34] In another ruling, the Constitutional Court, when commenting on the inborn nature of constitutional rights, gave the following explanation:

> "The inborn nature of human rights means that they are inseparable from an individual, that they are linked with neither a territory nor a nation. An individual possesses his inborn rights regardless of whether they are entrenched in legal acts of the state or not. These rights are enjoyed by every individual, and it means that they are enjoyed by the best and worst people alike ... The inborn human rights are inborn opportunities of an individual which ensure his human dignity in the spheres of social life. They constitute that minimum, that starting point from which all the other rights are developed and supplemented, and which constitute the values that are unquestionably recognised by the international community."[35]

More specifically, the Constitutional Court interpreted Article 3 of the UDHR (right to life, liberty and security) as predicting the perspective of the refusal of the death penalty, in line with the interpretations given by the UN

32 T. BIRMONTIENĖ, 'Žmogaus teisių konstitucinė samprata', in V. ADOMAITIENĖ (ed.), *Lietuvos konstitucinė teisė: raida, institucijos, teisių apsauga, savivalda* (Mykolo Romerio universitetas, Vilnius, 2007) pp. 327–328.

33 Lietuvos Respublikos Konstitucija (Žin., 1992, Nr. 33–1014).

34 The Constitutional Court of the Republic of Lithuania Ruling of 20 November 1996 'On the compliance of Article 5 of the Law of the Republic of Lithuania on the Privatisation of Apartments with the Constitution of the Republic of Lithuania', available in English at <www.lrkt.lt/dokumentai/1996/n6a1120a.htm>, visited on 25 May 2008.

35 The Constitutional Court of the Republic of Lithuania Ruling of 9 December 1998 'On the compliance of the death penalty provided for by the sanction of Article 105 of the Republic of Lithuania Criminal Code with the Constitution of the Republic of Lithuania', available in English at <www.lrkt.lt/dokumentai/1998/n8a1209a.htm>, visited on 25 May 2008.

Secretary General and General Assembly, and held unconstitutional a domestic legal norm providing for death penalty.[36]

5.3. THE UDHR IN THE ADJUDICATION OF INDIVIDUAL CASES

While the Constitutional Court of Lithuania is not competent to deal with individual complaints, issues of individual constitutional or human rights are examined by courts of general competence or by administrative courts. In adjudicating individual cases, these courts have so far not used the UDHR as an independent source of human rights. When the UDHR is referred to it is mentioned among other international legal acts providing for human rights, alongside with, for example, UN Charter, ICCPR, ICESCR, ECHR and the European Social Charter.[37] Occasionally applicants or their lawyers refer to the UDHR in more imaginative ways, for example, as providing for a prohibition of inconsistency of domestic laws and a requirement of a reasonable link between restrictions imposed by laws and actual needs of the society.[38]

5.4. THE UDHR IN POLITICAL DEBATE

All political parties in Lithuania declare their fidelity to the protection of human, individual or constitutional rights but do not specifically mention the UDHR in their charters or when forming their position on controversial issues (such as the notion of family, permissibility of abortions, and so on). The UDHR tends to attract most attention at its anniversaries. For instance, on the occasion of its 50th anniversary in 1998, the *Seimas* (Parliament) of the Republic of Lithuania held a solemn meeting in which politicians and public figures shared their views on the importance of the UDHR. The Chairman of the Parliamentary Committee of Human and Citizens' Rights and Ethnicity Matters E. Zingeris then observed that "by its importance the

---

36 *Ibid.*

37 *See* the Supreme Court of Lithuania Ruling of 25 June 2003 in civil case No. 3K-3-747/2003. The applicant alleged his illegal dismissal and failure by the employer to grant him parental leave. The Supreme Court quoted the abovementioned international legal acts as sources of the prohibition of discrimination and, having examined the facts of the case, ruled in favour of the applicant.

38 *See* the Supreme Administrative Court of Lithuania ruling of 8 January 2003 in case No. 49-03. The applicant used the UDHR to challenge the validity of a fine imposed on him for driving a vehicle with tinted windows. The Court was not impressed by the applicant's human rights arguments and upheld the decision to impose a fine.

UDHR was the fourth document in the world after Thomas Jefferson's Declaration, the Declaration of Rights of the Great French Revolution, and the 3 May 1791 Constitution of the joint state of Poland and Lithuania". Acknowledging the importance of the UDHR Mr. E. Zingeris nevertheless noted that at the time of the adoption of the UDHR the states occupied by the USSR were suffering from Soviet terror, and the voice of these states was heard by the international community only in 1991.[39] The Catholic priest J. Boruta noted that peaceful revolutions of Eastern and Central Europe in 1988 and 1989 were based on ideals enshrined in the UDHR.[40] These quotations illustrate a generally very positive attitude of the Lithuanian society towards the UDHR, which is somewhat reserved only due to Lithuanian experience of human rights for a long time having been merely remote hopes and ideals overshadowed by a different political reality.

One notable occasion when the UDHR was referred to in a political debate in a substantive manner stressing its importance as a yardstick for assessing the legality of treatment suffered by the Lithuanian nation as well as other nations under Communist rule was an International Congress on the Evaluation of Communist Crimes followed by the proceedings of the International Public Tribunal on the Evaluation of the Crimes of Communism held in Vilnius in 2000.[41] The Congress, attended by individuals and non-governmental organisations from 24 countries, appealed to the UN and to the Parliaments and Governments of all States urging them to establish the International Tribunal for the Prosecution of the Crimes of Communism in order to punish the perpetrators. At the same time the Congress agreed to set up the International Public Tribunal and authorised it to give a social, political and legal assessment of the Communist doctrine and the criminal acts committed by the Communist regimes. The latter tribunal held its proceedings in Vilnius and, relying, *inter alia*, on the UDHR (especially Article 3 providing for the right to life and essential for the protection against genocide) assessed the evidence submitted by public prosecutors from 15 countries, numerous witnesses and defence speakers and passed a judgment on the criminal nature of the Communist doctrine and on the crimes committed by the regime. The final operative clause of the judgment pointed

---

39 *See* transcript of Parliamentary proceedings at <www3.lrs.lt/pls/bis/doc_print.print?key=69717>, visited on 25 May 2008.

40 *Ibid.*

41 *See generally* A. ANUŠAUSKAS et al. (eds), *Anti-Communist Congress and Proceedings of the International Public Tribunal in Vilnius "Evaluation of the Crimes of Communism" 2000* (Ramona, Vilnius, 2002); *Vilnius International Public Tribunal on the Evaluation of Crimes of Communism*, <ok.w3.lt/cgi-bin/tribunal/En_Tr_program.htm>, visited on 30 July 2008.

to the necessity of submitting the evidence collected to an international criminal trial under the auspices of the UN.[42]

Reliance on the UDHR in the political debate related to issues of genocide may be explained by the insufficiency of the concept of genocide in the UN 1948 Convention on the Prevention and Punishment of the Crime of Genocide to address the issue of genocide against what the Communist regimes would prefer to define as a 'class' (that is, a political or social group) rather than a nation.[43] The issue of the insufficiency of the abovementioned Convention to evaluate genocide, politically re-emerged in Lithuania in the course of recent EU discussions on the proposed Council Framework Decision on Combating Racism and Xenophobia, which specifically addressed the Nazi but not the Soviet crimes of genocide even though the Communist crimes were felt by their victims to be racist or xenophobic as a significant portion of them were directed against "enemy nations" because of their association with the "enemy class".[44] Even though in the context of the debate on the abovementioned EU Framework Decision the UDHR has not so far played a significant role, it can be expected that the lack of attention in international and EU law to collective suffering might shift the discussion on the Soviet genocide in Lithuania back to individual rights and dignity protected by the UDHR.

5.5. THE UDHR AND HUMAN RIGHTS ISSUES IN THE MASS MEDIA

The UDHR is referred to in mass media when global human rights controversies are commented or analysed. For instance, some time after the 11 September 2001 attacks in the USA, the daily *Lietuvos rytas* commented that these events drew parallels between, on the one hand, those to whom the UDHR was important and, on the other those to whom it was not.[45] When domestic or European human rights issues are discussed, the ECHR is

---

42 *Judgement of the International Public Tribunal in Vilnius*, in ANUŠAUSKAS et al., *supra* note 41, pp. 900–1002.

43 *International Congress on the Evaluation of the Crimes of Communism Resolution Regarding the Extension of the Meaning of the Concept of Genocide, ibid.*, p. 483; also available at <ok.w3.lt/cgi-bin/2000.pl?En_rezo.htm>, visited on 30 July 2008.

44 A general approach on the Council Framework Decision on Racism and Xenophobia was reached on 19–20 April 2007 in the 2794th Council meeting (Justice and Home Affairs). *See* the relevant press release of the Council of the EU at <europa.eu/rapid/pressReleasesAction.do?reference=PRES/07/77&format=HTML&aged=1&language=EN&guiLanguage=fr>, visited on 30 July 2008.

45 'Interesų ir vertybių sankirtos aidai', *Lietuvos rytas*, 19 January 2002, available at <www.tspmi.vu.lt/files/tpkomentarai/LR%2001-19.htm>, visited on 25 May 2008.

usually referred to. Heated debate arose in the society, for example, around the ECHR cases on issues of a right to change one's sex (following the decision in *L.* v *Lithuania*[46]) and a right of homosexuals to adopt (following the decision in *E.B.* v *France*[47]), and various reactions were reflected in mass media. In general, the UDHR is viewed by Lithuanians as a catalogue of obvious, uncontested rights. It does not tend to directly give rise to controversial judicial or policy decisions and, therefore, it receives considerably less media attention than the ECHR.

6. THE INFLUENCE OF THE UDHR ON THE UNDERSTANDING OF HUMAN RIGHTS IN LITHUANIA

A question in which ways the UDHR has influenced thinking in Lithuania is a difficult one. When people's deeds are in line with UDHR it is still impossible to know where those people got their ideas from. As the UDHR in itself is a product of centuries of thinking and as it is never the only factor which influences people's thinking, tracing the UDHR in the thinking of a nation can be a cumbersome task.

A Lithuanian lawyer could say that the UDHR influenced the content of subsequent international human rights acts, notably the UN human rights treaties and the ECHR, and as a result of implementation of those treaties in Lithuania, as in any other country, the UDHR maxims became axiomatic. The most obvious sign of the UDHR in the legal system of Lithuania is the already mentioned constitutional provision providing for inborn nature of human rights. However, in this respect, the UDHR itself only repeated what natural law proponents put forwards centuries ago. Therefore, the influence of the UDHR on the content of the concept of inborn nature of rights in the Constitution of Lithuania can be questioned. Similarly one can question the importance of the UDHR for specific implementation of its right to liberty or to fair trial because the current content of relevant Lithuanian laws was directly influenced by the case law of the European Court of Human Rights, which is understandably far more specific than the respective UDHR provisions.

---

46 *L* v. *Lithuania*, 11 September 2007, ECHR, No. 27527/03, <cmiskp.echr.coe.int/tkp197/view.asp?item=7&portal=hbkm&action=html&highlight=Lithuania&sessionid=11603989&skin=hudoc-en>, visited on 12 July 2008.

47 *E.B.* v. *France*, 22 January 2008, ECHR, No. 43546/02, <cmiskp.echr.coe.int/tkp197/view.asp?item=15&portal=hbkm&action=html&highlight=France&sessionid=11603989&skin=hudoc-en>, visited on 12 July 2008.

A Lithuanian person interested in politics could find on a website of one of the Lithuanian political parties a section where thoughts of party members are published, and read an observation that 'globalism', that is, the ideology of the unification of the world (as distinguished from 'globalisation' which is the process of the application of this ideology), was formulated in the Communist Party Manifesto and that its actual implementation started with the adoption of the UDHR.[48] The same website publishes a presentation by one of the party leaders, philosopher R. Ozolas, where he voices concerns that the European Union poses a threat to the Lithuanian nation as the "Euro-nation" is being created.[49] Mr. R. Ozolas observes that one of the means for assimilating nations is the UDHR which creates legal opportunities for everyone to struggle against her state.[50] Again, it is quite difficult to assess to what extent such interpretations were influenced by the UDHR itself and to what extent they resulted from extraneous factors.

A Lithuanian person without any specific interest in law or in politics but with an artistic twist, could feel that her rights are accurately described in the so-called Constitution of the Republic of Užupis, the artists' district of Vilnius, often compared to Montmartre in Paris. The Constitution of the self-declared Užupis Republic (which, to dispel any possible doubts, does not aspire to international recognition or UN membership) can be found affixed on a wall in the area and is essentially a declaration of rights and obligations of a human person and some other beings. This constitution provides for, *inter alia*, a right to hot water, a right to love and take care of a cat, a right to be happy, a right to be unhappy, a right to believe, a right to cry, and a right not to have any rights.[51] Noticing that the form of the Užupis Constitution is similar to the UDHR one could ask whether the content of the catalogue of rights was influenced by the UDHR. There could be various sub-questions and various answers. Is it possible that the recognition of the presence and the absence of rights in the Užupis Constitution are somehow linked to the painful collective memory of the UDHR being out there for all but at the

---

48 *See '2006 08 23'*, <centropartija.lt/pamastymai(arch).html>, visited on 25 May 2008.

49 Such a view does not seem to prevail in Lithuania. According to the opinion research centre VILMORUS, in May 2008, 70 per cent of the population supported Lithuania's membership in the EU. The number of EU membership supporters has been rather stable. *See Lithuanian Public Opinion and the EU Membership*, <www.euro.lt/en/lithuanias-membership-in-the-eu/lithuanian-public-opinion/>, visited on 8 July 2008.

50 R. OZOLAS, *Nacionalinė valstybė kaip principas. Pranešimas konferencijoje "Lietuvių tautos atgimimas: praeitis, dabartis, ateitis" Kauno karo muziejuje 2007 m. lapkričio 26 d.*, <centropartija.lt/kronika.htm>, visited on 25 May 2008.

51 *See Užupis*, <en.wikipedia.org/wiki/U%C5%BEupis>, visited on 25 May 2008.

same time not being actually implemented in the Soviet era? Or is the catalogue merely a literary attempt to capture the multifaceted complexity of being, and to search for harmony with inner and outer world? Does the ambiguity of this particular catalogue of rights and obligations have anything to do with the memories of the "universal absurdity" of the Soviet world or the useful knowledge from that period that "having learnt ambiguity you find a way to avoid the moralising difference between black and white" as described in literary works and discussed by literary critics?[52] Could it be that the Užupis Constitution expresses the view of the Lithuanian nation that the catalogue of rights in the UDHR is not complete? Lithuanian dissidents in Soviet times regretted that the UDHR did not contain a peoples' right to create a state. The Chairman of the Supreme Council of Lithuania Mr. V. Landsbergis in his testimony given on 7 May 1991 to the Helsinki Commission of the US Congress said it was a pity that among human rights, with which modern democracies were preoccupied, a right to have a Motherland was seldom mentioned.[53]

The present author does not have any evidence that the UDHR or its interpretations by lawyers or politicians has inspired the artistic minds of Užupis to specifically deal with the issue of rights omitted from the UDHR, and merely observes that the Constitution of the Republic of Užupis in its first line provides for a right which is not found in the UDHR but which alleviates concerns related to the absence in it of a right to have a Motherland. Article 1 of the artists' district constitution proclaims "[a] human being has a right to live by the River Vilnelė, while the River Vilnelė has a right to flow by a human being".[54]

---

[52] I. VEDRICKAITĖ, 'Know your Place, Noisy Northerner', 21 *the Vilnius Review* (spring/summer 2007), <test.svs.lt/?Vilnius;Number(195);Article(4656)>, visited on 25 May 2008. For more on the impact of Communist rule on the understanding of the difference between truth and falsehood, *see* the International Congress on the Evaluation of the Crimes of Communism Resolution Regarding the Spiritual Consequences of Genocide, in ANUŠAUSKAS et al., *supra* note 41, p. 482, also available at <ok.w3.lt/cgi-bin/2000.pl?En_rezo.htm>, visited on 30 July 2008.

[53] 1991 m. gegužės 7 d. Liudijimas JAV Kongreso Helsinkio komisijos apklausoje in V. LANDSBERGIS, *Laisvės byla* ("Lietuvos aido" leidykla, Vilnius, 1992) p. 231.

[54] *See Užupis* at <en.wikipedia.org/wiki/U%C5%BEupis>, visited on 25 May 2008.

27. THE SLOVAK REPUBLIC: POLITICAL SIGNIFICANCE, NOT LEGAL

Mária Patakyová
Katarína Galdunová

1. INTRODUCTION

The Universal Declaration of Human Rights from 1948 has gone through a magnificent development. Having been adopted as a legally non-binding document to set a common standard of human rights protection, it has become a cornerstone of the international bill of human rights.[1] This article will discuss the position of the Universal Declaration of Human Rights (hereinafter UDHR) in the Slovak Republic in three respects. The first part will be a short introduction to the UDHR and the situation in Slovakia which at the time of the adoption of the UDHR was as a part of Czechoslovakia. The second part will describe the situation within judicial, governmental and legislative state bodies and governmental organisations established to promote the legacy of the UDHR. The third part will focus on the position of Slovak scholars. The conclusion will summarize the position of the UDHR in the Slovak Republic. The article focuses through a socio-legal methodology in relation to a historical approach on the position of relevant actors in the political and academic arena.

2. THE DECLARATION AND SLOVAKIA (AS A PART OF CZECHOSLOVAKIA) FROM 1948 TO 1989

The UDHR was adopted by the General Assembly as a Resolution. It was submitted as an annex to the General Assembly Resolution 217A (III) that was adopted on 10 December 1948 without any dissenting vote. However, apart from Byelorussian SSR, Poland, Ukrainian SSR, Yugoslavia, South Africa, Saudi Arabia, and the USSR, Czechoslovakia also abstained from voting. This was no surprise as the division of the international community

---

1 M.N. SHAW, *International Law*, 5th ed. (Cambridge University Press, Cambridge, 2003) p. 259.

into the Eastern and the Western bloc had already taken place. To find and transfer a commonly accepted concept of human dignity into words of an international agreement seemed to be difficult. Nevertheless, the UDHR was adopted and the date of its adoption is remembered and celebrated as the International Human Rights Day. It has become an example of a document that, despite not being legally binding, calls for strong attention to the protection of human rights. It stands firm against relativism by reaffirming the universality of interrelated human rights, and its basic principles of non-discrimination, equality, justice and human dignity support its importance. Most of the provisions in the UDHR have been incorporated into legally binding international treaty obligations and also into domestic law, especially at the national constitutional level.

The position of the UDHR in Czechoslovakia from 1948 to 1989 reflects the basic features of an authoritarian regime. The regime was introduced in what is now Slovakia in February 1948 to lead the country to a higher level of social development under the motto of everlasting cooperation with the USSR. The position of keeping all international commitments in good faith was very well described in the contribution of the Minister of Foreign Affairs of Czechoslovakia, Mr. Bohuslav Chňoupek, during the meeting of the Federal Assembly as a federal legislative body in 1977.[2] The contribution was meant to answer a question of deputy Kalkus about attempts of some Western countries to misuse the area of human rights protection in order to interfere into domestic matters. The Minister submitted that although some politicians had claimed that human rights protection was not a domestic matter any more, this must be rejected. According to the official position of the government of Czechoslovakia and the Communist Party that held the dominant position in the government of the country, such a proposition could not be entertained. The only correct position was supposed to be the one coming out of a free opportunity of every single state to claim its own political, social and cultural system, including its own legal norms and rules. The obligation of all other states was to respect mutually this choice. According to the Minister, such a position is supported by the Helsinki Final Act of 1975 and by other commonly accepted international norms. It was therefore natural that every state adopt such rules that corresponded to the principles of its own social structure. This should also be the case in the sphere of the protection of human rights.

---

2 Bohuslav Chňoupek, Minister of Foreign Affairs of the Czechoslovak Socialist Republic, shorthand record of the meeting No. 3, 5 April 1977, <www.nrsr.sk/dk/Download.aspx?MasterID=58418>, visited on 30 May 2008.

However, Minister Chňoupek contradicted himself. On the one hand, he emphasised that the human rights issue was entirely for the state to decide upon. The state as a sovereign is the most appropriate subject to govern the rights of its own citizens and people present in its territory. The Minister pointed out that there was nothing either in the United Nations (hereinafter UN) Charter or in the UDHR to put the concept of sovereignty against the concept of human rights of individuals. On the other hand, he admitted that massive and systematic violations of human rights and basic principles of international law may not entirely be a domestic matter. In such a situation, the protection of human rights became an interest of the international community as a whole. The reason for this is obvious; a violation of friendly relations could cause conflict situations which are able to threaten international peace and security.

According to Mr. Chňoupek, for example Chile could be dealt with by the UN and its agencies. However, the situation in Slovakia differed from the one in Chile. The protection and promotion of human rights have been said to be a part of the Socialist democracy, which followed entirely the purposes and principles set up in the UN Charter, the UDHR and other universal human rights treaties. The Minister focussed on the fact that different understandings of human rights resulting from different social structures cannot be an excuse to interfere with domestic matters of another state. Moreover, the Minister pointed out that a Socialist republic managed to provide the maximum and a sustainable promotion of all rights and freedoms for its people. This quality is said to be a fundamental basis of the Socialist social structure. This was the reason why the Czechoslovak Socialist Republic ratified all the relevant international treaties that guarantee human rights and fundamental freedoms. This had been the position not only concerning the UDHR but also concerning the legally binding International Covenant on Civil and Political Rights and International Covenant on Economic, Social and Cultural Rights. According to Chňoupek, the Socialist social structure was completely sufficient to protect human rights because it was able to provide for their practical realisation. He also emphasised that pre-ratification research showed that the Czechoslovak legal order provided even higher standards than any of the documents included in the International Bill of Rights.

It is submitted here that the pre-1989 regime kept claiming that the rules and principles of protection of human rights, as set up by the UDHR and elaborated in the 1966 Covenants, were thoroughly followed. However, the realities on the ground were, of course, quite different in comparison with the official position of the government.

3. THE DECLARATION AND THE INDEPENDENT SLOVAK REPUBLIC

After the fall of the Communist regime in Czechoslovakia in November 1989, it became necessary to implement standards set up by the UDHR in the legal and social norms of the country. The list of basic human rights and fundamental freedoms was adopted under a constitutional act[3] that was later included in the Constitution of the Slovak Republic (hereinafter Constitution).[4] The Slovak Republic itself has been an independent state since 1 January 1993. Although its Constitution does not explicitly mention the UDHR, the Reasoning report to the Constitution emphasised that it followed the ideas and the spirit of such important documents as the UDHR.[5]

The Slovak Constitution contains an interesting concept of self-executing treaties. It elaborates a theory according to which international treaties on human rights and fundamental freedoms take priority over Slovak legal acts under two conditions. Firstly, the treaties secure a greater extent of constitutional rights and freedoms. Secondly, Slovakia is a state party to these treaties. According to the official interpretation, these documents particularly include the UDHR, the European Convention for the Protection of Human Rights and Fundamental Freedoms (hereinafter ECHR), the International Convention on Civil and Political Rights (hereinafter ICCPR) and the International Covenant on Economic, Social and Cultural Rights (hereinafter ICESCR).[6] Slovakia has created a broad legislative and institutional framework through which the equality and freedom in rights and obligations have been approved for the entire population present on its territory.

Since the Slovak Republic is a party to the international treaties that are more easily presentable and justiciable in court, for example the aforementioned ECHR, the UDHR is not used in the Slovak jurisprudence very often and there is a lack of references thereto. However, the Constitutional Court of the Slovak Republic (hereinafter the Constitutional Court) was established by the Slovak Constitution as an independent judicial body to protect its constitutionality, including the protection of basic human rights. Indeed, there have been some rulings and findings containing

---

3 *See* Constitutional Act No. 21/1991 on Fundamental Rights and Basic Freedoms.

4 *See* Constitution of the Slovak Republic, Act No. 460/1992.

5 See Reasoning report of the Constitution, <www.nrsr.sk/dk/Download.aspx?MasterID=75408>, visited on 30 May 2008.

6 *See* Article 7 of the Slovak Constitution, *e.g.*, on <www.vlada.gov.sk/INFOSERVIS/DOKUMENTY/ACQUIS/en_npaa_kap_1_2.shtml>, visited on 30 May 2008.

reference to the UDHR, even though there were few of them.[7] However, these references have been presented by a person alleging the violation of his or her rights. To sum up those applications, most of them were found non-admissible on the basis of different reasons, especially manifestly ill-founded, or a *res iudicata* application or because of lack of jurisdiction or missing the deadline; in two admissible case it was found that there was no violation of fundamental human rights. The second case of the list was not only admissible, but a violation was found. Nevertheless, the violation was reasoned by a reference to the ICCPR and the Slovak Constitution. As for the UDHR, the Court reasoned the same as in the first case which was based solely on the UDHR, that is, that "[t]he Universal Declaration of Human Rights has the character of a political document. It was not adopted in accordance with Article 11[8] of the Constitution of the Slovak Republic and with Section 1 and Section 4 paragraph 3 of the Act of National Council of the Slovak Republic No. 1/1993 of the Collection of Law about the Collection of Laws of the Slovak Republic. This Declaration does not provide for constitutionally guaranteed rights and freedoms to individuals. This means that the Constitutional Court of the Slovak Republic may not open proceedings in respect of a complaint or part thereof filed by a person alleging the violation of a right protected under the Universal Declaration of Human Rights".[9] This part of the judgment has been quoted — if at all — in the cases that followed when an applicant referred to the UDHR.

The interpretative approach to the UDHR of the Constitutional Court as a political document has been used in the political area as well. Individual representatives of Slovakia use the UDHR in various situations; its moral strength is used in the political discussions and in reports. The presentation of them could be started by an annual report provided by the Slovak president at the beginning of each year in order to report on the position of the republic. The 1998 report submitted by the former president, Mr. Michal Kováč, discussed the basic meaning of human rights that lay in the value of the life of

---

7 Ruling of the Constitutional Court of the Slovak Republic, File Ref.: II. ÚS 18/97 from 25 March 1997, II. ÚS 28/96 from 12 May 1997, II. ÚS 230/03–27 from 26 November 2003, I. ÚS 158/05–24 from 23 August 2005, I. ÚS 213/05–32 from 5 October 2005, III. ÚS 325/05 from 23 November 2005, III. ÚS 16/06–37 from 11 January 2006, ÚS 18/06–45 from 18 January 2006, IV. ÚS 44/06–28 from 28 February 2006, II. ÚS 58/06–28 from 15 March 2006, I. ÚS 176/03, I. ÚS 18/06, III. ÚS 324/05–51 from 29 March 2006, I. ÚS 126/06–23 from 5 April 2006, III. ÚS 16/06, I. ÚS 127/06–37 from 5 April 2006, I. ÚS 134/06–35 from 11 April 2006, II. ÚS 149/06–28 from 4 May 2006, III. ÚS 215/06–32 from 27 June 2006, I. ÚS 11/07–31 from 15 March 2007.

8 According to the constitutional amendments, it is an article 7 of the Constitution now.

9 Ruling of the Constitutional Court of the Slovak Republic, File Ref. II. ÚS 18/97 of 25 March 1997.

a human being. The human rights law exists to ensure safety and freedom for all citizens. Furthermore, it is not state originated law; it stems from the universal natural law of man. According to Mr. Kováč, the Declaration derives from and refers to that type of law.[10]

There are two main reasons for why politicians talk publicly about the UDHR: firstly, to show a high level of compliance of Slovakia with international standards and its commitments by effective implementation of various international treaties dealing with human rights issues and secondly, to point out that Slovakia has to improve the protection of human rights even more.

Within the first group, there is an example of a speech given by former Vice-Prime Minister, Mr. Lubomír Fogas, during a session of the Commission of Human Rights on 22 March 2001.[11] Mr. Fogas considered the protection of human rights as a goal for all international organisations. It was not an economic demand but instead, ethical, cultural and social values were set up in the UDHR that are necessary to maintain and develop in the present world.

Another example could be a speech by Mr. Pal Czaky, former Vice-Prime Minister for human rights matters during a conference addressing human rights in a modern society. Mr. Czaky asked how we actually fulfil the purposes of the UDHR.[12] It was true that human rights had become an integral part of constitutional law in all democratic countries, which have also adopted numerous international treaties. Human rights helped in human and social development, it prevented extreme poverty, and they could be used to introduce democracy or to reinforce democratic institutions. Although Mr. Czaky submitted that because the world had been changing, also human rights must change: he asserted that the message of the UDHR was not tied to a certain time or a period. In addition, according to Mr. Czaky, Slovakia had already passed an examination of maturity in the area of human rights. By implementing the human rights treaties and by creating effective mechanisms to ensure realisation of human rights, Slovakia had provided a system where every human being may enjoy their human rights. Moreover, one cannot forget the other side of the same coin — every right includes a responsibility that makes the whole concept of human rights

---

[10] M. KOVÁČ, *Správa o stave Slovenskej republiky* (Bratislava, 1998) p. 10.

[11] *See* <www.government.gov.sk/aktuality_start.php3?id_ele=651>, visited on 30 May 2008.

[12] Pál Csáky: Význam ľudských práv v modernej spoločnosti: Slovensko rok po vstupe do EÚ, konferencia k Medzinárodnému dňu ľudských práv, Bratislava, 9. december 2005; Pál Czáky: Importance of human rights in a modern society: Slovakia a year later after entering the EU in 2004, *see* <www.mensiny.vlada.gov.sk/data/files/1561.doc>, visited on 30 May 2008.

workable. However, bearing in mind the complexity of human rights and current challenges for the present society, one could not see the development in understanding and promoting human rights. "We will not enjoy development without security, we will not enjoy security without development, and we will not enjoy either of the two without respect for human rights".[13]

It is the level of protection and rights securing human dignity that is decisive in relation to the development of the particular society, to its democratic and legal principles. The current Slovak Vice-Prime Minister Mr. Dusan Caplovic, focused on the Slovak Republic as a functioning democracy that fully respects and protects human rights and fundamental freedoms. [4] At the same time, there was still space for constant improvement. The message of the UDHR is about freedom and equality as a motto and as a symbol of the protection of human rights. The UDHR had acquired acknowledgement and it has become a source of codification of human rights law at the national, regional and universal level. According to Mr. Caplovic, the moral strength of the Declaration came from the fact that it also nowadays inspires actors in the process of protection and promotion of human rights.

Another point that has already been mentioned is the position of different deputies as members of Slovak legislative body who use the UDHR to point out that in Slovakia there have been systematic violations of human rights. The reasoning in itself is focused on the violation of the Constitution and the UDHR.[15] However, there are other deputies, who emphasise the importance of the UDHR only in relation to the values that are provided there. Otherwise they point out the legally non-binding character of the UDHR.[16] Moreover, some deputies dealing with the protection of children and women submitted that positive discrimination was included as a feature in the UDHR.[17]

In Slovakia, the human rights as an issue are covered by a special Vice-Prime Minister. Also, a Council of Slovak Republic for National Minorities and Ethnic Groups has been established. When the UDHR was drafted and adopted, the personalities attached with the project consciously set the issue of minorities aside. Therefore, there is no mention of minorities in the

---

13 K. Annan, In Larger Freedom, <www.un.org/largerfreedom>, visited on 30 May 2008.

14 *See* <www.caplovic.vlada.gov.sk/5591/prihovor-na-konferencii--medzinarodna-ochrana-ludskych-prav-a-slovenska-republika.php>, visited on 30 May 2008.

15 Ivan Hopta, a deputy, 40th meeting of the National Council of the Slovak Republic, 13 November 2002, 3rd meeting of the National Council of the Slovak Republic, 13 November 2006, 1 February 2005, 60th meeting in the National Council of UK, 15 March 2006.

16 Monika Benova, Reasoning report of the Antidiscrimination Act, October 2003.

17 Eva Rusnakova, 28th meeting of the National Council of the Slovak Republic, 30 June 2004.

UDHR, and therefore, the Council goes a little bit beyond the scope of the national implementation of the UDHR. However, it improves the general concept of human rights protection. Likewise, there also exists an institutional basis for a governmental representative for the Roma community. In 1993, the institutional basis for promotion of human rights was improved by the creation of a Slovak National Centre for Human Rights, which has been recognized by the UN as a national institution for human rights.

In 2008, Slovakia applied for membership in the Human Rights Council. In its application it proclaimed that one of its aims is the implementation of norms and standards derived from the UDHR and other international human rights treaties.[18] On 21 May 2008, a Slovak representative was elected to join the Human Rights Council, mainly to improve the institutional basis and individual national policies aimed at the protection of human rights, whilst focusing on vulnerable groups such as children, women and trafficked persons.

4. THE UDHR ACCORDING TO SLOVAK SCHOLARS

This part will present Slovak scholars' opinions concerning the UDHR as elaborated in their academic texts, conference contributions or other analytical pieces. Slovak scholars are usually active either at the university level or in the Slovak Academy of Sciences or exclusively working to protect and promote human rights in the human rights organisation established by law, the Slovak National Centre for Human Rights. The Centre is an independent legal person that performs tasks in the area of human rights and basic freedoms. In this respect, it in particular monitors and assesses the observance of human rights and the observance of the principle of equal treatment, gathers information on racism, xenophobia and anti-Semitism in the Slovak Republic and carries out research and surveys in the area of human rights. It also gathers and disseminates information in this area. Moreover, there are also non-governmental organisations that submit highly professional and well-elaborated analyses, such as the Institute for Public Affairs that is an independent non-governmental and non-profit organisation. The Institute has been established in order to reinforce values of an open society and democratic political culture in public affairs.

---

18 *See* <www.rokovania.sk/appl/material.nsf/0/DB13C517B271D343C12573F600317D81/$FILE/vlastnymat.rtf>, visited on 30 May 2008.

The scholars who have worked or who are working in these institutions constitute the Slovak academic community for the purposes of this article. As for their opinion on the UDHR, they have been interested in its various aspects. Professor Tomko considers the UDHR as a legally non-binding document that has only a recommending character.[19] Professor Klucka emphasises the position of the UDHR as the first document containing the list of human rights and fundamental freedoms and as a document that has become later a basis for a treaty and custom based international human rights law.[20] Klucka and Jankuv discuss the relevance of the fact that the UDHR had been adopted in the format of a General Assembly Resolution, which has acquired a specific reputation because of its qualities.[21] Thanks to its almost unanimous adoption, Klucka and Jankuv argue that these types of declarations affirm or form basic rules of international law.[22] Moreover, Jankuv adds that the Declaration is not legally binding.[23] The nature of a document which is legally speaking only a recommendation was discussed also by Mraz, Poredos and Vrsansky in a Slovak international law textbook for law schools in Slovakia.[24] They also argue that some parts of the UDHR have been continuously changing into legally binding treaty and customary law.[25] Professor Azud focused on the position of an individual at the international level that has been influenced by the UDHR, followed by other legal documents in the area of international law.[26] On the other hand, Svak pointed out the fact that the Declaration lacks any control mechanism.[27] Likewise, Straznicka and Sebesta see the aim of the Declaration as a determination of goals of the states in the area of human rights.

The UDHR has been used as a starting point to emphasise a common standard of the rights included in the contributions by Slovak scholars during

---

19 J. TOMKO, *Medzinárodné verejné právo* (Obzor, Bratislava, 1988) p. 241.

20 J. KLUČKA, *Medzinárodné verejné pávo* (Iura Edition, Bratislava, 2004) p. 75.

21 J. KLUCKA and J. JANKUV, *Medzinárodné verejné právo (všeobecná časť)* (Univerzita Pavla Jozefa Šafárika, Košice, 2000) p. 63.

22 *Ibid.*, p. 64.

23 J. JANKUV, *Medzinárodné a európske mechanizmy ochrany ľudských práv* (Iura Edition, Bratislava, 2006) pp. 30–31.

24 S. MRAZ, F. POREDOS and P. VRSANSKY, *Medzinárodné verejné právo* (Univerzita Komenského v Bratislave, Právnická fakulta, Vydavateľské oddelenie, Bratislava, 2003) p. 168.

25 *Ibid.*

26 J. AZUD, *Medzinárodné právo* (Veda, Bratislava, 2003) p. 23.

27 J. SVÁK, *Ochrana ľudských práv* (EuroKodex, Bratislava, 2006) p. 30.

several conferences.[28] It is often quoted in analyses dealing with different phenomena in the area of the protection of human rights.[29]

Most of the Slovak internationalists focus on the legally non-binding character of the UDHR. On the other hand, it has been submitted that individual parts of the UDHR have become either treaty or custom based international legal obligations. Such a position follows the research done by the International Law Association and its Committee on the Enforcement of Human Rights Law. In its Final Report on the Status of the Universal Declaration of Human Rights in National and International Law, the Committee has confirmed that although there is insufficient state practice to support acceptance of the UDHR as customary law, many individual provisions do reflect customary law. Therefore, in some instances, violations of the UDHR are violations of international law.[30]

5. CONCLUSION

Although Slovakia has a short history as an independent state, it has overcome several phases of its attitude towards the UDHR during the past 60 years after its adoption. The first phase, from 1948 to 1989, could be seen reflected in the formal position of the Communist regime in relation to the concept of human rights. It was a phase when Slovakia was a part of Czechoslovakia. The second phase took place during a transition period from 1989 to 1993. It was during that time when the basic principles of the UDHR and other universal human rights treaties were incorporated into the Slovak legal acts in order to establish an effective system for the protection and promotion of human rights. The third phase, in place since 1993, has been a period of constant improvement of the established system so that the standard

---

28 Nebývanie ako súkromný problém? (Poznámky k bytovej politike a právu na bývanie na Slovensku a vybraných európskych štátoch), Konferencia "Ľudia bez domova" 14.–15.11.2007, Liptovský Ján, Zuzana Kusá, SÚ SAV. Non-accomodation as a Private Problem? Some Notes to the Accomodation Politics and to a Right to a Standard of Living in Slovakia and chosen European States, Conference "People without Home", 14–15 November 2007, Liptovský Ján, Zuzana Kusá, Institute for Sociology, Slovak Academy of Sciences.

29 E. KRIGLEROVÁ, *Diskriminácia Rómov v prístupe k vzdelávaniu.* (Inštitút pre verejné otázky, Bratislava, 2004). E. KRIGLEROVÁ, Discrimination of Roma Population in the Access to Education (Institute for Public Affairs, Bratislava, 2004) <www.euractiv.sk/rovnost-sanci/analyza/diskriminacia-romov-v-pristupe-k-vzdelavaniu>, visited on 30 May 2008.

30 R.B. LILLICH and H. HANNUM (eds), *International Human Rights, Problems of Law, Policy, and Practice* (Little, Brown and Company, Boston, 1995) p. 167.

set up by the UDHR could become an integral part of the life of every human being.[31]

[31] General Secretary, International Human Rights Day, 10 December 2007, <www.unis.unvienna.org/unis/sk/pressrels/2007/unissgsm032.html>, visited on 30 May 2008.

28. SLOVENIA: INDIRECT BUT INCREASING IMPACT

Milan Brglez
Bojko Bučar

1. INTRODUCTION

At the end of World War II Slovenia was a federal unit within Communist Yugoslavia, firmly anchored within what then was considered as a Socialist (Communist) camp. There was optimism in high politics but also in large parts of the public that with the end of the war new and inevitably better times were dawning, especially in the area of human rights. The Communist revolution also promised the improvement of substantive rights for all working people within the country. This was welcomed by many who had experienced the legal and political system of the Kingdom of Yugoslavia between the two World Wars. Yugoslavia had been quite active in international politics during World War II and it stayed active after the war in the international labour (Communist) movement, in the Balkans and within the United Nations (UN) system. In the illusion that a new and more just world had been born, Yugoslavia tried to be active also in the field of human rights. Small wonder, then, that within the UN it became a member of the drafting committee entrusted with the International Bill of Human Rights while the issue either of a declaration or a convention and measures of implementation were still on the table.[1]

However, in the general debate on the draft of the Universal Declaration of Human Rights (UDHR) in the Third Committee, Yugoslavia was among the critics of the declaration claiming that "through lack of real substance, the Declaration might be forgotten even before the ink of the signatories affixed to the document had dried" and urged for "every possible effort to draw up a text which would fulfil the legitimate aspirations of the peoples".[2] Already the term 'peoples' showed attentiveness for collectivism which has been a feature of the Communist movement as opposed to individualism. In mid-1948 Yugoslavia had been expelled from the Information Bureau of

---

1 YUN 1948–49, p. 525.

2 YUN 1948–49, p. 529.

Communist Parties which constituted the first rift in the Communist movement (or labour movement as it was called at the time) and showed the antagonism between the Soviet Union (SU) on the one hand and Yugoslavia on the other (Stalin v Tito). Nevertheless, in the debate on the Declaration Yugoslavia supported the view of the SU, especially the issue of the alleged neglect of substantial economic and social rights. It was still a time when both states competed as champions for the authentic representation of Communist ideas.

One more issue has to be mentioned in connection with this debate which bears some relevance to the present. At the time the East European countries contested the unlimited right to the freedom of expression on the ground that it would include the right of spreading fascist ideas.[3] Much later, at the end of the 1980s, Dr. Vojislav Šešelj was sentenced to eight years of prison according to Article 133 of the Yugoslav Penal Code sanctioning hostile propaganda, or as we would say today, 'hate speech'. At that time in Slovenia a campaign among intellectuals had been launched in favour of the release of the convict and for the abolition of the notorious article on a simple 'verbal misdemeanour'. In 2007, the aforementioned individual appeared before the International Tribunal for the Prosecution of Persons Responsible for Serious Violations of International Humanitarian Law Committed in the Territory of the Former Yugoslavia since 1991 (ICTY).

All the above mentioned criticisms notwithstanding, the adoption of the UDHR on 10 December 1948 was considered as an important event at that time by the Federal Peoples Republic of Yugoslavia.[4] However, together with other East European members of the UN, Saudi Arabia and the Union of South Africa,[5] Yugoslavia abstained and justified its abstention mainly with a too individualistic view on the conceptualization of, and a too idealistic approach to the provisions of human rights.[6] Not surprisingly it also abstained from the resolution on the dissemination and publication of the UDHR (GA Res. 217 (III) D) which did have some effect in practice.

---

3 In a way this was understandable if we remember the speeches of Hitler, Mussolini, Göbbels, Schtreicher for example, and the fact that the Declaration has been adopted only three years after World War II. Having said that, we do not wish to deny the abuse of curtailing the freedom of speech by Communist regimes.

4 General Assembly, Adoption of the Universal Declaration of Human Rights, *Verbatim Record of the Hundred and Eighty-third Plenary Meeting* (UN Doc. A/PV.183), Palais de Chaillot, Paris, Friday, 10 December 1948; *see* a speech of the representative of Yugoslavia, Mr. Radovanović, at pp. 913–917.

5 *Ibid.*, p. 933.

6 General Assembly, *supra* note 4.

But time flew by and in the 1950s, to show its difference from the Soviet system, Yugoslavia introduced its unique political and social self-government and worker's self-management system, a system which in the 1960s became an interesting case study for many social scientists including those who were interested in studying and promoting human rights. Also, in the 1960s Yugoslavia became one of the founders of the non-aligned movement which in the 1970s became a proponent of the New International (Economic) Order within the UN. Moreover, Yugoslavia, *inter alia*, became interested in the third generation of human rights, especially the right to development.

Yugoslavia's own image of a society that highly respected human rights (especially the equality of men and women, non-discrimination, economic and social rights, minority rights, the right to peace and development etc.) created a favourable environment for a limited advocacy of human rights in general. Thus, for example, in 1964 the United Nations Association (UNA) of Slovenia (being part of the Federation of UNA Yugoslavia) started celebrating the 10 December by awarding on that day a special prize for BA Theses on the functioning of the UN and also on human rights. Needless to say it also started disseminating the UDHR.

But at that time there was still a prevailing belief that the UDHR was not a binding instrument. Once the International Covenant on Civil and Political Rights (ICCPR)[7] and the International Covenant on Economic, Social and Cultural Rights (ICESCR)[8] were open for signature, states started pondering on the limitations brought on them by firm legal obligations. It took ten long years before both covenants became binding in 1976 after being ratified by only 35 states. Holding in high esteem its self-image of being a society that highly respects human rights, Yugoslavia was in the forefront of those states. It signed both covenants already in 1967 and ratified them by 1971.[9] The story somewhat differs once it comes to the issue of the Optional Protocol allowing for individual complaints.[10] Yugoslavia never ratified the Protocol,

7 General Assembly, Resolution 2200A (XXI), 21 UN GAOR Supp. (No. 16) at 52, UN Doc. A/6316 (1966), 999 UNTS 171, entered into force 23 March 1976.

8 General Assembly, Resolution 2200A (XXI), 21 UN GAOR Supp. (No. 16) at 49, UN Doc. A/6316 (1966), 993 UNTS 3, entered into force 3 January 1976.

9 Mednarodni pakt o državljanskih in političnih pravicah – Pacte International relatif aux Droits Civils et Politiques (*Official Gazette of the Socialist Federal Republic of Yugoslavia* – Ur. l. SFRJ 1971/7, pp. 73–87) and Mednarodni pakt o ekonomskih, socialnih in kulturnih pravicah – Pacte International relatif aux Droits Economiques, Sociaux et Culturels (*Official Gazette of the Socialist Federal Republic of Yugoslavia* – Ur. l. SFRJ 1971/7, pp. 88–96). Slovenia notified its succession in 1992.

10 General Assembly, Resolution 2200A (XXI), 21 UN GAOR Supp. (No. 16) at 59, UN Doc. A/6316 (1966), 999 UNTS 302, entered into force 23 March 1976.

yet it also never claimed that it would not do so. On the contrary, at least in the 1980s, the dignitaries of the Foreign Ministry always found an excuse why the Protocol had (then) no legal force (for example, that by accident it was misplaced in the domestic legal process, that it always takes time and so on). Therefore, after becoming independent in 1991 Slovenia had to ratify the Optional Protocol by itself in 1993.[11]

Be this as it may, some provisions of the International Bill of Human Rights were included into the Constitution of the Socialist Federal Republic of Yugoslavia (SFRY) from 1963[12] and 1974,[13] which by itself speaks of the notion of the relation between international and national legal obligations. This does not mean that both covenants did not become the law of the land.

Being a constitutive part or federal unit of the SFRY, the Socialist Republic of Slovenia (SRS) also provided for some human rights in its own Constitution. Due to a more centralistic orientation of the federation the Constitution of the SRS from 1963 just added to the Constitution of the SFRY from 1963 some articles on cultural rights and the protection of the Italian and Hungarian minority on its territory.[14] On the other hand the Constitution of the SRS from 1974 enshrined a larger spectrum of human rights and the decentralization tendencies within the federation were clearly more visible.[15] Those facts provide a background for the beginning of our story of the gradual and indirect impact of the UDHR on Slovenia as the federal unit of SFRY. At that time one may speak about at least a kind of formal protection of (some) human rights but hardly about real processes of democratisation.

---

[11] Zakon o ratifikaciji Fakultativnega protokola k Mednarodnemu paktu o državljanskih in političnih pravicah, (*Official Gazette of the Republic of Slovenia – International Agreements –* Ur. l. RS, MP 9/93, p. 335).

[12] *Ustav Socijalističke Federativne Republike Jugoslavije sa ustavima socijalističkih republika i statutima avtonomnih pokrajina* [*The Constitution of the Socialist Federal Republic of Yugoslavia with the Constitutions of Socialist Republics and Autonomous Provinces*], (Novinske ustanove Službeni list SFRJ, Belgrade, 1963), Part 1: "Social and Political Arrangement", Chapter 3: "Freedoms, Rights and Duties of Man and Citizen", Articles 32–70.

[13] *Ustava Socialistične federativne republike Jugoslavije z obrazložitvijo* [*The Constitution of the Socialist Federal Republic of Yugoslavia with Comments*], (ČGP Delo, Ljubljana, 1974), Part 2: "Social Arrangement", Chapter 3: "Freedoms, Rights and Duties of Man and Citizen", Articles 153–203.

[14] Ustava Socialistične Republike Slovenije [The Constitution of the Socialist Republic of Slovenia], *Ur. l. SRS* [*Official Gazette of SRS*], No. 10/1963, Part 2: "Social Arrangement", Chapter 2: "Social-political Arrangement", Section a) "Social-political Communities", Articles 74-77.

[15] Ustava Socialistične Republike Slovenije [The Constitution of the Socialist Republic of Slovenia], *Ur. l. SRS* [*Official Gazette of SRS*], No. 6/1974, Part 2: "Social Arrangement", Chapter 4: "Freedoms, Rights and Duties of Man and Citizen", Articles 195–251.

The latter got momentum in 1991 with the independence of the Republic of Slovenia (RS) and thus the Slovenian story of human rights and democratisation continued. The UDHR has provided a background for the functioning of the human rights protection system, materialised most notably in the new Constitution of the RS[16] and the unreserved ratification of the European Convention for the Protection of Human Rights and Fundamental Freedoms (ECHR).[17] This has been an important shift from the previous system that had provided for the protection of the society (political system) and the state (federal) structure(s) ahead of human rights (for they were considered a guarantor of a perfect system of human rights) to a system that is normatively founded on human rights themselves.

To corroborate that story we firstly turn more analytically to the implementation of the UDHR in former Yugoslavia and then compare that with the situation after the independence of the RS. More emphasis is put on the second part since in Yugoslavia the UDHR was more or less assumed as a background for the implementation of human rights while in Slovenia paradoxically the Declaration is not so clearly visible in political, public and even legal discourses.

2. IMPACT OF THE UDHR IN THE SFRY

The hesitant attitude of the SFRY towards the UDHR is most easily understood as an indication of unwillingness to submit its own system for the protection and implementation of human rights under international supervision. There is little surprise in the fact that the SFRY neither signed nor ratified the Optional Protocol to the ICCPR and thus did not allow its own citizens to file complaints with the Human Rights Committee. Obviously, lacking such an intrusive control mechanism it was much easier for the SFRY to be bound by both international Covenants (the ICCPR and the ICESCR).[18]

---

16 Ustava Republike Slovenije, *Ur. l. RS* [*Official Gazette of RS*], No. 33/1991-I.

17 Zakon o ratifikaciji Konvencije o varstvu človekovih pravic in temeljnih svoboščin, spremenjene s protokoli št. 3, 5 in 8 ter dopolnjene s protokolom št. 2, ter njenih protokolov 1, 4, 6, 7, 9, 10 in 11 [The Law on the Ratification of the Convention for the Protection of Human Rights and Fundamental Freedoms Amended by Protocols Nos. 3, 5 and 8, and Completed by Protocol No. 2, and Its Protocols Nos. 1, 4, 6, 7, 9, 10 and 11], *Ur. l. RS* [*Official Gazette of the RS*], No. 33/1994, Mednarodne pogodbe [*International Agreements*], No. 7/1994.

18 This was exactly the reason why a separate instrument on the implementation of human rights had been drafted in the first place. According to Article 210 of the Constitution of SFRY

Therefore, the impact of the UDHR on state legislation — at both levels, on the federal level and on the level of federal units including the SRS — was indirect. In so far as the principles of human rights enshrined in the UDHR were specified and elaborated in the ICCPR and the ICESCR, the Yugoslav legislation was mostly in line with them. Because of its own conception of (social) ownership, it seemed to be ideologically most suitable for the regime of the SFRY that the right to property (Article 17 of UDHR) was not included in the Covenants. On the other hand, the right of self-determination recognized by both Covenants (common Article 1 of the ICCPR and the ICESCR) and not contained in the UDHR gradually became perhaps the most important principle for the conceptualisation of Slovenia's independence.[19]

The 1974 Constitution of the SFRY[20] thus included provisions on the human dignity (Article 179), prohibition of discrimination (Article 154), right to life (Article 175), liberty and security (Article 177), equality before the law (Articles 197–198), the right to effective legal remedy (Articles 180 and 199), prohibition of arbitrary arrest and detention (Article 177), the right to basic guarantees in criminal proceeding (Articles 178, 181 and 182), the right to privacy (Articles 176, 184 and 185), freedom of movement (Article 183), the right to asylum (Article 202), the right to nationality (Article 200), the protection of family (Article 190), the freedom of thought, conscience and religion (Articles 166 and 174), the freedom of opinion and expression (Articles 167 and 168), the freedom of assembly and association (Article 167), the right to take part in government and to equal access to public service (Articles 156–158), the right to social security (Articles 163 and 189), the right to work, equal pay and just remuneration (Article 159), the workers' rights (Articles 161–162), the right to an adequate standard of living (Article 189), the right to education (Article 165), the right to cultural life and the protection of intellectual property (Article 169), as well as the duties to the community (Articles 153 and 195). From the list of rights contained in the UDHR, the Yugoslav constitution did not include the prohibition of slavery, the right to recognition before the law, the right to fair hearing by an independent and impartial tribunal, or the right to own property, but it added the inalienable right to self-management (Article 155), the right to work (Article 160) instead of the freedom of trade unions, the right to a household (Article 164), the freedom of national identity, culture and use of language for

from 1974 only ratified and published international agreements were used by Yugoslav courts. Article 153 in the 1963 Constitution provided the same.

19 *See* E. PETRIČ, *Pravica do samoodločbe: mednarodni vidiki* [*The Right to Self-determination: International Aspects*] (Obzorja, Maribor, 1984).

20 *Supra* note 13.

persons belonging to nations and nationalities (Articles 170–171), the right and duty of state defence and social self-protection (Articles 172–173), the right to health protection (Article 186), the protection of children (Article 188), the right to abortion (Article 191), the right to a healthy environment and the duty of its protection (Articles 192–193), as well as the duty of solidarity (Article 196).

The same rights were included also in the constitutions of the Yugoslav republics. As already mentioned, the Constitution of the SRS just added the special protection of the Italian and Hungarian minorities and persons belonging to them.[21] However, such an excess of repetitive regulation as enumerated above was not also a guarantee that human rights would be respected and implemented.[22] Even a brief look at the structure of all those constitutions from socialist times provides an explanation why. Human rights have been treated as secondary to the protection of the existing social and political structure. Therefore it is no surprise that the analysed constitutional texts did not mention anything similar to "periodic and genuine elections" (Article 21, paragraph 3 of UDHR) which is considered to be a basic prerequisite for genuine democracy.

3. IMPACT OF THE UDHR IN THE RS

Thus genuine democracy only became possible with the first free elections in April 1990 which led to the independence and the adoption of the new Constitution of the RS at the end of 1991.[23] However, the process of constitution-building did not bring the UDHR clearly to the foreground. The UDHR has only been implicitly assumed in the drafting of the constitution which structurally turned over the priorities from the previous constitutions. This time human rights were emphasised before the organisation of the state. Perhaps a kind of path-dependency has continued to influence the new social, political, and legal environment. The first report of the new international recognised state to the Human Rights Committee set out its obligations:[24]

---

21 *See supra* note 15, Articles 250–251.

22 *See* L. ŠTURM, *Omejitev oblasti: ustavna izhodišča javnega prava* [*The Limitation of Government: Constitutional Departures of Public Law*] (Nova revija, Ljubljana, 1999), Chapter on the Infringements of Human Rights and Fundamental Freedoms in Slovenia in 1945–1990, pp. 246–302.

23 *See supra* note 16.

24 *Initial reports of States parties due in 1992: Slovenia. 22/12/93* (CCPR/C/74/Add.1), para. 4.

> "On the proclamation of the Republic of Slovenia as an independent state (June 1991), the country did not have its own complete legislation. For this reason Slovenia still makes use of legislation from the former Yugoslavia, which ratified the International Covenant on Civil and Political Rights (but not the Optional Protocol) in 1971. The Yugoslav legislation was therefore for the most part in line with the International Covenant on Civil and Political Rights. The Constitutional Law on the Implementation of the Constitution of the Republic of Slovenia determines that all regulations must be harmonized by the end of 1993. Since the human rights and basic freedoms guaranteed in the Constitution are realized directly on the basis of the Constitution, those provisions of current legislation which are contrary to the Constitution are not, or rather should not be, used in practice. This also holds for those provisions of current legislation which are at variance with the International Covenant on Civil and Political Rights, since according to the Constitution, ratified international agreements take precedence over internal legislation. The Constitution indeed determines that laws and other regulations must accord with the generally valid principles of international law and with international agreements which bind Slovenia, and also that ratified and published international agreements are used directly."

Browsing through the materials of the Commission for the Constitutional Questions of the Parliament one may even more clearly get the impression that implicit knowledge of the UDHR receded to the background, while other treaty-based parts of the International Bill of Human Rights and the ECHR were mentioned more often.[25] Indeed, the UDHR was explicitly mentioned only once in the general discussion on the placement and importance of human rights for the new Constitution.[26]

As a matter of substance, the Constitution of the RS comprises a special Chapter 2 that enshrines human rights and fundamental freedoms (Articles 14–65).[27] Compared to the constitutions of former Yugoslavia it contains all rights included into the International Bill of Human Rights and the ECHR, reaching even beyond those international standards. Thus, the prohibition of torture implicitly including slavery (Articles 18 and 21), the right to fair hearing by an independent and impartial tribunal (Article 23), the right to

---

25 M. CERAR and G. PERENIČ (eds), *Nastajanje slovenske ustave: izbor gradiv Komisije za ustavna vprašanja 1990–1991* [*The Evolution of Slovenian Constitution: Selection of Materials of the Commission for Constitutional Questions*], volumes I–III (Državni zbor Republike Slovenije, Ljubljana, 2001), especially volume II.

26 *Ibid.*, p. 349, discussion of Darja Lavtižar Bebler from the Socialist Party (now part of the Social Democratic Party – reformed Communists) defending the indivisibility of human rights against those who tried to limit human rights to the 'first generation' only.

27 *See supra* note 16.

own property (Article 33) which is limited by its economic, social and ecological functions (Article 67), and basic electoral rights (Article 43 linked with Articles 80 and 103) were included into the Constitution of the RS in 1991, while any mentioning of the right to self-management was excluded (instead we have a much narrower notion of co-management regulated by law in Article 75). Moreover, the Constitution maintained most other social and economic rights known in former Yugoslavia,[28] and it also raised and elaborated the standards of guarantees in criminal and other legal proceeding (Articles 19–31) clearly above the international recognised minimum (or maximum).[29]

Besides the above mentioned instances in the constitutional debate, issues of human rights including referrals to the UDHR have generally not been present in the political discourse. One notable exception has been the arguments of pressure groups (but not of political parties) in the process of denationalisation, for example, the return of nationalised property by the Communist regime to former legal owners or their heirs.[30] As a second instance we may refer to the argumentation of the Slovenian civil society and the Ombudsman against the conclusion of an agreement with the US, granting citizens of both states jurisdictional immunity before the International Criminal Court (ICC).[31]

Part of the explanation for the rather low attention to human rights including the UDHR may be attributed to the transition period of the RS that

---

28 Notably, the freedom of work (Article 49), the right to social security (Article 50) and the right to health protection (Article 51).

29 Indicative of this was a remark by Professor Dr. France Bučar, the first President of the National Assembly and the President of the Assembly Commission for Constitutional Questions, according to whom "there are much too much issues in this Constitution that actually belong to the Penal Code". *See supra* note 25, volume I, p. 336.

30 One of the most elaborated defences of property rights based on the UDHR was probably made by Martin Jakič, President of the Association of Owners of Nationalised Property. In M. ZVER (ed.), *Človekove pravice in svoboščine v tranziciji: primer Slovenije* [*Human Rights and Freedoms in Transition: The Case of Slovenia*] (Državni svet Republike Slovenije, Ljubljana, 1998) Part III, Discussion, pp. 103–105.

31 The public statement of the second Slovenian Ombudsman, Matjaž Hanžek who used the UDHR as a key argument against the conclusion of such an agreement in 2002. Reported in Varuh človekovih pravic, *Osmo letno poročilo* [*Eight Yearly Report*] (RS Varuh človekovih pravic, Ljubljana, June 2003) p. 118. Slovenia ratified the Rome Statute of the ICC in December 2001. Zakon o ratifikaciji Rimskega statuta Mednarodnega kazenskega sodišča [The Law on the Ratification of the Rome Statute of the ICC], *Ur. l. RS – mednarodne pogodbe* [*Official Gazette of the RS – International Agreements*], No. 29/2001.

called for other more demanding priorities.[32] There was also a general recognition that the international human rights standards and the most developed mechanisms of protection should be accepted without reservation and implemented (with the pressure or help of international supervision) in municipal law, changing Slovenian legislation wherever necessary.[33] Finally, at least for the political discourse it was relevant that the official Slovenian interpretation of human rights tends to separate the status of citizens and foreigners more neatly that the letter or spirit of the UDHR allows for.[34] Therefore, it has not been a surprise that the Constitutional Court's findings on the unconstitutionality of the administrative 'erasure' of the inhabitants from other republics (federal units) of former Yugoslavia from their legal residency in the RS have not been based on the UDHR,[35] despite the fact that the 'erasure' has been challenged precisely on the basis of the UDHR itself (in particular on Article 15).[36]

Constitutional lawyers and the Constitutional Court of the RS have, nevertheless, been much more conscious of the UDHR within the broader context of human rights. Most commentaries of the Constitution and other publications on the state of human rights in the RS contain also at least the translation of the UDHR.[37] The Constitutional Court, on the other hand, has widely recognized and mentioned the UDHR in its argumentation of cases or

---

32 This has been acknowledged also by the first Slovenian Ombudsman Ivan Bizjak in 1998. I. BIZJAK, 'Spoštovanje in varstvo človekovih pravic v Sloveniji – izkušnje in dileme' [Recognition and Protection of Human Rights in Slovenia – Experiences and Dilemmas]. In *supra* note 30, pp. 11–21.

33 This may clearly be seen in the ratification process of the ECHR and its Protocols without any reservations. *See supra* note 17.

34 This fundamental issue originates from Article 13 of the Constitution, which recognizes treaties as the sole international source of human rights for foreigners. And the UDHR of course is not a treaty.

35 Relevant decisions of the Constitutional Court on this issue are: U–I–266/95 from 20 November 1995, U–I–284/94 from 4 February 1999, Up–60/97 from 15 July 1999, U–I–89/99 from 6 October 1999, U–I–295/99 from 18 May 2000, U–I–246/02 from 3 April 2003, and Up–211/04–21 from 2 March 2006. They are available at <odlocitve.us-rs.si/usrs/us-odl.nsf/index_eng.htm>.

36 J. DEDIĆ, V. JALUŠIČ and J. ZORN, with the Post scriptum of Matevž Krivic, *The Erased: Organized Innocence and the Politics of Exclusion* (Mirovni inštitut, Ljubljana, 2003) pp. 34, 36, 69, and 135. Available also at <www2.mirovni-institut.si/eng_html/publications/pdf/MI_politike_erased.pdf>.

37 M. ZVER (ed.), *Človekove pravice in svoboščine v tranziciji: primer Slovenije* [*Human Rights and Freedoms in Transition: The Case of Slovenia*] (Državni svet Republike Slovenije, Ljubljana, 1998); L. ŠTURM (ed.), *Komentar Ustave Republike Slovenije* [*Commentary of the Constitution of the Republic of Slovenia*] (Fakulteta za podiplomske državne in evropske študije, Ljubljana, 2002).

as one of the justifiable reasons for constitutional complaints. There were 209 of such cases before the Constitutional Court of RS so far.[38] Since "[h]uman rights and fundamental freedoms shall be exercised directly on the basis of the Constitution" (Article 15, paragraph 1 of the Constitution), most of the cases before the Constitutional Court are in one way or the other related to human rights.[39]

In-between those political and legal discourses, the UNA Slovenia has continued to celebrate the 10th of December, but from 1997 also the first Slovenian Ombudsman started commemorating this day (and appropriating part of the public attention). However, the second Slovenian Ombudsman has used the UDHR also for much more substantial interventions — paradoxically in particular in the elaboration and justification of his focus on social rights.[40]

4. CONCLUSION

As we may see, the impact of the UDHR on the respect and implementation of human rights in national politics and law has been primarily indirect in the case of Yugoslavia as well as in the case of Slovenia. However, one may observe marked differences. In Yugoslavia the communist regime for ideological reasons considered that the national legislation was much more advanced in guaranteeing and implementing human rights than international

---

38 The first motion has been made by the Council for the Protection of Human Rights and Fundamental Freedoms against the constitutionality of the Law on Foreigners. Motion was denied (Decision of the Constitutional Court U–I–90/91–12 from 7 May 1992; unpublished, but available at <odlocitve.us-rs.si/usrs/us-odl.nsf/o/3C96E576D9E1EC92C125717200280B8D>, visited on 17 July 2008). The first motion that has been allowed was again made by the Council for the Protection of Human Rights and Fundamental Freedoms challenging the constitutionality of the Law on the Citizenship of the Republic of Slovenia. The contested part allowed for a discretional decision of administrative bodies without any justification (Decision of the Constitutional Court U–I–98/91–21 from 10 December 1992 published in Official Gazette of RS, No. 61/1992).

39 While in the first year after the adoption of the Constitution the Constitutional Court dealt mostly with "questions related with the organization of government, the principle of division of powers, the establishment of local self-government and typically transitional issues (denationalisation, ownership), recently it is more and more engaged … with … protection of human rights and fundamental freedoms". Constitutional Court of RS, *Poročilo o delu Ustavnega sodišča za leto 2000* [*Report on the work of the Constitutional Court for the Year 2000*], Su–139/00–1 from 18 December 2000, p. 2. Available at <www.us-rs.si/media/poro2000.pdf>.

40 *See* the *Annual Reports of Slovenian Ombudsman*, available at <www.varuh-rs.si/index.php?id=54>.

instruments. In the independent Slovenia — because of the transition and its ideological reasons — much more attention was paid to international instruments. The reasons for this can be sought in the historical perspective, mainly because of past negative experiences in Yugoslavia, as well as in the ongoing integration processes in Europe, which Slovenia strived to catch up with. However, in both cases international hard law instruments carried the flag and the UDHR has been more the context for devising a human rights protection system. Nevertheless, the use of the UDHR by the Constitutional Court of Slovenia in recent times may point to a development where the legal system will recognize the UDHR as customary international law.

PART VI

THE EUROPEAN ORGANISATIONS

29. THE COUNCIL OF EUROPE: FIRST STEPS AND THEN SOME — COLLECTIVE ENFORCEMENT OF THE UNIVERSAL DECLARATION

Antti Korkeakivi[1]

1. INTRODUCTION

The United Nations and the Council of Europe were born only three years apart, in the immediate aftermath of World War II. Given the horrors of the war and massive human rights violations witnessed in Europe and elsewhere, it was natural that protection of human rights emerged early on as a priority in both organisations. The UN Charter as well as the Council of Europe's Statute underlined respect for human rights, and both organisations launched almost immediately the drafting of instruments aimed to advance these rights.[2] The results of this commitment were first seen in the adoption of the Universal Declaration of Human Rights by the United Nations in December 1948, which was soon followed by the European Convention on Human Rights, opened for signature by the Council of Europe in November 1950.[3]

Bearing in mind this timeline and background, it is natural that the Universal Declaration was a key reference and influence for the framers of the European Convention on Human Rights. This is reflected in the preamble of the Convention, in which the State Parties express their resolve "to take the first steps for the collective enforcement" of the Universal Declaration.

---

1 The views expressed are those of the author.

2 The UN Charter, adopted on 26 June 1945, states, *inter alia*, in Article 1(3) that one of the purposes of the organisation is "to achieve international co-operation … in promoting and encouraging respect for human rights and for fundamental freedoms for all without distinction as to race, sex, language or religion". The Statute of the Council of Europe, opened for signature on 5 May 1949, provides in its Article 3 that "[e]very Member … must accept the principles of the rule of law and of the enjoyment by all persons within its jurisdiction of human rights and fundamental freedoms", ETS 1, 87 UNTS 103.

3 The European Convention for the Protection of Human Rights and Fundamental Freedoms, ETS 5, 213 UNTS 222, opened for signature on 4 November 1950.

In this contribution, I will first discuss how the Declaration influenced the drafting process and what are the main similarities and differences between these two seminal human rights texts. I will then examine how the European Court of Human Rights has drawn upon the Declaration and whether its jurisprudence has bridged any perceived or real differences between the two instruments.

In order to provide a comprehensive palette of human rights instruments, the Council of Europe has complemented the European Convention with a range of additional conventions or monitoring mechanisms, such as the European Social Charter. The final part of the present contribution will study to what extent the Universal Declaration has inspired and informed these efforts.

2. THE UNIVERSAL DECLARATION'S IMPACT ON THE EUROPEAN CONVENTION

2.1. ROLE OF THE DECLARATION IN THE DRAFTING OF THE CONVENTION

On 12 July 1949, only seven months after the adoption of the Universal Declaration, a draft European Convention on Human Rights was submitted to the Committee of Ministers of the Council of Europe by the European Movement, a non-governmental organisation with influential jurist members, such as Pierre-Henri Teitgen of France, Sir David Maxwell-Fyfe of UK and Fernand Dehousse of Belgium. This draft had no formal status, and some members of the Committee of Ministers had, at first, reservations about pursuing the matter further and agreeing to the inclusion of human rights formally in the agenda of the Council of Europe's Consultative Assembly (later to be called the Parliamentary Assembly). Interestingly, the advisability of taking up human rights in the Council of Europe was challenged, *inter alia*, on the grounds that the matter had already been extensively discussed at the United Nations.[4] However, as members of the Assembly and others continued

4 Some of the arguments in favour of drafting a European Convention seem, in retrospect, equally off the mark, including the statement that the added value of a European text in relation to the Universal Declaration would be in that it would cover those Council of Europe Member States whose UN membership was still pending. *See* <hrls.echr.coe.int/uhtbin/cgisirsi.exe/tE9mOAGv8M/102430009/18/X245/XTITLE/Collected+edition+of+the+%22Travaux+préparatoires%22+of+the+European+Convention+on+Human+Rights+%5e2F> *Collected edition of the*

to insist on the importance of the issue, these reservations soon quietened down and the work on the Convention started in the Consultative Assembly's Committee on Legal and Administrative Questions, with Pierre-Henri Teitgen in a leading role as the Rapporteur.[5]

The need to co-ordinate human rights activities of the Council of Europe with those of the United Nations was stressed from the beginning of the drafting work. The Committee on Legal and Administrative Questions highlighted early on the "the moral authority and technical value" of the Universal Declaration and concluded that the Council of Europe should make use "as far as possible" of the definitions set out in the Universal Declaration.[6] One of the main drafters of the Universal Declaration had been (together with John Humphrey) Teitgen's compatriot René Cassin, and this probably helped to make many of the formulations and approaches of the Declaration acceptable for the key draftsmen of the European Convention. Cassin himself, while reportedly an early critic of the Council of Europe's project,[7] eventually became a strong supporter of the Convention and the President of the European Court of Human Rights from 1965 to 1968.

The draft that emerged from the Consultative Assembly in September 1949 acknowledged the role of the Universal Declaration as the main basis for the European standards, by referencing each of the substantive rights directly to the corresponding provisions of the Declaration. For example, Article 2 of the draft provided that Member States shall undertake to ensure to all persons residing within their territories "[s]ecurity of person, in accordance with Articles 3, 5 and 8 of the United Nations Declaration".[8] The Assembly's proposed method of expressly referring to the Universal Declaration for details was, however, subsequently rejected, as some Government experts, including those of Luxembourg, the Netherlands and the United Kingdom,

---

"Travaux préparatoires" of the European Convention on Human Rights, Vol. 1 (Martinus Nijhoff, The Hague, 1975) pp. 5–6 and 10–12.

5 *See, e.g.*, M. JANIS et al., *European Human Rights Law: Text and Materials* (Oxford University Press, New York, 1995) pp. 18–22.

6 *See* <hrls.echr.coe.int/uhtbin/cgisirsi.exe/tE9mOAGv8M/102430009/18/X245/XTITLE/Collected+edition+of+the+%22Travaux+préparatoires%22+of+the+European+Convention+on+Human+Rights+%5e2F> *Collected edition of the "Travaux préparatoires" of the European Convention on Human Rights, Vol. 1, supra* note 4, p. 194.

7 *See* P.-H. TEITGEN, *Faites entrer le témoin suivant: 1940–1958: De la Résistance à la Ve République* (Rennes, 1988) pp. 489–490.

8 *Collected edition of the "Travaux préparatoires" of the European Convention on Human Rights, Vol. 2* (Martinus Nijhoff, The Hague, 1975) p. 276.

argued for a self-standing instrument with more detailed formulations and legal precision.[9]

While all references to the Universal Declaration were thereby erased from the substantive articles, the Declaration eventually found its way back to the text of the Convention, thanks to a preamble proposed by the Committee on Legal and Administrative Questions at a rather late stage. The draft preamble was briefly discussed by the Consultative Assembly during its meeting in August 1950, and it eventually became the final version with only minor modifications.[10] The first two recitals of the short preamble mention the Universal Declaration, but the most important reference is in the fifth recital which provides as follows: "Being resolved, as the Governments of European countries which are like-minded and have a common heritage of political traditions, ideals, freedom and the rule of law to take the first steps for the collective enforcement of certain of the Rights stated in the Universal Declaration". This recognition of the role the Universal Declaration is more prominent than corresponding paragraphs in the preambles of other regional human rights instruments, such as the African Charter on Human and Peoples' Rights or the American Convention on Human Rights. Indeed, even many of the Council of Europe's own human rights treaties have since been less explicit about the role of the Declaration.

Although the substantive articles of the Convention do not explicitly refer to the Declaration, it is clear that many of them were inspired by, and essentially derived from, the text of the Declaration. In some cases, the Convention repeats the wording of the Declaration virtually *verbatim*. For example, Article 7, paragraph 1, of the Convention, prohibiting retroactive penal legislation, is identical with Article 11, paragraph 2, of the Universal Declaration. It is, however, important to note that the drafters of the Convention also had at their disposal first drafts of a UN Covenant on human rights, which was at that point still envisaged as a single document. The draft Covenant was explicitly invoked and drawn upon during the Convention's

---

[9] *See Collected edition of the "Travaux préparatoires" of the European Convention on Human Rights, Vol. 3* (Martinus Nijhoff, The Hague, 1976) pp. 190–192 and 252–262. For an in-depth look at the evolution of the UK's position in this respect and its early opposition to the introduction of a European Court of Human Rights, *see* G. MARSTON, 'The United Kingdom's Part in the Preparation of the European Convention on Human Rights 1950', 42 *International and Comparative Law Quarterly* (1993) pp. 796–826.

[10] *See* T. VAN BOVEN, 'Convention de sauvegarde des droits de l'homme et des libertés fondamentales', in L.-E. PETTITI et al. (eds), *La Convention européenne des droits de l'homme; commentaire article par article* (Economica, Paris, 1999) pp. 125–128.

preparation, including by the Secretariat and by a representative of the United Kingdom.[11]

While the preamble of the Convention (together with the formulation of a number of its substantive articles) clearly affirms the tight link between the Declaration and the Convention, it also acknowledges the limits of the European Convention as a vehicle for enforcing the rights contained in the comprehensive Declaration. The Convention represented only a "first step" in the enforcement of "certain rights" stated in the Declaration. In a number of comments, the drafters argued that such selectivity was necessary, bearing in mind that the Convention was going to be a legally binding document with a collective enforcement mechanism. For example, according to Teitgen, the possibility to impose on States "sanctions for violations" meant that the Council of Europe had to choose only those rights of the Declaration that were "indisputably fundamental".[12]

The most obvious victims of the drafters' "pick-and-choose" approach were economic, social and cultural rights, which constitute a significant part of the Declaration (Articles 22 to 27). Their inclusion in the Declaration had been relatively uncontroversial,[13] but the drafters of the Convention pursued a different approach. Despite some attempts, notably by a number of socialist members of the Consultative Assembly, to go beyond civil and political rights framework, the dominant thinking amongst the key drafters was early on that the European Convention should be, by and large, restricted to civil and political rights. It was argued that the inclusion of economic and social rights would be "too controversial and difficult" and it would "jeopardize the acceptance of the Convention".[14] The opponents of the inclusion of social and economic rights also invoked the fact that, while such rights were contained in the Universal Declaration, they were not, at that point, included in the draft UN Covenant on human rights that was being circulated.[15] They

---

11 *See, e.g.*, A.A. CANCADO TRINDADE, 'Co-existence and Co-ordination of Mechanisms of International Protection of Human Rights (At Global and Regional Levels)', 202 *Academy of International Law, Collected Courses* (1987) pp. 155–157.

12 *See* TEITGEN, *supra* note 7, p. 481.

13 *See, e.g.*, A. SAMNØY, 'The Origins of the Universal Declaration of Human Rights', in G. ALFREDSSON and A. EIDE (eds), *The Universal Declaration of Human Rights: A Common Standard of Achievement* (Martinus Nijhoff Publishers, The Hague, 1999) p. 11.

14 Statement by Sir David Maxwell-Fyffe, *Collected edition of the "Travaux préparatoires" of the European Convention on Human Rights, Vol. 3, supra* note 9, p. 10.

15 *Ibid.* The Human Rights Commission had at first decided not to include such rights in a covenant, although these rights subsequently made a comeback, eventually resulting in two covenants. *See, e.g.*, M.A. BADERIN and R. MCCORQUODALE, 'The International Covenant on Economic, Social and Cultural Rights: Forty Years of Development', in M.A. BADERIN and R.

accepted that the "professional freedoms and social rights" should also be addressed, but that the Council of Europe, should, the argument went, "begin from the beginning" by focusing on civil and political rights.[16]

As the adoption of the final version approached, the line advocating strict focus on civil and political rights easily won the day — with no vocal opposition from any of the Member States. True, the right to education and the right to property were, after lengthy debates, eventually introduced through the First Protocol to the European Convention in 1952 and the European Court of Human Rights later stressed that "the mere fact that an interpretation of the Convention may extend into the sphere of social and economic rights should not be a decisive factor against such an interpretation" and that "there is no water-tight division separating that sphere from the field covered by the Convention".[17] But these and other developments towards a wider acceptance of economic and social rights have not changed the fact that the European Convention remains to this day a treaty heavily dominated by civil and political rights, as envisaged in the early drafts.

In addition to putting aside most economic, social and cultural rights, the drafters of the Convention decided not to borrow some other provisions of the Declaration. They omitted, for instance, the right to seek and enjoy asylum as well as the right to a nationality (Articles 14 and 15 of the Declaration), and disagreements over the inclusion of the right to free elections meant that this right was introduced only in the First Protocol to the Convention in 1952. Moreover, the Member States of the Council of Europe limited the scope of the Convention in ways not employed in the Universal Declaration, including by expressly allowing for restrictions on political activities of aliens in relation to certain rights contained in the Convention.[18] While there are such substantial differences between the two

---

MCCORQUODALE (eds), *Economic, Social and Cultural Rights in Action* (Oxford University Press, Oxford, 2007) pp. 1–5 and R. CASSIN, 'La Déclaration Universelle et la Mise en Oeuvre des Droits de l'Homme', 79 *Academie de Droit International, Recueil des Course* (1951) pp. 297–305.

16 *See* Report of the Committee on Legal Administrative Questions in *Collected edition of the "Travaux préparatoires" of the European Convention on Human Rights, Vol. 1, supra* note 4, p. 194.

17 *Airey* v *Ireland*, 9 October 1979, ECHR, Series A No. 32, para. 26, <www.echr.coe.int/ECHR>.

18 Article 16 of the Convention provides that nothing in Articles 10, 11 and 14 of the Convention "shall be regarded as preventing the High Contracting Parties from imposing restrictions on the political activity of aliens". This article has not had a substantial impact on the case law of the Court, and its relevance has been further limited by the fact that Protocol 12 on non-discrimination does not refer to it. For more details, *see* J. SCHOKKENBROEK, 'A New

texts, it is important to note that the Council of Europe has continued to abolish or reduce some of them through additional protocols to the European Convention, including Protocols 7 and 12. Indeed, the explanatory report of Protocol 12, when contextualising why a new protocol was needed to strengthen the European non-discrimination guarantees, clearly recognises that the protection provided by Article 14 of the Convention with regard to equality and non-discrimination was limited in comparison with Article 7 of the Universal Declaration (and Article 26 of the International Covenant on Civil and Political Rights).[19] Furthermore, the European Court of Human Rights has through its jurisprudence (examined in more detail in the below section) helped to advance consistency between the European Convention standards and those of the Universal Declaration in certain areas where there was a risk of the Convention falling short of the material contents of the Declaration.

There are also areas where the Universal Declaration contained shortcomings or gaps that travelled to the European Convention. One "shared gap" in the substantive coverage concerns the protection of minorities, which is addressed in both instruments merely through non-discrimination guarantees. In both cases, attempts were made during the drafting process to include specific provisions on minority rights, but these failed, first at the United Nations[20] and then in the Council of Europe, where notably a Danish representative attempted unsuccessfully to introduce minority rights in the European Convention. In both venues, minority rights eventually found their way to the normative arsenal of the organisations, but in different ways. Whereas at the UN, Article 27 of the Covenant on Civil and Political Rights was devoted to minorities,[21] attempts to include minority rights in a protocol

European Standard Against Discrimination: Negotiating Protocol No. 12 to the European Convention on Human Rights', in J. NIESSEN and I. CHOPIN (eds), *The Development of Legal Instruments to Combat Racism in a Diverse Europe* (Brill Academic Publishers, Leiden, 2004) pp. 61–79.

19 Explanatory Report of Protocol No. 12 to the Convention for the Protection of Human Rights and Fundamental Freedoms, para. 1, ETS 177, opened for signature on 4 November 2000.

20 On the debates leading to the omission of a special minority rights article, *see* J. MORSINK, *The Universal Declaration of Human Rights: Origins, Drafting and Intent* (University of Pennsylvania Press, Philadelphia, 1999) pp. 269–280 and A. EIDE, 'The Non-inclusion of Minority Rights: Resolution 217C (III)', in G. ALFREDSSON and A. EIDE (eds), *The Universal Declaration of Human Rights: A Common Standard of Achievement* (Martinus Nijhoff Publishers, The Hague, 1999) pp. 701–723.

21 International Covenant on Civil and Political Rights, 6 ILM 368, opened for signature on 16 December 1996.

to the European Convention have so far failed.[22] The Council of Europe has, however, adopted a separate treaty, the Framework Convention for the Protection of National Minorities, with a non-judicial monitoring mechanism.[23]

2.2. UNIVERSAL DECLARATION IN THE STRASBOURG CASE LAW

While the actual formulation of the substantive rights of the European Convention contain only a limited number of innovations, the Convention's legally binding nature and, in particular, its enforcement machinery represented a truly unprecedented step in international human rights law. The European Commission and the Court of Human Rights, later replaced by a single Court, have provided an essential international remedy to individual victims and a source of significant case law guiding domestic policies and practices in Europe. In its jurisprudence, questions related to inter-linkages between the Convention and the Universal Declaration have been addressed a number of times. The present section will provide an overview of some of the pertinent cases, but it is by no means exhaustive. First of all, we will not dwell upon the significant *indirect* impact that the Universal Declaration has had on the Strasbourg case law through other international treaties, that is, cases where international human rights treaties (and the findings of their monitoring bodies) that were at least partially inspired by the Declaration — such as the UN Covenant on Civil and Political Rights or the Council of Europe's Social Charter — have in turn been invoked by the European Court of Human Rights.[24] Secondly, the limited space available here allows us to

---

22 A recent attempt to draw up such a protocol was launched in 1993, but the Member States were unable to agree on a number of pertinent concepts, including as regards the nature and scope of rights included, and in January 1996 the Committee of Ministers decided to suspend the work of the pertinent committee. For details on the Council of Europe's wide-ranging work in the area of minority rights, *see* P. THORNBERRY and M.A. MARTÍN ESTÉBANEZ, *Minority Rights in Europe* (Council of Europe, Strasbourg, 2004).

23 Framework Convention for the Protection of National Minorities, ETS 157, 34 ILM 351, opened for signature on 1 February 1995.

24 The UN High Commissioner for Human Rights recently stressed that "[g]iven the wide degree of overlap of substantive protection between the European Convention and, in particular, the International Covenant on Civil and Political Rights, the Court's use of UN materials diminishes the risk of inconsistent jurisprudence and enhances the likelihood of a better result in both venues". L. ARBOUR, *Address at the Opening of the Judicial Year 2008 of the European Court of Human Rights*, Strasbourg, 25 January 2008. On the Court's increasing willingness to take such an inclusive approach in non-discrimination cases, *see* A. KORKEAKIVI, 'Introductory Note — European Court of Human Rights Grand Chamber: D.H. v. Czech Republic', 47 *International Legal Materials* (2008) p. 35.

cover but a small sampling of the varied cases in which the Strasbourg organs have invoked the Universal Declaration. Even though it has been argued that the Commission and Court could use the Declaration more frequently, references to the Declaration are rather common.[25] The first such citation by the Commission of Human Rights dates back to 1958,[26] and in 2007 alone, the Declaration was mentioned in 13 judgments of the Court.[27] It is true that most of these references did not involve the Court's own assessment of the case at issue but concerned only brief citations of domestic law mentioning the Declaration or applicants invoking the Declaration to bolster their legal arguments.

Some cases, however, involve more in-depth analysis of the Declaration. These include consideration of the implications of the preambular phrase "to take the first steps for the collective enforcement of certain of the Rights stated in the Universal Declaration" and argumentation as to whether the said phrase dictates the inclusion (or exclusion) of a particular right. The Governments concerned have at times stressed that the phrases "first steps" and "certain rights" place clear limits on the reach of application of the Convention. In the *Golder* case, for example, the UK Government referred to the above-mentioned recital when arguing that Article 6, paragraph 1, of the Convention does not secure the right to have claims relating to civil rights and obligations brought before a court or tribunal. According to the Government, the preamble illustrates the "selective process" adopted by the draftsmen and that the Convention does not seek to protect human rights in general but merely "certain of the Rights stated in the Universal Declaration".[28] In its judgment, the Court also attached importance to the preamble of the Convention. But instead of stressing the sentence on "first steps" and "certain rights", the Court referred to the preamble's emphasis on

---

25 Upon the introduction of the single Court, Tavernier argued that the Universal Declaration could be invoked by the Court more often as a common reference, especially as the Council of Europe expanded to cover so-called new democracies of Europe. P. TAVERNIER, *La jurisprudence de la Cour européenne des droits de l'Homme dans le prolongement de la déclaration universelle des droits de l'Homme*, Cahiers du CREDHO, No. 5, 1999, p. 172.

26 The Commission of Human Rights noted that there was a "striking difference" between Article 9 of the Universal Declaration of Human Rights and paragraph 1 of Article 5 of the European Convention in that the latter did not cover exile, and it concluded that this omission was deliberate. *Greece* v *United Kingdom*, App. No. 176/56, 2 Yearbook of the European Commission on Human Rights 174 (1959).

27 According to the results of a ECHR portal search (HUDOC) on 6 May 2008 <www.echr.coe.int/ECHR>.

28 *Golder* v *UK*, 21 February 1975, ECHR, No. 4451/70, 1 EHRR 524 <www.echr.coe.int/ECHR>.

the rule of law and concluded that a right of access to the court, while not explicitly mentioned in the Convention, is inherent in Article 6(1).

There are also other cases where the Court's interpretation of certain rights has helped to ensure that the Convention's coverage is similar to the express guarantees contained in the Universal Declaration. In some cases, this has involved a gradual evolution of the Court's jurisprudence. One prominent example is the right not to join a trade union. The right not to be compelled to join an association is guaranteed in Article 20, paragraph 2, of the Declaration but not mentioned *per se* in Article 11 of the Convention, which deals with freedom of association and assembly. The UK Government, invoking the *travaux préparatoires* of the Convention, argued in the *Young, James and Webster* case that the omission was deliberate and that, consequently, Article 11 did not guarantee any right not to be compelled to join an association. In the said case, the Court avoided taking a firm position on the issue, although it stated, *inter alia*, that to construe Article 11 of the Convention as "permitting every kind of compulsion in the field of trade union membership would strike at the very substance of the freedom it is designed to guarantee".[29] In its more recent case law, the Court has developed its position and recognised in explicit terms that Article 11 encompasses a negative right of association.[30]

The above examples show how the Strasbourg Court has advanced consistency between the Declaration and the Convention. It has taken steps in that direction also in respect of rights that, the Court accepts, are not covered by the Convention, including in the area civil and political rights. For example, the Court has recognised that, although a "right to nationality" similar to that in Article 15 of the Universal Declaration of Human Rights is not guaranteed by the Convention or its Protocols, an arbitrary denial of citizenship might in certain circumstances raise an issue under Article 8 of the Convention because of the impact of such a denial on the private life of the individual.[31] Similar developments can be seen in relation to the protection of asylum-seekers. Although the Convention, unlike the Universal Declaration, does not contain a right to seek and enjoy asylum, the Court has through its case law ensured that (also) asylum-seekers receive substantial

---

29 *Young, James and Webster* v *the United Kingdom*, 13 August 1981, ECHR, No. 7601/76 and 7806/77, Series A No. 44, paras. 51–52, <www.echr.coe.int/ECHR>.

30 *See, e.g., Sigurdur A. Sigurjónsson* v *Iceland,* 30 June 1993, ECHR, No. 16130/90 and *Chassagnou and Others* v *France*, 29 April 1999, ECHR, No. 25088/94, <www echr.coe.int/ECHR>.

31 *See, e.g., Karassev* v *Finland,* 12 January 1999, ECHR No. 31414/96, <www.echr.coe.int/ECHR>.

protection under the Convention in certain matters, including against expulsion or extradition that would amount to inhuman treatment within the meaning of Article 3 of the Convention.[32] Moreover, the Declaration's provisions on the right to seek asylum have been invoked in the Court's judgments under the "applicable law" rubric. For example, in the important *Saadi* case of January 2008 — in which the Court ruled that the absolute prohibition of torture under Article 3 prohibits Italy from returning a Tunisian national deemed a security risk to his country of origin because he faced a real threat of torture — the Court not only mentioned Articles 3, 9 and 13 of the Declaration but also recalled, under the section "relevant international law documents", that Article 14(1) of the Declaration declares that "everyone" has the fundamental right "to seek and to enjoy in other countries asylum".[33]

The Court's jurisprudence has also ironed out, or at least diminished, certain conceptual differences that some originally perceived as existing between the Convention and the Court. For example, the question as to whether, and to what extent, the implementation of the Convention requires positive measures has been repeatedly addressed by the Court. Back in 1968, in the so-called *Belgian linguistic* case, the Belgian Government argued that the Convention and its First Protocol are "inspired on the whole by the classic conception of freedoms, in contrast to rights, differing in this respect from the Universal Declaration of Human Rights ... The commitments undertaken by the States by virtue of the Convention and the Protocol possess therefore an essentially negative character".[34] Gradually building a strikingly different approach, the Court has affirmed increasingly often — including in relation to Articles 2, 3 and 8 — that the Convention imposes in many cases positive obligations on the State Parties.[35] While the Court has not expressly rooted this development in the text of the Declaration, it is in

32 *See generally*, Council of Europe and UNHCR, *Proceedings of the 2nd Colloquy on the European Convention on Human Rights and the Protection of Refugees, Asylum-seekers and Displaced Persons* (Council of Europe Publishing, Strasbourg, 2000).

33 *Saadi* v *Italy*, 19 January 2008, ECHR, No. 37201/06, paras. 29–30, <www.echr.coe.nt/ECHR>.

34 *Case "relating to the certain aspects of the laws on the use of languages in education in Belgium"* v *Belgium (Belgian Linguistics case)*, 23 July 1968, ECHR, No. 1474/62; 1677/62; 1691/62; 1769/63; 1994/63; 2126/64, Series A No. 6, 1 EHRR 252 <www.echr.coe.int/ECHR>.

35 *See generally*, A. MOWBRAY, *The Development of Positive Obligations under the European Convention on Human Rights by the European Court of Human Rights* (Hart Publishing, Oxford, 2004). On positive obligations in relation to the right to life, *see* P. VAN DIJK et al. (eds), *Theory and Practice of the European Convention on Human Rights*, 4th ed. (Intersentia, Antwerpen, 2006) pp. 353–386.

keeping with the basic tenets of the Declaration and it can to some extent palliate the lack of explicit social and economic rights in the Convention.

Furthermore, the Strasbourg organs have been prepared to draw on certain concepts expressly included in the Declaration. Perhaps the most prominent example is the notion of human dignity, which is referred to several times in the Universal Declaration but which is altogether absent from the text of the European Convention.[36] The Court affirmed in the 1978 *Tyrer* case — concerning corporal punishment in the UK — that one of the main purposes of Article 3 was to protect a "person's dignity and physical integrity".[37] Since then, the concept of dignity has been a factor in the interpretation also of many other articles of the Convention, and the Court has even concluded that "[t]he very essence of the Convention is respect for human dignity and human freedom".[38]

In certain situations, the Court has suggested in its jurisprudence what the Universal Declaration does *not* include or imply. In the recent *Al-Adsani* case, the Court first invoked leading legislative and jurisprudential authorities as well as the Universal Declaration to conclude that prohibition against torture is accepted as a peremptory norm of international law, but the Court then went on to conclude that it does not follow from the pertinent texts (such as Article 5 of the Declaration) that international law now bars a state from enjoying immunity from civil suit in the courts of another state in respect of alleged acts of torture.[39]

In addition to its judgments of the merit, certain admissibility decisions contain interesting references to the Universal Declaration. In its recent *Behrami* and *Šaramati* admissibility decisions, the Court found that it had no jurisdiction over the action of states acting in Kosovo on behalf of the UN under Chapter VII of the UN Charter. In analysing the relationship between the Convention and the UN acting under Chapter VII, the Court recalled, *inter alia*, that "one of the aims of the Convention was the collective enforcement of rights in the Universal Declaration of Human Rights of the

---

36 For an overview of the development of the concept of dignity and its application in domestic and international jurisprudence, *see* C. MCCRUDDEN, 'Human Dignity', *University of Oxford Faculty of Law Legal Studies Research Paper Series*, Working Paper No. 10/2006, April 2006.

37 *Tyrer* v *the United Kingdom*, 25 April 1978, ECHR, No. 5856/72, para. 33, <www.echr.coe.int/ECHR>.

38 *Pretty* v *the United Kingdom*, 29 April 2002, ECHR, No. 2346/02, para. 65, <www.echr.coe.int/ECHR>.

39 *Al-Adsani* v *United Kingdom*, 21 November 2001, ECHR, No. 35763/97, paras. 60–61, <www.echr.coe.int/ECHR>. *See also* L. WILDHABER, 'The European Convention on Human Rights and International Law', 56 *International and Comparative Law Quarterly* (2007) pp. 225–226.

General Assembly of the UN".[40] This reference to the Declaration was not at the centre of the Court's assessment, and the Court did not go on to analyse separately the implications of this particular phrase in its decision. However, the context suggests that the preambular phrase was seen as lending support to the view that there is a need for the Strasbourg organs to grant a degree of deference to the UN and that the Convention mechanism should play a supporting rather than a controlling role when the UN — the author of the "master text" on human rights — pursues its activities, in particular under Chapter VII.

3. IMPACT OF THE UNIVERSAL DECLARATION BEYOND THE CONVENTION

3.1. THE EUROPEAN SOCIAL CHARTER

While the European Convention on Human Rights is no doubt the Council of Europe's most prominent contribution to the enforcement of the Universal Declaration, the Council's human rights work goes well beyond the Convention. The Convention standards have been complemented by treaties ranging from social rights to minority rights, and the Court's work on individual cases is being added to by a number of treaty mechanisms looking at a range of human rights issues.

The Council of Europe Commissioner for Human Rights recently noted that "[i]n an ideal world there would not have been a European Social Charter. Its important provisions would have been part of the European Convention on Human Rights".[41] But, as was discussed above, the drafters of the Convention thought otherwise. The process that eventually led to the adoption of the European Social Charter[42] started only a year after the signature of the European Convention, with a Consultative Assembly's recommendation that the Council of Europe Member States adopt a "common

---

40 *Behrami and Behrami* v *France*, 2 May 2007, ECHR, No. 71412/01 and *Saramati* v *France, Germany and Norway*, 2 May 2007, ECHR, No. 78166/01, <www.echr.coe.int/ECHR>.

41 Remarks by Thomas Hammarberg, Commissioner for Human Rights, to the seminar to mark the tenth anniversary of the Revised European Social Charter CommDH/Speech(2006)5, <wcd.coe.int/ViewDoc.jsp?id=995347&BackColorInternet=99B5AD&BackColorIntranet=FABF45&BackColorLogged=FFC679>, visited on 30 May 2008.

42 The European Social Charter, ETS 35, opened for signature on 18 October 1961. A revised version of the Charter (ETS 163), which updates and extends the rights protected, was adopted on 3 May 1996.

policy in the social field". The Secretariat's proposal to follow this recommendation up with a charter was first met with reservations in the Committee of Ministers. The idea gradually gained traction, however, and in 1954 a new committee was tasked to draw up a charter.[43]

During the preparatory stages, those defending the Charter initiative recalled that the Universal Declaration was not confined to political and civil rights and that the Charter would be an opportunity to expand the "more limited framework" of the Council of Europe.[44] Individual provisions of the Universal Declaration, including those on the right to work and leisure, no doubt also inspired and informed the preparation of the Charter, but there were also other key UN standards to draw on. In particular, the ILO conventions and recommendations provided valuable guidance to the drafters. Furthermore, they had access to drafts of the UN Covenant on Economic, Social and Cultural Rights, although these reportedly did not influence the text significantly.[45] It is, nevertheless, somewhat surprising that neither the preamble nor the substantive articles of the final version of the Charter mention the Universal Declaration. The Charter's substantive provisions do, however, clearly echo some of the provisions of the Declaration and provide more detailed guarantees relating, for example, to the implementation of the right to work and the right to rest and leisure, contained in Articles 23 and 24 of the Declaration. Moreover, while the Declaration does not figure expressly in the country-specific conclusions of the European Committee of Social Rights — the body responsible for the monitoring of the Charter — the Committee has recognised the central influence of the Declaration by stating, *inter alia*, that the purpose of the Charter "is to apply the Universal Declaration of Human Rights within Europe, as a complement to the European Convention on Human Rights. It reflects the concern of countries that have ratified it to give real meaning to the notion of the indivisibility and interdependence of human rights".[46]

Furthermore, it is important to recall that the Social Charter's monitoring mechanism has at times been a European pioneer in pursuing certain

---

43 *See* D. HARRIS and J. DARCY, *European Social Charter*, 2nd ed. (Transnational Publishers, Ardsley, 2001) pp. 1–4.

44 *See* the comments by the Chair of the Parliamentary Assembly's Committee on Social Questions, in *European Social Charter, Collected Travaux Préparatoires* (provisional edition), Vol. 1 (1953–1954), Section IV, p. 16.

45 HARRIS and DARCY, *supra* note 43, pp. 23–24.

46 The European Committee of Social Rights, Conclusions XVIII–1, Vol. 1, Council of Europe, December 2006, p. 8, <www.coe.int/t/e/human_rights/esc/3_reporting_procedure/2_recent_conclusions/2_by_year/XVIII1Vol1_en.pdf>, visited on 30 May 2008.

concepts contained in the Universal Declaration that have been accepted only step by step by other Council of Europe mechanisms. For example the European Committee of Social Rights concluded early on that freedom to organise — contained in Article 5 of the European Social Charter — guarantees also a negative right to organise, whereas, as discussed above, the European Court of Human Rights moved only gradually towards a similarly explicit position in respect of negative right of association under Article 11 of the Convention.[47]

3.2. OTHER TREATIES AND MECHANISMS

The Universal Declaration continues to have an impact on the Council of Europe standard-setting activities. Some of the relatively recent normative work of the Council of Europe contributes directly to the implementation of certain of those provisions of the Declaration that were not incorporated in the European Convention on Human Rights or in the Social Charter. For instance, the European Convention on Nationality of 1997 and the Convention on the Avoidance of Statelessness in Relation to State Succession of 2007 recognise the right to a nationality and their explanatory reports refer in this respect to Article 15 of the Universal Declaration of Human Rights.[48]

Furthermore, references to the Declaration can be found in the preambles of certain new treaties, such as the Convention on Human Rights and Biomedicine.[49] One of the most recent conventions, the Framework Convention of the Council of Europe on the Value of Cultural Heritage for Society, not only mentions the Declaration in its preamble but also in its substantive provisions. According to Article 1 of the said Convention, the Parties "recognise that rights relating to cultural heritage are inherent in the right to participate in cultural life, as defined in the Universal Declaration of

---

47 For an account of the development of the Committee's and Court's respective positions on this issue, *see* J-K. AKANDJI-KOMBÉ, 'The Material Impact of the Jurisprudence of the European Committee of Social Rights', in G. DE BURCA and B. DE WITTE (eds), *Social Rights in Europe* (Oxford University Press, Oxford 2005) pp. 100–103.

48 *See* Article 4 of the European Convention on Nationality, ETS 166, opened for signature on 6 November 1997, and Article 2 of the Council of Europe Convention on the avoidance of statelessness in relation to State succession, ETS 200, opened for signature on 19 May 2006. *See generally*, I. ZIEMELE and G. SCBRAM, 'Article 15', in G. ALFREDSSON and A. EIDE, *supra* note 13, pp. 297–324.

49 The Convention for the Protection of Human Rights and Dignity of the Human Being with regard to the Application of Biology and Medicine: Convention on Human Rights and Biomedicine, ETS 164, opened for signature on 4 April 1997.

Human Rights".[50] It is interesting to note that, almost 60 years after the proposal by Pierre-Henri Teitgen to do so in the draft European Convention on Human Rights, a Council of Europe convention now refers to the Universal Declaration for a definition of a particular right.

Finally, there are linkages between the Universal Declaration and the Council of Europe's wide-ranging information and training activities in the area of human rights. For example, the Council of Europe has organised a range of special events on the Human Rights Day — observed every year on 10 December to commemorate the day in 1948 the General Assembly adopted the Universal Declaration of Human Rights — on current human rights themes, ranging from human trafficking to extraordinary renditions.

4. CONCLUDING REMARKS

The Universal Declaration was a key influence and source of inspiration for the framers of the European Convention on Human Rights. For them, the Convention represented "first steps" in the collective enforcement of the Universal Declaration. These have turned out not to be baby steps but major leaps, as the Convention and the European Court of Human Rights have acted as main motors of Europe's human rights protection system. The significance of this system has only increased with the expansion of the Council of Europe into a truly pan-European organisation with 47 Member States.

The drafters of the Convention borrowed, however, only selectively from the Universal Declaration, leaving aside most economic, social and cultural rights. While the Court has through its case law reduced some of the perceived differences between the two texts, at times drawing directly on the Declaration, the reach of the Declaration continues to be markedly broader. Therefore, it is important to keep in mind that the Council of Europe's human rights arsenal goes beyond the Convention. Starting with the European Social Charter, the Council of Europe has adopted a range of additional human rights treaties, some of which refer expressly to the Universal Declaration. Although their monitoring mechanisms are not as strong as that of the European Convention, these treaties are a valuable element of the Council of Europe's on-going efforts to ensure regional implementation of the broad and inclusive human rights protection design envisaged by the Universal Declaration of Human Rights.

---

50 The Council of Europe Framework Convention on the Value of Cultural Heritage for Society, ETS 199, opened for signature on 27 October 2005.

30. THE EUROPEAN UNION: IN SEARCH OF LEGITIMACY

Allan Rosas

1. FROM COAL AND STEEL TO HUMAN RIGHTS

The European Union (hereinafter EU) has its origins in economic integration communities, starting with the European Coal and Steel Community, founded in 1951. Perhaps it is symptomatic that the Coal and Steel Community is not with us anymore but ceased to exist as a separate entity in 2002.[1] And the European Economic Community, founded in 1957, later changed its name to European Community (hereinafter EC) to reflect the broadening of the integration agenda brought about by the Single European Act of 1986 and the Treaty of Maastricht of 1992. The concept of the EU, introduced by the Treaty of Maastricht, would completely replace the EC if the Treaty of Lisbon, signed on 13 December 2007, were to enter into force.[2] These name changes attest to the fact that the EU has become an economic and political union of States, which even displays some features of a federal state, or at least of a federative community or association.[3]

The EU today deals with a wide range of subjects, from a more traditional emphasis on economic freedoms and the internal market, including a common agricultural policy and an external trade policy, to fields such as the environment, social and labour affairs, immigration, judicial cooperation and even issues of police cooperation, penal law and defence policy. The EU is a far cry from intergovernmental organisations such as the Council of Europe or the United Nations. Intergovernmental organisations do not have

---

1 The Treaty establishing the European Coal and Steel Community entered into force in 1952 and was, according to its Article 97, concluded for a period of 50 years from its entry into force.

2 Treaty of Lisbon amending the Treaty on European Union and the Treaty establishing the European Community, OJ C 306, 17 December 2007. Consolidated versions of both Treaties (the latter being renamed Treaty on the Functioning of the European Union) have been published in OJ C 115, 9 May 2008, p. 1. The Treaty of Lisbon was scheduled to enter into force on 1 January 2009, but the negative outcome of a referendum in Ireland in June 2008 has rendered entry into force highly uncertain.

3 A. ROSAS, *The European Union as a Federative Association: European Law Lecture 2003* (Durham European Law Institute, Durham, 2004).

legislative powers over a given territory, a concept of citizenship, a common currency or a common defence policy. The Treaty of Lisbon would, if it were to enter into force, further strengthen the supranational and state-like character of the EU.

While human rights and fundamental rights played a marginal, if any, role in the early days of the Communities, they are already today high on the agenda of the EU. It could not be otherwise. A fundamental rights-free-zone at the EU level would engender clashes with the national constitutions and national fundamental rights regimes of the Member States, given the primacy (or supremacy) and direct effect of EU law, coupled with the wide-ranging broadening of the integration agenda.[4] As human rights have become an important subject for international relations, they must be — and indeed have become — an important part of an EU external relations strategy as well.[5]

With respect to the internal EU situation (the EU and its Member States), it has become commonplace to speak of *fundamental rights*. This dimension, which is of a constitutional nature, concerns the protection of fundamental rights through, *inter alia*, provisions in written primary and secondary EU law, the Charter of Fundamental Rights of the European Union,[6] the case-law of the Court of Justice of the European Communities (hereinafter ECJ) and the new EU Agency for Fundamental Rights.[7] The notion of *human rights* is mainly used in the context of EU external relations, including human rights clauses contained in cooperation agreements with third countries, human rights assistance programmes in favour of third countries and international

---

4 *See, e.g.*, A. ROSAS, 'The European Court of Justice and Fundamental Rights: Yet Another Case of Judicial Activism?', in C. BAUDENBACHER and H. BULL (eds), *European Integration Through Interaction of Legal Regimes* (Universitetsforlaget, Oslo, 2007) pp. 33–63. *See more generally* the articles on EU fundamental rights in P. ALSTON (ed.), *The EU and Human Rights* (Oxford University Press, Oxford, 1999).

5 *See, e.g.*, B. BRANDTNER and A. ROSAS, 'Human Rights and the External Relations of the European Community: An Analysis of Doctrine and Practice', 9 *European Journal of International Law* (1998) pp. 468–490. *See more generally* the articles on EU external human rights policies in ALSTON, *supra* note 4.

6 The Charter was originally proclaimed in December 2000 by the European Parliament, the Council and the Commission as a 'soft law' document, OJ C 364, 18 December 2000, p. 1. An adapted version of 12 December 2007, OJ C 303, 14 December 2007, p. 1, will, if the Treaty of Lisbon enters into force (*supra* note 2), be made legally binding and be included in EU primary law through Article 6, paragraph 1, of the Treaty on European Union as amended by the Lisbon Treaty.

7 Council Regulation (EC) No. 168/2007 of 15 February 2007 establishing a European Union Agency for Fundamental Rights, OJ L 53, 22 February 2007, p. 1.

and non-governmental organisations and the coordination of EU Member States' human rights policies.

The Universal Declaration of Human Rights (hereinafter UDHR) has been an important source of inspiration, mainly in the development of an EU external human rights policy,[8] but to some extent also for the protection of fundamental rights in the EU itself. There is, in fact, a special reason why the UDHR has played a relatively significant role for the EU, as compared to many nation-states: Until recently, the EU[9] has not been able to adhere to binding international human rights conventions, including the European Convention on Human Rights (hereinafter ECHR) and the legally binding parts of the International Bill of Rights, namely the International Covenant on Economic, Social and Cultural Rights and the International Covenant on Civil and Political Rights, both of 1966. These conventions, as will be explained below, have thus not been applied directly as binding sources of law but have rather been used as 'guidelines' and points of reference in the development and application of EU law. This means that the border-line between 'soft law' instruments such as the UDHR and binding treaties becomes less relevant.

This situation may to some extent change if and when the EU starts to adhere to international human rights conventions. The first human rights convention to admit EU accession is the UN Convention on the Rights of Persons with Disabilities, adopted by the UN General Assembly in December 2006.[10] The Convention was opened for signature on 30 March 2007, when it was also signed by the EC. The Convention entered into force in May 2008 but has not yet been formally confirmed by the EU.[11] As to the ECHR, while the ECJ in 1996 held that as Community law stood at the time, the EC lacked

---

8 A. ROSAS, 'The Role of the Universal Declaration of Human Rights in the Treaty Relations of the European Union', in P. BAEHR et al. (eds), *Innovation and Inspiration: Fifty Years of the Universal Declaration of Human Rights* (Koninklijke Nederlandse Akademie van Wetenschappen, Amsterdam, 1999) pp. 201–209.

9 The term 'EU' is here used as a broad umbrella term, to include the European Communities and notably the EC (often referred to as the 'First Pillar' of the EU). Most international agreements are still concluded in the name of the EC but as was noted above, the entry into force of the Treaty of Lisbon would extinguish the EC as a separate Community.

10 According to Article 44 of the Convention, it is open for adherence not only by States but also by 'regional integration organizations', meaning essentially the EU.

11 <www2.ohchr.org/english/issues/disability/index.htm>, visited on 24 May 2008. According to Article 43 of the Convention, while signatory States may ratify the Convention, the corresponding term for regional integration organisations is formal confirmation. Of the EU Member States, the Convention (as of 24 May 2008) had been ratified by Hungary, Slovenia and Spain.

competence to accede to the Convention,[12] the entry into force of the Treaty of Lisbon would change the situation. According to Article 6, paragraph 2, of the Treaty on European Union (hereinafter TEU), as amended by the Treaty of Lisbon, the EU "shall accede" to the ECHR. EU accession would also require an amendment to the ECHR itself. This has, in fact, been prescribed in Article 59 of the Convention, as amended by Protocol No. 14, but the Protocol has not yet entered into force.[13] In this context it should also be mentioned that Article 53 of the Charter of Fundamental Rights presupposes that the EU, including the EC, can become a party to international human rights treaties, referring as it does to "international agreements to which the Union, the Community or all the Member States are party, including the [ECHR]".

2. EU FUNDAMENTAL RIGHTS AND THE UDHR

While the UDHR seems to have played a greater role in the development of EU external human rights policies than in the formation of an internal EU fundamental rights regime, I shall first provide an outline of the fundamental rights dimension, as it was introduced long before one can speak of any EU external human rights policy. The extensive case-law of the ECJ relating to fundamental rights is here of crucial importance. In fact, it was the case-law of the ECJ which set the ball rolling. In its landmark judgment of 1969 in *Stauder*, the Court for the first time declared that fundamental rights form part of the general principles of Community law whose observance the Court ensures.[14]

While in *Stauder* the ECJ did not mention any external sources, and in *Internationale Handelsgesellschaft* only referred to the "constitutional traditions common to the Member States",[15] the 1974 judgment in *Nold* sets out a broader formula:[16]

---

[12] Opinion 2/94 *European Convention on Human Rights* [1996] ECR I–929.

[13] Protocol No. 14 to the Convention for the Protection of Human Rights and Fundamental Freedoms, amending the control system of the Convention, Strasbourg 13 May 2004. At the time of writing, the Protocol has been ratified by 46 Member States of the Council of Europe but its entry into force is barred by the lack of Russian ratification, <ww.conventions.coe.int/Treaty/Commun/ChercheSig.asp?NT=194&CM=8&> visited on 24 May 2008.

[14] Case 29/69 *Stauder* [1969] ECR 419.

[15] Case 11/70 *Internationale Handelsgesellschaft* [1970] ECR 1125, paras. 3–4.

[16] Case 4/73 *Nold* [1974] ECR 491, para. 13.

> "As the Court has already stated, fundamental rights form an integral part of the general principles of law, the observance of which it ensures.
>
> In safeguarding these rights, the Court is bound to draw inspiration from constitutional traditions common to the Member States, and it cannot therefore uphold measures which are incompatible with fundamental rights recognized and protected by the Constitutions of those States.
>
> Similarly, international treaties for the protection of human rights on which the Member States have collaborated or of which they are signatories, can supply guidelines which should be followed within the framework of Community law."

This formula has been followed in subsequent case-law, including quite recent case-law, of the ECJ (apart from a variation in the English text of judgments which will be explained below).[17] It is to be noted that the Court, while stating that the ECHR has "particular relevance", has continued to refer to other international human rights instruments as well, despite the fact that Article 6, paragraph 2, TEU, which in other respects can be seen as a codification of the case-law of the ECJ in the field of fundamental rights, mentions the ECHR only. Since 1974, the ECHR and other international human rights instruments have been used by the ECJ as guidelines when applying fundamental rights as *general principles of Community law*.

International human rights instruments have also inspired the references to fundamental rights or human rights which have been added to the basic Treaties by the Treaties of Maastricht (1992), Amsterdam (1997) and Nice (2001). Already the Preamble to the Single European Act of 1986 referred to the ECHR and the European Social Charter of 1961. Today, not only does Article 6, paragraph 2, TEU contain an explicit reference to the ECHR, but Article 63, paragraph 1, of the Treaty establishing the European Community (hereinafter ECT)[18] mentions the Geneva Convention of 1951 and its Protocol of 1967 relating to the status of refugees, while a reference to the European Social Charter of 1961 is to be found in Article 136 ECT. Similar references

---

17 *See, e.g.*, Opinion 2/94, *supra* note 12, para. 33; Case C–540/03 *Parliament* v *Council* [2006] ECR I–5769, para. 35; Case C–244/06 *Dynamic Medien*, judgment of 14 February 2008, para. 39. *See also* Case C–438/05 *International Transport Workers' Federation*, judgment of 11 December 2007, para. 43, and Case C–341/05 *Laval an Partneri*, judgment of 18 December 2007, para. 90.

18 As was noted *supra* note 2, the ECT will be renamed Treaty on the Functioning of the European Union (TFEU) if the Treaty of Lisbon enters into force.

appear in a number of acts of secondary law[19] and in the Charter of Fundamental Rights.[20]

It will be noted that these references do not mention specifically the UDHR. However, the Universal Declaration does appear from time to time in the case-law of the ECJ and the other EU courts, namely the Court of First Instance and the EU Civil Service Tribunal,[21] and including the opinions of the Advocates-General of the ECJ.[22]

There are very few references to the UDHR in judgments, and some of these references pick up an argument of a party without ruling explicitly on the meaning and status of the provision of the UDHR invoked.[23] But in two well-known judgments relating to sanctions against alleged terrorists, the Court of First Instance went further in referring to Article 17 of the UDHR as a possible indication that the right of property has become part of peremptory international law (*jus cogens*).[24] After having cited Article 17, the Court went on to say that "in so far as respect for the right to property must be regarded as forming part of the mandatory rules of general international law, it is only an arbitrary deprivation of that right that might, in any case, be regarded as contrary to *jus cogens*". In a judgment of the Civil Service Tribunal, the interpretation of Article 21, paragraph 2, of the UDHR ("Everyone has the right of equal access to public service in his country"), is discussed, but without prejudice to its binding force in the Community legal order.[25]

---

19 Just to mention one example, *see* Council Directive 2003/86/EC of 22 September 2003 on the right to family reunification, OJ L 251, 3 October 2003, p. 12, and Case C–540/03, *supra* note 17, in which the legality of this Directive was at issue.

20 The Charter refers to the ECHR, the European Social Charter and, in Article 53, to "international agreements to which the Union, the Community or all the Member States are party, including the [ECHR]".

21 The latter Tribunal has, by application of Article 225a ECT, which enables the establishment of such special tribunals, been established by Council Decision 2004/752/EC, Euratom, of 2 November 2004 establishing the Civil Service Tribunal, OJ L 333, 9 November 2004, p. 7.

22 A. ROSAS, 'The European Union and International Human Rights Instruments', in V. KRONENBERGER (ed.), *The European Union and the International Legal Order: Discord or Harmony?* (T.M.C. Asser Press, The Hague, 2001) pp. 53–64, at p. 58.

23 Case C–76/93 P *Scaramuzza* [1994] ECR I–5173, paras. 14, 18 and 29–31; Case T–37/97 *Forges de Clabecq* [1999] ECR II–859, para. 122.

24 Case T–306/01 *Yusuf* [2005] ECR II–3533, paras. 292–293; Case T–315/01 *Kadi* [2005] ECR II–3649, paras. 241–242. *See also* para. 342 of the first judgment and para. 287 of the latter judgment, which refer to Article 8 of the UDHR in the context of the right of access to justice. At the time of writing, these cases are pending on appeal before the ECJ as Cases C–402/05 P and C-415/05 P, *see* Opinions of Poiares Maduro AG of 16 and 23 January 2008 (the Advocate-General does not mention the UDHR).

25 Case F–43/05 *Olivier Chassagne*, judgment of 23 January 2007, para. 53.

The reason for the Court of First Instance to cite, in the context of universal human rights standards and *jus cogens*, Article 17 of the UDHR is probably to be found in the fact that the right of property recognised in this provision does not appear in the legally binding parts of the International Bill of Rights, the two Covenants of 1966.[26] At the universal level, Article 17 of the UDHR is the only provision recognising the right of property generally (without taking into account its protection in special contexts, such as the prohibition of racial or gender discrimination). The reason why the Civil Service Tribunal, again, was faced with Article 21, paragraph 2, of the UDHR may be explained by the fact that equal access to public service does not figure in the ECHR (although it is true that a provision akin to Article 21 is to be found in Article 25 of the International Covenant on Civil and Political Rights).[27]

References to the UDHR are much more common in the opinions of the Advocates-General of the ECJ.[28] In some instances, it is simply a question of referring to the arguments of one of the parties.[29] More often, it is a footnote reference, usually citing a provision of the UDHR alongside provisions of binding human rights conventions and/or the EU Charter of Fundamental Rights,[30] or a similar short reference in the main text of the opinion.[31] While

---

26 A. ROSAS, 'Property Rights', in A. ROSAS and J. HELGESEN (eds), *The Strength of Diversity: Human Rights and Pluralist Democracy* (Martinus Nijhoff, Dordrecht, 1992) pp. 133–157.

27 A. ROSAS, 'Article 21', in G. ALFREDSSON and A. EIDE (eds), *The Universal Declaration of Human Rights: A Common Standard of Achievement* (Martinus Nijhoff, The Hague, 1999) pp. 431–451 at p. 438.

28 According to Article 222 ECT, it is the duty of the Advocate-General (who is a member of the Court but not a judge), "acting with complete impartiality and independence, to make in open court, reasoned submissions on cases which, in accordance with the Statute of the Court of Justice, require his involvement".

29 Opinion of Jacobs AG of 9 June 1994, paras. 12 and 23–25, in Case C–76 P *Scaramuzza* [1994] ECR I–5173; opinion of Bot AG of 1 March 2007, para. 109, in Case C–76/06 P *Britannia Alloys & Chemicals* v *Commission* [2007] ECR I–4405.

30 Opinion of Gerven AG of 15 September 1993, note 22, in Case C–116/92 *Charlton et al.* [1993] ECR I–6755; opinion of Tesauro AG of 22 January 1998, note 6, in Case C–200/96 *Metronome Musik* [1998] ECR I–1953; opinion of Ruiz-Jarabo Colomer AG of 19 September 2002, note 46, in Joined Cases C–187/01 and C–385/01 *Gözütok and Brügge* [2003] ECR I–1345; opinion of Ruiz-Jarabo Colomer AG of 26 May 2005, note 48, in Case C–176/03 *Commission* v *Council* [2005] ECR I–7879; opinion of Ruiz-Jarabo Colomer AG of 12 July 2005, note 3, in Case C–14/04 *Abdelkader Dellas* [2005] ECR I–10253; opinion of Ruiz-Jarabo Colomer AG of 15 November 2005, note 37, in Case C–499/04 *Werhof* [2006] ECR I–2397; opinion of Ruiz-Jarabo Colomer AG of 6 September 2007, note 32, in Case C–267/06 *Tadao Maruko*, judgment of 1 April 2008.

31 Opinion of Warner AG of 22 September 1976 in Case 130/75 *Prais* [1976] ECR 1589; Opinion of Darmon AG of 14 July 1994, para. 10, in Case C–68/93 *Shevill* [1995] ECR I–415;

in these cases there is no explicit discussion of the legal status and relevance of the UDHR in the EU legal order, the fact that a provision of the Declaration is cited and often alongside provisions of human rights conventions seems to suggest that the Advocates-General in question have considered that the Declaration expresses generally recognized principles which can be used as guidelines in the search for fundamental rights as general principles of Community law. At least in two opinions of Advocate-General van Gerven, this assumption is made explicit. According to him, the UDHR is a declaration of principle which contributes to defining the contents of the general principles of Community law[32] and that according to the Court's case-law, it may draw inspiration from guidelines such as a provision of the Declaration.[33]

The readiness of the Advocates-General of the ECJ, and in some instances of the EU Courts themselves, to cite provisions of the UDHR as guidelines which contribute to defining the contents of the general principles of Community law is nothing extraordinary in view of the fact that the fundamental rights case-law from time to time makes reference to other 'soft law' instruments as well.[34] It is on the other hand true that most of the 'soft law' instruments cited by the EU Courts are declarations made by the EU institutions themselves rather than by intergovernmental organisations such as the UN and the Council of Europe. The most important and recent example is provided by the EU Charter of Fundamental Rights, which has become a source of inspiration used on an almost regular basis by the EU Courts.

The first ones to cite the Charter as a guideline were the Advocates-General of the ECJ as well as the Court of First Instance.[35] Subsequently,

---

opinion of Tizzano AG of 8 February 2001, para. 23, in Case C–173/99 *BECTU* [2001] ECR I-4881; opinion of Stix-Hackl AG of 18 March 2004, para. 82, in Case C–36/02 *Omega Spielhallen* [2004] ECR I–9609; opinion of Kokott AG of 11 November 2004, para. 56, in Case C–105/03 *Pupino* [2005] ECR I–5285; opinion of Mengozzi AG of 16 October 2006, para. 80, in Case C-354/04 P *Gestoras Pro Amnistía* v *Council* [2007] ECR I–1579; opinion of Trstenjak AG of 24 January 2008, para. 35, in Case C–350/06 *Schultz-Hoff* (pending); opinion of Trstenjak AG of 24 January 2008, para. 48, in Case C–520/06 *Stringer et al.* (pending).

32 Opinion of van Gerven AG of 22 October 1992, paras. 10–13, in Case C–206/91 *Poirrez* [1992] ECR I–6685.

33 Opinion of van Gerven AG of 18 February 1993, para. 42, in Case C–17/92 *Federación de Distribuidores Cinematográficos* [1993] ECR I–2239. The ECJ cases cited by the Advocate-General are Case 4/73 *Nold*, *supra* note 16, and Case C–260/89 *ERT* [1991] ECR I–2925.

34 ROSAS, *supra* note 22, p. 58.

35 Opinion of Tizzano AG in Case C–173/99 *BECTU* [2001] ECR I–4881, para. 28. Already in Case C–340/99 *Traco* [2001] ECR I–4109, the Charter had been mentioned by Alber AG in an Opinion of 1 February 2001, para. 94.

references to the Charter in opinions of Advocates-General have become almost a matter of routine[36] and the Court of First Instance, too, began at an early stage to cite individual provisions of the Charter as 'confirming' or 'reaffirming' the existence of specific fundamental rights protected under Community law.[37] While the ECJ at first chose not to cite the Charter in its judgments, it changed its practice in a case decided in June 2006.[38] In subsequent judgments, the ECJ has cited a provision of the Charter by mentioning that a given fundamental right has been 'reaffirmed' by that Charter provision.[39] It thus seems that the ECJ, in line with the case-law of the Court of First Instance, has started to use the Charter as a kind of authoritative interpretation for determining what fundamental rights constitute general principles of Community law.

The reasoning behind the frequent use of the Charter of Fundamental Rights in the case-law of the EU Courts may to some extent apply to the UDHR as well, although it has to be born in mind that the Charter stands out as a 'soft law' instrument of particular relevance, in view of the fact that it was prepared by an EU Convention displaying constitutional features,[40] was

---

36 *See, e.g.*, the Opinion of Kokott AG of 8 September 2005, para. 98, footnote 58, in Case C-540/03 *Parliament* v. *Council*, *supra* note 17.

37 *See* Cases T–112/98 *Mannesmannröhren-Werke* [2001] ECR II–729, para. 76T–77/01; *Territorio Histórico de Álava*, order of the Court of First Instance of 11 January 2001 (not reported), para. 35; T–54/99 *Max.mobil* [2002] ECR II–313, para. 48; T–177/01 *Jégo-Quéré* [2002] ECR II–2365, para 42; T–116/01 and T–118/01 *P & O European Ferries* [2003] ECR II–2957, para. 209; Joined Cases T–67/00, T–68/00, T–71/00 and T–78/00 *JFE Engineering Corp.* [2004] ECR II-2501, para. 178, and as an example of more recent case-law, Case T–170/06 *Alrosa Company*, judgment of 11 July 2007, para. 188.

38 Case C–540/03 *Parliament* v *Council*, *supra* note 17, paras. 38, 58. In this case the European Parliament (unsuccessfully) challenged the validity of Council Directive 2003/86/EC of 22 September 2003 on the right to family reunification, OJ L 251, 3 October 2003, p. 12.

39 Case C–432/05 *Unibet* [2007] ECR I–2271, para. 37; Case C–303/05 *Advocaten voor de Wereld* [2007] ECR I–3633; Case C–438/05 *International Transport Workers' Federation*, *supra* note 17, paras. 43–44; Case C–341/05 *Laval an Partneri*, *supra* note 17, paras. 89–90; Case C-275/06 *Promusicae*, judgment of 29 January 2008, paras. 33, 41–42, 46, 61, 64; Case C–450/06 *Varec*, judgment of 14 February 2008, para. 48; Case C–244/06 *Dynamic Medien*, *supra* note 17, para. 41. *See also* Case F–1/05 *Landgren*, judgment of 26 October 2006, paras. 70–72 (not reported), in which the EU Civil Service Tribunal seems to have given considerable weight to a provision in the Charter as a tool for interpreting the personnel legislation of the EU.

40 The Convention consisted of representatives of the European Parliament (16), the national parliaments of the then 15 Member States (30), the Governments of the Member States (15) and the European Commission. It was succeeded by another Convention preparing the draft Treaty establishing a Constitution for Europe, signed in Rome on 29 October 2004 (OJ C 310, 16 December 2004) but never entered into force. The Treaty of Lisbon (*supra* note 2) is meant to replace the constitutional Treaty.

adopted by consensus, was "solemnly proclaimed" by the three main EU political institutions and would, if the Treaty of Lisbon were to enter into force, achieve legally binding force.[41]

The use of 'soft law' human rights instruments such as the UDHR as guidelines is related to a variation in the English versions of the judgments of the ECJ. While the French text of the *Nold* formula, referred to above,[42] makes reference to 'instruments internationaux', the English version has until recently referred to 'international treaties' and thus instruments of a legally binding character. As from 2006, however, the English text in most cases refers to 'international instruments'.[43] It is submitted that this broader expression better corresponds to the French text and also the inclination of the EU Courts not to make any sharp distinction between international treaties and other international instruments.

Finally, it should be noted that references to the UDHR can be found in EU secondary law as well. Examples are provided by two non-discrimination directives adopted in 2000, one on equal treatment between persons irrespective of racial or ethnic origin and the other on equal treatment in employment and occupation.[44] The preamble of both directives states that the right to equality before the law and protection against discrimination "constitutes a universal right recognised by the Universal Declaration of Human Rights" as well as by some legally binding human rights conventions.

3. EU HUMAN RIGHTS POLICIES AND THE UDHR

Especially during the 1990s, human rights have become an important subject in the external relations of the EU.[45] But it has to be remembered that the integration intensity in external relations varies greatly, ranging from an

---

[41] Article 6, paragraph 1, TEU, as amended by the Treaty of Lisbon. *See also supra*, notes 2 and 40.

[42] *Supra* note 16.

[43] Case C–540/03 *Parliament* v *Council*, *supra* note 17, para. 35; Case C–305/05 *Ordre des barreaux* [2007] ECR I–5305, para. 29; Case C–244/06 *Dynamic Medien*, *supra* note 17, para. 39.

[44] Council Directive 2000/43/EC of 29 June 2000 implementing the principle of equal treatment between persons irrespective of racial and ethnic origin, OJ L 180, 19 July 2000, p. 22; Council Directice 2000/78/EC of 27 November 2000 establishing a general framework for equal treatment in employment and occupation, OJ L 303, 2 December 2000, p. 16.

[45] *See*, *e.g.*, D. NAPOLI, 'The European Union's Foreign Policy and Human Rights', in N. NEUWAHL and A. ROSAS (eds), *The European Union and Human Rights* (Martinus Nijhoff, The Hague, 1995) pp. 297–312; BRANDTNER and ROSAS, *supra* note 5, pp. 468–490.

exclusive Community competence in matters of international trade and some other areas, a 'shared' or 'parallel' Community competence in fields such as development cooperation, transport and environmental policy to a co-operation framework of a more intergovernmental nature in matters of foreign, security and defence policy regulated by Title V TEU (the Common Foreign and Security Policy – CFSP, or the 'Second Pillar' of the EU).[46] As far as Treaty provisions of relevance for external relations are concerned, Articles 177 and 181a ECT stipulate that Community policies in the area of development cooperation and in the area of economic, financial and technical cooperation with third countries shall contribute to the "general objective of developing and consolidating democracy and the rule of law" and the objective of "respecting human rights and fundamental freedoms". In the same vein, Article 11 TEU provides that one of the objectives of the CFSP is to "develop and consolidate democracy and the rule of law, and respect for human rights and fundamental freedoms".

Especially before the addition of these Treaty clauses, there was disagreement as to whether, and to what extent, human rights were part of the policies and activities that the Communities could lawfully promote and undertake within the framework of the supranational 'First Pillar'. One of the most contentious issues was whether the EC could adhere to the ECHR. Opinion 2/94 of the ECJ, which held that as Community law stood at that time, the EC had no competence to accede,[47] was probably due to the specific features of the ECHR, involving as it does a compulsory control system, and should not be seen as a denial of any Community competence in the external human rights field.[48]

In any case, Opinion 2/94 did not stop the increasing activities of the EU in the field of human rights, as witnessed, *inter alia*, by the inclusion of human rights clauses in bilateral trade and cooperation agreements concluded with third countries and in legislation dealing with development cooperation and financial and technical cooperation with such countries, including the adoption of two human rights regulations of a general nature in 1999.[49] A human rights clause included in a trade and cooperation agreement concluded with India was in fact explicitly approved by the ECJ in the same

---

[46] *See, e.g.*, P. EECKHOUT, *External Relations of the European Union: Legal and Constitutional Foundations* (Oxford University Press, Oxford, 2004) *passim*.

[47] Opinion 2/94, *supra* note 12.

[48] BRANDTNER and ROSAS, *supra* note 5, pp. 471–472.

[49] Council Regulation 975/1999/EC of 29 April 1999, OJ L 120, 8 May 1999, p. 1, and Council Regulation 976/1999/EC of 29 April 1999, OJ L 120, 8 May 1999, p. 8.

year as it handed down its Opinion on the lack of competence to accede to the ECHR.[50]

There can be no doubt that the UDHR has played an important part in the development of an EU external human rights policy. It will be recalled that the EU has not, until recently, been in a position to adhere to international human rights conventions and that the UDHR, as a universal proclamation of principles not subject to formal ratification or other adherence procedures, has, on the one hand, compensated for this lack of adherence to legally binding conventions and, on the other, backed up the EU emphasis on universal values and principles, applying to all members of the international community, whether or not they have adhered to specific human rights conventions.

The basic philosophy was outlined in a Communication from the European Commission of 1995.[51] The human rights policies of the EU are based on the principles of *universality*, *indivisibility* and *interdependence* between human rights, democracy and development.[52] These three principles, in the view of the Commission, are "arising from the Universal Declaration of Human Rights" and they are reaffirmed by the Vienna Declaration and Programme of Action adopted by the UN World Conference on Human Rights of June 1993. There are a number of subsequent pronouncements of the European Parliament, the Council and the Commission on the importance of the UDHR as an important frame of reference for the EU.[53]

Since the early 1990s, the EC has systematically included a so-called human rights clause in its trade and cooperation agreements concluded with third countries, including so-called association agreements such as the Europe agreements concluded with the candidate countries (before their accession to the EU in 2004 and 2007, respectively), agreements concluded with a number of Mediterranean countries and the Lomé/Cotonou agreements concluded with African, Caribbean and Pacific (ACP) countries.[54] It should be noted that

---

50 Case C-268/94 *Portugal* v *Council* [1996] ECR I-6177.

51 *The European Union and the External Dimension of Human Rights Policy: From Rome to Maastricht and Beyond*, Communication from the Commission to the Council and the European Parliament, COM(95) 567, 22 November 1995.

52 *Ibid.*, p. 10.

53 *See, e.g.*, ROSAS, *supra* note 8, pp. 203–204.

54 *See* the *Communication from the Commission on the inclusion of respect for democratic principles and human rights in agreements between the Community and third countries*, COM(95) 216 final of 23 May 2005; NAPOLI, *supra* note 45, pp. 306–308; BRANDTNER and ROSAS, *supra* note 5, pp. 473–477; F. HOFFMEISTER, *Menschenrechts- und Demokratieklauseln in den vertraglichen Aussenbeziehungen der Europäischen Gemeinschaft* (Springer Verlag, Berlin,

all such agreements have been concluded in the name of the EC, and in the context of the 'First Pillar'.

According to a standard formula, the principal human rights clause stipulates that respect for fundamental rights and democratic principles, as laid down or proclaimed "in the Universal Declaration of Human Rights", inspire the internal and external policies of the parties and constitute an "essential element" of the agreement.[55] In a European context, reference has also been made to the Helsinki Final Act of 1975 and other Organisation for Security and Cooperation in Europe instruments, but especially more recent agreements with European countries refer to the UDHR as well. As an example can be cited Article 2 of the Stabilisation and Association Agreement with the Republic of Croatia of 2000:[56]

> "Respect for the democratic principles and human rights as proclaimed in the Universal Declaration of Human Rights and as defined in the Helsinki Final Act and the Charter of Paris for a New Europe, respect for international law principles and the rule of law as well as the principles of market economy as reflected in the Document of the CSCE Bonn Conference on Economic Cooperation, shall form the basis of the domestic and external policies of the Parties and constitute essential elements of this Agreement."

Another provision normally to be found among the final provisions of the agreement deals with the possibility of taking measures in cases of non-execution of the agreement (that is, of any provision of the agreement and not just of the human rights clause) by the other side, including suspension of the operation of the agreement, and requires each party to consult the other

---

1998); M. BULTERMAN, *Human Rights in the Treaty Relations of the European Community: Real Virtues or Virtual Reality?* (Intersentia - Hart, Antwerpen, 2001); E. FIERRO, *The EU's Approach to Human Rights Conditionality in Practice* (Martinus Nijhoff, The Hague, 2003).

55 *Inventory of Agreements Containing the Human Rights Clause*, European Commission, External Relations, DG RELEX/B2 – Treaties Office, 16 May 2008. *See also EU Annual Report on Human Rights 2007* (Council of the European Union, European Commission, Brussels, 2007) p. 24, and BULTERMAN, *supra* note 54, pp. 151–184.

56 Council and Commission Decision 2005/40/EC, Euratom of 13 December 2004 concerning the conclusion of the Stabilisation and Association Agreement between the European Communities and their Member States, of the one part, and the Republic of Croatia, of the other part, OJ L 26, 28 January 2005, p. 1. For an example of a human rights clause concluded with a non-European country, *see* Article 1 of the Economic Partnership, Political Coordination and Cooperation Agreement with Mexico, which does not refer to the European instruments mentioned in the above quotation but cites the UDHR only ("[r]espect for democratic principles and fundamental human rights, proclaimed by the Universal Declaration of Human Rights"), OJ L 267, 28 October 2000, p. 46.

party before taking measures, save in cases of special urgency. There is normally also an interpretative declaration, specifying that cases of special urgency include breaches of an "essential element" of the agreement, that is, of the human rights clause.

As has been recognised by the ECJ, an important reason for including the human rights clause in agreements with third countries is to spell out the right of the EU (and of the other Contracting Party concerned) to suspend the operation of the agreement or to take other countermeasures in case of non-respect of the clause.[57] The human rights clause thus does not seek to transform the basic nature of an agreement otherwise concerned with trade, development cooperation, and so on, or to establish new standards in the international protection of human rights.[58] The EU's approach to these matters, as spelled out in the first EU Annual Report on Human Rights adopted in 1999, is based on the assumption that the basic terms of reference for the human rights clause, the UDHR, reflects general international law on the subject. Its treaty practice, accepted by the third countries parties to these agreements, accordingly contributes to the reaffirmation of the Universal Declaration as an expression of general international law.[59] It will be recalled that the EU, as a subject of international law, is bound by general international law in the field of human rights, whether seen as customary international law or general principles of law recognized by civilized nations.[60]

Human rights clauses have also been included in legislation establishing Community assistance programmes with third countries or groups of third countries. Such clauses can be used to suspend cooperation with a partner State in case of serious human rights violations. They can also be used as a basis for certain positive measures aimed at promoting human rights and democracy in a partner country which depart from the normal assistance programme in providing, for instance, for special direct support to non-governmental organisations. Apart from the human rights-related activities which can be supported under various geographical and sector programmes,

---

57 Case 268/94 *Portugal* v *Council* [1996] ECR I–6177.

58 BRANDTNER and ROSAS, *supra* note 5, p. 474.

59 *European Union Annual Report on Human Rights 1998–1999* (Council of the European Union, Brussels, 1999) p. 22; *European Union Annual Report on Human Rights 2000* (Council of the European Union, Brussels, 2000) p. 34. *See also* ROSAS, *supra* note 8, pp. 201–209.

60 *See, e.g.*, BRANDTNER and ROSAS, *supra* note 5, pp. 473–477; A. ROSAS, 'With a Little Help from my Friends: International Case-Law as a Source of Reference for the EU Courts', 5 *The Global Community YILJ* 2005 (2006) pp. 203–230, at p. 220.

two human rights regulations of 1999[61] have provided the legal basis for an European Initiative for Democracy and Human Rights (EIDHR), which has had an allocation of more than 100 million euros in the EU budget.

The Community instruments for the provision of financial and technical assistance to third countries have recently undergone a major re-structuring, with the adoption of several new instruments in 2006.[62] The package includes a new financing instrument for the promotion of democracy and human rights worldwide, which replaces the two Regulations of 1999, allowing for assistance to non-governmental organisations and projects independent of the consent of the third country government concerned.[63] According to Article 1, paragraph 2(b), of this Regulation, EU assistance shall aim at enhancing, *inter alia*, "the respect for and observance of human rights and fundamental freedoms, as proclaimed in the Universal Declaration of Human Rights and other international and regional human rights instruments".[64]

4. CONCLUDING REMARKS

The fact that the EU, unlike nation-States, has not been able to adhere to international human rights conventions such as the two Covenants of 1966 and the ECHR can be seen as a handicap on its ability to constitute itself as a global human rights actor.[65] As the EU is not a Contracting Party to these conventions, it cannot participate, in its own right, in conferences of the High Contracting Parties, is not required to submit periodic reports to the monitoring bodies set up under the conventions and cannot submit

---

61 *Supra* note 49.

62 *See* notably Regulation (EC) No. 1905/2006 of the European Parliament and of the Council of 18 December 2006 establishing a financing instrument for development cooperation, OJ L 378, 27 December 2006, p. 41. Other financial instruments include Regulation (EC) No. 1638/2006 of the European Parliament and of the Council of 24 October 2006 laying down general provisions establishing a European Neighbourhood and Partnership Instrument, OJ L 310, 9 November 2006, p. 1 and Regulation (EC) No. 1717/2006 of the European Parliament and of the Council of 15 November 2006 establishing an Instrument for Stability, OJ L 327, 24 November 2006, p. 1.

63 Regulation (EC) No. 1889/2006 of the European Parliament and of the Council of 20 December 2006, OJ L 386, 29 December 2006, p. 1.

64 *See also* Article 2, paragraph 1(b).

65 An even more serious handicap consists of the fact that the EU is not a member of the United Nations. *But see* Article 302 ECT, according to which the Commission shall "ensure the maintenance of all appropriate relations with the organs of the United Nations and of its specialised agencies", and Article 19, paragraph 2, TEU, which contains certain obligations for EU Member States which are members of the UN Security Council.

candidates for membership of the monitoring bodies. Non-adherence to these conventions also invites criticism alleging that the EU practices 'double standards', preaching human rights to the rest of the world and insisting on human rights clauses in bilateral agreements while refraining from adhering to the multilateral instruments most States have committed themselves to.[66]

The UDHR, together with the fact that most human rights conventions are binding on all the EU Member States, has offered a useful tool to mitigate this deficit. By citing the Universal Declaration, the EU has asserted and articulated a common universal platform of generally accepted standards, applicable to all countries and also to the EU itself. The Declaration has in this respect served not only a 'defensive' aim, designed to counter criticism for double standards, but also a more 'offensive' objective, promoting the principle of universality. The UDHR has served another purpose, too. As it covers both civil and political rights and economic, social and cultural rights, it has strengthened the EU's insistence on the principles of indivisibility and interdependence and the equal value of both categories of rights.[67]

As the case-law of the EU courts, in the absence of EU adherence to legally binding conventions, draws upon international human rights instruments as 'guidelines' rather than directly applicable sources of law, it is understandable that 'soft law' instruments, too, such as the UDHR have played a role in the development of EU fundamental rights. The fact that the UDHR is also mentioned in EU secondary law, and in legislation of both internal and external relevance, can only add to this picture.

As the EU now may be entering into a new phase, enabling it to adhere to international human rights conventions in its own right, it is possible that the relative importance of 'soft law' instruments will diminish in the future. But as adherence to the main universal instruments, such as the 1966 Covenants, is not likely in the foreseeable future, it may well be that the UDHR will retain its relevance as an interpretation of universally accepted values and standards. In this context, it may be noted that the TEU, as amended by the

---

66 Such a criticism was at the forefront when Australia in 1996 refused to conclude a bilateral agreement with the EC containing a human rights clause, *see* BRANDTNER and ROSAS, *supra* note 5, p. 474.

67 According to the *EU Annual Report on Human Rights 2007*, *supra* note 55, p. 46, the EU "attaches the same importance to economic, social and cultural rights as to civil and political rights, bearing in mind the universality, indivisibility, interdependence and interrelatedness of all human rights and fundamental freedoms, as confirmed by the 1993 World Conference on Human Rights held in Vienna". *See also* BRANDTNER and ROSAS, *supra* note 5, pp. 484–487; A. ROSAS, 'Economic, Social and Cultural Rights in the External Relations of the European Union', in A. EIDE et al. (eds), *Economic, Social and Cultural Rights: A Textbook*, 2nd rev. ed. (Martinus Nijhoff, Dordrecht, 2001) pp. 479–492.

Treaty of Lisbon, contains important references to the need to promote and respect the objectives and principles of the UN Charter and international law.[68] While the TEU and the ECT, whether in their existing form or as amended by the Lisbon Treaty, do not cite specifically the UDHR, the Declaration can be seen as a specification and authoritative interpretation of the references to human rights and fundamental freedoms contained in the UN Charter.[69] By its commitment to the objectives and principles of the Charter, the EU maintains, and perhaps even reinforces, its commitment to the UDHR as well.

---

68 Article 3, paragraph 5, Article 21, paragraphs 1 and 2, TEU. *See also* Article 220 ECT. It will be recalled, however (*supra* note 2), that the entry into force of the Treaty of Lisbon is uncertain, in view of the negative outcome of a Irish referendum.

69 BRANDTNER and ROSAS, *supra* note 5, pp. 475–476, with references.

31. THE OSCE: A COMMITMENT TO HUMAN RIGHTS

Robert-Jan Uhl
Bernhard Knoll

1. INTRODUCTION

This article analyses the reception of the Universal Declaration of Human Rights (hereinafter UDHR) into the Organisation for Security and Cooperation in Europe (hereinafter OSCE) human rights system. It sketches the origins of the Helsinki process and the manner and importance of its incorporation into the OSCE's normative framework and discusses the parallels between the creation of the UDHR and the normative framework of the OSCE. A red thread through its history, as with the history of the UDHR itself, has been the involvement of human rights defenders: those who take up the struggle to make the rights in documents such as the UDHR a reality.

2. ORIGINS AND NATURE OF THE CSCE PROCESS

Before analysing the relationship between the UDHR and the OSCE, it may be worthwhile to look back at how the Conference on Security and Cooperation in Europe (hereinafter CSCE) process evolved and became an international mechanism in support of human rights.

The CSCE process started in the early 1970s as a forum for dialogue between the East and the West. A series of conferences served to enumerate principles on which both Eastern (Warsaw-pact) states and Western states could agree. After two years of negotiations in a series of conferences in Geneva and Helsinki, the 'Helsinki Final Act' was concluded in 1975. Its 'Decalogue' set out the ten key principles, that all participating States could agree on, governing their actions towards their own citizens and towards each other. The key principles included respect for territorial integrity, peaceful resolution of disputes and, crucially, respect for human rights.

This process has continued ever since, with a major peak of activity around the fall of the Berlin Wall and the collapse of the Communist system, which resulted in the well-known Vienna (1989), Copenhagen (1990) and Moscow (1991) documents. It was in these documents that all OSCE participating States agreed that democratic government with the rule of law and respect for human rights was the only acceptable form of government in the OSCE region, and elaborated key norms and principles required for this form of government in binding commitments. Crucially, they also acknowledged, in 1991, that commitments undertaken within the OSCE's 'human dimension' were matters of direct and legitimate concern to all participating States, rather than matters belonging exclusively to the internal affairs of the State, and promised to hold each other responsible for their implementation.

The result is a wide body of commitments on democratic government, human rights and the rule of law which may be referred to as the OSCE *acquis*, to which all participating States must agree upon joining the organisation. There are now 56 participating States in Europe, North America and Central Asia, the most recent member being Montenegro. One of the crucial characteristics of the CSCE and, subsequently, of the OSCE, has been the process approach: norms are gradually expanded upon and refined, with the norms already agreed upon remaining equally binding. While these commitments are not founded on a multilateral treaty and do not create direct legal obligations in themselves, they are considered to be "politically binding". This formulation has had the advantage of an OSCE-wide acceptance of standards without the need for the time-consuming and sometimes controversial process of formal ratification by each participating State.

The CSCE process, a series of more or less informal conferences, has over the years grown ever more structured. A number of different structures and bodies have been created. The CSCE evolved into a permanent organisation, the OSCE, with a permanent decision-making body, the Permanent Council. In the 1990s, several bodies were created to assist participating States in upholding their commitments. These include the Office for Free Elections, later renamed the Office for Democratic Institutions and Human Rights, which has moved from election observation into a wide variety of human rights-related areas, with programmes aiming at strengthening many different aspects of democratic government. Other important bodies include the High Commissioner on National Minorities, set up to assist states with minority issues through quiet diplomacy, and the Representative on the Freedom of the Media, who monitors and assists states in the area of press freedom. OSCE Missions, with widely differing mandates, also exist in many countries, mainly in Central Asia, Southern Caucasus and the former Yugoslavia.

3. THE STATUS OF THE UDHR IN THE OSCE SYSTEM

As a resolution of the UN General Assembly, the UDHR was not as such a binding instrument of international law to begin with. Its importance to the CSCE process and the development of the OSCE's normative framework can, however, not be overstated.

A careful reading of the wording of the OSCE commitments indicates that OSCE participating States have considered the UDHR a binding document from the inception of the Helsinki process. As participating States stated in the Helsinki Final Act's Decalogue, "[i]n the field of human rights and fundamental freedoms, the participating States will act in conformity with the purposes and principles of the Charter of the United Nations and with the Universal Declaration of Human Rights. They will also fulfil their obligations as set forth in the international declarations and agreements in this field, including *inter alia* the International Covenants on Human Rights, by which they may be bound".

The importance of the UDHR was reaffirmed in the 1983 Madrid document, which also referred to the "particular significance" of the UDHR and the international Covenants on Human Rights and other relevant international instruments. Referring to their "joint and separate efforts to stimulate and develop universal respect for human rights and fundamental freedoms" all participating States were called on to act in conformity with those international instruments. Those participating States which had not yet done so were called on "to consider the possibility of acceding to the covenants".

That the UDHR is binding on OSCE participating States is not in doubt. What is the nature of this obligation? Upon the adoption of a wide variety of human rights in the 1989 Vienna document and 1990 Copenhagen document, participating States stated there that the UDHR was a body of international commitments, as opposed to the international Covenants (that is, the International Covenant on Civil and Political Rights, hereinafter referred to as ICCPR, and the International Covenant on Economic, Social and Cultural Rights, hereinafter referred to as ICESCR), which they described as an obligation under international law. Specifically, participating States promised they would ensure that the exercise of the human rights they had agreed to abide by in these documents would not be subject to any restrictions "except those which are provided by law and are consistent with their obligations under international law, in particular the [ICCPR], and with their international commitments, in particular the Universal Declaration of Human

Rights. These restrictions have the character of exceptions". Participating States also promised to ensure that these restrictions would not be abused and would not be applied in an arbitrary manner, "but in such a way that the effective exercise of these rights is ensured".[1]

The UDHR has also been used in the OSCE commitments as a specific normative source. In the 1989 Vienna document, participating States promised to "facilitate the freer and wider dissemination of information of all kinds, to encourage co-operation in the field of information and to improve the working conditions for journalists", and referred in this connection to the need to act "in accordance with the [ICCPR], the Universal Declaration of Human Rights and their relevant international commitments concerning seeking, receiving and imparting information of all kinds", and promised to ensure that individuals can freely choose their sources of information. In this context they promised to ensure that radio services operating under the ITU Radio Regulations could be directly and normally received in their States; and that they would allow individuals, institutions and organisations, while respecting intellectual property rights, including copyright, to obtain, possess, reproduce and distribute information material of all kinds.[2]

Similarly, in the Sofia 2004 document, participating States promised to take action to ensure that the Internet remains an open and public forum for freedom of opinion and expression, "as enshrined in the Universal Declaration of Human Rights", and to foster access to the Internet both in homes and in schools.[3]

We may conclude from the above that the UDHR is regarded as a binding commitment engaged in by OSCE participating States which is on a par with their other, more specific commitments engaged in under the CSCE and OSCE process, and also that the UDHR serves as a normative reference point for participating States.

4. THE SIGNIFICANCE OF THE UDHR IN THE OSCE PROCESS AND SYSTEM

With the UDHR being a binding instrument for OSCE participating States, what does this mean for the functioning of the OSCE system as a whole?

---

1 Vienna 1989, para. 21.

2 Vienna 1989, para. 34.

3 Sofia 2004, para. 1.

What is the function and significance of the UDHR in the OSCE's normative framework?

There are a number of reasons for why the UDHR is important in the CSCE/OSCE context. First, during the Cold War, there were political challenges within the CSCE process in achieving agreement on norms, including human rights norms. The clashes on issues like economic, social and cultural rights 'favoured' by the communist bloc and the civil and political rights emphasised by the West reduced the possibility of coming to substantive agreements on many human rights issues. This meant that a large number of human rights did not make their way into the OSCE commitments directly. The effect of the UDHR in the CSCE process during the years between the adoption of the Helsinki document and the tryptichon of the Vienna, Copenhagen and Moscow documents was therefore vital: without the reference to the UDHR, many of the values enshrined in the commitments, such as many of the civil and political rights like freedom of assembly and association, would not have been the subject of agreement. Without the reference to the UDHR, and the promise in the Helsinki Final Act that individuals would be allowed to know and act upon their rights, human rights defenders throughout the OSCE region would have had one less tool to use in their struggle to turn the human dimension commitments into a reality. And that civil society activists did see the value of human rights commitments is beyond doubt: organisations such as Charta 77 and many of the Helsinki organisations, including the organisation that would later become Human Rights Watch, all had their origin in the process of monitoring human rights in the CSCE framework.

The significance of the UDHR as a normative reference point did not cease with the fall of the Berlin Wall, however. For a variety of reasons, not all rights in the UDHR were or are enshrined in specific OSCE commitments, and not all States are parties to all international conventions. This makes the UDHR an important document, setting the normative baseline for all OSCE participating States, and allowing States to hold one another to account on the full spectrum of UDHR rights.

It should be noted that the UDHR — now often considered a norm of customary international law — was a controversial document and was not rapidly accepted as a binding obligation, requiring nearly two decades of negotiation to be turned into the two main human rights conventions, the ICCPR and the ICESCR. There are, indeed, still some rights it enshrines which are not explicitly contained in the conventions drafted under the UN system. The lacunae within the UN system and the slowness of the process of adoption of these instruments were and are to a large extent filled by organisations such as the Council of Europe, with its European Convention on Human Rights and many other treaties and declarations, and the OSCE, which adopted many new and more specific human rights commitments.

5. PARALLELS BETWEEN THE OSCE PROCESS AND THE UDHR

This brings us to another point: though there are many differences between the approach of the UN, the Council of Europe and the OSCE, there are a number of parallels as well. Differences between the Council of Europe and the OSCE are mainly that the OSCE takes a comprehensive security approach to human rights issues, and the Council of Europe's approach is more based on setting legally binding standards. The main difference between the OSCE and the UN system is its relative flexibility: whereas it took many years to agree on binding agreements elaborating the UDHR in conventions, decision-making within the OSCE is much less cumbersome. The lack of enforceability in court of OSCE commitments might be seen as a weakness: what, after all, is a right without a court to enforce it in? Yet this apparent disadvantage is in fact a strength when combined with the binding nature of commitments: as already mentioned, it allows states to agree relatively quickly on binding norms without having to go into great detail and specifics which would be necessary in a legally enforceable treaty. An example of such flexibility would be the OSCE's reaction to the increase of violations of minority rights in the 1990s. The OSCE reacted first to these issues, drafting a comprehensive set of standards in the field of minority protection. Later, these political standards served as basis for the legally binding Council of Europe Framework Convention for the Protection of National Minorities.

This reveals the first parallel: the way the UDHR was adopted and the way the CSCE and later the OSCE system functions are somewhat similar. In contrast to the long process required to adopt the ICCPR and ICESCR, the UDHR, as a non-binding instrument, was explicitly designed as a statement of principles which would not be considered formally legally binding, and could therefore be adopted much more quickly and easily.

Another way in which principles from the UDHR have influenced the CSCE process and where we can thus speak of a parallel is the recognition very early on in the Helsinki process of the importance of respect for human rights as a key element of the maintenance of international peace and security. This principle is perhaps most clearly stated in the 1990 Copenhagen document, in which the OSCE participating States expressed their conviction that "full respect for human rights and fundamental freedoms and the development of societies based on pluralistic democracy and the rule of law are prerequisites for progress in setting up the lasting order of peace, security, justice and co-operation that they seek to establish in Europe".[4]

This link between security and human rights forms the basis of the OSCE's comprehensive concept of security, and is closely matched by the UDHR's preamble which states: "Whereas recognition of the inherent dignity and of the equal and inalienable rights of all members of the human family is the foundation of freedom, justice and peace in the world".[5] The recognition of the vital link between human rights and security is thus key to appreciating the commonalities between the UDHR and the founding documents of the OSCE.

6. THE MORAL FORCE OF THE UDHR AND HUMAN RIGHTS DEFENDERS

One key issue recognised early on in the OSCE framework was that rights may be formally granted and recognised, but can only be made real from below. As the Helsinki Final Act puts it, the individual has the right to know and act upon his rights.[6]

In this connection, it is perhaps of interest to note a document adopted at the last major anniversary of the UDHR, its fiftieth birthday. To celebrate this occasion, the General Assembly passed the Declaration on Human Rights Defenders, recognising that without protecting the organisations and individuals who stand up for human rights, there can be no lasting progress in this area. The OSCE has also recognised these principles, and enshrined them in various relevant commitments.[7] Under OSCE commitments, all individuals

---

4 Copenhagen 1990, Preamble.

5 UDHR, Preamble.

6 Helsinki 1975 (Questions Relating to Security in Europe: 1.(a) Declaration on Principles Guiding Relations between Participating States) Principle VII.

7 *See* in particular Budapest 1994, paragraph 18: "The participating States ... emphasize the need for protection of human rights defenders and look forward to the completion and adoption, in the framework of the United Nations, of the draft declaration on the 'Right and Responsibility of Individuals, Groups and Organs of Society to Promote and Protect Universally Recognized Human Rights and Fundamental Freedoms'". For a further overview of relevant commitments, *see* OSCE/ODIHR, OSCE Human Dimension Commitments (Vol. 1-Thematic Compilation), 2nd ed. (Warsaw, 2005). The issue of human rights defenders has been a controversial one in the OSCE in recent years, with several proposals for more specific commitments being rejected at successive Ministerial Council meetings.

have the freedom of assembly, the freedom of association, the right to receive funding from abroad, the right to help others protect their rights and many other rights required for the defence of human rights and the operation of human rights NGOs.

Many of these rights, of course, can also be found in the UDHR itself, but the UDHR lacks specifics on these 'implementation' issues. This was in fact something for which it was criticised by some states at the time. With the Defenders Declaration, the UDHR was crowned with at least the principal means by which its implementation could be achieved. Based on existing commitments, the OSCE has since taken up the cause of protecting the rights of human rights defenders, which are currently being challenged in a variety of ways.[8]

Another parallel between the UDHR and the Helsinki Final Act is their moral force and encouragement for the civil society. Just as organisations throughout the world still cite the UDHR as a morally binding instrument, so too did many civil society organisations in the former Eastern bloc start to invoke the rights they had been promised in the document. Needless to say, the UDHR, cited in the Helsinki Final Act itself, formed a key and integral part of this process. Helsinki Organisations played a vital part in fostering change in society and bringing down the systems of oppression in the former Eastern bloc. As mentioned above, without the Helsinki Final Act, they would not have had a politically binding document to cite, and without the UDHR, they would not have had a clear moral and normative compass to turn to within the Helsinki Final Act.

Today, the OSCE's commitment to civil society is also demonstrated in the constant dialogue with non-governmental organisations, which was recognised by the OSCE early on and is still today practised in the OSCE process. For many years, the OSCE has held an annual review conference in Warsaw, now known as the Human Dimension Implementation Meeting, to review the process of implementation of commitments. Many NGOs are represented at these meetings at the same level as governments, which form a vital 'reality check' for OSCE participating States to see to what extent those under their jurisdiction have actually benefitted from the high-minded documents adopted in their name. These conferences are open to all civil society organisations which do not condone or commit terrorism or violence, and the conferences serve as a vital means of holding governments to account. In addition, major OSCE conferences and meetings have come to be

---

8 OSCE/ODIHR, *Our Collective Conscience-Human Rights Defenders in the OSCE Region* (Warsaw, 2007).

preceded by preparatory NGO meetings, with key recommendations on how implementation can be improved emerging from these fora for civil society.

All this would not have been possible without the UDHR, the normative binding documents based upon it, and the inspiration offered by this most simple yet visionary historical document. It is in the work of human rights defenders that we see its daily practical significance, and a daily inspiration to help them make the rights it enshrines a reality for all individuals in the OSCE region and throughout the world.

PART VII

FINAL COMMENTS

32. A VIEW FROM THE OUTSIDE

Hurst Hannum

Europe is home to the most sophisticated systems for the promotion and protection of human rights in the world. The primary instrument, of course, is the European Convention on Human Rights, but this rather conservative document is complemented by a host of others. The latter include, for example, the European Framework Convention for the Protection of National Minorities, European Social Charter, European Convention for the Prevention of Torture and Inhuman or Degrading Treatment or Punishment, and the various activities of the Council of Europe, European Union, and Organisation for Security and Cooperation in Europe. In all, quite an impressive array. In addition, every EU member has ratified both the Covenant on Civil and Political Rights and the Covenant on Economic, Social, and Cultural Rights.

Given this plethora of legally binding commitments and organisational initiatives, it is not surprising that the Universal Declaration of Human Rights (UDHR) appears in the preceding chapters primarily as a source of moral and political inspiration. Indeed, the subtitles of many of the chapters reveal a surprising degree of skepticism or caution when analysing the Declaration: "without binding force … content without reference … little domestic impact … low profile … not legal … a legal puzzle … tenuous … political significance, not legal …".

While there are exceptions — Latvia, Poland, Portugal, and Spain, for example — few claims are made that the UDHR constitutes customary international law or, indeed, that its principles should necessarily be taken into account by domestic courts. This reluctance of courts to rely on international law to provide rules of decision is common to many jurisdictions, not only those in Europe.

First, courts tend to interpret narrowly those articles of their national constitutions that import international law into the local systems, thereby reducing their own opportunities to interfere with governmental policies in the light of international law. Second, national courts tend to interpret international rules so as not to upset their governments' interests, sometimes actually seeking guidance from the executive for interpreting treaties. Third, courts use a variety of 'avoidance doctrines', either doctrines that were specifically devised for such matters, like the act of state doctrine, or general doctrines like standing and justiciability, in ways that give their own governments, as well as other governments, an effective shield against judicial review under international law.[1]

Outside Europe, the UDHR has served directly and indirectly as a model for many domestic constitutions, laws, regulations, and policies that protect human rights. These domestic manifestations include direct constitutional reference to the Universal Declaration or incorporation of its provisions; reflection of the substantive articles of the UDHR in national legislation; and judicial interpretation of domestic laws (and applicable international law) with reference to the Universal Declaration.

At least 24 national constitutions in the world contain specific reference to the UDHR, although the legal effect of the Declaration varies.[2] Most of these states are African, perhaps reflecting their greater appreciation of the potential importance of the Declaration on a continent in which human rights protections are often minimal at both the regional and national levels. In addition, as exemplified by the ultimately successful battle against apartheid, African states have tended to rely more upon international or global norms to support their political goals, as opposed to inward-looking Europeans.

While there is no evidence to suggest that more frequent invocation of the UDHR outside Europe has led to any discernable improvement in human rights, the broader substantive scope of the UDHR does reflect the wider understanding of human rights that generally exists in Africa, Asia, and Latin America. The distinction between 'traditional' and 'newer' rights still found in Europe[3] does not find much support outside Europe (apart from the United States, which is discussed further below). Indeed, the somewhat stereotypical observation that many developing countries prioritise economic, social and cultural rights above civil and political rights does contain more than a kernel of truth.[4]

In theory, such debates about relative priorities were laid to rest at the 1993 World Conference on Human Rights held in Vienna, in which a push

---

1 E. BENVENISTI, 'Judicial Misgivings Regarding the Application of International Law: An Analysis of Attitudes of National Courts', 4 *European Journal of International Law* (1993) pp. 159 and 161.

2 *See* H. HANNUM, 'The Status of the Universal Declaration of Human Rights in National and International Law', 25 *Georgia Journal of International and Comparative Law* (1995/1996), p. 287 Annex 1.

3 *See* Concluding Remarks, p. 454.

4 For a persuasive contrary view, *see* A. SEN, *Development as Freedom* (Oxford University Press, Oxford, 2000).

by Asian states for recognition of greater cultural relativism was largely rebuffed. While adding some rhetoric about selectivity, the Final Document of that conference returned to the holistic concept of rights found in the UDHR:

> "All human rights are universal, indivisible and interdependent and interrelated. The international community must treat human rights globally in a fair and equal manner, on the same footing, and with the same emphasis. While the significance of national and regional particularities and various historical, cultural and religious backgrounds must be borne in mind, it is the duty of States, regardless of their political, economic and cultural systems, to promote and protect all human rights and fundamental freedoms."[5]

In light of the fact that no global human rights treaty has been universally ratified (although the Convention on the Rights of the Child is close), the UDHR remains the only articulation of human rights norms that is implicitly accepted by all states in the world. It is interesting that, despite the recognition that the UDHR is not legally binding, the European Union bases its human rights foreign policy on that instrument. Since diplomacy is perhaps the ultimate political game, utilising the moral and political influence of the UDHR both lends universalist credibility to the EU's efforts to influence human rights in other states and offers the requisite vagueness on which diplomacy thrives. Relying on more legalistic documents would be less satisfying in many respects, not least because of the inconveniently generous limitations on most rights that are explicitly permitted under most treaties.

There is nonetheless a danger in interpreting a universal instrument through a regional lens, particularly in the context of foreign policy, and many of the 'human rights' asserted by the EU and its member states appear to go far beyond the original intention of the Declaration's drafters. European human rights standards on sensitive issues such as sexuality, abortion, capital punishment, and judicial procedures cannot automatically be applied to regions with different legal and social systems, and a regionally influenced definition of human rights risks creating a backlash within states for which European (and American) hectoring on human rights remains offensive. There is nothing inappropriate about offending human rights violators, but the goal should be to emphasise effective implementation of shared values, not simply to impose one particular view of those values on the rest of the world.

---

5 Final Document of the 1993 Vienna Conference, para. 5.

Article 29 of the UDHR recognises that "duties to the community" and limitations on rights are consistent with both the essence of human rights and their universality. Supervisory bodies such as the European Court of Human Rights and the Human Rights Committee have emphasised that a state's ability to limit rights is not absolute, but the margin of appreciation frequently referred to by the European Court is not insignificant. Even with limitations on the limitations,[6] Europeans should not expect every state's view of morality to be like Sweden's or the degree of gender equality to be the same as that found in Iceland or Norway.

Europeans also should be wary of linking other issues to human rights and thus implicitly seeking to shift the debate on how major global concerns should be addressed. While there may be human rights implications in designing trade policies or dealing with the global financial crisis that erupted in 2008, the norms of the UDHR cannot provide the answer as to the best or most equitable means of dealing with such issues. Similarly, Europe's attention to the global environment is welcome, but it is not helpful when Mary Robinson, the well-respected former UN High Commissioner for Human Rights, states baldly that "climate change causes human rights violations".[7] Such hyperbole may resonate well in Europe, but it runs the risk of making environmental concerns seem to be simply another example of Europeans using their particular view of human rights to force other countries to change their behavior.

On the 40th anniversary of the adoption of the UDHR, China described the Declaration as a significant international document whose influence "has increased with the continuous enrichment and development of its original content".[8] However, China continues to reject direct criticism of its human rights record as constituting interference "in the internal politics of China under the pretext of human rights".[9] One need not accept this discredited argument at face value, but it is difficult to avoid giving some credence to

6 Article 29 permits limitations "solely for the purpose of securing due recognition and respect for the rights and freedoms of others and of meeting the just requirements of morality, public order, and the general welfare in a democratic society".

7 International Council on Human Rights Policy, 'Climate change and human rights: a rough guide' (Geneva, 2008), quoted in Oxfam International, *Climate Wrongs and Human Rights* (September 2008) p. 2.

8 Statement of Ding Yuanhong, Deputy Permanent Representative of China to the UN, at the UN General Assembly session celebrating the 40th anniversary of the Universal Declaration of Human Rights, as quoted in 'Human Rights Declaration Reflects World People's Aspirations, says Chinese ambassador', Xinhua General Overseas News Service, 8 December 1988.

9 'China Lashes Out at U.S. Human Rights Report', *China Daily*, 2 March 2005.

criticisms about the 'selective' or 'politicized' use of human rights norms in ways that, coincidentally, also suit other foreign policy goals.

To a degree, this is unavoidable, and no one asserts that compliance with human rights norms should be the sole, or even most important, component of foreign policy, which may legitimately take into account economic, security, and other concerns that fall within the 'national interest'. Many so-called 'anti-terrorist' initiatives both within and beyond Europe are extremely problematic from a human rights perspective, for example, as are calls by Muslim countries for prohibiting criticism of religion.

If it is true, as the Concluding Remarks observe, that "there is neither general, uniform and consistent state practice nor *opinio juris* to support the claim that the UDHR as a document could be placed in the category of customary law",[10] demands that China and other countries comply with 'norms' that they have not formally accepted may begin to resemble other political demands based on national interest, not principle. While this may appear to be an overly legalistic quibble, it reminds us that human rights norms are not set in concrete, nor are they immune from change — whether that change may be positive or negative, from a European perspective.

The degree to which Europeans have internalised human rights is remarkable, and it is impossible to imagine a European legal or political space in which the human rights of the UDHR do not play a central role. This is not the case in the rest of the world, with the possible exception of Latin America, where memories of coups and generals remain fresh and a commitment to human rights (theoretically, at least) remains strong.

It is, of course, dangerous to generalise about continents, particularly when they are as vast and diverse as Asia and Africa (not to mention much of the former Soviet Union). Nonetheless, the immediate relevance of human rights is more difficult to perceive in countries that suffer from near anarchy, violent conflict, extreme poverty, gross economic disparities, and a history of governments that are corrupt or despotic or both. Singapore's authoritarian capitalism continues to be an attractive model for China and other Asian countries, although it is doubtful that countries much larger than the Singaporean city-state will be able to manage to balance a free economy with a lack of freedom in the political sphere.

The UDHR certainly remains an important ideal in such countries, but creating respect for the rule of law in a context of widespread lawlessness is likely to take decades. Europe's fixation on democracy as a panacea has not been successful, and it may be time to focus more on civil and economic

10 P. 462.

rights than on splashy, well-monitored elections. Political engineering has not worked well in Bosnia and Herzegovina, despite billions of euros and tens of thousands of troops, and it is unrealistic for Europe to expect to be able to transplant its emotional as well as political attachment to human rights into young countries in which human rights remains a slogan rather than a principle. Only a true cynic would believe that Asia and Africa need to endure the equivalent of European history from 1848 to 1948 before human rights can take root, but Europeans would do well to reflect on the catastrophes that preceded the UDHR's adoption in their own region before becoming too impatient with its slow implementation in other parts of the world.

While many of the same reflections apply to the United States, this volume is a refreshing change from discussions of 'Western' values that simplistically conflate European and American norms. Although the administration of George W. Bush may be remembered as the worst in U.S. history, the smug rejection of human rights as something relevant primarily to 'others' has been present in the U.S. for at least decades. U.S. courts (and military lawyers) deserve credit for attempting to rein in the lawless treatment of terror suspects in Guantànamo and elsewhere, but the anti-internationalist bent of most Americans could not be more different than the commitment to multilateralism that is today natural for most Europeans.

The good news is that George W. Bush almost never used the term 'human rights', preferring instead to promote democracy and free markets. A new administration may be expected to rekindle the impression that the United States does take human rights seriously, but the U.S. view of human rights is notoriously narrow. There is little likelihood that even an Obama administration will publically accept the full panoply of human rights set out in the UDHR (although there does seem to be some movement on the right to health), let alone consider ratifying the Covenant on Economic, Social, and Cultural Rights. Nonetheless, the annual human rights reports issued by the Department of State may gain credibility, and it is to be hoped that the United States will become more active in the UN Human Rights Council and other multilateral forums.

There is a great deal of commentary directed at the notion of 'American exceptionalism', but it may be Europe that is exceptional when it comes to human rights. If one views the European Union as a single country (fanciful, of course, but perhaps permissible in light of the EU's proclaimed common foreign policy), it is clear that only the European Union both practices and preaches, even if imperfectly, the international human rights set forth in the UDHR. The other major powers — including the United States, Russia, China, and India — maintain varying degrees of commitment to the ideal of human rights, but their interpretation and application of that ideal varies widely.

Europe is not without hypocrisy, and it does share some of the arrogance with which the United States often views the rest of the world. EU or Council of Europe pronouncements are often not followed up by effective action, and compliance even with the judgments of the European Court of Human Rights is not perfect. The circumspection with which most European countries view the legal impact of the UDHR matches the views of the rest of the world, but one should not be too cynical about the depth of political and moral commitment to the UDHR that does, indeed, exist in European foreign ministries, law faculties, and civil society. Let us hope that even fears of terrorism, whether well-founded or not, will not result in abandoning the principle that every human being has inherent rights.

At 60 years old, the UDHR is still in its early middle age, and European countries and institutions need to ensure that it matures gracefully. Its impact on the rest of the world will be based on consent, not force; persuasion, not moralising. It is time to embark even more seriously on the difficult task of nurturing acceptance of the Declaration in one country at a time outside Europe, while ensuring that Europeans of the 21st century continue to view the Declaration as a living instrument, not a fossil.

33. CONCLUDING REMARKS ON EUROPE: DIVERSITY WITHIN THE UNITY

Vinodh Jaichand
Markku Suksi

1. INTRODUCTION

In 1948 and long afterwards, it was clear both at the level of international law and at the level of national law that the Universal Declaration of Human Rights (UDHR) was not a document that contained legally binding obligations for the states. Therefore, it is not surprising that the UDHR has been treated as a non-binding set of principles, guidelines or standards, rather than as a type of law that could be used in courts for the judicial resolution of individual cases or before administrative authorities when making decisions. That started to change during the 1970s, when new constitutions in Portugal and Spain were trying to cast off the authoritarian heritage and looked for suitable ways to cut the cords to the past by creating a new basis for legal and social legitimacy. A similar phenomenon took place in Central and Eastern Europe, where a number of countries, most notably the Baltic states, used the UDHR to politically motivate their independence and to lay claim to their re-emergence as authentic states in the post-Cold War Europe. The extremes on this dimension could be Austria, France, Sweden and the United Kingdom, on the one hand, and Latvia, Poland, Portugal and Spain, on the other, ranging from virtual indifference towards the UDHR to creative use in legislation and court decisions for giving binding legal effect to the UDHR, even in the resolution of individual cases. Therefore, it seems that the chronology of contact that a state had with the UDHR has a relatively strong explanatory force.

Interestingly, it seems that the countries that were involved in the drafting and adoption of the UDHR as well as the countries that joined the UN in the 1950s and 1960s were, and in most cases still are, generally speaking very consistent in not acknowledging any domestic legal force to the UDHR (Poland excluded from the 1990s, of course). For instance, the courts in these countries, when confronted with a claim involving the UDHR, tend to be very clear about the fact that the UDHR does not have the force of law. The argument often made is that these countries were founding members of the Council of Europe and parties to the European Convention on Human

Rights (ECHR), opened up for ratification in 1950. As the European human rights system was created under the heavy influence of the UDHR and because the ECHR was not only made binding upon the states but also furnished with an implementation mechanism containing a Commission and, in particular, the Court of Human Rights, the western European members of the UN of those times felt that they had certainly fulfilled any expectation with regard to giving effect to the idea of human rights as embedded in the UDHR. It was recognized from a European point of view that the absence of a global implementation mechanism was a disappointment, and therefore, a regional one had to be created. The complacency with regard to the UDHR was compensated through adherence to the ECHR.

The states which instituted the European system of human rights of course also participated in one of the grand debates that dealt with human rights, namely in the debate about the nature of the rights and about what could and what could not be a right. Back in 1948, most of the European members of the UN, the newly emergent Socialist bloc excluded, felt that only the so-called traditional freedoms and liberties, that is, the civil and political rights, could be regarded as human rights, because they were justiciable in a way relevant for an individual. The exceptions to this approach were Belgium and Luxembourg. As a result, these countries were opposed to the so-called economic, social and cultural rights promoted in particular by the Socialist bloc. The point was made that such rights were only declaratory aims that could not be brought to court by individuals; those rights were not real rights. Consequently, the ideological divide that characterised the international political arena resulted in the 1950s in the adoption in Europe of a set of human rights that contained only a more traditional set of civil and political rights. Europe in those days was the western part of Europe, and it made the claim of freedom and human rights against the authoritarian states behind the so-called Iron Curtain. The ideological divide between two different blocs of states in Europe has since disappeared and some of the structural imbalances between different categories of rights have been remedied in separate conventions, but it is still possible to detect a distinction between the 'traditional' rights, on the one hand, and the 'newer' rights, on the other. Despite the fluxion of sixty years, this divide is artificially justified in many domestic legal systems in Europe and the continued justification is anachronistic. However, from the point of view of the UDHR, such a distinction is not valid. This is more so since "almost no state has specifically rejected the principles proclaimed in the

Universal Declaration of Human Rights"[1] and social, economic and cultural rights are a part of the UDHR.

The range of human rights in the ECHR was and still is limited in comparison with the UDHR. Therefore, it is not convincing that many of the original western European members of the UN, and also states that joined later, make the claim that they received the UDHR indirectly, via the ECHR. The argument of the indirect reception of the UDHR via the binding regional document is, of course, strong with regard to the issue of the binding nature of the ECHR and of the existence of an implementation mechanism that facilitates individual complaints. However, materially speaking, the argument from the national point of view concerning indirect reception is unconvincing, because many of the substantive rights of the UDHR are not included in the ECHR. Of the UDHR rights not included in the ECHR, most belong to the category of economic, social and cultural rights. Without going into detail about the scope of each right, the *lacunae* contains such important human rights as the right to asylum (Article 14 of the UDHR), right to nationality (Article 15), the right to social security and entitlement to the realisation of economic, social and cultural rights (Article 22), the right to work (Article 23), the right to rest and leisure (Article 24), the right to a certain standard of living (Article 25), the right to education (Article 26) and the right to participate in cultural and scientific life (Article 27) as well as certain intellectual (property) rights (Article 28). Of course, it has to be recognised that many of these rights have been included in other treaties of the Council of Europe.

A somewhat similar claim is sometimes made in a number of countries, such as Ireland, France and Sweden, against the background of their national constitutions: because the constitution of a country guarantees the rights of the individual, there is no need to revert to the UDHR. This is not a coherent argument because a right protected more than once remains a right: it is not a lucid conclusion that a right protected in several documents is a more important right than another, is deserving of more protection or even dilutes the protection of others. Even a country without a written constitution, such as the United Kingdom, made the self-assessment that human rights were better protected there and in the colonies than in other parts of the world. Ironically some of those colonies, when they became independent, promulgated constitutional protection through a bill of rights, based on the UDHR. Here, the implication may be that the constitution of the country or

---

1 H. HANNUM, 'The UDHR in National and International Law', 3:2 *Health and Human Rights* (1998) p. 149.

the judicial system catered for a very broad coverage of individual rights, but the claim may also be based on the understanding that the UDHR lacks the binding force of law. Another explanation is the chauvinism of many states in Europe who believed their national laws to be superior and that human rights were to be implemented elsewhere.

2. STATES' DOMESTIC RECEPTION, IN THE UN AND BY THE PRESS

Although information about the UDHR and sometimes also the text of the UDHR itself was relatively widely published after its adoption in the various western European countries, for example, Belgium, Denmark, France and Sweden, and even in some eastern European countries, like Poland, as well as in Bulgaria, Slovenia and Slovakia when their new constitutions were being drafted, it is difficult to ascertain just how much governments of the different countries did to disseminate the UDHR and to inform the inhabitants of the countries of the UDHR and its contents. What is clear is that newspapers, in particular, were engaged in following up on the decision-making of the UN in 1948 and assumed often a critical tone towards the activities of the organisation, while leaving the detail of the adoption of the UDHR in a secondary role. In addition, most of the newspaper coverage dealt with the UDHR in general terms, without printing the entire text. One newspaper in the Netherlands was the exception: in that paper, the whole text was reproduced. The United Kingdom, together with France and Belgium, was concerned that the publication and dissemination of the UDHR should be controlled and limited in its colonies generally: as a result, Cyprus, Malta and Ireland were the specifically affected states in Europe under this colonial response. Indeed, the presence of this concern is still manifested in former colonies outside Europe. A full discussion of that is outside the brief of this research.

Attention in the independent news media is, of course, mostly positive, but it does not follow from such attention that the government of a country should be directly credited for the fulfilment of the dissemination recommendation. However, at least in France and Belgium, the UDHR was published in the official journal, that is, in the same forum in which legislative enactments and ratified treaties are published. This was an exceptional measure considering the fact that the UDHR was not a normative enactment in the two countries and that it therefore lacked the force of law.

In some countries, NGOs and other organisations belonging to the civil society, such as the UN Association in Finland published the text for wider distribution very soon after it had been adopted by the UN General Assembly, and later, different organisations in, for instance, Germany made the text available for the general audience. In addition to the regular press, information and analysis concerning the UDHR was earlier on published in a multitude of professional journals and literary works, for instance, in those of the legal community, as in Greece and the Netherlands, and it should not be entirely wrong to conclude that such professional groups that traditionally have been engaged in the defence of individual rights received information about the UDHR at an early stage. It seems, however, that the positive human rights message included in the UDHR was at least to some extent overshadowed by the criticism that was directed towards the activities of the UN during and after the adoption of the UDHR. The UDHR also faced a certain amount of unintended rivalry from the ECHR. Later on local NGOs and Amnesty International in Europe continued to celebrate each anniversary of the UDHR with a view to disseminating the content of the rights to the citizens. In some countries it is debatable whether the state voluntarily plans national celebrations of the anniversaries of the UDHR or is persuaded by the campaigns of NGOs to do so.

Earlier on the governments of the states involved made it abundantly clear that the UDHR is not a binding set of human rights. Nevertheless, a solemn declaration made by states that steps would be undertaken to introduce legislation to protect those rights must have some value in international law and perhaps also in national law. Therefore, it is probably possible to distinguish between two directions of the binding nature, namely the domestic sphere, on the one hand, and the international sphere, on the other. While the denial of the binding character seems to be consistent with regard to the domestic sphere, the governments and the political debate have certainly made use of the UDHR in the international sphere in relation to third states. It seems that the norms of the UDHR become convenient for an argument when the human rights situation of a third country is discussed: the human rights are now part and parcel of the foreign policies of all European states and of the European Union itself. Therefore, the governments of the states included in this review may have recognised the value of the UDHR at least in their external relations, but many, if not all of these governments are also aware of the domestic or internal implications of the UDHR which should be directed to the legislative branch, that is, the parliaments.

3. THE UDHR IN CONSTITUTIONS, LAWS AND POLITICAL DEBATES

As mentioned above, three European constitutions make explicit reference to the UDHR, namely the constitutions of Portugal, Romania and Spain. Because of the references, the UDHR holds a strong position at least in Portugal and Spain. The position is strong in Spain in particular, where provisions of the UDHR have many times been used as a legal basis for deciding individual cases. In Romania, again, the UDHR is at least formally recognised in the soft-law role of influencing a decision, made on the basis of 'black-letter law', in favour of human rights, but the Romanian legal order has not yet started to explore the potential of the UDHR in the same way as the other two countries, although the formulation of the constitutional provisions are very similar.

A general reference to human rights is often found in constitutions and legislation of other countries, but it seems as if ordinary legislation adopted by parliaments of the different countries, did not refer to the UDHR in a formal way, except in the secondary legislation of the European Union in some instances. The legal orders of all countries contain laws, and also provisions in individual pieces of law, that transform the material contents of the UDHR into national law, as the case seems to be in Lithuania. Such transformation often takes place without reference to the UDHR, but in a good number of countries, for example in Estonia and Luxembourg, parliamentary debates or *travaux preparatoires* leading to the adoption of an act of parliament may mention the UDHR as a source of inspiration or even as a point of departure. In such contexts, a moral or political obligation is often attached to the UDHR. An approach of this kind seems to be very much in line of the original intention of the UDHR where the political discourse inside a country may recognise the connection between a social phenomenon and the UDHR and advance its regulation against the background of a provision in the UDHR.[2] If the solution chosen is in harmony with the principle established in the UDHR, the domestic implementation of the UDHR and its reception into the national legal and political order may be regarded as sufficient.

It does not, however, seem as if the political parties stood out as great champions of UDHR-based argumentation: the charters of political parties or their party programmes are often not human rights sensitive to any greater extent (with at least the notable exception of two political parties in Luxembourg), and one should not expect to find too many references to the

---

2 This reflects a similar outcome in the research undertaken in twenty different countries on the implementation of international human rights treaties, not the Universal Declaration of Human Rights, where human rights norms are likely to become part of the domestic legal order where there is a local need, like law reform. *See* C.H. HEYNS and F. VILJOEN, 'The Impact of the United Nations Human Rights Treaties on the Domestic Level', 23 *Human Rights Law Quarterly* (2001) pp. 483–535, at pp. 487–488.

UDHR in those documents. Hence there exists space for improvement in the context of the political discourse which should not be left to anniversaries of the UDHR. In some countries, opposition parties have used the UDHR norms in their parliamentary debates to reveal the short-comings of the ruling party, as in Ireland and the United Kingdom.

4. THE UDHR IN THE COURTS

In a good number of jurisdictions, especially in those where the UDHR is mentioned in the constitution of the country, direct references to the UDHR can be found in individual judgments by courts of law. Hence it is not surprising that references to the UDHR are found in Portugal and Spain, but unexpectedly, courts in a number of other jurisdictions, too, seem to use the UDHR in different ways. The experiences of Latvia and Poland stand out as very special, because in those countries, the courts have accorded the UDHR the binding status of law through their own decisions. This means that the UDHR, or at least the provision that was relevant in a case, has actually been incorporated by way of judicial decision so as to make it the legal basis for the resolution of the case.

Yet in some other jurisdictions, such as the European Union and the Council of Europe as well as Hungary, the UDHR is, from time to time, used as a reference document that can enhance the argument of the court when there is a human rights dimension involved in a case. However, some jurisdictions have internal difficulties in agreeing upon whether or not to allow the usage of the UDHR. In the Czech Republic, one chamber of the Supreme Court, on the one hand, and the Constitutional Court on the other, have adopted different positions on the issue: the former denied that the UDHR had those legal effects that the latter had confirmed, although both seem to agree that the UDHR has at least some domestic legal effects, while the Supreme Administrative Court in the same country would seem to accord legal effects only to formal treaties. In France, administrative courts have denounced the use of the UDHR as a basis of argumentation, while the ordinary courts seem to allow the use of the UDHR. From the point of view of the legal theory and the expectation of harmony and coherence of a legal order, such a division is normally not a tolerable situation. At the same time the division creates so-called 'hard cases' that call for argumentation for and against the usage of the UDHR, with an eventual resolution to be expected sometime in the future. The role of precedents in some of the courts is unclear and more research is required to ascertain this for it might have a bearing on the UDHR jurisprudence in certain civil law countries.

Finally, the courts in a relatively large number of states, such as Denmark, Estonia, Finland, Ireland, the Netherlands, Slovenia, Sweden and the United Kingdom, do not treat the UDHR or its provisions as a relevant source of law, but require a more definite political decision, such as a legislative enactment or a ratification of a treaty, for a norm that can be applied in individual cases. From the point of view of incorporation as international law, the position of the last group of countries would be the expected one as the UDHR is just a resolution of the General Assembly of the United Nations, while the open position of the courts in the countries mentioned earlier with regard to the applicability warrants a short comment on different mechanisms of implementation of international law in the domestic legal orders of the various states, which basically is a constitutional issue.

5. IMPLEMENTATION OF THE UDHR

Implementation of international law in national jurisdictions can be done by means of several formal mechanisms, such as adoption, reference, incorporation, transcription and transformation.[3] A formal incorporation decision, taking on the form of an act of parliament or a government decree, regarding treaties according to the constitutional rules of each state is probably the ordinary method of implementing international law in such domestic jurisdictions which are based on a dualist perspective concerning the role of international law in domestic law.

However, in the case of the UDHR, there was no treaty to be incorporated, although a specific document existed. The same should be the case concerning adoption, the mechanism used by so-called monist states with a view to the position of international law in the domestic legal order, because there was no treaty of international law that the state could ratify.

---

3 *See*, for example, M. SCHEININ, *Ihmisoikeudet Suomen oikeudessa* (Suomalainen Lakimiesyhdistys, Helsinki, 1991) pp. 18–21, and M. SCHEININ, 'International Human Rights in National Law', in R. HANSKI and M. SUKSI (eds), *An Introduction to the International Protection of Human Rights: A Textbook* (Institute for Human Rights at Åbo Akademi University, Turku/Åbo, 2000) pp. 418–419, for an elaboration of the different relationships between the national and international legal orders in the context of national applicability of international norms. In the latter piece, the point is made that the incorporation discussion (in the context of human rights treaties) may be largely outdated, while the main focus is shifting from formal status issues to more concrete problems of implementation. This shift of focus is probably to some extent visible in the inclination of courts in some countries to use the UDHR in different ways in resolving practical issues that involve human rights perspectives in spite of the fact that the UDHR is just a resolution of the UN General Assembly.

The fact that a state may have been a member state of the UN in 1948 and voted for the UDHR is not an act of adoption by ratification.

Transcription has probably been used to some extent by way of recording the position of the UDHR in constitutions of different countries in the form of constitutional provisions, because in some instances, such as Bulgaria and Germany, it seems that constitutional provisions may be more or less direct translations of articles found in the UDHR. Reference is also a mechanism used at the level of constitutional law when the country in question wants to create a holistic human rights approach by way of making a direct reference to the entire UDHR in the constitution, as is the case in, for instance, Portugal, Romania and Spain.

Transformation is likely to be common not only at the level of constitutional law, as in Portugal, but also at the level of ordinary legislation, where legal provisions in, for instance, criminal codes, may be fashioned in a manner which is materially congruent with an article in the UDHR. In such situations, a reference to the UDHR might be found in the *travaux preparatoires*, indicating a link between the domestic provision and the provision in the UDHR. In cases of transformation, the political process and the political discourse has recognized the need to link the regulation of a social phenomenon to the UDHR and, ideally, to follow the UDHR by adopting national legal rules that are congruent with the relevant provisions of the UDHR.

Constitutional rules concerning implementation of international law normally presuppose legislative or executive action on the matter, that is, at least one decision by the parliament, the president or the government of the country that marks the formal entry point of a norm of international law in the domestic legal order. This should be the case both concerning monistic and dualistic legal orders. This is, however, not the case in jurisdictions where the courts have accorded the UDHR a legally binding character. In such countries, the legal construction seems to be that of customary law, but of a dual nature, as if the operation of granting the force of law to the UDHR first required the conclusion that the UDHR, or a provision thereof exists as a norm at the level of customary international law and then, at the second instance, the conclusion that the UDHR consequently also constitutes customary national law at the domestic level and that it can be used in individual cases. While the above implementation mechanisms vary as to their relationship to the issue of monism and dualism, direct implementation by courts of the UDHR seems to indicate a strong monistic orientation of the court system either with or without enabling provisions in national constitutions.

In some countries, constitutional provisions make explicit statements about the binding nature of the general principles of international law, while in other jurisdictions peremptory norms (*jus cogens*) of international law are regarded as binding domestic law. Even some other positions are possible. Under such circumstances, a reference to customary law or similar constructions by national courts may make it possible for them to circumvent the constitutionally prescribed formal implementation and incorporation mechanisms and accord the UDHR the force of law or at least some legal effect through their own judgments in individual cases or in abstract cases of constitutional review. It is, however, normally quite difficult to know what is and what is not a general principle of international law, a peremptory norm of international law or a legal norm recognised by all civilised countries. What is relatively clear is that the UDHR as such, that is, as a document, is not a general principle of international law, nor a peremptory norm or a legal norm recognised by all civilised countries. Also, there is neither general, uniform and consistent state practice nor *opinio iuris* to support the claim that the UDHR as a document could be placed in the category of customary law. Therefore, it would seem somewhat odd to regard the document as such as constituting customary international law.

As a consequence, a distinction should probably be made between the formal document, on the one hand, and the material contents of the document, on the other. That, in turn, necessitates a closer look at the different provisions, because it seems clear that not all the articles of the UDHR are binding on the states as norms of customary international law. For instance, it is probably not possible to regard the right to a nationality in Article 15 of the UDHR as a customary norm of international law (admittedly, the provision does not say that there is a right to nationality of a particular state), because it is clear on the basis of another customary rule that each state has the sovereign right to prescribe rules concerning its own citizenship, as long as the granting of citizenship is done on a non-discriminatory basis. At the same time, the UDHR contains provisions that can be regarded as customary international law, such as the prohibition of torture in Article 5 of the UDHR. In addition, there may be provisions in the UDHR that are in a state of emergence into customary international law, although they have not reached that level as of yet. The extent to which the different provisions of the UDHR constitute or do not constitute customary international law is thus variable. The national court cases, in their turn, indicate that the national courts may regard the UDHR in its entirety as a binding norm or some specific provisions of the UDHR as binding. The latter should probably be the preferred course of action. However, the exact reasoning of the domestic courts that use the UDHR should be studied much more in detail than is possible in this context, although the phenomenon in itself is extremely interesting and opens up new avenues for the domestic application of human rights norms.

How the national courts have used the UDHR would also require a deeper study, but it seems in light of the experience so far that national courts may relate to the UDHR mainly in three different ways: firstly, not use the UDHR at all; secondly, use it as a soft-law document to influence the decision in some direction while the decision itself is based on a more solid norm in domestic or treaty law; or thirdly, find the legal basis for a decision in a provision of the UDHR. With regard to the last alternative, it might be possible to ask whether the national court, when using the UDHR as a basis of its decision, is using customary *international* law or whether it is making or finding customary *national* law. As the application of the UDHR is done by a national court, the latter conclusion is probably the appropriate one, although the rule may be found in a document that has been created at the level of international law.

In case only individual provisions of the UDHR may assume the nature of customary law, which is the position submitted here, the customary law obligation towards the rules contained in the UDHR becomes patchy from the point of view of the entire set of rules or principles. This may not be an ideal situation with a view to the indivisible and interdependent nature of human rights, and it would be much more practical and convenient for the application of human rights if the provisions could be found in one coherent document. However, even with a dispersed point of departure indicating a possible applicability of at least some provisions of the UDHR as customary law, the normative effect of the UDHR in relations between the individual and the state exceeds the legal position accorded to it back in 1948.

In this context, it is interesting to pause at the question of the binding character of the UDHR or of the provisions thereof. The states deciding on the adoption of the UDHR in the General Assembly of the United Nations in 1948 thought that the UDHR, as a resolution of the General Assembly, would not be legally binding upon the states, and most governments have since maintained the same position. The decisions by the highest court of states may have a bearing on the position of a state on this issue (depending also to some extent on the role of precedents in that legal system). If the highest court (a constitutional court or a supreme court) of a state makes the determination that the UDHR is binding, at least in individual cases establishing an individual provision of the UDHR as a binding source of law, that determination may change or affect the position of the state at the international level. The judiciary may, in this context, become the actor that defines state practice of a particular state in a manner which cannot be countered by at least the executive representatives of the state, neither domestically nor internationally.

6. CIVIL SOCIETY AND NATIONAL INSTITUTIONS

It would be entirely wrong to confine the impact of the UDHR to the realm of the state powers, that is, to the legislative, the executive and the judiciary, because the UDHR has clearly had a role also outside of these public institutions. As was explained above, individuals and different associations, the so-called NGO sector, have had an important role in making the UDHR and its provisions known not only in relation to a general audience, but also in relation to the state institutions. While labelling the discussions concerning the possible customary law status of the UDHR as "futile scholarly exercises" (a contention that can be repudiated on the basis of this research), although at the same time recognising the fundamental importance of the UDHR, it was concluded already a decade ago that the resort to the content of the UDHR by non-governmental actors has been no less significant than the references to the UDHR in some constitutions of European states: "The domestic impact of the Declaration has thus been much wider than might have been expected of a non-binding instrument".[4] This is certainly true in light of our review.

Much has been said about the role of Amnesty International already in this book, as one leading example of the work of international NGOs without diminishing the role of local ones. This organisation which achieved its fame, and a Nobel Peace Prize, through the protection of prisoners of conscience, has begun to focus on social, economic and cultural rights as part its global programme of action, through highlighting the right to dignity, for example. As a result there will be a greater reference to the UDHR in many of their actions and campaigns internationally and in European countries because it constitutes the only compendium of all rights.

There are other examples of the effectiveness of civil society where organised action has permitted the embedding of human rights. The role of the resistance movements, such as in Latvia, cannot be underestimated in the location of human rights into their new found independence. In a similar vein the United Nations Association of Bulgaria aimed to ensure UN membership for Bulgaria as early as 1948 but which was only achieved in 1955. The organised Jewish community in Denmark has been able to remind us of the need for human rights by recalling the atrocities of the past.

---

4 K. DRZEWICKI, 'The United Nations Charter and the Universal Declaration of Human Rights', in R. HANSKI and M. SUKSI (eds), *An Introduction to the International Protection of Human Rights: A Textbook* (Institute for Human Rights at Åbo Akademi University, Turku/Åbo, 2000) pp. 74–75.

The importance of the human rights message of the UDHR in authoritarian states cannot be overstated. The UDHR was used as a platform for arguments for change in many Central and East European countries between 1948 and 1990. Examples from what used to be Czechoslovakia and what is now the Czech Republic and Slovakia as well as from Lithuania bear witness of individuals who truly believed in the UDHR and in the power of human rights. In the former Czechoslovakia Charta '77 and other dissident organisations can be credited with establishing a firm foundation for a culture of human rights that was carried over after the Socialist government had collapsed, and in Lithuania, while the nation was a part of the Soviet Union, the UDHR was published by the underground movement. Similar examples can be found also from other states. Supported by the Organisation for Security and Cooperation in Europe, the message of human rights of which was written into the 1975 Final Act of the Conference on Security and Cooperation in Europe and by the individual strides that were made for the cause of human rights these rights have now become part and parcel of governance in all European states. This position of the rights guarantees the individual the possibility to file complaints at the European Court of Human Rights and helps to specify the application of concrete cases of those human rights protected in the ECHR.

Although authoritarian regimes do not, and cannot, exist in the European Union, their demise in the southern parts of Europe in the 1990s does not mean that the message of the UDHR has become obsolete. On the contrary the examples of Germany and Italy are of particular relevance here, because they show that the UDHR may have an energising message for the civil society in countries where the political process already meets the formal test of realisation of human rights and where life is, by and large, good. It should be the case in other countries, too, that the UDHR is put to creative use by organisations of civil society. In any country there are blind spots that the policies of the state do not reach or cover well and in those instances, human rights defenders and activists are needed to detect the deficiencies and to react to the direction of the authorities.

Not all the contributions in this book have referred to national institutions in the respective EU country which promote and protect human rights and provide human rights education as articulated in the Paris Principles of 19 August 1991. The anniversaries of the UDHR usually provide a useful platform for these national institutions, where they exist, to showcase their human rights concerns in their communities. But they also respond to everyday concerns relating to the violation of human rights in that state. Today, they are important institutions which measure the implementation of international human rights standards at the national level. They constitute an integral part of civil society oversight. At the same time they provide strong networks and act as mediators between certain NGOs and government.

It is disconcerting to note that for instance in Belgium, there is no such institution. Recent research has revealed that Europe has only eight countries whose national human rights institutions comply with the Paris Principles and are accredited by their peers: France, Denmark, Greece, Republic of Ireland, Luxembourg, Northern Ireland, Germany and Norway.[5] There are various reasons for this phenomenon, including that some states believe that there is no need to have such institutions as human rights are adequately protected in their respective countries. The flaw in this logic has already been pointed out in the discussion on a state's self-assessment that its constitutions adequately protect human rights in this chapter.

A survey of some of the European Union states' national institutions reflects a patchwork response to the major human rights issues of the time within the countries without a holistic view of national human rights institutions or what constitutes human rights. Finland has a parliamentary ombudsman while Hungary has a commission on national and ethnic minorities. Sweden has an ombudsman for children, one for ethnic discrimination, one for disability and finally, one for equal rights. Poland has an institution for civil rights protection while the Netherlands has an equal treatment commission. In one case such a national institution was the outcome of a negotiated political settlement rather than a national desire to provide the best human rights service for its people. A Northern Ireland Human Rights Commission was established in 1998 through the Good Friday Agreement which required the Republic of Ireland to also have a Human Rights Commission. In 2006, the UK established the Commission for Equality and Human Rights which amalgamated with the previous Commission on Racial Equality, the Disability Rights Commission and the Equal Opportunities Commission.

This brief overview of national institutions that protect human rights indicates that some European states have responded to the political pressures of the day in a piece-meal approach to human rights and reproduces, without advancing, that state's understanding of their human rights obligations. While the Paris Principles provide broad guidelines for the establishment of such institutions, there is no single model for Europe but a set number of parameters which need to be met for an authentic national human rights institution. Any human rights commission established to promote, protect and educate the norms of the UDHR could create a broad umbrella of

---

5 G. DE BECO, 'National Human Rights Institutions in Europe', 7:2 *Human Rights Law Review* (2007) p. 332.

protection for all human rights without taking away the specialised competency of an existing institution. As a result civil society would be better served.

7. CONCLUSIONS

The UDHR has, as a document and as a collection of norms, that is, of rules and principles, started to live its own life, exceeding by far the formal implications of a resolution of the General Assembly of the United Nations or the expectations of the original states who voted it into existence. It is completely clear that the UDHR has influenced legal and political thinking in the European states and organisations in many ways. The civil society has made use of the UDHR in its advocacy, the governments consider the UDHR when drafting legislation, the parliaments make use of the UDHR in political argumentation, and the courts may sometimes invoke the UDHR as an argument or even as a source of law. All international human rights conventions, since the genesis of the UDHR, have cited it in their preambles by acknowledging its foundational nature. Many European states are parties to such international human rights conventions and are bound by their provisions although they have not been canvassed in this research.

At the same time, there is, of course, general acceptance of the UDHR as a leading document in the area of human rights. Undoubtedly, this variable landscape at the national level will continue to be such also in the future. One generalised view of the European Union, sometimes masked by the presence of an efficient and effective regional human rights protection system in what is a more economically stable region, may be that all human rights in the UDHR have been respected and protected by all European states from inception or before. That view belies the fact that the reception of the UDHR in the 27 member states of the European Union and in the three European organisations is very varied and the differences between the states and the organisations are great. The creation of the European Union has melded the various human rights histories of each member state into what appears to be a common view of the protection of human rights, as presented in the ECHR. The research undertaken in this book reveals that history of individual member states of the European Union from the perspective of today, sixty years after the adoption of the UDHR: the European story of human rights and also of democratisation in the broad sense of the term is one of diversity within the unity. While the subject of this book is the reception of human rights in Europe, the approach it has taken has value for the rest of the world because it reveals the individual states' pre-occupations at that time, and since then, when human rights started to become mainstreamed. That the UDHR has become the benchmark of human rights globally, one of its original intentions, is supported by this research.

SUBJECT INDEX

Adequate standard of living (right to) 34, 37, 80, 175, 235, 390, 455
Amnesty International 17, 37, 38, 82-83, 108, 123, 209, 210, 223, 242, 284, 286, 288, 457, 464
Arbitrary arrest 107, 233, 390
Asylum (right to) 16, 18, 34, 59, 69, 79, 170-171, 203, 234, 290–291, 390, 404, 408-409, 455

Cassin, René 8, 19-21, 22, 23, 208, 401
Children (protection of) 80, 154, 169-170, 236, 309, 391
Cold War 3, 9, 21, 49, 51, 114, 148, 150, 168–169, 211, 213, 215, 253, 269, 283–284, 287, 291, 437, 454
Council of Europe 61, 102, 165, 169, 200, 242, 243, 255, 334, 335, 337, 344, 365, 399–414, 437, 438, 445, 451, 455, 459
Customary international law 13, 19, 24–25, 31, 35, 61, 65, 66, 105, 131, 176, 207, 209, 210, 217, 218, 221, 238, 259, 276, 347, 348, 353, 354, 381, 382, 396, 428, 437, 445, 449, 461-463

Declaratory 66, 182, 205, 206, 219, 276, 328, 340, 350, 351, 454
Dignity 22, 79, 87, 105, 108, 141, 149, 151, 154, 155, 170, 180, 182–183, 184, 187, 189, 190, 195, 206, 217, 224, 233, 238, 244, 256–257, 281, 316, 366, 374, 390, 410, 439, 464
Disabled persons 9, 62, 155, 206, 225, 315, 417
Discrimination (prohibition of) 18, 35, 55, 62, 79, 104, 126, 128, 148, 155, 163, 171–172, 183, 184, 196, 215, 296–297, 338, 352, 353, 379, 390, 405, 424, 462

Education (right to) 45, 46, 79, 104, 148, 151, 155, 162, 206, 236, 258, 309, 315, 328, 390, 404, 455
Effective remedy (right to) 140, 233, 390
European Committee of Social Rights 412–413
European Convention on Human Rights 9, 11, 12, 14, 21, 24, 30-36, 52, 56, 66, 67, 71, 76, 96, 97, 98, 119–123, 125, 126, 127, 130–131, 138, 139, 142, 145, 157, 169, 175, 182, 200, 202, 204, 206, 207, 218, 219, 220, 244, 255, 257, 277, 278, 289, 294–300, 335, 337, 339, 340-341, 353, 365, 369–370, 376, 389, 392, 399–406, 410, 412, 414, 417–418, 419, 425, 445, 453–455, 467
European Court of Human Rights 109, 194–195, 218, 276, 289, 290, 297, 298, 299, 341, 370, 404, 405, 406, 413, 414, 448, 451
European Court of Justice 192, 220, 416, 417, 418–424, 425-426, 428
European Social Charter 11, 36, 98, 125, 257, 277, 406, 411-413, 419
European Union 70, 76, 131, 172, 191–192, 217, 218, 219, 220, 295, 301, 337, 369, 371, 415-431, 445, 447, 450, 451, 457, 458, 459, 465, 467

Fair trial (right to) 68, 105, 107, 140, 157, 205, 206, 233, 298-299, 353, 370, 390, 392, 407–408
Family (protection of) 81, 86, 151, 157, 183, 206, 221, 390
Forced labour (*see* slavery)

Freedom of assembly and association 28, 53–54, 128, 148, 152, 181, 191, 234, 251, 269, 390, 408, 413, 437, 439
Freedom of movement 128, 152, 234, 244, 390
Freedom of opinion and expression 68, 76, 105, 106, 170, 179–180, 185–196, 215, 234, 244, 251, 269, 309, 361, 386, 390, 436
Freedom of religion and conscience 37, 54, 67, 70, 104, 109, 117, 148, 157, 173, 180, 215, 234, 251, 320, 390

General principles of international law 24, 61, 63, 207, 259, 276, 302, 329, 461–462

Housing (right to) 80–81, 339
Human rights commissions 31–32, 69, 79–80, 84, 141–142, 154, 202, 203, 222, 228, 379–380, 466
Humphrey, John 20, 45, 116, 198-199, 401

Indivisibility and interdependence (of human rights) 20, 40, 59, 140, 143, 147, 149–150, 159, 281, 312, 315, 412, 426, 430, 447, 463
International Court of Justice 8, 61, 117, 197, 208
International Covenant on Civil and Political Rights 9, 11, 66, 71, 76, 81, 98, 102, 103, 125, 138–140, 154, 157, 175, 182, 208, 209, 218, 255, 257, 294, 301, 310, 314, 326, 332, 334, 339, 340, 349, 362, 364, 375, 376, 377, 387, 388, 389, 390, 392, 417, 435, 436, 438, 445
International Covenant on Economic, Social and Cultural Rights 9, 11, 36, 98, 102, 103, 125, 138–139, 175, 209, 218, 236, 255, 257, 277, 294, 301, 310, 314, 326, 332, 334, 339, 340, 364, 375, 376, 387, 388, 389, 390, 412, 417, 435, 438, 445, 450
Iron Curtain (*see* Cold War)

jus cogens 35, 36, 238, 410, 420, 421, 461–462

Legislation 9–10, 28, 30–31, 54-55, 76, 80, 129, 139, 169–173, 176, 182, 207–208, 218, 221, 243, 277, 291, 299–300, 337–338, 390, 392, 394, 446, 458, 461, 467
Life (right to) 29, 35, 37, 107, 109, 157, 158, 170, 182, 183, 233, 290, 309, 312, 316, 366, 368, 390

Malik, Charles 86, 116, 208
Minorities (protection of) 7, 9, 18, 27, 28, 46, 126, 138, 139, 148, 151, 156, 158, 189, 190, 195, 196, 245, 309, 314, 337, 354, 363, 379–380, 387, 388, 391, 405–406, 434, 438

Nationality (right to) 8, 36, 234, 390, 394, 404, 408, 413, 455, 462

Ombudsman 69, 79, 109, 171, 176, 193, 393, 395, 466

Paris Principles 17, 223, 228, 465, 466
Participation rights 34, 37, 70, 152, 162, 195, 236, 309, 330, 349, 391, 413, 420, 421, 455
Peremptory norms (*see jus cogens*)
Privacy (protection of) 34, 70, 81, 104, 105, 109, 157, 170, 234, 277, 390, 408
Property rights 34, 36, 75, 104, 152, 183–184, 234, 236, 244, 276, 296, 314, 320, 322, 390, 393, 404, 420, 421, 436, 455

Roosevelt, Eleanor 19, 20, 44, 93, 208

Self-determination 29, 117, 197, 200, 231, 265, 282, 293, 309-310, 317, 327, 390
Slavery 35, 67, 205, 233, 267, 309, 390, 392
Social security (right to) 25, 80, 151, 170, 235, 310, 315, 328, 351, 390, 455

Terrorism 29–30, 54, 285, 286, 420, 440, 449, 451
Torture (prohibition of) 33, 35, 80, 144, 152, 157, 170, 203, 290, 309, 353, 392, 409, 410, 462

UN Charter 2, 8, 46, 70, 73, 76, 88, 98, 150, 153, 162, 168, 206, 231, 249, 250, 293, 301, 302, 361, 367, 375, 399, 410, 431, 435
UN Human Rights Commission 7, 8, 44, 45, 74, 85, 86, 87, 111, 116, 154, 306
Universality (of human rights) 14, 19, 20, 21, 22, 59, 143, 144, 210, 233, 322, 323, 374, 426, 430, 448

Vienna Declaration and Programme of Action 61, 140, 143–144, 286, 426, 447

Women (rights of) 8, 18, 20, 43-46, 50, 56, 79, 109, 144, 151, 154, 173, 184, 198, 228, 248, 309, 315, 328, 387
Work related rights 8, 11, 34, 46, 52, 68, 104, 151, 172, 203, 235, 307, 309, 310, 315, 316, 319, 328, 329, 349, 359, 390, 412, 455